MILITARY OBJECTIVES
IN SOVIET FOREIGN POLICY

D0733609

Michael MccGwire

MILITARY OBJECTIVES IN SOVIET FOREIGN POLICY

DOMINICAN COLLEGE LIBRARY
Blauvelt, New York 10913
DISCARDED

THE BROOKINGS INSTITUTION
Washington, D.C.

110659

Copyright © 1987 by

THE BROOKINGS INSTITUTION

1775 Massachusetts Avenue, N.W., Washington, D.C. 20036

Library of Congress Cataloging-in-Publication data

MccGwire, Michael.
Military objectives in Soviet foreign policy.
  Includes bibliographies and index.
    1. Soviet Union—Military policy.   2. Soviet Union—
Foreign relations—1945—   .   I. Title.
UA770.M399 1986   355′.0335′47   86-24932
ISBN 0-8157-5552-X
ISBN 0-8157-5551-1 (pbk.)

1 2 3 4 5 6 7 8 9

Board of Trustees

Louis W. Cabot
Chairman
Ralph S. Saul
Vice Chairman;
Chairman, Executive
  Committee;
Chairman, Development
  Committee

Samuel H. Armacost
J. David Barnes
Rex J. Bates
Frank T. Cary
A. W. Clausen
William T. Coleman, Jr.
Lloyd N. Cutler
Thomas R. Donahue
Charles W. Duncan, Jr.
Walter Y. Elisha
Robert F. Erburu
Roberto C. Goizueta
Robert D. Haas
Philip M. Hawley
Amory Houghton, Jr.
Roy M. Huffington
B. R. Inman
Vernon E. Jordan, Jr.
James A. Joseph
James T. Lynn
Donald F. McHenry
Bruce K. MacLaury
Mary Patterson McPherson
Donald S. Perkins
J. Woodward Redmond
James D. Robinson III
Robert V. Roosa
Henry B. Schacht
Howard R. Swearer
Morris Tanenbaum
Phyllis A. Wallace
James D. Wolfensohn
Ezra K. Zilkha
Charles J. Zwick

Honorary Trustees
Vincent M. Barnett, Jr.
Barton M. Biggs
Eugene R. Black
Robert D. Calkins
Edward W. Carter
Bruce B. Dayton
Douglas Dillon
Huntington Harris
Andrew Heiskell
Roger W. Heyns
John E. Lockwood
William McC. Martin, Jr.
Robert S. McNamara
Arjay Miller
Charles W. Robinson
H. Chapman Rose
Gerard C. Smith
Robert Brookings Smith
Sydney Stein, Jr.
Phyllis A. Wallace

THE BROOKINGS INSTITUTION is an independent organization devoted to nonpartisan research, education, and publication in economics, government, foreign policy, and the social sciences generally. Its principal purposes are to aid in the development of sound public policies and to promote public understanding of issues of national importance.

The Institution was founded on December 8, 1927, to merge the activities of the Institute for Government Research, founded in 1916, the Institute of Economics, founded in 1922, and the Robert Brookings Graduate School of Economics and Government, founded in 1924.

The Board of Trustees is responsible for the general administration of the Institution, while the immediate direction of the policies, program, and staff is vested in the President, assisted by an advisory committee of the officers and staff. The by-laws of the Institution state: "It is the function of the Trustees to make possible the conduct of scientific research, and publication, under the most favorable conditions, and to safeguard the independence of the research staff in the pursuit of their studies and in the publication of the results of such studies. It is not a part of their function to determine, control, or influence the conduct of particular investigations or the conclusions reached."

The President bears final responsibility for the decision to publish a manuscript as a Brookings book. In reaching his judgment on the competence, accuracy, and objectivity of each study, the President is advised by the director of the appropriate research program and weighs the views of a panel of expert outside readers who report to him in confidence on the quality of the work. Publication of a work signifies that it is deemed a competent treatment worthy of public consideration but does not imply endorsement of conclusions or recommendations.

The Institution maintains its position of neutrality on issues of public policy in order to safeguard the intellectual freedom of the staff. Hence interpretations or conclusions in Brookings publications should be understood to be solely those of the authors and should not be attributed to the Institution, to its trustees, officers, or other staff members, or to the organizations that support its research.

Foreword

WESTERN INTERPRETATION of Soviet foreign policy is strongly influenced by Soviet military developments, which are usually analyzed in terms of Western interests and vulnerabilities. This book represents a major departure from that approach. Rather than viewing the Soviet military posture from the perspective of the West, Michael MccGwire focuses on the Soviet viewpoint and way of thinking. He shows how the need to plan for the contingency of world war has shaped Soviet policy, resulting in a force structure often perceived as far in excess of legitimate defense needs.

According to the author, a change in Soviet military doctrine in late 1966 about the possible nature of world war led the Soviets to adopt a radically new hierarchy of strategic objectives. Consequently, they had to restructure their forces, adopt a new approach to arms control, and adjust their policy in the third world. The process of changing from one set of strategic concepts and objectives to another took almost ten years, producing the evidence on which MccGwire bases insights into Soviet military requirements and the motivations underlying military developments during the past thirty years. The cut-off date for this evidence is mid-1985.

Michael MccGwire is a senior fellow in the Brookings Foreign Policy Studies program. The author wishes to express his appreciation to the many people who offered specialized advice or helpful comments at various stages of the analysis. In particular, he thanks Raymond L. Garthoff for his fund of knowledge and advice, and John D. Steinbruner for supporting the lengthy process of analytical discovery and helping to shape the argument. John Hines, Thomas L. McNaugher, William B. Quandt, and Ted Warner made important contributions to the study as a whole. Karen Dawisha, Jonathan Dean, Ellen Mickiewicz, Cynthia Roberts, Matthew Evangelista, Andrew Goldberg, John McDonnell, Alan Neidle, Jack Snyder, Gael Tarleton, and James Westwood contributed valuable comments on various chapters.

Stephen Wegren verified the factual content of the book and also provided research assistance, as did Nancy Ameen, Lisa Mages, and Christine Potts. Thomas Somuah produced the many drafts, and Judith Longley prepared the index. The author is especially grateful to Theresa Walker for judicious editing of the manuscript.

Brookings gratefully acknowledges the financial support for this book provided by the Rockefeller Foundation, the Ford Foundation, the Carnegie Corporation of New York, and the John D. and Catherine T. MacArthur Foundation.

The views expressed here are those of the author and should not be ascribed to the persons or foundations whose assistance is acknowledged above, or to the trustees, officers, or other staff members of the Brookings Institution.

BRUCE K. MAC LAURY
President

January 1987
Washington, D.C.

Contents

TABLES

FIGURES

Abbreviations and Acronyms

ABM	antiballistic missile
APC	armored personnel carrier
ASAT	antisatellite
ASW	antisubmarine warfare
BMD	ballistic-missile defense
BMEWS	ballistic-missile early warning system
BPK	large antisubmarine ship
CTOL	conventional takeoff and landing
GLCM	ground-launched cruise missile
ICBM	intercontinental ballistic missile
INF	intermediate-range nuclear forces
MBFR	mutual and balanced force reductions
MIRV	multiple independently targeted reentry vehicle
MPK	small antisubmarine ship
MTVD	maritime theater of military action
OTVD	oceanic theater of military action
SAC	Strategic Air Command
SALT	strategic arms limitation talks
SAM	surface-to-air missile
SDI	Strategic Defense Initiative
SKR	escort ship
SRF	strategic rocket forces
SSB	ballistic-missile submarine
SSBN	nuclear-powered ballistic-missile submarine
SSG	cruise-missile submarine
SSGN	nuclear-powered cruise-missile submarine
SSM	surface-to-surface missile

SSN	nuclear-powered torpedo-attack submarine
SS	torpedo-attack submarine
START	strategic arms reduction talks
TVD	theater of military action
VRBM	variable-range ballistic missile
VTOL	vertical takeoff and landing

CHAPTER 1

Know Your Enemy

THE IMAGE of Russia as a riddle, wrapped in a mystery, inside an enigma, is immensely compelling to the West. It is not, however, applicable to the modern Soviet state. Despite being a partly closed society, the Soviet Union produces a vast amount of evidence and is unusual in the way it publicly articulates ideology, doctrine, and plans. Although the Soviets do conceal the details of the decision process, the outcomes of major decisions are largely visible. This evidence is highly revealing of the underlying policy.

The difficulty in understanding Soviet policy does not stem from any dearth of information, but from the problem of interpreting it. Here the difficulty lies as much with the lens of reasoning and logic through which Westerners are accustomed to viewing the world, as with any inherent obscurity of the evidence. In most cases this lens is different from the one used by the Soviets, which is an amalgam of Marxist-Leninist theory and traditional Russian instincts. But in one area, military thought, the reasoning and logic of both Russia and the West stem from the same roots. These shared principles allow Westerners to view Soviet military developments through Russian eyes.

In an immediate sense, this ability is important because it enables the West to identify the reasons that underlay the buildup in Soviet ground and air forces during the 1970s and the naval buildup that started in 1980. It also provides a window on other policy areas, including arms control and Soviet involvement in the third world. Such understanding is important in a broader sense because it provides insight into Soviet motivations. To handle an opponent successfully, one must know both what he does and why he does it. In dealing with the Soviet Union, the matter of why is the West's weakest suit.

In the military field one can discern the reasons underlying Soviet policy through deducing Soviet objectives. The idea of objectives is a universal concept central to the military planning process in all countries, and the Soviets apply the concept with systematic rigor. This reflects the structured way they think about war and the traditional influence of the German General Staff approach, as well as the Marxist belief in the existence of basic regularities in all aspects of human endeavor.

If one can deduce the hierarchy of Soviet military objectives, one can begin to understand the why of Soviet policy rather than being limited to the what. In military terms this understanding provides an insight into Soviet war plans and allows one to infer Soviet policy in areas in which little or no evidence is available. In analytical terms it allows one to develop a model of the Soviet mission structure and related military requirements. Such awareness enables one to forecast developments and identify areas in which the Soviets may run into problems, making one sensitive to shifts in policy and their likely implications.

The most important advantages, however, are in foreign policy analysis. An understanding of Soviet military objectives highlights how Russian behavior in peacetime is shaped and distorted by the need to prepare for the contingency of world war, a war the Soviets wish to avoid but whose possibility they see as inherent in the prevailing structure of international relations. The immediate purpose of this study is, therefore, to identify Soviet strategic objectives in a world war. The broader purpose is to assess how these objectives shape Soviet military requirements and the effect they have on Soviet foreign policy. This effect is important in Soviet policy in the third world and is most obvious in the field of arms control.

The Soviets see a world war as war between opposing social systems. This concept stems from the early days of the Soviet state, when Lenin concluded that it was only a matter of time before the imperialists would be driven to attack the Soviet Union, turning on the socialist system in a last desperate attempt to avoid the demise of capitalism. This basic dogma of Marxism-Leninism persisted until the mid-1950s, when it was decided that such a war was no longer "fatalistically" inevitable because the Soviet Union's military capability was by then sufficient to deter a deliberate Western attack. Nevertheless, the possibility of world war remained, and this worst-case contingency continues to shape Soviet threat assessments.

The Soviets' definition of world war does not mean that they exclude the possibility of more limited conflicts between the superpowers. The ultimate threat remains, however, world war, precipitated in some way by the imperialists. This possibility need not imply a deliberate Western attack, and in recent times the Soviets have seen the greater danger to lie in some third-party conflict, which could lead to a Sarajevo-type situation such as preceded World War I. How a world war might come about is not, however, the critical condition. Rather in such a war the imperialist objective of destroying the Soviet system provides the impetus for Soviet military requirements. In response to this perceived Western objective, inferred from Western statements over the years and from the logic of Marxism-Leninism, the Soviets formulate their own objectives.

These military objectives have evolved over the years, reflecting changes in the strategic environment, the correlation of forces, and Western concepts of military operations. The contemporary set of objectives dates from 1967–68, a period that represents a watershed in Soviet defense policy and in certain aspects of foreign policy, particularly the approach to arms control. The restructuring of Soviet objectives that took place at that period was necessitated by a change in doctrine about the nature of a future war and the way it should be fought.

On the face of it, the change was fairly subtle. The Soviets moved from the prevailing assumption that a world war would inevitably escalate to an intercontinental nuclear exchange, to the new assumption that it might be possible to avoid such an exchange. In reality this doctrinal adjustment had immense consequences, the evidence for which started to appear in the late 1960s and became fully apparent during the mid-1970s and early 1980s. The changes in national policy and force structure that stemmed from the 1966 adjustment were more fundamental than any since the postwar reevaluation of 1947–48, and the substance of these changes persists today.

The Soviet conclusion that escalation to an intercontinental exchange was not inevitable meant that, for the first time, the Soviets could adopt the objective of *avoiding the nuclear devastation of Russia*. The adoption of this fairly obvious objective had far-reaching consequences. How could that be so?

Consider the Soviets' previous reasoning. As long as they believed that escalation to a large-scale intercontinental exchange was inevitable, then not losing the war meant getting in the first nuclear strike in the hope of limiting the damage of the inevitable American attack. In other words, the decision that world war was inevitable and imminent was, at least in theory, synonymous with a decision to launch a preemptive strike on the United States. This course of events changes if the objective is to avoid the nuclear devastation of Russia. A nuclear strike on the United States would mean nuclear retaliation, which is what the Soviets are seeking to avoid.

The implications of the new objective were numerous and far reaching, ranging from naval building programs to the relative priority of air defense, from the number of divisions facing China to Soviet interests in the Horn of Africa, and from arms control policy to the role of force in the third world. One of the more obvious implications could be inferred from the radical restructuring of Soviet forces in Europe. The Soviet Union would need to redesign the concept of operations in that theater to minimize the danger that war in Europe would precipitate an intercontinental exchange.

A less obvious implication of the new objective was that if it were to be achieved, then the U.S. military-industrial base would have to remain untouched. The ramifications of an intact U.S. economy were immense. The Soviets would have to assume that even if they defeated NATO in Europe and evicted U.S. forces from the Continent, America would still carry on the war. In turn the Soviets must plan for a two-phase war, the first fairly short and sharp, and the second long-drawn-out and of unknown duration.

The Analytical Approach

Given the Soviet Union's obsession with secrecy, how is it possible to infer its strategic objectives as has been done in this book? Russia's geostrategic situation, the scale of its military requirements, and the Marxist-Leninist approach to solving problems yield abundant evidence that enables one to develop a well-supported hypothetical hierarchy of military objectives.

Two kinds of direct evidence are readily available. There are authoritative doctrinal statements about the likely nature of a future war and the methods of waging it, and these can be fleshed out by the professional debates in the military press. There is also a great deal of concrete evidence provided by the structure, disposition, and deployment of forces; the weapons procurement programs; and Soviet operational concepts. A direct relationship exists between these two bodies of evidence, and the theoretical link that joins them and makes sense of that relationship is the hierarchy of objectives. Doctrine determines objectives, and these objectives determine missions, which determine requirements, which become manifest as weapons systems and operational behavior.

Other evidence reflects the implications of specific objectives at different levels of the hierarchy. As one reconstructs this hierarchy, a series of testable hypotheses emerges. Proof for these hypotheses lies in the details of weapons programs, military exercises, and policy pronouncements.

The structured way of thinking that permeates the Soviet system allows one to impose coherence on this mass of evidence. In the military the emphasis is on the ordering of objectives and on the importance of identifying the main objective, the main theater of military operations, and the main axis of advance. This thinking reflects sound military practice, and, consequently, one can use deductive logic to reconstruct the policy framework that explains the evidence.

Finally, the fact of change in Soviet policy is crucial. Because the Soviet system is tightly planned, any serious change of policy, perceptions, or requirements reverberates throughout the system. Even fairly minor change in a higher-order objective can precipitate a cascade of changes that result in observable differences in operational concepts and force structure and anomalies in established patterns of production. Comparison of the evidence from before and after a change throws light on both the old and the new policy, a fact that underscores the importance of the "decision period" as a tool in this analysis.

The Decision Period

The process of coming to a decision on the need for a major change of policy can be pictured as a wave form. The rear slope of the wave represents the period when perceptions of the need for change build up to the crest of a top-level agreement-in-principle. The front slope of the wave represents the series of implementing decisions that stem from this acceptance of the need for change, and it constitutes what can be called the decision period.

The analytical process of identifying decision periods works backward in time and involves three stages. First comes the alert that something has changed, which could be sounded by observable changes in the pattern of military operations or production programs, which may not appear until several years after the decision-in-principle. Stage two is the process of dating the underlying decisions, using estimated lead times, pipeline inertia, and, when appropriate, analysis of published material. Stage three is the search for the most likely causes of the changes.[1]

If one can establish the primary causes of a change in policy and also

---

1. Appendix A details the process of identifying the decision periods. The decision period is conceptually distinct from the decisionmaking involved in preparing the five-year economic plan that figures so prominently in Soviet political and economic life, although sometimes the two may mesh in time. The five-year planning process is primarily incremental, but decision periods reflect the need for major, and often out-of-cycle, changes to existing policies and plans.

know some of its effects (that is, the evidence that sounded the initial alert), one can then postulate the new or amended objectives that will thereafter shape Soviet policy. This awareness allows one to infer the full range of policy changes that would logically result from the redefinition of objectives.

Firm evidence exists for five significant decision periods in Soviet foreign and defense policy in the twenty-five years following World War II. Each of these was unique in its effects and they all differed in the type of primary cause that prompted the central decision and in the significance of the consequences, which ranged from major changes in weapons programs and operational concepts to fundamental shifts in defense and foreign policy. These decision periods were 1947–48, 1953–54, 1957–58, 1959–62 (which is a double period), and 1967–68. In 1976–77 a review of the practical effects of the policy decisions made in 1967–68 apparently took place, resulting in a sixth decision period. It is also possible that major decisions were taken in 1983–85 in response to the deterioration in Soviet-American relations that occurred in the 1978–83 period.

The dating of decisions also establishes cutoff points for evidence. Soviet pronouncements, military operations, and weapons programs that originate from a time before a decision period can not be adduced as evidence when analyzing Soviet policy in the wake of that decision. The neglect of this rule explains many of the more fundamental disagreements over the substance of Soviet military doctrine as people use evidence from the past to support their assertions about the present.[2]

Meanwhile the analytical process of identifying decision periods highlights those circumstances in the present and recent past that could have precipitated a major policy decision. It also makes one more sensitive to the types of evidence that provide early indications that a change of policy has taken place.

Comments on Methodology

The end product of this analysis is an explanation of contemporary Soviet defense policy that is comprehensive in scope, if not in detail, and the outline of a Soviet plan of military operations for the contingency of world

---

2. The use of Soviet pronouncements to explain Soviet policy is an imprecise art, and it can be downright misleading if statements dated prior to a decision period are offered as evidence of the relevant Soviet policy after that date. Old-style pronouncements may persist after a decision to change has been made because it takes time to achieve the necessary restructuring of forces that will allow the implementation of the new policy. Until that has been done, the old policy will remain in force.

war. These explanations, like any interpretation of Soviet policy, are hypotheses. They do have inherent strengths provided by the two hierarchies of objectives, and the shift from one to the other explains much of the change in force posture and operational concepts observed in the 1970s. It also explains the changes in Soviet arms control policy in the 1968–75 period.

Another strength of the central hypothesis of the fundamental shift in doctrine is that the geostrategic analyses forced the hypothesis to the surface. The original intention had been to carry out a straightforward assessment of Soviet military requirements in the three main geographical regions. But to explain the results of the initial assessment it was found necessary to embark on the quite different type of analysis that underlies the first part of this book, which then led to the central hypothesis in its final form.

The hypothesis that a hierarchy of strategic objectives underlies Soviet military policy and the structure of its forces does not require particular assumptions about the Soviet political process. The focus of the study is on why certain policies were adopted rather than on how they came to be decided. To identify why, the study applies the principles of objectives analysis and its derivative, requirements analysis. It recognizes the likelihood of interorganizational conflict but only dwells on that when such conflict is important to understanding particular developments, for example, Soviet naval policy in the 1970s. It acknowledges that personalities can be important, for example, when Dmitriy F. Ustinov took over as minister of defense in 1976, or in 1981–84 when Marshal Nikolay V. Ogarkov disagreed with the political leadership on the priority of preparations for possible war. Collective terms such as "the military" or "the Soviets" are, however, deemed adequate for most purposes. The study assumes that Soviet leaders strive to make rational decisions, but ones that conform to a military criterion of common sense rather than to an abstract concept of rationality.

Requirements analysis uses the hard evidence of weapons characteristics, force structure, and patterns of operation and deployment to develop a concrete frame of reference against which to interpret the often ambivalent evidence of Soviet professional writing and public pronouncements.[3] The value of this published material is enhanced by establishing decision periods that decree what can and can not be adduced as evidence. The

3. Requirements analysis is also called mission analysis. For an explanation of this methodology see Michael MccGwire, "The Turning Points in Soviet Naval Policy," in MccGwire, ed., *Soviet Naval Developments: Capability and Context* (Praeger, 1973), pp. 176–209.

requirements approach also means that the geostrategic analysis is carried out in terms of Soviet strategic requirements and not from the viewpoint of Western interests and vulnerabilities.

The extent to which the defense policy and supporting plan of military operations that are outlined in this book are likely to match the realities of Soviet thinking can be assessed by responding to several questions. Can the hypothesis explain all the known evidence, or do so with minor adjustments, and predict other kinds of evidence? Is there a better explanation that can meet these requirements? Does the hypothesis meet the criteria of internal coherence and logical consistency?

The hypothesis does explain all the evidence known to me and is largely derived from that evidence. Although this information is not all that would be available to the intelligence community, it seems unlikely that there is concealed evidence so significant that it could derail my central argument. Of course one might improve on the hypothesis by considering new information or the results of further research and analysis. But currently, alternative hypotheses that could accommodate the same body of evidence are scarce, and none exists with the comprehensive scope of this study. The few alternative explanations are mainly partial hypotheses, and only some meet the criteria of coherence and consistency.

Meanwhile the objectives' analysis generates a number of lesser hypotheses, many of them testable. For some of these, the evidence is already well known, although not always well understood. For others, testing will require systematic research. The remaining hypotheses that depend on war for validation provide a logical basis for estimating Soviet behavior in these opaque policy areas.

The postulated hierarchy of objectives establishes what the Soviets must seek to achieve in the event of a world war, not how they will choose to do so. There may be more than one way of achieving the objective, there can be disagreement about the best way, and the Soviets may start with one approach and later change to another. The hypothesis can therefore predict the thrust of Soviet policy but not the specific details, although it provides a ready-made explanation once the details can be discerned. As long as the Soviets do not reverse the 1966 decision about the possibility of avoiding escalation to an intercontinental exchange, the basic structure of their strategic objectives should remain intact.

The focus is on what the Soviets hope to achieve and does not assess their probability of success. Nor does it consider what preparations the Soviets have made to cover the possibility that they will be unable to achieve some or most of their objectives. This focus disarms the criticism that the analysis assumes a logic, order, and successful implementation in the military field that is contradicted by evidence from the civilian field. The military analog of the actual performance of the domestic economy in relation to the central economic plan would be the wartime performance of Soviet forces in relation to the strategic plan. The wartime peformance is not, however, the focus of this study. The mismatch between economic performance and plan is not therefore relevant as evidence. However, the Soviet emphasis in the civilian economy on central planning and performance objectives does support the assumption that a hierarchy of strategic objectives shapes military policy and the structure of Soviet forces.

This study concentrates on the military roots of Soviet policy. Obviously, other policy dimensions, particularly the economic one, are essential for a full understanding of the Soviet Union, but that is not the purpose of this study. Rather this study concentrates on how planning for the contingency of a world war shapes and distorts Soviet policy while producing a military posture and structure of forces that appear to the West as being far in excess of any legitimate defense needs. The focus is on the military-technical aspects of doctrine, which is the responsibility of the military to implement. The study does not dwell on the decisions that the Soviet political leaders would face in the course of a war except to note how the hierarchy of objectives would influence those decisions.

Organization of the Book

The study is organized in three parts. In part one chapters 2 through 5 identify the watershed in Soviet military doctrine and explore its general implications. Chapter 2 reviews the course of events that led to the decision in December 1966 that the established doctrine would have to be changed. Chapter 3 starts by inferring the two sets of objectives that are implied by the old and new doctrines. It then considers the broader consequences of the shift from one hierarchy of objectives to the other, looking at issues ranging from the policy regarding nuclear preemption and escalation to the relevance of the military-industrial base. Chapters 4 and 5 discuss specific implications of the new objectives for the land battle and for war at sea. Discovery of the new structure of objectives required a fundamental re-evaluation of Soviet naval developments since the late 1960s, and these are analyzed in appendixes B and C.

Part two of the book considers Soviet military requirements in the various theaters of military action in the light of the new hierarchy of objectives; these are discussed for three broad regions: Euro-Atlantic, Asian-Pacific, and Indo-Arabian. These three chapters are an exercise in geostrategic analysis of the kind that would be done by military planners on the General Staff in Moscow. The analysis goes beyond the generally accepted conclusions about the Soviet concepts of military operations in these different regions.

In part three chapter 10 reviews the implications of the new objectives for the role of Soviet military force in the third world. Chapter 11 considers the implications for Soviet arms control policy; the new structure of objectives required a reanalysis of Soviet strategic missile programs, which is contained in appendix D. Chapter 12 discusses significant international developments since the Soviets adjusted their military doctrine in 1966 and whether they would have prompted changes in the underlying direction of Soviet foreign and defense policy. Chapter 13 focuses on 1983–85 as a potential decision period affecting foreign and defense policy and postulates the major questions that would have been at issue. The final chapter provides an overview of the study's findings, discusses the analytical bases of the difficulty the West has in understanding Soviet motivations, and considers the implications of this analysis for Western policy.[4]

---

4. The following system is used in citing Russian publications throughout this book. If the author read the article in Russian, the Russian title and its English translation are given. If only the English translation of an article was read, then only the English title is used. The English translations are from various U.S. government publications.

PART ONE

The Genesis of Soviet Strategic Objectives

CHAPTER 2

The Evolution of Soviet
Military Doctrine

IN 1966 the Soviets made a basic change in their assumptions about the nature of a world war, which led them to modify their military objectives should such a war prove unavoidable. The years 1961 through 1966 were the gestation period for these basic changes, but to understand the evolution of Soviet thinking, a consideration of the postwar years, 1945–60, is also important. This outline focuses exclusively on the Soviet view of events. Given the different concerns and perceptions of the wartime allies, it is hardly surprising that the viewpoint was little understood in 1945–47, and the Soviet Union's boorish behavior in negotiating forums and ruthless behavior in occupied territories further diminished comprehension. The history of the last forty years and the continued subjection of Eastern Europe also make it understandable that any appreciation of the complex alliance relationships in the 1944–48 period has now been superseded by the beliefs that justified the foundation of NATO and the strategic arms race.

Nevertheless, the Soviets did have a point of view, whose essence was "never again." And while the United States hoped to hurry home to North America, having made the world safe for democracy, the Soviet Union set about restoring its shattered economy and ensuring its security against future military aggression.

The Postwar Years: 1945–60

As World War II drew to a close, the Soviets had a reasonably sanguine view of the future and no very clear policy for the countries of Eastern Europe. General Secretary Josef V. Stalin even hoped that there would be

13

a sufficient compatibility of concerns to enable wartime collaboration with the Western allies to carry over into the postwar years. The United States seemed set on withdrawing its forces to North America, and reluctance to become involved in European problems made an Anglo-American anti-Soviet coalition unlikely, while Britain's obvious hostility to Russia presented no real problem on its own.

Stalin was most concerned about the possible resurgence of a powerful Germany, the country that had inflicted partial dismemberment on Russia in the final years of World War I and 20 million dead in World War II.[1] He prepared to meet this potential threat by exacting punitive reparations designed to destroy Germany's war-making potential; establishing a protective barrier of Soviet-oriented buffer states; and building up the Soviet Union's military capability to counter a German threat if it ever did emerge. He hoped to achieve security for the Soviet Union within fifteen to twenty years.[2]

This rather reassuring assessment of Germany as the main but future problem persisted well into 1947, despite mounting evidence of an emerging threat that was both more serious and more immediate. As early as the second half of 1945, Soviet analysts of the Western scene were seeing two competing tendencies in Britain and America. One school favored continuing Franklin D. Roosevelt's wartime collaboration with the Soviet Union, while the other, which reflected the ideas of John Foster Dulles and Winston S. Churchill, seemed to indicate that the Anglo-Saxon powers sought to retain world domination. A sharp change in the U.S. style of negotiation after March 1946 reinforced the second interpretation.[3] Nonetheless, until July 1947 Stalin kept hoping that some kind of collaborative relationship

1. Stalin is described as being obsessed by the thought of future German revenge, a theme he repeated to nearly every one of his numerous visitors in the Kremlin. Isaac Deutscher, *Stalin: A Political Biography* (Harmondsworth, England: Penguin Books, 1966), p. 524. Stalin returned to this theme several times at the Tehran conference and also talked about it to Milovan Djilas in April 1945. William Taubman, *Stalin's American Policy: From Entente to Détente to Cold War* (W.W. Norton and Co., 1982), pp. 80, 134.

2. In April 1945 Stalin told Milovan Djilas, "We shall recover in fifteen or twenty years." In his electoral speech on February 9, 1946, Stalin talked of ambitious fifteen-year industrial targets, whose achievement would "guarantee our country against any and all circumstances." Taubman, *Stalin's Policy*, p. 134.

3. Taubman, *Stalin's Policy*, pp. 120–21, itemizes the Soviet commentary on the struggle between the two tendencies in Western policy. Daniel Yergin discusses these sharply conflicting tendencies in the U.S. government in *Shattered Peace: The Origins of The Cold War and the National Security State* (Houghton Mifflin, 1978); and John Lewis Gaddis describes the evidence of a "bitter anti-Soviet bloc in the State Department" as early as April 1945. Gaddis also concludes that American leaders embarked on a new Russian policy during the first months of 1946. See *The United States and the Origins of the Cold War, 1941–47* (Columbia University Press, 1972), pp. 226, 313, 356.

was still possible. After the Marshall Plan, however, he accepted that the lines of battle were irrevocably drawn. The "two tendencies" assessment of Western policy was replaced by a "two camps" interpretation of international relations, and Andrey F. Zhdanov elaborated this doctrine at the organizing conference of the Communist Information Bureau in September 1947.[4]

The two camps view seems to have led to a basic reassessment of the threat facing Russia. This process probably included a reworking of all the data since 1944 and even earlier, a winnowing out of the evidence that reflected the collaborationist tendency in Western policy (because that point of view had clearly lost), and a focusing on the evidence suggesting hostile intent. By viewing the world through this misanthropic prism and taking the evidence of subsequent Soviet behavior into account, it can be inferred that Moscow now believed the following objectives were shaping U.S. policy: denying the Soviet Union an atomic delivery capability; containing the influence of communism within Soviet borders; and effecting a basic change in the nature of the Soviet state.[5]

What lengths the Soviets believed the United States would go to in pursuit of these objectives is another matter, but from their viewpoint the omens were not reassuring. One notable feature of the immediate postwar period was how speedily American policy toward erstwhile enemies, the Axis powers, moved from hostility to friendship. The Soviets were deeply disturbed because the development matched the Marxist prognosis so well and because Germany, Italy, and Japan were not just former enemies of the wartime Grand Alliance, but the three founding members of the Anti-Comintern Pact. These three nations' expansionist ambitions in the 1930s had led to the carnage of World War II, and both Germany and Japan were long-standing enemies of Russia. Yet the United States had insisted that Italy be considered a founder-member of the United Nations, while vetoing the membership of Poland. By 1948 U.S. policy had moved from exacting reparations to rehabilitating Germany and Japan.

It is difficult to recapture the rancorous tone of international discourse at that period or the outspoken hostility in Western leadership circles to the Soviet Union, driven mostly by fear of communist encroachment. But

4. The Zhdanov doctrine echoed the characterization of East-West relations by Harry S. Truman in a speech on March 12, 1947, as a global struggle "between alternative ways of life." See John C. Campbell, *The United States in World Affairs, 1945–1947* (Harper, 1948), p. 480.

5. For a recent Soviet example of defining the threat to Russia through the use of U.S. objectives, see Marshal Ustinov's speech to senior officers, *"Za vysokuyu boevuyu gotovnost'"* (For high battle preparedness), *Krasnaya zvezda* (Red star), November 12, 1983.

however much Western hostility may have been justified by Russian behavior, that has no bearing on the Soviet Union's perceptions of threat.

The war-weary Soviets were particularly worried by the West's depiction of communist Russia as relentlessly bent on territorial aggression, a
characterization then used to justify gearing up the U.S. military-industrial
base for a possible war.[6] Indeed, it is often overlooked that during this
period many American officials and commentators were propagating the
idea that conflict with Russia was inevitable. As early as May 1945 Assistant Secretary of State Archibald MacLeish noted that "explicit reference to the possibility of a war with Russia is becoming more common in
the American press from day to day." In July 1946 Secretary of Commerce
(and former Vice-President) Henry Wallace wrote a 5,000-word letter to
President Harry S. Truman, saying it appeared that "we are preparing our-
selves to win the war which we regard as inevitable." In 1947 the option
of bombing Moscow was openly discussed and in October of that year,
former Secretary of State James F. Byrnes asserted that if the Russian army
did not leave Germany, the United States and other nations should band
together to take measures of last resort. In early 1948 a group of scholars
noted increasing talk about the inevitability of war with Russia, while in
March 1948 Drew Pearson reported that U.S. military leaders were study-
ing how to drop the atomic bomb on strategic Russian cities.[7]

Furthermore, the idea of a preventive war against Russia was common
currency in the United States. In November 1945 Senator Edwin C. Johnson of Colorado suggested that the United States "with vision and guts and
plenty of atomic bombs . . . [could] compel mankind to adopt the policy
of lasting peace . . . or be burned to a crisp." General Leslie R. Groves,
the director of the Manhattan Project, said that the U.S. atomic monopoly
could be used "as a diplomatic bargaining point to lead to the opening up
of the world so that there will be no opportunity for a nation to arm se-
cretly." In his classified statements, which were probably available to Mos-

6. The postwar cutback in defense expenditures was checked in 1947 when total obligation
authority for the air force and for procurement was increased over the previous year. Manpower
limits and the defense budget as a whole bottomed out in fiscal 1948 and rose in fiscal 1949. See
Office of the Assistant Secretary of Defense (Comptroller), *National Defense Budget Estimates
for FY 1983* (Department of Defense, 1982), pp. 21, 24. See Paul Y. Hammond, "Super Carriers
and B-36 Bombers: Appropriations, Strategy, and Politics," in Harold Stein, ed., *American Civil-
Military Decisions: A Book of Case Studies* (University of Alambama Press, 1963), pp. 480, 482.

7. Gaddis, *Origins of the Cold War,* p. 229; Yergin, *Shattered Peace,* p. 249, 5; D. F. Fleming, *The Cold War and Its Origins, 1917–60,* vol. 1, 1917–50 (Doubleday, 1961), p. 486; The
Staff of the International Study Group of the Brookings Institution, *Major Problems of United
States Foreign Policy, 1948–49* (Brookings, 1948), p. 27; and Fleming, *Cold War,* vol. 1, p. 497,
citing the *Nashville Tennessean,* March 22, 1948.

cow through the British spy Donald Maclean, Groves included the possibility of a preemptive nuclear strike against foreign atomic research facilities to guarantee continued exclusive supremacy. In 1947 Senator Brian McMahon, a Democrat of liberal views, proposed that Russia's failure to agree to the Baruch Plan (a U.S. proposal for an international authority to own and manage all atomic materials) should, of itself, constitute an "act of aggression." And in October 1948 Senator Eastland proposed dropping an atomic bomb on a Russian city if the blockade on Berlin was not lifted.[8] To Russia the sustained and largely successful efforts to persuade U.S. opinion that Soviet communism was a threat to the survival of the United States argued for worst-case assumptions.[9]

The Emerging Threat

Russia thought the most immediate threat was a possible preventive air strike against its atomic research and development facilities. Initially, the immediacy of the threat was limited by the well-publicized American belief that the Soviets could not develop a weapon before 1953. However, this complacency was shattered by the Soviet atomic test in August 1949. The Soviets then had to assume that new pressures would emerge to take action against their nascent capability. They considered themselves vulnerable to an air strike until they could develop a crude intercontinental delivery capability of their own, which they achieved in the mid-1950s.

A less immediate but equally serious threat was implicit in the other two U.S. objectives. To contain communist influence within the borders of the Soviet Union implied the replacement of Soviet-oriented governments in Eastern Europe with Westward-leaning regimes. To change the nature of the Soviet state implied the demise of the Communist party apparatus, something that could only come about as the result of war between the two systems. Such a war might be an outgrowth of a Western attempt to roll

8. Gaddis, *Origins of the Cold War*, p. 245; Gregg Herken, *The Winning Weapon: The Atomic Bomb in the Cold War* (Alfred A. Knopf, 1980), pp. 111–13, citing the *New York Times*, September 22, 1945; Gaddis, *Origins of the Cold War*, p. 388–89; and Peter Calvocoressi, *Survey of International Affairs, 1947–48* (London: Oxford University Press, 1952), p. 60.

9. For example, the September 9, 1946, issue of *Newsweek* reported flatly that those in the know in Washington feared they had confirmation that "the Soviet Government has made up its mind that capitalism must be destroyed if Communism is to live." This was the conclusion of the Clifford memorandum, which was prepared for Truman during the summer of 1946 and was based on the views of senior officials throughout his administration. The report concluded that the very existence of the Soviet Union threatened American security. Yergin, *Shattered Peace*, pp. 241–45; and Gaddis, *Origins of the Cold War*, pp. 318–23.

back Soviet influence in Europe or a by-product of a preventive strike on the Soviets' nascent atomic delivery capability. Possibly, rising anticommunist fervor in the United States and the fear of a growing Soviet military capability might lead to popular demand in America for a preventive war against Russia, especially if the brunt of the land battle was to be borne by others.

Evidence of U.S. preparations for such a battle was particularly disturbing. By July 1946 Reinhard Gehlen, formerly intelligence chief of the eastern military division of the German armed forces, had reassembled many of his former staff and was providing the U.S. Army with current and background intelligence on Russia and Eastern Europe. The Americans also had senior German generals recording and analyzing their experiences fighting the Russians. During 1946–47 the United States was known to be assembling experts on Eastern Europe, particularly Ukrainians, as potential leaders of partisan forces. Most ominous of all, between 1948 and 1950, the political leaders of most of the puppet regimes established by the Nazis in Eastern Europe and occupied Russia were moved to the United States. These developments were contrary to Allied agreements on how to handle collaborators and war criminals (the latter including the German generals) and suggested that the United States had future plans for these people.

Meanwhile the reparations process, which was intended to disarm Germany and restore Russia, had been halted in the American and British zones. By the end of 1947 the Anglo-Saxon powers were concentrating overtly on establishing a German state that would comprise the three western occupation zones (which encompassed the great bulk of Germany's industrial capacity), and binding that state to the European Recovery Program. At this same period, Churchill, an outspoken enemy of the Soviet Union and still influential, was seeking to weld the West European states into an anticommunist bloc, the core of which would be a radical new partnership between France and Germany, the recognized proponents of large ground forces. This development posed a double threat. It would turn France from a traditional ally of Russia into a latent enemy, while rehabilitating Germany and placing it at the center of a hostile and potentially powerful coalition. Britain would be freed for a global role in partnership with the United States.

These developments paralleled the steady militarization of the movement for European unity; its fusion with the European Recovery Program, thus confirming the Soviets darkest suspicions about the purpose of the

Marshall Plan; and finally, its extension and transformation into the North Atlantic Treaty Organization (NATO), bringing in Canada and the United States. The U.S. accession to NATO signaled a basic shift in American foreign policy, sanctioning active involvement in entangling alliances and was the prelude to a flow of armaments from America to many countries around the Soviet periphery. Even more serious, as *Le Monde* commented on April 6, 1949, "The rearmament of Germany is present in the Atlantic Pact as the seed is in the egg."

Drawing together this evidence, it was not hard for the Soviets to envision the scenario they might be faced with in the not too distant future, even if President Truman could resist internal pressures for a preventive strike against Soviet atomic facilities. The Soviets believed that in the same way that Germany had justified aggressive incursions in 1938–41, some pretext, opportunistic or contrived, would be found to justify a capitalist-imperialist intervention in the name of freedom. The details might vary from picking off a single country currently under Soviet control to intervention across the board. Such intervention could well be limited to the Western European continental armies, with the Anglo-Saxons standing back to deter a Soviet reaction, or it might include the full panoply of Western military power from the start. The Soviets would have to plan for the worst case, which would involve a combination of land assaults across the German plain and through the Balkans; major amphibious landings on the Baltic and Black Sea coasts, opening up new fronts in the rear and linking up with partisan forces; and massive air attacks by conventional and atomic bombers throughout the Soviet Union.[10]

War therefore became a distinct possibility and the Soviets had to take strategic preparations seriously. Their recent experience in World War II defined the nature of the anticipated land battle and the necessary scope of Soviet objectives. It dictated a forward strategy in Europe, which had the objective of deterring Western incursions and, if unsuccessful, of repelling such aggression and then going on to achieve victory over the enemy.

The threat of nuclear weapons delivered by long-range aircraft presented a new dimension. The scope of the air threat was spelled out for the Soviets in a magazine article by General Carl Spaatz, published the week he retired as chief of the U.S. Air Force in mid-1948. He talked of destroy-

10. From 1948 onward evidence of a sustained Western attempt to establish a partisan capability in Poland, Albania, the Baltic States, the Soviet Ukraine, Byelorussia, and Georgia mounted. None of these were successful, and the last of the Ukraine partisans was finally destroyed in late 1952. Thomas Powers, *The Man Who Kept the Secrets* (Alfred A. Knopf, 1979), pp. 29–32, 39–43; and John Loftus, *The Belarus Secret* (Alfred A. Knopf, 1982), pp. 79–110.

ing "a few hundred square miles of industrial area in a score of Russian cities." He also stressed acquiring forward bases for U.S. bombers, from which the United States could mount an air offensive against Russia's industrial heartland until the introduction of intercontinental supersonic bombers and guided missiles carrying atomic warheads made the bases unnecessary.[11]

The initial Soviet response to this air threat included the establishment of a national air defense system. As the American Strategic Air Command (SAC) developed a system of staging bases around the periphery of the Soviet Union, a Soviet doctrine of preemptive attacks against these bases also emerged.[12] Initially, the Soviets had to rely on the use of medium-range aircraft carrying conventional weapons. The concept of preemption became operationally more attractive at the end of the 1950s, however, when the Soviet medium-and intermediate-range missiles armed with nuclear warheads began to enter service. These Soviet missiles were also the most appropriate response to the qualitatively new threat posed by the emplacement of Thor and Jupiter missiles in European NATO.[13]

From Threat of Aggression to Danger of War

Once they were recognized as serious possibilities, the land battle in Europe and the threat of nuclear strikes on Russia became central, enduring elements of the military problem facing the Soviet Union. However, Soviet perceptions of the source of the problem have evolved over time. Until at least the middle 1950s, the Soviets took the threat of premeditated capitalist aggression seriously, while the inevitability of war with the West remained a dogma until at least 1952. The dogma was formally revised in

11. "If We Should Have To Fight Again," *Life Magazine* (July 5, 1948), pp. 34–44; and "General Spaatz on Atomic Warfare," *Life Magazine* (August 16, 1948), pp. 90–104. Although the discussion was pitched in terms of responding to a Soviet attack, the logic of the analysis was equally valid for a war initiated by America.

12. PVO strany (air defense of the country) was established as a separate branch of service in 1948. M.V. Zakharov, ed., *50 let vooruzhennykh sil USSR* (Fifty years of the armed forces of the USSR) (Moscow: Voenizdat, 1968), p. 477; see also the article by Marshal P. Rotmistrov, "On the role of surprise in contemporary war," *Voennaya mysl'* (Military thought), no. 2 (February 1955), pp. 18–19, which Raymond L. Garthoff analyzes in *The Soviet Image of Future War* (Washington D.C.: Public Affairs Press, 1959), p. 65.

13. Robert P. Berman and John C. Baker, *Soviet Strategic Forces: Requirements and Responses* (Brookings, 1982), pp. 41–50. Andrew Goldberg discusses the importance of U.S. staging bases in the Soviets' development of this concept of operations. See Andrew C. Goldberg, "Nuclear Escalation in Soviet Theater Warfare Strategy" (Ph.D. dissertation, Columbia University, 1985), pp. 39–43.

1956 when First Secretary Nikita S. Khrushchev announced that such a war was no longer inevitable because of the buildup in Soviet military strength; by 1960 the possibility of a deliberate American attack had been largely discounted.[14]

The reformulation did not mean that the Soviets believed the danger of war had evaporated. They continued to see Western intervention to exploit an opportunity in Eastern Europe as a possibility, and they believed the seeds of global conflict were inherent in the antagonisms of the two social systems. Similarly, the central elements of the military problem persisted, although the specifics of military requirements changed in response to what the Soviets refer to as the military-technological revolution. During the second half of the 1950s the emerging implications of nuclear weapons forced a basic reassessment of established military theory and concepts of military operations. Much of this reassessment focused on how to integrate nuclear weapons into traditional ground force operations at the theater level and what this meant for force structure and the balance between arms. The Soviets were also rethinking the nature of a war involving the superpowers.[15]

They concluded that armed conflict would inevitably develop into a full, intercontinental nuclear exchange. In its initial stages each power would carry out massive nuclear-missile strikes on the other's territory to deprive its enemy of the military, political, and economic means of waging war.

14. Before 1956 Marxist-Leninist doctrine decreed that conflict within the capitalist system would spill over and draw the Soviet Union into war, as happened in 1938 with Japan and in 1941 with Germany. In 1956 Nikita S. Khrushchev announced a reformulation of doctrine, reflecting the physical rehabilitation of the Soviet Union and the emergence of a powerful communist bloc. He now decreed that the contradiction *between* the capitalist and socialist systems was the primary source of conflict. The reformulation had an important corollary: world war was no longer inevitable because the growing strength of the socialist system would make the imperialists realize the futility of launching an attack on the Soviet Union in an attempt to halt the progress of history. War could, of course, come about through other circumstances.

In assessing Soviet views on the likelihood of an American attack one must distinguish between statements in military publications, where the threat was ritualistic, and the opinion of the political leadership. The military was focusing on Soviet vulnerability to an American attack, which was high at this period and increased during the early 1960s. The political leadership was more concerned with the probability of such an attack.

15. Their thinking would have been shaped in part by Western statements. For example, a study carried out by the Office of the Supreme Allied Commander Europe (SACEUR) in 1954 concluded that a future war would inevitably be atomic. See David N. Schwartz, *NATO's Nuclear Dilemmas* (Brookings, 1983), p. 32, citing Robert E. Osgood, *NATO: The Entangling Alliance* (University of Chicago Press, 1962), p. 109; and *Mutual Security Act of 1958,* Hearings before the Senate Committee on Foreign Relations, 85 Cong. 2 sess. (Government Printing Office, 1958), pp. 186–87.

The results of the reassessment were accepted at the end of 1959 and announced publicly by Khrushchev in January 1960. Debate about the implications continued into the early 1960s.[16]

Military Doctrine in Flux: 1960–66

The decisions that emerged from the reassessment that culminated in December 1959 were doctrinal decisions. In Soviet parlance military doctrine is an officially adopted system of views on basic questions about war, including the nature of a future war, the appropriate objectives in such a war, and the likely way it would be waged. The fact that it was a doctrinal decision did not mean that all the loose ends were tied up; there was ample room for argument about implications for force structure. But the basic decisions were not in question and, because of them, substantial changes were effected in the size and shape of frontal and naval aviation.

In 1966 a very different set of conclusions about the nature of a world war and the inevitability of nuclear strikes on Russia replaced the 1959 doctrine. The fact that new conclusions emerged rather suddenly during the last six months of the period, and were not the outcome of a prolonged debate, reflects the convoluted nature of Soviet military developments in the seven years 1960 through 1966.

The reasons for the complexity are easy to understand. Most important, the Soviet Union, like the United States before it, was coming to grips with the full implications of nuclear war. During the second half of the 1950s the Soviets had been focusing mainly on the problems of integrating nuclear weapons into existing strategic concepts, as the United States had done a few years previously.[17] The Soviet Union's fairly simple extrapolations were brought into question, however, by the scale of the American

16. See Marshal V.D. Sokolovskiy, ed., *Military Strategy: Soviet Doctrine and Concepts* (Praeger, 1963), pp. 189, 195–97; and N.S. Khrushchev, "Razoruzhenie—put' k uprocheniyu mira i obespecheniyu druzhby mezhdu narodami" (Disarmament—the path to strengthening peace and ensuring friendship between peoples), *Pravda*, January 15, 1960.

17. In a public address to the Royal United Service Institution in late 1954, Field Marshal Bernard Montgomery, then Deputy SACEUR said, "We at SHAPE [Supreme Headquarters Allied Powers Europe] are basing all our planning on using atomic and thermonuclear weapons in our own defense" Schwartz, *NATO*, p. 32. The National Security Council directive 162/2 of October 1953 had established that "in the event of hostilities, the United States will consider nuclear weapons to be as available for use as other munitions." In 1956 the Basic National Security Plan decreed, "It is the policy of the United States to integrate atomic weapons with other weapons in the arsenal." *The Pentagon Papers: The Defense Department History of United States Decisionmaking on Vietnam*, vol. 1, the Senator Gravel edition (Beacon Press, 1971), p. 426.

nuclear buildup in the first half of the 1960s, which the Soviets would match in due course.

During the 1960s significant adjustments to U.S. strategic policy occurred, undermining some of the premises that had shaped the Soviets' 1959 doctrinal decisions. For instance, the change of U.S. administration in January 1961 brought a shift from a declaratory policy of massive retaliation to one of flexible response. Flexible response though was primarily meant to enhance the credibility of deterrence in Europe by improving NATO's conventional capability, thereby providing an alternative to the early and virtually automatic use of nuclear weapons. In 1964 the United States also introduced the concept of assured destruction, which defined a strategic delivery capability that could absorb a surprise attack and still inflict unacceptable damage on the aggressor.[18]

The controversy in the Soviet Union over the role and utility of traditional forces in the circumstance of nuclear war further complicated decisionmaking. Some Soviet analysts claimed that nuclear-armed missiles could do almost everything, replacing artillery and strike aircraft on land and ships and submarines at sea; at the other extreme were those who thought that little had changed in war besides the ordnance. Meanwhile a separate argument persisted about whether a nuclear war would demand fewer forces, being short, sharp, and decisive, or more forces because of the unprecedented scale of casualties.

In certain respects the United States had grappled with these same problems five to seven years earlier, that being the lead it had in the availability of nuclear weapons. However, the United States and the Soviet Union emerged from their periods of reassessment with very different conclusions, largely determined by how they envisioned the danger that faced them. The Soviets, who had originally seen the threat as a premeditated attack on Eastern Europe and perhaps Russia itself, progressively adjusted their perception. By the 1960s they were discounting the likelihood of a deliberate attack but still had to prepare for the contingency of a world war that they would be unable to avoid and that they could not afford to lose. The United States originally saw the threat as premeditated communist

18. Flexible response became a practical option when it was discovered that Soviet capabilities had been considerably overestimated and that the real disparity in East-West strength could be remedied with increases in NATO defense budgets. Schwartz, *NATO,* pp. 150–52. Unacceptable damage was first defined as the destruction of 20 percent of the Soviet population and 50 percent of its industrial capacity. Secretary of Defense Robert S. McNamara introduced this concept as a way of capping the unconstrained buildup of U.S. strike forces. See Lawrence Freedman, *The Evolution of Nuclear Strategy* (London: Macmillan Press, 1981), pp. 246–47.

aggression, particularly in Western Europe. This perception did not evolve over time because it was encased in the doctrine of nuclear deterrence, which the West had adopted in the early 1950s.[19]

During the period from 1960 to 1966 the Soviets were trying to digest the implications of the 1959 doctrinal decision that war would inevitably be nuclear. They were also conducting an internal debate about the impact of the nuclear-missile revolution on their military operations, deciding how to respond to the Kennedy administration's defense initiatives, and slowly coming to grips with the implications of escalating weapons inventories on the two sides. Inevitably, the evidence is confused, and developments over the seven years can best be grasped by seeing the period as four successive stages, although this procrustean approach means simplifying a complex picture.[20]

Stage One, 1960–61

The new Soviet policy decided at the end of 1959 and announced in January 1960 shifted the emphasis from large-scale conventionally armed ground forces to greater reliance on nuclear missiles. This was reflected in the formation in December 1959 of the strategic rocket forces (SRF) as a separate branch of service; its designation as the primary arm of the nation's defense; and the plan to reduce the size of the armed forces from 3.6 million to 2.4 million over the next two years. The continuing importance of tanks was clearly perceived for the land battle, but the Soviets also concluded that the role traditionally played by massed infantry and artillery in breaching the enemy front could in the future be assigned to nuclear weapons.[21] Whether the changes would result in force economies was a different matter, and many argued that any economies would be canceled by the need to replace the heavy casualties of the nuclear battlefield.

19. The relevance of deterrence theory depends on the presence of an adversary with a compelling urge to take the action being deterred, hence the question of enemy intentions is a given rather than a subject for analysis.

20. I am grateful to Andrew Goldberg, who contributed to my understanding of this period.

21. The cut in manpower would be the third one since 1955. The first, which was completed by June 1956, reduced the size of the armed forces from 5.7 million to about 3.9 million and echoed the United States' post-Korean reduction from 3.2 million to 2.8 million. A further Soviet cutback of 0.3 million occurred in 1958–59. The third reduction was only about half complete when it was halted in mid-1961 in response to the U.S. call-up at the time of the Berlin crisis. Thomas W. Wolfe, *Soviet Power and Europe, 1945–70* (Johns Hopkins Press, 1970), pp. 164–65. The delivery rate of tanks rose sharply in 1962–65. See Goldberg, "Nuclear Escalation," pp. 54–55.

The implication of the doctrinal decision that nuclear strikes on Russia were inevitable was more basic. The conclusion that any superpower conflict would involve all-out nuclear war put a premium on getting in the first blow, a concept already firmly established in Soviet military thought. Indeed preemption was the only feasible response to the qualitatively new threat of intercontinental ballistic missiles emplaced in North America. The Soviets' limited intercontinental capability during the first half of the 1960s did not undermine a first-strike strategy. If an exchange was inevitable, Russia would be slightly less worse off if it could get in the first blow, even if only a modest strike. At least in theory, the decision that war with the West was inescapable would be synonymous with the decision to launch nuclear strikes on North America, as well as against nuclear bases on the continental and maritime periphery of the Soviet Union.

Stage Two, 1962–63

The ideas of Khrushchev and his supporters in the military had shaped the policy announced in January 1960, and these ideas prevailed through mid–1961. However, the terms of the internal debate had been changed by the far-reaching defense initiatives introduced by President John F. Kennedy after taking office in January 1961 and his vigorous response to the growing crisis over Berlin in the summer of that year. These developments provided ammunition for those who believed that Khrushchev and his supporters had greatly exaggerated the extent to which nuclear missiles could replace, rather than supplement, traditional weapons systems.

By July 1961 a compromise was apparently made on this aspect of the debate. An agreement was reached that while strategic nuclear strikes would be decisive, a war could only be won through the combined operations of all arms.[22] The reduction in the size of the armed forces was halted, and Minister of Defense Marshal Rodion Malinovskiy announced the revised policy at the Twenty-second Party Congress.[23]

During this time the Soviets generally agreed on the doctrine that the land battle in Europe would be nuclear from the start, despite their awareness of the new U.S. concept of flexible response and the steps being taken

22. John McDonnell, "Khrushchev and the Soviet Military-Industrial Complex: Soviet Defense Policy, 1959–1961" (Halifax, Nova Scotia, Dalhousie University, Center for Foreign Policy Studies, 1979), pp. 73–82; and Wolfe, *Soviet Power*, p. 196.
23. See Marshal V.D. Sokolovskiy, ed., *Voennaya strategiya,* 1st ed. (Military strategy) (Moscow: Voenizdat, 1962).

to strengthen NATO's conventional capability.[24] The Soviets saw flexible response, initially, as an American attempt to enhance its capability to fight a nuclear war in Europe (the only kind NATO was in a position to win), a conclusion fostered by the introduction of a complete new family of tactical nuclear systems throughout NATO in the 1962–64 period.[25]

The impact of the Kennedy initiatives on the threat of nuclear strikes on Russia was much more substantial, but they served to reinforce rather than undermine the 1959–60 basic doctrine that a world war would inevitably be nuclear and would mean massive strikes on Soviet territory. The Soviet military assumed that the large and rapid buildup of America's intercontinental delivery capability implied the United States was seeking the capability for a disarming first strike.[26]

This buildup, combined with the inadequacies of the Soviets' own intercontinental ballistic-missile programs, prompted the attempt to deploy shorter-range missiles in Cuba as a stopgap measure. America's vehement response provided an important lesson in U.S. crisis behavior, but in military terms, it told the Soviets nothing they did not already know. It did reinforce their resolve to at least match the U.S. capability to devastate its opponent's homeland.

Stage Three, 1964–66

During this period the Soviets came to a clearer appreciation of what flexible response implied for the land battle in Europe. A flurry of Soviet articles appeared in 1964, discussing the possibility that a war might start

24. Sokolovskiy refers to flexible response and to Maxwell Taylor's *Uncertain Trumpet* in the first edition of *Voennaya strategiya*. U.S. officials publicly asserted the importance of improved conventional capabilities after the 1961 Berlin crisis, and McNamara gave a detailed exposition of the new defense policy at Ann Arbor in June 1962. Much of the debate within NATO took the form of public statements. Schwartz, *NATO*, pp. 165–73; by January 1962, spurred on by the Berlin crisis, SACEUR's strength on the Central Front had increased from about 16 real division equivalents to about 25. Meanwhile the United States announced its intention to increase active military strength worldwide from 11 to 16 divisions and from 16 to 21 tactical air wings; to improve combat readiness and logistic support; to increase the airlift capability and to preposition 2 divisions' worth of equipment in Europe; and to streamline the mobilization system. Ibid., pp. 150, 156.

25. Goldberg notes that "far from being interpreted as a search for alternatives to nuclear war, flexible response was initially seen by the Soviets as augmenting and refining the continued interest in nuclear war fighting." "Nuclear Escalation," p. 63. NATO's new nuclear systems comprised two types of surface-to-surface missile (Sergeant and Pershing), two types of self-propelled cannons, the Davy Crockett small rocket, and nuclear mines. Berman and Baker, *Soviet Strategic Forces*, table C-1, p. 133.

26. In a retrospective interview with Robert Scheer, former Secretary of Defense McNamara noted that in 1963 he had formally recorded his opinion that this assumption must have been the Soviet perception, and that furthermore, the U.S. Air Force had been pressing to acquire a first-strike capability at that period. *Los Angeles Times*, April 4, 1982.

with a conventional phase of indeterminate duration and even speculating on the possibility of a protracted conventional war. The new appreciation was facilitated by the ouster of Khrushchev in October 1964, and in 1965 the Warsaw Pact exercise "October Storm" began with a conventional phase. In 1966 a Soviet textbook on general tactics in conventional warfare (but within the shadow of nuclear escalation) was published at the secret level.[27]

The new emphasis on conventional warfare did not, however, represent a basic shift in policy; the military exercise "Vltava" in 1966 was nuclear from the start. The Soviet doctrine concerning NATO's central front still held that "one must regard the conduct of military operations with nuclear weapons as being the basic version," although it was acknowledged that in other sectors the campaign might remain nonnuclear.[28]

That acknowledgment was part of a growing recognition in 1965–66 that a nuclear war might be limited in geographic scope and scale of weapons used. This idea would have been prompted in part by the U.S. adoption in 1964 of an assured second-strike capability as the criterion for sizing its strategic nuclear forces.[29] Although this concept could be explained as covering the contingency of a surprise disarming strike, it could also be read as evidence that the United States now thought the defense of NATO Europe could be left to the nuclear forces deployed in the theater and did not require automatic strikes on Russia.

In these assessments the Soviets were responding to changes in Western strategic concepts rather than initiating their own changes. After all the United States had originally embraced the policy of resorting to massive nuclear attacks on Russia at the onset of hostilities, and NATO had decided to rely on nuclear firepower rather than on conventional forces in Europe. There was also the disparity in nuclear inventories between the United States and the Soviet Union in 1964–66. So it is not surprising the Soviets

27. A few articles appeared in 1963. See Wolfe, *Soviet Power,* pp. 211–14, 451–58; and Goldberg, "Nuclear Escalation," p. 83. Further impetus to the evolution of Soviet policy would have been added by the reemergence in mid-1965 of the debate within NATO over flexible response. It had dropped from sight between late 1962 and mid-1965, a period when NATO was preoccupied with the idea of a multilateral (nuclear) force. The United States had proposed the force partly to assuage the doubts over extended deterrence raised by flexible response. Schwartz, *NATO,* pp. 82–135. General-Major V.G. Reznichenko, *Taktika* (Tactics) (Moscow: Voenizdat, 1966). Translated in 1982 by the U.S. Army Intelligence and Threat Analysis Center, Arlington Hall Station, and declassified in September 1983, this textbook discusses conventional operations at the division (or brigade) level while under the threat of nuclear attack.

28. Malcolm Mackintosh, *The Evolution of the Warsaw Pact,* Adelphi Paper 58 (London: Institute for Strategic Studies, 1969), p. 8, citing *Defensive Operations in the Course of an Offensive* (Moscow: Voenizdat, 1966).

29. In Western strategic circles the possibility of conducting limited nuclear war was being discussed. See Morton Halperin, *Limited War in the Nuclear Age* (John Wiley and Sons, 1963).

assumed that the choice about whether operations in Europe would be conventional, and whether a world nuclear war would be limited, lay with the United States and not with the Soviet Union.

This assumption conditioned Soviet thinking. Although the trend in the West to restrict reliance on nuclear weapons was correctly perceived, the Soviets had still to appreciate that they were in a position to reinforce this trend since it favored their interests should they become embroiled in a world war.

Stage Four, July–December 1966

During the second half of 1966 the full realization emerged that, given the appropriate Soviet strategy and contrary to the doctrinal conclusions of 1959, it was no longer inevitable that a world war would lead to a nuclear strike on Russia. This break with the prevailing mind-set required a fundamental change in assumptions. The catalyst of change was probably the announcement by the French in March 1966 that they planned to withdraw from NATO at the end of July. This would effect a significant diminution of NATO's military capability, including not only the loss of forces in being, but also the loss of defensive depth and of the extensive logistical infrastructure within and across France's borders.[30]

Such a shift in the military balance in the central region was bound to have set in motion within the Soviet General Staff the formal process of reestimating the situation.[31] Only at this late stage did the Soviets appreciate that they could exploit developments for their own purposes instead of just adjusting to NATO policy. This critical realization was quite different in substance and implications from the Soviets' recognition in 1964 of the emerging trend toward conventional operations in the theater. The Soviet response to that trend did, however, prepare the ground for the more fundamental change of 1966. The process of developing the necessary tac-

30. The decision that was formally approved in December 1966 was apparently reached in a fairly short time and without open debate. The evidence also indicates that in the summer of 1966, following the Twenty-third Party Congress, the key elements of the new doctrine had yet to be perceived. However, all the objective factors enabling change had been present or foreshadowed since 1964. One must therefore postulate an appropriate catalyst that could explain this timing, and the French decision is the only known development that fits.

31. An estimate of the situation is a method of systematically evaluating a military problem at any level of analysis—politico-military, strategic, operational, or tactical—which leads to making the appropriate plans. The estimate (or "appreciation" in British parlance) embodies an analytical approach universal in application and taught in most staff colleges of the world. The Soviets certainly use this method, and the logic of the estimate underlies their approach to automating operational planning and decisionmaking.

tical doctrine would have highlighted the near-insuperable problems of conducting conventional offensive operations in Europe while under threat of imminent nuclear attack.

By the end of 1966 the Soviets had reformulated their doctrine on the nature of a world war, reversing the 1959 conclusion that such a conflict would inevitably be nuclear and would mean massive nuclear strikes on the Russian homeland. For the first time the objective of *avoiding the nuclear devastation of Russia* might be achievable in a world war. Adopting the objective led to the basic restructuring of Soviet military strategy and the reshaping of their concepts of military operations. The underlying reason for these changes was, however, obscured because many of their effects, particularly in the European theater, could be mistaken as a natural extension of developments since 1963.

The Reformulation of Military Doctrine

There is convincing evidence that the change to less cataclysmic assumptions than those adopted in 1959 was decided during the second half of 1966 and seems likely to have been made formal at the Central Committee Plenum in December 1966. This change did not stem from the Twenty-third Party Congress, which merely reaffirmed established policy. (Appendix A contains detailed evidence about the substance and timing of the reassessment.)

Specific changes in doctrinal assumptions can be inferred from a comparison of successive editions of authoritative works on military doctrine published on either side of that date, and these differences are summarized in table 2-1. Linking the changes is the underlying shift from the fundamental assumption that a world war would inevitably be nuclear and would mean massive strikes against the homelands of the two superpowers to the idea that nuclear escalation was not inevitable, that a world war might be waged with conventional weapons, and that the homelands of the United States and the Soviet Union might be spared nuclear attack.

As already noted, the shift in Soviet assumptions was made possible by the West's adoption of the policy of flexible response in NATO Europe and by the U.S. emphasis on an assured second-strike capability.[32] Flexible response was by far the more significant, and from the Soviet viewpoint,

32. Although NATO did not formally adopt flexible response until May 1967, the concept had been under renewed discussion since mid-1965. Schwartz, *NATO*, pp. 186–87.

Table 2-1. *Soviet Positions on World War, before and after December 1966*

Aspect	Before December 1966	After December 1966
Scope of the war	Inevitably global	. . .
Length of the war	Short and swift moving	. . .
Use of nuclear weapons	Inevitable	Not inevitable
Intercontinental nuclear exchange	Inevitable	Not inevitable
Strategic preemption	Vital	. . .
Simultaneous strategic strikes	The basic method	A method
Victory through traditional operations	Not possible	Possible but slow
Operational-tactical use of nuclear systems	Essential	. . .
Concept of limited war	Invalid	Valid
Protracted limited war	. . .	Possible
Level of casualties	Accept massive	Cause for concern
Mobilization	Forfeits surprise	Important
Reserves and stockpiles	. . .	Important
Shift balance of strength during war	Most unlikely	. . .
Economic potential after war starts	Not important	Important
Experience of World War II	Not relevant	Very relevant
Relevance of local wars	Misleading	Should be studied

Source: See the various extracts from Soviet texts quoted in appendix A.

there were two aspects to this U.S. initiative. First, the policy indicated that if NATO had a choice, the early stages of a war in Europe would be conventional. Second, the debate within NATO that preceded the policy's adoption had certain implications about the U.S. nuclear guarantee of Europe.[33]

Flexible response had been justified on two grounds. One was that mas-

---

33. There were basic disagreements within the alliance over the place of nuclear escalation in NATO plans. The Europeans believed that the credibility of deterrence lay in the readiness to escalate, and NATO must therefore be demonstrably willing to cross the nuclear threshold at an early stage of any engagement. The Americans, particularly Secretary of Defense McNamara, were more sensitive to the dangers of crossing that threshold and sought a conventional capability

sive retaliation was not only an inappropriate response to a range of possible minor incursions by Warsaw Pact forces, but it was also so clearly incommensurate that it had no credibility as a deterrent against coup de main operations or other methods of presenting the West with a fait accompli. The other ground was that a NATO capability to check a Warsaw Pact offensive for several days, first relying on conventional forces and then resorting to theater nuclear weapons, would allow the West time to be certain that it was faced by deliberate aggression and allow the Soviets time to have second thoughts and mend their ways.

Although the U.S. proposal was rationalized in terms of credibility and flexibility, it could also be read as reflecting a reluctance to make good on the nuclear guarantee of Europe, now that the United States was vulnerable to nuclear attack. The French, certainly, interpreted the proposal in that way, and while the Germans were less explicit, they too saw this implication. Even the British expressed doubts about the continued validity of the nuclear guarantee.[34] This impression was reinforced by the concept of assured destruction, which suggested a deeper reluctance to resort to strategic nuclear weapons, except in response to a direct attack on the United States.[35]

The buildup of the Soviet intercontinental missile capability was working in the same direction as the U.S. policies of flexible response and assured destruction. Some 210 SS-7s and SS-8s had been deployed in 1962–64, but the surge in U.S. capability announced by President Kennedy had required the restructuring of Soviet missile programs.[36] The twenty-megaton SS-9 and the one-megaton SS-11 ICBM began to enter service in 1965–66. By the early 1970s, 288 SS-9s and 1,030 SS-11s would be deployed, bringing the numerical force levels of the two sides roughly into balance. The combination of the emerging Soviet capability and the apparent U.S. reluctance to escalate offered the possibility of deterring the United States from initiating an intercontinental exchange in the event of a world war.

---

sufficient to check a conventional Warsaw Pact attack, placing the onus of escalation on Soviet shoulders. To some Europeans flexible response reinforced doubts about the U.S. strategic guarantee, now that Russia could strike directly at America. Schwartz, *NATO*, pp. 176–77.

34. Ibid., pp. 168–71.

35. Andrew Goldberg contributed this insight.

36. Besides the rapid buildup in the number of U.S. missiles, which supplanted the bomber as the primary means of strategic delivery, the basing mode of land-based missiles was shifted from soft launch pads to hardened silos.

However, the problem of NATO Europe remained. The Soviets had always been convinced that, in a world war, they would have to take over Western Europe if they were to avoid ultimate defeat. But the West's defense of NATO was predicated on the use of nuclear weapons. The Soviets did not subscribe to Western theories of escalation ladders and graduated response, and at this period they held to the common-sense view that if war in Europe involved nuclear weapons, it would inevitably lead to an intercontinental exchange. The Soviets also believed that if NATO were facing defeat in Europe, the United States would certainly strike at Russia. Under the assumption that, one way or another, a world war would inevitably mean a massive nuclear attack on Russia, the lesser evil was to focus on achieving strategic preemption. Such was the Soviet mind-set in the middle 1960s and to break it the Soviets had to change three beliefs and recognize one major opportunity.

First, the Soviets had believed that a preemptive nuclear attack against North America would yield some notional advantage, or more precisely, would represent a lesser evil. However, the increase in the size and survivability of the U.S. strategic inventory and the U.S. adoption of assured destruction as a strategic concept meant that even if preemption were achieved, the Soviet Union would sustain an intolerable level of devastation. Thus the idea of a notional advantage or even of a lesser evil became meaningless.

Second, the Soviets had thought that the United States would not hesitate to strike at Russia if American forces in Europe were going down to military defeat. However, the evidence that could be inferred from the concepts of flexible response and the emphasis on an assured second-strike capability argued that a U.S. attack on Russia in such circumstances was considerably less than certain. The Soviets presumed a growing U.S. reluctance to take any action that would provoke a nuclear strike on the continental United States.

Third, the Soviets had assumed that it was inevitable that NATO would resort to the use of theater nuclear weapons in the defense of Europe. However, for five years the United States had been arguing for a basic shift in NATO strategy away from the automatic or even early resort to nuclear weapons in the European theater to a reliance instead on strengthened conventional forces to halt a Soviet attack. Nuclear weapons were to be held in reserve and as a deterrent to Soviet escalation in the theater.

If these three beliefs were no longer valid, then the Soviets were faced with a situation very different from the one predicated by the 1959 doctrinal decision. In these different circumstances, a policy of strategic preemption at the onset of a world war not only was less likely to yield any significant military advantage, but it would also guarantee the nuclear devastation of Russia. Meanwhile if U.S. wishes prevailed within NATO, the use of nuclear weapons in a war in Europe was by no means inevitable. Furthermore, whether or not NATO did resort to the use of nuclear weapons and even if American forces were going down to defeat, the evidence was growing that the United States would be extremely reluctant to initiate an intercontinental exchange.

Not only was this scenario significantly different from the one envisaged by the Soviets in 1959, but the NATO doctrine of flexible response offered them an opportunity that had not existed earlier. NATO was moving to adopt a defense posture in Europe that, even though perhaps not relying exclusively on conventional weapons, would seek to enforce a conventional pause on the battle for Europe before it became necessary to resort to nuclear weapons. If, during this pause, the Soviets could neutralize NATO's theater nuclear forces by nonnuclear means, they would have removed the critical first rung of the ladder of escalation. Alternatively, if the Soviets could knock European NATO out of the war during the pause by using conventional forces only, then the question of escalation might become moot. A combination of both courses of action would increase the chances of taking over Western Europe without precipitating escalation to an intercontinental exchange.

The reshaping of these three beliefs and the opportunity provided by NATO's adoption of flexible response added up to saying that in a world war, an intercontinental nuclear exchange might be avoided by a combination of adopting the appropriate strategy in Europe and changing the role of intercontinental nuclear systems from strategic preemption to nuclear deterrence.

A crucial corollary of this assessment was that, for the first time since the advent of nuclear missiles, it was possible to think realistically of avoiding the nuclear devastation of Russia in a world war and to contemplate making plans and developing strategic concepts based on this critical assumption. Although the avoidance of such devastation had always been highly desirable, it had appeared unachievable and therefore, by the axioms of military planning, it could not serve as a strategic objective. Hence the prevailing strategy became one of preemptive intercontinental strikes should war become inescapable. But it would now be possible to adopt the objective of avoiding the nuclear devastation of Russia, and the Soviets would have to develop new strategic concepts to maximize the chances of achieving that objective.

The Soviets made an important change in their approach to the land battle in Europe; they switched from a passive response to NATO policy to an active policy of their own. Conventional ground force operations had always been in the Soviets' best interests, but before 1964, NATO's policy and posture had ruled out that possibility. The possibility of a conventional phase did emerge in 1964, and during the next three years the Soviets adjusted their operational and tactical doctrine so that if war should start conventionally, they could exploit that favorable development. However, the decision on how long the battle in Europe would remain conventional lay largely with NATO, which always had the option of escalating. After 1966 the Soviets set out to develop a concept of operations that was designed to deny NATO that option or at least degrade it.

The 1966 adjustment in doctrine did not mean that the Soviet Union had concluded that a world war could not or, indeed, was unlikely to escalate to a nuclear exchange. Rather the advantages of avoiding such an exchange were so great that it was worth the considerable cost of restructuring Soviet forces to enable a strategy that would make such avoidance more likely. The Soviets, however, are sensitive to the unpredictability of conflict and how wars take on their own momentum. It seems unlikely that their formal plans have ever assumed that the odds of avoiding an intercontinental exchange were as good as even.

Soviet forces and the Soviet strategy for the contingency of world war have been structured to maximize the chances of avoiding escalation to an intercontinental nuclear exchange. Because there is no certainty that they will be successful in this endeavor, the Soviets must also be prepared for a world war that does mean significant strikes on Russia and America and one in which nuclear weapons are used in some or all theaters. In other words, the new strategy that emerged from the 1967–68 decision period did not replace the previous strategy designed to wage global nuclear war. Both strategies remain in force, with the original one to be resorted to if escalation becomes unavoidable.

The new strategy is the preferred Soviet option in the event of world war and would be followed as long as circumstances allowed, circumstances that would largely depend on Western behavior. If the West appeared unwilling to accept the constraints of this strategy and seemed poised to escalate to nuclear strikes on Russia, then, in theory, the Soviets would revert to their original preemptive strategy for global nuclear war.

In practice the Soviet strategies, rather than abutting, mesh to produce a combined strategy designed to respond to changing circumstances in a world war. Because the two underlying strategies have different hierarchies of objectives, the combination is not a simple continuum. It is therefore misleading to think of escalation as a linear process, a point that is elaborated in chapter 4.

The Soviets' need to plan and train to fight a primarily conventional war, while also being ready for the contingency of nuclear war, means that the evidence of how they intend to wage a world war is contradictory. Although the preferred strategy is conventional, the relative emphasis the Soviets place on that plan, compared with various nuclear strategies, will reflect changing views on the likelihood of escalation or concern that one concept of operations has been neglected at the expense of another.

As a rule it is unwise to impute a preferred Soviet strategy (for example, nuclear) based on the Soviets' military writings or even on their military exercises. The Soviets prepare for the full range of contingencies that may face them. Other evidence must be weighed to identify the strategy they would prefer to follow should a world war become inescapable.

CHAPTER 3

The Restructuring of Soviet Objectives

BEFORE 1966, the Soviets had believed that a world war would inevitably escalate to include nuclear attacks on Russia, but in late 1966 they concluded that nuclear escalation was no longer inevitable. As a logical corollary of the adjustment in doctrine, the Soviets could, for the first time, adopt the objective of *avoiding the nuclear devastation of Russia.*

Because this aim is obviously desirable, there is a tendency to assume that it had always been a Soviet objective, but that is not so. Desirability and achievability are very different matters. Even when the U.S. threat was limited to long-range bombers, the best the Soviets could hope for was to dilute the weight of attack with preemptive strikes and air defenses. Given the U.S. capability and concept of operations, avoiding such an attack was not an option. In the early 1960s, when the main threat shifted from bombers to intercontinental missiles, the Soviets went even further and accepted the idea that massive nuclear strikes on Russia were inevitable, acknowledging this inescapable fact in their doctrinal pronouncements.

In doing so, the Soviets were obeying a universal axiom of military planning, which says that success in war depends on choosing an objective that is optimal in the prevailing circumstances. One should never specify a clearly unachievable objective because the outcome is bound to be less favorable, or more unfavorable, than if one's objective was less ambitious but achievable. Before December 1966 Soviet military doctrine decreed that a world war would be nuclear and would escalate to an intercontinental exchange. By definition, if war was unavoidable, so was the devastation of Russia.

The fact that *avoiding the nuclear devastation of Russia* was a new objective tends to be obscured because developments prior to the 1966 decision merged with those that flowed from that decision. Thus the Soviets' gradual acceptance in the mid-1960s of the likelihood that a world war would start conventionally merged with their progressive adjustment of statements as they worked toward adopting the new hierarchy of objectives. But while it is possible for statements and even operational behavior to change gradually, doctrine about the inevitability of war being nuclear and escalating to an intercontinental exchange can not change gradually. Either escalation is inevitable, or it is not; either there is no chance of avoiding the nuclear devastation of Russia, or there is some chance of doing so. December 1966 was therefore a true watershed.

It is, however, one thing to note that the Soviets were in a position to adopt the new objective and quite another to claim that they did so. Even if it is accepted that the Soviets did adopt the new objective, it is not intuitively obvious that they would then fundamentally reshape their defense policy. To demonstrate that the new objective had far-reaching implications for defense policy, one must reconstruct the Soviet hierarchy of objectives as it would have existed before December 1966 and then analyze the effects of introducing the new objective. This analysis will show that a revised hierarchy of objectives is fully compatible with the evidence of the changed operational concepts and force structure that now prevail, but the pre-1967 hierarchy is not.

The Hierarchy of Strategic Objectives—The 1960s

To reconstruct a hierarchy of objectives, one must start at the top. On the basis of what the Soviets have said and done during the past sixty-five years, it is possible to infer the implicit overarching objective that guides Soviet leaders in their conduct of national affairs. Inevitably, an objective of this type is expressed somewhat generally but is nonetheless a powerful influence on national action. The Soviets' overarching objective is *to promote the long-term well-being of the Soviet state*. The term state rather than people reflects the idea that the welfare of the people stems from the well-being of the state. It has important implications for decisions concerning war and peace.

Three first-order objectives that are both necessary and sufficient directly support the overarching national objective. They are equally important, but an inherent tension among them will at times cause them to come into conflict with each other. The Soviet Union's first-order objectives are to ensure the retention of power by the Communist party; retain independence of action in the international arena; and avoid world war.

The three objectives are implicit in Soviet pronouncements, but their identification also derives from the internal logic of the Soviet situation. *Retention of power by the Communist party* is, by definition, essential to the well-being of the Soviet state. This core dogma of Marxism-Leninism serves the interests of those who hold power in the Soviet Union, so there can be little argument about it being a first-order objective.

Preserving the capacity for independent action underlies the concept of national sovereignty. It provides the rationale for investing in a military capability, something to which the Soviets accord a high value. *Promoting the long-term well-being of the state* would be difficult if, through intimidation or military defeat, the Soviet Union lost its capacity for independent action.

Avoiding world war also qualifies as a first-order objective although the reasons for its ranking may not be immediately apparent. A moment's reflection will justify its place. The Soviets believe in historical inevitability and declare that socialism is the wave of the future. Nuclear war is one of the few developments capable of derailing or seriously retarding the inexorable progress to a socialist world. Marxism-Leninism decrees that war is only to be seen as an instrument of policy if victory is virtually ensured and if the certain benefits greatly outweigh the possible costs; neither of these criteria can be met by world war. The Soviets are also very conscious of the disruptive effects of war on the party's control of the populace. The harrowing experience of the last seventy years, with 20 million Russian dead and a devastated homeland from World War II, not to mention the carnage of World War I and the civil war that followed, haunts the Soviet leaders.

Other clearly desirable objectives such as raising the Soviet standard of living or improving the efficiency of the Soviet economy do not rank in the first order. Although raising the standard of living might help the Communist party retain power, it could make war more likely by diverting resources from defense, and it might limit independence of international action because of the need for imports to meet raised expectations. Similarly, making the economy more efficient would probably require greater reliance on Western technology and include organizational changes that would undermine the power of the Communist party. Thus the pursuit of these domestic objectives is constrained by the need to avoid undermining the three first-order objectives.

In the same way, increasing the socialist system's share of world influence is not a first-order objective. In the first flush of postrevolutionary fervor there was talk of spreading socialism on the points of Red Army bayonets, but that was sixty-five years ago, and the failure of the Polish campaign in 1920 put a stop to that idea. Since those early days, the evidence is clear that increasing the Soviet Union's international influence is not a first-order objective. It has invariably yielded precedence to the objective of avoiding world war, and no evidence suggests any change in the foreseeable future. Of course, an increase in Soviet world influence can work in support of the other two first-order objectives, but it remains subordinate to all three.

The primary tension among the three first-order objectives is between avoiding world war and preserving the capacity for independent action, since the second aim could itself lead to war. World war is therefore a continuing possibility, and should it be inescapable, the objective must be *not to lose*. If the Soviet Union were to lose such a war, not only would it lose independence of international action, but the Communist party would also be removed from power, meaning a failure to sustain all three first-order objectives and hence the overarching national objective. Not losing is a minimum objective and, of course, if the Soviets could "win," "prevail," or "achieve victory" in some way, they would prefer such an outcome. But in a world war, it is difficult to specify exactly what those terms imply, and the objective of not losing is sufficient as well as necessary.

In this analysis, the top three levels of national objectives are, therefore, to promote the well-being of the Soviet state, to avoid world war, and if war cannot be avoided, do not lose (figure 3-1).

This series leads to the specialized hierarchy of Soviet strategic objectives that apply to the contingency of a world war, at whose apex is the objective of not losing the war. The higher-order national objectives continue to influence the selection of consequential policies and supporting objectives. For example, avoiding war has precedence over not losing. This aim rules out a resort to preventive war, and it also constrains the pressure to preempt if war seems near.

The supporting objectives that must be achieved in order not to lose a world war depend on the nature of such a war. In the doctrinal statement that flowed from the reassessment at the end of the 1950s, the Soviets were specific. A world war would be short, swift moving, and global (that is, intercontinental) in scope. It would mean nuclear strikes on the home territories of the two superpowers and the use of nuclear weapons in the con-

Figure 3-1. *The Hierarchy of National Objectives*

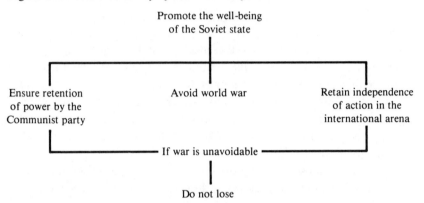

tinental theaters. Massive casualties and physical destruction would occur. Although this clear-cut description was shaded in the 1964–66 period by allowing for the possibility of a conventional phase at the start of a world war and by considering restraint on the use of nuclear weapons in some regions, the key assumptions were not affected. Both Russia and America would be devastated and, although hostilities might drag on, the outcome of the war would be decided by the initial nuclear exchanges.

The political nature of a world war would be as important as its physical features. A world war would represent the decisive clash between the capitalist and socialist systems, and the victor would destroy the vanquished.[1] In other words, a world war would be a fight to the finish in which defeat would be synonymous with extinction. Two primary objectives were implicit in this definition, which had to be achieved if the Soviets were not to lose such a war. Each primary objective has a set of supporting objectives.

The primary objective of *preserving the socialist system* would be supported by the objectives of protecting the physical structure of government and securing its capacity for effective operation throughout the Soviet state; ensuring the survival of a certain proportion of the nation's industrial base and working population; and securing an alternative base to contribute to the rebuilding of a socialist society in Russia. The primary objective

1. See Peter H. Vigor, *The Soviet View of War, Peace, and Neutrality* (London: Routledge and Keagan Paul, 1975), pp. 39, 121–126; and Robert L. Arnett, "Soviet Attitudes toward Nuclear War: Do They Really Think That They Can Win?" *Journal of Strategic Studies,* vol. 2 (September 1979), pp. 175–77.

of *destroying the capitalist system* would be supported by the objectives of destroying enemy forces in being, destroying the system's war-making potential, and destroying the system's structure of governmental and social control.

The three supporting objectives that had to be achieved to destroy the capitalist system were spelled out in Soviet military publications of this period.[2] The three supporting objectives needed to preserve the socialist system were not specified as clearly, but they were implicit in Soviet behavior during this period. For example, an antiballistic-missile system was built around Moscow, the center of government, rather than located to protect ICBM fields as was the U.S. preference.[3] A major reorganization of civil defense occurred in mid-1961. The Soviets instituted a nationwide system with central headquarters within the Ministry of Defense, headed by Marshal Vasily Chuikov who at that time was commander in chief of the ground forces.

Evidence of the objective of securing an alternative economic base that would help preserve the socialist system was circumstantial and could be inferred from the Soviet concept of operations in Europe. Given the requirement to destroy the capitalist system, one would expect the Soviets to have planned to destroy NATO Europe in the same way that they clearly planned to destroy North America—with massive nuclear strikes. Yet Soviet ground forces were postured for a rapid offensive into Western Europe, breaking through to the enemy's rear with projected rates of advance of over sixty miles a day and airborne operations reaching from one hundred to two hundred miles behind the lines. The concept of operations was clearly designed to seize and hold territory rather than devastate the region, and the accepted use at that period of chemical weapons as an alternative to nuclear ones meant that physical destruction could be limited in key areas.[4]

2. For example, Marshal V.D. Sokolovskiy, ed. *Voennaya strategiya,* 2d ed. (Military strategy) (Moscow: Voenizdat, 1963), p. 380.

3. The Soviets began construction of the Galosh antiballistic-missile system around Moscow in 1964, and all four complexes had been installed by 1968. Robert P. Berman and John C. Baker, *Soviet Strategic Forces: Requirements and Responses* (Brookings, 1982), p. 148.

4. See Professor J. Erickson, "The Soviet Concept of the Land Battle," in *The Soviet Union in Europe and the Near East: Her Capabilities and Intentions* (London: Royal United Service Institution, 1970), pp. 28–30, and *Soviet Military Power* (London: Royal United Services Institute for Defence Studies, 1971), pp. 66–67, 72. Erickson noted that the Soviets talked of nuclear or chemical warheads, both of them being classified as weapons of mass destruction. Information dated to 1960–61 makes it clear that the Soviets planned to use chemical weapons at that period in the event of a world war. See Oleg Penkovskiy, *The Penkovskiy Papers* (Doubleday, 1965), pp. 249–50.

This plan implied that the Soviets wanted to make use of NATO Europe in some way. Obviously, they intended to exploit its economic resources to replace those lost to Russia in the intercontinental exchange, a concept that reflected their approach to Germany at the end of World War II.[5] This conclusion also provides the only satisfactory explanation for the Soviet navy's shift to forward deployment in the first half of the 1960s. The primary objectives of destroying the capitalist system and preserving the socialist system, with their supporting objectives, formed the core of the 1960s hierarchy of objectives.

The Shift in Strategic Objectives–The 1970s

In 1966 the Soviets concluded that nuclear strikes on Russia were no longer inevitable in the event of world war. However, they could not pursue the logical corollary and fully adopt the objective of avoiding the nuclear devastation of Russia until they had reshaped their policies and restructured their forces. In other words, their immediate decision would have been to work toward adopting the objective of avoiding the nuclear devastation of Russia.

It seems likely that the Soviets set a target date of 1975–76 for the full adoption of a new hierarchy of objectives for military operations. The date can be inferred from changes in Soviet force structure and the entry into full operational service of weapons systems that had been designed specifically for the new strategic and operational concepts. In May 1974 the chief of the General Staff noted that the Soviet armed forces had "entered upon a new stage of their qualitative development.[6] In 1975 the preparation of a new textbook on military strategy was completed, containing "new views on the nature and methods of waging war, and also of strategic actions of the branches of the Armed Forces."[7] In 1976 evidence appeared

5. For a Soviet reference to the intention of preserving NATO Europe, see Colonel M. Shirokov, "Voennaya geographiya na sovremennom etape" (Military geography at the contemporary stage), *Voennaya mysl'* (Military thought), no. 11 (November 1966), p. 49, last para.

6. In an article in *Krasnaya zvezda* (Red star) on May 9, 1974, Army General V. Kulikov, chief of the Soviet General Staff, claimed that the Soviet armed forces had "entered upon a new stage of their qualitative development" and that the increase in mobility, striking power, and fire power meant the Soviets were now "abreast contemporary requirements." "The Invincible Force of Socialism," in Foreign Broadcast Information Service, *Daily Report: Soviet Union,* May 10, 1974, p. A2. (Hereafter FBIS, *Daily Report: SU.*)

7. V.G. Kulikov, ed., *Akademiya General' nogo Shtaba* (The General Staff Academy) (Moscow: Voenizdat, 1976), p. 205.

that the Soviets were prepared to renounce the need for superiority in strategic nuclear systems and to forgo first use of nuclear weapons. Both these changes were logical corollaries of a new hierarchy of objectives.

However, in nonoperational areas such as negotiations over arms control, the new objectives could begin to shape policy as soon as the politico-military leadership had worked out the implications. With hindsight one can see the new hierarchy begin to take effect in the late 1960s. In other words, the move from one hierarchy to the other was incremental, although the major shift involving the application of new strategic and operational concepts did not take place until 1975–76. Thus it is convenient to talk of the old 1960s hierarchy of objectives and of a new hierarchy that took effect in the 1970s.[8]

The 1967–75 period was a time of transition for strategic and operational concepts. For three to five years after the critical decision in December 1966 the 1960s objectives would have been in force, as would the 1960s concepts of operation and the policies for preemption and nuclear release. The final shift to the new set of objectives would only have taken place toward the end of the period, although from 1972 to 1975 there could have been incremental adjustments. This process was confusing, and interpreting the evidence is further complicated because the Soviets might have been discussing, or conducting military exercises for, a contingency in the immediate, near, or distant future, each of which would evoke a different response.

Thus considerable care is required when drawing inferences from pronouncements made in the 1967–75 period. Equally important, pronouncements before the December 1966 watershed can not be adduced as evidence when analyzing Soviet policy in the years after the watershed.

The 1960s and 1970s hierarchies of strategic objectives stem from the same national objectives. At the apex of both hierarchies is the military objective of not losing the war. Each hierarchy has two primary objectives in support of not losing the war, one designed to protect the socialist system and the other designed to defeat the capitalist one. The 1960s and 1970s primary objectives are different from each other because they relate to different circumstances. The 1960s hierarchy was designed to make the best of a situation in which nuclear attacks on the Soviet homeland and an

8. These labels reflect the periodization adopted for the first time in a 1985 publication by Marshal Nikolay V. Ogarkov, chief of the General Staff. See N.V. Ogarkov, *Istoriya uchit bditel' nosti* (History teaches vigilance) (Moscow: Voenizdat, 1985), p. 51, cited by Mary C. Fitzgerald in "Marshal Ogarkov on Modern War: 1971–85," paper prepared for the Center for Naval Analyses of the Hudson Institute.

intercontinental nuclear exchange were considered inevitable; the 1970s hierarchy was designed for a situation in which such nuclear warfare might be avoided.

Once the Soviets believed it possible to avoid a nuclear exchange it became necessary for them to adopt that aim as a primary objective. To promote the well-being of the Soviet state, the Soviets would adopt the aim as long as it did not risk losing the war. Within that constraint the new objective would be most precisely expressed as avoiding the nuclear devastation of Russia. This formulation does not exclude the possibility of nuclear weapons being used elsewhere in the course of a war and recognizes that it might be necessary to absorb limited nuclear strikes on Russia rather than escalate automatically. The formulation also serves as an umbrella objective, permitting a variety of supporting military strategies.

The more demanding objective of avoiding the nuclear devastation of Russia replaced the 1960s aim of preserving the socialist system as one of the two primary objectives in the strategic hierarchy. As a logical corollary, the Soviets would have to refrain from launching nuclear attacks on the United States since this would invite retaliatory strikes on Russia. But if the bastion of capitalism was to be spared, then the 1960s primary objective of destroying the capitalist system was no longer achievable. Therefore, the Soviets had to replace it with a less radical objective such as *gravely weakening the capitalist system.*

Because of the decision that it was no longer inevitable that a world war would mean a nuclear exchange, the Soviet Union's primary strategic objectives underwent basic change. In the 1960s the objectives of preserving the socialist system and destroying the capitalist system were equally important, but in the 1970s hierarchy these two primary objectives were not equal. As a result, *avoiding the nuclear devastation of Russia* became the governing objective in the strategic hierarchy, constrained only by the need *not to lose the war.*

The fundamental change in primary objectives would also have necessitated a shift in doctrine concerning the political nature of a world war. As long as a nuclear exchange was seen as inevitable, such a war was defined as a decisive encounter between two social systems. But this definition could not apply to a war in which the governing objective would be to avoid the nuclear devastation of Russia, the price for which was sparing North America. Such a war could be described more accurately as a critical campaign in the ongoing struggle between the two social systems (table 3-1).

Table 3-1. *Soviet Doctrine on the Nature of World War*

Aspect	The 1960s	The 1970s
	Nature of world war	
Military	Inevitably nuclear, including nuclear strikes on Russia.	May not be nuclear. Strikes on Russia are not inevitable.
Political	A fight to the finish between two social systems.	A critical campaign in the ongoing struggle between the two systems.
	Primary military objectives	
Own survival	Preserve the socialist system.	Avoid the nuclear devastation of Russia.
Enemy's defeat	Destroy the capitalist system.	Gravely weaken the capitalist system.

The logic of the change in objectives is clear, but does the evidence support these deductions? This study will show that major shifts in the Soviet Union's force structure and operational concepts can be related to change in its hierarchies of objectives. Further evidence reflects the fact that strategic objectives in a war and how that war is fought are inextricably bound together. While the Soviets made no public announcements of new wartime objectives, they did alter their descriptions of how a future war would be fought.

Because the Soviets still had to allow for the contingency of a nuclear exchange as well as the preferred strategy of avoiding escalation, statements after the December 1966 decision were ambivalent about nuclear war, and the omission of certain earlier assertions was most significant. There was a clear change in the Soviet position about the importance of mobilization, of reserves and stockpiles, and of the country's economic potential once war was engaged. There was also a change regarding the relevance of the experience of World War II and the lessons of local wars. These positive changes only made sense in terms of a war in which escalation to an intercontinental exchange was avoided.

Besides these changes related to a world war's physical nature, there was also a change concerning its political nature. Before 1967, Soviet doctrine had asserted that a world war would be the decisive encounter between the two social systems. It would mean massive devastation on both sides; the capitalist system would collapse and be destroyed, and the socialist system would survive. Such a war could be characterized as a fight to the finish between two social systems. But starting in the early 1970s, Soviet writing began to suggest that a world war did not have to be waged for such fundamental ends, and after 1972 there was a sharp decline in references to "victory," which had previously been routine in discussing wartime objectives.[9] If the ends were to be less than fundamental, then so must the means, which implied that the Soviets had moved away from the cataclysmic primary objectives of the 1960s strategic hierarchy. The change in ultimate aims also implied changes in the supporting objectives of the 1970s hierarchy.

How were the Soviets to avoid the nuclear devastation of Russia given that there was no effective means within sight of preventing ballistic missiles from striking Russia, once they had been launched? Two approaches were possible. One focused on averting the type of military situation that would precipitate escalation to an intercontinental exchange, and the other focused on deterring the West from striking at Russia.

The situation most likely to lead to intercontinental escalation was the land battle in Europe, which would be a central feature of any world war. Averting escalation in the European theater would require active steps to hamper NATO's resort to nuclear weapons in the theater. The best way to deter nuclear strikes on Russia was to pose a credible threat of massive retaliation against North America. The Soviets already had the necessary missiles to pose such a threat, and the inventory of warheads would steadily increase in the years ahead. But could they be certain that the United States would not make some technological breakthrough that would render the fixed-silo systems impotent? To cover against this contingency, the Soviets had to take active steps to ensure against technological outflanking.

How were the Soviets to gravely weaken the capitalist system given that nuclear strikes on North America were ruled out? The most practical way would be to dismember it, bringing Europe and Japan within the Soviet orbit and isolating the United States in the Western Hemisphere. This would require the defeat of NATO's ground-air forces, as part of the process of establishing control of Europe. Thereafter, steps would have to be taken to deny the United States access to the Eurasian continent, with particular emphasis on the part lying to the west of the Central Siberian Plateau. Meanwhile in East Asia, the Soviet Union would, if possible, establish hegemony over Japan and South Korea.

9. Vigor, *Soviet View,* p. 39; and Raymond L. Garthoff, *Détente and Confrontation: American-Soviet Relations from Nixon to Reagan* (Brookings, 1985), p. 780.

Table 3-2. *A Comparison of the 1960s and 1970s Strategic Hierarchies*

The 1960s hierarchy	The 1970s hierarchy
Objectives	
Preserve the socialist system.	Avoid the nuclear devastation of Russia.
Protect the physical structure of government and secure its capacity for effective operation throughout the Soviet state.	Hamper NATO's resort to nuclear weapons.
Guarantee the survival of a proportion of the nation's industrial base and working population.	Deter nuclear strikes on Russia.
Secure an alternative economic base to contribute to the rebuilding of a socialist society in Russia.	Insure against the fixed-silo deterrent being rendered impotent.
Destroy the capitalist system.	Gravely weaken the capitalist system.
Destroy enemy forces in being.	Establish physical control of Europe.
Destroy the system's war-making potential.	Deny America access to the western parts of Eurasia.
Destroy the system's structure of governmental and social control.	Establish hegemony over Japan and South Korea.
Type of war	
Short, all-out nuclear war, including intercontinental nuclear exchange.	Two-phase war; no intercontinental exchange I- Short, high-intensity offensive operations in Europe, preferably nonnuclear II- Long-drawn-out, primarily defensive; course unpredictable.

To compare the hierarchies is not to suggest that the 1970s one replaced the 1960s one (table 3-2). The new strategic concepts that took effect in the 1970s did not replace the previous strategy designed to wage global nuclear war, but meshed with it to produce a flexible strategy designed to respond to changing circumstances. The Soviets would prefer to remain within the 1970s hierarchy of objectives, but they are prepared for the full range of contingencies, including nuclear war limited to the theater and the full-scale global nuclear war.

Implications of the Shift in Strategic Objectives

The implications that are discussed at this stage of the study can help one to understand Soviet planning for the contingency of world war and Soviet concepts of operation in such a war. Some of the changes resulting from the shift are also implicit in the various Soviet statements indicating that an important doctrinal decision had been made at the end of 1966. Concrete evidence of this kind of change can be found if one knows what to look for. But other changes in key strategic concepts are logically implied, for which evidence is unlikely to be available or else very hard to discern because of its nature. However, although these doctrinal changes can only be hypothesized, the hypotheses provide a more valid basis for Western planning than relying on pre-1967 evidence or assuming that the Soviets mirror-image Western concepts.

The Nature of a World War

As already discussed, two very different kinds of war underlie the different objectives hierarchies, but two implications of the change in objectives were particularly far reaching in their effects. One, which had the broadest consequences in terms of force structure, concerned the operational concept for the land battle in Europe. The other, which had the broadest consequences for grand strategy, concerned the likely duration of a war fought in these changed conditions.

In the 1960s it was assumed that a world war would mean massive nuclear strikes on the home territories of the two superpowers, and once war escalated to an intercontinental exchange, the conflict would most probably be short and violent.

In the 1970s if the Soviets were successful in avoiding an intercontinental exchange, there would be no inherent limit to the duration of a world war because both the Russian and the American industrial bases would remain intact. For planning purposes, such a war had to be seen as comprising two distinct phases. The focus of the first phase would be the ground and air battle in Europe, in which the Soviets would hope to defeat NATO on land by using conventional weapons only and rid themselves of the U.S. military presence on the continent. That achieved, the Soviets would suggest peace talks, in the faint hope that America might agree, but they would have to assume that the conflict would move on to a long-drawn-out second phase. Evidence that the Soviets think in these terms can be found in the articles by the commander in chief of the Soviet navy that were published in 1972–73.[10]

In the second phase of a world war, the circumstances of both sides would be approximately that of the United States in World War II. A major problem facing the Soviets would be how to prevent the United States and its allies from regaining a foothold on the western half of the Eurasian continent. If the United States were to achieve a foothold it would then be able to build up its forces until they could roll back the socialist system and secure its ultimate defeat. Denying the United States access to the Continent would therefore be a strategic imperative and would mean establishing a defense perimeter taking in Europe, Southwest Asia, and the northern part of Africa. The need to carry the war to the enemy by denying the United States access to raw materials from outside the Western Hemisphere was more debatable.

Deterrence

In the 1950s and 1960s, deterrence of a premeditated attack on the Soviet Union had depended on the capacity to absorb such an attack and then go on to fight and win the subsequent war. This capability also served to make the West more sensitive to the dangers of accidental world war, a sensitivity that increased as the Soviets developed the capability to strike directly at North America.

This type of generalized deterrence persisted in the 1970s, but the objective of avoiding the nuclear devastation of Russia generated a new and far more demanding requirement for full-scale deterrence during the course of a global war. The West now had to be deterred from attacking Russia with nuclear weapons even when faced by the impending defeat of NATO forces in Europe. This requirement, combined with the new constraints on preemption, would have heightened the Soviets' concern about the survivability of their ICBM force in face of a disarming strike, the effectiveness of command and control, and the dangers of their deterrent forces being rendered impotent (technologically outflanked) by the United States.

10. See chapter 5 and appendix C.

Intercontinental Nuclear Preemption

As long as escalation to an intercontinental exchange was inevitable, the destructive capacity of nuclear weapons placed a premium on getting in the first blow, particularly against the primary opponent. A successful preemptive strike against the United States would serve the objective of *destroying the capitalist system* while also working to *ensure the survival of the socialist system* by diminishing the weight to the U.S. strategic attack on Russia. In the 1960s the military arguments for nuclear preemption were therefore very high. On the other hand, the first-order objective of avoiding world war placed considerable constraints on the military urge to preempt. Nevertheless, military-technical doctrine in the 1960s was premised on intercontinental preemption. [11]

In the 1970s the pressure against intercontinental nuclear preemption would have been strong because the objectives of avoiding world war and avoiding the nuclear devastation of Russia both argued against preemption. In these circumstances the Soviets would need a second-strike capability. They would have to be able to launch on warning but would also need to be able to ride out a surprise attack. The pressure against nuclear preemption at the theater level would also be strong because of the inherent danger of escalation, particularly if it were the Soviets who initiated the use of nuclear weapons.

In terms of evidence, this pressure implies that prior to 1967, one would expect the Soviets to emphasize, either openly or in euphemisms, the vital advantage of nuclear preemption at the strategic and theater level, as indeed they did. From 1967 onward one would expect to see a progressive shading of this emphasis until some time in the mid-1970s when it might be dropped altogether, [12] which would indicate that the Soviets felt the restructuring of their forces had placed them in a position to adopt the new objective of avoiding nuclear strikes on Russia. That would mean they no longer considered nuclear preemption a realistic option.

Of course the Soviets were not excluding the use of conventional means to destroy NATO's nuclear capability. As noted, conventional attacks are

11. For a discussion of Soviet views on preemption in the 1950s, see Raymond L. Garthoff, "BMD and East-West Relations," in Ashton B. Carter and David N. Schwartz, eds., *Ballistic Missile Defense* (Brookings, 1984), p. 290.

12. Starting in 1969 (with one important precursor in 1967), Soviet pronouncements indicated a shift from a policy of preemption to one of launch on warning. Raymond L. Garthoff, "Mutual Deterrence and Strategic Arms Limitation in Soviet Policy," *International Security,* vol. 3 (Summer 1978), pp. 129–32.

a central feature of the 1970s Soviet concept of operations, and the evidence of this emerging capability was among the developments that sounded the alert that something had changed. The possibility remained that any conflict might escalate to theater nuclear war and then to an intercontinental exchange. But the emphasis in Soviet pronouncements was on the danger of being surprised by the West's resort to nuclear weapons rather than on the advantage of achieving surprise by initiating the use of nuclear weapons.[13]

Strategic Superiority

If a world war was to be a fight to the finish between two social systems, with massive nuclear strikes on each other's territory, then the side that started off with an advantage in nuclear delivery systems was likely to have some left when the other's had run out. The requirement for superiority was also a logical corollary of a strategy premised on intercontinental preemption, since it would be necessary to destroy all the enemy's strategic delivery systems and have other weapons with which to attack administrative, economic, and remaining military targets. Of course superiority did not have to be numerical, and in the 1950s the Soviets apparently intended to achieve such superiority through the use of large warheads and a policy of area devastation. When, however, the United States deployed the Minuteman ICBMs in hardened silos in the Middle West, remote from centers of population, a requirement for numerical superiority emerged. Until the Soviets realized that they could achieve comparable results by striking at the Minuteman launch-control centers (there was one for every ten launchers), they had to plan to target each Minuteman silo with at least one missile. But whatever the means of achieving it, the doctrinal requirement for superiority was never in doubt, and the Soviets regularly insisted that they needed nothing less than qualitative superiority over their true enemies.

The new strategic premise of deterring U.S. nuclear strikes on Russia had different implications. The shift from a strategy of intercontinental preemption to one of launching on warning of a U.S. attack meant that a large proportion of the original target set would cease to have military significance, since the birds would already have flown. Superiority was therefore no longer a logical corollary, and the sizing of the strategic nuclear forces would reflect other criteria. Nor was superiority implicit in the

13. See, for example, Marshal V.D. Sokolovskiy, ed., *Voennaya strategiya*, 3d ed., 1968, p. 390; and the analysis in appendix A.

definition of a world war as a critical campaign in the ongoing struggle. After the Twenty-fifth Party Congress in February–March 1976, reference to the doctrinal requirement to maintain "qualitative superiority over the armies of our true enemies" all but disappeared from Soviet public pronouncements. In his Tula speech in January 1977, Leonid Brezhnev formally denied it was Soviet policy to seek such superiority "with the aim of delivering a first strike."[14]

Nuclear Release

An implication of the 1959 doctrine was that a decision that world war was unavoidable would have been synonymous, at least in theory, with the decision to launch preemptive nuclear strikes against North America and against strategic targets in the theaters adjacent to the Soviet Union. A corollary was that the release of nuclear weapons at the strategic level automatically meant their release at the theater level, and the actual orchestration of nuclear strikes could logically be left to the military.

The political leaders would have determined the scope for diplomatic maneuver and whether certain enemies should be spared nuclear attack. Apart from that, decisions on the use or nonuse of nuclear weapons on land or sea would be made by the military on operational grounds. The sole constraint would be the need to preserve certain areas to serve as socioeconomic bases for the rebuilding of the devastated socialist economies.

The simple dichotomy between military and political decisionmaking may have begun to blur after 1964 as the Soviets came to acknowledge that the use of nuclear weapons might be limited in scale and geographic scope and that war might start with a conventional phase.[15] Nevertheless, the idea that theater nuclear weapons would be used as a matter of course at the discretion of the army high command prevailed throughout most of the 1960s.

In the 1970s the concern to avoid the nuclear devastation of Russia, and

14. William V. Gardner, *Soviet Threat Perceptions of NATO's Eurostrategic Missiles* (Paris: Atlantic Institute for International Affairs, 1983), p. 72. For a wider discussion of the shift in Soviet military doctrine about the need for superiority, see Garthoff, *Détente and Confrontation*, pp. 76–85, and "Leonid Brezhnev's Speech in Tula," FBIS, *Daily Report: SU*, January 18, 1977, p. R9. Brezhnev's denial is limited by implication to intercontinental nuclear systems. The "Tula line" was duly repeated in statements by other members of the party and military leadership.

15. See N.Ya. Sushko and T.R. Kondratkov, eds., *Metodologicheskie problemy voennoy teorii i praktiki*, 1st ed. (Methodological problems of military theory and practice) (Moscow: Voenizdat, 1966), pp. 107–08.

the possibility that any use of nuclear weapons might inadvertently escalate to an intercontinental exchange, meant that the question of nuclear release became increasingly critical. The concern did not imply that nuclear weapons would not be used at the theater level. Rather authority for nuclear release would be held tightly by the political leadership, and decisions on use would be made on a case-by-case basis. A Soviet book that analyzes the factors considered decisive in a nuclear war notes, "The decision to employ . . . nuclear weapons has become the exclusive prerogative of the political leadership. It is primarily the political, not the military leaders, who determine the necessity of employing weapons of mass destruction, who specify the principal targets and when they are to be hit."[16] The dangers of escalation would be balanced against the immediate operational advantages of resorting to nuclear weapons. Perceptions of this balance will continually evolve.

Arguments against initiating the use of nuclear weapons in most mediums and theaters would be strong and would extend to forgoing the option of preemption. But in many cases an even stronger argument might be made for responding in kind to any Western use of nuclear weapons.[17] The Soviets would carefully choose the type of target and level of response to match the particular circumstances. In some cases, response might mean a straight tit-for-tat; if possible, the Soviet action would have equivalent target symbolism but more damage to the enemy's military operations. In other cases, particularly in the land battle, the response might mean a sharp increase in scale, designed both to cauterize the trend to nuclear escalation and to reap specific benefits of nuclear use.

It seems likely that the range of possible Soviet responses would be planned ahead of time in detail, including the designation of the type of target and the weapons to be used in various circumstances. The promptness and appropriateness of response would therefore be ensured, but release of nuclear weapons would be a political decision made at the very top, since it would directly involve the governing objective of avoiding the nuclear devastation of Russia.

16. Colonel M.P. Skirdo, *The People, the Army, the Commander: A Soviet View* (Moscow: Voenizdat, 1970), p. 97, translated by the Ottawa, Canada, Secretary of State Department, Translation Bureau, and published by the U.S. Government Printing Office.

17. Some Soviets would argue in favor of a nuclear response out of concern that a failure to respond might foster the impression that the Soviet Union was intimidated, thus encouraging America to strike at more important targets. Others might argue for the use of nuclear weapons to strike at certain U.S. targets because of a desire to profit from such opportunities without risking immediate escalation to a full-scale attack on Russia.

If, however, the Soviet leaders were to conclude at some stage of a war that there was no longer any chance of achieving that objective because escalation to a full intercontinental exchange had become inevitable, then Soviet policy would revert to the 1960s mode. In theory, that would require them to seek to gain the advantage of getting in the first strike against North America. In practice, this is unlikely to be seen as a realistic option. The priority of avoiding escalation would militate against adopting the appropriate operational posture, and, even if that were not so, the chance of successful preemption in such circumstances would be extremely low, even negligible.

These multiple requirements would require extremely effective command, control, and communications, and the architecture for a considerably improved system began to appear in the early 1970s.

Limited War and No First Use

Before 1967, the possibility of any kind of limited war was generally denigrated by the Soviets, while the emphasis on a strategy of preemption implied the Soviets would be the first to resort to nuclear weapons.

The 1970s hierarchy of objectives required that the Soviet Union take active steps to keep a future war limited, and diplomatic measures were those immediately available to further this aim. In December 1970 members of the Soviet delegation at the strategic arms limitation talks took informal soundings about the possibility of a mutual agreement not to be the first to resort to nuclear weapons.[18] In April 1972 Brezhnev proposed a treaty that would have the superpowers renounce the use of nuclear weapons against each other. In effect the superpowers would be agreeing to treat each other's territory as sanctuary in the event of war.[19] But even if the Soviets could have concluded such agreements, there was no certainty that they would hold in war. The Soviets' main requirement had to be avoiding escalation in Europe.

By the mid-1970s the Soviets had a two-pronged military strategy, designed to defeat NATO forces in Europe while inhibiting the resort to

18. The Soviets were warned by their U.S. counterparts that such a proposal would be rejected if broached formally. Garthoff, *Détente and Confrontation*, p. 182.

19. Henry Kissinger deflected these proposals into what he saw as the innocuous "Agreement on the Prevention of Nuclear War," signed in June 1973 at the Washington summit. According to Kissinger, the agreement transformed "the original Soviet proposal of an unconditional renunciation of the use of nuclear weapons against each other into a somewhat banal statement that our objective was peace." Henry Kissinger, *Years of Upheaval* (Little, Brown, 1982), pp. 275–86.

nuclear weapons in the theater. To implement this strategy the Soviets depended mainly on the new concept of operations, which their new conventional capability enabled. They also made politico-military statements to promote the same results. They ridiculed the idea that NATO could resort to nuclear weapons without precipitating an international exchange, and one would expect their observable military exercises to reinforce this idea.[20] The Soviets also pressed for a mutual agreement on the no first use of nuclear weapons, and, finally, Brezhnev made a unilateral pledge that the Soviet Union would not be the first to resort to nuclear weapons.[21]

As the earlier discussion on preemption made clear, the Soviets have good reasons not to initiate the use of nuclear weapons in the European theater, and there is every reason to assume that Brezhnev's declaration of no first use was as genuine as such a pledge can be. Equally important, the Soviets are correct in pointing to the probability that a nuclear war in Europe would escalate to an intercontinental exchange. They also intended their pronouncements to bolster NATO's self-imposed constraints on initiating the use of nuclear weapons.

Weapons Procurement

The 1966 decision clearly caused changes in the structure of naval and ground and air forces, and evidence of that first alerted the West to the change in objectives. A review of the implications of the new objectives across all five branches of service will lead to a better understanding of Soviet procurement policy throughout the 1970s.

GROUND FORCES. The Soviets had to reshape the ground and air forces facing NATO. They would have to be able to launch a massive German-style conventional blitzkrieg at the onset of war while carrying out simultaneous conventional attacks against theater nuclear facilities. To carry out preventive attacks, deep in the enemy rear, they also needed a kind of aircraft different from those in service. Breaking through NATO defenses

20. See A.S. Zheltov, T.R. Kondratkov, and E.A. Khomenko, eds., *Metodologicheskie problemy voennoy teorii i praktiki,* 2d ed. (Methodological problems of military theory and practice) (Moscow: Voenizdat, 1969), p. 326.

21. This no-first-use proposal was initially made publicly at the meeting of the Warsaw Pact Consultation Committee in Bucharest, October–November 1976. See also "Leonid Brezhnev's Speech in Tula," FBIS, *Daily Report: SU.* In June 1982 at the United Nations Second Special Session on Disarmament, Brezhnev announced a unilateral Soviet commitment not to use nuclear weapons first, and the declaration appeared in *Pravda* on June 16. Dmitriy F. Ustinov, minister of defense, subsequently repeated the pledge. Raymond Garthoff notes that the principle had been enunciated previously in *Whence the Threat to Peace* (Moscow: Military Publishing House, 1982), p. 12. The Russian language version was sent to the printer in December 1981.

without nuclear weapons demanded a considerable local preponderance of force and would need a substantial increase in the firepower, mobility, and sustainability of individual ground force units.

These new demands came on top of the separate requirement to build up the ground and air forces facing China, which emerged in the middle 1960s and became increasingly pressing by the end of the decade. The procurement programs to meet these new requirements abutted directly with the introduction of new aircraft and armored fighting vehicles that stemmed from the 1961–62 decisions. The combination of these three separate impulses resulted in a sustained buildup in the number and quality of Soviet ground forces and frontal aviation, from the late 1960s throughout the 1970s, tapering off toward the end of the period.

NAVAL FORCES. The implications of the new objective were even more fundamental for the Soviet navy. The long lead time for major naval units meant that most of the newly designed classes did not begin to enter service until the beginning of the 1980s. The Delta ballistic-missile nuclear submarine was only an exception because it involved the reconfiguration of an existing program.[22]

PVO STRANY. The new emphasis on deterrence to help avoid the nuclear devastation of Russia implied that, if anything, territorial air defense would become somewhat less vital. Hence the priority of the national air defense troops (PVO strany) in comparison with other branches of service would drop during the 1970s. In terms of relative investment, this did indeed happen.[23] The never-ending process of replacing older systems with more modern ones would have to continue, but the delivery rate of new systems might slow, particularly if PVO strany were competing for aircraft with frontal aviation. This slowdown also happened.[24]

STRATEGIC ROCKET FORCES. In considering the implications of the new objective for the strategic rocket forces, one must distinguish between in-

---

22. See appendix B.

23. PVO-*protivovozdoshnaya oborona* (antiair defense) *strany* (of the country); in 1967 PVO strany received 14 percent and the air force 17 percent of Soviet investment and operating expenditure. In 1977 the proportions were 12 percent and 22 percent. See Andrew C. Goldberg, "Nuclear Escalation in Soviet Theater Warfare Strategy" (Ph.D. dissertation, Columbia University, 1985), table IV-7, using Central Intelligence Agency data.

24. The number of aircraft in frontal aviation exceeded those in the PVO for the first time in 1973. The annual delivery rate of fighter/interceptors exceeded that of ground attack aircraft before 1971–72, but then fell below. In the period 1972/73–1978/79 the delivery of fighter/interceptors averaged about 110 a year, and ground attack averaged about 310. Goldberg, "Nuclear Escalation," graphs IV-5 and IV-7.

tercontinental and continental, or regional, systems. The requirement to possess a fully credible ICBM deterrent force meant that existing intercontinental missile development programs would proceed unchecked. Soviet ICBMs lagged badly behind U.S. systems in accuracy, number of independent warheads, readiness factors, and, probably, reliability. The intercontinental ballistic missiles in service when the accords of the first session of the strategic arms limitation talks (SALT I) were signed in May 1972, the SS-9 and SS-11, were essentially adaptations of earlier designs. Only when the next generation of missiles (SS-17, SS-18, SS-19) began to enter service in the mid-1970s would the Soviets have the basic systems that could be progressively modified to match the U.S. capability in the carriage of independently targetable warheads and in accuracy. However, having reached this plateau of capability and in the absence of any new initiative from the U.S. side, there would be no great pressure to go further, except to convert at least part of the force to solid-fuel propulsion to provide for improved launch on warning.

As for continental, or regional, strategic missiles, the new concept of a large-scale, conventional, preventive campaign against NATO's nuclear capability at the outbreak of a war would have reduced the relative importance of these Soviet systems and hence the priority given to replacing the SS-4 and SS-5 missiles. This may account in part for the fact that the SS-14 and SS-15 were never deployed, the SS-4 and SS-5 being replaced later by the more capable SS-20. Meanwhile the emphasis on avoiding escalation in the NATO theater would raise a new requirement for a different type of medium-range missile. The missile would need to be highly survivable and, should NATO resort to nuclear weapons, be capable of striking at dispersed targets whose location and even existence might not be known much in advance.[25]

AIR FORCES. After World War II, development of long-range aircraft was accepted as one of several ways of delivering nuclear weapons on North America. Toward the end of the 1950s, two different types of bomber were in series production, and a third, follow-on type, was at the prototype stage. It was, however, decided that the ICBM was the most effective means of striking at North America, and the bomber and submarine programs were curtailed or canceled. Having lost the mission of intercontinental delivery, there was no important role left for the long-range

25. See appendix D.

bomber, particularly since the Soviets' 1960s concept of operations assumed that their airbases would be destroyed in the initial nuclear exchange.

The 1970s hierarchy of objectives reopened the question of the long-range bomber's utility. If the nuclear devastation of Russia could be avoided, then the bombers' bases would remain available throughout the war. Meanwhile the concept of a two-phase war generated a range of general-purpose roles for the long-range bomber or strike aircraft. In a long-drawn-out war fought mainly with conventional ordnance, the aircraft's heavy payload and reusability offered considerable advantages over missiles. Its likely targets would include Western invasion forces and threatening troop formations and military bases that were established outside the defense perimeter.

The Military-Industrial Base

In the 1960s the inevitability of escalation to an intercontinental exchange, even if preceded by a period of conventional conflict, meant that the Soviet military-industrial base would be of little importance once war broke out. The forces on both sides would have to rely on weapons already at hand and supplies already in the pipeline, and the potential contribution of factories and shipyards (to the extent they survived) would be to rebuilding the shattered socialist state.

This thinking changed in the 1970s, with the war now being thought of in two phases. In the first phase NATO would be defeated in Europe and U.S. forces would be ejected from the Continent. The scope, duration, and intensity of the second phase could only be guessed at. But the Soviets could be absolutely certain of one thing. Both sides, their military-industrial bases undamaged, would embark on an intense and sustained arms race. The U.S. system had demonstrated its ability to build up industrial capacity rapidly when challenged. If the Soviets were to compete in such a race, they would need to have most of the industrial plants already in place.

In the 1970s, therefore, one would expect to see a significant expansion in the productive capacity of the Soviet military-industrial sector of the economy. The increased capital investment would not necessarily result in a corresponding increase in output, except in cases in which the new concept of operations required a buildup in forces of the kind noted for the ground forces and frontal aviation. Sometimes it might be possible to use the additional capacity for civilian production, but in more specialized facilities (for example, nuclear submarine production) one might expect to see plants producing below their nominal capacity, even on a one-shift basis.

There is some evidence that production floor space did increase in the 1970–1980 period and, starting in the 1980–82 period, production of several weapons systems, including tanks and fighter aircraft, dropped below the established rate.[26]

Civil Defense

In the 1960s the primary objective of *preserving the socialist system* and its supporting objective of *ensuring the survival of a proportion of the nation's industrial base and working population* meant that civil defense measures received very high priority. The new importance of civil defense was indicated by its reorganization in 1961 and the institution of a nation-wide system with central headquarters in the Ministry of Defense and the commander in chief of the ground forces at its head.

In the 1970s the governing objective of avoiding the nuclear devastation of Russia and the growing hope that this aim would be achieved through a mixture of détente and deterrence would mean that the priority given to civil defense would fall, in practice if not also in theory. This would particularly be true if it meant allocating scarce resources, whether money, men, or matériel.

The Shaping of Policy since 1976

Much, of course, has changed since the flow of implementing decisions that stemmed from doctrinal decisions in December 1966. As early as 1967–68 new developments would have been shaping consequential policies and operational concepts. For example, in April 1967, Marshal Andrey A. Grechko, previously the commander in chief of Warsaw Pact Forces, was appointed as minister of defense in preference to Dmitriy F. Ustinov. In June the Israelis demonstrated in the six-day Arab-Israeli war

26. See the figure entitled "Soviet Military Production Facilities-Growth of Floorspace," in U.S. Department of Defense, *Soviet Military Power, 1984,* 3d ed. (Government Printing Office, 1984), p. 91. (Hereafter *SMP.*) It describes a noticeable increase in production floor space, the largest being for ground-force weapons; see also the list of annual production rates in *SMP, 1984,* p. 98.

that the Egyptian air force could be knocked out on the ground by preemptive air strikes. The Prague spring came in 1968, ending that fall with the invasion of Czechoslovakia by Warsaw Pact forces and the permanent stationing of five Soviet divisions on Czech territory for the first time.[27]

In 1969 Egyptian President Gamal Abdel Nasser started a war of attrition against Israel, which drew Soviet air defense forces into Egypt and tested the relative effectiveness of ground-based air defense. Further experience was gained in the October War of 1973, which also provided information about the survivability of armored fighting vehicles. During this whole period, the move toward East-West détente and the series of agreements that culminated in SALT I occurred. All the events took place against the backdrop of the ongoing American military experience in Vietnam, in which the diverse potential of helicopters was demonstrated.

These and other developments would undoubtedly have influenced the evolution of Soviet military policy in the 1970s. Nevertheless, it is not possible to identify any one event or series of events that could challenge the validity of the governing objective of avoiding the nuclear devastation of Russia. One can therefore be reasonably confident that the main structure of the 1970s hierarchy of objectives will still serve as a framework for analyzing both the politico-military and the military-technical aspects of Soviet military doctrine concerning world war.

However, various assessments of practicality, effectiveness, cost, and risk are likely to have changed over the years. In the 1967–68 period the Soviets made far-reaching long-range policy decisions concerning future concepts of operation and appropriate weapons systems. In many cases these policies not only entailed completely new ideas but were projected against an evolving Western capability. By the mid-1970s the Soviets had a far clearer idea of the emerging situation and could make midcourse corrections if their assessments had been seriously wrong or if new developments warranted a change. One would therefore expect at least one major adjustment of policy to have occurred since the 1967–68 decision period, particularly since five militarily significant decision periods had occurred in the preceding twenty-two years.

The Soviets have also noted how the process of weapons development

27. Karen Dawisha argues that well before the Prague spring, the Soviet military command was unhappy about the military capabilities of the Czechoslovakian divisions who were holding this important part of the front line. Karen Dawisha, *The Kremlin and the Prague Spring* (University of California Press, 1984), pp. 52–54. With the shift to a policy of a conventional blitzkrieg, the quality of the troops in the first echelon became much more critical.

imposes a periodicity on the methods of waging war. Although the lead time for new weapons systems is ten to fifteen years, they are superseded by improved systems within five to seven years of entering service, and the rate of technological obsolescence has been steadily increasing.[28] However, the structural nature of the policy changes decided in 1967–68, the resulting shifts in weapons programs, and the fact that the doctrinal reorientation was taking place in a context of fairly stable East-West relations, do, however, make it likely that the basic structure of decisions persisted until the mid-1970s without major change. After that, one would expect a major reevaluation and subsequent adjustment.

1976–77: A Review of Progress

A major review of policy probably took place in about 1976–77. This period coincided with the appointment of Dmitriy F. Ustinov as minister of defense after Marshal Grechko's death in April 1976, and the appointment of Nikolay V. Ogarkov as chief of the General Staff in January 1977.

Anomalies in the naval building programs and changes in the balance of deployments between the Northern and Pacific fleets are the most persuasive evidence of a major reevaluation. At this time the Soviets probably downgraded the importance of the Arctic Ocean as a deployment area for the bulk of their ballistic-missile submarine force.

There is also circumstantial evidence that a new concept emerged at this period for targeting the strategic rocket forces. Nuclear weapons are categorized as tactical, operational, and strategic, according to the range of the weapons system. The strategic element was originally divided between continental (or regional) systems and those which had an intercontinental reach. Strategic targets were defined according to their geographic relationship to the Soviet Union, and target sets were separate for continental and intercontinental systems.

But at this period it seems likely that the Soviets decided that in the future target sets would no longer be distinguished according to geography. Instead targets would be defined according to the type of conflict in which the target would be struck. There would still be two "strategic" target sets. One would cover the contingency of a nuclear war that was limited to the continental theaters and did not escalate to an intercontinental exchange;

28. V. D. Sokolovskiy and Major-General M. Cherednichenko, "Military Strategy and its Problems," *Voennaya mysl'* (Military thought), no. 10 (October 1968), p. 40.

and the other would cover the contingency of global nuclear war. The distinction followed the logic of the two hierarchies of objectives. The 1970s hierarchy, the preferred one, applied as long as an East-West conflict did not escalate to an intercontinental exchange; the 1960s hierarchy would take effect if conflict escalated to global nuclear war.

Probably the new requirement for a long-range bomber for use in a general purpose role, particularly in the second, drawn-out phase of a world war, was decided at this period.[29]

The Soviets also streamlined the higher command structure to provide a better balance between coordination and delegation. At the same time the Soviets were reassessing developments in NATO operational doctrine and concluding that they would have to resuscitate the World War II concept of the mobile (now operational maneuver) group.

The Changing Risk of Escalation

The Soviet assessments of the risk of escalation have probably changed since their 1967–68 assessments. With the passage of time the Soviets' perceptions of how the West would be likely to respond in various crises are likely to have evolved. They have observed U.S. behavior in a wide range of international involvements and have participated in strategic arms limitations talks, which have given them a most unusual insight into the way the U.S. politico-military establishment thinks about these matters. The insight would have been fleshed out and crosschecked by the network of nonofficial contacts in the United States, which burgeoned in the late 1960s and continued throughout the 1970s.

The Soviets have probably decided that in the past they overestimated the danger of escalation stemming from superpower confrontation in the third world. Their conclusions about the danger of escalation because of conflict in Europe are not obvious because they are faced with contradictory evidence.

On the one hand, it seems increasingly unlikely that the United States would launch a nuclear attack on Russia except in response to an imminent strike on North America. Assertions by former senior government officials, European complaints about decoupling, and statements such as the

29. See the report of Harold Brown, secretary of defense, in *Department of Defense Annual Report, Fiscal Year 1979*, p. 51. Flight testing of this aircraft began in August 1982, and it is expected to enter operational service in 1986–87. "Soviet Bomber," *Aviation Week and Space Technology*, vol. 117 (August 23, 1982), p. 13. The existence of this program was first referred to in February 1978.

Schlesinger Doctrine of 1974 and Presidential Directive 59 in August 1980 seem to support that assumption.[30]

On the other hand, the attempt to develop limited nuclear options could be read as evidence that the United States plans to exercise the options in the event of war. The Soviets see that endeavor as highly escalatory and likely to precipitate an intercontinental exchange, whether intended or not. Some evidence suggests that the United States is seeking a disarming strike capability, embodied in the hard-target-kill qualities of the MX ICBM, the D-5, Trident II submarine-launched ballistic missile, and the Pershing II intermediate-range ballistic missile. The illusion that the United States had such a first-strike capability could encourage Washington to strike at Russia if faced by defeat in Europe.

Renewed Soviet Discussion on the Use of Nuclear Weapons

A conviction that the U.S. was certain to escalate to an intercontinental exchange could explain the new section added to the 1981 edition of *V.I. Lenin and Soviet Military Science*. The author, N.N. Azovtsev, advocated, in effect, a return to the 1960s hierarchy of objectives and a strategy predicated on nuclear preemption at the theater and intercontinental levels.[31] The book can be seen as a last attempt to reverse the December 1966 doctrinal decision before it was authoritatively reaffirmed at the Twenty-sixth Party Congress in 1981. The party congress decreed that to count on victory in a nuclear war was "dangerous madness" and thereby ruled out a strategic concept predicated on initiating the use of nuclear weapons.[32]

30. Walter B. Slocombe, a member of the National Security Council in the Carter administration and a deputy under secretary of defense, 1979–81, has noted that "distinguished U.S. spokesmen have joined in questioning the credibility of the U.S. making any nuclear response to a Soviet attack in Europe." See his "Extended Deterrence," *Washington Quarterly,* vol. 7 (Fall 1984), p. 97. Henry Kissinger, "NATO-The Next Thirty Years" (Washington, D.C., Center for Strategic and International Studies, 1979), p. 11; Samuel P. Huntington, "Correspondence," *International Security,* vol. 9 (Summer 1984), p. 212; Paul Warnke, "The Illusion on NATO's Nuclear Debate," in Andrew J. Pierre, ed., *Nuclear Weapons in Europe* (New York: Council on Foreign Relations, 1984), p. 79; and Diana Johnstone, *The Politics of Euromissiles: Europe's Role in America's World* (London: Verso, 1984), p. 182.

31. N.N. Azovtsev, *V.I. Lenin i sovetskaya voennaya nauka* (V.I. Lenin and Soviet military science) (Moscow: Izdatel'stvo Nauka, 1981), pp. 299–301. This book was sent for typesetting in June 1980. Azovtsev invokes the Twenty-second and Twenty-third Party Congresses (1961 and 1966) when he discusses the contemporary development of the armed services and military science.

32. Leonid I. Brezhnev, "Brezhnev's Report to Congress—I," in *Current Digest of the Soviet Press,* vol. 33 (March 1981), p. 11. According to information gleaned by Raymond Garthoff while in Moscow, it was not until the Twenty-sixth Party Congress that the party officially accepted the doctrine of the impossibility of victory in nuclear war.

What is apparently a direct rebuttal to Azovtsev's line of argument subsequently appeared in a book by the deputy chief of the General Staff.[33]

However, despite this rejection of Azovtsev's argument there has been renewed emphasis in Soviet military writing since 1982 on the role of nuclear weapons.[34] The explanation for this renewed emphasis could be simple. The Soviets had recently introduced nuclear delivery systems in the shape of dual-capable artillery at the level of the tactical maneuver unit. Soviet officers had to begin thinking of what was involved in using such systems.[35] The Soviets had focused discussion for the best part of a decade on how to replicate the effect of nuclear strikes with the integrated use of conventional weapons. It was now time for them to redress the balance of emphasis in training and indoctrination. The Soviets had to reemphasize that, whatever their preference, the likelihood that war in Europe would become nuclear was ever present, and Soviet forces had to be thoroughly prepared for the worst case. It was probably not coincidental that the renewed emphasis became apparent after General Secretary Leonid I. Brezhnev's unilateral pledge that the Soviet Union would not be the first to use nuclear weapons.[36]

Possibly the Soviet military was responding to what it perceived as America's increased readiness to resort to nuclear weapons in the event of war in Europe. The evidence for this readiness lay in the aborted attempt to deploy enhanced radiation weapons, the plans to deploy ground-launched cruise missiles and the Pershing II intermediate-range ballistic missile, and perhaps also in the adoption of Presidential Directive 59, which talked of fighting a nuclear war, albeit at the strategic level. It was the United States that had pushed for the adoption of flexible response and the idea of a conventional pause in the event of a Soviet offensive, but the Europeans in general and Germany in particular had always favored the almost automatic resort to nuclear weapons. The shift in U.S. policy could mean that the "conventional window of opportunity," which the Soviet

33. M.A. Gareev, *M.V. Frunze—voennyy teoretik* (M.V. Frunze—military theoretician), (Moscow: Voenizdat, 1985), pp. 239–40. The book makes statements to the effect that Marshal Sokolovskiy's *Military Strategy* (1962, 1963, and 1968) contained outdated propositions about the use of nuclear weapons.

34. Stephen M. Meyer, *Soviet Theater Nuclear Forces, Part I: Development of Doctrine and Objectives*, Adelphi Paper 187 (London: International Institute for Strategic Studies, 1983–84).

35. Phillip A. Petersen and John G. Hines, "The Conventional Offensive in Soviet Theater Strategy," *Orbis*, vol. 27 (Fall 1983), pp. 726–27.

36. The pledge was a major step beyond the 1977 proposal from the Warsaw Treaty Organization for a multilateral treaty on "no first use." Ustinov's defense of the pledge suggests considerable internal debate over this self-denying ordinance. See D. Ustinov, "Otvesti ugrozu yadernoy voyny" (Avert the threat of nuclear war), *Pravda*, July 12, 1982.

1970s operational concept sought to exploit, was now being closed, and that any war in Europe would almost certainly be nuclear.

The least likely explanation for the Soviets' renewed discussion of nuclear weapons is that they were reconsidering the role of nuclear weapons in the theater to compensate for perceived deficiencies in their conventional capabilities.[37] They might have been concerned about the Western air threat to their second-echelon forces and lines of communications, as well as about their ability to draw down NATO's long-range interdiction capability rapidly enough. The Soviets might also have doubted the ability of their ground and air forces to breach NATO's defenses and break through to the rear. Whatever the reasons, the Soviets had concluded that they could not be certain that in all circumstances they would be able to meet their operational objectives in the Western theater of military action, by using conventional weapons only.

However, that explanation runs counter to the evidence that the Soviets believe that the resort to nuclear weapons in offensive ground operations hinders rather than helps the attacking force. In mountainous terrain it actually slows the advance.[38] Nevertheless, given the extreme views put forward by Azovtsev, it is possible that there was some Soviet debate about whether conventional forces could achieve the operational objectives within the Western theater of military action, and about the probability that Soviet first use of nuclear weapons in the theater would lead to strategic strikes on Russia.

In such a debate the spectrum of opinion would probably encompass two main tendencies. Some would argue that the danger of escalation continued to be substantial. They would think that, given the right combination of intellectual ingenuity and military resources, the Soviets could meet their operational objectives by using nonnuclear means only. Others would hold grave doubts about the ability of conventional means to disable NATO's theater nuclear capability in a short enough time span. They would question the capacity of the ground forces to achieve the necessary breakthrough by using conventional fire only. They would argue that the

37. Christopher N. Donnelly summed up articles in the Soviet military press by saying, "The reader could be forgiven for coming to the conclusion that in 1978 the Soviet army considered that a frontal attack, at high speed against a well-prepared defense in conventional war, in fact was virtually bound to fail." See "Ground Force," in David R. Jones, ed., *Soviet Armed Forces Review Annual*, vol. 3 (Gulf Breeze, Fla.: Academic International Press, 1979), p. 18.

38. John G. Hines, "Soviet Front Operations in Europe—Planning for Encirclement," paper prepared for "Spotlight on the Soviet Union," a conference at Sundvollen, Norway, April 25–27, 1985.

dangers of escalation were overrated, that the availability of subkiloton high-precision nuclear ordnance reduced the likelihood even further, and that the first use of nuclear weapons should be reinstated.

To an extent, the arguments are circular and reflect emphases on two different objectives. One focuses on avoiding the nuclear devastation of Russia, thus stressing the dangers of escalation in Europe. The other focuses on the objective of not losing the war, thus stressing the ability to achieve the operational objectives in the Western theater of military action. Disagreement is not surprising; it reflects the complex and demanding nature of Soviet military requirements. In a world war the Soviets will face continuing tension among their objectives as they strive to win in Europe while avoiding the nuclear devastation of Russia.

CHAPTER 4

Shaping the Land Battle

THE NEW objectives stemming from the 1966 decision, and embodied in the 1970s hierarchy, affected military requirements in all the continental theaters of war. Nevertheless, the threat of nuclear strikes on Russia and the land battle in Europe continued to be the dominant strategic problem facing the Soviet Union. Despite the emergence of a new threat from China in the 1960s, the land, air, and sea battle for Europe absorbed the lion's share of Soviet defense resources and professional attention.

Europe was and is the main theater. To perceive the overall strategic concept that underlies the 1970s operational plan for the contingency of world war, one must understand the conditions that shaped Soviet military policy toward Europe in the postwar years and the problems that will face them in that theater if war is unavoidable.

Postwar Military Objectives

In 1947–48 the Soviets reworked their threat assessments and concluded that an emerging threat was more serious and more immediate than the prevailing estimate of "Germany in twenty years time, with Japan in the rear." The reassessment at this period perceived an imminent threat of U.S. preventive air strikes against Russian atomic research and development facilities, following the first Soviet test in mid-1949. The Soviets would also have seen a more traditional threat of Western military invasion five to six years in the future.

A Western invasion would have the objective of overturning the fledgling socialist regimes in Eastern Europe and bringing down the communist government in Russia. The ensuing war would constitute the decisive encounter between the two social systems and, as such, worst-case scenarios were prudent and appropriate. The Soviet leaders had therefore to prepare to repulse massive land attacks across the German plain and up through the Balkans, spearheaded by the rebuilt armies of Germany and France. The Soviets had to be ready to defend against major amphibious landings on the Baltic and Black Sea coasts by American and British forces, which would thrust inland to link up with Polish, Belorussian, Ukrainian, and Rumanian partisans and so open up new fronts in the Soviet rear. The Soviet Union had to gird itself to endure massive air attacks on military, transportation, and industrial targets throughout the Soviet Union.

In considering how best to respond to this emerging threat, some thought may have been given to consolidating the Soviet defense perimeter on Russia's boundaries as defined after World War II. The idea might have made sense if the Soviets could have been confident that if they withdrew to their borders, they would be left in peace. But everything pointed to the opposite conclusion, especially the experience of the previous thirty years.

After the Bolshevik Revolution, Russia had suffered invasion and partial dismemberment at the hands of Germany and its protégés. Following Germany's defeat on the Western front, Russia had to withstand armed intervention by significant British, French, and Japanese forces, and a coordinated attack by Polish and Ukrainian armies. In World War II Russia was again invaded and dismembered by Germany, and Rumania advanced its borders one hundred miles to the River Bug. In this history the Soviets found reason to fear that the pressure to dismember Russia was strong and would reemerge, and this time it would be reinforced by the U.S. urge to change the nature of the Soviet state. If history had not provided sufficient reason, Marxist theory ruled that a capitalist attack on the Soviet Union, the embodiment of socialism, was inevitable.

If an assault on the Soviet Union was inevitable, all the arguments favored a forward defense. The Eastern European states must not be counted on the Western side, which would happen if the existing regimes were overthrown. Given the history of those countries, most of the new regimes would be rabidly anti-Soviet, thus turning a defensive buffer zone into a springboard for subversion and invasion. Relative numbers argued even more strongly for the same conclusion. It had been difficult enough to defeat the Germans when they had forces tied down on other fronts and only had the Rumanians, Hungarians, and Finns in significant numbers on their side. If the Soviets were now to be faced with Germany and the combined armies of the other European states, the odds on the ground would be impossible, without even considering American air power or whether U.S. and Commonwealth ground forces would also be involved.

The de facto boundary between the Soviet Union and its potential enemies happened to be drawn across the narrowest part of Europe, running from Lubeck Bay in the Baltic to the head of the Adriatic Sea. This offered a much shorter front line than the borders of Russia, and although the open German plain in the north constituted less than half the front, the southern part was mountainous and lent itself to defense. The situation compared favorably with the Russian borderlands, where the Carpathian Mountains in the south offered the only obstruction to a ground offensive.

The harsh experience in 1941 provided further arguments for a forward defense. Once again, space had turned out to be vitally important. Axis forces had advanced six hundred miles in four months on their whole front and were only held at the outskirts of Moscow. They were finally checked in August 1942, when their southern armies had advanced about one thousand miles. Leningrad would certainly have fallen to the Germans if they had not had to cover four hundred miles (the Baltic states) before launching their assault. Distance was itself a defense and if war did come and the Soviets should be forced to retreat, the five hundred miles of Eastern Europe could be critical in providing time to mobilize the full defense effort.

Forward defense also meant the battle would not be fought on Russian soil, much of which still lay devastated because of the hugely destructive war that had been waged over it from 1941 to 1944. In 1948 the possibility of disaffected populations in Eastern Europe is unlikely to have been seen as much of a problem. Bulgaria was traditionally pro-Russian; free elections in Czechoslovakia had given the Communist party 38 percent of the poll; and in Yugoslavia the rift with Russia had yet to come. In Poland, as in Czechoslovakia, the Soviets could claim to be liberators and believed that a communist government would prove acceptable to the mass of people and be naturally pro-Soviet.[1] The same reasoning applied to the ex-enemy states of Hungary and Rumania, where the workers and peasants had had little or no effective representation in the interwar years.

A final reason for rejecting the option of concentrating the defense on the borders of the Soviet Union was the future of Germany, a country that

---

1. Peter Calvocoressi makes the point that the communist parties of East European states were not alone in wanting the foreign policies of their countries to be based on an alliance with Russia. Other political groups agreed that the Soviet Union was a surer safeguard against renewed German aggression than the Anglo-Saxons. See *Survey of International Affairs, 1947–48* (London: Oxford University Press, 1952), p. 150.

still dominated Soviet fears. The total exclusion of the Soviets from any say in Allied policies toward the ex-enemy states of Italy and Japan made it clear to the Soviets that only by continuing as one of the four occupying powers would they have any influence, however slight, over policies in the three western zones of Germany. Only by continuing to occupy their own zone could the Russians ensure that when war came, they would not be faced again by the weight of the whole German state.

All these arguments make good sense, but probably the most persuasive consideration was the fact that Soviet troops were already deployed as occupation forces in Germany, Austria, and Hungary, and they were also manning the lines of communications through Poland. The question of withdrawal just did not arise.

In the face of the emerging threat, the Soviet objective would have been to deter Western attempts to overthrow the newly established regimes in the Eastern European states, and this aim required forces well forward. If deterrence failed, the objective would be to repel the attack and then go on to defeat the aggressor. Given the recent experience of World War II, blocking a land attack would not present too great a problem, although the expected buildup of Western ground forces would have to be monitored with care. Repelling the air and maritime assaults presented new problems of a different order, and in 1948 PVO strany was established as an independent branch of the armed services for national air defense. The Soviets also set about strengthening their navy's capability against maritime invasion.[2]

To be able to repel such assaults was a minimum requirement; the larger requirement was to defeat the capitalist bloc, which implied going on the offensive. In large part, the idea of victory reflected the cast of mind that emerged during the last years of the war against Hitler. It also stemmed from the Soviet perception of the West's objective in a future conflict, namely, the overthrow of the socialist system. Just as it had been necessary to defeat Germany to bring World War II to an end, so would it be necessary to defeat the capitalist bloc if it initiated war. To achieve victory and a durable peace would require a major offensive into Western Europe and the accession to power of pro-Soviet or genuinely neutral regimes through-

2. Between 1948 and 1953 the Soviets perceived a serious threat of maritime assault on the Baltic and Black Sea coasts. The reasons for concluding that the large submarine force was designed for defense against amphibious assault forces, particularly in the Baltic and Black Seas, rather than for commerce war against trans-Atlantic shipping are given in Michael MccGwire, "The Turning Points in Soviet Naval Policy," in MccGwire, ed., *Soviet Naval Developments: Capability and Context* (Praeger, 1973), pp. 184–85.

out the area. The offensive operations would have the dual purpose of defeating NATO forces and denying the United States a bridgehead in Europe, an objective that was clearly articulated as early as 1950.[3]

As the Soviets responded to the reassessment of threat that took place in 1947–48, the ground forces in Europe had to develop an offensive concept of operations. Soviet forces would be postured to repel an initial attack and then move over to the offensive. The concept made good sense, but it also reflected the bias of Soviet military theory and the conviction that victory could only be achieved through offensive operations. Both beliefs had been reinforced by the successful campaign against Germany.

The offensive also meant that war would be waged on enemy territory, rather than on one's own or that of one's allies. To the extent that the Soviets were concerned about the reliability of the Eastern European population, offensive operations would make defections less likely. The capability for offensive operations into Europe had the ancillary advantage of posing a counterthreat that might deter the United States from exploiting its atomic monopoly to launch a preventive strike on Soviet atomic facilities.

The Evolution of Objectives

The idea of forward defense and the concept of offensive operations have persisted to the present day. During the intervening years the Soviets have changed their perceptions of the nature of the threat in the European theater, the place of Europe in their strategic plans, and their capability to implement an offensive concept of operations.

At least through Stalin's death in early 1953, the Soviets took the threat of military aggression by the West very seriously. The West's failure to press ahead with the buildup of a Franco-German army meant that the threat was still not imminent, but it remained the contingency for which the Soviets shaped their forces. That threat included the likelihood of large-scale landings on the Baltic and Black Sea coasts.

The reassessment that followed Stalin's death downgraded the threat of premeditated territorial aggression by land or sea, and the West's inaction

3. See Raymond L. Garthoff, *Soviet Strategy in the Nuclear Age* (Praeger, 1958), pp. 136–37, citing Major-General V. Khlopov, *Voennaya mysl'* (Military thought), no. 6 (June 1950), pp. 75–76. The article refers to the liquidation of the U.S. bridgehead in Europe by "powerful offensive operations on a large scale with a high tempo of advance."

during the Hungarian crisis in the fall of 1956 probably persuaded the Soviets, finally, that premeditated Western aggression was not a serious danger. Earlier in that same year First Secretary Nikita S. Khrushchev had
decreed that a capitalist attack on the Soviet Union was no longer inevitable. Soviet military capability was now sufficient to make any such attack
a fruitless exercise, and capitalist aggression in the European theater was
now effectively deterred.

This development did not mean that the Soviets thought that the U.S.
urge to change the political complexion of Eastern Europe had evaporated.
The danger of Western intervention to exploit a perceived opportunity
would persist and remained a potential cause of war. However, over the
years the perceived danger of a war caused by Western military intervention steadily diminished as the status quo in Europe gained de facto acceptance. The danger of war from other causes gradually increased as the
Soviet Union's growing involvement on the world scene broadened the
scope of superpower competition. The nuclear arms race was also introducing new tensions to the relationship.

In the 1950s the contingency to be covered in the European theater was
still seen as Western territorial aggression that had to be deterred or re-
pelled. By the 1970s the contingency to be prepared for was a world war,
involving multitheater conflict. This evolution of Soviet military objectives and operational concepts in the European theater can be described in
terms of the developments of successive decades. Allowance must be made
for the lags inherent in reassessing changing circumstances, initiating new
policies, and adjusting force structures and postures.

The 1950s

The type of military objectives and operational concepts that would
have been generated by the 1947–48 reassessment and then refined during
the 1950s can be described as "improved World War II." The basic principles, strategies, and tactics that had proven so successful in driving the
Germans out of Russia and back across the eastern half of Europe could
be used to repulse a future aggressor and drive him back across the other
half of Europe. But at this period, a thrust into Western and southern Europe would be primarily a by-product of offensive operations to defeat the
enemy and destroy his forces, rather than an end in itself.

A Soviet victory and military presence in those regions would provide
the opportunity for "progressive" forces to take power and ensure regimes

friendly to the Soviet Union. In countries such as France, Italy, and Greece, which had large communist parties that had been the backbone of the resistance against the Germans, communist-controlled governments would probably result. There is no evidence that the Soviets had an urge to territorial expansion at this period or thought of taking over large tracts of Europe as the Germans did during World War II.

The 1960s

As noted earlier, the introduction of nuclear weapons into the Soviet arsenal led to a basic reassessment of established military theory and operational concepts during the late 1950s and to the doctrinal ruling that a war would inevitably be nuclear and mean massive attacks on the Soviet homeland. In one sense the Soviets had been responding urgently to the threat of nuclear strikes on Russia since 1948. What was new in the 1960s was the overwhelming scale of such attacks and the absence of any means to dilute, let alone rebuff, them. This threat had major implications for Soviet military objectives in the European theater.

Soviet authorities acknowledged that by 1966 the United States was planning to have about 1,800 missiles capable of striking targets in the Soviet Union. There were no real means of defending Russia against such missile attacks. The Soviets, without even considering the weapons carried by strike aircraft, were under no illusions about the devastation that would result from missiles alone. The survival of the Soviet state as a functioning entity was brought into question. The Russians were striving to build up their own capability to strike at North America, but it would avail them nothing to be able to destroy the United States if the Soviet state did not survive. Should world war be inescapable, the objective was not to lose, but this aim could not be achieved by mutual destruction.

Survival implied the continued existence of some kind of governmental apparatus and of an economic and social base on which to rebuild a socialist society. Antiballistic-missile systems were therefore built around Moscow, rather than located to protect intercontinental ballistic-missile fields. A major reorganization of civil defense occurred, including the institution of a nationwide system with strong military participation.

But after a nuclear exchange, the Soviets would not have to rely entirely, or even mainly, on the economic capacity that survived the strikes on Russia. Around the Soviet periphery were potential socioeconomic bases from which to rebuild their shattered economy, most notably Western Europe and Manchuria. How much these areas would be damaged by war would largely depend on Soviet decisions concerning the use of nuclear weapons and what concept of operations the Soviets adopted.

The areas adjacent to the Soviet Union differed from those adjoining the United States. The United States had no control over the damage that would occur in Canada and Mexico. These two countries came within the Soviet target set. To the extent they were important to U.S. survival, they would share the general devastation of North America, giving the Soviet Union one advantage to compensate for the preponderance of U.S. nuclear weapons. The Soviet Union also had the infrastructure for centralized social control provided by the Communist party, the internal troops of the Committee for State Security and Ministry of Internal Affairs, and the nationwide enterprise systems such as transportation and communications, with their military styles of organization.

The requirement to use the adjacent areas for rebuilding a socialist society would obviously seriously influence nuclear targeting policy and the overall pattern of military operations.[4] It would be desirable to limit the extent of devastation through selective weapons' policies, confining the battle to essential areas and using the diplomatic tools of bribery, blackmail, and coercion to the fullest extent. The concept of operations would favor high mobility and deep penetration. The Soviets would seize and hold areas in the enemy's rear and, where facilities needed to be preserved, rely on chemical rather than explosive weapons.

Thus the military objective in Europe would be to *destroy NATO's forces* and to *gain access to the area's economic resources*. Besides the major constraint of needing to preserve those resources, there would be no inherent restrictions on the employment of nuclear weapons in the theater. Such weapons could be used to break through NATO's forward defenses, attack its nuclear assets, and destroy its forces in the rear. The value of specific industrial resources would have to be weighed against the military problems of gaining access. For an area like Britain it might be more cost-effective to devastate the country than to attempt to exploit its economic potential.

Because the United States would have been rendered impotent by the intercontinental exchange and would be in no condition to mount a transoceanic assault, the Soviets would not have to establish political control over Europe, beyond that needed for economic exploitation. Survival

4. See Colonel M. Shirokov, "Voennaya geografiya na sovremennom etape" (Military geography at the contemporary stage), *Voennaya mysl'*, no. 11 (November 1966), p. 49, last para.

would be the name of the game, with the people of the Warsaw Pact having first call on resources. Concern for the people of NATO would be directly related to their capacity to produce such resources and their willingness to join the communist fold. Soviet economic theory and methods would be well suited to extracting the maximum current production from recalcitrant economies.

The 1970s and 1980s

The Soviet concept of offensive operations in NATO Europe is not so much an intellectual decision based on self-evident principles as it is a habitual frame of mind, based on prewar tenets of Soviet military science, the viewpoints induced by World War II, the threat perceptions of the early 1950s, and the evolving requirements of the 1960s. When the Soviets reviewed the implications of the December 1966 decision on their contingency plans for world war, it is unlikely that any alternative to offensive operations in Europe was even considered. The only question addressed was how best to carry out such operations within the new constraints.

But even if the Soviets had started from self-evident principles, there is no reason to suppose that they would have reached any different conclusions. The 1947–48 arguments that favored a forward defense posture and offensive operations in the event of war were still valid twenty years later and had been reinforced. East European forces now formed a significant component of the overall Soviet capability facing NATO, and their reliability in war was an important issue and would be affected by the nature of the war. Historical experience and common sense argued that the reliability of individual national units and the passivity of the population in the East European states would be reinforced by successful offensive operations on the territory of NATO nations. This would be undermined if Warsaw Pact forces had to make strategic withdrawals or sustain defensive operations on their own territories.

A more important argument stemmed from the new governing objective of avoiding the nuclear devastation of Russia. Its achievement assumed a situation of mutual strategic deterrence, implying that the North American continent would be untouched and its vast production capacity undamaged. In such circumstances the defeat of NATO forces and the eviction of the United States from the European continent became a strategic imperative.

If NATO forces were not defeated, the West would possess a bridgehead on the Continent, into which the North American military-industrial complex could pour its products. NATO could then build up sufficient strength to move onto the offensive and battle the Soviets to defeat. The danger of a two-front war also existed. It would no longer be possible to eliminate the Chinese threat with nuclear strikes at the outbreak of war, and the deteriorating relationship and growing Chinese military capability made the threat increasingly serious.

The defeat of NATO in Europe had to be accomplished without precipitating an intercontinental exchange. Thus the immediate objective was to inhibit NATO from resorting to nuclear weapons. The possibility of being able to do so was based in large part on NATO's adoption of flexible response, which meant that NATO would initially resist a Soviet offensive with conventional means only. If during this conventional pause the Soviets could neutralize NATO's nuclear forces by nonnuclear means, they would have removed the critical first rung of the ladder of escalation. Alternatively, if during this pause the Soviets could knock European NATO out of the war with a conventional blitzkrieg, then the question of escalation might become moot as Washington faced a fait accompli. A combination of both courses of action, with additional action designed to disrupt or paralyze the NATO decisionmaking process, would increase the chances of taking over Europe without precipitating escalation to a full-scale nuclear strike on Russia.[5]

Successful models of these operational concepts were already at hand. The German offensive in Western Europe in May–June 1940 and the Ardennes offensive in December 1944 showed what could be achieved using conventional blitzkrieg combined with daring raids, deception, and fifth-column diversions. The preemptive Israeli air strikes that neutralized the Egyptian air force in June 1967 indicated what might be possible against NATO's nuclear delivery systems.

Clearly, there could be no certainty that operations in Europe would not escalate to an intercontinental exchange. But where world war is concerned, there are no ideal solutions, only lesser evils. The nuclear devastation of Russia would be such an overwhelming catastrophe that if war could not be avoided, it was still worth investing considerable resources to pursue a fairly small possibility of avoiding escalation, even if chances were as low as 10 to 20 percent.

5. See Major General V. Zemskov, "Characteristic Features of Modern Wars and Possible Methods of Conducting Them," *Voennaya mysl'*, no. 7 (July 1969); and Charles J. Dick, "Soviet Operational Concepts," *Military Review*, vol. 65 (September 1985), pp. 29–45.

Moreover, the Soviets were not balancing the costs and benefits of an initiative aimed at taking over the rest of Europe as is implied by Western deterrence theory. Rather they were trying to decide on the best policy should world war become inescapable. A crucial consideration was whether the United States would launch a massive nuclear strike on Russia if American forces faced defeat on the ground in NATO. If such a probability seemed high, then the best policy was to concentrate on securing any benefits available from strategic preemption. But if there was a significant possibility that the United States might not escalate, then the best policy would be to concentrate on shaping Soviet force structure and operational concepts to reinforce that possibility. This policy meant eschewing strategic preemption.

In 1966 the possibility of managing to avoid escalation to an intercontinental exchange was not insignificant and appeared to be increasing. Although Western strategic theorists talked of crossing the nuclear threshold as if it were just another rung in the ladder of deterrence, comments by past and present Western decisionmakers made it increasingly evident that there were strong psychological constraints on taking this portentous step into the unknown. John Foster Dulles had spoken almost casually about resorting to massive retaliation, but that was before the Soviets were able to strike at the United States. As the Soviets acquired that capability, there were adjustments to, and rationalizations of, U.S. strategic nuclear policy. All were designed to fend off the final decision that would almost certainly bring nuclear weapons raining down on North America.

Many Europeans, including General Charles de Gaulle of France, were openly skeptical that the president of the United States, if faced by the impending defeat of U.S. forces in Europe, would order a strike on Russia. A strike would not save Europe and would certainly bring about the devastation of America's cities. In this situation it was in Soviet interests to invest the additional resources required for conventional operations and to forgo the uncertain advantages of strategic preemption in order to increase the possibility of avoiding the nuclear devastation of Russia.

Contemporary Considerations

Soviet forces are structured to be able to fight and win a world war. However, the first-order objective is to avoid such a war. A possible cause of war would be an outbreak of internal unrest in Eastern Europe, leading to a Western incursion of some kind. The least unlikely of such scenarios would involve conflict between the two parts of Germany. A primary military objective in the European theater is therefore to avoid such a situation by deterring and, if necessary, preventing external involvement in Eastern Europe. Meanwhile the Soviets use force as necessary to suppress internal insurrection.

The Onset of War

Should a world war become unavoidable, the military objective would then shift to not losing the war and, among other things, this aim would require a full-scale ground and air offensive against NATO Europe. As already discussed, the necessary operations would have to combine speed with precision; the use of conventional weapons and sabotage to mount disarming strikes and special operations against nuclear delivery systems stationed in the theater; deep, disruptive operations to paralyze NATO command and control and, if not too late, to prevent full mobilization; and offensive blitzkrieg operations to outflank, destroy, or capture NATO ground forces would be necessary.

It should not be assumed that the problems caused for such an offensive by unrest in the Warsaw Pact would necessarily cause the Soviets to re-double their efforts to avoid world war. At a certain stage the prospect of such problems is likely to have the opposite effect. If war were a real possibility, and if it seemed that the capability for a successful offensive would be placed in jeopardy by civil turmoil in the rear, then the pressure to launch the offensive while still possible would be considerable.

This potential highlights a difference between the way the two opponents envisage the onset of war. In the West escalation tends to be seen as a linear process. Starting from a state of relative relaxation, one moves progressively up the scale of hostility, through heightened tension, to increasingly serious confrontation until finally there is an exchange of blows somewhere on the periphery of the Soviet bloc. From there one moves to conventional war in Europe, the use of tactical and then theater nuclear weapons, progressing to intercontinental strikes on increasingly larger numbers of carefully selected targets in the superpowers' home territories. The time scale can be stretched out or compressed, but the process is envisaged as inherently linear, allowing a series of graduated decisions.

The Soviets have consistently made it clear that they think the concept of controlled nuclear escalation is dangerous nonsense. It seems likely that the Soviets envisage the progression as a series of disjunctions or "catastrophe folds"[6] rather than as a simple gradient. The change from one situation to another would be large and sudden because at each stage they would be faced by conflicting pressures. As war becomes more likely, they must continue to do everything in their power to avoid it, until they deem it inescapable. At that moment they must switch to pursuing the objective of not losing, which places a high premium on surprise and shock.

This "catastrophic" change of policy would be less acute today than it would have been before 1966, when doctrine required the Soviets to seek the benefits of strategic nuclear preemption. Nevertheless, the switch from peace to war is likely to be considerably more abrupt than is envisaged by Western theorists. Similarly, there would be other potential catastrophe folds as the war progressed, such as the resort to nuclear weapons in different theaters or the decision that escalation to an intercontinental exchange was unavoidable.

Catastrophe theory warns one not to expect the Soviets to obey the notional rules of some theoretical escalation ladder, although this does not exclude "tit-for-tat." Rather one should expect the Soviets to anticipate a coming shift from one behavioral surface to the other and then move to that new surface suddenly and with maximum force.

Policy toward Nuclear Escalation

This concept underlay the Soviet emphasis on preemption in the 1960s and would still pertain in a wide range of circumstances today. However, in the contemporary period, the objective of avoiding the nuclear devastation of Russia has introduced a complication because of the danger that a preemptive nuclear attack on the West at any level could precipitate escalation to an intercontinental exchange. At the same time the Soviets' higher-order objective of not losing the war continues in force. It can be inferred therefore that Soviet policy toward escalation is complex. Their operational decisions would depend on judgments made at the time about U.S. reactions in the prevailing circumstances. At least through the mid-

6. Catastrophe theory is a mathematical method for dealing with discontinuous and divergent phenomena and can cover a wide range of situations requiring decisionmaking. The situations can be modeled by a folded surface; the double fold explains the abrupt shift of policy as one moves across the surface. See E.C. Zeeman, "Catastrophe Theory," *Scientific American*, vol. 234 (April 1976), pp. 65–83. The folded surface is a more plausible model of the development of hostilities between nations than the simple gradient of escalation theory and shows how a small change in the situation can trigger a catastrophic change of policy.

1970s, lectures at the Soviet General Staff Academy assumed that the introduction of nuclear weapons into a conventional strategic operation would occur as a result of NATO, rather than Soviet, first use. Throughout this period, Soviet military theorists saw little advantage to be gained from a Soviet first use of nuclear weapons.[7]

In comparing this brief discussion with the conclusions of other more specialized analyses of Soviet theater nuclear doctrine, it must be borne in mind that the other analyses rely heavily on pronouncements from the 1960s, which can not be adduced as evidence for the contemporary period.[8]

THE THEATER LEVEL. At this level two main types of situation must be covered. The simplest is the one in which the Soviet offensive is going well. Then the arguments would be strong for resisting the military urge to preempt a NATO resort to nuclear weapons. The Soviets would tend to allow the West the advantage of initiating the use of nuclear weapons, but the Soviet response would be shaped to yield the maximum military return while discouraging further escalation. This type of restraint would be particularly appropriate if the West's declared policy was to start on the lower rungs of an escalation ladder or with some demonstration shot. Soviet skepticism about the military utility of nuclear weapons suggests that they might choose to respond asymetrically (for example, by striking at an aircraft carrier) rather than resorting to nuclear weapons on land.

The more difficult situation would be one in which the Soviet offensive in Europe had been held up by NATO conventional forces. Then the Soviet leaders would have to decide whether, by using conventional means only, they could achieve the local preponderance required to break through. If the answer were no, in order not to lose the war they might then resort to nuclear weapons to achieve their objective in the Western theater of military operations. If the Soviets believed that Europe was effectively decoupled from the U.S. strategic deterrent, this would present no new problems. But if they had concluded otherwise, they would then have to assess the probability of escalation to an intercontinental exchange.

If the probability were low, the sensible policy would be to try to finesse

7. Notra Truelock III, "Weapons of Mass Destruction in Soviet Military Strategy," paper presented at a conference on "Soviet Military Strategy in Europe," Oxfordshire, England, September 24–25, 1984, pp. 70, 91.

8. See Stephen M. Meyer, *Soviet Theater Nuclear Forces—Part I: Development of Doctrine and Objectives,* Adelphi Paper 187 (London: International Institute for Strategic Studies, 1983–84); and Paul K. Davis and Peter J.E. Stan, *Concepts and Models of Escalation,* R-3235 (Santa Monica, Calif.: Rand Corp., 1984), pp. 20–31.

the danger. If the probability were high, verging toward certainty, the lesser evil might be to seek whatever advantage could be gained from strategic preemption. Given Soviet policy decisions of the past fifteen years, it seems likely that they are biased toward finessing escalation. But should the Soviets have to decide on initiating nuclear use in the theater, one must assume that they would also review the option of full-scale intercontinental preemption.

THE STRATEGIC LEVEL. At this level a major problem is how to respond to the American concept of escalating "limited nuclear options." Under this plan, the United States strikes at selected targets inside the Soviet Union. The objective of avoiding the nuclear devastation of Russia argues against any automatic policy of escalating to an intercontinental exchange. On the other hand, the Soviets must demonstrate that they are not open to coercion by the threat of escalation and that such attacks will not yield the United States any relative military advantage.

In deciding on the appropriate response, the Soviets have no reason to assume that because the United States thinks it can make selective strikes on the Soviet Union without provoking a full-scale attack on North America, the reverse is necessarily true. Indeed the thrust of Soviet writing and the scorn they heap on the idea of controlling strategic nuclear war implies that they believe that any kind of nuclear attack on North America has a high probability of provoking a massive nuclear strike on Russia, a judgment that seems well founded in common sense. There are a range of important military facilities outside the continental United States, such as islands, other bases, and aircraft carriers. These not only provide appropriate targets for a selective response, but their destruction would almost certainly yield the Soviets a relative military advantage.[9]

THE TENDENCY TO ESCALATION. What do all these considerations say about the Soviet tendency toward escalation in the event of a world war? On the one hand, the objective of avoiding the nuclear devastation of Russia imposes strong constraints on resorting to nuclear weapons at both the theater and the strategic level, although this does not preclude the appropriate response to Western nuclear initiatives at either level. On the other hand, the higher-order objective of not losing the war means that if the main Soviet offensive in Europe is bogged down, there could be strong

9. The pressure to escalation would be a function of the target's location and its politico-military significance. The high symbolism of a target inside the Soviet Union dictates that, if the United States hoped to avoid escalation, the military significance of such a target would have to be fairly low.

pressure to use nuclear weapons to achieve a breakthrough. The argument would then focus on whether the resort to nuclear weapons was essential to avoiding defeat rather than on the dangers of escalation. If the Soviets were faced with the failure of their offensive in Europe, they would have to choose between the possibility of escalation then and there, and the near certainty of escalation later, in extremely unfavorable circumstances.

The near certainty of "escalation later" reflects the following reasoning. At least for planning purposes, the Soviets would have to assume that if NATO were left with a viable bridgehead in Europe, it would only be a matter of time before the United States, supported by the other capitalist states, would build up an overwhelming preponderance of military power. This assumption would reflect Marxist beliefs about the nature of the struggle between capitalism and socialism and be reinforced by the experience of World Wars I and II. Once the United States had built up its strength, it would then move to overthrow the Soviet state and destroy the socialist system, in the same way that it had moved to overthrow the facist systems in World War II. At this stage intercontinental escalation would become almost inevitable.

In the worst case the United States would have developed some means of weakening the Soviet deterrent force or rendering it impotent and would be able to strike at Russia with relative impunity. Even in circumstances less unfavorable to Russia, the pressure on both sides to escalate preemptively would be almost irresistible. If Russia were faced by certain defeat and dismemberment, the United States would be likely to assume that, rather than surrender, the Soviet leaders would gamble on launching a full strike on America. The United States would therefore choose to strike first.

If the Soviets were faced by failure in Europe during phase I of a world war, the forces constraining them from escalating would therefore be much weaker than the forces constraining the United States if it were faced by eviction from the Continent. If the United States allowed NATO to go down to defeat without launching a nuclear attack on Russia, it would certainly have suffered a serious military setback. But because the American homeland would still be intact, the United States would still be able to carry on the war. Then ultimate victory achieved by industrial might and technological ingenuity would still be conceivable. Although the United States would have lost a major battle, it would still be a long way from having lost the war. Meanwhile there would be every reason to assume that the American homeland would continue to be spared nuclear devastation.

The Soviet concern to avoid escalation is demonstrated by the resources they invested in developing the potential to knock NATO out of the war by using conventional forces only.[10] Nevertheless, the Soviets remain skeptical that escalation can be avoided, and their armed forces are prepared to fight by using conventional or nuclear weapons as the circumstances may require. At the same time the thought patterns that shaped the 1960s hierarchy of objectives are unlikely to be far below the surface.

A strong measure of fatalism permeated the policy and operational concepts formulated in the 1959–66 period. The experience of World War II had conditioned the Soviets to think of massive casualties as the price of rebuffing the enemy, and well into the mid-1950s the United States had a virtual monopoly on deliverable nuclear weapons. It seems likely that this ingrained fatalism would continue to play its part in shaping Soviet decisions. If at any stage of the war the Soviets concluded that events were leading inexorably to a major nuclear attack on Russia, then it remains possible that the Soviets would launch a preemptive strike on North America.

Neutralizing NATO Forces in Europe

What are the Soviet plans in a world war that does not escalate to an intercontinental exchange? If the Soviet Union is not to lose such a war in the long run, it must neutralize NATO forces in Europe and deny America a future bridgehead on the Continent. The question of what the term neutralizing implies must still be answered. Operations in Europe will be crucial to the final outcome of the war, which the Soviets see as one episode in the struggle between two social systems. Does neutralizing therefore imply the total destruction of NATO forces, or might one expect a more carefully differentiated policy?

There is little doubt that the Soviets would seek to destroy all nuclear weapons and means of delivery in the theater, including most types of fixed-wing aircraft. One would also expect considerable destruction as the Soviets strove to break through NATO's defenses. Assuming that the Soviets were successful and NATO acknowledged defeat on the ground in

---

10. In December 1984 General Bernard Rogers, the Supreme Allied Commander Europe, was reportedly convinced that the Soviet Union does not want to be the first to resort to tactical nuclear weapons because of fear of a quick escalation to a strategic exchange with the United States. William Beecher, "General Outlines Plan to Avert Nuclear War," *Boston Globe*, December 16, 1984.

Europe, there would be strong arguments for a nondestructive and conciliatory policy toward the remaining NATO forces. Soviet interests would
be served best by an immediate armistice, followed by a peace treaty that
upheld some new status quo.

Protracted war would impose massive social and economic costs on the
Soviet system while the final outcome could not be foreseen. The unilateral destruction of the United States would be no more of an option after
the defeat of NATO in Europe than before, because it would result in the
reciprocal destruction of the Soviet Union.

The Soviets, having achieved the immediate military objective of not
losing the war, would resume giving prominence to the first-order national
objectives of avoiding world war while preserving the capacity for independent action. Whether these objectives would be attainable is question-
able, but to the extent they were, Soviet policy concerning the disposal of
the defeated forces in general, and U.S. forces in particular, would be critical in determining the outcome.

The British and French Strategic Nuclear Capability

The British and French strategic nuclear forces jeopardize the governing
objective of avoiding the nuclear devastation of Russia. The ultimate rationale for their existence is that the United States can not be relied on to
destroy itself for the sake of Europe, but Britain and France can be expected to sacrifice themselves.

The Russians can address the threat in two ways. Disarming these systems with conventional attacks is not feasible because both Britain and
France have submarine-launched missiles that at least in the short term are
largely invulnerable. Riding out a strike from either or both of these countries is also not a satisfactory answer. Although the weight of a British or
French attack would be only a fraction of what the United States could
deliver, there would be a strong possibility that a European strike would
trigger a full-scale preemptive strike by the United States, since the United
States would reason that the Soviets would be unlikely to limit their response to European targets. A European attack might also incapacitate Soviet command, control, communications, and intelligence sufficiently to
prompt a U.S. disarming strike.

These unattractive possibilities leave the Soviets one other alternative.
They could try to invalidate, by threat or inducement, the claim by Britain

and France that they would be willing to suffer nuclear devastation if NATO were to go down to defeat. The Soviets can not be sure of the success of such efforts, but clearly they have room for maneuver.

Although the security of Britain and France is more dependent on the fate of Europe than is America's, the United States undoubtedly has more numerous and closer cultural ties to the rest of Europe than do either of them. Traditionally, Britain has stood aloof from the rest of Europe and her involvement on the Continent has been strictly pragmatic and directed at serving fairly narrowly construed interests. Over the years, the British nuclear capability has been justified more on the grounds of political influence than military utility, and the latter has always focused on deterring a Soviet urge to expansion and ignored the question of what should be done if deterrence fails in the face of a Soviet strategic imperative. Physically, France is more part of Europe, but its history, traditional enmity for Germany and contempt for Italy, and arrogant policy toward NATO, argue that it is France's fate and not the rest of Europe that is the issue. Furthermore, France's performance in 1940 showed a willingness to compromise to preserve some kind of national entity, even if severely truncated and heavily circumscribed.

In other words, if the United States did not escalate to avert defeat in the field, it would be most unlikely that Britain and France would do so until their territories were directly threatened. In such circumstances the Soviets should be able to adapt their operational strategy and diplomatic demands to reinforce the inherent constraints on Britain and France from escalating to nuclear war. After all, it would make little sense in pragmatic terms to compound the disaster of military defeat by acting to ensure the nuclear devastation of one's homeland. Soviet policy would therefore focus on developing outcomes for Britain and France that avoided escalation and could be rationalized as serving the two countries' long-term interests.

Establishing Political Control

Even if NATO forces in Europe were defeated and the European governments sued for peace, America would be likely to carry on the struggle. This would present the Soviet Union with the demanding requirement to maintain political control throughout the theater during a protracted war. The Soviets however would have several advantages over the Germans, who faced much the same situation in the 1939–44 period. In purely practical terms, the Soviets can draw on the German experience, their own experience in Eastern Europe, and even their "nationalities" problem. The Soviets now have a more sophisticated understanding of the dynamics of national cultures and the limitations of transnational concepts such as the international proletariat. They also have a much keener awareness of how to manipulate these forces to ensure control, as well as a more subtle appreciation of what that requires.

The natural antagonism between victor and vanquished would be inevitable, but the Soviets would have the advantage that, unlike national socialism, Marxism is a universal ideology, and Marxist theory is not far from the roots of most left-of-center parties in Europe. In the same way, the concept of the USSR as a multiethnic union of socialist republics and of the Warsaw Pact as a brotherhood in arms, is very different from the national socialist idea of an Aryan master race.

The existence of substantial communist parties in most Western European countries would also work in the Soviet interest once the battle was over. In many of these countries, communists have held electoral office with distinction at the local and regional levels of government, while rank and file members would provide important administrative cadres, and they would all be reasonably well attuned to Soviet expectations. The Soviets should also be able to appeal to the members of the broader working class, exploiting their latent envy and distrust of political and bureaucratic elites to refashion the infrastructure of governance to better serve the interests of the socialist system. At the same time, by encouraging the separatist tendencies of the cultural nationalists and of those who seek regional autonomy, the Soviets should be able to weaken the remaining influence of the established state structures.

Soviet political objectives would be largely determined by whether they were faced with the prospect of protracted war or had been able to conclude some kind of peace with the United States. The situation would be comparable with that in Eastern Europe in the 1945–47 period. In a protracted war the Soviets would seek to incorporate the countries of Western Europe into the greater socialist bloc as rapidly as possible, implying massive political purges and forced-draft communization. The military situation might also require the wholesale removal or exchange of populations in key strategic areas. If, however, the Soviets were able to reach some kind of peace agreement with America, they would be more inclined to be relaxed about the political complexion of West European states, allowing many of them to adopt a Finland-type stance.

Denying America Access to Europe

If the Soviets were successful in defeating NATO forces in Europe, but were then unable to make peace with America, they would be faced with the prospect of a protracted war between the two social systems.

In planning against such a contingency, the history of World War II offers some analogies. Defeated on the Continent, the British withdrew across the English Channel and provided a rallying point for the scattered remnants of their allies' forces and their governments in exile. Although it was four years before Commonwealth troops returned to the Continent, within eight months of the defeat at Dunkirk, they were engaging Axis forces elsewhere in the world.

America, caught by surprise at Pearl Harbor in December 1941, proceeded to build up its forces and drive west across the Pacific and by 1945 had closed in on Japan and was girding itself for the final assault on those islands. Within eleven months of Pearl Harbor, U.S. forces sailed directly from America to land in North Africa, fought their way eastward to link up with the British in Tunisia, from where the Allied armies launched their assault on Sicily and on up through Italy. At the same time Allied forces were being built up in Britain, and within a year of the invasion of Sicily, the Allies recrossed the English Channel with continental-scale armies.

The Soviets would draw at least two lessons from this record. One, distance would be no deterrent to the projection of U.S. military power. Two, if the United States were allowed to gain a secure foothold on the Continent, it would only be a matter of time before its industrial capacity allowed it to build up sufficient forces to overpower its opponent.

The Soviets have therefore to think of establishing a defense perimeter that would deny America the use of such bridgeheads. The need for some kind of "Atlantic wall," this time to include the British Isles, would seem self-evident, but the more interesting question is where the Soviets should draw the southern perimeter. The problems involved in defending the northern littoral of the Mediterranean and the experience of World War II argue strongly for denying the West access to the Mediterranean during the second phase of a world war, and this implies having control of the Gibraltar Straits.

The fatal danger of allowing the Western Allies to gain a foothold in North Africa had also been demonstrated in World War II and would argue in favor of using the Sahara Desert as the southern boundary. The eastern end of that boundary would angle down to meet the Indian Ocean at the Horn of Africa, which would serve the extra purpose of covering the sea line of communication between the Black Sea and the Soviet Far East. From the Horn the defense perimeter would run northeast along the inhospitable shores of the Arabian Peninsula, past the Gulf of Hormuz, and then up through Baluchistan to Afghanistan. Such an alignment would make maximum use of the obstructive nature of oceans and deserts and would also encompass the bulk of the petroleum resources lying outside the Western Hemisphere.

From Afghanistan the defense perimeter could follow the Sino-Soviet border to the Pacific, and the threat of a U.S. invasion of western Russia by way of Siberia is unlikely to be of major concern to Soviet military planners. They would have to cover a much more dangerous contingency that could emerge at a later stage of a world war—an alliance between the United States and China. This would have the effect of outflanking the central and eastern parts of Siberia. In their long-range planning therefore the Soviets would have to allow that they might have to sacrifice those sparsely populated parts of the Soviet Union and concentrate on holding the West Siberian Plain, with the defense perimeter following the general north-south alignment of the Yenisey River.

The Overall Concept of Operations

In planning for a world war in which they are able to avoid escalation to an intercontinental exchange, the Soviets have to think of two phases. A first phase of initially intense operations would lead to the defeat of NATO forces in Europe, followed by some kind of peace agreement if possible. If peace were not possible, the war would then move into a second phase of protracted struggle on a global scale, whose course is hard to predict.[11]

For planning purposes, phase I would be divided into three separate stages, which will be called phase I-1, I-2, and I-3. Phase I-1 would cover

11. In 1969 General Zemskov noted that, assuming a conventional war, "there can obviously be an initial and subsequent periods. The initial period will obviously encompass a short period of time during which the most immediate strategic goals of the war will be achieved in the theaters of military operations and the mobilization deployment of the armed forces will continue. Characteristic of this period is the great dynamic nature and rapid change of forms of combat operations. The subsequent periods will encompass combat operations directed towards achievement of the final goal of the war." See "Characteristic Features of Modern Wars," p. 9.

the period of the offensive into Western Europe, including the operations designed to defeat the main body of enemy forces and knock NATO out of the war. Attempts to negotiate peace would be initiated at the completion of this stage. Phase I-2 would cover the redeployment of forces and the completion of offensive operations on the secondary axes of advance, as well as the rapid occupation of territories to the rear of the defeated enemy's main forces. Phase I-3 would cover the establishment of a defensive perimeter. The planners might think of achieving phase I-1 in twelve to twenty days; phase I-2 in another twenty to thirty days; and phase I-3 within another two to three months, depending on the alignment of the perimeter.

During the first two stages of phase I, the Soviets would be on tripwire alert for indications that the United States intended to escalate to strategic strikes on Russia. If they decided that escalation was inevitable, the Soviets would revert to the 1960s hierarchy of strategic objectives and the associated concepts of operation.

CHAPTER 5

The Implications at Sea

THE DOCTRINAL decision made in December 1966 and embodied in the 1970s hierarchy seriously affected Soviet naval policy.[1] Shifting from the objective of preserving the socialist system to that of avoiding the nuclear devastation of Russia resulted in two changes. One, ballistic-missile submarines would now have to provide insurance against the Soviet land-based intercontinental ballistic-missile (ICBM) force, the primary deterrent to a nuclear attack on the Soviet Union, being rendered impotent. Two, the shift in hierarchies reduced the relative importance of the Soviet navy's mission of countering the West's sea-based nuclear delivery systems. These changes in mission priorities meant that the Soviets had to adopt new concepts of operation throughout the fleet and restructure their surface and submarine forces.

A third change stemmed from the fact that if a world war did not escalate to an intercontinental exchange, the U.S. military-industrial base would then remain undamaged. What would the Soviet navy's role be in phase II, the protracted global struggle, of such a war? Finally, as an indirect result of the shift in objectives, a major internal debate about the role of navies in war and peace occurred. As a consequence of the debate, the concept of sea power came for the first time within the purview of Soviet military science.

The Soviet Approach to Deterrence

The objective of avoiding the nuclear devastation of Russia introduced a completely new requirement to deter the United States from launching a nuclear strike on the Soviet Union, even when America was faced with the

1. Appendixes B and C develop the evidence for the conclusions drawn in this chapter.

impending defeat of its forces in Europe. During the 1950s and 1960s Soviet military doctrine did not separate nuclear deterrence from the general concept of defense. Defense of the homeland depended on the ability to repel, or at least absorb, any attack and then go on to win the subsequent war. Obviously, the Soviets hoped that this capability would be sufficient to dissuade (or hold back, as the Russian term literally has it) an aggressor, which is deterrence in the generic sense. If war should nevertheless come, the Soviet emphasis has always been on defense through war fighting and on the capacity to wage war rather than simply on "inflicting punishment."

By 1956 the Soviets apparently felt that within a couple of years they could achieve this kind of deterrent capability. Thus they saw the introduction of intercontinental nuclear weapons into their inventory as part of the normal process of upgrading the armed forces. The weapons were not primarily related to nuclear deterrence in the Western sense. The West thought in terms of credibility, argued about the merits of counterforce or countervalue, and worried about stabilizing and destabilizing developments. The Soviets focused on not losing a war. The Soviet Union's readiness to fight and win a nuclear war was spelled out in the first edition of Marshal V.D. Sokolovskiy's *Military Strategy*. The public release of this book in 1962 may have even been intended as a deterrent statement to the West, in response to what the Soviets saw as an alarming buildup of U.S. strategic systems.[2]

The Soviet type of generalized deterrence against Western intervention or attack still pertains, but adoption of the new governing objective introduced a demanding requirement for a specialized form of Western-style deterrence. If world war was unavoidable, the Soviets would have to evict the United States from Europe. But according to NATO doctrine, an impending defeat of Western forces would trigger strikes on Russia by the three nuclear powers. The only thing likely to deter the United States, Britain, and France from such action was the certainty of devastating counterattacks on their homelands. The certainty of Soviet retaliation would be critical because the criteria for credibility would rise sharply once war was in progress. It would also be harder to achieve. Under the 1970s hierarchy the Soviets would have to forgo the option of preemption in order to promote the objective of avoiding the nuclear devastation of Russia. With the launch of its ICBMs dependent on indisputable evidence of a U.S. attack,

---

2. Marshal V. D. Sokolovskiy, ed., *Voennaya strategiya*, 1st ed. (Military strategy) (Moscow: Voenizdat, 1962).

the Soviet land-based missile force would be more vulnerable to a disarming strike.

In 1967 the Soviets were just beginning to build up their operational ICBM force in response to the surge in U.S. strength during the preceding five years. In numbers they would be able to balance the U.S. ICBM capability by about 1972. But could they be certain that the United States would not be able to render these land-based systems impotent, either by a disarming strike or by some technological breakthrough? Past experience of the American capacity to apply the latest scientific developments rapidly and successfully in the military field argued otherwise.

On the U.S. side, greatly improved missile accuracies and increased throw-weight could be achieved fairly easy. The development of warheads carrying multiple independently targeted reentry vehicles (MIRVs) was well in hand. The United States maintained the Minuteman force on high alert, and it was highly responsive to decisions. A functioning ballistic-missile defense system was clearly within grasp. On the Soviet side technological inadequacies meant difficulty in maintaining a large proportion of the ICBM force on combat alert. The embryonic antiballistic-missile system had severe limitations and was designed to protect the centers of government, not the ICBM fields. The Soviets probably had serious doubts about the effectiveness of their command, control, and communications system.

Besides this unfavorable balance, the United States had repeatedly demonstrated the technological capacity to "outflank" sucessive Soviet attempts to defend Russia against strategic attack.[3] All in all, the Soviets could have had little confidence that the United States would not be able to, in the next five to ten years, somehow render the Soviet ICBMs impotent. How that might be achieved was less important than the record of American success in achieving such objectives. The most obvious danger was the potential for a U.S. disarming strike. In principle a disarming strike could be countered by a policy of launch on warning, but the American satellites that now passed over the Soviet Union on a routine basis offered the means of neutralizing the command, control, communications, and intelligence (C³I) system that made such a policy practical. In the fu-

3. The United States successively developed the high- and low-altitude penetrating bombers and then the missile-armed stand-off strike bomber. At sea the strategic threat from the United States moved from the off-shore zone to distant sea areas such as the eastern Mediterranean and south Norwegian Sea and then graduated from carrier-borne strike aircraft to Polaris submarines.

ture lay the possibility of U.S. space platforms carrying exotic systems capable of disabling the ICBM force without warning.[4]

The future possibility of technological outflanking meant that, in war, the Soviets might not be able to rely completely on their land-based ICBMs to deter a U.S. strike on Russia. The most immediate requirement was to diminish the vulnerability of the ICBM force to foreseeable developments in U.S. capability. The Soviets could achieve their aim by increasing the hardness of the launch silos and by improving the certainty and survivability of the C³I system, both of which were undertaken during the 1970s.[5]

The Soviets also needed insurance against the possibility of being surprised by U.S. technological developments. They had to develop an alternative to the fixed-silo ICBM. Deploying mobile land-based missiles was ruled out as an immediate option because of problems with solid-fuel propulsion systems. The only readily available alternative was the submarine-launched ballistic-missile system.

The Development of Sea-based Strategic Delivery Systems

The Soviets were quick to perceive the submarine's potential for strategic delivery and have long stressed the value of its survivability. However, the present ballistic-missile submarine force is not the end product of a long-range plan, projected in the late 1940s. It is not just the result of incremental product improvement, a generation-by-generation upgrading of the submarine's hull-propulsion unit and the associated missile system. Rather today's Soviet force reflects three developmental periods: 1947–58, 1961–67, and 1968 to the present. In each period, the submarine's capability for the intercontinental delivery of nuclear weapons was intended to

4. It was technically feasible for reconnaissance satellites to carry a nuclear device that could be exploded on command over the Soviet Union. The electromagnetic pulse from such an explosion could disable Soviet command, control, communications, and intelligence. If necessary, satellite orbits could be adjusted to allow a simultaneous multiple explosion.

The Soviets' concern about space-based weapons had been demonstrated by their readiness in 1963 to conclude a treaty banning the stationing of weapons of mass destruction in space. See Raymond L. Garthoff, "Banning the Bomb in Outer Space," *International Security,* vol. 5 (Winter 1980-81), p. 25.

5. Third-generation intercontinental ballistic missiles were hardened to 200–400 pounds per square inch (psi). Fourth-generation missiles were hardened to 4,000 psi. Robert P. Berman and John C. Baker, *Soviet Strategic Forces: Requirements and Responses* (Brookings, 1982), pp. 91–92.

serve a significantly different strategic purpose. Between the first and second of these periods, the navy's role of strategic strike was eliminated.

This conclusion is partly based on Soviet pronouncements, but it is also based on major anomalies and discontinuities in the submarine building programs, for which some explanation must be found.

1945–57: Strategic Reach

After World War II the Soviets placed high priority on breaking the U.S. atomic monopoly. Developing a means of delivery was as important as building the bomb, and to ensure success, the Soviets adopted three lines of attack: the intercontinental missile, the long-range bomber, and the submarine.[6] Pursuit of the three approaches proceeded apace during the remainder of the 1940s and through the 1950s. The Soviets steadily increased the range of ballistic missiles, from the 150-mile SS-1, flight tested in 1947, to the 3,200-mile SS-6 tested ten years later; the first operational ICBMs, the SS-7 and SS-8 (a range of 5,000 to 6,000 miles) were flight tested in 1961. They developed two long-range bombers, the turbo-prop TU-20 Bear A and the jet MYa-4 Bison, which entered service in 1957 and 1956.[7] And they developed submarine systems.

The Soviets had initially planned to develop a large-type diesel submarine that would carry torpedoes armed with nuclear warheads and be capable of sustained operations off the American coast.[8] About 1947 they decided to allocate nuclear propulsion to the navy's strategic delivery mis-

---

6. The Soviets had always been in the forefront of ballistic theory and rocketry, but they had no practical experience in longer-range missiles and had to build on German experience. They lacked a long-range bomber force, but they had a well-developed aircraft industry and several innovative design bureaus. After World War II the Soviets had access to German design and production technology, were able to purchase jet engines from the British, and had available the American experience incorporated in the B-29 bomber. The one field in which Soviet technology and experience were already developed was the diesel submarine armed with a long-range torpedo. This system could deliver an atomic warhead close to, or even in the middle of, the many cities that lined the American coast.

7. Berman and Baker, *Soviet Strategic Forces*, pp. 96, 104–05; and Robert P. Berman, *Soviet Air Power in Transition* (Brookings, 1978), p. 25.

8. According to a Soviet naval history at the beginning of the 1950s, the Soviets applied atomic weapons in the form of warheads for rockets and naval torpedoes. N. A. Peterskiy, *Boevoy put' sovetskogo voenno-morskogo flota*, 2d ed. (The combat path of the Soviet fleet) (Moscow: Voenizdat, 1967), p. 544. In accuracy and ability to penetrate enemy defenses sea-based delivery would be at least as good as the next most certain means of delivery, the long-range bomber. A shallow-water burst in New York harbor or Hampton Roads was something to be reckoned with. Admiral L. Vladimirskiy pointed to the possibility of delivering mines and torpedoes with nuclear warheads into the harbors of major ports and naval bases. See Raymond L. Garthoff, *Soviet Strategy in the Nuclear Age* (Praeger, 1958), p. 204.

sion, and then in about 1949 they accepted that the launching of ballistic missiles from submarines was a realistic possibility. Both decisions involved untried technologies. Once more the Soviets had hedged their bets, just as they had when they decided to pursue three means of delivering a nuclear weapon; assigned two design bureaus to develop ICBMs; and developed both a jet and a propellor-driven bomber.

For submarines this diversified approach meant the development of two different hull-propulsion systems and two different weapons systems, resulting in a four-track program. Delivery to the navy of all four types was due to begin in 1958. Two would be nuclear-powered classes: the November attack submarine (SSN), armed only with torpedoes; and the Hotel SSBN, carrying three SS-N-4 350-nautical-mile ballistic missiles in the fin.[9] Two would be diesel-powered classes: the torpedo-armed Foxtrot SS and the missile-armed Golf SSB. Delivery of the first-generation, large-type diesel submarine, the Zulu-class SS, had begun in 1952, and these submarines had probably started carrying nuclear-armed torpedoes during 1955–56.[10]

Because of this major development effort, the Soviet Union would have been capable of delivering nuclear weapons on the United States by ICBM, bomber, and submarine by the early 1960s. But in about 1957–58 the Soviet leaders decided to concentrate on the land-based ICBM (whose development is outlined in appendix D). They halted the production of Bear and Bison long-range bombers and stopped the development of the Bison's successor, the MYa M-50 Bounder.[11] They also disrupted their submarine programs.

9. I am referring to the date of delivery (*sdacha*) of a ship by the building yard to the navy after acceptance trials have been successfully completed. Delivery of the first of a class is important to understanding the pattern of shipbuilding programs, and this term avoids the wider ambiguities of "entered service."

10. The Soviets have tended to make public claims for a capability about two years before it was due to become operational. In a "Statement of the Soviet Government concerning President Eisenhower's Address of 8 December 1953" a reference to "torpedoes with atomic heads" was linked to "rocket weapons which . . . can cover thousands of kilometers," in *Pravda,* December 22, 1953. See H. S. Dinerstein, *War and the Soviet Union: Nuclear Weapons and the Revolution in Soviet Military and Political Thinking* (Praeger, 1962), p. 71.

11. About 110 Bears and 85 Bisons were delivered from 1957 to 1960. Berman, *Soviet Air Power,* p. 25. After that, Bear production facilities concentrated on the civilian version of the aircraft (TU-114 Cleat) that was introduced on the Moscow-Khabarovsk run in 1961. In later years the production facilities produced Bear aircraft in reconnaissance (Bear D), antisubmarine warfare (Bear F), and airborne early-warning (Moss) configurations for the Soviet navy. Most recently the Bear aircraft has been adapted to carry a long-range air-launched cruise missile. There was no commercial version of the Bison. The Soviets' development of a follow-on to the Bison, but not the Bear, suggests that they concluded that jet propulsion was essential for long-range strategic delivery. The Bounder embodied the full development of this new design technology.

The relative success of Soviet land-based ballistic-missile programs, the development by the United States of substantial air and antisubmarine defenses, and the demands of the domestic economy were among the reasons for the Soviet decision. The submarine programs were disrupted for two more reasons: the nuclear submarines turned out to be technologically inadequate for the strategic delivery mission, and their hull-propulsion units were needed to counter the new threat posed by the U.S. development of long-range, carrier-borne nuclear-strike aircraft.[12] These aircraft were now capable of attacking the Soviet Union's industrial heartlands from the eastern Mediterranean and the south Norwegian Seas.

The allocation of nuclear hull-propulsion units in the Soviet navy was therefore shifted abruptly from the mission of strategic delivery to one of countering the aircraft carrier. By the end of the 1950s the mission of contributing to the main nuclear bombardment of the United States had been taken away from the navy, although it retained some capability for destroying coastal targets.[13]

The Yankees: A Matching Force

In 1961 the Soviet perception of strategic priorities changed again in response to the sharp increase in the U.S. defense budget and the accelerated production of U.S. strategic nuclear delivery systems after President John F. Kennedy took office. The Soviets were now seeing an apparent shift in U.S. emphasis from land-based to sea-based strategic forces. The United States was embarking on the rapid buildup of Polaris submarines, and this coincided with the entry into service of the large attack carriers ordered after the Korean War.

Unlike land-based missiles and bombers, the naval forces had a good chance of surviving the nuclear exchange with which, at that time, war was expected to start. If the United States chose to hold back the sea-based systems for use at a subsequent stage of the war, it was essential that the Soviet Union should have a comparable capability. This need generated the requirement for the Yankee ballistic-missile nuclear submarine (SSBN),

12. The reactor plants were noisy, making the nuclear variants easy to detect; the range of the SS-N-4 missile required the submarine to penetrate U.S. antisubmarine defenses; and the complex method of surface launch limited the certainty of response. Only the diesel-powered torpedo-armed Foxtrot came near the planned operational requirement.

13. See Robert W. Herrick, *Soviet SSBN Roles in Strategic Strike,* Report KTR 119-79 (Arlington, Va.: Ketron, 1979), pp. 6–7, 19. In July 1960 Admiral Sergey Gorshkov claimed the capability for destroying coastal objectives.

which would be able to match the capability of the U.S. carriers and Polaris submarines.

Fortuitously, key design and production processes were already moving in the right direction, which allowed the Soviets to schedule the Yankee program to start delivery to the navy in 1968. They probably planned a ten-year production run of 70 units (including the usual midterm upgrade), which would have roughly matched the combined nuclear delivery capability of the U.S. carrier force and the Polaris submarines. The Yankee would carry missiles with a 1,350-nautical-mile range, which would subsequently be extended to 1,600 nautical miles.

The Soviets were also faced by a surge in U.S. land-based strategic delivery systems, accompanied by a shift in U.S. basing policy toward hardened silos. The new U.S. policy largely invalidated the targeting philosophy that underlay existing plans for the Soviet ICBM force, and this occurrence necessitated radical changes in Soviet missile programs. The Soviets attempted to emplace medium-range missiles in Cuba to mitigate the impending gross U.S. advantage in intercontinental range systems. But the U.S. advantage would not have been the reason that led the Soviets, starting in 1964, to deploy Hotel-class SSBNs, armed with improved missiles, in closing distance of the U.S. coast. The targets of these submarines are likely to have been the aircraft carriers and Polaris submarines that were still in port at the onset of war.

By March 1966 the Yankee program was close enough to starting delivery for the SSBN force to be linked with the Soviet strategic rocket forces as "the main means for deterring an aggressor and for decisively defeating him in war."[14] At this date the United States was completing the deployment of its strategic nuclear forces, and the Soviet deployment had yet to get properly under way. The inclusion of the SSBN was more a demonstration of Soviet resolve than of capability, since the first Yankee was more than two years from entering service.

As originally conceived in 1961–62, the Soviets' requirement for a matching force stemmed from their prevailing doctrine that war with the West would inevitably be nuclear. If war seemed inescapable, then the Soviets would try to get in the first blow. This step would mean launching the full inventory of land-based intercontinental missiles against the United States because few of the silos for these missiles could be expected to

---

14. Marshal R. Malinovskiy at the Twenty-third Party Congress, cited in Herrick, *Soviet SSBN Roles*, p. 46. The SSBN force was linked with the strategic rocket forces throughout the third edition (1968) of Sokolovskiy's *Voennaya strategiya*.

survive an American strike. The Soviets would withhold the great majority of the Yankee force for use by the Soviet Supreme High Command during the subsequent stage of the war.[15] Except for a few Yankees needed to target any carriers and Polaris submarines that were in port at the outbreak of war, the force would not be deployed forward in peacetime or in a crisis, but could move to within range of likely targets after the initial exchange.

Delta and Typhoon: An Insurance Force

The 1970s hierarchy of objectives generated the requirement for a sea-based deterrent to provide insurance against the fixed-silo ICBM force being technologically outflanked by the United States. Should deterrence fail and war escalate to an intercontinental exchange, then these SSBNs would revert to the 1960s role of matching the West's sea-based nuclear delivery capability.

THE OPERATIONAL REQUIREMENT. It is useful to draw a sharp distinction between the SSBNs' functions as an insurance force and as a matching force to highlight the difference between the corresponding operational requirements. In deciding to build the Yankee matching force, one can assume that the Soviets did not overlook its potential as a hedge against some unforeseen inadequacy of the land-based missiles. This was, however, a secondary consideration: a bonus and not a factor in shaping operational requirements. In 1957–58 when the Soviets decided to concentrate on ICBMs to the exclusion of bombers and submarines, they had deliberately eschewed the U.S. policy of a strategic triad because it was not relevant to the Soviet concept of intercontinental preemption. Successful preemption depended on a timely political decision that war was imminent and unavoidable, and not on the military decision that the United States was about to launch an attack. To have to launch on warning was the worst case. It had to be provided for, but the certainty of such warning was a reasonable assumption in the 1960s. Insurance was not therefore an issue.

The different roles dictated different design specifications, which also reflected the different stages at which the missions would need to be discharged in war. The mission of the matching force would only become operative after an intercontinental nuclear exchange, when the force would

15. The concept of "withholding" stems from the 1961–62 decision period. The first Yankee was delivered in the fall of 1967, and the concept would therefore have been part of the "united views with respect to the tasks the fleet will have in modern war." See S. G. Gorshkov, "XXIII s'ezd KPSS i Zadachi voennykh moryakov" (The twenty-third congress of the CPSU and the tasks of navy men), *Morskoy sbornik* (Naval journal), no. 5 (May 1966), p. 8

constitute the major element of the remaining Soviet nuclear war-fighting capability. It was not essential for the matching force to be able to strike immediately at targets in North America, and the Soviets could assume that the majority of the force would be able to deploy within range of likely target areas after this exchange. The West's antisubmarine warfare (ASW) capability would have been seriously degraded by the loss of shore-based facilities for the bottom-mounted sound surveillance system, maritime patrol aircraft, and command, control, and communications.

The mission of the insurance force would become operative with the onset of war and would persist as long as the conflict did not escalate to an intercontinental nuclear exchange. The 1970s objective of avoiding the nuclear devastation of Russia meant that the insurance force would have to endure Western attempts to degrade its capability; survivability would be a vital characteristic of the SSBN in the insurance force. The Soviets could achieve the aim by designing the submarine to withstand battle damage and by providing defenses against Western attackers. The defenses could comprise on-board systems and external systems such as fixed defenses or supporting naval forces. The potential contribution of external defenses put a premium on the insurance SSBN being able to discharge its mission while close to home waters, where Soviet power gradients would be at their height and Western ones at their lowest. This ability reinforced a requirement that stemmed from the deterrent function of the insurance force.

Effective deterrence required that retribution be reasonably swift as well as certain. Neither could be ensured if the SSBNs had to make lengthy transits before they were in missile range of their targets. The insurance force would only be needed if the United States had developed some means of rendering the land-based ICBM force impotent. In that case the Soviets had to assume that the West's comprehensive ASW capability would be undamaged and fully operational. There could therefore be no certainty that Soviet SSBNs would be able to survive an ocean transit. Effective deterrence required that the insurance force be able to reach its targets from waters in which the SSBN had the greatest chance of surviving until it was ordered to launch its missiles.

THE 1967–68 DECISION PERIOD. The Soviets' immediate requirement was for a submarine-launched ballistic missile with the range to reach North America from Soviet home waters. As part of the normal process of product improvement the Soviets were already working toward such a capability, with a 4,300-nautical-mile missile due to enter service in 1978. However, that missile was not yet in the development pipeline. The adaptation of existing programs needed to produce such a missile and then fit it into the available hull-propulsion unit in time to allow a new class of SSBNs to begin delivery in 1973 provide classic indicators of a major change in policy.

The Soviets' end product was the Delta SSBN program, comprising three successive adaptations of the Yankee hull-propulsion system. The Delta I and II represented the initial response to the new requirement, and the Delta III was the interim response. At the same time, work was proceeding on the final response, a newly designed submarine tailored to the demanding new mission. The operational requirement was for an SSBN that could endure and survive concerted enemy attacks during a world war that did not escalate to an intercontinental exchange. The submarine had meanwhile to remain in continuous contact with the Soviet Supreme High Command and be ready to launch a strike on the United States at short notice. The Typhoon, which began delivery in 1982, was designed to meet these requirements.

The Typhoon may also have been designed to fulfill another role. If the Soviets should succeed in evicting U.S. forces from Europe without precipitating intercontinental escalation, the requirement for insurance against technological outflanking would lapse. The requirement might reemerge in later years, should the United States succeed in developing the means of rendering the land-based force impotent. In the intervening period the SSBN force would be unable to make any significant contribution to war at sea during phase II, unless, that is, the design of the SSBN incorporated a general purpose capability. Given that the surface displacement of the Typhoon class SSBN is comparable to that of the Kirov-class battle cruiser, this possibility is real.

PROTECTING THE INSURANCE FORCE.   The requirement to provide protection to the SSBN force was qualitatively new. A matching force required no special protection beyond that provided by the area defenses of the fleet. If a "matching" SSBN was attacked in home waters, that would signal the onset of war and trigger a full-scale nuclear strike on North America and targets throughout NATO. After the nuclear exchange, the matching force would need to deploy to within range of likely targets. The severe degradation of Western ASW, particularly its ocean surveillance capability, would facilitate such deployment. Surface combat support would probably be needed to gain the open ocean, but thereafter the matching SSBN could operate independently, perhaps with an attack submarine as outrider.

The insurance force would require sustained and heavy protection from the onset of hostilities until either a peace was negotiated or the conflict escalated to an intercontinental nuclear exchange. This demanding requirement was underlined by the information that the United States was developing a nuclear-powered attack submarine designed to operate against Soviet SSBNs.[16] The Soviet answer to this requirement was to plan to deploy SSBNs in defensible bastions. It seems likely that, originally, it was intended that the bastions would be located mainly in the Arctic Ocean, which the Soviets planned to turn into enclosed waters by establishing command of the Norwegian Sea. However, in the second half of the 1970s, emphasis shifted to the Pacific and the potential of the Sea of Okhotsk as a natural bastion.

The Soviets' general approach to the problem reflected long-established operational preferences, but the requirement to conduct sustained defensive operations for the duration of a conventional war was new. It represented a radical shift in operational concepts and generated a basic change in naval design criteria, particularly for distant-water surface forces.

Previously, the Soviet emphasis had been on the surface ships' ability to weather a preemptive attack long enough to discharge their primary mission of striking with nuclear weapons at Western carriers and Polaris submarines, after which they were expendable. But now, these same surface ships had to ensure the security of the SSBN force for an indeterminate time, through crisis, conventional war, and probably crisis again. Surface ships had to be capable of the sustained operations needed to gain and maintain command of substantial maritime defense zones. This capacity required long endurance, large magazine loads, and the ability to replenish supplies while under way. Since the war might well escalate, all units would require a full load of nuclear as well as conventional ordnance.

All distant-water surface ships and certain types of submarines would need to be considerably larger than previously. The Soviets therefore scaled up the various types that constitute the surface force, roughly doubling the size of the follow-on classes that would be programmed to begin delivery in 1980. However, the first of the Delta class would be ready for operational deployment in 1974, which meant that existing surface

---

16. Raymond V. B. Blackman, ed., *Jane's Fighting Ships, 1968–69* (McGraw-Hill, 1969), p. 522, reported that the SSN 685 electric-drive boat was planned as a superquiet submarine to track Soviet SSBNs. By early 1968 it was also clear that the U.S. Navy was proposing a very fast submarine. *Department of Defense Appropriations for Fiscal Year 1969*, Hearings before the Senate Committee on Appropriations, 90 Cong. 2 sess. (Government Printing Office, 1968), pt. 3, p. 1505; and *Department of Defense Appropriations for 1969*, Hearings before the House Committee on Appropriations, 90 Cong. 2 sess. (GPO, 1968), pt. 6, pp. 102–03, 337–38.

forces—already overstretched—would have to defend the Deltas. The defense could only be undertaken at the expense of other commitments. Forward strategic defense, the capability that the Soviet navy had been developing laboriously since 1961, was the most obvious choice for cutting.

Implications for the Navy's Mission Structure

The navy's move to forward deployment, which had begun in 1963–64, had been the other half of the Soviet response to the apparent U.S. shift in emphasis to sea-based strategic forces in 1961. The Yankee SSBN program would meet the general requirement to match the potential role of these U.S. naval forces as a strategic reserve. But the Yankee program would do nothing to counter the threat the U.S. systems could pose to the use of Western Europe as an alternative socioeconomic base from which to rebuild the shattered socialist economies. Because there was no way of physically defending an occupied Europe against U.S. strikes from the sea, some method had to be found of denying the United States the option of using its sea-based nuclear delivery systems for that purpose.

Thus the Soviets sought the capability to pose the United States with the choice of either using its sea-based nuclear delivery systems at the outbreak of war or losing them to Soviet attack. The Soviet navy would be deployed forward so that forces would be in weapon range of U.S. strategic delivery units at the onset of war. If the Soviet forces could to some extent prevent the U.S. units from launching strikes against Russia, so much the better. Their specific mission was, however, to deny the United States the option of withholding these nuclear weapons from the initial exchange for use at a subsequent stage of the war. To the extent this aim could be achieved, it would also support the broader objective of drawing down the U.S. strategic reserves.[17]

In 1961 the Soviets had already embarked on a distant-water response to the aircraft carrier, relying primarily on nuclear submarines, but Polaris presented them with a problem of a different order. The Soviets could directly counter U.S. ballistic-missile submarines in three possible ways: area exclusion, trailing, and ocean search and surveillance. The last two

17. In discussing the need to destroy all kinds of military reserves as a way of retaining a favorable correlation of forces, Major General Kh. Dzhelaukhov noted, "In a modern war the most important objectives in the reserves are, of course, nuclear rocket means which have not yet been brought into action." See "Combating Strategic Reserves in a Theater of Military Operations," *Voennaya mysl'* (Military thought), no. 11 (November 1964), pp. 2–15.

would require the development of new systems. A start could be made on the incremental process of excluding Polaris submarines from the more threatening sea areas by trying to raise to unacceptable levels the probability of their detection. This would require an extension and elaboration of the operational concepts that had been successfully developed for defense of the Soviet offshore zone. At the same time the Soviets would be contributing to countering the U.S. carrier threat.

In 1963–67 the initial response to the new requirement extended the outer defense zone to the 1,500-nautical-mile circle from Moscow. This took in the Norwegian Sea and the eastern Mediterranean and covered the threat from carrier-borne strike aircraft as well as from the early Polaris systems.[18] In the interim response, planned to start in 1967–68, the Soviets began the slow process of consolidating the newly established defense zones while extending the area of naval concern to take in the 2,500-nautical-mile circle of threat, including the northwest quadrant of the Indian Ocean. The Soviets probably originally hoped that a ten-year period would be time enough to develop measures that, beginning in 1972–73, would allow some kind of final response to the Polaris threat, along all three lines of attack.

It was in these circumstances that the Soviet military leaders reevaluated naval priorities and decided, in the wake of the December 1966 decision, that strategic delivery and hence the protection of the SSBN force must receive precedence in the naval mission structure. Given the new objective of avoiding the nuclear devastation of Russia, the decision was logical. The mission of countering U.S. sea-based strategic strike systems was directed primarily at a threat that would emerge after a nuclear exchange. In contrast the new objective was intended to deter the United States from initiating such an exchange. To the extent that deterrence was effective, it would cover sea-based systems as well as land-based ones. The new role of the SSBN force was to serve as an insurance force to guarantee the deterrent capability of the Soviet ICBM force. If this objective could be achieved, then postexchange threats would never materialize.

A further argument in favor of pulling back naval forces deployed in distant sea areas and concentrating them closer to home was the question of their survival. Under the 1960s concept of operations, the forces were only required to survive long enough after the outbreak of war to launch their nuclear weapons against Western attack carriers and Polaris subma-

18. The range of Polaris A-1 was 1,250 nautical miles; Polaris A-2 was 1,500 nautical miles.

rines. Under the 1970s concept of operations those weapons could not be used in that way unless escalation was considered inevitable. Meanwhile Soviet forward-deployed units would be subjected to sustained attack by greatly superior Western forces.

Clearly, the Soviet naval leadership could not challenge the requirement to ensure the security of the SSBN bastions during the conventional phase of a world war. There were, however, good reasons, other than institutional, why naval leaders should resist meeting the new commitment at the expense of the navy's forward deployment. Furthermore, the political circumstances existed for the navy to argue the case before a broader audience.

The Navy's Argument

The American proposal in 1967 to embark on strategic arms limitations talks considerably widened the internal Soviet debate on the implications of the ability to avoid nuclear attacks on Russia. The Soviet discussion ranged over the whole field of peace and war, including the desirability and possibility of stabilizing the strategic military competition, arguments about missions and force levels, and the allocation of resources.[19] The debate extended to the goals of Soviet foreign policy, the likelihood of world war, the nature of military objectives, and the potential role of Soviet military force in the third world. Disagreement ran not only between institutions and sectors of the body politic but also within the groups. Opinion reflected differing attitudes toward the dangers of war and the role of force in foreign policy.[20] In this atmosphere of open disagreement and debate the Main Naval Staff now challenged the General Staff on how best to handle the problem of securing the SSBN bastions.

The public vehicle for the navy's challenge was a series of articles entitled "Navies in War and Peace," which were published in the navy's journal during 1972–73, under the name of Sergey G. Gorshkov, commander

19. See Marshall D. Shulman, "Toward a Western Philosophy of Coexistence," *Foreign Affairs*, vol. 52 (October 1973), pp. 41–49; Thomas W. Wolfe, *Soviet Power and Europe, 1945–1970* (Johns Hopkins Press, 1970), pp. 273, 456, 508; and John Erickson, "Soviet Defense Policies and Naval Interests," in Michael MccGwire, Ken Booth, and John McDonnell, eds., *Soviet Naval Policy: Objectives and Constraints* (Praeger, 1975), pp. 60–61.

20. For a listing of how opinion divided, see MccGwire, "The Overseas Role of a Soviet Military Presence," in Michael MccGwire and John McDonnell, eds., *Soviet Naval Influence: Domestic and Foreign Dimensions* (Praeger, 1977), pp. 49–53.

in chief of the Soviet navy.[21] The major thesis was a contemporary exposition of classical seapower theory. It concluded that naval strength had always been a necessary attribute of great power status and claimed that Russia had always suffered when it neglected naval strength. In terms of the immediate debate, the argument had three main strands, one defending forward deployment in peacetime, a second concerning the operational requirements for ensuring the security of the SSBN force in war, and a third, longer-term argument about the importance of navies in influencing the course and outcome of wars.

In defending forward deployment, Admiral Gorshkov stressed the party's role in reshaping the navy so that it could defend the homeland against the threat of attack by sea-based strategic delivery systems while also deterring imperialist aggression in distant parts of the world.[22] He listed the task of countering sea-based delivery systems as one of the three that make up the basic naval mission in a nuclear war.[23] He stressed that the shift to forward deployment had fundamentally altered the correlation of forces in this sphere of peacetime confrontation and noted the navy's role as an ambassador of the socialist system.

However, the greater part of the series was taken up with a selective historical analysis of the role of navies in war, leading to the conclusion that they had always been important to the outcome. He wrote that nations had invariably paid a price for naval inferiority and defeat at sea. Furthermore, naval forces had become increasingly important because their inherent attributes had projected them to the forefront of contemporary combat.

His argument went far beyond advocating a greater role for the navy in Soviet strategy to criticism of how naval policy was formulated by the army-dominated military leadership. If the Soviet Union was to be able to exploit the potential of seapower as an instrument of state policy, the navy had to have a greatly improved worldwide general purpose capability. It

21. Sergey G. Gorshkov, "Voenno-morskie floty v voynakh i v mirnoe vremya" (Navies in war and peace), *Morskoy sbornik*, nos. 2–6 (February–June 1972), nos. 8–12 (August–December 1972); and no. 2 (February 1973). (Hereafter for the series entitled "Navies in war and peace": *Msb* year/month/page/para.)

22. The case is made most succinctly in the penultimate article *Msb* 72/12/20/5 through 21/5.

23. "Under today's conditions the basic mission of navies of the great powers in a world-wide nuclear war is their participation in the attacks of the country's strategic nuclear forces, the weakening of the nuclear attacks by the enemy navy from the direction of the oceans, and participation in the operations conducted by ground forces in the continental theaters of military action." *Msb* 73/2/21/8.

needed a broader range of types of surface ships, including aircraft carriers, and effective afloat support.

The Navy's Role in Phase II of a World War

More explicit statements of later years make it clear that Gorshkov was addressing the naval implications of the new objective of avoiding the nuclear devastation of Russia. On land the Soviet Union had to develop the capability to knock NATO Europe out of the war, a fairly short and finite operation that would end with Europe under Soviet control and the United States without a viable foothold on the Continent. But America would not just give up the struggle and retire to sulk in the Western Hemisphere. The U.S. military-industrial base would be undamaged, and NATO's navies could regroup in American ports. If history was any guide, Western naval forces would be a primary means of continuing the struggle and carrying the war to Russia.

Gorshkov's analysis of naval operations in the two world wars has to be interpreted with these circumstances in mind. In reviewing the basic tasks discharged by navies in World War II, Gorshkov focuses on the battle for sea communications and on strategic amphibious operations. His discussion of the battle for sea communications accounts for about 60 percent of the space devoted to operational analysis in the series. He concludes that the German submarine campaign had a significant effect on both world wars. He says that the reason it was less effective in World War II was because of German inadequacies and not any inherent limitation of the submarine weapon system. Furthermore, the diesel submarine was never driven from the sea, despite the massive buildup of Western ASW forces; imagine, then, the impact of nuclear submarines in such a campaign.

In his discussion of amphibious operations, Gorshkov brings out the almost universal success of landing operations during World War II and is concerned to draw lessons from the failure of the defenses against such assaults. He notes that not once during the war was a continuous attack mounted against a landing force, from the time of its initial assembly to its entry into the assault zone.

In both these discussions, Gorshkov was arguing the strategic significance of disrupting sea lines of communications, whether they were being

---

24. When talking with Western naval officers in the early seventies about balanced forces, Gorshkov commented that although it was easy to defend the requirement for submarines, it was much harder to justify the need for surface ships.

used to convey goods and people or to project force at a distance. He wanted to demonstrate that past limitations in this operational area could be overcome. He discussed two different kinds of operation. One was defense against seaborne invasion and the need to attack such forces from the moment of their initial assembly. The other was the blockade of North America.[25] A blockade would be feasible if the Soviet Union had sufficient submarine forces at the outset of a war and did not allow the United States time to build up its merchant fleet and ASW forces.

A major focus of Gorshkov's criticism was the military leaders preoccupation with the continental theaters of action. He decried the military's inability to perceive the central importance of the Soviet navy's role in a war in which the primary opponent was a maritime power such as the United States. In his analysis of naval operations in World War II, he concluded that task-specific fleets, such as the German and Japanese, were severely handicapped in comparison to those, such as the British and American navies, that had the broad and more balanced capability needed for large-scale strategic missions. Gorshkov was arguing against cutting back on forward deployment and against forcing the navy to concentrate on the mission of protecting the SSBN force. He wanted Soviet military leaders to extend the scope of naval missions to cover the requirement of protracted war at sea.

Compromise

Gorshkov's public challenge to basic policy decisions was unprecedented.[26] It indicates the cleavage in opinion in the Soviet politico-military establishment; the strength of the forces ranged on Gorshkov's side of the broader argument. The public debate was closed in May 1973, and some kind of compromise biased in the navy's favor seems to have been reached by April 1974. Marshal A. A. Grechko, the minister of defense, acknowledged that the function of Soviet armed forces was no longer restricted to defending the homeland and other socialist states. This policy fell into line with those endorsed by the Twenty-fourth Party Congress in 1971. Gorshkov acknowledged that the main naval mission was operations against tar-

25. The vulnerability of the U.S. military-industrial base to a sustained maritime blockade is evident from the tabulations compiled by the Bureau of Mines, U.S. Department of the Interior. See, for example, *Materials Policy, Research and Development Act,* Hearings before the Subcommittee on Energy Resources and Materials Production, Senate Committee on Energy and Natural Resources, 96 Cong. 2 sess. (GPO, 1980), pp. 37, 78, 209.

26. See Erickson, "Soviet Defense Policies," p. 60.

gets on land rather than combating the enemy fleet. Thus he accepted the leadership's order of formal mission priorities and the overriding importance of securing the SSBN bastions against enemy attack.

Certain constraints were apparently imposed on the navy's capacity for public dissent, but significant additions to naval building programs were approved. In addition the preparation of a book expounding the concept of seapower was authorized, with the restriction that it would have to reflect the interests of other ocean users besides the navy. Gorshkov's series of articles had largely ignored those interests.

Of course compromise does not mean agreement. While paying lip service to the new policy, the naval leaders continued to press their point of view in *Seapower of the State*, which appeared shortly before the Twenty-sixth Party Congress in 1976.[27] In a section that purported to be expounding the new priority of the fleet-against-shore mission (that is, the role of the SSBN and its supporting forces), most of the comments were really illustrating the importance of the traditional fleet-against-fleet role. A thinly veiled attack on the inability of military leaders to understand the importance of the navy in war was included. Although the book toed the line on the definition of a balanced fleet, a new section on command of the sea provided powerful arguments in support of the traditional role.

The book was well received; reviews stressed its contribution to military science, noting that the role of maritime power had for the first time been given a scientific formulation. The impression that the navy's political clout had increased considerably seemed to be reinforced by the appearance of a second edition of the book within four years. Meanwhile three of the contributing authors had been promoted. However, the trend toward greater naval autonomy had by then already peaked, and the General Staff had managed to reassert its authority in the field of military thought and the formulation of Soviet defense policy.

It may not be coincidental that the downturn in the Soviet navy's political fortune occurred not long after it became clear that a decision-in-principle had been reached about the future size of the U.S. Navy. The U.S. fleet was to be reduced to 12 carrier battle groups rather than the 15 it had averaged since the middle 1950s. Total numbers would stabilize at about 475 ships, compared with the 900 to 1,000 of the 1960s.

The downturn in the Soviet navy's fortunes was confirmed by a series of articles in *Morskoy sbornik* between April 1981 and July 1983 on the

27. S. G. Gorshkov, *Morskaya moshch' gosudarstva*, 1st ed. (Seapower of the state) (Moscow: Voenizdat, 1976).

"Theory of the Navy." They constituted a structured debate on the purpose of such a theory and what it should comprise; the discussion closed with an article by Admiral Gorshkov. The debate can be construed as an attempt to mark out the navy's legitimate turf within a unified system of military science and strategy, while setting up a theoretically legitimate vehicle for arguing the naval case in that system. Gorshkov did not forgo the opportunity to stress the importance of the naval element of a unified military science and to reemphasize the importance of a properly balanced fleet. Nevertheless, he did not challenge the central verities of Soviet military thought.

The Navy's Share of Resources

Despite Gorshkov's strictures, it is fair to say that since the early 1920s, Soviet leaders have persistently shown awareness of naval requirements. Josef Stalin and Nikita Khrushchev both took a personal interest in naval matters, and given the geostrategic circumstances and the scale of competing priorities, the navy appears to have had at least a fair share of scarce resources. The basic procurement and strategic policies have been well founded, if not always fully successful.

After the war, when the Soviet Union was faced by the "traditional maritime powers," the leaders responded with mass production warship building programs to cover the threat of invasion. Stalin also allocated nuclear reactors to submarines intended for strategic delivery. Military publications have constantly acknowledged the importance of the navy's role. The 1962 edition of *Military Strategy* emphasized the great changes in maritime warfare since World War II. It stressed that in a future war the navy's primary theater of operations would be the open ocean and that it must not be tied to ground force theaters of operations. In 1971, that is, after the decision to work toward the 1970s concept of operations, Marshal Grechko noted that maritime combat was achieving a special significance and that navies could have an enormous impact on the entire course of a future war.[28] It would be wrong therefore too interpret the naval debate in the 1970s as evidence that Soviet political leaders were insensitive to the maritime elements of a world war.

It may have been true that in working out the ramifications of the 1970s

28. A. A. Grechko, "The Fleet of our Homeland," in Foreign Broadcast Information Service, *Daily Report: Soviet Union,* August 11, 1971, pp. M1–6. (Hereafter FBIS, *Daily Report: SU.*)

hierarchy of objectives, the General Staff concentrated too exclusively on phase I of such a war, whose outcome would be determined by the success of ground and air operations in the European theater. The staff may have neglected what would be needed in phase II, the protracted struggle. Thus the Ninth Five-Year Plan that was under preparation in the 1969–70 period and was adopted by the Twenty-fourth Party Congress in the spring of 1971 apparently allocated less than the navy considered necessary to meet the new requirements generated by the 1966 decision, namely, to secure the SSBN bastions and to carry out a range of missions in phase II of a world war.

The General Staff was prepared to stick by its original decision, but after the Gorshkov articles, some additional construction of surface ships was apparently authorized as part of the compromise reached in 1973–74. An increase in the allocation of nuclear reactors for the next generation of attack submarines may have been agreed on at that time, only to be re-scinded before the end of the decade.

The Shaping of Naval Policy since 1975

The downturn in the navy's political fortunes that can be inferred from the evidence in publications coincided with the appointment of Dmitriy F. Ustinov as minister of defense and the subsequent appointment of Nikolay V. Ogarkov as chief of the General Staff. It is therefore unlikely to have been coincidental that 1977 saw a 15 percent reduction in the scale of naval deployment in the Mediterranean, which fell back to the level first achieved in the 1970s.[29] This was part of a general decline in the political use of the Soviet fleet in the third world that occurred in the late 1970s, a use that Gorshkov had strongly supported in the penultimate article of his 1972–73 series.[30]

A reassessment of the significance of the Arctic Ocean was a more se-rious blow to the importance of the navy's place in national plans. While

29. The Mediterranean deployment fell back from the 1972–76 average of 19,400 ship days a year to about 16,500 and remained close to that figure at least through September 1982. Robert G. Weinland, *Soviet Strategy and the Objectives of Their Naval Presence in the Mediterranean,* Professional Paper 410 (Alexandria, Va.: Center for Naval Analyses, 1982), pp. 32–33.

30. N. Bradford Dismukes and Kenneth G. Weiss, *Mare Mosso: The Mediterranean Theater,* Professional Paper 423 (Alexandria, Va.: Center for Naval Analyses, 1984), p. 2; and S. G. Gorshkov, "Navies as Instruments of Peacetime Imperialism," *Morskoy sbornik,* no. 12 (Decem-ber 1972), pp. 14–22.

the General Staff may have undervalued the navy's role in phase II of a world war in which the opponent would be a coalition of maritime states, it seems that the staff was overoptimistic about the cost-effectiveness of SSBNs as insurance against the technological outflanking of the land-based ICBM deterrent force. Although the evidence is still somewhat fragmentary, it strongly suggests that a major shift in policy occurred in the 1976–77 period, after Ustinov's appointment as minister of defense in 1976. Apparently, it was concluded that there were better and cheaper ways of insuring the land-based ICBM force than deploying submarines in heavily defended bastions in arctic waters.

One reason, and possibly the main reason, for placing the insurance force at sea was the relative failure of the SS-13 solid-fuel and potentially mobile ICBM. Clearly, the Soviets have now mastered the problem of producing viable solid-fuel missile propulsion systems, which means that they can deploy an insurance force carried by mobile launchers on land. There would be many ways of achieving mobility, ranging from an extension of the SS-20-type launcher system to use of the existing railroad network. Conceivably, mobile launch platforms of the future could be air-cushion vehicles or large crawler-tractors, each with a self-contained reactor power plant and ability to exploit the empty expanses of the Russian hinterland.

A land-based force has several advantages over a sea-based one. The first advantage is physical security. In times of tension, and during a world war that has yet to escalate, national territory will remain largely a sanctuary, but sea areas are always open to enemy intrusion. The second advantage is command and control because communication with launchers ashore is likely to be more certain. The third is the cost of supporting forces. Sea-based launchers like the SSBNs need heavy protection and are open to attack in peacetime and throughout a conventional war. But in a conventional war land-based forces are protected against attack by the sanctuary factor and by territorial defense systems such as PVO strany. Meanwhile a land-based force that can rely on dispersion and mobility can provide effective insurance against the technological outflanking of the fixed-silo ICBM.

It therefore seems likely that the Soviets have come to question the cost-effectiveness of an insurance force that has to be deployed in defended ocean bastions. A sea-based insurance force would remain a viable option in the Pacific, where the Kurile Islands provide a defensive barrier to the Sea of Okhotsk, but it is much harder and much more expensive to secure such bastions in the Greenland and Barents Seas. Effectiveness not only requires a large number of highly capable naval forces, but also demands specially mounted military operations to seize key islands and stretches of coast to gain command of the Norwegian Sea. Even then, the prospects of totally excluding enemy SSNs from the Arctic Ocean would be remote.

The evidence that the Soviets have had second thoughts along these lines is of two kinds, both dating from 1977–78. One involves changes in the Pacific, where there has been a buildup of the Soviet military presence on the Kurile Islands and a significant shift in the proportions of SSBNs and supporting forces between the Northern and Pacific Fleets. The other involves apparent changes in submarine and surface-ship building programs, including several that were apparently designed to support the new concept of operations in the Norwegian Sea. There is also the surprisingly low delivery rate of the Typhoon-class SSBN, coupled with the unexpected introduction of a fourth variant of the Delta SSBN. It was in January 1977 that Leonid Brezhnev offered to "refrain on a mutual basis from the development of new types of submarines and strategic bombers,"[31] and in the fall of 1982 the Soviets proposed that the number of Typhoon and Trident SSBNs be limited to four to six units.

If the Soviets have decided to move to a mix of land-mobile ICBMs and Okhotsk-based SSBNs, it could be well into the 1990s before a truly dispersible land-mobile component could be deployed and fully operational. For the next several years SSBNs will continue to be deployed in the Greenland and Barents Seas and will need to be held secure against Western naval intrusion. Even after that, the Soviets will almost certainly continue to deploy SSBNs in arctic waters, both for strategic dispersion and to complicate the U.S. Navy's problems. These units will depend largely on concealment and dispersal for their survival, operating within the protection of the fleet area defense zone.

An important implication of such a change is that command of the Norwegian Sea would no longer be essential to the safety of the SSBN force. If the Soviets moved the Northern Fleet's defense perimeter back from the Iceland-Faeroes Gap to some line running from northern Norway, the effect on Soviet naval requirements in that area would be significant.

A separate development that is compatible with the downgrading of the requirement to gain command of the Norwegian Sea is the greater use of Soviet naval forces in direct support of ground force operations within the continental theaters of military action.

31. See "Leonid Brezhnev's Speech in Tula," FBIS, *Daily Report: SU,* January 18, 1977, p. R8.

The Future

Questions about the importance of the Arctic Ocean and about establishing command, as opposed to denying command, of the Norwegian Sea have apparently been settled for the time being. The scope of the navy's role in phase II of a world war is a much more contentious subject. There is also room for disagreement about the navy's relative priority in the competition for scarce resources. Predicting the long-term effects of the 1970s objectives on Soviet naval requirements is therefore difficult.

One development that could influence the outcome of the wider debate on the navy's role in peace and war is the theoretical acceptance of the concept of seapower. Authoritative reviews of the first edition of Gorshkov's book, *Seapower of the State,* acknowledged that, for the first time in Soviet literature, seapower had been formulated as a scientific category, implying that the concept had become established in the mainstream of Soviet analytical discourse.[32] Previously, Soviet theorists had had an ideological aversion to the concept, which they equated with Mahan, capitalism, and colonialism. Just as John Maynard Keynes "General Theory" legitimized the idea of deficit financing and induced a shift in national economic policies, so may this scientific formulation have engendered a shift in Soviet perceptions of the navy as an instrument of national policy.

Such a shift could be important, both to the perceived contribution of the Soviet navy in a world war, particularly phase II, and for the navy's role in peacetime. The role of Soviet military presence in the third world was constrained throughout the 1960s and 1970s by the danger that superpower confrontation might escalate to global nuclear war. The conjunction of three possible developments in the first half of the 1980s could bring about a change.

One would be a downgrading by the Soviets of the perceived danger of escalation in third world confrontations; another would be a Soviet conclusion that the emergence of progressive regimes in the third world, and hence the progress of history, was being consistently checked by the U.S. use of military force; and third would be a surplus of naval capability over Soviet requirements as a result of redefining the strategic role of the Arctic Ocean. Such naval forces could project force in peacetime and could also make an important contribution in phase II of a world war.

32. Review of *Morskaya moshch' gosudarstva* (Seapower of the state) by Rear Admiral F. Savel' ev, *Krasnaya zvezda* (Red star), May 25, 1976.

A narrower question concerns the effect that the disruption of the arms control process that occurred in the 1979–83 period will have, or has had, on the allocation of resources to naval construction. At the time of the 1976–77 decision period the Soviets claimed that détente was irreversible, and the U.S. Navy seemed set to stabilize at some 475 ships and 12 carrier battle groups. With the subsequent crumbling of détente, the resurgence of U.S. naval strength, and the Reagan administration's approach to arms control negotiations, the Soviet leaders may have had to review some of the decisions made in 1976–77, and to assess how they stand up in the changed international circumstances.

PART TWO

The Operational Plan

CHAPTER 6

Governing Concepts

WHEN REVIEWING the evidence of the Soviet plans for the contingency of world war, one must distinguish between *structure* and *level of resources*. The structure of Soviet requirements is shaped by the contingency of world war; the level of resources allocated to meeting the requirements is conditioned by the Soviet assessment of the likelihood of war. The concept of structuring the armed forces is an important aspect of Soviet military thinking.[1] It reflects the truism that the force structure and supporting infrastructure that are established in peacetime are major determinants of what is possible in war.

Much of the evidence described in this book reflects the restructuring of the Soviet armed forces in response to the doctrinal shift decided in late 1966 on the nature of a future war and how it would be waged. Force structure had to be brought into line with the new doctrine. Priority differed among and within the three regions bordering Russia. In the more vital areas, for example, the central front in Europe, Soviet capabilities more closely match requirements, yielding concrete evidence of their structure. In less crucial areas, for example, the Horn of Africa, only some of the necessary capabilities are in place, and the structure of requirements has to be largely inferred.

The following three chapters develop the outline of an operational plan for the contingency of war in each of the main geographical regions bordering Russia. For all three regions the geostrategic analysis concentrates on assessing Soviet requirements, and the allocation of resources to meet

1. Structuring, *stroitel' stvo*, is often rendered less accurately as "development." See *Sovetskaya voennaya entsiklopediya*, vol. 7 (Soviet military encyclopedia) (Moscow: Voenizdat, 1979). (Hereafter *SVE*.) See also *Voennyy entsiklopedicheskiy slovar'* (Military encyclopedic dictionary) (Moscow: Voenizdat, 1983); "structuring the armed forces" rates as one of the six bodies of theory that now make up "military science."

the requirements is only implied and not discussed directly. The focus is on military concepts of operation designed to achieve the 1970s hierarchy of objectives that is posited in this book. No attempt has been made to assess the chances of Soviet success in achieving those objectives, nor is there any discussion of what the Soviets might do if their plans should go seriously awry. In particular no consideration has been given to the question of how the Soviets might seek to end a war, beyond assuming that once they had achieved victory in Western Europe, they would try to negotiate peace with the United States at the end of phase I-1.

In developing such hypothetical operational plans, many factors must be considered. Some of these, such as the Soviet emphasis on surprise and on offensive operations, or the need to select and maintain the main objective or the main axis of advance, are important, but they also reflect good military practice and generally accepted principles of war and are not particularly noteworthy. However, three factors are peculiar to the Soviets and significantly influence their operational plans: the concept of theaters of military action, the principle of combined arms, and the theory of deep operations.

Theaters of Military Action

The analysis of the operational requirements that stem from the post-1975 strategic objectives is organized for three regions: the Euro-Atlantic, the Asian-Pacific, and the Indo-Arabian. The geostrategic groupings reflect military logic rather than some Soviet classification. There is no Russian-language equivalent for "region" in the sense it is used here. The Soviets are loath to discuss geostrategic parameters openly, and to the extent they do, the discussion is based on either the Western organization of its military boundaries or the Allied experience in World War II.

The Soviets use World War II precedents to illustrate the concept of a theater of war (*teatr voeny*), which they describe as a broad geographical concept that does not have strictly defined boundaries. Such theaters of war are smaller than the three regions used in this book, nevertheless, they usually encompass a whole continent and its adjoining waters or an ocean and its coastline. The Soviets name the European, North African, Atlantic, and Pacific theaters as examples of how the West used the term in the second World War. It is generally assumed that the Soviets have divided the Eurasian land mass and its approaches into three theaters of war, which they may have labeled European, Far Eastern, and Southern.[2]

The Soviets distinguish between a theater of war and a theater of military action (*teatr voennykh deystviy*), which will henceforth be called a TVD.[3] A theater of war may contain several TVDs or it may be a single TVD, which leads to a confusion of terminology. However, unlike the theater of war, the TVD is a precise concept and its historical roots go back to 1815. In a TVD the operations of two or more large strategic groupings of forces are based on a single strategy, concept, and plan.[4] What has changed over the years is the breadth and depth of a TVD; the depth, in particular, was increased radically with the advent of long-range missiles and aircraft. There are two main categories of TVD: continental and oceanic (OTVD). The sea areas in the continental TVDs are called MTVDs (*morskoy* = sea).

The orientation and geographic scope of a theater of military action will reflect the existing disposition of forces and most likely areas of engagement. Currently the Soviet defense perimeter is divided into five continental TVDs (Western, Southwestern, Northwestern, Far Eastern, and Southern), and the Arctic OTVD (*okeanskiy* = ocean), but these boundaries are not immutable, and adjacent TVDs can overlap the same territory (figure 6-1). Besides the Arctic Ocean there is at least one other OTVD, the Atlantic Ocean.

For military operations, a continental TVD is deemed to extend from inside Russia to as far beyond its borders as makes military sense. It is a construct for planning in peacetime as well as for conducting operations in war. Each one has definite politico-military, military, economic, geographic, ethnographic, and engineering features that influence the preparation for, and the conduct of, military operations.[5] The Soviets talk of preparing and fitting out a TVD in peacetime for the ultimate contingency of war.[6]

2. U.S. Department of Defense, *Soviet Military Power, 1984*, 3d ed. (Government Printing Office, 1984). (Hereafter *SMP*.)

3. The literal translation of *voennykh deystviy* is "military actions." Until recently the Soviet term has often been rendered in the West as "theater of military operations" (TMO), which is an accurate reflection of the underlying concept. TMO can however lead to misunderstanding because the Soviets distinguish the strategic, operational, and tactical levels, and they classify the TVD level as strategic. Hence the literal translation.

4. Entries for *teatr voennykh deystviy* and *teatr voyny,* in *SVE*, vol. 8, 1980, pp. 8–9.

5. *SVE*, vol. 8, p. 8.

6. The Soviets even have a separate entry in the *SVE* under "P" (*podgotovka*) for "preparing a TVD." *SVE*, vol. 6, 1978, p. 384.

Figure 6-1. *Theaters of Military Action (TVDs)*

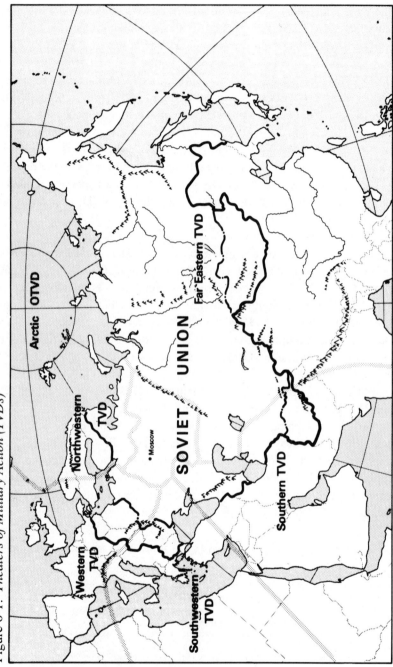

The basic operation in a future war is seen as a strategic operation within a TVD, encompassing two or more fronts and/or fleets.[7] However, the forces in each TVD will not necessarily have their own high command interposed between the Supreme High Command in Moscow and the front or fleet level. It is generally accepted that a high command for the forces of the Far Eastern TVD was established in the late 1970s, an organizational innovation that could be justified because of the TVD's remoteness and strategic objectives. In the fall of 1984 high commands were established for the forces assigned to the Western, Southwestern, and Southern TVDs.[8] The existence of a Northwestern TVD is unlikely to warrant the establishment of a high command in peacetime since there is only one front and one fleet active in the area. This arrangement, however, could change in the course of the war.

The Soviets value centralized control, and the creation of an intermediate command authority at the TVD level, which is based on the practice developed in World War II, reflects the need to provide operational flexibility rather than a belief in the intrinsic merits of such delegation. In World War II the Soviets also used other methods of ensuring coordination between fronts, such as the appointment of a Stavka representative (for example, Marshal G. K. Zhukov), and comparable expedients could again be brought into play.

The Principle of Combined Arms

The Soviet concept of combined arms embodies the sensible idea that military tasks are best discharged by the combined use of all appropriate arms, without regard to branch of service. There is nothing radical about this principle for ground and air warfare, but the Soviets apply it across all three mediums: land, sea, and air. They succeed in doing so for two reasons, one institutional and the other intellectual.

For traditional geostrategic reasons, the Soviet military is dominated by the ground forces. Russia was and is predominantly a continental power and, until the advent of nuclear weapons, the only threats to its territorial

7. N. Ogarkov, "Na strazhe mirnogo truda" (Guarding peaceful labor), *Kommunist,* no. 10 (July 1981), p. 86. Before 1978 a front was rated as the highest strategic formation of the armed forces, but it was then reclassified as an operational-strategic formation. Jack Sullivan and Major Tom Symonds, *Soviet Troop Control: Challenging Myths* (Maryland: Fort George G. Meade, Air Force Intelligence Services, 1985), p. 7.

8. *SMP, 1985,* 4th ed., p. 19; and Sullivan and Symonds, *Soviet Troop Control,* pp. 8–13.

existence had come by land. The army ground forces have therefore been the basis of security at home and of influence abroad, and the navy has been used primarily in support of operations on land. The support has often been far reaching and ambitious, but there was never any doubt about the primacy of the ground forces. Nor was this primacy put in question by the progressive emergence as separate branches of service of the Soviet air force, troops of national air defense (*PVO strany*), and the strategic rocket forces.

The extent of domination by the ground force is indicated by the fact that of the twenty military officers who are full members of the Central Committee of the Communist party, fifteen come from the ground forces. The other four branches of service and the main political administration only rate one place each.[9] The minor role played by the navy in the development of Soviet military thought is suggested by the relative number of service academies at the command and staff level and of book titles in the Officers' Library series.

The dominance by one branch of service has fostered a coherence of military thought, strategic priorities, and operational concepts. In the United States, three roughly equal branches of service are jealous of their prerogatives and missions; and it is not unusual for the different services to have discordant strategic concepts. The Soviets' army-dominated leadership can be more autocratic in the way it makes and implements decisions. This does not preclude genuine debate about controversial developments, but such debates are driven to some kind of conclusion, and the results are made to stick.

The Marxist belief in the existence of fundamental laws covering all aspects of human behavior, including war, reinforces the focused approach to military analysis. This orientation has led to the development of a unified body of knowledge called military science, which is concerned with preparing for and conducting armed conflict. Science is understood in its original sense of "knowledge" and "disciplined inquiry."

Soviet military science now comprises six main elements, the most important of which is referred to in the West as military art.[10] However, the established translation of *iskusstvo* as art is misleading because of the word's connotations in English, particularly the tendency to contrast the

9. See John McDonnell, "The Soviet Defense Industry as a Pressure Group," in Michael MccGwire, Ken Booth, and John McDonnell, eds., *Soviet Naval Policy: Objectives and Constraints* (Praeger, 1975), p. 104. His figures applied to the 1952–71 period, but the same pattern has been maintained since then.

10. Military art comprises military strategy, operational art, and tactics.

colloquial meanings of art and science. The sense in Russian is conveyed better by the original meaning of art as technics or applied knowledge, which is a subset of science or knowledge. The Russian term is perhaps best translated as the military craft or the craft of war. The semantics are important because they highlight the very different way that Westerners and the Soviets approach the problem of waging war. The Soviets tend to see it as an applied science with immutable laws; Westerners tend to see it as an art form executed by great captains.

One implication of this approach to strategic analysis is that, in the Soviet Union, neither maritime strategy nor the strategy of air power exists as subjects separate to military strategy or even as subsets of this unified theory. For example, it is not until one steps down to the level of "operational art," which deals with the theory and practice of operating major formations, that the naval aspects of war are treated as a separate theory. Even at the subsequent level of tactics, naval theory does not stand independently of the general theory of tactics or of the tactical theory of the other four branches of service.

Soviet emphasis on the combined arms approach and on a single body of military thought has increased in recent years. The navy's attempt to develop a more particular body of maritime thought was squashed in the second half of the 1970s, and the Soviets discontinued the separate doctorate in naval (rather than military) science in April 1979.[11] The major reorganization of the air forces in the late 1970s, in which most of PVO strany's assets were divided among the TVDs, has served to consolidate the combined arms approach even further. It is probably the inevitable outgrowth of an increasingly systematic approach to the complex problems of waging contemporary war. It may also be associated with Dmitriy F. Ustinov's appointment as minister of defense in April 1976 and the reintroduction of high commands at the TVD level.

Combined Arms and Naval Operations

A good case can be made that the principle of combined arms has invigorated Soviet naval thought, not least by saving it from the fallacy that naval strategy is a universal science whose rules were discovered for all time by Colomb, Corbett, and Mahan. A pragmatic approach, combined

---

11. Noted by Charles Petersen under the entry for *Doktor voennykh nauk* in the *Voennyy entsiklopedicheskiy slovar'*, p. 240.

with strictly limited resources, introduced a healthy realism to naval planning, and naval procurement has been tailored to Russia's particular requirements and not to some idealized perception of what a navy should be.

What is more, the army-oriented leadership has required the navy to undertake tasks that have violated traditional assumptions about naval operations and forced the development of radical concepts. A particular example was the shift to forward deployment in the early 1960s, so that ill-armed Soviet naval units were required to maintain close company with U.S. forces in the Mediterranean, where the West enjoyed overwhelming maritime preponderance. The idea of relying on "the protection of peace" to safeguard such exposed deployments was a daring concept, given the tenor of the Western strategic debate at the time.[12] The decision to ignore the survivability of such units and exploit the characteristics of nuclear-missile war was a major departure from traditional naval thought.

The dominance of the ground force way of thinking can be seen in the concept of close shadowing Sixth Fleet carriers with a gun-armed destroyer. The unit was acting as a forward observation post, and in the event of war would call down fire on the carriers. The fire would probably have included medium- and intermediate-range ballistic missiles emplaced in southwest Russia,[13] a concept that was spelled out by Defense Minister Andrey A. Grechko in December 1972. He stated that the wartime mission of the strategic rocket forces included the destruction of "enemy means of nuclear attack, and troop and naval groupings in land and sea theaters of military action."[14]

The idea of territorial defense, of defending "areas" of sea and of defense in depth, rather than securing the use of the sea, also reflects a ground force way of thinking, as well as the influence of Russia's geostrategic circumstances. For good historical reasons, the Russian perception

12. As part of their response to renewed Soviet pressure on Berlin in 1958, the Western powers (United States, United Kingdom, France) developed plans for naval reprisals to any restriction of access to the city.

13. Although there was no firm evidence of such targeting, it was inferred at the time from the persistence of close shadowing, whether or not there was any seaborne countercarrier capability present; such a countercarrier capability was not achieved on a sustained basis until the end of the 1960s. Russia-based aircraft were not suitable for this strike role, since their response time was too long, and they first had to breach the NATO air defense barrier. There were sufficient land-based missiles to cover this requirement, and the task was technically feasible. The existence of such a concept is supported by the subsequent claim for a more extensive capability of this type. See appendix D.

14. A. A. Grechko, "Armiya sotsialisticheskaya mnogonatsional'naya" (A socialist multinational army), *Krasnaya zvezda* (Red star), December 12, 1972.

of the sea's strategic quality is the exact opposite of the West's. The Western maritime powers view the sea as a means of access to nonadjacent areas; the Russians view the sea as a potential buffer zone, which can keep the enemy away from their homeland. However, Russia's opponents have often been able to concentrate their forces to achieve local superiority against any one of the four widely separated Russian fleets. In the Baltic and Black Seas the Soviets addressed the problem by developing the capability to seize the exits at the outbreak of war. Their objective is to keep NATO forces out, and not, as the West assumes, to allow the Soviet navy to "burst forth" onto the ocean expanses.

On balance the injection of army concepts and the common development of weapons systems like missiles and aircraft have been beneficial to the navy. Even when a new idea was initially unsuccessful, as, for example, the long-range antiship missile, it often served to break traditional concepts and open new avenues for development. The Soviet leadership's perception of the navy as an expensive necessity has often led to the definition of naval requirements in narrow terms of countering specific threats, instead of more general capabilities. This emphasis has restricted the navy's flexibility. On the other hand, the unquestioned primacy of the opinion of the ground force engenders clearly defined priorities and a readiness to apply the combined resources of all relevant branches of the armed forces to meet any serious threat, including those that come from the sea.

Theory of Deep Operations

The theory of deep operations, or battle, was developed by Marshal M. N. Tukhachevskiy and others in the late 1920s as a way of escaping the danger of positional, that is, trench, warfare. This theory is based on the principle of offensive operations throughout the entire depth of a TVD.

The theory was extended in the postwar period to take account of the qualitative change in the reach and devastation of contemporary weapons and the greatly increased mobility of ground forces. The concept of deep operations is now integral to the principle of "the offensive," to the extent that deep operations has not been used as a special category in Soviet publications since the 1960s and is as central to Soviet strategic thinking as the concept of combined arms.[15]

15. *SVE*, vol. 2, 1976, p. 578; see also Earl F. Ziemke, "The Soviet Theory of Deep Operations," *Parameters*, vol. 13 (June 1983), pp. 23–33.

The theory of deep operations applies equally to oceanic TVDs. It meshes with the emphasis on surprise and the concept of diversionary operations designed to pin down enemy forces or to draw them away from areas of importance to the Soviet Union, such as the ballistic-missile submarine bastions.

The Soviet Approach to War

The Soviets are Clausewitzian in the broad sense that Carl von Clausewitz's theorizing about war is congenial to their general approach to social problems. They are also Clausewitzian in the narrow sense that they accept his precepts about the primacy of the political over the military, the significance of the center of gravity in war, and the importance of a carefully thought out hierarchy of objectives that balances strategic importance against timeliness. V. I. Lenin extolled Clausewitz's ideas, and they provide the basic substance of the Leninist approach to war. Like Clausewitz, the Russians emphasize historical experience, from which they seek to draw general principles. At one time they believed the "nuclear missile revolution" made past experience irrelevant, but this thinking changed after the December 1966 decision, and in 1973, after a twenty-five year hiatus, the training of military historians was resumed at the General Staff Academy.[16]

The stress on history means that the Soviet approach to war is both theoretical and practical. The Soviets seek general principles at the higher level of analysis and try to derive combat norms at the tactical level. They also base their approach on numerous examples of what happened in comparable situations in the past rather than on postulated scenarios in the future.

The Soviets attach great importance to ranking objectives and hence to establishing priorities among theaters, TVDs, and strategic axes.[17] At any one time there can be only one main TVD and one main axis of advance

16. This was after a twenty-year hiatus. Marshal V. G. Kulikov, *Akademiya General'nogo Shtaba* (The General Staff Academy) (Moscow: Voenizdat, 1976), p. 202.

17. The Russian term *strategicheskoe napravlenie* is sometimes rendered as "strategic direction."

in a TVD. This TVD and axis will take precedence in the allocation of forces in peace and war. Priorities are not immutable and, assuming that resources can be redeployed, they may change during the course of a conflict or campaign. The concept of a main objective and a main axis of advance is central to understanding the Soviet conduct of war.

CHAPTER 7

The Euro-Atlantic Region

THE EURO-ATLANTIC region includes the European and Atlantic theaters of war. The European theater covers the same general area that was fought over in Hitler's war and extends from the Barents Sea to the Mediterranean (figure 7-1). In the event of a world war it would be the main theater.

This chapter seeks to explain the rationale for the strength and structure of Soviet forces in Europe and their concepts of operation. It focuses on what the Soviet General Staff hopes will happen if its plans work out. The analysis does not consider how realistic the military's plans are in terms of the capabilities of the Soviet Union versus the West, nor does it consider how the political leaders might adjust the plans under duress. The analysis follows the logic of the 1970s hierarchy of objectives and focuses on the military-technical aspects of the problem, largely ignoring the sociopolitical aspects.

On the Russian side of the East-West divide the main theater includes the five East European members of the Warsaw Pact and the six westernmost military districts in the Soviet Union. Ninety-six Soviet and 55 East European divisions and about 3,500 tactical aircraft, 200 major surface combatants, and 250 submarines are deployed in the area. The continental defense perimeter is divided into three theaters of military action (TVDs): the Western TVD, which is the main one, followed in order of importance by the Southwestern TVD and the Northwestern and Arctic Ocean TVDs.

The Western TVD

On the Soviet side, the Western TVD takes in Czechoslovakia, East Germany, Poland and the Baltic, and the Carpathian, Belorussian, and Baltic military districts. On the Western side this theater covers the NATO

128

central region, and the Baltic exits, and extends to include Britain, France, Spain, and their maritime approaches. The northern boundary cuts across the southern part of Sweden and Norway and westward toward Iceland. The southern boundary runs along the Alps and then curves south across the Mediterranean to the Algerian coast (figure 7-2).

Ninety-three Warsaw Pact divisions are concentrated on the Soviet side of the frontier. Sixty-two of the divisions are Soviet (31 tank, 28 motor rifle, and 3 airborne) and 31 non-Soviet (12 tank, 17 motor rifle, and 2 airborne and amphibious). Of the 93 divisions, about 50 are assessed to be combat ready.[1] The Warsaw Pact forces assigned to the Western TVD constitute more than 60 percent of all ground forces in the European theater, including more than three quarters of the tank divisions, and comprise the great bulk of combat-ready units.

The disposition of Soviet forces in this theater is mainly determined by operational plans for the contingency of world war, but it is also influenced by the requirement to suppress any major insurrection in Eastern Europe and to deter or prevent any Western involvement in such an insurrection. The Soviet estimate of the relative threats from this quarter is probably reflected in the relative size and structure of the Polish, East German, and Czechoslovakian armed forces.

The military quality of the East German units is reputed to be as high if not higher than any other East European unit. One might therefore expect East German armed forces to constitute a major component of the strength of the Warsaw Pact. But even though East Germany has been among the more docile satellites during the last twenty-five years, the Soviet Union allows it to have only 6 army divisions, compared with the 10 divisions allowed Czechoslovakia, which has a smaller population. More pertinent, East Germany has only 2 tank divisions compared with Czechoslovakia's 5 divisions; and 4 fighter and ground attack squadrons, compared with Czechoslovakia's 13.

---

1. See U.S. Department of Defense, *Soviet Military Power, 1984,* 3d ed. (Government Printing Office, 1984), p. 50. (Hereafter *SMP.*); and the International Institute for Strategic Studies, *The Military Balance, 1983–84* (London: IISS, 1983), pp. 15–24. These figures assume that the divisions in the Kiev military district (6 tank and 4 motor rifle) are intended for use in the Southwestern TVD. They could be committed in either direction. See also William W. Kaufmann, "Nonnuclear Deterrence," in John D. Steinbruner and Leon V. Sigal, eds., *Alliance Security: NATO and the No-First-Use Question* (Brookings, 1983), table 4-6. Warsaw Pact divisions can be at three levels of readiness: 1: the division is at 75–100 percent of its authorized strength and considered combat ready; 2: reduced strength, 50–75 percent; and 3: cadre strength, less than 50 percent.

Figure 7-1. *The Euro-Atlantic Region*

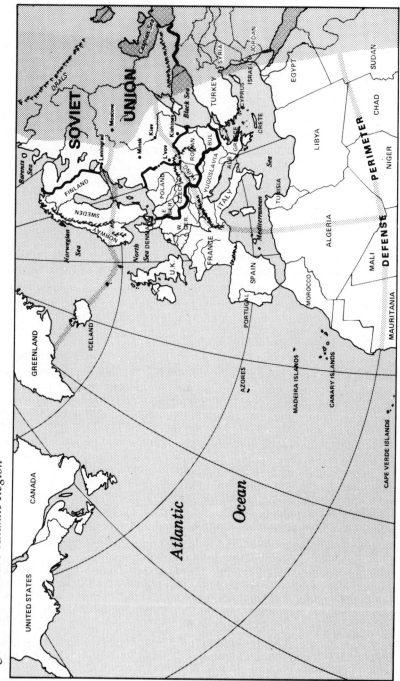

Figure 7-2. *The Western Theater of Military Action*

This arrangement suggests that any advantage that might accrue to the Soviet offensive against NATO from additional East German forces is outweighed by the danger the Soviets perceive in the existence of formed military units. The Russians persist in this fear even though they have an overwhelming preponderance of military power in East Germany, where 19 Soviet divisions are deployed, compared with only 5 Soviet divisions in Czechoslovakia. Furthermore, Poland has the same size of army relative to population as East Germany does (although Poland has twice as many ground attack aircraft), but there are only 2 Soviet divisions stationed inside Polish borders.

Phase One, Stage One

The Soviet objective in phase I-1 of a world war would be to defeat the forces concentrated in NATO's central region, which constitute the bulk of NATO's combined ground and air capability. If possible, the victory must be achieved without resort to nuclear weapons because nuclear action could escalate to a nuclear strike on Russia.

To this end, the Soviets have sought to replicate their nuclear capability in the theater with nonnuclear means. Accordingly, the Soviet capability for deep interdiction against NATO's command and control centers, nuclear weapons, and means of delivery includes conventional air strikes, airborne and special force operations, and breakthroughs by large "raiding" detachments of up to divisional size. To replace nuclear weapons in ground force maneuver, the Soviets have developed the concept of "integrated fire destruction" of the enemy. Fire includes air- and missile-delivered conventional ordnance, as well as tube-artillery. The critical factor is the density of fire in time, as well as space. The Soviets now talk of a troop strike by airborne assault and a fire strike by high-density fire. Formerly, the term strike (*udar*) was used exclusively in a nuclear context.[2]

The concept of operations the Soviets have developed to achieve their objective in phase I-1 reflects their doctrinal emphasis on the offensive, on deep operations, and on the combined use of all arms, and their plans incorporate the requirement to carry out the operations in a very short time span. Speed is important to the objective of avoiding the nuclear devastation of Russia.

At the strategic level, a successful high-speed offensive would make it clear that NATO was destined to be defeated in Europe within a few days. The situation would cause decisionmakers in Washington to hesitate to launch a nuclear strike on Russia because that would precipitate a nuclear strike on the United States. Refraining from intercontinental nuclear strikes would allow an undamaged America to carry on the struggle. At the theater level, the rate at which NATO's nuclear delivery capability can be put out of action, the rapidity with which NATO's command, control, and communications can be disrupted, the promptness with which Soviet operational maneuver groups can begin operations in NATO's rear areas, and

2. See Phillip A. Petersen and John G. Hines, "The Conventional Offensive in Soviet Theater Strategy," *Orbis,* vol. 27 (Fall 1983), pp. 695–739; and John G. Hines and Phillip A. Petersen, "The Soviet Conventional Offensive in Europe," *Military Review,* vol. 64 (April 1984), pp. 2–29.

the speed with which the battlefront can be advanced into NATO territory will determine whether NATO can resort to nuclear weapons in the theater.

Developing the capability to defeat the enemy in a short time span brings with it other advantages. If used successfully, the capability considerably reduces the requirements for ordnance and other supplies. A high-speed offensive would boost Warsaw Pact morale and should result in fewer casualties, allow enemy facilities to be taken intact, and complicate the enemy's targeting. A high-speed offensive would also play havoc with the enemy's morale, not only that of the defending forces but also that of the populace at large and their political leaders, a point the Germans demonstrated only too well in 1940 and again in 1941.

If NATO resorted to nuclear weapons in the theater the Soviets would have two primary concerns. One would be to confine the use of nuclear weapons to the theater and avoid escalation to a strategic strike on Russia. The other would be to effect a successful transition from a conventional to a nuclear mode of operation in the theater. The continued functioning of command, control, communications, and intelligence facilities would be critical, particularly at the TVD and front levels.

The nuclear balance in the theater would depend on the success of the Soviets' conventional air and antiair operations. The air operation (*aviatsionnaya operatsiya*), one of the six possible components of the strategic offensive operation, includes strikes by conventionally armed surface-to-surface missiles and artillery and attacks by airborne air-assault, and special purpose troops coordinated with strikes by frontal and strategic aviation. The antiair operation (*protivovozdushnaya operatsiya*), focuses on protecting Warsaw Pact forces and gaining air superiority, and it dovetails with the air operation.[3] However, the Soviets' operational concepts and their weapons and equipment are as appropriate as any for the prospect of nuclear war. Despite the large amount of intellectual and material resources they have invested since 1970 in acquiring the weapons and developing the operational concepts required to achieve their objective in the Western TVD by using conventional weapons only, the Soviets have never neglected the likelihood of nuclear escalation in the theater. Their design of weapons and equipment and their development of operational concepts and tactical procedures testify to their readiness.

The more interesting question is what the Soviets would do if NATO managed to block their westward advance. To address the question one

3. Phillip A. Petersen and Maj. John R. Clark, "Soviet Air and Antiair Operations," *Air University Review*, vol. 36 (March–April 1985), pp. 36–54.

must go back to their first-order objective of avoiding world war. A Soviet offensive in the Western TVD would imply that they had decided that a world war was inescapable and that they now had to act so as not to lose the war. In order not to lose, the Soviets would have to defeat the bulk of NATO forces in Europe, evict the United States from the Continent, and prevent its return. If NATO defenses held against the Soviets, they would be unable to achieve any of those objectives. It would be only a matter of time before the West built up military capability around the Soviet periphery and then moved on to the offensive to destroy the socialist system.

In other words, a Soviet offensive into Western Europe would be a strategic imperative and would have to succeed if the Soviets were not to lose the war. This point must be stressed because the West has a tendency to assume that a Soviet offensive would be in response to some irresistible temptation to make territorial gains. This belief promotes the assumption that if a Soviet offensive could be checked, then it should be possible to negotiate some kind of withdrawal to the status quo ante. This is unlikely to be the assumption that Soviet planners work on today although one cannot tell how Soviet political leaders would respond if faced by such a situation. The Soviet military would stress that the offensive on the main axis of the main TVD must succeed if war is not to be lost ultimately. Even a severe hold-up in the Western TVD would imperil operations in the adjacent TVDs, preventing the timely redeployment of forces and drawing down national reserves.

The Soviets have done their best to ensure success in the western TVD by building up conventional forces there to meet the Leninist requirement for "a crushing preponderance of force at the decisive moment and at the decisive point."[4] They have developed the concept of operational maneuver groups to counter the NATO doctrine of active defense. But given the varied circumstances in which they might have to launch their high-speed offensive, which range from a "standing start" to both sides being fully mobilized, the Soviets cannot be certain that they can succeed in all circumstances by using only conventional weapons.

If all else failed, the Soviets would have to consider the selective use of nuclear weapons. Many considerations would shape their decision, including the effect of NATO's theater response on the Soviets' own capability. Overall the Soviets would have to choose between two evils: the possibility of escalation to an intercontinental exchange; and the possibility of losing

---

4. N. N. Azovtsev, *V. I. Lenin i sovetskaya voennaya nauka* (V. I. Lenin and Soviet military science) (Moscow: Izdatel'stvo Nauka, 1981), p. 299.

the war in the longer term, which could lead to the nuclear devastation of Russia.

If the Soviets decided against resorting to nuclear weapons and chose to grind down NATO defenses, the disruption of NATO's sea lines of communication would assume critical importance. Obviously, the Soviets have to plan to cover the contingency of finding themselves bogged down in the Western TVD. This development, however, would represent a serious setback to their plans and can not be seen as the preferred approach.

Phase One, Stages Two and Three

In the Western TVD the process of occupying the areas to the rear of NATO's defeated forces during phase I-2 contributes to meeting the requirement to establish a defense perimeter in phase I-3. The situation is complicated because it mainly involves the territories of the minor nuclear powers, Britain and France.

It is unlikely that the Soviets' estimate of French resistance is as sanguine today as in the late 1960s. It is generally accepted that at that time the Soviets assumed France would capitulate as soon as Russian troops crossed the Rhine. Circumstances are different now, but even so, the problems are unlikely to be insuperable. One is not talking of a situation in which NATO has managed an orderly withdrawal through Germany by using each river barrier in turn and pivoting the southern end of its line on Switzerland, swinging it counterclockwise from a north-south to a west-east alignment along the Seine. The Soviet concept of operations in the Western TVD is designed to frustrate such a plan and to force NATO to fight in place and facing enemy forces both to its front and rear.[5] Phase I-2 implies that NATO has been defeated in the field, and there is no prospect of resupplying French forces.

The Soviets would be seeking to establish the necessary control over France without provoking a nuclear strike on Moscow. To the extent that military operations rather than political negotiations would be involved, geography allows for an incremental approach that avoids the sudden actions that would force a decision by France on whether to strike at Russia. It would not matter to the Soviets if significant French forces holed up in the mountainous parts of the country; they could be dealt with at leisure, once the political situation had stabilized. Similarly, the process of establishing an Atlantic Wall could wait until things settled down.

5. Petersen and Hines, "The Conventional Offensive," p. 729.

Britain presents a more difficult problem because of the water barrier, which removes the option of incremental military action. The Soviets would have to decide whether they would delay dealing with the problem until some later stage or move immediately to resolve it.

It would be hard to know in advance the effectiveness of diplomatic overtures and whether the defeat of NATO in Europe would induce in British decisionmakers the paralysis of despair or the rage of Samson. In purely military terms the German experience of the summer of 1940 would argue for an immediate invasion with no more than a pause to assemble some kind of lift, which could draw on the Soviet and European river fleets. The Soviets pride themselves on their capacity for this type of assault, which they demonstrated several times in the Black Sea during World War II, and it is now reinforced by the capability the ground forces have developed for the assault-crossing of rivers, virtually on the march.

The Russian talent for improvisation is at its best in such circumstances. In view of what the Soviets would have been through to get to the English Channel, they would not hesitate to accept heavy casualties from drowning and on the beaches should they decide that the invasion of Britain was essential.

Maritime Operations

In war the Baltic Fleet is subordinate to the high command of the Western TVD and shares the main objective of ensuring the defeat of NATO's combined ground and air forces in the central region.[6] The fleet's primary mission therefore is to support Soviet operations in the continental TVD and to prevent the West from using the sea to frustrate these operations.

PHASE I, STAGE 1. The traditional forms of naval support for land operations along a maritime axis include amphibious hooks to outflank the enemy's line, the movement of supplies by sea right up to one's own front line, and support with direct fire of one's troops ashore.

In the Western TVD the Baltic coast offers little opportunity for amphibious hooks in support of the main axis of advance. The front line is already close up against Schleswig-Holstein, the neck of Denmark, and the direction of the Soviet advance would be westward, across the German plain to the North Sea coast. The Soviets would, however, need to establish control of the Danish Straits, partly to prevent Western naval incursions

---

6. The evidence for this arrangement, which makes military common sense and follows the precedents of World War II, comes from the pattern of exercises during the last ten years or so.

into the Baltic but also to support ground force operations along the axis of the North Sea coast. Thus the straits must be open for passage. The Danish peninsula is off to one side of the main axis of advance, but its strategic location requires its seizure at an early stage of the war.

The primary naval missions in the Baltic are to establish command of the sea area and to participate in a combined arms *desant*[7] against the Danish peninsula and archipelago to seize key areas, hamper the mining of narrow waters, and facilitate the advance of ground forces through Schleswig-Holstein. A major objective of the *desant* would be to secure the Kiel Canal intact. Its availability would considerably simplify the provision of the maritime support on the North Sea flank.

Beyond these traditional activities, long-range missiles mean that naval forces can also contribute to nuclear strikes in the continental theater. The role of submarine-launched ballistic missiles for this mission has long been established and was apparently confirmed by the deployment of six Golf-class ballistic-missile submarines to the Baltic in 1976.[8] The nuclear-powered Yankee SSBN can cover the Western TVD from Northern Fleet waters.

Soviet naval units with conventional weapons could also contribute to neutralizing NATO's theater nuclear capability, thus reducing the requirement for land-based missiles and deep interdiction aircraft to do so. The ability of the sea-launched cruise missile to outflank or pass under NATO's air defense system offers an important advantage, and the SS-N-24 may have been designed for this role. This supersonic missile, which is due to enter service in 1987, is large enough to carry the necessary conventional payload. Its 1,900-nautical-mile range would allow it, from the northern Norwegian Sea, to cover targets in Britain and the whole central region of NATO. With a submarine as launch platform, the response time for a conventionally armed cruise missile could be as little as two to three hours, and terminal homing could be provided by on-board sensors or by homing beacons in the target area, which would be activated by undercover agents.

Naval forces can also help to prevent NATO from using the sea to supply and reinforce NATO or to intervene directly in the land battle with carrier-based air strikes. However, the principle of combined arms means that this mission is not the sole responsibility of the navy. All the air assets

7. The Russian word *desant* covers any operation in which forces are projected a distance by sea or by air.

8. Some analysts argue that these submarines are used primarily for crew training rather than nuclear fire support. Given the upgrading of theater nuclear forces in terms of accuracy, and the limitations of the SS-N-5 missile, this assessment may be true.

available to the TVD high command, and those held in reserve by the Supreme High Command, will be taken into account, with a keen appreciation of timing. For example, a convoy carrying supplies that could not reach the battle in time to affect the outcome would be disregarded, but a carrier moving to augment NATO's tactical air capability or a combat-loaded marine force within two days of the beach would be liable to attack.

The air threat to NATO at sea will not be limited to aircraft of the naval and long-range air forces, which are liable to be pinned down in other parts of Russia. NATO would also be threatened by Soviet frontal aviation, which the West may tend to think of as tied to the land battle. The establishment of Strategic Aviation, a new arm of the air force that is directly subordinate to the Supreme High Command in Moscow, facilitates the Soviets' flexible approach. This arm includes five air armies. Two of the air armies were formerly part of frontal aviation, and another is made up of medium-range strike aircraft. All three of these armies are available to the Western TVD.[9]

The use of land-based ballistic missiles against naval forces is a live possibility also. If the Soviets thought that a particular naval intervention could tip the balance and imperil the achievement by conventional means of their objectives in the Western TVD, they might even decide to use nuclear weapons against those naval forces. The move would be less escalatory than initiating the use of nuclear weapons on land. The Soviets would also be sensitive to the potential of carrier-borne aircraft should NATO resort to nuclear weapons. They would hope to have decimated NATO's land-based nuclear delivery systems by their air offensive, and the sea-based systems are likely to represent a substantial proportion of NATO's remaining theater capability.

Clearly, the geographical scope of the maritime theater of military action (MTVD) must reach well beyond the Baltic, and the Soviets' guiding principle would be the possibility that NATO naval forces might affect the outcome of the land battle in the Western TVD. This possibility argues that the MTVD must include at least the North Sea and English Channel. The MTVD probably extends westward to include the waters bounded by an arc centered on West Germany; it curves down from the Faeroe Islands, to the west of Ireland and into the southeastern corner of the Bay of Biscay.

---

9. Of the two frontal aviation armies, each comprising about 350 fighters, one is headquartered in Poland and the other in southwest Russia. A third army of more than 300 medium bombers is based in Belorussia, with headquarters in Smolensk. There is a fourth air army for strategic bombing and a fifth one based in the Far Eastern TVD.

PHASE I, STAGE 2. The major maritime activity in phase I-2 would be the assault on Britain, and as noted, an immediate invasion would make the best military sense. Assembling the necessary sealift might pose problems, particularly if all the continental fishing vessels, coasters, ferries, and so forth had fled to ports in the British Isles, as many did in World War II. But it would not take long to press enough of the large, self-propelled river barges into service, bringing them from the Soviet inland waterways system if necessary.

A separate and even more critical factor would be whether NATO's air forces had been effectively destroyed during phase I-1 or had been able to withdraw to British airfields. If they had withdrawn, they would be able to contest command of the air and hence of the sea, and the Soviets might have to launch a major air operation before they could start their assault on Britain by sea.

The Southwestern TVD

The Southwestern TVD is oriented toward the Balkans, Turkey, and the Mediterranean. In strategic priority it is a poor second to the Western TVD, where the main battle with NATO will take place, but it would assume increasingly greater importance during subsequent stages of a world war.

On the Soviet side of the East-West divide the Southwestern TVD includes Bulgaria, Hungary, Rumania, and the Odessa and Kiev military districts. On the Western side the southwestern TVD covers NATO's southern region, and the boundary with the Western TVD would run along the line of the Alps and then south across the Mediterranean to the Algerian coast. The boundary with the Southern TVD (to the east) cuts through the middle of Turkey and runs south between Cyprus and the Levantine coast to Egypt. Italy, Greece, and half of Turkey are in the Southern TVD, as well as most of the Mediterranean (figure 7-3).

There are 46 Warsaw Pact divisions in the Southwestern TVD, of which 20 are Soviet (8 tank, 11 motor rifle, and 1 airborne) and 26 non-Soviet (5 tank and 21 motor rifle), and of these 46 divisions at least one quarter and perhaps as many as one-half are cadre units.[10] Except for 2 divisions in

10. IISS, *Military Balance, 1983–84*, pp. 24–27; and Kaufmann, "Nonnuclear Deterrence," table 4-6.

Figure 7-3. *The Southwestern Theater of Military Action*

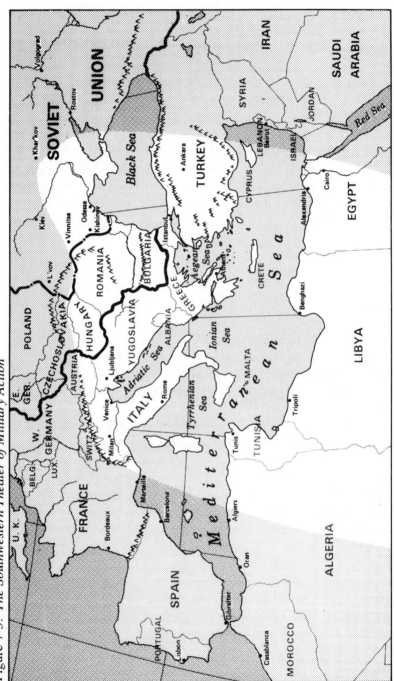

Hungary, all of the Soviet units are stationed inside Russia, which means that the Soviet posture is very different here than in the Western TVD.

Military Objectives

There are three different axes of advance in the Southwestern TVD. One provides direct support to operations in the Western TVD. The other two provide indirect support. The objectives in the Southwestern TVD could assume prominence only when it was certain that operations in the Western TVD would be successful.

PHASE I, STAGE 1. In the northern part of the TVD, two axes run westward out of Hungary. One follows the Danube through Austria and Bavaria to link up with operations in the Western TVD. The other angles southwest through the Lubljana Gap to the head of the Adriatic (Gulf of Venice) and the north Italian plain. The immediate objective is to pin down NATO forces in the area, particularly tactical air units, so that they can not be redeployed to reinforce NATO's central region, while at the same time bringing direct pressure to bear on Italy.

To the south, the axis runs through the Turkish Straits and the Aegean, down into the eastern Mediterranean. The immediate objective is to secure the straits against NATO incursions. The Soviets want to cover the contingency that their advance in the Western TVD may bog down. NATO might then try to seize the initiative by shifting the strategic center of gravity away from the central region by a major amphibious assault in the Black Sea, directed at Rumania and the Ukraine. A secondary objective of this Soviet axis of advance would be to occupy western Thrace. This action which would provide access to the Aegean and allow some direct support to be provided to ships of the Soviet Mediterranean squadron.

On both the axes that focus on the Southwestern TVD, Soviet objectives are compatible with the interests of their Warsaw Pact allies. In the north, Hungary would welcome regaining the direct access to the Adriatic that it enjoyed as a part of the Austro-Hungarian Empire, when Trieste was its principal port. In the south, Bulgaria would welcome the chance to regain control of western Thrace and with it access to the Aegean, which it sees as a natural entitlement. Bulgaria enjoyed such control from 1913 to 1918 and again from 1941 to 1944. If the allies believed that world war was inescapable, their support should be reliable. Bulgaria, in particular, sees

Russia as protector and friend. However, given the low operational readiness of the Warsaw Pact forces, timing might be a problem.[11]

A more serious problem of timing faces Soviet forces. Until it is reasonably confident of success in the Western TVD, the Supreme High Command must avoid committing to other axes any resources that could be used to turn the tide of battle in the west. Sixteen divisions of the strategic reserve would be readily available.[12] Nevertheless, the 10 divisions (6 of them tank) stationed in the Kiev military district and the air army headquartered at Vinnitsa in the southwest Ukraine, comprising about 350 fighters, including 5 regiments of SU-24 (Fencer) deep-interdiction aircraft, are critical because of their composition and relative location. The 2 Soviet tank divisions deployed in Hungary are probably earmarked for the Danube axis, and in the initial days of a war, the high command of the Southern TVD might have to cover the other two axes with the 7 motor rifle divisions (and 1 airborne) stationed in the Odessa military district. Soviet planners would also have to assume that Rumanian forces could not be counted on at the very start.

It is probable that Warsaw Pact forces in the Southwestern TVD would launch an assault along all three axes, immediately following the initiation of hostilities in the Western TVD. Offers of a separate peace would likely be made to Italy, Greece, and Turkey at the outset, in the hope of neutralizing these fairly isolated members of NATO. In the drive toward Italy, Pact forces would have to cross from 150 to 200 miles of Yugoslav territory, and, given Yugoslavia's refusal to allow the Germans uncontested transit in 1941 and the Hungarians' obvious territorial aspirations, the Soviets would have to plan that they might have to fight their way through Yugoslavia. A major campaign would not, however, be inevitable because the Soviets' transit would mainly affect only Slovenia and a small part of Croatia and, given the stakes involved, the country as a whole might prefer to sit this war out.

On the southern axis the most effective way of preventing NATO incursions into the Black Sea would be to gain control of the Turkish Straits. This operation would also serve longer-term objectives in the TVD. However, the operation would have to yield priority to the Western TVD. Pos-

11. Bulgaria: seven category 1 divisions; three category 3 divisions; Hungary: three category 2 divisions, three category 3; Rumania: two category 1; four category 2; and four category 3. IISS, *Military Balance, 1983–84*, pp. 24–27.

12. The 16 divisions (3 tank, 12 motor rifle, and 1 airborne) are stationed in the Moscow military district. In all, there are 24 divisions in the central strategic reserve. IISS, *Military Balance, 1983–84*, p. 16.

itive control of the straits would be critical only if that offensive failed. Meanwhile small-scale NATO incursions into the Black Sea could be prevented by naval countermeasures. In other words, the offensive on the southern axis would probably have to rely initially on forces from the Odessa military district who were operating with the 10 Bulgarian divisions (2 tank and 8 motor rifle), a Soviet airborne division, and marine infantry regiment. However, depending on the military situation in the Southern TVD, it might well be practical to sealift the 8 divisions (1 tank and 7 motor rifle) from the North Caucasus military district directly to Bulgarian ports. Most arms shipments to the third world sail from Odessa and Nikolaev, hence shipping would be readily available to lift such forces.

PHASE I, STAGE 2.   By this stage, operations in the Western TVD would have been all but successfully completed, and some forces would be available for redeployment to the other TVDs in the Western theater. On the Italian axis of advance, if it had not already been achieved as a by-product of negotiations in phase I-1, the Soviet objective would be to force Italy out of the war and to establish effective political control over the country. On the southern axis, sufficient force would be brought to bear to gain physical control of both sides of the Turkish Straits, but again this effort would parallel political attempts to force Greece and Turkey out of the war. Because Turkey is militarily the more significant of the two by far, its acquiescence and future support might be sought at the expense of Greece in the Aegean and in Cyprus.

PHASE I, STAGE 3.   The primary objective in this phase would be first to expel the United States from the Mediterranean and then to establish the means for preventing it from returning. The difficulty of defending the northern littoral of the Mediterranean, combined with the unsuccessful German experience in World War II, argues strongly for securing the Gibraltar Straits against U.S. attempts to return by sea and for establishing an embryonic defense perimeter along the northern edge of the Sahara.

The perimeter, which might follow roughly the Tropic of Cancer, could cut across as many as seven different African states. To simplify the establishment and maintenance of such a defense line, the Soviets might decide to rearrange the colonially defined boundary between Mali, Niger, and Chad to the south, and Algeria and Libya to the north. The Soviets would then transfer territory to Algeria and Libya, with whom they would need to establish some form of alliance.

A secondary Soviet objective would be to open up the route from the

Black Sea to the Far East by way of the Suez Canal. The Soviets would have to assume that the canal would probably already be blocked; if it was not, they would have to be prepared to protect it against attempts to do so. If the canal remained unobstructed during phase I-2, the Soviets might think of jumping in airborne forces to secure it as soon as resources became available, following up with air defense systems.

The Soviets could assume that the psychological impact of their success in the earlier phases of the war would create the political conditions that would allow such an operation, despite the presence of substantial Egyptian forces, including an army of more than 300,000 men and a potentially hostile Israel on the flank. This type of requirement, and the need to establish a defense perimeter across north Africa, makes one look twice at the inventory growth of Soviet-built tanks and armored personnel carriers (APCs) in Libya.

Between 1971 and 1983 the Libyan inventory grew from 115 tanks and zero APCs to a total of 2,800 tanks and 1,600 APCs. During this same twelve-year period, the number of men in the army only increased 2.75 times from 20,000 to 55,000. Besides the Soviet-built armored fighting vehicles, the Libyans have another 100 tanks, 500 armored cars, and about 500 APCs. Undoubtedly, the Libyan leader Muammar Muhammed el-Qaddafi had his own reasons for acquiring the large numbers of armored fighting vehicles and can rationalize them as a defense against the combined strength of his neighbors, Algeria and Egypt. The Soviets have, nevertheless, prepositioned a large number of these hard-to-ship fighting vehicles where they could be extremely useful in phase I-3 of a world war.[13]

Maritime Operations

During the first two stages of phase I, Soviet naval forces would contribute to achieving the objectives of the Southwestern TVD in two main ways. One, they would participate in the seizure of the Turkish Straits, which is a reasonably straightforward requirement. Two, they would prevent NATO from using the sea to frustrate operations on either axis of advance, a mission that divides into two elements.

13. This concept of prepositioning heavy equipment for use in a world war is quite different from Haselkorn's contention that the equipment is evidence of a Soviet collective security system. See Avigdor Haselkorn, *The Evolution of Soviet Security Strategy, 1965–75* (Crane, Russak, 1978).

The Soviets would have to prevent any kind of maritime support from being provided to NATO forces defending the straits, whether it be direct support by carrier aircraft or indirect support by securing the passage of reinforcements to the battle zone. The Soviets could achieve this objective by establishing a submarine barrier across the entrance to the Aegean, and the framework for such a defense zone has been in place since at least the late 1960s. The Aegean is also in reach of Soviet frontal aviation, although Soviet aircraft would be operating in heavily defended NATO air space.

The Soviets would also have to focus directly on the threat posed by the U.S. carriers, whose aircraft can be used for other tasks besides intervening in the battle for the Turkish Straits. For instance, aircraft could attack airfields in Bulgaria and Rumania. Moreover, the carriers have a significant capability for nuclear delivery, and although their reach could be strategic, the Soviets are likely to consider them as theater systems. In principle, therefore, the U.S. carrier would be a prime target in the Southwestern TVD and liable to attack by the full range of weapons available to the high command, as well as longer-range systems at the disposal of the Supreme High Command. In practice, the Soviets would have to consider both the carrier's political symbolism and whether a successful attack at an early stage of the war might precipitate nuclear escalation.

Another problem facing the Soviets would be preserving the units of the Mediterranean squadron that were not committed to engaging the U.S. Sixth Fleet or to manning the Aegean barrier. Given the extent of Western maritime predominance, the prospects of survival would be low. However, the Soviets could seek the protection of land-based air cover, such as Libya might provide. The Soviets' strategic position in the Mediterranean would be considerably enhanced if they could enjoy the kind of shore-based air support that the facilities in Egypt allowed them from 1968 to 1972, and this prospect suggests that the Soviets might seek to establish comparable facilities in Libya at the outbreak of a war.

The primary objective in phase I-3, if it had not already been achieved as a by-product of operations during the earlier stages of the war, would be to establish command of the Mediterranean. Soviet success in the continental TVDs would have denied NATO naval forces their shore support while providing forward airfields for Soviet strike aircraft. Besides the shore-based aircraft, the maritime forces available to the Soviets would be the ships and submarines of the Black Sea Fleet. Depending on the time of the year, the fleet might be reinforced by submarines and smaller surface units that would redeploy from the Baltic through the inland waterways.

After the Soviets cleared the Mediterranean of NATO forces, they would then need to establish an effective defensive barrier across the Gibraltar Straits at the western end while readying the Suez Canal for passage at the eastern end.

The Northwestern and Arctic Ocean TVDs

It is customary to talk of the Northwestern TVD and the Arctic OTVD as two separate regions. However, in geostrategic and operational terms it is more sensible to think of them as a single entity, with the continental TVD being a part of the OTVD. The relationship between the two may well be a bone of contention between the Soviet navy, which probably favors such an arrangement, and the General Staff, which is probably not prepared to concede the subordination of a continental TVD (or even a strategic axis) in this way.[14] Nevertheless, the combined approach is the one adopted here. The focus is on the Arctic Ocean, and the surrounding land is seen as an integral part of the OTVD (figure 7-4).

To perceive what is implied by this OTVD, one needs to look down from above the North Pole onto the Arctic Ocean. The boundary of this ocean is described as crossing the Bering, Davis, and Denmark Straits at about the Arctic Circle, roughly 66.5 degrees north, and then running southeast through Iceland and the Faeroes to the Shetlands, where it turns northeast to Norway's Stadlund Peninsula at about 62.0 degrees north.[15] If, as seems likely, the Arctic OTVD covers roughly the same waters, which include the Norwegian Sea, it would make sense for the southern boundary to continue eastward across Norway from Stadlund, leaving the Swedish coast north of Stockholm to run along the southern shores of the Gulf of Finland to Leningrad at 60.0 degrees north.

The full Arctic OTVD would comprise a roughly circular area centered on the North Pole, with a mean radius of about 1,500 nautical miles and a perimeter of about 10,000 nautical miles that runs around the globe between latitudes 60 degrees and 70 degrees north. This area is predominantly water, and since 90 percent of its perimeter is land, it can be en-

14. This disagreement is suggested in the second edition of *Seapower of the State*. S. G. Gorshkov, *Morskaya moshch' gosudarstva* (Moscow: Voenizdat, 1979), p. 317.

15. *Severnyy ledovityy okean* (Arctic Ocean) in *SVE*, vol. 7, p. 291. For a map showing the Arctic TVD as coterminous with the Arctic Ocean, see Charles C. Petersen, *The "Stalbo Debates": Their Point of Departure*, Professional Paper 404 (Alexandria, Va.: Center for Naval Analyses, 1984), p. 10.

visaged as a largely enclosed sea. In this OTVD, the Northwestern TVD includes those parts of Norway and Sweden to the north of 60 degrees; the whole of Finland; and the Leningrad military district, which extends north to the Barents Sea.

In a world war the military significance of this OTVD, or rather, of those parts that lie in the Eastern Hemisphere, is twofold. The OTVD provides a potentially secure means of communication between the western and eastern parts of the Soviet Union and between the Atlantic and the Pacific. It also offers a potentially secure haven for the deployment of ballistic-missile submarines (SSBNs). A primary strategic objective in the Arctic OTVD would be to deny Western forces access to the area so that it could be used without hindrance for these and other Soviet purposes.

Russia's maritime geography and history have led the Soviets to seek the exclusion of the enemy from a particular sea area to secure unhindered use for themselves. This approach to security was particularly relevant to the enclosed waters of the Black Sea and the Baltic, which for a long time were the two main fleet areas. In 1967–68 the Soviet navy naturally based its concept of operations on this idea when faced with the requirement for an SSBN force to be held secure as insurance against the technological outflanking of the land-based, fixed-silo ICBM deterrent.

There are three maritime access routes to the Arctic OTVD. Two of these, the Bering Strait between Siberia and Alaska, and the straits through the Canadian arctic archipelago, are fairly narrow and/or shallow and lend themselves to being blocked in some way or another. The third route lies between Greenland and Norway and presents a problem of a different order. Although Iceland and the Faeroes and Shetland Islands lie across the southern approaches to this route, the so-called gap still comprises 800 miles of stormy ocean, located about 1,200 nautical miles from the nearest Soviet base. The concept of a gap is misleading because it suggests something that can be plugged fairly easily. But the task is to prevent passage through a sea area that is about 900 nautical miles square with depths down to 12,000 feet, in other words, the whole Norwegian Sea.

The best way for the Soviets to prevent access to the Arctic OTVD by this route would be to gain command of the Norwegian Sea. It would allow the establishment of fairly impenetrable antisubmarine barriers across the Greenland-Iceland-Faeroes shelf, thus denying submarine intruders any surface or air support. This would not be a radical departure from existing policy. The Soviets would merely be reinforcing the existing status of the Norwegian Sea as an outer defense zone of the Northern Fleet area. They

Figure 7-4. *The Northwestern and Arctic Ocean Theaters of Military Action*

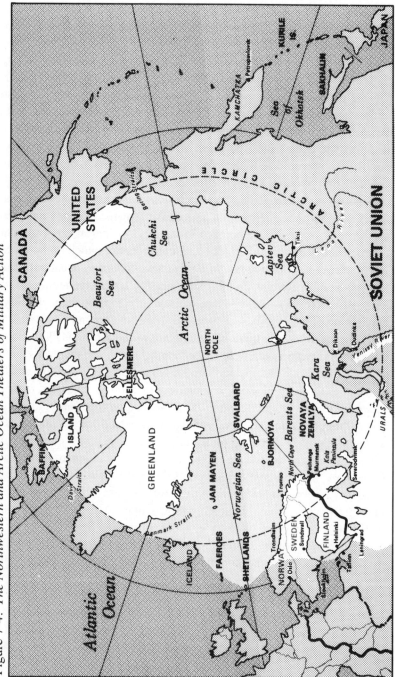

would also be extending their existing requirements to deny the use of the Norwegian Sea to U.S. sea-based strategic delivery systems, whether nuclear-strike carriers or Polaris submarines. Meanwhile the SSBNs could be deployed in ways to further enhance their security. Most of them, perhaps, could be grouped for mutual support in strongly defended bastions. Others could rely on dispersal, concealment, and stealth for individual protection, and some could use the shelter of the coastal fjords.

This approach was apparently considered cost-effective in 1967–68. By the end of the 1960s the Soviets had begun to speak of "command of the sea" in favorable terms. Previously, it had been condemned as an imperialist geopolitical concept. By 1975 the concept was fully reinstated and was referred to in the open literature as an essential precondition to the success of the strategic mission of the SSBN force.[16] However, by 1978 evidence was emerging that the Soviets no longer considered command of the Norwegian Sea essential.

In the wake of the 1976–77 decision period the relative importance of the Arctic as a secure haven for deploying SSBNs was apparently downgraded, and priority shifted to the Pacific and to land-based mobile systems. A major reason for the decision is likely to have been growing doubts about the feasibility of excluding Western attack submarines from the Arctic. The evidence suggests that another major reason was the operational costs of gaining and maintaining command of the Norwegian Sea.

The Evolving Concept of Operations

There seems little doubt that a major shift in the operational concept for the Arctic TVD occurred toward the end of the 1970s. Possibly, the concept of operations evolved through three stages, each one less ambitious than its predecessor.

THE 1967–76 PERIOD. Soviet discussion of command of the sea in 1970 was in general terms and did not tie it to any specific area, but three points were particularly relevant to the Arctic OTVD: the need to prepare extensively in peacetime for the task of gaining command in war, the fact that the West would be seeking to gain command at the outset of a war, and the importance of controlling adjacent coastal regions.

16. See the first edition of *Seapower of the State*. S. G. Gorshkov, *Morskaya moshch' gosudarstva* (Moscow: Voenizdat, 1976), pp. 378–79. For an early favorable discussion of command of the sea, see N. Petrov, "Gospodstvo na more" (Command of the sea), *Voennaya mysl'* (Military thought), no. 6 (June 1970), pp. 51–61.

This suggests that the Soviet navy saw a requirement to seize key islands and stretches of coast around the Norwegian Sea to provide the necessary strategic leverage in the drawn-out process of establishing command of the area. Furthermore, the seizures should take place in the early days of the war. If a delay occurred, the Soviets would be faced with a much tougher problem because NATO would have strengthened its hold on these assets to ensure its own command of the Norwegian Sea.

Speed would be a costly requirement. NATO Norway in the 1970s was a very different proposition than neutral Norway in 1940; the geography of the situation had also changed. Germany had had direct access by sea to the crucial southern parts of Norway, but the Soviets had first to secure the Baltic exits. To seize key stretches of the Norwegian coast at the outset of a war would therefore require a complex series of operations, including a land offensive along two axes of advance. The northern axis would run through the Finnish wedge to Tromso and Narvik; the southern one would run across Sweden from Sundsvall to Trondheim.[17] The land offensives would link up with a series of amphibious hooks along the Norwegian coast, which would be mounted from the Northern and the Baltic Fleet areas.

One important objection to this ambitious naval plan was simply the competition for scarce resources; the Western TVD had overriding priority. Besides that consideration, offensive ground operations in the Northwestern TVD could be carried out at considerably lower military cost at a later stage of the war and in some cases might not be necessary.

There were both psychological and military reasons for delaying the main operation against Norway until phase I-2 of the war. At the start of the war, no one could be certain of the outcome, and resistance in Sweden, Norway, and Finland would be at its strongest. There would also be political disadvantages to breaching Swedish neutrality in that particular way. By phase I-2 however the great bulk of NATO's ground forces would have gone down to defeat in the central region, and the weight of Soviet military power could be brought to bear against NATO's northern flank. The odds would be overwhelming and Soviet ruthlessness evident, generating strong domestic pressures in Sweden and Norway for negotiations, whether for the Swedes to provide transit rights or for the Norwegians to allow the Soviets to take over key installations.

Militarily, in phase I-2 the Soviets would have the advantage of being

17. There is a road and rail link between Sundsvall and Trondheim, following one of the few routes across the Scandinavian peninsula. It is probably not coincidental that Sundsvall is one of the areas where the Swedes have firm evidence of intruding Soviet submarines.

able to ship forces from the south, either through the Baltic exits or from Germany's North Sea ports. In the unlikely event that the Swedes and Norwegians did put up a strong resistance, the preponderance of Soviet force would allow a short operation and hence fewer casualties.

The operational plan in force in the mid-1970s is likely therefore to have deferred the main operation against Norway until phase I-2 of a world war. During phase I-1 the Soviets would be content with securing a limited number of footholds such as Svalbard, Bjørnøya, and perhaps Jan Mayen Island. They could push a couple of hundred miles into Finmark, perhaps as far west as Hammerfest, and possibly take up position in the Finnish wedge, depending on whether military opposition could be expected to such a move. Meanwhile the Soviets would concentrate on neutralizing the shore facilities and land-based systems that support NATO operations in the Norwegian Sea. It would be prudent to divert significant assets to seizing coastal regions and other islands of the Norwegian Sea only when the objective in the Western TVD was close to achievement. The additional weight of force that would then be available would more than compensate for any reinforcement achieved by NATO.

In such a concept of operations, the doctrine of combined arms, reinforced by the principles of concentration and economy of force, argue that the Soviet navy would not attempt to establish command of the Norwegian Sea during phase I-1. Instead the Soviets would restrict themselves to denying such command to NATO until they were ready to move over to the offensive. The plan implies heavy reliance on submarines while holding surface forces back until they could be provided with shore-based air cover in phase I-2 or I-3. The navy's mission of countering incursions into the Norwegian Sea by NATO carrier forces and amphibious assault groups would continue unchanged.

The concept of delaying the main operation against Norway and simply denying command of the Norwegian Sea to NATO is less demanding than the original naval requirement of speedily gaining control of the sea and coastal regions. Nevertheless, the military costs that would be incurred during phase I of a world war would be substantial. The requirement to maintain command of the Norwegian Sea would also incur significant costs in phase II. One such cost would be the need to occupy substantial parts of Norway. In phase II of a world war, Soviet forces would be stretched to their limits because of manning the extended defense perimeter and holding down occupied territories. There are bound to be pressures to limit that requirement to essential areas.

Norway's geographic situation means that it would be of little use as a bridgehead to returning Western forces. This suggests that Soviet purposes would be adequately served if in phase I-2 and I-3, Norway could be induced to settle for a political status akin to Finland's. Such acceptance could be expected, given that the main forces of NATO would have just gone down to defeat and that the alternative would be brutal occupation. By sidestepping the occupation of Norway, the Soviets would also avoid having to face partisans in a mountainous territory, covering as large an area as West Germany, Denmark, and the Benelux countries combined.

THE CONCEPT SINCE 1976–77.   It seems probable that the requirement to establish command of the Norwegian Sea has been relaxed and that a major reason for the change is the need for military economy. Thus the prevailing concept of operations in the Arctic OTVD is likely to be considerably less demanding than the previous requirement to seize key islands in the Norwegian Sea and large stretches of the surrounding coastline. Instead the Soviets have probably reverted to their traditional concept of the Norwegian Sea as the outer defense zone of the Northern Fleet area.

At sea the Soviets could establish their main defense perimeter on a line running north from about Hammerfest, through Bjørnøya and Svalbard and thence to Greenland. On land they would only need to move into sparsely populated Finmark, stopping well short of the main Norwegian defense line in the Troms province, a heavily defended area that is considered a natural fortress. While avoiding engagement with Norway's land forces, the Soviets would still need to prevent the arrival of NATO military reinforcements by sea. The task would fall largely to the navy, whose longstanding mission of preventing Western incursions into the Norwegian Sea would be unaffected. At the same time, policy regarding attacks on shore facilities and land-based systems in central Norway and the means used in such attacks would be as much a political as a military decision, reflecting the objective of avoiding the need to occupy the country.

At some time, but probably not until phase I-3, the Soviets would need to take over Iceland and the Faeroes and Shetland Islands. These would be garrisoned, and the precedent of the Baltic states in 1939–41 suggests that some or all of their population would be moved elsewhere and perhaps be replaced by Soviet citizens.

The important difference between this concept of operations and the earlier one lies in the requirements generated for ground and air forces, both in phase I-2 and in phase II of a world war. The overall requirement for naval forces is also affected, but not to the same extent. The increased priority of the Pacific as a deployment area for SSBNs means an increase of forces in that area, which absorbs some of the savings in the North; meanwhile protection must still be provided for SSBNs in the Arctic. Relaxing the requirement to establish command of the Norwegian Sea does not imply that command would be conceded to NATO. The Soviet navy would be striving to prevent the use of the Norwegian Sea by U.S. carriers, NATO reinforcements, and intruding submarines, and although the Soviets might not be able to establish command of the area during phase I, they would certainly expect to be able to deny command to NATO.

The Role of the Ballistic-Missile Submarine Force

At first sight there might seem to be a contradiction between the undisputed priority that the Soviet navy now gives to ensuring the security of the SSBN force and the concepts of operation just outlined. In the earlier plan, command of the Norwegian Sea would be deferred to phase I-2. In the more recent plan the requirement to establish command is relaxed, the Norwegian Sea reverts to its former role as an outer defense zone of the Northern Fleet area (whose defense perimeter is reestablished closer to home), and greater reliance is placed on ensuring the security of the SSBN force through concealment and dispersion. The fact that security of the SSBN force would be less than complete is implicit in both of these plans.

The apparent contradiction illuminates important aspects of Soviet policy. The Soviets emphasize the concept of "balance," both among and within branches of the armed forces and among military objectives. In order not to lose the war, the Soviets have to achieve several subsidiary objectives, including defeating NATO in Europe, evicting U.S. forces from the Continent, and then preventing them from returning. A separate Soviet objective is to deter the United States from striking at Russia as U.S forces go down to defeat in Europe. The SSBN force constitutes part of that deterrent capability. But although striking at targets in the North American continent may now be the most important mission of the Soviet navy, it does not follow that this naval mission has the same priority in the mission structure of the armed forces as a whole. The navy's claims have to be balanced against other missions and against other forces contributing to the same mission, in regard to both timing and the allocation of resources.

The function of SSBNs as an insurance force covers the possibility that the United States could somehow render the land-based deterrent force impotent. In the absence of such a breakthrough, once war is engaged, the insurance force loses its importance in the short term. The land-based ICBM force would be more than adequate to perform the "deterrent" function to the extent that such deterrence is likely to be effective. As the war continued, the insurance function would regain importance, since it could be assumed that the United States would invest heavily in devising ways to outflank the land-based ICBM deterrent. In the interim, however, the importance of the SSBNs would be limited to their potential role should war escalate to an intercontinental exchange.

Given this situation, the Soviets can obviously afford to lose a number of SSBNs during the initial stages of a war and it is not therefore essential that the force be held secure at any cost. Furthermore, the Soviets would expect the West to attempt to draw down the force; the sinking of an SSBN would not precipitate a nuclear strike on the United States. Under the 1960s hierarchy of objectives a U.S. attack on a Soviet SSBN would have signaled the outbreak of general war and thus a nuclear strike on the United States because Soviet strategy in such a war meant striking first. But this perspective changed with the adoption of the 1970s hierarchy of objectives and with the shift in the SSBN's primary role from a postexchange war-fighting force to a deterrent force. If the purpose of the SSBN force was to contribute to deterring America from striking at Russia during the course of a war, then, clearly, the sinking of an SSBN would not justify an attack on the United States because that would defeat the objective.

This line of thinking raises the question of whether there is some predetermined limit to the number of SSBNs the Soviets can afford to lose. The short answer is no, as can be seen by rephrasing the question to ask whether the cumulative loss of SSBNs would, on its own, justify escalating the war to an intercontinental exchange, thus discarding the governing objective of avoiding the nuclear devastation of Russia and reverting to the 1960s hierarchy. Clearly, the significance of SSBN losses can only be assessed in a much broader strategic framework. Two considerations would be particularly important. One would be the continuing viability of the ICBM fixed-silo deterrent and the availability of other types of insurance against outflanking. The other would be the overall likelihood of avoiding escalation to global nuclear war. The answer to that question would determine whether the SSBN's postexchange capability was critical to the final outcome of the war.

The modern SSBN force has two roles, a present one that supports the 1970s hierarchy of objectives and a potential role in support of the 1960s hierarchy. The present role is to insure against the technological outflanking of the fixed-silo deterrent force, thus contributing to deterring the United States from intercontinental escalation in the course of a world war. This function is most critical in peacetime and during phase I of a world war, particularly in the war's first stage. After that it becomes less important, as the likelihood of escalation wanes. The potential role, which stems from the 1960s hierarchy, lies in the ability of the SSBNs to largely survive an intercontinental exchange. Should the Soviets be unsuccessful in deterring escalation, the SSBN force could constitute an important part of the nation's postexchange nuclear capability.

These clear-cut roles have been obscured in Western discussion by the notion of some new "withholding strategy" that the Soviets are claimed to have adopted when the Delta-class SSBN began to enter service in the mid-1970s. It is misleading to talk of withholding as a strategy rather than an option that is inherent in the characteristics of the SSBN. It is also misleading to imply that the concept of withholding had not existed before the Delta force. The Yankee program was prompted by the requirement to match the capability for withholding that was already embodied in Western sea-based strategic delivery systems, a requirement that dates back to 1961. What was new about the Deltas was their role as an insurance force and the need to hold them secure for a protracted period while hostilities were actively engaged.

Should wartime deterrence fail, the SSBN force would become part of the Soviet Union's war-fighting arsenal to be used when the Supreme High Command saw fit. Some limits are imposed on the use of the SSBN force because of the difficulty of ensuring instantaneous communications with the SSBNs, an inherent problem that becomes greater in arctic latitudes. The difficulty means that should the Soviet leadership decide that escalation to an intercontinental exchange is inevitable, the SSBN force could not be counted on to participate in a preemptive strike on the United States, unless the Soviets had overcome the communication problem in some way. By default the force is likely to be withheld from such a strike, but beyond that, decisions on the use or nonuse of these assets would depend on the circumstances.

In this context the notion of a predetermined withholding strategy is especially misleading. It implies constraints on Soviet decisionmaking that are unlikely to exist, particularly on the arctic component of the SSBN force. Decisions on the use of nuclear weapons in the postexchange phase of a global war would be determined by what assets were still in existence and how much longer they were likely to remain available. For SSBNs, the number of assets would depend on how long hostilities had been under way before intercontinental escalation and how successful the West had been in drawing down the force during that period. For land-based systems, and for the part of the SSBN force in port at the time, availability of weapons would depend on what assets were used in the initial Soviet strikes and how effective were the West's initial strikes. None of these questions could be answered definitely before the event, and the answers would also determine how long the various systems would be likely to remain available.

It is possible that if the West succeeded in drawing down the SSBN force in the Arctic during the preexchange phase of a world war, the Soviets might hasten to use the SSBNs in the postexchange phase rather than lose them to Western attack. The Soviets might, for instance, decide to use the weapons aboard the arctic SSBNs, but hold back those aboard the Pacific force, which is inherently more defensible. But the latter decision is only a matter of degree, and a situation could emerge in which the Soviets were left with land-based missiles, which the United States had no means of targeting. Then the Soviets would choose to use the missiles aboard the SSBNs, withholding the land-based systems to the last.

Interfleet Deployment

The concept of the Arctic OTVD as a semienclosed sea draws attention to the possibility of redeploying forces between the Northern and Pacific Fleets by way of the Arctic to achieve naval superiority in one area or the other. The Soviets can already redeploy aircraft and nuclear submarines between the fleets, but they are striving, with the use of nuclear-powered icebreakers, to develop the capability for the year-round redeployment of surface ships. The distance by way of the pole is about 3,500 nautical miles. This can be compared with about 18,000 nautical miles from the Aleutians to the Iceland-Faeroes Gap by way of Drake Passage, the 600 nautical-mile stretch of water between Cape Horn and Antarctica, which is the most likely route for U.S. carriers.

The Atlantic OTVD

The North Atlantic serves as an antechamber to the other TVDs in the European theater for war, and all U.S. support for the battle in Europe would have to pass through this antechamber. Naturally, the Soviets want to prevent NATO from using this sea area to frustrate their plans in other parts of the region, especially the Western TVD. The time line of operations elsewhere in the theater is critical in deciding whether action needs to be taken in this OTVD.

Phase One, Stages One and Two

An important Soviet maritime objective in the main Western TVD is to prevent the arrival of seaborne supplies and reinforcements that could affect the outcome of the battle in Europe, and the MTVD extends far enough into the Atlantic to cover this requirement. In the Arctic OTVD the main objective is to prevent incursions by NATO naval forces, thus securing the operational availability of the Northern Fleet's SSBN force and preventing the reinforcement of northern Norway. Both these objectives can be supported indirectly by long-range interdiction operations in the Atlantic OTVD, designed to divert NATO naval forces away from these critical areas and tie them and other forces down in sea areas that are of no immediate strategic interest to the Soviet Union. Such operations would also help relieve the pressure from antisubmarine forces on the forward-deployed Yankee SSBN.

In other words, assuming that operations were going according to plan, the Soviets would attach little importance to the traditional naval mission of "preventing the enemy from using the sea" in the North Atlantic. The objective of interdiction operations would be to relieve the pressure in the other more important TVDs and only incidentally to disrupt sea communications or draw down NATO naval forces. Such operations would need to prevent the seaborne reinforcement of NATO's northern flank. Should, however, the ground offensive in the Western TVD get bogged down, then interrupting the flow of seaborne supplies would become a matter of prime importance.

The U.S. carrier force is an important exception to the general rule that the Soviets would not be concerned about preventing the use of the Atlantic during phase I-1 and I-2. Because of versatility, mobility, firepower, and nuclear capability, each carrier represents a significant proportion of America's total military capability in all circumstances and would constitute a critical component in the wake of a nuclear exchange. This capability promotes the carrier from a problem to be dealt with at the TVD level, if or when it threatens to disrupt operations in a particular TVD, to one that must be addressed from the outset of a war and irrespective of the carrier's location in the world.

The challenge would, however, have to be addressed in the context of the 1970s hierarchy of objectives, with the emphasis on avoiding escalation to an intercontinental exchange. The carrier has high political symbolism and also counts as part of the United States strategic arsenal, which gives it an indeterminate status between U.S. theater forces and strategic systems located on U.S. soil. In planning operations to draw down the carrier force, the Soviets would have to weigh how the United States would view the sinking of a carrier and in what circumstances it might be seen as strategic escalation rather than the fortune of theater war. To some extent the problem would resolve itself. There would be no immediacy about launching an actual attack, except when a carrier could directly influence the battle in a continental TVD. The overall Soviet concept of operations would be to develop favorable opportunities for engaging each carrier with a reasonable chance of success at a reasonable cost. The Soviets would use the most appropriate system, which would not be limited to the conventional array of forces and could include sea mines, land-based missiles, and space systems.

Drawing down the carrier force and preventing the redeployment of battle groups among theaters of war would both require the same type of military response. U.S. Pacific Fleet carriers could redeploy to the North Atlantic in time to affect the outcome of the Soviet operation in the Northwestern TVD, which would not be launched until phase I-1 was drawing to a close and possibly somewhat later. The Soviets are aware of this possibility, and the fairly narrow waters of Drake Passage might be one of the places in which they would choose to offer battle.[18]

Phase One, Stage Three

Once the main objectives in the three continental TVDs had been achieved, the North Atlantic would assume a new importance, as the Soviets moved to establish a defense perimeter. In deciding which of the island groups should be included in the perimeter, the Soviets would consider the Japanese experience in World War II. In particular, they would have to consider whether Japan's fairly rapid defeat stemmed from the

18. In an article discussing the role of straits in naval warfare, the Soviet authors link the Bering Straits, the straits through Canada's arctic archipelago, and Drake Passage (referred to by the Soviets as a strait) in a reference to their heightened importance in a future global war because of the West's need to redeploy forces between "oceanic theaters of military action." See G. Morozov and B. Krivinskiy, "Rol' prolivov v vooruzhennoy bor'be na more" (The role of straits in the armed struggle at sea), *Morskoy sbornik* (Naval journal), no. 8 (August 1982), p. 22.

length of the perimeter it tried to defend and the distance the perimeter lay from its main bases. The extended perimeter flouted the principle of concentration, and its length and distance from bases meant that logistic support was costly and supply lines were very vulnerable.

The Madeira and the Canary Islands, which lie between 60 and 400 nautical miles from the coast of Morocco and the general area of the North African landings in World War II, would probably serve a useful purpose as outposts and be taken over. The Azores, about 800 nautical miles due west of Lisbon, are really too distant for outposts, but their position on the mid-Atlantic ridge and their importance to antisubmarine surveillance and airborne reconnaissance would argue that control of these islands was essential.

The Cape Verde Islands, which lie from 350 to 500 nautical miles off the African coast, are roughly abreast the former French base of Dakar in Senegal. The arguments for establishing physical control of these islands, which have relatively poor facilities, are really no stronger than for establishing control of the more fertile West African states that lie to the south of the Saharan belt. The defense perimeter would define the area in which Soviet control was deemed essential. Beyond that, there would be an indefinite zone in which the Soviets would seek to ensure that their political influence predominated. However, they would be wary of becoming overextended in places like the Cape Verde Islands.

Phase Two

The Soviets agree on the necessity of establishing a defense perimeter. However, the best way of conducting the continuing global struggle must be one of the more contentious questions that plague the General Staff. It is most open to disagreement between the navy and the rest of the Soviet armed forces. Could the Soviets afford to sit tight behind their defense perimeter? Is there a requirement to carry the war to the enemy in order to disrupt American trade and deny it raw materials, and to challenge U.S. attempts to build up hostile coalitions in other parts of the world? The second requirement has major implications for naval forces in general and for the capability to project force in distant parts of the world.

If the Soviets decided just to rely on a defense perimeter, then how would the perimeter be best secured? Would Soviet naval forces have to attack amphibious assault groups in their assembly and staging areas, harass them as they cross the oceans, and confront them in the landing zone, as Admiral Sergey G. Gorshkov argued in his articles? Or would the Soviets be able to exploit their interior lines of communication and rely on land-based systems, including intermediate-range ballistic missiles, to disrupt the buildup and prevent the passage of assault forces? The answer to this question, in turn, depends on decisions about the use of nuclear weapons in phase II. It could be argued that, by this stage of a world war, it would be both safe and credible for the Soviets to threaten to use nuclear weapons against any group of ships that crossed a specified demarcation line.

CHAPTER 8

The Asian-Pacific Region

THE ASIAN-PACIFIC theater encompasses the Far Eastern theater of military action (TVD) and extends to include the Philippine and China Seas and the Northwest Pacific Basin. The Far Eastern TVD focuses on China to the south and looks eastward to Japan and the Northwest Pacific. The territorial expanse of this theater is vast, spanning at least one hundred degrees of longitude (well over half the breadth of Russia), and it encompasses most of the Central Asian, Siberian, Trans-Baikal, and Far Eastern military districts, and Mongolia. It also includes maritime theaters of military action (MTVDs) that cover the Seas of Japan and Okhotsk and the waters off Kamchatka (figure 8-1).[1]

Establishment of this theater was the culmination of a significant strengthening of the Soviet defense posture opposite China and elsewhere in the area, which took place during the late 1960s and early 1970s.[2] By 1978 Western analysts had identified a large, new, and somewhat autonomous Far Eastern command structure. The relative autonomy of this command is significant in terms of the TVD's military objective.

1. Phillip A. Petersen, "The Soviet Conceptual Framework for the Application of Military Power," *Naval War College Review,* vol. 34 (May-June 1981), pp. 18, 20; and "Sowjetunion: Zum Kraftestand in Zentralasien und in Fernost" (Soviet Union: Capabilities in Central Asia and in the Far East) *Osterreichische militarische zeitschrift,* Vienna, no. 3 (1983), pp. 255–58; and James T. Westwood, *Power in the Pacific: An Assessment of Security Issues between the USSR and Japan,* SA-013 (Falls Church, Va.: E-Systems, 1983).

2. This was the period of the most rapid buildup, but the strengthening continued throughout the 1970s and into the 1980s. The number of divisions grew from 20 in 1965 to 53 in 1985, and fixed-wing tactical aviation went from less than 300 aircraft in 1965 to almost 1,700 in 1985. See U.S. Department of Defense, *Soviet Military Power, 1984,* 3d ed. (Government Printing Office, 1984), pp. 50, 57 (Hereafter *SMP*); and *SMP, 1983,* 2d ed., p. 52.

Figure 8-1. *The Asian-Pacific Region*

Major Strategic Considerations

There are only 55 divisions, 2 of them Mongolian, deployed throughout the vast expanse of the Asian-Pacific theater, including the 4,500 mile border with China. Ninety-three Warsaw Pact divisions face the 500-mile gap between the Baltic and the Alps. The disparity sums up the relative standing of the Western and Far Eastern TVDs and is what would be expected from Soviet military doctrine, which is adamant that priority must be established among objectives, TVDs, and main axes of operations. Priority obviously has to be given to the theater in which significant territorial objectives have to be secured at the outbreak of a war. As already noted, such objectives loom large in the Western and Southwestern TVDs, but there are no comparable time-critical objectives in the Far Eastern TVD.

The lower priority of the Far Eastern TVD, its relative autonomy and vast geographic scope, and the absence of time-critical territorial objectives, would lead one to expect that the overall strategic objective of this theater would be defensive. This assessment is confirmed by the fairly low density of Soviet ground forces, the high proportion of motorized rifle (rather than tank) divisions in the Far Eastern TVD compared with the European ones, and the way the Soviet units are deployed in relation to Chinese forces.

But the objective is likely to be more specific than that. The Soviets want, if possible, to avoid combat, particularly ground combat, on their western and eastern borders simultaneously.[3] It can therefore be inferred that in a world war the main objective in the Far Eastern TVD is to persuade China to remain neutral or, expressed in specifically military terms, to deter China from trying to take advantage of a war in Europe.

This objective covers the worst case, and it also covers the lesser contingency of China initiating war when Russia is not already embroiled in conflict. In both cases, the immediate threat from China is territorial aggression (it is assumed that China would not attempt a disarming nuclear strike), and the Soviet objective is to deter such a conventional attack with the minimum expenditure of resources.

---

3. See Banning N. Garrett and Bonnie S. Glaser, *Soviet and Chinese Strategic Perceptions in Peacetime and Wartime*, prepared for the Defense Nuclear Agency, DNA 001-81-C-0923 (Burlington, Ma.: Harold Rosenbaum Associates, 1982), pp. 137–45.

China

The threat of war with China may seem overblown to outside observers, but it is sufficiently real to Soviet leaders to justify the deployment of 53 divisions and almost 2,000 aircraft in the Far Eastern TVD.[4] However, only some of the Soviet buildup since 1965 can be attributed to the perception of an increased threat from China. The major part of it probably stems from the December 1966 decision about the likely nature of a world war. The number of divisions went from 20 in 1965 to 45 in 1973. The addition of another 8 divisions in the first half of the 1980s would have been in response to the Sino-U.S. rapprochement. It has been argued that although the original purpose of the buildup was to protect the frontier, other purposes such as discouraging China from embarking on military adventures to its south and ensuring that the Soviet Far East can support geopolitical advances in South and Southwest Asia have overlaid the original purposes. Although the Soviet Union may seek to exploit the existing military deployment for these and other purposes, these purposes do not determine force requirements in the Far Eastern TVD. Indeed, if China were to compose its differences with India and Vietnam, Soviet requirements might well increase. In 1983 some 20 Chinese divisions (about 300,000 troops) were deployed opposite Vietnam and Laos (only 2 less than the number of Chinese divisions in Manchuria), a diversion of Chinese military strength that the Soviets must welcome.[5]

By the end of the 1950s, the Soviets must have been having doubts about China as a loyal ally in the event of a world war. By the middle of the 1960s it seems likely that Soviet war plans assumed that at best China would remain neutral and might even seek to profit at Soviet expense. However, throughout the 1960s, it was still assumed that war with the West would lead inevitably to an intercontinental exchange, and there is every reason to suppose that, in such a war, the Soviet Union planned to disable China with nuclear weapons at the same time as it devastated the West. Not to have done so would have jeopardized the primary objective of preserving the socialist system (of which the Soviet Union was the essential core), since an undamaged China could physically take over a devastated Russia by virtue of China's vast population.

However, after the 1966 decision, the Soviets hoped to achieve a situa-

4. See Bonnie S. Glaser and Banning Garrett, *Peacetime/Wartime*, vols. 2 and 3, DNA 001-83-C-0928 (Washington, D.C.: Palomar Corp., 1984), pp. 5–7.
5. Japan Defense Agency, *Defence of Japan, 1983* (Tokyo: Japan Times, Ltd., 1983), pp. 26, 42.

tion in which escalation to an intercontinental exchange could be avoided. This aim implied that in a world war, the Soviets had to cover against two additional contingencies in the Far Eastern TVD. In one, China would remain neutral; in the other, China would seize the opportunity of Soviet preoccupation in Europe to seek military gains in Asia. In either case the Soviets would have to decide what to do about China in the course and aftermath of such a war. These circumstances, and a 4,500-mile shared border, prompted the massive buildup of Soviet forces in the TVD.

Should war with the West not escalate and should China remain strictly neutral, the details of Soviet policy are imponderable. The Soviets would almost certainly retain the option of initiating a limited war against China at some time after the first phase of a world war was over. The contingency of Chinese belligerence is more demanding in terms of planning, but many of the same considerations would shape Soviet policy if China were neutral. Why, however, would the Chinese allow themselves to be drawn into a world war as opponents of Russia? At least two reasons appear plausible to Soviet planners. The Chinese may believe that Soviet forces were doing badly in the Western TVD, or they may believe that the Soviet Union would ultimately turn on China, irrespective of what stance it adopted.

The Soviet Union has to cover the possibility that China will choose to initiate hostilities when Soviet forces and reserves are totally committed in the European TVDs and may be facing defeat. Obviously, Russia could respond by resorting to tactical nuclear weapons on the battlefield and striking hard at key targets in the Chinese rear. However, the governing objective of avoiding the nuclear devastation of Russia is as relevant to strategic concepts in the Far Eastern TVD as in the European theater, and the concern that Beijing might be tempted or provoked to initiate a "catalytic" nuclear war will always be present. This fear dictates a mainly defensive posture on the ground, supplemented by the capability for deep operations against China's nuclear weapons facilities, without the use of nuclear weapons.

The defeat of China would depend on events in the European theater, although this still leaves the question of how to achieve victory over 1 billion people. Military occupation is clearly impractical as a general policy. While the Soviet Union might like to see the People's Republic broken up into many autonomous and mutually hostile political entities, it seems unlikely that the Soviets would put much weight on such a possibility. The Soviets could aim to limit China's capacity to regenerate its strength; they had the same objective for Germany at the end of World War II, which they hoped to achieve through reparations. But one can only extract reparations if one occupies the enemy's territory, and since this is impractical, the Soviets would have to find some other way of crippling China.

If Russia found itself in a conventional war with China, just before, or even after, agreeing to make peace, Soviet leaders might consider it prudent to devastate key industrial centers and other critical facilities with nuclear strikes. The fact of a world war would completely change the political calculus of such a decision, and the key consideration would be the extent to which China's nuclear retaliatory capacity had been, or could be, spiked. If that were certain, the Soviets could even give extended warning of their intentions to allow time for the evacuation of target areas.

Whether or not Russia found itself at war with China in phase I, Soviet military planners would have to allow for the possibility that at some stage in phase II, the United States might make an arrangement that would allow it to use China as the avenue for an assault on the Russian heartlands, following the path of the Mongol hordes. By advancing through China, U.S. forces would outflank eastern and central Siberia, gaining access to the Kirghiz steppes and the West Siberian Plain.

MANCHURIA. The Soviet Union is likely to treat Manchuria as a special case because of its long history of political separation from China, special links with Russia, and what Manchuria is today.[6]

In the event of a Soviet-U.S. intercontinental exchange, this heavily industrialized area could serve as an alternative socioeconomic base for rebuilding the socialist system. In a conventional war initiated by China, all or part of what used to be called Manchuria could be prised away from China and set up as a semiautonomous state akin to Mongolia.[7] In any event, Manchuria would need to be spared nuclear strikes and would have

6. Chinese penetration of central and northern Manchuria did not take hold until the seventeenth century, and colonization was then accelerated to counter the eastward march of Russian power. By 1860 Russia had been ceded the lands to the east of the Ussuri and looked on Manchuria as a legitimate sphere of interest. Russia backed China against Japan in 1895. Consequently, Russia received the right to build the Chinese Eastern railway across Manchuria and a twenty-five-year lease on the Liao-tung Peninsula, Port Arthur, Dairen. In 1900, during the Boxer Rebellion, Russia occupied the whole of Manchuria, but after the Russian defeat in 1905, Russia ceded its interests in southern Manchuria to Japan. Russia retained influence in the rest of the area until the revolution in 1917, when joint management with China of the railway was agreed on. Manchuria was under Japanese control from 1932 to 1945.

7. The Soviets hoped for such a state in the 1949–53 period. In August 1949, following the defeat of the Kuomintang forces, the Northeast People's Government was formally established over what used to be Manchuria. Kao Kang, who exercised virtually autonomous powers and had frequent contact with the Soviets, headed the government. This government was abolished by Beijing in 1953, and Kao Kang was purged in 1955.

to be physically occupied, an operation the Soviets carried out successfully in 1945 against the defending Japanese forces.[8]

Manchuria, in friendly and malleable hands, would yield significant long-term benefits to the Soviet Union. It would seriously weaken China by depriving it of its industrial heartland. It would deny China land access to North Korea and provide additional means of bringing Soviet pressure to bear on North Korea. It would give the Soviet Union a substantial defensive buffer and at the same time provide a potential springboard for military operations against China's political heartland. Furthermore, Soviet access to the ports on the Liao-tung Peninsula would expose China's most vulnerable maritime flank while denying the U.S. Seventh Fleet the use of the Yellow Sea to bring targets in the Lake Baikal area range of carrier-borne aircraft.[9]

Just taking over the two-thirds of Manchuria lying north of the line joining the Soviet-Korean border with the Mongolian salient would be useful to the Soviets. That would return control of the Vladivostok-Harbin-Chita rail link to friendly hands, put four hundred miles between the redrawn Chinese frontier and the Trans-Siberian railway, and still deprive China of a large part of its industrial base.

Given the potential importance of Manchuria, it could be argued that the Soviets' most appropriate strategy would be to plan, should war be inevitable, to launch an offensive to seize the area at the same time as, or even before, they made their move in the Western TVD. By moving early, the Soviets could divert attention from the European theater. They would be more likely to catch the Chinese less well prepared, while denying them the lessons they could draw from a European campaign. Such an offensive would, however, ensure Russian involvement in ground combat in the west and east simultaneously, and possibly in the south as well.[10] Such an offensive also ignores the larger strategic picture. The optimum situation from the Soviet viewpoint is for China to remain neutral in the east while Russia is waging war in the west. When the outcome of Russia's war in the west

8. The Chinese have a more pessimistic estimate of Soviet capabilities and objectives. They assume that the Russians will attempt to take over the part of China that is north of the Yangtze.

9. The Yellow Sea allows carriers to come four hundred miles closer to targets in the Irkutsk-Chita area. In 1957 the Soviets proposed a joint Sino-Soviet Air Defense and antisubmarine command for this area, which China refused. The supply of Whisky submarines to China at that period can be seen as providing an obstacle to Seventh Fleet carriers as well as a counter to the threat of U.S. amphibious assault on the northern plains.

10. If the Chinese were to cut the Trans-Siberian railway, the Soviets would have to establish a southern sea line of communication, which might require that supplies be shipped across Iran.

has been satisfactorily resolved, there will be time and resources enough to deal with the secondary problem of Manchuria.

THE OVERALL CONCEPT.   In the initial stages of a world war, this action would be a holding operation, with Manchuria as an exception in the longer term. The primary Soviet objective is to deter attacks on their territory, but, should they come, the Soviets would want to repulse them with the minimum expenditure of resources so as not to weaken the Soviet posture in the west. Should China take the opportunity of a world war to attack the Soviet Union, the Soviets' long-term objective would be to *cripple China's war-making capacity,* probably with nuclear strikes and also by depriving it of Manchuria. Should the war escalate to an intercontinental nuclear exchange, China would be struck, whether or not it had attacked, and Manchuria would be occupied to serve as an alternative socioeconomic base. Should war with the West not escalate and China remain neutral, the details of Soviet military policy toward China are imponderable and would be determined by the prevailing circumstances.

Assuming that the Soviets had been successful in the Western TVD and that the United States had not escalated to an intercontinental exchange, Russia would be able to bring a much greater proportion of military strength to bear on China and thereby force a resolution in the Far East. The objective would be to achieve a reasonably stable political situation that could be sustained at not too great a cost in military resources, and which would deny China to the United States as a potential ally in the ongoing global struggle between the two social systems.

Japan

Japan on its own poses no direct threat to Russia, nor do these islands with their limited natural resources, dense population, and difficult terrain offer the Soviet Union any temptation to territorial expansion. The attraction of Japan lies in its advanced technological capacity and modern industrial base, and military occupation would likely destroy both.

Ideally, the Soviets would like to supplant the United States as Japan's primary ally so that Japan could be a counterbalance to China and provide basing rights that would extend the Soviet Union's offshore defense zone against the threat of U.S. naval power. This is clearly not a practical option in the foreseeable future, and it can therefore be assumed that, in a world war, the immediate Soviet objective would be to limit the military value of Japan to the United States.

This aim argues for a policy of threats and inducements designed to persuade Japan to declare itself neutral in such a conflict, or if that can not be achieved, to deter Japan from actively participating in the war on the U.S. side. There is little purpose in speculating on the modalities of such a policy once war was in progress and on how the Soviets would respond if Japanese bases were used to support U.S. attacks on Russia. It is worth reflecting on how military developments in Europe would shape Japanese perceptions and decisions. If the Soviets were successful in seizing NATO Europe without precipitating a U.S. intercontinental strike, then the notion that Japan was protected by the shield of extended U.S. nuclear deterrence would be discredited. In other words, in phase II of a world war, Japan would have to take Soviet threats of punishment at face value, because there would be no other recourse. However, during phase I the Soviets would have to walk that difficult line between dissuasion through punishment, and driving Japan to cast its lot with the West.

It is hard to predict how the Russians would handle Japan should world war escalate to an intercontinental nuclear exchange. One option would be to strike it at the same time as China so as to deny Japan a position of residual dominance. But it is perhaps more likely that the Soviets would choose to spare Japan so as to use its industrial capacity for rebuilding the socialist system. They might well reckon that the Japanese would be prepared to accept a quasi-vassal status rather than suffer nuclear devastation, an alternative which by then would be only too credible.

The Korean Peninsula

The optimum Soviet policy toward the Korean Peninsula is less obvious. On the face of it, a North Korean offensive against the South would distract U.S. attention and tie down its forces. Furthermore, assuming that North Korea was successful, it would bring one side of the Tsushima Strait into friendly hands. There are, however, several disadvantages to such an offensive.

It could jeopardize the governing objective of avoiding escalation to an intercontinental exchange. The United States is committed to using tactical nuclear weapons in defense of South Korea, and the Soviets would have to assume that there is a high probability that the United States would act on this commitment in this particular area. But crossing the nuclear threshold on the ground in the Far East would make it just that more likely that the United States would resort to the use of nuclear weapons in Europe, thus increasing the danger of escalation.

A North Korean offensive could also jeopardize the main objective in the Far Eastern TVD, which is to deter China from entering the war against Russia. If the North Koreans were successful, could the Chinese stand by and watch the United States go down to defeat, or would China decide to intervene against North Korea? If the Chinese did choose to intervene, the Soviet Union would either have to leave North Korea to its fate or embark on an offensive into Manchuria. The latter would not only precipitate a Sino-Soviet war, but it would also mean that the Manchurian campaign would have to be initiated in circumstances that were not of Soviet choosing, thereby prejudicing its success.

If North Korea succeeded in unifying the peninsula without Russian involvement, the Soviets would probably end up with another Yugoslavia or mini-China on their southern flank rather than a subservient ally. All in all, the prospects argue that the Soviet Union would seek to prevent North Korea from launching an offensive during the first phase of a world war.

The optimum policy would provide for North Korea to coordinate plans with the Soviet Union and to launch an attack shortly after the initiation of a Soviet offensive into Manchuria, which would probably not be mounted until phase II, although its launching in phase I-3 is possible. This would mean that the North Korean rear was covered and that U.S. forces would be fully occupied in Korea and unavailable to support the Chinese in Manchuria. The most likely Soviet contribution to a Korean offensive would be air support, which could include the reinforcement of the North Korean air defense capability in the period between the outbreak of world war and the start of operations in the peninsula, and possibly an amphibious assault on the eastern coast of South Korea.

The Maritime Zones of the Far Eastern TVD

The maritime geography of this area and the existing base structure suggest that the Far Eastern TVD includes at least two maritime theaters of military action (MTVDs). One, controlled from Vladivostok, would encompass the Seas of Japan and Okhotsk. The other, controlled from Petropavlosk, would cover the maritime approaches east of the Kurile chain and Kamchatka Peninsula, and reach north to the Bering Strait, where it would abut with the Arctic OTVD. The boundary between these two MTVDs is likely to run along the Kurile chain, with the defensive barrier of the islands coming under Petropavlosk.

It is also possible that the Sea of Okhotsk comprises a third MTVD, with headquarters at Sakhalin.[11] For the purpose of this discussion it will be convenient to analyze naval requirements in terms of these three separate zones.

Naval Objectives

The primary objectives in the maritime areas of the Far Eastern TVD are the traditional ones of securing the use of the sea for Soviet purposes and denying its use to the enemy. These objectives translate into four primary missions. The most important is to ensure the security of the ballistic-missile submarine force, primarily the Delta-class ballistic-missile submarines (SSBNs) targeted on the United States. The safety of the Yankee SSBNs and the Golf SSBs, whose targets lie mainly within the theater and would include U.S. military installations is also included in this mission.[12]

The other missions are more traditional: the most basic one is to protect the homeland against attacks from the maritime axes. In this context the Seas of Japan and Okhotsk serve as inner defense zones, with outer defense zones extending eastward as far as carrier strike range, perhaps three hundred to four hundred miles beyond Japan and the Kuriles. Similar inner and outer defense zones will extend eastward from the southern part of the Kamchatka Peninsula. A third mission is to prevent enemy forces from penetrating the Arctic OTVD by way of the Bering Strait, while at the same time ensuring access to the OTVD from Pacific Fleet bases, and vice versa. A fourth mission would be to support any invasion of South Korea and the seizure of islands in the Tsushima Straits, both of which would involve amphibious operations. These four missions translate into specific requirements for each of the MTVDs.

The Sea of Okhotsk

In the naval mission structure, there is an overriding requirement to secure the physical integrity of the Sea of Okhotsk as a maritime bastion. The Soviets already control the Kurile Island chain, and all of the sur-

11. There have been reports of large-scale construction of a naval base, including submarine, facilities on Sakhalin in the Sea of Okhotsk. Lim Joo-Jock, "Southeast Asia, Northeast Asia, and the Geopolitics of Global Balance," *Contemporary Southeast Asia,* vol. 3 (March 1982), pp. 395–96.

12. Westwood, *Power in the Pacific,* pp. 13–14.

rounding shoreline except for about 150 nautical miles of Japanese coast. The natural barrier of the Kuriles can be augmented by the use of fixed detection systems, mines, and diesel submarines.[13] A maritime defense screen (or outer defense zone) to seaward of the island chain should also be assumed. Although this zone would rely primarily on submarines, they would be supported by maritime air and by surface ships operating in easy range of shore-based fighter cover. Meanwhile the islands need strong defenses to cover the threat of an American amphibious assault designed to breach this physical barrier.[14]

Even with the seaward defenses secure, there remains the stretch of Japanese coast at the southern end of the Sea of Okhotsk. The political objective of keeping Japan neutral, or at least nonbelligerent, argues against seizing the southern shores of Nemuro and Soya (La Perouse) Straits. It is not militarily essential to do so because both straits lie over the continental shelf, with depths of one hundred fathoms or less. They can be blocked fairly easily by mines, and the fields can be defended from the northern side of the straits. This plan seems likely to be the preferred solution, although the Soviets must cover the possibility that Japan will be dragged into the war on the side of the West. That might lead to a decision to occupy the two horns of Hokkaido. In any event, it will be necessary to gain air superiority over the two straits or at least deny it to the West.[15]

The Sea of Japan

By denying Western naval forces access to the Sea of Okhotsk, the Soviets achieve de facto command of that area. Command of the whole Sea of Japan is not, however, a realistic Soviet objective because the Japanese will already have naval forces operating in the eastern part of the area, combined with local air superiority. If, however, the Soviets can limit ac-

13. Most of the channels between the islands are between one hundred and five hundred fathoms deep, and their combined breadth is more than one hundred nautical miles. However, the Soviets have developed the capability for mining at such depths, and the distances involved are also manageable. *Hearings on Military Posture,* Department of Defense Authorization for Appropriations for Fiscal Year 1979, before the House Committee on Armed Services, 95 Cong. 2 sess. (GPO, 1978), pt. 5, p. 4314.

14. The Soviets began deploying troops to the four southern islands of the Kurile chain in 1978 and building military support facilities. Currently about 10,000 troops, including a coastal defense division, are on the islands. *SMP, 1983,* p. 51.

15. A squadron of MiG-23s was deployed to Iturup in the summer of 1983, and the number of aircraft rose to about 40 in the spring of 1984. Drew Middleton, "Soviet Strategic Region," *New York Times,* September 2, 1983; and *Aviation Week and Space Technology,* vol. 120 (May 7, 1984), p. 7.

cess by other Western naval forces to the Sea of Japan, their efforts to gain command of as much of the area as they can, and to deny command to the West of as much of the rest as possible, will be facilitated. To the extent the Soviets can achieve these aims, they will be better able to accomplish their primary missions in the area: to secure the safety of the Yankee SSBNs deployed in the north and west parts, to counter attempts by U.S. aircraft carriers to support the Chinese in the battle for Manchuria, and to prevent U.S. surface forces from interfering with the invasion of South Korea.

There are three ways into the Sea of Japan: Soya Strait at the northern tip of Hokkaido; Tsugaru Strait between the Japanese mainland islands of Honshu and Hokkaido; and Tsushima Strait between Japan and Korea. Soya Strait is already covered by the requirement to seal off the Sea of Okhotsk. It is probably not practical to close Tsugaru Strait completely with mines, even by using specially built delivery vehicles. But it would not be unrealistic for the Soviets to plan on forcing the West to keep to swept channels. This would make life somewhat more difficult for Western submarines, but the major impact of such action would be on carrier battle groups. These would, of course, have the benefit of shore-based air cover, but constraining the force's ability to maneuver would make it vulnerable to two other kinds of attack: long-range torpedoes fired by submarines; and tactical ballistic missiles fired from Soviet territory, about three hundred nautical miles to the west.

Tsushima Strait presents the greatest problem to the Soviets because both sides could be in potentially hostile hands. It is both the broadest and the furthest away from Russian bases. Initially, the Soviets would have to rely on mining and submarine barriers; their primary objective would be to prevent the passage of carrier battle groups. Subsequently, if or when the takeover of South Korea had given the Soviets control of the northern side of the strait, a more effective closure could be attempted, aimed at intruding submarines as well as the carrier battle groups. This action might require occupation of Tsushima and other Japanese islands that lie in the strait area.

In timing, the situation is comparable with that in the Euro-Atlantic region, where operations in the Northwestern and Arctic Ocean TVDs would have to yield precedence to those in the Western TVD. It would be easier to gain command of the southern part of the Sea of Japan if South Korea were in friendly hands. But again this aim has to yield precedence to the Western TVD and to the need to avoid precipitating U.S. nuclear escalation on the Korean Peninsula, which might spread to the European theater. Operations in Korea also have to yield precedence to the possibility of a campaign to seize Manchuria. However, as the war continues, it becomes increasingly important to ensure the integrity of the SSBN bastions. This necessity argues that whether or not China enters the war, South Korea will be taken over in due course in order to secure the southern approach to this MTVD.

The Bering Sea

As the Soviet focus moves north to the Bering Sea and its approaches, requirements become less extensive. Primary missions are controlling passage through the Bering Straits to and from the Arctic and securing the sea line of communication between the strait and Soviet Pacific ports. If there are only two MTVDs in the Far East, then this one is likely to extend south to include responsibility for the seaward and territorial defense of the Kurile Island barrier.

The MTVD as a Buffer Zone

As was true in the Western TVDs, the central concept of the MTVDs as defense and support zones is again apparent. The requirement is not to provide for the "break out" of Soviet naval forces but to prevent the intrusion of Western naval forces. In discharging this mission the Soviets will in the main be operating in range of shore-based air cover and will be able to deploy air, surface, and subsurface assets. The carrier battle group poses the main threat. The Soviets must face the strategic aspect, primarily nuclear strike, against which they can deploy submarines and missile-armed aircraft of the naval and long-range air forces. But carriers might also become directly involved in the land battle, whether by supporting the seizure of islands in the Kurile chain or by reinforcing the defense of Manchuria or South Korea. In either case, the carrier would become the concern of frontal aviation, a well as all the longer-range forces.

The Importance of the Okhotsk SSBN Bastion

In the Sea of Okhotsk, the opportunities for denying physical access to the area are much greater than they are in the Northern Fleet area, which means that its potential as an SSBN bastion is greater and the cost of achieving such security is less. Since the missiles that are currently carried by the Delta SSBNs can cover two-thirds of the continental United States from the Sea of Okhotsk, it would make sense to favor the Pacific bastion at the expense of the Arctic Ocean. Traditionally, only 30 percent of Soviet ballistic-missile units were deployed in the Pacific, but the numbers began to change in the late 1970s and by 1984 the proportion of Deltas was more than 40 percent.[16] In the late 1970s the Soviets began reinforcing the defenses of the Kurile Islands, a process that continued in the 1980s.

During this period, the size of the surface force also increased. Although the new importance of the Okhotsk bastion may have been partly responsible, other factors like the sustained U.S. naval presence in the Indian Ocean, following the Iranian hostage crisis, and the Soviet invasion of Afghanistan were probably more important. The Soviets also had to demonstrate tangible support for Vietnam, following the Chinese punitive attack in 1979. The Chinese navy was improving slowly but steadily, increasing the threat to the southern sea route linking the Soviet Far East with western Russia. Soviet access to Cam Ranh Bay in Vietnam presented the opportunity to pose a direct counter to U.S. naval forces based on Subic Bay in the Philippines. The Pacific Fleet is now the largest of the four, but the initial impetus for its size goes back to the mid-1960s when the Indian Ocean deployment was first planned, a deployment that would be mounted and sustained from the Pacific bases.

Maritime geography and the scale of threat would primarily determine the requirement for forces to defend the Okhotsk bastion. Except for submarines providing direct protection, numbers would not be directly related to the number of SSBNs. One should not, however, ignore the possibility of additional attack submarines being made available to the Pacific in wartime, by way of the Arctic. If the immediate threat to the Northern Fleet seemed low (for example, if the U.S. Navy gave initial priority to the Mediterranean), the Soviets might find it practical to redeploy certain types of submarines to the Pacific to achieve a concentration of force in that area without jeopardizing the defense of the arctic bastions against U.S. attack submarines. If the U.S. carriers in the NATO theater headed north, the Northern Fleet submarines would still be able to get back in time across the Pole.

16. In June 1983 the proportion of Delta SSBNs in the Pacific was 38.8 percent, and the proportion of missiles aboard Delta was 37.3 percent. Defense Intelligence Agency, *Unclassified Communist Naval Orders of Battle*, DDB-1200-124-83 (DIA, 1983), p. 1. In early 1984 the proportion of Delta SSBNs had risen to 41.6 percent; *SMP, 1984*, p. 26. Since then the Typhoon has entered service in the North, which will reverse the trend unless Deltas are redeployed.

The U.S. Concept of Horizontal Escalation

What, if any, are the implications for Soviet military requirements of the U.S. concept of horizontal escalation? The idea behind this concept is that in a world war, or some lesser contingency such as a Soviet thrust toward the head of the Persian Gulf, offensive operations by U.S. naval and Marine forces in the Far Eastern TVD would serve to pin down existing forces in the TVD and might even draw in reinforcements from other TVDs.

The last idea greatly exaggerates the scale of force the U.S. Navy could project ashore at short notice and completely ignores Soviet strategic theory and the central importance of the main objective, the main TVD, and the main axis of advance. If the Soviets go to war, they will have considered the range of possible U.S. responses and allowed for such diversionary attacks in their calculation of costs and benefits. The Soviets will not be deflected from the main objective and main axis of advance by pinpricks in the Pacific.

The real question is, how redeployable are the Soviet forces in the Far Eastern TVD? With one exception, the answer is that they are not. Ground forces and their air support are sized to cover the Chinese threat and to defend the Soviet coastline, including the Kurile chain, against U.S. amphibious assault. Air defense forces are sized to cover the strategic air threat, of which carrier-borne aircraft are a relatively small component. The number of naval forces is largely determined by the requirement to secure command of the MTVDs. In other words, almost all these forces are already pinned down.

The one exception is the missile-armed medium-range strike aircraft, which contribute to countering the carrier threat. These Badgers and Backfires can be redeployed among TVDs fairly easily, and indeed the Soviets exercise such redeployments on a regular basis. However, pinning down the aircraft in the Far East does not require the United States to launch carrier strikes against Vladivostok or Petropavlosk.[17] The United States could best achieve the desired result by operating the carriers in an area that lies outside the Backfire's radius of action but within forty-eight

17. In congressional testimony highlighting "the advantage of airpower carriers" when attacking bases ashore, Admiral Turner, deputy commander of naval operations, used a map of East Asia, where the illustrative target was Vladivostok. *Hearings on Military Posture*, Department of Defense Authorization for Appropriations for Fiscal Year 1980, before the House Committee on Armed Services, 96 Cong. 1 sess. (GPO, 1979), p. 941.

hours' steaming of the launch position for air strikes against such targets, which would be, of course, the classic concept of a fleet in being.

The pin-down effect would not be increased by attacking targets ashore. Look at it from the Soviet viewpoint. The primary mission of Soviet naval Badgers and Backfires is to attack and disable the carrier to counter the threat posed by the carrier's aircraft; once that mission is accomplished, the Badgers and Backfires are free to redeploy. But this particular threat can also be countered directly by destroying the aircraft, which the Soviet air defense system is specifically designed to do, particularly around high-value targets such as naval bases and airfields.

In the broader strategic picture, it therefore seems likely that the Soviets would welcome the opportunity to blunt the U.S. capability for carrier strikes with air defense forces rather than their naval air force. Then the Soviets could turn the Pacific Fleet's Badgers and Backfires into an inter-theater reserve, which could be used in several ways. Such a reserve could reinforce the Northern Fleet in the battle for the Norwegian Sea. It could also contribute to the conventional ground and air battle in other TVDs. Medium bombers will suffer heavy attrition in the early stages of any war, and these naval aircraft could be used to rebuild depleted air force units.

The potential role of the aircraft as an intertheater reserve could affect Soviet willingness to use nuclear weapons against U.S. carriers in the Pacific. The advantages of doing so would be considerable. The odds on a conventional attack succeeding in disabling a carrier are at best even, and in most circumstances much lower, and it is inevitable that Soviet naval aircraft would suffer heavy attrition in the process. The result could be the worst of both worlds for the Soviets. They would face a depleted medium-range bomber force and a continuing carrier threat to the security of the Kurile Island barrier, the amphibious operations against South Korea, and the strategic targets in the Soviet mainland. In contrast, a nuclear attack on the carriers would have a high chance of success, and bomber attrition would be minimized because greater reliance could be placed on other delivery systems.

Only the danger of escalation constrains the Soviets from using nuclear weapons against the carrier. These constraints would probably disappear if the United States were to initiate the use of nuclear weapons in the TVD, especially if this step took the form of a limited strike against some significant but fairly isolated military target as part of an explicit policy of horizontal escalation or as some kind of "demonstration" shot for purposes of "signaling." Because these American concepts are the antithesis of uncontrolled escalation, such a strike would probably embolden Moscow rather than intimidate it. Indeed the Soviets might welcome such a U.S. attack. It would allow them to reap the benefits of sinking the carrier, with little fear of escalation to general nuclear war.

Distant Theaters of Maritime Operations

The Far Eastern TVD, with its subordinate MTVDs, is a continental TVD with an autonomous high command. But Soviet interest in the Asian theater of war extends beyond these boundaries to include the situation in the Pacific Ocean and in the South China and Philippine Seas. The forces for use in these waters will be drawn from the Soviet Pacific Fleet, but command and control might lie with the Supreme High Command in Moscow rather than with the Far Eastern TVD.

To perceive the nature of Soviet requirements in these distant sea areas a brief review of the overall strategic picture is needed. In the European theater, phase I of a world war would mean defeating NATO on the ground, evicting the United States from the Continent, and establishing a defense perimeter. The primary concern in phase II would be preventing the Western alliance from regaining a foothold on the Continent as the first step toward an invasion of the Soviet Union. The situation in the Asian-Pacific theater is rather different. China provides a permanent bridgehead on the Eurasian continent, and there is little the Soviets can do about that. And the Far East is a poor starting place for an assault on Russia, whose center of gravity lies west of the Urals. The Soviets would, however, want to close off the Sea of Japan, which means that they must take over South Korea.

The Soviet Union would enter phase II of a world war with its maritime flank buffered by semienclosed seas. By taking over Manchuria, the Soviets would also deny access by sea to the north China plain and prevent it from being used as a gateway to Mongolia and the west. With this situation in mind we can now turn to look at Soviet requirements in the broad Pacific and in the waters surrounding Southeast Asia.

Southeast Asian Waters

The Soviets want to be able to use the Southeast Asian waters, if need be, to ship supplies from western Russia to the Far East. The waters are not important as an access to China's southern flank because the impact of Soviet naval forays against the Chinese mainland would be negligible. Similarly, although the Soviets might assign a few older submarines to harass Chinese coastal shipping in the event of war, this would be a diversionary operation without major strategic significance.

The southern sea route does have vital strategic significance for the Soviets because of the vulnerability of the Trans-Siberian railway to physical disruption in the event of war with China. If that happened, military supplies for the Far Eastern fronts would have to be shipped by sea to arrive before stockpiles and local production were exhausted.

If it were merely a Sino-Soviet conflict, with the United States remaining neutral, the Soviets should be able to handle the threat from Chinese submarines in the South China and Philippine Seas with a mixture of evasive routing and active defensive measures. Having gained access to Cam Ranh Bay in the wake of China's military thrust into northern Vietnam in 1979, Soviet naval forces are now well positioned to interpose themselves between Chinese submarine bases and the flow of shipping. The Soviets could establish antisubmarine barriers and carry out offensive operations, and they would also be in a blocking position to prevent the Chinese from closing off the straits through the Indonesian archipelago.

In a world war the situation would be much more difficult, with U.S. naval and air forces based on the Philippines and Okinawa and carrier battle groups roaming the area. The ubiquitous U.S. presence would severely limit the opportunities for evasive routing, and it seems likely that the Soviets would be forced to fight convoys through the South China and Philippine Seas, as the British did in the Arctic and Mediterranean in World War II. The Soviets would draw what support they could from forces operating out of Vietnam. Whether they would be successful is another matter.

The U.S. threat to the southern sea route provides another important reason why the Soviets will strive to persuade China to remain neutral in a world war. The threat of U.S. carrier battle groups to Soviet plans provides yet another argument for trying to remove the carriers from the board as early in a war as is politically prudent.

The Pacific Ocean

In a world war Soviet strategic interests in the broader expanses of the Pacific are limited and primarily directed toward countering those U.S.

naval forces and their support groups that could threaten the Soviet home-land, the security of the SSBN bastions, and the southern sea route.

Embarking on a sustained effort to disrupt the flow of shipping to Japan would not serve the Soviet Union's overall strategic objective.[18] In a world war, the Soviets hope to persuade Japan to remain neutral or at least to refrain from active belligerence. To that end they will use a combination of inducements, threats, and punishments. In the circumstances envisaged, an antishipping campaign would be an ineffective instrument of persuasion because of its indeterminate and drawn-out nature. During phase I of a world war, the Soviets do not want to be thinking in terms of defeating Japan, which would be the long-term purpose of such a campaign. How-ever, if Soviet policies were to go disastrously wrong, and Japan should join the West as a fully committed belligerent, then the Soviets would surely resort to rapid, brutal, and certain methods, rather than the oblique approach of commerce war, to defeat Japan.

In any case, the Soviets would assign a small number of submarines to deep interdiction attacks on shipping in order to tie down U.S. forces that might otherwise be available to support offensive operations against Soviet vital interests and to divert antisubmarine assets away from forward-deployed Yankee SSBNs. The Soviets would also want to prevent substan-tial reinforcement of U.S. forces in Japan and Korea and the importation of aviation fuel. With hostilities raging in Europe, however, it seems un-likely that significant U.S. resources would be spared to reinforce Japan and Korea. The Soviets could find other ways of attacking critical supplies shipped by sea besides an indiscriminate campaign against shipping.

The Soviets could plan that if the war progressed to phase II, the Japa-nese would evict U.S. forces under threat of Soviet surgical nuclear strikes on the air bases used by them. By definition, phase II implies that the United States had not resorted to intercontinental strikes when facing de-feat in Europe, and a U.S. threat to do so in response to an attack on Japan would not be credible. Should America threaten limited nuclear strikes on remote targets in the Far Eastern TVD, of a kind that would be unlikely to escalate to a full exchange, the Soviet Union might welcome the opportu-nity to take out U.S. island bases and launch nuclear strikes against carriers in the western Pacific, without fear of escalation.

18. Western assumptions about the threat of such a campaign seem to be based on the expe-rience of Britain in the very different circumstances of World Wars I and II.

Phase Two of a World War

With Japan neutralized, the Soviets would have no special interest in the broader expanses of the Pacific Ocean. Japan's experience in World War II would surely dissuade Russia from occupying islands as a forward defensive screen. The Soviets' traditional approach suggests that they would concentrate on securing the defense of their maritime buffer zones and on ensuring that China could not be used as a bridgehead by the West.

They would, however, want to deprive the United States of any advantage it might gain from forward bases in Okinawa and Guam and in the Philippines at Subic Bay and Clark airfield. How this could best be achieved would depend upon the political situation at this stage of the war and the forces available to the two sides. If the Soviets were to focus initially on preventing or limiting the constructive use of these bases, rather than seeking to evict the United States by force of arms, a wide range of cost-effective approaches would be available to them. The objective could be to have these facilities wither on the vine until they were of little military significance.

By fairly early in the second phase of the war, it could be assumed that hostilities with China would either have been terminated or would be under control. In any event, it should no longer be necessary to ship military supplies by way of the southern sea route to the Far Eastern TVD. This would reduce the military importance of Cam Ranh Bay in Soviet plans and raises the question of how the Soviet Union would view Vietnam in phase II of a world war. Some Soviets would argue that Vietnam had the military capacity to take over Thailand and Malaya. This would consolidate the socialist position in Southeast Asia, as well as reinforce the threat to China from the south. Alternatively, the Soviets could argue that concentrating on Vietnam would generate heavy demands for armaments and logistic support, commit the Soviet Union to sustaining an exposed salient by sea, and bring more costs than benefits.

It could be argued that confining the United States to the Western Hemisphere would be sufficient to ensure the early demise of the capitalist system, that the socialist defense perimeter needed to be kept as short as possible, and that neutrality was a satisfactory state for the rest of the Eurasian landmass. In other words, the political objective in Southeast Asia should be to persuade the states of the area, including Australia and New Zealand, to accept the defeat of NATO in Europe as a fait accompli and to opt for neutrality rather than the horrors of war.

Soviet analyses of the Pacific campaign in World War II and the lessons that could be applied to contemporary circumstances would serve as a backdrop to these arguments. In World War II, the United States was able to fight its way back across the Pacific by using armadas of surface ships. But that was before the days of space surveillance systems, over-the-horizon radars, nuclear submarines, long-range homing missiles, and nuclear weapons. The Asian-Pacific region is likely to figure greatly in the Soviet debate about the best way of preventing the return of the United States to the Eurasian landmass, and the Soviet navy's mission will be a special focus of concern.

CHAPTER 9

The Indo-Arabian Region

THE SOUTHERN theater of war is said to encompass Southwest Asia, including the Arabian Peninsula.[1] The geography of the region suggests that it probably extends to take in the Indian subcontinent and the Indian Ocean, with the coastline of Southeast Asia forming the eastern perimeter.

The Southern theater of military action (TVD) forms part of this theater and looks south from the Caucasus and Turkestan, out across the eastern half of Turkey, Iran, Afghanistan, and Pakistan.[2] The western boundary of this TVD cuts through the middle of Turkey and runs south between Cyprus and the Levantine coast to Egypt, and it may include the Suez Canal. In the east, the boundary is likely to follow the line of the Himalayas flanking Pakistan and then turn south, following the west coast of India to Cape Comorin. The southern boundary is likely to follow that of the Arabian Sea, which runs southeast from the Horn of Africa to the southern tip of the Maldives, and the boundary of the Laccadive Sea, which runs northeast from the Maldive Islands to Sri Lanka (figure 9-1).

The character of this theater differs fundamentally from the others that have been discussed. In both the European and the Asian theaters of war, the Soviets are faced by in-place military capabilities of their potential enemies. In the Far East, the Soviets' main objective is to counter the threat of Chinese territorial aggression. In Europe, the threat is more complex, but the Soviets must seize substantial tracts of NATO territory in the early stages of a general war if they are to avoid ultimate defeat. None of these circumstances pertain in the Southern TVD. The Soviets are not faced by an in-place threat of territorial aggression across their southern borders, and it would not be easy for an opponent to mount such a threat.

1. U.S. Department of Defense, *Soviet Military Power, 1983,* 2d ed. (Government Printing Office, 1983), p. 34. (Hereafter *SMP.*) See also *SMP, 1984*, 3d ed., p. 50.
2. *SMP, 1984*, p. 50.

Figure 9-1. The Indo-Arabian Region

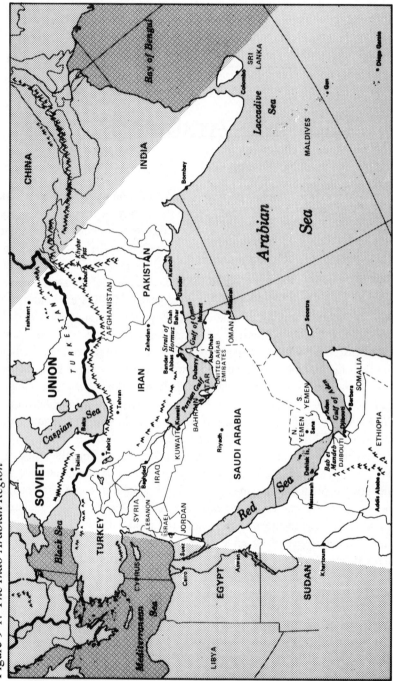

And there is no inherent requirement for the Soviets to seize strategic objectives beyond their borders in the early stages of a war with NATO or China.

This means that the Southern TVD comes in a poor fifth to the other TVDs in strategic priority. The Soviets can not, however, afford to ignore this TVD in wartime, and in peacetime its political fluidity provides its own kind of danger. The Southern TVD covers a large area, but the absence of a major capabilities threat does allow the Soviet Union a flexibility in formulating missions that is not possible in other TVDs. In view of the diverse nature of potential requirements in the Southern TVD, this advantage is important.

These diverse requirements differ sharply, depending on the type of circumstance and the part of the TVD in question. Geographically, this theater can be divided into three main areas, with the Arabian Sea as one and the other two lying northeast and southwest of a line running down the middle of the Arabian Peninsula. Each area must be considered separately.

Peacetime contingencies, threats to sea communications through the area, and the situation in a world war must also be considered. Although I am primarily concerned with identifying Soviet objectives in a world war, the Soviets' military posture will be strongly influenced by the need to cover against these other circumstances.

The Persian Gulf and Surrounding Territory

Russian involvement with the Persian empire dates from the beginning of the eighteenth century. To the west of the Caspian Sea, the Russians established the present boundary along the Aras River in 1828; the boundary to the east of Caspian was agreed on in 1881. To the south of the boundaries, Russia has been interested primarily in wielding influence and not in gaining terrritory, and the nineteenth century was characterized by Anglo-Russian rivalry in both Persia and Afghanistan.

This competition continued into the twentieth century, until the rising threat of Germany persuaded the imperial rivals to compose their differences. The Anglo-Russian Convention of 1907, which acknowledged a Russian sphere of influence reaching south to the city of Isfahan, gives some indication of Russia's aspirations at that time, and Russia's interest in northern Iran was again recognized by the British-Soviet agreement in

1941.[3] This interest, however, has nothing whatsoever to do with some "historical Russian drive for warm water ports."

There was a historical drive for warm water ports, but it occurred in the ninth through eighteenth centuries, and the ports in question were on the northern shores of the Black Sea. For at least ten centuries the Russians and their forebearers strove repeatedly to gain trading access to these waters. Russians also faced the equally long-standing problem of securing free passage for the produce of the steppes through the Black Sea exits, which were controlled by the Ottoman empire.

The oft-quoted assertion about the drive for warm water ports originates in the nineteenth century, a period of intense Anglo-Russian imperial rivalry, which was sharpened by British sensitivity to perceived threats to its maritime supremacy. By that date, the Russians were interested in controlling passage through the Turkish Straits, as the only practical way of preventing the British and French from using their fleets to determine the outcome of events on the Black Sea littoral, as they had done in 1856 and 1877. This traditional Russian interest in the Black Sea exits was reaffirmed during the Nazi-Soviet negotiations in November 1940. The Germans proposed that the Russian vector of interest should be Southwest Asia, in the direction of the Persian Gulf and the Arabian Sea. The Russians kept returning to the question of the Balkans and the Dardanelles. Consequently, no agreement could be reached.

Outside the circumstances of world war or extreme turbulence in Iran or Afghanistan, are there good reasons for the Soviet Union to want to thrust south of its border? Occupying the oil fields at the head of the gulf and establishing a Baluchistan republic as a Soviet satellite on the Indian Ocean are frequently mentioned inducements. They do not stand up to close inspection.

The notion of a Soviet urge to seize the oil fields surfaced in the wake of the Iranian revolution, and Western analysts saw it as a way for the Soviets to hurt the West while helping themselves. It was believed that the Soviet Union was about to become a net energy importer; this would cause it to seek direct control of additional resources. Neither belief was justified, but more serious, the notion ignored a whole range of certain costs

---

3. In August 1941, Britain and the Soviet Union, by mutual agreement and with a coordinated drive, occupied Iran. The Russians took control of the area to the north of thirty-five degrees latitude (running through Tehran), and the British took everything to the south. George Lenczowski, *The Middle East in World Affairs,* 4th ed. (Cornell University Press, 1980), pp. 50, 168, 179.

and never explained why the Soviets would not be able to acquire additional oil supplies by commercial agreement.

Two especially difficult problems argue against a Soviet drive for territory. One, the Soviets would face the military problem of gaining and maintaining control over a politically volatile area, located at the end of long lines of communication that run through difficult terrain.[4] Two, the West has a vital interest in the oil fields. A Soviet occupation of the region would not be accepted by the West as a fait accompli but would become a source of dangerous instability to the Soviet Union.

The objections to attempting to establish a Baluchistan satellite, outside the circumstances of a world war, follow the same general lines. Such a move would almost certainly involve the Soviet Union in military operations against both Iran and Pakistan, and the Soviets would have to rely on lines of communication through Afghanistan. It would alienate most third world nations, including all the Muslim states; encourage countries in the region to seek U.S. support; and probably persuade India and Pakistan to settle their differences and present a united front to the intruder. The Soviets would still not know whether the Baluchs would prove to be any more politically tractable than the Afghans or, for that matter, the Iranians.

A case can be made that Russia's long-term security would be improved if Soviet control were extended from 150 to 300 miles southward to take in Persian Azerbaijan, and perhaps Kurdestan as well. The Soviets would gain a land corridor giving them direct access to Syria and Iraq.[5] The head of the gulf would be brought within tactical air range of Soviet-controlled territory, a strategic advantage that would greatly increase Soviet leverage while threatening U.S. plans for rapidly deploying military force into the area.

Although the Soviets would have to use forces to gain control, their primary method could well be political. The Autonomous Republic of Azerbaijan, which enjoyed a brief twelve months' existence in 1945–46,

4. For a discussion of the military problems involved in carrying out such an operation, see Thomas L. McNaugher, *Arms and Oil: U.S. Military Strategy and the Persian Gulf* (Brookings, 1985), pp. 23–46. See also Keith A. Dunn, "Constraints on the USSR in Southwest Asia: A Military Analysis," *Orbis*, vol. 25 (Fall 1981), pp. 607–29; and see Joshua M. Epstein, "Soviet Vulnerabilities in Iran and the RDF Deterrent," *International Security*, vol. 6 (Fall 1981), pp. 126–58.

5. See Gerold Guensberg, *Soviet Command Study of Iran (Moscow 1941): Draft Translation and Brief Analysis* (Arlington, Va.: SRI International, 1980), pp. 113, 127. The study described Iranian Azerbaijan as the main theater of war. It also described the main operational axis as running through Tabriz, pointing out that this line opened up the possibility of moving against Tehran and against the most important centers in Iraq.

could be resuscitated. The Kurds might be tempted into cooperation by the prospect of an independent republic, taking in parts of Turkey, Iran, and Iraq, which could enjoy a status akin to that of Mongolia.

To note that Russia's long-term security would be improved is not to say that Soviet overall interests would be served by extending its control southward. That would depend on the prevailing circumstances, which would determine the balance of costs and benefits.

Internal developments in Afghanistan and Iran and their effect on Soviet Turkestan to the north, which now includes the republics of Turkmenistan, Uzbekistan, Tadzhikistan, and Kirgiziya, present a broader problem. Turkestan is not only the most recent major addition to the Russian empire (1864–81), but it is also the most typically "colonial." European military and administrative power was used to subjugate this Asian region of settled agricultural economy and ancient civilization and then bring it under a colonial rule that was not much different from its British and French counterparts. There was substantial settlement by Russian peasants, an intrusion that lay at the root of the widespread Muslim revolt in 1916. Elsewhere in the world, almost all such recent colonies have regained their independence under indigenous leaders, but Turkestan remains part of Russia.

This circumstance, memories of the Bashmachi rebellion during the 1920s, and the fact that Russia's borders with Afghanistan and Iran cut through a single ethnic area make the Soviet Union particularly sensitive to Muslim irredentism. This does not, however, imply a strategic imperative to turn Afghanistan and Iran into communist satellites. Rather the reverse. The historical record suggests that Russian interests have, on balance, been well served by having these more-or-less independent buffers to the south, whereas the pro-communist coup in Kabul, Afghanistan, in 1978 was followed by a slide toward anarchy.[6] This led to Russian military intervention, which was a major setback to Soviet policy.

The fact that the Russians considered it essential to intervene at that stage, despite the obvious political and military costs, highlights the nature of their concerns.[7] The threat from the south is not military nor is it really

6. In other words, Russia intervened to preserve Afghanistan's role as a buffer. See Raymond L. Garthoff, *Détente and Confrontation: American-Soviet Relations from Nixon to Reagan* (Brookings, 1985), p. 928.

7. The Soviets have had the military capability to invade Afghanistan at any time since the mid-1950s. This argues that the geostrategic advantage of occupying Afghanistan was not the primary determinant of the decision to invade, although such an advantage may have been seen as mitigating the invasion's costs.

ideological; rather it is the subversive combination of religious fervor and an absence of political control.

U.S. Military Intervention

The Soviets must wrestle with the question of how to react to U.S. military intervention in the area, particularly in the region of the Persian Gulf. U.S. intervention could take several forms: flying in tactical air assets, deploying army divisions, landing a marine force, or carrying out various kinds of carrier operation. Intervention could take place in the course of a general war, in a Sino-Soviet war, or in response to some peacetime contingency in the area.

The type of Soviet response required would depend on the combination of form and circumstance. Take, for example, the landing of a marine amphibious brigade (about 15,000 men) on the northern side of the Strait of Hormuz. If the Soviets were at war with China, U.S. control of the north sides of the strait could, in certain circumstances, pose a direct threat to the potential sea line of communication with the Far Eastern TVD. In other circumstances, such a landing would serve to tie down a significant portion of the available American forces while having few adverse consequences for the Soviet strategic posture.

Persian Gulf Oil

In a general war with the West, the Soviets have to consider the desirability of cutting the supply of petroleum products from the Middle East, and how best that can be accomplished. The issues are not clear-cut. If the Soviet land campaign in the Western TVD goes according to plan, products that are upstream of Middle East tanker terminals at the outbreak of war can have no impact on the outcome of that battle. Middle East oil is not essential to the United States if it withdraws from Europe to fight on from fortress America. The United States can mobilize the substantial petroleum resources in the Western Hemisphere to its own advantage while continuing to exploit access to other sources of supply that lie at a distance from the Soviet Union.

Of course, if the Soviet advance in Europe were checked and the front stabilized, Middle East oil could then be the critical factor in allowing continued NATO operations, assuming that the petroleum products could be landed and distributed. Even then, the military arguments for disrupting the supply at source are not overwhelming, and there are substantial political and strategic costs to consider. A sharp drop in revenue in the producing countries could lead to political unrest and a new surge of Muslim fundamentalism, something the Soviets do not see as being in their interests. Cutting off Middle East oil would cause significant economic distress among third world countries, which would be faced with sky high prices as well as an acute shortage of petroleum products, and the political fallout would hit friend (India, for example) and foe alike. Depriving a country such as Japan of its primary source of supply would ipso facto provide the United States with a powerful lever for ensuring Japan's active participation in the war on the Western side. The military cost to the Soviet Union of such a development could be considerable.

Sea Lines of Communication

The Soviets want to secure an alternative line of communication with the Far Eastern TVD, where ammunition and fuel stocks are sufficient to sustain two months of conflict.[8] The Trans-Siberian railway is vulnerable to long-term disruption, as is the Baikal-Amur loop that is now under construction. Although the Soviets have been steadily increasing the availability of the Northern Sea route, and air transport may be feasible for certain categories, they would have to rely primarily on the southern route across the Indian Ocean for a sustained supply of large quantities of stores and equipment.

Ideally, the route would run out of the Black Sea, by way of the Suez Canal and through the Red Sea. Since this option will not necessarily be available, the Soviets must be prepared to use some variant of the route that was used to supply Russia in World Wars I and II, by shipping overland to the Persian Gulf or the Arabian Sea. This requirement is neither immediate nor inevitable. Undoubtedly, the Soviets have substantial stockpiles throughout the Far East, and they may well be able to keep the rail link functioning. Nevertheless, they would have to allow for an alternate route in their war plans.[9]

8. *SMP, 1984*, p. 79.//
9. The southern sea route's importance to the Soviet economy, to the fishing industry, and to supplying North Vietnam had long been recognized, but after 1971 its military importance emerged in the event of war with China.

Phase Two of a World War

As noted, the Soviets must assume that, even if they defeat NATO on land in Europe, the Western alliance will carry on the struggle. The Soviets must allow that the alliance will regroup in North America, Australia, and elsewhere and then seek to reestablish itself on the Eurasian continent as the first step toward building up forces for an assault on the Soviet Union and the defeat of the socialist system. Two of the established approaches to Russia pass through the Southern TVD. The route through western Iran was used to ship supplies to Russia in the first two world wars and could serve as an axis for an invasion in World War III. The traditional invasion and trade route into India that runs through Afghanistan and over the Khyber and Khojak passes could be used in the reverse direction.

In both cases, the harsh terrain presents formidable problems for invading forces, but the Soviets cannot afford to ignore either approach. Both routes are accessible by sea and provide the possibility for a massive buildup of military strength ashore to the south of the natural defensive barriers, before invading forces attempt an assault on Russia. Furthermore, there is less sacrificable space to the south of the Soviet industrial heartlands than in most other directions.

Soviet Military Requirements

In most cases in the Persian Gulf region, the Soviets are not faced with imperatives, and immediate responses are not called for. The choice of timing of particular actions lies with the Soviets, as does the choice of whether to take action or not. Outside the circumstances of world war, political considerations will be at least as important as the military ones. This flexible situation is, however, distorted by the ever-present possibility of U.S. military intervention, a contingency that has to be considered in all contemporary planning for the region. Soviet military requirements have to be assessed with this fact in mind.

THE CAUCASUS-GULF AXIS. In the event of U.S. military intervention in the gulf area, the buildup of American ground forces can be expected to take place around the head of the Persian Gulf. Operational and logistic constraints dictate that it cannot be much further to the north, and it makes sense to deploy the forces initially as a shield around the oil-producing areas. The Soviets would find it difficult to prevent such a deployment.[10] Their incentive to do so is low because their position in relation to Middle East oil supplies would not be affected. After all, the Soviets do not need the oil themselves, and they can still deny the oil to the West by other means.

Soviet interests could, however, be threatened if they failed to counter U.S. intervention, implying that Soviet forces would move south of the Russian border and take up a blocking position. As already noted, Russia's long-term geostrategic posture, for other reasons, would be enhanced by extending Soviet control over Iranian Azerbaijan and possibly Kurdestan as well. It seems likely therefore that the Soviets will have made a virtue out of necessity and will have established the military requirement to be able to advance their defense perimeter some three hundred miles southward, should they have to.

The modalities of such an operation would depend on prevailing political alignments and the extent to which the Soviets could manipulate them to their benefit. A full three hundred-mile advance would allow the use of airfields in northern Iraq, but in many circumstances it might be necessary to halve the depth of advance and consolidate south of Tabriz. Whatever happened, the logistic demands would be heavy. The Soviet air defense system would have to extend southward rapidly, an evolution that requires substantial airlift. Obviously, the Soviets would prefer not to have to fight their way south, and their problems would be considerably increased if their advance were also subject to U.S. air attack. If that seemed a real possibility, the Soviets would have to be ready to launch interdiction strikes against air bases in eastern Turkey and the Arabian Peninsula.

The need for airlift and medium-range air strike, and the value of an additional airborne division, highlights the extent that operations in northwest Iran depend on the availability of central assets, which in turn depends on the politico-military situation in the European and Asian theaters.[11] However, the Soviets do have the advantage of forces in place and interior lines of communication, which gives them a measure of flexibility.

10. The problem is reaction time. The Soviets could drop an airborne division, but such a long-range operation would run counter to their well-founded doctrinal tenets, and it could only disrupt, not prevent, a U.S. deployment of forces. See McNaugher, *Arms and Oil,* pp. 23–46.

11. There is one airborne division stationed in the Caucasus, but all seven divisions are strategic resources controlled by Moscow, as is Military Transport Aviation. These assets are allocated to theaters of military action as the Supreme High Command deems appropriate. Medium-range strike aircraft have recently been reorganized into four air armies, three in the European theater and one in the Asian theater. Mark L. Urban, "Major Re-organization of Soviet Air Force," *International Defense Review,* vol. 16, no. 6 (1983), p. 756.

Thus, although this TVD yields precedence to all others, in the event of NATO war, the Soviets might choose to launch an offensive as if they were moving toward the Persian Gulf, in the hope of drawing U.S. forces away from what the Soviets rank as the main theater. In a peacetime crisis in the gulf area, the same flexibility gives the Soviets the option of waiting for U.S. military intervention and evaluating the political fallout from it before deciding on a response.

THE SEA LINE OF COMMUNICATION. The requirement to ship military supplies to the Far Eastern TVD is mainly tied to the contingency of a protracted war with China but could also arise in the event of a world war. America's military stance would be critical in deciding which overland route to use and, outside the circumstances of a world war, one determinant of that stance would be Iran's willingness to allow the Soviets to establish such a line of communication through its territory. If Iran were reluctant to do so, there would be little purpose in the Soviets establishing it by force, since the probability of provoking a U.S. reaction would be high. The United States has the military capability to block land access to the head of the gulf with ground forces, but its response could be simpler than that. If American air units were ensconced along the southern shore of the gulf, it would be extremely costly, if not impossible, for the Soviets to secure a flow of shipping through the gulf, even if they controlled the whole northern shore.

There are two sets of circumstances, therefore, when the Soviets could sensibly consider shipping out of the head of the gulf. They could do so in a war with China, given Iranian and U.S. acquiescence, and they could do so in a world war if U.S. forces were already fully committed elsewhere or could be prevented from being redeployed to the gulf. In the latter case, the Soviets would have to weigh the pros and cons of taking control of Azerbaijan; the alignment of the overland route, which could pass through Iraq as well as Iran, would depend on both political and military factors.

If the Soviets were faced with the likelihood of Iranian and U.S. opposition to this western route, there would be distinct military advantages to using a route through eastern Iran, even though it is considerably more circuitous. This route would run down through Afghanistan and Iranian Baluchistan, using the port facilities at Chah Bahar, located about three hundred miles east of the Strait of Hormuz. Establishing this route would require a thrust out of southwest Afghanistan, with a three hundred-mile advance through a harsh environment. This might well be simpler, in military terms, than establishing a route through the western part of Iran, since the terrain is less mountainous and constricting, the area is remote and sparsely populated, and there are sufficient airfields to support such an operation.

The immediate objective would be to seize the port and airfield at Chah Bahar. The likelihood of U.S. ground force intervention would determine the concept of operations, particularly the need for airborne troops. However, given the allocation of sufficient forces, the Soviets should be able to establish themselves securely on the shores of the Arabian Sea within twenty days of launching their offensive out of southwest Afghanistan.[12] Shipping out of Chah Bahar has the advantage of bypassing the hazardous passage through the Persian Gulf and Strait of Hormuz. The port gives directly on to the Arabian Sea and is not too close to potential enemy facilities, namely, the Pakistani naval base at Karachi, about four hundred nautical miles to the east, and Muscat airfield, two hundred nautical miles across the Gulf of Oman.

PERSIAN GULF OIL. There is a possible requirement to stop the flow of oil at the source. As noted, there would be unavoidable political costs in such action, some of which could have significant military repercussions. Although this undifferentiated approach would only be adopted because more selective methods (such as sinking NATO-bound tankers as they near their destination) were impractical, it seems likely that the Soviets would seek to minimize these costs. One way of doing so would be to restore the flow of oil as soon as the military situation allowed. This rules out the indiscriminate destruction of oil facilities (loading terminals, refineries, pumping stations, and so on) as the primary means of disrupting supplies and favors a type of action that can be reversed fairly easily.

Mining the oil terminals, by using bottom mines with firing mechanisms that could be deactivated by remote control, could fit the requirement for reversible action. Such an operation would be practical in the Persian Gulf but much harder to carry out against the distant terminals on the Mediterranean and Red Sea coasts. There, it would be appropriate to attack the distribution system near its point of origin.

---

12. Chah Bahar is six hundred miles as the crow flies from the Soviet airbase at Shindand, the Iranian field at Zahedan lies midway between the two, and there are two smaller airfields between Zahedan and the coast and one to the north of it. An existing road links Chah Bahar and the airfields with the strategic road that rings Afghanistan. Despite the rugged terrain and harsh climate, an average rate of advance from the Afghan border of twenty miles a day is not unrealistic. The Soviets would have to be ready to seize Chah Bahar with airborne troops to preempt U.S. intervention.

WESTERN LODGEMENTS.   In the early days of a world war, the Soviet Union would be happy to see significant air and ground forces drawn into the gulf, since it would divert them from the main TVDs in the European theater. In the longer run, however, the Soviets do not wish to have Western forces ensconced in the area, particularly not an effective air defense capability because this would facilitate the West's return in the second phase of such a war. The Soviets therefore need to be able to deny the West the use of airfields throughout the area and also to prevent them from establishing the kind of lodgement that would facilitate a Western military buildup.

Soviet control of the base at Chah Bahar could be important to achieving this objective. Indeed, within this strategic context, a strong military argument can be made for establishing a heavily defended bridgehead on the Arabian Sea, extending from Chah Bahar to the port of Gwadar, one hundred miles to the east.[13] A key factor in such a decision would be the political stance of Pakistan. If Pakistan seemed likely to allow its territory to be used as the main staging area for a Western invasion across the Hindu Kush mountain range, then nothing would be lost if the Soviets seized Gwadar. In other circumstances, the political costs and military benefits would have to be carefully weighed.

SUMMARY OF GROUND AND AIR REQUIREMENTS.   On the basis of these different considerations the immediate Soviet requirements for ground and air forces in the northeastern part of the Southern TVD can be summarized. In terms of military capability, the Soviets must be able to carry out the following tasks: advance the Soviet defense perimeter southward 150–300 miles into northwest Iran in the face of U.S. air interdiction;[14] carry out deep penetration air strikes and special forces' operations throughout the area;[15] mine the oil terminals in the gulf within ten days; and establish a secure overland supply route from western Afghanistan to Chah Bahar on the Arabian Sea within twenty-one days. That period covers the contingency of war with China, but in a world war, the Soviets could take much longer.

13. Gwadar was developed as a major fishing port by the Soviets in the 1960s and could have been seen as a strategic stepping-stone that might be useful at some future date.

14. Estimates of the U.S. ability to deploy ground and tactical air forces to the area would determine the Soviets' reaction time. See McNaugher, *Arms and Oil,* pp. 47–86. The most demanding Soviet requirement, in terms of response time as well as logistics, is to extend the air defense umbrella southward to cover the advance of Soviet ground forces.

15. The Soviets' minimum response time would be determined by the need to disrupt the deployment of U.S. tactical air units.

The Red Sea and Surrounding Territory

Soviet strategic interest in the southwestern part of the Southern TVD is comparatively recent, and the focus of concern has shifted during that period.[16]

The Initial Concern: 1967–71

The initial involvement came as part of the second phase, 1968–72, of the Soviet navy's move forward in strategic defense that began in 1963. There was specific evidence in the first half of the 1960s that the United States intended to deploy and probably base submarines in the Indian Ocean, which is the best area in the world from which to target both Russia and China with submarine-launched ballistic missiles.[17] The Soviets clearly appreciated the potential threat, and March 1968 saw the first deployment of combatants to the area, with the choice of Somalia as the *pointe d'appui* by mid-1969.[18]

Somalia's hostile relationship with immediate neighbors and other African states indicated that the Soviet navy's interest was in the Horn's geostrategic location, rather than in political influence building. There is evidence that this deployment was planned well before the British decided to withdraw from east of Suez, supporting the conclusion that the Soviet Union was responding to the problem posed by U.S. Polaris submarines.[19] The Soviets were under no illusion that they had the capability to counter

16. The Soviets gave political support to the government of North Yemen during the civil war, 1962–67, and some indirect military support through Egypt's involvement in the war. This activity was part of the general pattern of influence building in the area and was not related to the Soviet Union's own military requirements. See Lenczowski, *Middle East in World Affairs*, pp. 626–34.

17. The Australian government announced on May 17, 1963, that it had signed an agreement with the United States to build a very low frequency (VLF) communications facility at North West Cape in Western Australia. A VLF implies communication with submerged submarines, and the location of the station could only mean that the U.S. Navy wished to communicate with units operating in the Indian Ocean. These units could only be ballistic-missile submarines. In December 1965, a fifty-year agreement for the joint United Kingdom-United States use of Diego Garcia was signed, the Chagos archipelago having been hived off from Mauritius before it was given its independence.

18. The 1964 proposal by the Soviets to the United Nations on the creation of nuclear-free zones included only two seas: the Mediterranean and the Indian Ocean.

19. The hydrographic precursors to the main deployment appeared in the spring of 1967, indicating that the Soviets had made an operational decision at least by 1966. At that period the British were committed to remaining east of Suez, and this intention did not change until the economic crisis in the fall of 1967 forced a drastic restructuring of British defense policy.

Polaris in the Indian Ocean at this stage. They wanted to develop the operational and physical infrastructure to support measures that they hoped would gradually become available after 1972–73. By the end of 1970, Soviet facilities in Berbera and Mogadishu were supporting a modest but steady deployment of three naval combatants.

The Change in Focus after 1972

A change in the focus of Soviet concern was evidenced by the visit to Somalia in February 1972 of the Soviet Minister of Defense Andrey A. Grechko who signed an agreement for the construction of new facilities at Berbera. This provided for extending or constructing airfields, building missile-handling and storage facilities and a communications station, and enlarging the fuel tank farm.[20] Why was the decision taken, at this juncture, to make substantial improvements? Although the changes were followed by a higher level and quality of Soviet naval deployment, the explanation can not be related to the original counter-Polaris mission.[21] The relative priority of that mission had been downgraded in the wake of the December 1966 decision.

The answer must be sought in the events of that period: the fact that it was Marshal Grechko who went to Somalia in February 1972, the withdrawal of Soviet forces from Egypt later that year, and the dangerous state of Sino-Soviet relations.

Some evidence suggests that the Soviets sharply increased their investment in Somalia in the knowledge that Soviet troops would soon be out of Egypt. In the spring of 1970 substantial air defense forces had been deployed to Egypt to prevent its collapse in the face of Israel's deep penetration raids; the number of Russian troops was built up to more than 20,000. Indications are that the original decision to intervene had been finely balanced, and it seems likely that during the second half of 1971 the Soviets

20. Charles C. Petersen, "Trends in Soviet Naval Operations," in Bradford Dismukes and James M. McConnell, eds., *Soviet Naval Diplomacy* (Pergamon Press, 1979), pp. 71–72; and *Soviet Military Capability in Berbera, Somalia,* Committee Print, Report of Senator Bartlett to the Senate Committee on Armed Services, 94 Cong. 1 sess. (GPO, 1975).

21. Petersen, "Trends in Soviet Naval Operations," pp. 37–87, particularly tables 2.5, 2.7, 2.8, 2.10, 2.11, and 2.14. Until late 1971, the regular deployment usually consisted of a gun-destroyer, a landing ship, a diesel submarine and its "safety" ship, and six or seven auxiliaries. After 1972, the deployment rose to perhaps five or six warships and eight or nine auxiliaries. Numbers increased during periodic flag-showing cruises, and specially formed groups would be deployed from the Pacific Fleet in times of crisis. See Michael MccGwire, "The Evolution of Soviet Naval Policy," in MccGwire, Ken Booth, and John McDonnell, eds., *Soviet National Policy: Objectives and Constraints* (Praeger, 1975), p. 526.

decided that the political and military costs of direct involvement out-weighed the benefits, which were now considerably reduced.[22]

By this time the air defense situation had been stabilized, and the primary military benefit was the Soviet access to Egyptian naval facilities and airfields to support the Mediterranean deployment. However, this deployment was under attack because of the change in mission priorities. Heikal's comment that the Russians were not surprised at the eviction order and the Soviets' refusal to subscribe to a face-saving joint communiqué suggest that the Soviets were waiting for an opportunity to extricate their troops from Egypt.[23] But the most persuasive evidence is the Soviet navy's objections to the impending withdrawal. These objections were expressed in the second article of the Gorshkov series, which went to typesetting in January 1972, six months before the eviction.[24] These objections in conjunction with Grechko's visit to Somalia in February 1972 suggest a policy decision some time in the fall of 1971.[25]

What did that decision imply for Soviet objectives? Admiral Sergey G. Gorshkov had been directly involved from 1961 to 1966 in pressing Egypt for the use of port facilities. He visited the Indian Ocean area for the first time in 1967 and 1968, before the initial deployment in spring 1968.[26] His lack of involvement in the 1972 agreement with Somalia, combined with the Soviet withdrawal from Egypt, argues that the original naval mission

22. See Michael MccGwire, "The Overseas Role of a 'Soviet Military Presence'" in Mcc-Gwire and John McDonnell, eds., *Soviet Naval Influence: Domestic and Foreign Dimensions* (Praeger, 1977), pp. 32–34, 42–43.

23. General Secretary Leonid I. Brezhnev is quoted as saying to Anwar Sadat, "You asked for the experts. If you want them to leave that is your decision, and we will comply with it. But we . . . will not take the responsibility before history of suggesting that they are being withdrawn at our request." As Heikal comments (although in a different context) "Brezhnev . . . was brilliant at public relations." Mohamed Heikal, *The Road to Ramadan* (New York: Quadrangle, 1975), pp. 176, 89.

24. See Sergey G. Gorshkov, "Voenno-morskie floty v voynakh i v mirnoe vremya" (Navies in war and peace), *Morskoy sbornik* (Naval journal), no. 3 (March 1972), pp. 20–32; and see appendix C in this book.

25. In the wake of the Soviet eviction in July 1972, the navy lost the use of installations ashore, most notably the airfields, but the original five-year agreement on access to port facilities ran its full course to March 1973. The agreement was even renewed for another five years, possibly as the quid pro quo for the new arms deal concluded in late 1972–early 1973. Richard B. Remnek, "The Politics of Soviet Access to Naval Support Facilities in the Mediterranean," in Dismukes and McConnell, *Soviet Naval Diplomacy,* pp. 373–77.

26. Gorshkov made four visits to Egypt in just over five years. He visited Massawa, Ethiopia, in January 1967 to attend its annual Navy Day celebration, and India in February 1968. The initial deployment of Soviet combatants to the Indian Ocean was from March 22 through July 15, 1968, and the second was from November 1968 through April 29, 1969. See Michael MccGwire, "The Pattern of Soviet Naval Deployment in the Indian Ocean, 1968–71," in MccGwire, ed., *Soviet Naval Developments: Capability and Context* (Praeger, 1973), pp. 425–26.

that had justified the bases in Somalia and Egypt was being superseded by a new one. Gorshkov's absence also highlights the fact that he and Grechko were on opposite sides of the debate about the role of a military presence outside the Soviet Union. Gorshkov was arguing for an assertive overseas policy based on military power. Grechko limited his description of the internationalist duty of the Soviet armed forces to their commitment to other socialist states, that is, members of the Warsaw Pact. Grechko's interest in Somalia is therefore likely to have been directly related to the territorial defense of the Soviet Union.

Finally, Grechko's new interest in the Horn of Africa underlines events involving China. In the mid-1960s, the Sino-Soviet dispute had moved from the ideological and political plane toward military confrontation, reaching a climax in 1968–69 "when there was a real danger of war."[27] Armed clashes occurred at Damansky Island on the Ussuri River and at Dzungarian Gate, along the Sinkiang border. In June 1969, Brezhnev's proposal for an Asian collective security zone evoked no enthusiasm. The American counterpoise to China was removed in July when Richard M. Nixon enunciated the Nixon Doctrine while visiting Guam, which limited the scope of U.S. involvement in future Asian conflicts.

The trend was clearly adverse, and the Soviets accelerated their buildup along the Chinese border. But worse would come. There were growing indications that two decades of Sino-American confrontation were coming to an end, and this prospect was confirmed by the announcement in the summer of 1971 that President Richard M. Nixon would visit China early the next year.

The Soviet military leadership, evaluating the situation in the fall of 1971, could only have concluded that the Chinese threat was assuming new dimensions. The rash of border clashes had shown that the possibility of conflict was real, and the unpredictability of the Beijing government and its bellicosity toward the Soviet Union greatly increased the likelihood of war. China's military capability in comparison with Russia's would steadily increase as it lowered its guard against America, and its acquisition of an effective nuclear delivery capability was only a matter of time.

In immediacy, the threat of war with China took precedence over the possibility of war with the West. Although the latter remained the most serious contingency, its probability had diminished with the initiation of the strategic arms limitation talks and the trend toward détente.

27. A. Doak Barnett, *China and the Major Powers in East Asia* (Brookings, 1977), pp. 9–10, 49–50, 194–95.

The Southern Sea Route

The likelihood of war with China, combined with the vulnerability of the Trans-Siberian railway to disruption, would inevitably have focused the Soviet General Staff's attention on the need to be able to supply the Far Eastern front by sea. But the military interest in a sea line of communication between the eastern and western parts of Russia extended beyond the contingency of conflict with China to the possibility of world war with the West. As if to underline what all this implied for the projected southern sea line, the United States seized the occasion of the Indo-Pakistani war in December 1971 "to prove . . . [the United States] a factor in an arena of interest to the Chinese."[28] America took a strong stand in support of Pakistan, branded India an aggressor and cut off military and economic aid to it, and deployed a carrier battle group to the Indian Ocean. In May 1972, in another demonstration of the capability to prevent the use of the sea, the United States used air-delivered mines to close the port of Haiphong in North Vietnam.

In 1971 the Suez Canal was still closed so the Soviets would have had to think of shipping across Iran; the auguries were not unfavorable in that direction. The British had declared their intention of leaving the Persian Gulf by the end of the year, and the American buildup of Iran was only incipient. However, the supply lines by way of Iran were clearly second best, and the simplest and fastest route for large-scale military shipments was to load out of Black Sea ports and go by way of the Suez Canal and Red Sea. The canal had been closed for four years, and the Soviet Union was among the countries most seriously affected by the closing. However, it was unlikely that this situation would persist forever. Preparing the MTVD would include preparations for using this route.

The Soviets could assume that, unless they were at war with the West, a common interest in transit rights would ensure the safe passage of their merchant ships through the Turkish Straits and the Suez Canal. The Straits of Bab el Mandeb at the southern end of the Red Sea were another matter. These straits were the single choke point between Suez and Russian waters in the Pacific, which Soviet ships had no means of avoiding.[29] The six-mile wide shipping channel could be controlled fairly easily by forces

28. James McConnell and Anne M. Kelly, "Superpower Naval Diplomacy in the Indo-Pakistani Crisis," in MccGwire, *Soviet Naval Developments,* pp. 445–46, citing James Reston, *New York Times,* January 12, 1972.

29. There are many alternative ways through the Indonesian archipelago, and the Soviets have the further option of sailing south around Australia.

afloat or ashore.[30] Even if the Soviets were at war with the West, these straits could still be vital because if the campaign in Europe had been successful, the Soviets would have control of the Turkish Straits. While the status of the Suez Canal could not be foreseen in such circumstances, unless Soviet ships were able to exit the Red Sea, a usable canal would not profit them. It was therefore important that control of the Straits of Bab el Mandeb should not be in hostile hands, and this priority focused Soviet attention on the littoral states: Ethiopia, the Territory of the Afars and Issas, and North and South Yemen. South Yemen also had sovereignty over the Island of Perim, which divides the straits in two.

The Soviets had to deal with political as well as military problems. The Chinese formed a significant presence in the area of the Horn. In 1968 the pro-Chinese National Liberation Front had emerged as the dominant party in South Yemen. This influence predominated, even after the front split into Chinese and Soviet factions. There was also evidence of Chinese involvement in North Yemen and Oman. This factor would have dictated the decision in 1971 to build on the existing Soviet presence in Somalia rather than seek the advantages of South Yemen's optimal geostrategic location and of the superior facilities available at the former British base at Aden. The Soviets gained important access to those facilities only after the coup in mid-1978. The coup brought the pro-Soviet faction to power, ousting Salem Rubayr Ali, president and leader of the pro-Chinese faction. Ali had been seeking to draw closer to the anti-Soviet Arab states.[31]

The less radical Arab states, who were encouraged by the West, also offered general resistance to Soviet intrusion into the Red Sea area. Relations with the other Red Sea states steadily deteriorated during the first half of the 1970s.[32] The danger that Arab solidarity against Israel would be used to pursue policies inimical to Soviet strategic interests, such as declaring the Red Sea an "Arab lake," increased.[33] To counter this trend the Soviets made a brief but unsuccessful attempt to forge a confederacy

30. Egypt blockaded the Straits of Bab el Mandeb during the October 1973 war. Passage can easily be denied to selected shipping by cruise missiles emplaced ashore.

31. Garthoff, *Détente and Confrontation*, pp. 654–56.

32. Saudi Arabia was already firmly anticommunist and was willing to provide financial support to states that resisted Soviet influence. Egypt had ousted the pro-Soviet faction in May 1971, demanded the immediate withdrawal of Soviet ground-based forces in July 1972, turned toward America in the wake of the 1973 war, and abrogated the treaty of friendship with the Soviet Union in March 1976. A rift had already developed in Soviet-Sudanese relations during 1971, and a sharp deterioration in 1976 was followed by the expulsion of the Soviet military mission in May 1977. In 1976 South Yemen's relations with Saudi Arabia began to improve.

33. In March 1977 a meeting, fostered by Saudi Arabia, of North and South Yemen, Somalia, and Sudan to discuss the "Arab lake scheme" took place. The Soviets took the initiative seriously enough to alter their proposals for a Middle East settlement to include the right of all ships,

of Marxist states at the southern end of the Red Sea. By the end of 1978 somewhat fortuitous developments in Ethiopia and the outcome of the Ogaden war had stabilized the political situation around the Straits of Bab el Mandeb in the Soviet Union's favor.

Soviet Military Requirements

A major difference between the northeastern and southwestern parts of the Southern TVD is that contingencies in the Persian Gulf can be dealt with by forces based in the Soviet Union, but the distance to the Red Sea and its environs (about 1,800 nautical miles by air and perhaps eleven days by sea) means that the Soviets need a cadre of forces in place and some kind of supporting infrastructure if they are to be able to take military action in the area.

The process of establishing this infrastructure, political and military, underlies much of the Soviet activity in this area, as it does elsewhere. The process is implicit in the Soviet concept of preparing a TVD in peacetime for use in war, which involves a "system of measures" that is organizational, operational, and material. The Soviets refer to this process as outfitting a TVD.[34] This same process had underlain the navy's initial involvement in Somalia, but the increased scale of preparation that followed Grechko's visit reflected the change in the primary mission and the more concrete nature of the requirement.

The types of military operation the Soviets might need to conduct in the general area of the Red Sea and Horn of Africa can be grouped under three categories of requirement. One encompasses primarily maritime operations, which are discussed in the next section, while the other two involve operations ashore.

To be certain that passage through the Red Sea and Gulf of Aden in time of need is not impeded by hostile local forces, the Soviets must be able to control the situation ashore, should that prove necessary. They would obviously prefer to rely on political instruments, which could include the

---

including Israeli ones, to free passage through the region's waterways. Kenneth G. Weiss, *The Soviet Involvement in the Ogaden War,* Professional Paper 269 (Alexandria, Va.: Center for Naval Analyses, 1980), pp. 16, 20; and Remnek, *Soviet Policy in the Horn of Africa,* pp. 16, 17.

34. The term *outfitting* is drawn from the Soviet General Staff Academy 1965 *Dictionary of Basic Military Terms.* It is used by A. Alkhimenko, "Operativnoe oborudovanie okeanskikh i morskikh teatrov voennykh deystviy" (The operational fitting out of ocean and maritime theaters of military action), *Morskoy sbornik* (Naval journal), no. 1 (January 1980), pp. 15–20.

provision of internal security and other support to threatened friendly regimes, but the Soviets must also be prepared to intervene with military
force if necessary. The Territory of the Afars and Issas, which flanks the
south side of Bab el Mandeb and includes the French base at Djibouti,
presents a particular problem. Another problem is Berbera, with its Soviet-
developed base facilities. In a conflict the Soviet naval forces would like
access to these facilities, but ensuring that the bases do not remain available to the United States is of much greater importance.

The other category of requirements is solely related to the contingency
of world war. The Soviets will not have forgotten that the British were
evicted from the European continent in June 1940, but by February 1941
they had launched an offensive out of Kenya. This led to the conquest of
Somalia, Ethiopia, and Eritrea, and the surrender of the Italian forces by
November of the same year, allowing the linkup with Commonwealth
forces in the Middle East. The Soviets will also have noted that Kenya has
agreed to let the United States make greater use of the port and airfield at
Mombasa. The Soviets will therefore have to plan for the possibility that
in phase II of a world war the West would choose the east coast of Africa
as one line of advance.

Neither land-oriented requirement demands a rapid-reaction military
capability. In a war with China, at least two months would elapse before
the Soviets might have to secure the passage of supplies through the Straits
of Hormuz. With one exception, the response time in the event of a world
war could be even longer. This absence of operational immediacy does not,
however, diminish the potential importance of the Horn of Africa in phase
II of such a war. Geostrategically, the Horn can be seen as the eastern flank
of the socialist system's southern defense perimeter and the southern flank
of its eastern perimeter. The priority the Soviets will accord to this latent
requirement will depend on their assessment of the probability that such a
war will occur and, if it does, that America will continue the struggle after
it has been evicted from Europe. This assessment will change in response
to changes in the international environment.

The Arabian Sea

The maritime portion of the Southern TVD, which the Soviets may refer
to as the Arabian MTVD, would seem to be well defined by the parameters

of the Arabian Sea, as described in Soviet military publications. This MTVD includes the Gulfs of Oman and Aden and also appears to take in the Laccadive Sea, which lies between the Maldives and the west coast of southern India and Sri Lanka.[35] This MTVD can be seen as a large triangle, with its southeast corner on Addu Atoll, a barely populated group of islands lying at the southern extremity of the Maldives Republic, which includes the island of Gan. Gan has an eight thousand-foot runway and lies about three hundred nautical miles north of Diego Garcia.[36] The northern corner is on Chah Bahar, and the western one on the Straits of Bab el Mandeb. Each corner has the potential to provide naval support facilities, including maritime air, but up to now the only facilities available to the Soviet navy have been in the western corner of the MTVD. An operational command center is now apparently located in the Aden area.[37]

The initial Soviet naval presence in the MTVD was related to the problem of sea-based strategic delivery systems and the apparent U.S. intention to deploy ballistic-missile submarines in the Indian Ocean. The Soviets primarily intended to become familiar with the maritime geography and operational characteristics of the area, especially its oceanographic, meteorological, and climatological conditions. The Soviets had no practice in operating and maintaining ships in hot and humid climates, far away from main-base support facilities, and there was much that could only be learned by experience.

This peacetime purpose continues to be important and is part of preparing the MTVD for the contingency of war, but these forward-deployed forces have discharged other tasks as well. Omani rebel forces were sealifted from Aden to the border with Oman during the summer of 1973. Soviet naval units escorted the shipment of supplies from Aden to Ethiopia

35. In contrast to the International Hydrographic Organization (IHO) definition of the Arabian Sea, the *Sovetskaya voennaya entsiklopediya* (Soviet military encyclopedia) (Moscow: Voenizdat, 1979), p. 227, includes both gulfs. The *SVE* only includes the area north of about ten degrees north latitude, but the more recent *Voennyy entsiklopedicheskiy slovar'* (Military encyclopedic dictionary) (Moscow: Voenizdat, 1983), p. 41, gives the area of the Arabian Sea as 4,832 thousand km², compared with the *SVE's* 3,683 thousand km². This one-third increase would bring the southern boundary in line with the IHO definition. Neither Soviet publication gives the Laccadive Sea as a separate entity, but the *SVE* does include the Laccadive Islands in the Arabian Sea, contrary to the IHO definition.

36. In 1977 the Russians offered to lease the island for 1 million dollars per annum, but this and subsequent offers were turned down. Ostensibly, the Soviets wanted to use Addu Atoll as a fishing base, and the airfield would allow them to rotate the vessels' crews.

37. Soviet headquarters were originally located at the Khormaksar airfield in Aden, but in 1981, it was reported that the Soviets were building a new command center at Jabal Hal, overlooking Aden. Reuter's report, dateline Bahrain, December 20, 1981.

during the Ogaden war and thereafter, primarily to discourage third-party interference. Submarines armed with cruise missiles have been routinely deployed to match the deployment of U.S. attack carriers to the region.[38] A naval unit, providing early warning, has patrolled the Strait of Hormuz since 1974.

This does not, however, tell one much about Soviet naval objectives in the event of a world war or other major contingencies. Such aims are best considered in light of the two classic naval missions: securing the use of the sea for the Soviets' own purposes and preventing its use to their disadvantage.

Preventing the Use of the Sea to Soviet Disadvantage

The Soviets want to prevent the United States from using the sea to project force ashore in the Southern TVD. There are four main variants of such an operation. Two pose direct threats that have to be defended against, and the other two are contingencies that may need to be countered directly or indirectly.

THE SUPPLY ROUTE THROUGH CHAH BAHAR. The United States could attempt to prevent the Soviets from establishing a supply route through Chah Bahar, either by carrying out carrier air strikes against advancing Soviet forces or by landing U.S. ground forces to prevent the Russians from seizing the port and airfield. This kind of intervention presents a fairly standard problem to the Soviets, which is replicated to some extent in all the other TVDs. The Soviet response would follow the established pattern of a combination of attacks from the air and by naval forces at sea. The air attacks would include frontal as well as naval and long-range aviation, and perhaps shore-based missiles would also be used. The primary naval forces would be submarines. Since the readiness in peacetime for operations to establish the overland route is unlikely to be fewer than forty-five days, there should be enough time to bring in naval reinforcements from the Pacific unless the United States decided on a preemptive seizure. The capability required to respond to this particular threat would also cover the threat of carrier strikes against the Russian homeland.

THE THREAT TO DISTANT SUPPORT FACILITIES. Soviet maritime support and staging facilities that may be established in distant parts of the Southern TVD can also be threatened. The only existing facilities of this

---

38. Dismukes and McConnell, *Soviet Naval Diplomacy,* pp. 81, 137.

kind are in the northwestern corner of the MTVD, in the Bab el Mandeb area, but the Soviets have shown interest in gaining access to facilities on Addu Atoll, with its airfield on Gan. The most immediate threat is from air strikes, whether by carrier-based aircraft, sea-launched cruise missiles, or B-52 bombers, but the projected threat also includes the forcible seizure of such facilities by U.S. Marines supported by other specialized forces. The Soviets' most immediate requirement is for point air defense; longer-range defense against surface forces (strike and amphibious assault) can be provided by submarine screens and coast-defense missile systems.

There have been reports that the Soviets have installed surface-to-air missile (SAM) sites around Aden,[39] and it seems likely that the infrastructure for a much denser system is already in place, and additional weapons and equipment can be flown in if needed. Providing for the effective air defense of facilities at Aden is practical because there is sufficient space for layered defenses. Providing for the defense of Addu Atoll in the southeastern corner of the MTVD would be much harder, and the potential utility of facilities would depend greatly on the alignment of forces in the region.

U.S. SEIZURE OF ADVANCED BASES. The contingency that in the event of war the United States would move to seize or otherwise acquire additional base facilities in the Arabian Sea region is a closely related threat. The most serious variant of this contingency would be a U.S. move to take over the Soviet-developed facilities in the Berbera area, to which the United States already has naval access. This development would threaten Soviet access to the MTVD. To cover this contingency the Soviets would have to plan for the preemptive seizure of Berbera, or at least for the neutralization of the facilities by offensive demolition and mining. The latter action might still be appropriate, even if peacetime developments meant that the United States was already ensconced in the base.

When the separate requirements to deal with Berbera, to neutralize Djibouti, to control the situation on both sides of Bab el Mandeb (at least as far north as Massawah and Dahlak Island), and to provide for the defense of all base facilities in the northwest corner of the MTVD are combined, a substantial military requirement emerges. It might be possible to meet some of the requirements by political means. For example, the Soviets could cut a deal with Somalia at the expense of the Ethiopians and the Afars and Issas. But there would still remain a large residual requirement

39. Reuter's report, dateline Bahrain, December 20, 1981.

for men and equipment that could only be brought in by air.

The priority the Soviets accord to this geostrategic fulcrum in their war plans is unclear. Final calculations would depend on the extent to which the Soviets had built up effective defenses in peacetime. An argument could be made that if the Soviets did not make a preemptive move to consolidate their position in the area, it would surely fall to the U.S. Navy and Marines. A preemptive move would also have the merit of confusing Western perceptions, perhaps causing the West to start moving its forces in the wrong direction, away from the Soviets' main axis in the Western TVD.

U.S. INTERVENTION IN THE PERSIAN GULF. The other major contingency facing the Soviets in this MTVD is U.S. maritime intervention at the head of the Persian Gulf. Such intervention could be a preemptive response to the possibility of a Soviet advance into northwest Iran, or it could be reaction to such an advance. The appropriate Soviet course of naval action is not obvious in either case.

Although the ships involved in a U.S. intervention would be particularly vulnerable to submarine and other attack as they funneled into the Gulf of Oman, such attacks would not necessarily serve the Soviet Union's broader interests. Despite the military advantages of disabling a carrier or sinking shiploads of men and equipment, the appropriate course of action will depend on more complex considerations such as the level of East-West tension, the prevailing state of conflict, the likelihood of escalation, and the nature of Soviet objectives. These same considerations will apply to attacking the U.S. ships elsewhere in the MTVD.

It would be advantageous to attack such military reinforcements only in a general war or when it was clearly inevitable that U.S. ground forces would engage Russian troops for important objectives. If, however, the Soviets had limited objectives in northwest Iran, such as those outlined earlier in this chapter, and if they were trying to contain the conflict, avoid any kind of escalation, and exploit latent political divisions, domestic and international, then the adverse consequences of a successful attack would probably outweigh the immediate military advantages. Similar considerations would apply to the question of attacking a U.S. carrier, even if its aircraft were carrying out air strikes against a Soviet advance in northwest Iran.[40]

Using mines to prevent timely U.S. access to the Persian Gulf is another option and might be politically acceptable when direct attacks on ships

40. Unless the carrier dared to operate inside the gulf, the ranges involved would limit the value of the carrier aircrafts' contribution.

were not. But other military considerations come into play here. There are circumstances in which it would serve Soviet purposes to have the United States tie down its readily available forces at the head of the gulf.[41] For example, if the Soviets wanted primarily to avoid a preemptive U.S. occupation at Chah Bahar, they might choose to provoke a U.S. intervention at the head of the gulf, and once the men and equipment were committed ashore, work to prevent their redeployment. The underlying concept of tying down U.S. forces in the gulf also has wider applications.

Securing the Use of the Sea

The Soviets may want to use the sea in the Southern TVD to convey supplies and equipment to the Far Eastern TVD in the event that overland communications are disrupted. As noted, one possible shipping route would originate from the northern part of the Arabian sea, being fed either from the Persian Gulf or overland through eastern Iran. The other would originate from the Gulf of Aden and mean shipping out of the Black Sea and through the Suez Canal.[42]

In 1971, when the Soviets first responded to this newly perceived requirement, they were hedging against war with China. They were concerned about a fairly small number of diesel-powered, torpedo-armed submarines that could be deployed to the area and might possibly be forward based on Aden and Karachi. This potential threat still exists and has increased in terms of the number of Chinese submarines that could be deployed.[43] In the meanwhile, the threat has emerged that the United States could become directly involved in opposing Soviet passage through the area. This threat ranges in intensity from covert attacks by U.S. nuclear submarines during a Sino-Soviet war, to the circumstances of a world war in which the Soviets must expect concentrated air, surface, and subsurface attacks against their sea communications.

41. The weapons and equipment for a marine amphibious brigade, and certain stores for army and air force units, are loaded aboard maritime prepositioning ships stationed at Diego Garcia. There is also an eight-ship thirty-knot sealift designed to transport a fully equipped mechanized division from the United States.

42. A third route, which will not be considered further, could originate from the Cape of Good Hope.

43. In 1971 the Chinese had only about 32 ocean-going submarines. However, the Romeo-class program, which had started delivery in about 1968, was adding to the force at about 9 units a year. The Chinese were also set on developing nuclear submarines. In 1983 the Chinese had 2 Ming, 78 Romeo, and 21 Whisky diesel attack submarines. They also had 2 Han-class, nuclear-powered, cruise missile submarines. International Institute for Strategic Studies, *The Military Balance, 1983–84* (London: IISS, 1983), p. 84.

The last time the flow of Soviet shipping is focused (until funneled into its destination in the Soviet Far East) is as it leaves the Red Sea, the Persian Gulf, and Chah Bahar. That increases the attraction to the enemy of attacking Soviet shipping in the Arabian Sea. There the Soviets cannot provide a corresponding concentration of protective resources, as they can in the Pacific.

THE THREAT FROM CHINESE SUBMARINES. The Soviets can handle the threat from Chinese submarines by limiting its scale and by countering it directly. The Soviets should be able to deny the Chinese access to forward-base facilities in the Indian Ocean region. They have already supplanted the Chinese in South Yemen, and they have the political leverage to dissuade Pakistan from allowing China to use its facilities. The Soviets can also deny Chinese submarines the option of a fast transit on the surface through the South China Sea, by virtue of the Soviet presence at Cam Ranh Bay. The combination of both factors would drastically reduce a submarine's time on patrol and hence the size of force that could be sustained on station from a given number of submarines. This given number could be further reduced by posing a naval threat to the Chinese mainland that would require the bulk of their submarines to be committed to area defense. Only a small number of China's submarines would then be available for use against sea communications, and of necessity these would have to work closer to home.

This pattern means that in the event of a war limited to China, the Soviets only have to protect their shipping against a fairly modest submarine threat in the Arabian MTVD. The likely opposition would comprise a small number of diesel submarines of Soviet design that stems from the mid-1950s, with relatively inexperienced crews. If the Soviets shipped out of Chah Bahar, it would be impossible to conceal the identity of Soviet freighters, necessitating close escort on departure. In other areas there would be every reason to rely on concealment, camouflage, and distant antisubmarine support for protection. Peacetime patterns of shipping would prevail, making it difficult for the submarine to pick out Soviet vessels from the flow of shipping.

If the Soviets had access to airfields at each corner of the MTVD, Aden, Chah Bahar, and Gan, they could provide maritime air support throughout the area, but it is more likely that they will be restricted to Aden. Even if Chah Bahar did become available, most of the ships from the head of the Arabian Sea would still join the stream of shipping heading down the Arabian coast and would only turn east when abreast of the Gulf of Aden in order to remain within the ambit of the antisubmarine forces in that area. Thereafter the Soviet ships would make their way across the Indian Ocean and through the Indonesian archipelago, each ship choosing a different strait and most of them making their transit at night. It would be difficult for the Chinese to impose heavy casualties on such shipping, even if they had access to U.S. surveillance data.

U.S. THREAT TO SEA COMMUNICATIONS. If in a Sino-Soviet war the United States provided covert support to China with nuclear attack submarines, the loss rate of the Soviets' merchant ships would be much higher. It seems likely that the Soviets' same general strategy would prevail but with greater emphasis on offensive antisubmarine operations in the approaches to the shipping routes' origins.

The Soviets would be faced with a completely different problem in a world war. Shipping patterns would be largely disrupted, and the threat would include carrier aircraft and surface ships, as well as submarines. On the other hand, in a world war in which there had been no intercontinental nuclear exchange, and in which China had not been drawn into the struggle, there might be no requirement to establish a southern line of sea communication with the Far Eastern TVD. If the requirement did emerge, then the objective would shift from "securing the use of the sea" for Soviet purposes, to "preventing its use" to Soviet disadvantage, particularly by U.S. aircraft carriers.

The carrier, of course, loomed large in the other threats and contingencies discussed earlier, but in those cases the Soviets had to counter it directly and immediately. In the struggle for sea communications, however, the carrier can be countered indirectly and over time, suggesting that the appropriate target would not be the heavily defended carrier battle group but the ships in the less heavily defended under way replenishment group or the supply ships even further up the line. These considerations also draw attention to the importance of the forward base at Diego Garcia.

The Soviet position in the Arabian MTVD would be greatly enhanced if Diego Garcia could be neutralized, which could easily be done with a single nuclear weapon but which would take a considerable amount of conventional ordnance and would then probably be only partly successful. Despite its remoteness the Soviets would probably not risk initiating the use of nuclear weapons on Diego Garcia, except in dire need. However, as already discussed, the Soviets are likely to be poised to make such a strike in response to any U.S. demonstration shot or comparable nuclear initiative.

PART THREE

Contemporary Concerns

CHAPTER 10

Military Objectives in the Third World

BOTH geostrategic and ideopolitical conditions shape Soviet policy in the third world. The geostrategic factors, which can be labeled war-related requirements, stem from the objective of not losing a world war, should it prove unavoidable. The restructuring of objectives that followed the doctrinal adjustment in December 1966 directly affected these requirements.

The ideopolitical factors reflect the concept of competing social systems, which can be labeled intersystem competition. The Soviets characterize it as peaceful competition. In this area, the Soviets' primary impulse is the peacetime struggle for world influence, both as one of the superpowers and as leader of the socialist system. The 1966 decision that it was not inevitable that a world war would be nuclear also had potential implications for the role of military force in this struggle. The Soviets would debate about the use of military power in the third world and whether it would endanger the objective of avoiding world war.

In an ideal world, geostrategic and ideopolitical factors would be mutually reinforcing, resulting in clearly defined policies designed to promote Soviet interests in the third world. In practice, this is not always or even usually true. War-related requirements may clash with the more subtle demands of building influential relationships with particular countries. And clearly defined, if sometimes conflicting, objectives are not the only basis of Soviet policy in the third world. The Soviets must also consider the opportunity costs of inaction. Soviet policy is based on a complex balancing of interests, ideology, and concerns about war and peace. In this chapter, the focus is on geostrategic considerations, the role of the military instrument, and how the change in strategic objectives affected Soviet thinking about the third world.

War-Related Requirements

There is nothing new in war-related requirements shaping a nation's policy in distant parts of the globe, although in earlier years these considerations fell into the domain of naval strategy. In the 1960s, Soviet war-related requirements in the third world stemmed directly from the primary strategic objective of preserving the socialist system. At that period, doctrine decreed that a world war would inevitably escalate to a full-scale intercontinental exchange and would mean a fight to the finish between the two social systems. The Soviets would seek to destroy the capitalist system by nuclear strikes on the American homeland and its overseas facilities. If the Soviets were not to lose ultimately, they would need somehow to rebuild their own social system.

The Soviet response to this dilemma was to adopt a concept of operations in Europe, and probably Manchuria as well, that would preserve rather than destroy the productive capacity of these regions so that they could serve as socioeconomic bases for rebuilding the devastated Soviet homeland. The successful execution of such a concept would, however, not profit the Soviets if the United States responded by devastating these economic bases with nuclear weapons. That threat was latent in the U.S. strike carriers and Polaris submarines, which, unlike land-based systems, could be expected to survive the initial exchange.

If these seaborne systems were withheld from the initial exchange, they would pose a double threat to the Soviet objective of not losing the war. They would constitute an invulnerable and unmatched strategic nuclear reserve, and they could deny the Soviet Union the use of Europe and Manchuria as alternative socioeconomic bases. The requirement therefore was to remove the U.S. option of withholding such systems from the initial exchange. As one element of their response the Soviets deployed naval forces to those sea areas from which nuclear strikes could be launched against the Soviet Union and Europe. The Soviets wanted to maintain forces within weapon range of U.S. nuclear strike platforms, posing Washington with the choice of using them at the onset of war or losing them.

The shift to forward deployment presented the Soviet navy with immense problems. Its forces had not been designed with distant-water operations in mind, but more serious, the Soviets lacked a forward-base structure, of the kind enjoyed by the Western maritime powers. Although the Soviets looked into the possibility of relying on open-ocean support, their experience during the early years of the Mediterranean deployment made it clear that shore-based support facilities were essential. It was not until the Soviets gained access to Egyptian ports in the wake of the June 1967 war that they were able to sustain year-round deployment. The number of ship-days deployed increased by roughly three times, and air support was flown from Egyptian fields.

The war-related requirement that stemmed from the 1960s hierarchy of objectives was to establish the physical, political, and operational infrastructure that would enable the Soviet navy to pose a permanent counter in peacetime to Western sea-based strategic delivery systems that were deployed in distant waters. The requirement seems likely to have provided the primary impulse for Soviet actions in a number of countries in the third world. Activity ranged from preventing or promoting a coup in a client state to acquiring base rights by barely concealed coercion, as happened with Egypt in June 1967.[1]

Adoption of the 1970s hierarchy modified the focus and relative priority of the war-related requirement. The naval mission of countering U.S. sea-based strategic delivery systems yielded precedence to the missions of ensuring the security of the Soviet ballistic-missile submarines and of supporting ground and air operations in the continental theaters of military action. As a result, the requirement to establish the supporting infrastructure in distant sea areas also dropped in relative importance. The 1970s hierarchy did, however, raise additional war-related requirements for phase II of a world war. The Soviets had to secure sea lines of communication between the eastern and western parts of Russia, and to be able to repulse transoceanic invasions. The 1970s concept of operations gave a new importance to the Horn of Africa and also made it desirable to arrange for heavy weapons to be prepositioned in large quantities on the southern side of the Mediterranean.

These new requirements differed from the existing ones in timing and importance. In the 1960s concept of operations, denying the United States the option of withholding sea-based strategic nuclear systems from the initial exchange was critical to the objective of not losing the war. The avail-

---

1. Examples of preventing or promoting a coup are Guinea and Somalia in 1970 and Sierra Leone in 1971. See James M. McConnell, "The Soviet Navy in the Indian Ocean," in Michael MccGwire, ed., *Soviet Naval Developments: Capability and Context* (Praeger, 1973), p. 398. For the Egyptian case see Mohamed Heikal, *The Road to Ramadan* (New York: Quadrangle, 1975), pp. 47–48; and George S. Dragnich, "The Soviet Union's Quest for Access to Naval Facilities in Egypt Prior to the June War of 1967," in Michael MccGwire, Ken Booth, and John McDonnell, eds., *Soviet Naval Policy: Objectives and Constraints* (Praeger, 1975), pp. 237–77.

ability of the infrastructure required to support that mission had a similar priority, which pertained equally in peacetime. As a consequence, the Soviets were prepared to accept significant political and economic costs to gain peacetime access to the necessary facilities.

Under the 1970s war-related requirements, the prepositioning of heavy weapons was considered a convenience rather than a necessity. They would not be needed until phases I-3 of a world war. It would be nice to have various *pointes d' appui* already under Soviet control at the onset of war, but most of them would not become critical until phase II. This meant that the Soviets could plan to acquire the necessary facilities by force once war was under way, while guarding against the possibility of preemptive seizure by the West.

In other words, as determinants of Soviet policy toward the third world in peacetime, the 1970s war-related requirements are less important than were the 1960s ones. On the other hand, the shift from the concept of a brief nuclear war to the possibility of a long-drawn-out conventional conflict against a maritime coalition increases the attraction of a more far-flung foward-base system, as long as access can be gained at minimal political and economic cost.

The Competition between Social Systems

A major constraint on the role of Soviet military force in the struggle for influence in the third world has been the fear of escalation to global nuclear war. In the 1960s and before, the prevailing view was that local wars involving the nuclear superpowers were likely to lead to a world war. First Secretary Nikita S. Khrushchev had always been adamant that such escalation was inevitable. Although some of the Soviet military writers preferred just to say that escalation was possible rather than unavoidable, none denied the real danger of escalation.[2]

The December 1966 decision that nuclear war between the superpowers was not inevitable, and the new concept of operations that flowed from the doctrinal adjustment, provided new grounds for arguing another point of view on wars in the third world. If the Soviets could deter the United States from striking at Russia in the course of a world war, even when it faced the defeat of its forces in Western Europe, then surely they could deter the

2. Mark N. Katz, *The Third World in Soviet Military Thought* (Johns Hopkins University Press, 1982), pp. 18–21, 38–39.

escalation of a local conflict to global nuclear war. By 1969 the consensus on the dangers of escalation began to break. Those who downplayed the dangers of local war escalating to world war stressed the favorable change in the correlation of forces in the international arena.[3] Others continued to argue that the danger of world war would increase because of the escalation of military operations involving new states.

Two books published in 1972 reflected the opposing sides of the debate. The Institute of World Economics and International Relations (IMEMO) published each of them. *Military Force and International Relations,* edited by V. M. Kulish, was linked to the 1971 Twenty-fourth Party Congress and discussed the question of a "Soviet military presence" in the third world in terms that implied the authors were really discussing direct intervention by Soviet forces.[4]

The other book, *International Conflicts,* was a scholarly work edited by V. V. Zhurkin and E. M. Primakov. Zhurkin was a leading commentator on American foreign policy at the Institute for the Study of the U.S.A., and Primakov specialized in Middle East Affairs at IMEMO.[5] The book explicitly discussed the dangers that stemmed from the independent action of third parties. Although it referred to the U.S. Navy's role in the Middle East conflict and the 1971 Bangladesh crisis, it made no mention of the presence of Soviet naval forces in either case, or of the direct Soviet military involvement in Egypt in that period.

International Conflicts did, however, contain a chapter by Anatoliy Gromyko (the foreign minister's son) on the Cuban missile crisis, which was almost identical to his two-part journal article published in mid-1971.[6] The subject of the Cuban missile crisis had been virtually ignored by So-

3. The 1969 date derives from a 1974 article, which tied the new point of view directly to a statement made at a party conference in June 1969. See Colonel G. Malinovskiy, "Lokal'niye voini v zone natsional'no-osvoboditel'nogo dvizheniya" (Local wars in the zone of national liberation movements), *Voenno-istoricheskiy zhurnal* (Military historical journal), no. 5 (May 1974), p. 97, quoted by Katz, *Third World,* p. 68.

4. V. M. Kulish, *Voennaya sila i mezhdunarodnye otnosheniya* (Military force and international relations) (Moscow: Izdatel'stvo Mezhdunarodnye Otnosheniya, 1972), pp. 135–37. The authors of this collection were all members of the military-political section of the Institute of World Economics and International Relations.

5. V. V. Zhurkin and Ye. M. Primakov, *Mezhdunarodnye konflikty* (International conflicts) (Moscow: Izdatel'stvo Mezhdunarodnye Otnosheniya, 1972). This book and the Kulish book were released to the press within a month of each other.

6. Anatoliy A. Gromyko, "Karibskiy krizis" (The Caribbean crisis), *Voprosy istorii* (Problems of history), no. 7 (1971), pp. 132–44; and no. 8 (1971), pp. 121–29, reproduced in English by Ronald R. Pope, *Soviet Views on the Cuban Missile Crisis* (Washington, D.C.: University Press of America, 1982), pp. 161–226.

viet academics prior to the 1971 article and continued to be ignored after it until at least 1980.[7] One must therefore ask why Gromyko's account was published at this particular time. The answer appears to lie in the thrust of his argument.

As a commentary on the Cuban missile crisis, the article was not particularly interesting. As a cautionary tale of how easily a crisis can get out of hand, it was compelling. Gromyko repeatedly stressed three points in his analysis. The U.S. political leadership had a preference for confrontation and crisis and was on the alert to manufacture crises, the "legitimacy" of Soviet interests or actions was not a factor in American calculations, and the military leadership in the United States was bellicose and blinkered. Gromyko doubted that, once a crisis was under way, the U.S. political leadership could restrain its military from taking action that would inevitably lead to escalation.

The article included a short disquisition on crises in general. Gromyko argued that U.S. military preeminence in the world was diminishing, in response to which the United States had adopted a policy of political blackmail, threatening nuclear escalation whenever an undesirable situation arose. The discussion of this tactic was linked directly with an alleged quotation from Robert Kennedy that "President Kennedy charted a course of events, set them in motion, but was no longer able to control them."[8]

The Soviet authors who stressed the continuing danger of escalation from military involvements in the third world ultimately prevailed in the debate. Within a couple of years of his book's publication, Kulish's career with IMEMO was terminated and the ideas advanced in his book were not repeated in either the party or the military literature.[9] Primakov went on to become head of the Institute of Oriental Studies, and Zhurkin continued as a deputy director of the Institute for the Study of the U.S.A. Anatoliy Gromyko, who was a section head at the institute when he wrote his pieces on the Cuban crisis, was posted to Washington in 1973 as minister-counselor and later became director of the Institute of African Affairs.

It seems likely that the debate was set aside, rather than resolved, in mid-1974.[10] The pre-1967 doctrine stressing the dangers of escalation re-

7. Pope, *Soviet Views*, pp. 153–161.

8. Gromyko, *Voprosy istorii*, no. 8, p. 125.

9. Mark N. Katz, "On the Significance of V. M. Kulish," *Studies in Soviet Thought*, vol. 25 (1983), p. 196, note 21.

10. The article by Malinovskiy on "Local wars in the zone of national liberation movements" clearly defines the two points of view discussed in mid-1974. The publication of Malinovskiy's article in May 1974 coincided with publication of the article by Minister of Defense Andrey A.

mained largely intact. The argument had probably peaked in 1971–72, and the evidence suggests that between 1969 and 1973, the development of the policy about the involvement of Soviet forces overseas was the product as much of external events as of theoretical considerations. Among other developments, this period saw what was probably a finely balanced decision in the fall of 1969 to deploy 20,000 Soviet troops to Egypt, who would provide air defense against the Israeli deep interdiction raids. By the fall of 1971, the evidence suggests that the Soviets were debating the advisability of this deployment. Finally, they decided to extricate the forces when the opportunity arose, as it did in July 1972.[11]

The more cautious counsel had prevailed. The established policy of avoiding superpower confrontation continued with minor adaptation, as did the general reluctance to commit Russian forces outside the Soviet national security zone. Furthermore, the failure of the Soviet attempt to conclude an agreement with the United States renouncing the use of nuclear weapons outside of a NATO-Warsaw Pact conflict made the Soviets even more wary of potential escalation.[12] They were especially concerned about the Middle East, and their cautious attitude would have been reinforced by American behavior during the Arab-Israeli war in October 1973. To deter the Soviet Union from contemplating unilateral action in support of the U.N.-sponsored ceasefire, the United States had placed its strategic forces on alert.

The policy that emerged from this process still enabled the Soviet Union to affect the outcome of overseas conflicts with direct support on the battlefield, but their political commitment would remain strictly limited. The Soviets would restrict their involvement to providing advisers, weapons, and strategic logistic support; the combat role would be delegated to the Soviet-equipped forces of "revolutionary" states such as North Korea, Vietnam, and Cuba. The first example of this policy was provided by the Arab-Israeli war in October 1973. Between April and July, a Moroccan expeditionary force had been sealifted to Syria in Soviet landing ships,

---

Grechko, accepting an extended international role for the armed forces. Grechko's article, together with the one by Admiral Sergey G. Gorshkov, commander in chief of the navy, apparently indicated that some kind of compromise had been reached on the overseas role of the armed forces, if not on all the implications. See appendix C in this book.

11. See Michael MccGwire, "The Overseas Role of a 'Soviet Military Presence,'" in MccGwire, *Soviet Naval Influence,* pp. 32–34, 42–53.

12. The proposal, which Leonid I. Brezhnev made in September 1972, was ultimately watered down by Henry M. Kissinger into the "Agreement on the Prevention of Nuclear War." Brezhnev and Richard M. Nixon signed it in June 1973.

escorted by Soviet naval units in combat formation. During the war, North Korean pilots flew base defense missions in Egypt, and Cuban and North Vietnamese military personnel may have been active in Syria.[13]

The Role of the Military Instrument

When considering the role of the military instrument in Soviet policy toward the third world, it is necessary to exclude from discussion the Soviet "national security zone." This universal concept is somewhat fluid. A nation's perceptions of what constitutes its national security zone is conditioned by its capabilities, but it can be defined as "the area surrounding a state's borders, which it sees as critical to its well-being and security." Although the scope of a state's national security zone can change over time, it can be fairly clearly delineated at any one time. By the 1950s the Soviet primary national security zone encompassed the members of the Warsaw Pact, and Mongolia, Finland, and Afghanistan.[14] Thus the use of Soviet military force in Afghanistan has to be viewed in the same context as Soviet action in Hungary, Czechoslovakia, and Poland. Such action has little bearing on how the Soviets might use the military instrument in areas of the third world that are nonadjacent to their borders.

Outside its national security zone, the Soviet Union has two kinds of interest in the third world. One, the Soviets want to establish the necessary political, physical, and operational infrastructure needed to meet Soviet military requirements in the event of a world war. As just discussed, their specific nature and relative priority are likely to have evolved in the wake of the December 1966 decision, but these war-related requirements remain a significant factor in Soviet policy toward the third world.

The remaining interests come under the rubric of intersystem competition. This catch-all category, whose primary impulse is the Soviet struggle for world influence, extends to cover Sino-Soviet rivalry in the third world and the Soviets' need for access to certain raw materials.[15] Soviet policies

13. Avigdor Haselkorn, "The Soviet Collective Security System," *Orbis,* vol. 19 (Spring 1975), p. 245. Karen Dawisha has questioned whether Cuban and North Korean forces were in Syria, and if they were, whether they were active.

14. Afghanistan would have come into the Soviet national security zone by the end of the 1950s. Since 1980, northern Iran may have been reincluded in the zone.

15. The Soviet Union imports large quantities of bauxite and alumina (60 percent), barium (50 percent), flourine (47 percent), cobalt (43 percent), tin (10 percent) and antimony (10 percent); the number in parentheses shows the net import reliance as a percentage of consumption in 1980. See V. V. Strishkov, "The Mineral Industry of the U.S.S.R. in 1980" (U.S. Department of the Interior, Bureau of Mines, Branch of Foreign Data, 1981), tables 7 and 8.

can be intended to enhance their own position or damage that of their opponents.

Sometimes Soviet interests conflict, as happened in Somalia in 1968. The geostrategic requirements for a naval base in the northwest quadrant of the Indian Ocean led the Soviet Union to develop a political relationship with Somalia that carried costs to their broader goals of building influence in Africa as a whole.[16] But even when the political and strategic factors coincide, acquiring and exploiting base rights will usually consume influence rather than preserve it. Basing is only likely to increase Soviet political influence if the presence of Soviet forces is perceived by the host state as enhancing its security in the face of an immediate threat. Even the presence of Soviet forces in a directly supportive role (as were the 20,000 air defense troops in Egypt during 1970–72) can lead to antagonisms and a rapid erosion of influence, once the immediate threat is past.

In the colonial era, military bases (forts, ports, garrisons, and later airfields) were the nodal points of a web of administrative and commercial control that relied on latent force. That infrastructure was an instrument of imperial policy. But in the postcolonial era, the concession of base rights provides the host country with leverage over the tenant rather than the other way round. The Soviet military objective of establishing a strategic infrastructure to meet war-related requirements and the utility of that infrastructure as an instrument of policy in peacetime are two separate considerations.

Use of the Military Instrument

The military instrument can be used to persuade, to support, or to coerce a target state. Since the Soviet objective is to gain influence in the third world, it is not surprising that through 1984 (with one minor exception), the Soviet Union had not used actual or latent military force to coerce a state outside its national security zone.[17] The Soviets exercised restraint even when base rights were at stake, and they had significant

---

16. By becoming heavily committed to Somalia, the Soviet Union found itself on the opposite side of Kenya and Ethiopia. This involvement also provoked adverse reactions among the many francophone states that identified with Franco-Ethiopian interests in northeast Africa.

17. For the rather odd case of the two Russian vessels seized by the Ghanaian navy, see David K. Hall, "Naval Diplomacy in West African Waters," in Stephen S. Kaplan, *Diplomacy of Force: Soviet Armed Forces as a Political Instrument* (Brookings, 1981), pp. 521–31. The Arab-Israeli war of June 1967 is a possible example of indirect coercion. Some argue that the Soviets sparked the conflict in the hopes that Egypt would get a bloody nose and turn to Moscow for support, conceding the naval base rights that the Soviets desperately needed.

forces on the ground and control of air terminals in that country. Similarly, when the Soviets have applied supportive military force, either directly or through proxies, it has been defensive and not punitive, since it is counter-productive to generate unnecessary hostility. The provision of air defense has been the most typical form of supportive intervention. In response to the Somali invasion of Ethiopia, the Soviets and Cubans gave direct sup-port to the defense of Ethiopia but did not carry the war to Somalia.[18]

The Soviets have primarily used the military instrument in the third world to build influence through persuasion. Mostly, they have supplied arms and trained personnel, both in Russia and the home country. How-ever, the Soviets are not only concerned with building influence.[19] They have also tried to increase the client's ability to defend itself against exter-nal intervention, thus raising the costs to the West of using military force to rectify unfavorable political developments.

Their other, unstated, objective is to complicate the West's strategic sit-uation by introducing threats that draw Western capability away from the Soviet Union. In the mid-1950s, the Soviets provided the Egyptians with a submarine force, introducing a new factor into Sixth Fleet calculations. Indonesia, astride the straits linking the Indian and Pacific Oceans, was provided with a navy at the end of the 1950s, from cruisers to submarines and including missile-armed strike aircraft. This development drew a siz-able part of the British fleet, including its strike carriers, east of Suez and away from the NATO area.

After the Cuban debacle in 1962, Soviet attention once more focused on the threat from the Mediterranean. The Egyptian submarine force was upgraded, and the air force was provided with missile-armed strike air-craft. At the other end of the Mediterranean the Algerians were provided with missile-armed patrol craft that could threaten passage through the Gi-braltar Straits. Today, Soviet-supplied submarines and missile-armed pa-trol craft in Cuba and Libya complicate U.S. operational plans and divert

18. A similar principle seems to underlie the use of Soviet naval forces. Besides serving as an earnest of Soviet commitment, they seem to have been used primarily as a deterrent and shield against attacks by third parties (for example, Israel in 1973, South Africa in 1975, and Somalia in 1978) on the external lines of supply, or against the country itself (Israel vs. Egypt in 1967, Israel vs. Syria in 1974).

19. A third objective, to earn hard currency, has emerged in the last ten years. Cynthia A. Roberts, "Soviet Arms-Transfer Policy and the Decision to Upgrade Syrian Air Defense," *Survival*, vol. 25 (July-August 1983), p. 159. When this aim results in arms sales to a country like Libya, it also serves the purposes of prepositioning equipment on the far side of the Mediterranean for use in phase II of a world war.

resources that would otherwise be concentrated against the Soviet Union and its forces.

Although the Soviets had provided arms for strategic diversion and to raise the costs of Western military intervention, and although they arrange for the supply of arms to liberation movements, they do not see their interests as being served by undifferentiated conflict, fueled by the supply of arms. The evidence indicates that policy toward individual countries has generally been well thought out and implemented. The Soviets have been careful not to supply arms that would allow the client to achieve large results in relation to the international status quo, and rather than urge a client to resort to force against another state, the Soviets have usually only acceded to the state's determination to do so.

The Soviets have clearly used the military instrument in their attempts to increase their share of world influence, although without conspicuous success. Their behavior does not, however, support the hypothesis that the world is faced by a communist variant of traditional imperial colonialism based on military force. Soviet bases in third world countries have not been used to retain Soviet control over host countries. Somalia and Egypt provide two such examples. Somalia is particularly relevant because the circumstances of the Ogaden war would have allowed the Soviets to impose a military solution on the Horn, which is of great strategic interest to them in the event of a war. Their withdrawal from Somalia, before they had a secure alternative to Berbera, compares favorably with Britain's drawn-out attempt to retain Aden in in the 1960s.

Soviet or Soviet-controlled forces in third world countries have been used to protect a state against external attack, but outside the Soviet national security zone (which includes Afghanistan) they have not been used to overthrow a regime or keep a regime in power. At first sight, Angola might seem an exception to the latter, but while the Popular Movement for the Liberation of Angola had Cuban advisers, substantial Cuban forces were only committed in response to the South African invasion, and the initiative appears to have come from the Cubans rather than the Russians.[20]

The final element of the "imperial" hypothesis is the direct use of Soviet force against Western interests, in circumstances short of global war. The closest the Soviets have come to have such action has been their response to the West's projection of force. In 1972 Sergey Gorshkov claimed that

20. Raymond L. Garthoff, *Détente and Confrontation: American-Soviet Relations from Nixon to Reagan* (Brookings, 1985), pp. 502–19, 533–36, and 1112.

the Soviet navy had a role of deterring imperialist aggression and disrupting the plans of aggressors.[21] In practice, the Soviets have postured rather than interposed their forces to thwart Western plans.

In the early days of the Soviet navy's shift to forward deployment in the 1960s, it was difficult to disentangle the war-related mission of countering the carrier's nuclear-strike capability from this peacetime mission of deterring Western aggression in the third world. In any case, the former had overriding precedence in times of mounting tension in the eastern Mediterranean. But since 1971 and the restructuring of strategic objectives, a series of deployments has occurred that can be tied to local circumstances rather than to the contingency of global war. The Soviets matched the U.S. deployment of a carrier force to the Indian Ocean during the Indo-Pakistani crisis in 1971. This coincided with the height of the debate about the role of military force and the dangers of escalation arising from confrontation in the third world. There was the more intrusive behavior of the Mediterranean squadron during the October 1973 Arab-Israeli war.[22] There was also the precautionary deployment to the South Atlantic during the Angolan affair and the reinforcement of the Mediterranean squadron after the Israeli invasion of Lebanon in 1982.

During Middle East crises in 1967, 1973, and 1982, the Soviets implied that they might bring in airborne forces. But in all those cases the Soviet objective was to protect a client against Israel, and there was no attempt to prevent the projection of U.S. force. To the contrary, the Soviet threat of action was designed to persuade the United States to bring pressure to bear on Israel.

The naval evidence must remain inconclusive since in none of the cases did the United States move to project force ashore.[23] But nor were there any indications that the Soviets would be willing to engage U.S. forces in combat to prevent them from intervening. The impression is left that Soviet action was intended to demonstrate an interest in the outcome and to serve as a psychological constraint on U.S. behavior. The effectiveness of that constraint depended on an American belief that the Soviet Union was willing to order an unprovoked attack on U.S. naval forces. There was no such American belief, nor were the Soviets willing to go that far.

21. Sergey G. Gorshkov, "Voenno-morskie floty v voynakh i v mirnoe vremya" (Navies in war and peace), *Morskoy sbornik* (Naval journal), no. 12 (December 1972), p. 21.

22. Robert G. Weinland, *Superpower Naval Diplomacy in the October 1973 Arab-Israeli War,* Professional Paper 221 (Arlington, Va.: Center for Naval Analyses, 1978).

23. The U.S. Marines in Lebanon were initially lauded as a peacekeeping force, and the slow escalation of U.S. involvement provided no obvious opportunity for Soviet interposition.

The Sources of Soviet Policy

Given the roots of their policy, it is not surprising that the Soviets' military behavior in the third world does not conform to the pattern established by the European states during the period of colonial imperialism. For a start, the Soviet historical tradition is transcontinental expansion rather than maritime colonialism. During the era of exploration, the Russians were reluctant to take possession of distant islands or territories or even to retain possession of an adjacent but noncontiguous territory such as Alaska.[24] While the Europeans, living on the western fringes of the Eurasian continent and competing among themselves, were driven by "gold, glory and the gospel," the Russians were conducting a never-ending search for secure frontiers. While the Europeans won and lost empires and traded possessions like poker chips at the peace treaty negotiations, the tsar was preoccupied with control, both of the Russian colonialist-explorers and his new subjects encompassed by the expanding frontier.

More recent attitudes that stem from Marxist-Leninist theory and the Soviet experience since 1917 are superimposed on historical attitudes. The dogma of historical inevitability and the belief that the Soviet Union is on the side of historical progress are important. According to communist ideology, third world countries should inevitably evolve toward socialism. The objective of Soviet policy should be to accelerate the process by identifying and then opening the appropriate political stopcock, which at various times has been seen as the charismatic leader, the national bourgeoisie, the military radical, or the vanguard party. In such circumstances, the primary role of military force is to protect the fledgling regime from attempts by antiprogressive forces, supported directly or indirectly by the capitalist bloc, to overthrow them.

Various factors inhibit the use of Soviet military force to hasten the progress of history. The political utility of coercive intervention has diminished steadily since World War II. Large-scale coercive intervention by major powers has been successful only within their national security zones, where power gradients and political commitment are high. Elsewhere in the postcolonial world, the coercive use of force has yielded negative returns, except for short, sharp, rectifying operations, or *coups de main*.

The historical link between the projection of force and traditional capi-

---

24. Sergey G. Gorshkov, "Voenno-morskie floty v voynakh i v mirnoe vremya," *Morskoy sbornik*, no. 4 (April 1972), p. 11.

talist imperialism reinforces these pragmatic considerations. Just as the Soviets' theoretical aversion to the geopolitical theories of Alfred Mahan inhibited them from acknowledging "command of the sea" as a useful operational concept, so are they likely to have been inhibited from espousing Western assumptions about the value of projecting force in distant parts of the globe. The Soviets insist that the war-related support facilities they have established in distant sea areas in no way resemble the West's worldwide base structure. And well they might. The idea that far-flung bases bring prestige is very much a nineteenth-century notion, and by espousing it the Soviets would lose a stick with which to beat the imperialists, while handing one to the Chinese.

The Soviets' general approach also accords with the broader principles of Marxist-Leninism, which is primarily a socioeconomic theory. I am not implying that the Soviets undervalue military power. There is no doubt in their minds that matching military power persuaded the United States to mute its insistence on "positions of strength" in dealing with the Soviet Union and brought America to the negotiating table in 1970s. However, the Soviets focus not on the military balance but on the correlation of forces, which is a more extensive concept. While "in the final analysis, military might is decisive," in the broader scheme of things, military power plays a partial and indirect role.[25]

Military power and the use of force must be distinguished in the same way that one distinguishes between a family's wealth and the way it spends its money. The Soviets firmly believe in the political leverage that stems from military power, but this belief does not mean they are profligate in the use of force. Rather the reverse, because the use of force usually incurs political costs. The Soviets are sensitive to these costs even within their national security zone, as evidenced by the delay in moving against Hungary, Czechoslovakia, and Afghanistan, and by their military restraint in respect to Poland. The Soviets did use force in the first three cases, but that only emphasizes the difference in their concepts about the use of force in their national security zone and in the third world. Military power is central to the security of the Soviet Union and in the superpower relationship. It has only limited value as a lever for Soviet interests in the third world.

25. Robert Legvold, "Military Power in International Politics: Soviet Doctrine on its Centrality and Instrumentality," in Uwe Nerlich, ed., *The Soviet Asset: Military Power in the Competition over Europe,* vol. 1 (Ballinger, 1983).

Grounds for a Change in Policy

Through 1984, Soviet military forces had not been used coercively outside their national security zone, either to establish a position or to retain one, even when strategic bases were involved. The Soviets had been reluctant to go beyond political manipulation in preserving their position in a country, and this policy of "win some, lose some" made good sense, since they were confident that the historical trend was on their side. President Richard M. Nixon reinforced this confidence when he accepted the formula of peaceful coexistence as part of the "Basic Principles" adopted in May 1972.[26] The muted behavior of the United States in the wake of Vietnam made it reasonable to conclude that the military threat to the emergence of socialist states was on the wane.

In the mid-1970s the Soviets expected the role of the military instrument in the third world to diminish in the years ahead. However, the course of events during the late 1970s would have argued otherwise, and the policy of win some, lose some may have come under critical review in the 1983–85 period.

Through the mid-1970s, the Soviets were persuaded that the Marxist prognosis of history was being borne out at an accelerating rate, and the general secretary's report to the Twenty-fifth Party Congress in 1976 reflected a sense of optimism about the status of the ongoing struggle between socialism and capitalism.[27] This belief in the acceleration of the trend in the correlation of forces could not, however, have been based primarily on the balance of Soviet gains and losses in third world countries during the previous five years.[28] The Egyptian request to withdraw Soviet troops in 1972 was followed by the loss of naval support facilities in 1975, and Henry Kissinger's diplomatic maneuvering squeezed the Soviet Union

26. The "Basic Principles of Relations between the United States of America and the Union of Soviet Socialist Republics" were signed at the U.S.-Soviet summit in May 1972. See *Department of State Bulletin*, vol. 67, no. 1722 (Government Printing Office, 1972), pp. 898–99.

27. The connection between the socialist world and national liberation movements was seen as "invincible." The shift in the correlation of forces had allowed and strengthened détente, and this would also lead to reduced imperialist pressure on these movements in the third world.

28. Legvold explains the correlation of forces as "a sweeping concept, incorporating virtually all critical trends in international politics . . . a device for commenting on the underlying pattern of change." "Military Power in International Politics," p. 130. Historical materialism decrees that the long-term trend in the correlation of forces is by definition favorable. What has to be determined is the rate of change at a particular period, whether this rate is changing, and if so, in what direction.

out of the Middle East negotiations. A rift had developed with Sudan after a failed communist coup in 1971; in Chile, Salvador Allende was overthrown and killed in 1973; and while Angola and Mozambique could be counted as developments in the right direction, they had to be weighed against the more far-reaching implications of the U.S. rapprochement with China.

The balance of gains and losses did not improve during the second half of the 1970s. The Soviets steadily gained influence in Vietnam, but thereby increased the distrust of members of the Association of Southeast Asian Nations. The Soviets were forced to choose between Ethiopia and Somalia, losing their investment in Somalia and acquiring large political problems in Ethiopia. Although South Yemen had come their way, they now had to face a new American influence in Egypt, Sudan, Somalia, and Kenya. Angola became enmeshed in a drawn-out civil war, tying down significant Cuban forces; Zimbabwe gained its independence and turned a cold shoulder to Moscow; and by the end of the period Mozambique had begun to ease its way to accommodation with South Africa. In Southwest Asia there was a progressive loss of influence in Iraq; Syria demanded Soviet arms but gave little in return; and after the fall of the shah of Iran, the Soviet Union was reviled by the revolutionaries almost as much as was the United States. To cap it all, the Soviet invasion of Afghanistan incurred significant political costs, not only among the thirty-eight Muslim states but in the third world at large. A United Nations resolution condemning the takeover was supported by an unprecedented 104 votes.

This record was not so different from the three previous five-year periods and on its own could have been shrugged off as win some, lose some. But the sharp deceleration in the rate of change in the correlation of forces could not be shrugged off, and by 1981 the mid-1970s optimism had largely evaporated. The United States had emerged from its post-Vietnam depression in a more combative mood. Eventually, the election of Ronald Reagan as president led to a rejection of most of the assumptions that had underlain American policy toward Russia during the previous fifteen years. Instead the administration seemed bent on reestablishing a position of strength (that is, military superiority) and returning to the confrontational style of the 1947–1953 period. These developments were clearly reflected in the tone of the general secretary's report to the Twenty-sixth Party Congress in 1981, even though the adverse implications of the Reagan administration's policies had yet to be fully perceived.

The U.S. policy on the third world that could be inferred from public statements and practical action was one of intolerance toward the emergence of Marxist or socialist regimes. The United States seemed ready to use coercive military force to support its perceived interests, including the overthrow of governments deemed unfriendly. This was a radical reversal of the policy that had prevailed a decade earlier and had serious implications for the trend in the correlation of forces. In the face of this change, the Soviets would have had to address the question of whether they could afford to persist with their win-some lose-some policy or whether more positive steps were required.

During the 1970s the Soviets had already moved in the direction of consolidating the internal authority of Soviet-oriented regimes in the third world and strengthening Soviet control of such regimes. This was being achieved through encouraging the establishment of "vanguard parties," which provided an administrative structure capable of surviving the vagaries of individual rulers. At the same time links were created between the Soviet Communist party and the client Communist party, allowing the Soviets multiple access to the client's top leaders. The internal authority of such regimes was being further enhanced by the establishment of internal security apparatus that was organized, trained, and sometimes administered by the East Germans.[29]

The more difficult question was how the Soviet Union should respond to an American use of force to overthrow a socialist or pro-Soviet regime, or to prevent the accession to power of a national liberation movement. The accumulating evidence indicated clearly that the Soviet hope that the United States no longer saw military force as a primary instrument of foreign policy had been unfounded. This realization raised the question of whether or not to develop a countervailing military capability.[30]

This concern went right back to the substance of the earlier debate about the role of a Soviet military presence in the third world. In considering how the Soviets might have answered the question in 1983–85, two developments must be borne in mind. The 1969–74 Soviet debate had been colored by optimism, almost euphoria, about the accelerating trend in the correlation of forces. This optimism meant that the proponents of the use of force could be countered with the argument that force was unnecessary as well as dangerous. But in 1983–85 the question of necessity would

29. Francis Fukuyama, *The Military Dimension of Soviet Policy in the Third World*, P-6965 (Santa Monica, Calif.: Rand Corp., 1984), pp. 21–22.

30. Legvold makes the point that the Soviets consider military power and the use of force to be the primary instrument of U.S. military policy. "Military Power in International Politics," p. 137.

have been at the nub of the argument. The need to preserve independence of action had to be balanced against the objective of avoiding world war.

The Soviets were also concerned about the risk of escalation. During the earlier debate about the danger of escalation resulting from superpower confrontation in the third world, the Soviet Union was in transition from the 1960s hierarchy of military objectives to the 1970s hierarchy, and military thought was largely conditioned by the ideas and attitudes that had prevailed before December 1966, including the belief in inevitable escalation. The Soviet navy had only embarked on forward deployment in 1964, and its active use as an instrument of policy in peacetime had only begun in 1967, slowly building up after that time. The Soviets therefore had little experience of how the United States would react to armed confrontation in the third world, although the readiness with which the United States brought strategic nuclear forces on alert during the 1973 Arab-Israeli war was not reassuring.

By 1983–85 the Soviets had new sources of evidence on which to base their assessments of the danger of escalation. They saw the endless debate in NATO about whether or not Europe had been decoupled from the U.S. nuclear deterrent. A new element had been introduced by Henry Kissinger's 1979 address in Brussels on "NATO and the Next Thirty Years," in which he ridiculed the idea that the United States would be willing to invite immolation by launching a strategic strike on Russia in defense of NATO. The deployment of Pershing IIs and GLCMs appeared to support Kissinger's statement. It was hard to see the military utility of these missiles unless the United States had decided that it no longer intended to honor its commitment to intercontinental escalation.[31] Such a decision would explain why the United States was willing to jeopardize the cohesion of the NATO alliance, as well as the domestic support for members' national defense policies.

To the Soviets, the Kissinger address was particularly noteworthy since Kissinger was the man who as Nixon's national security adviser had flatly rejected the Soviet proposal for a bilateral agreement renouncing the use of nuclear weapons against each other's territories.[32] But it was only part of a growing body of evidence that the U.S. declaratory policy of deliberate escalation had been "a Grand Illusion or Great Lie."[33] Robert S.

---

31. Richard K. Betts, "Compound Deterrence vs. No-First-Use: What's Wrong is What's Right," *Orbis*, vol. 28 (Winter 1985), p. 704.

32. This rejection occurred in 1972. Henry Kissinger, *Years of Upheaval* (Little, Brown, 1982), pp. 274–86.

33. Betts, "Compound Deterrence," p. 702.

McNamara, the secretary of defense under John F. Kennedy and Lyndon B. Johnson, averred that he had "recommended [to both presidents], without qualification, that they never initiate, under any circumstances, the use of nuclear weapons," and he believed that his recommendation had been accepted.[34] Samuel Huntingdon, a member of Jimmy Carter's National Security Council, wrote of the "virtual certainty . . . that no American President will authorize the use of nuclear weapons in response to a conventional attack on Europe."[35]

If this was how U.S. officials felt about nuclear escalation in defense of Europe, where the United States had about 325,000 men on the ground and close cultural links, they would be even more reluctant to risk escalation in support of less tangible interests in the third world. Nor was there any evidence of U.S. domestic support for such a policy; rather the reverse. The response to the perceived increase in the danger of war with Russia had been the emergence of the ground zero and nuclear freeze movements in the United States and the declaration by individual communities that they were nuclear-free zones. Although the American public on the whole approved of the administration's readiness to resort to force in the third world, this support had limited staying power and little tolerance for significant costs in men or major military units.

In reassessing the danger of military involvement in the third world in the mid-1980s, the Soviets are therefore likely to have concluded that the probability of escalation to global nuclear war had been greatly exaggerated in the 1969–74 debate. It was true that the United States had designated a Rapid Deployment Force and was adopting a more interventionist policy. But there was also the evidence of Vietnam, the Iranian hostage crisis, and the marines in Beirut. When the evidence was viewed in the context of statements by former U.S. officials and the response of the American people to the increased danger of war, it argued that the inherent constraints on U.S. escalation were strong.

34. Robert S. McNamara, "The Military Role of Nuclear Weapons: Perceptions and Misperceptions," *Foreign Affairs,* vol. 62 (Fall 1983), p. 79.

35. Samuel P. Huntington, "Correspondence," *International Security,* vol. 9 (Summer 1984), p. 212. This statement was made two years after four eminent former U.S. officials advocated that NATO adopt a no-first-use policy for nuclear weapons. See McGeorge Bundy, George F. Kennan, Robert S. McNamara, and Gerard Smith, "Nuclear Weapons and the Atlantic Alliance," *Foreign Affairs,* vol. 60 (Spring 1982), pp. 753–68.

CHAPTER 11

Military Objectives and Arms Control

THE 1966 CHANGE in military doctrine about the nature of a future war had fundamental implications for the role of arms control in Soviet policy. The restructuring of objectives that stemmed from the December 1966 decision changed the Soviet calculus of costs and benefits, resulting in a shift of Soviet policy on the limitation of strategic systems.

Although arms control proposals, negotiations, and agreements can serve a range of political, economic,[1] and military purposes, two objectives are at the core of Soviet arms control policy: the first-order national objective of avoiding world war, and the military objective, should war be inescapable, of not losing. Although the Soviets may decide to embark on arms control negotiations in search of specific political benefits, these two objectives will shape the seriousness and substance of such negotiations.

Before 1967 the requirements of the two objectives were in conflict with each other. On the positive side, it was intuitively plausible that an arms control agreement with the United States would help to avoid world war, although the empirical evidence was ambiguous. On the negative side, the Soviets lagged behind America in tactical, theater, and intercontinental nuclear delivery systems, and although they had larger numbers of conventional forces, in key areas the quality of those forces was significantly lower. If the Soviet Union was not to lose some future war, it would need to remedy these disparities, but arms control was likely to prevent them from doing so.

An arms control agreement could lock the Soviet Union into a position

---

1. In his speech to the Twenty-fourth Party Congress Leonid I. Brezhnev explicitly recognized the economic benefits of arms control agreements. See "Brezhnev's Report to the Twenty-fourth Congress-I," in *Current Digest of the Soviet Press,* vol. 23 (April 1971), p. 12.

of military inferiority to the United States. Not only would this jeopardize the objective of not losing a world war, but by perpetuating the American advantage of being able to deal with the Soviet Union from a "position of strength" in world affairs, it would undermine the first-order national objective of preserving the capacity for independent action. Given its uncertain contribution to making war less likely, arms control could not therefore promote the well-being of the Soviet state, except by helping to prevent the spread of nuclear weapons through agreement on nonproliferation policies or nuclear-free zones.

The doctrinal adjustment decided in December 1966 directly affected this cost-benefit calculus. However, the doctrinal adjustment was only one of several developments that coincided in the 1967–68 period to reshape the Soviet approach to arms control. It seems unlikely that it would have been the predominant influence on Soviet thinking in the initial stages of the reevaluation of Soviet policy on arms control. The doctrinal change would, however, have become increasingly important and its consequential logic progressively accepted by the Soviet politico-military establishment.

The Objective of Avoiding World War

The United States' overtures in December 1966 and January 1967 that led ultimately to the strategic arms limitation talks (SALT) were seen by Moscow as important to the Soviet objective of avoiding world war. By 1966 deployment of the third generation of Soviet intercontinental ballistic missile (ICBM) had begun (the SS-9, SS-11, and SS-13), and development of the fourth generation was proceeding. Washington was apparently coming to recognize that the trend in the overall correlation of forces was favoring the Soviet Union and that the Soviet military component in particular was moving toward rough strategic parity with that of the United States.

During 1967–68 it would have become increasingly clear that constructive negotiations on limiting strategic arms could contribute significantly to the objective of avoiding world war. Although never adopted by the United States as official policy, the concept of Mutual Assured Destruction had emerged as the basis of U.S. nuclear deterrence. In America, bipartisan acceptance of the idea that the appropriate U.S. goal was strategic sufficiency rather than superiority was growing. Although the full flowering of détente that occurred in the early 1970s was probably not foreseen by the Soviets, it did appear to them that the United States was moving to recognize the concept of peaceful coexistence and to acknowledge that arms racing increased tension and hence the danger of unintended conflict.

The potential advantages of entering into arms control agreements that would constrain Soviet military capabilities were not immediately accepted throughout the Soviet politico-military establishment. During the 1967–68 period, the Soviets debated the inherent desirability of such negotiations as well as their appropriate substance. But in due course the arms control skeptics fell silent and, in the wake of SALT, numerous Soviet commentators stressed SALT's contribution to détente and hence to a reduction of the risks of war.[2] Furthermore, the U.S. acceptance of strategic nuclear parity did imply a weakening of the doctrine that the United States should always deal from a position of strength, and to that extent it also enhanced the Soviet capacity for independent action.

However, while successful arms control negotiations might help relax international tension and hence make war less likely, the Soviets still faced the requirement not to lose, should a world war prove inescapable. Consequently, the 1966 decision had one set of implications for Soviet arms control policy toward intercontinental systems, but a different set for the weapons that would be used in the adjacent continental theaters of war.

Wartime Requirements—Intercontinental Systems

Nuclear weapons were initially introduced into the Soviet inventory as part of the process of upgrading the armed forces' capability for waging war with new technologies as they became available. Offensive intercontinental systems, mainly ICBMs, were for bombarding the U.S. continent and striking at America's forces in being, war-making potential, and structure of government and social control in the attempt to destroy the capitalist system. Defensive weapons worked in support of preserving the socialist system in the face of intercontinental nuclear attack, and the development of antiballistic-missile (ABM) systems was a natural consequence of the appearance of ballistic missiles that could reach the Russian heartland.

This symmetry was broken by the doctrinal adjustment in December 1966. The shift generated consequential changes in supporting objectives,

2. Raymond L. Garthoff, "BMD and East-West Relations," in Ashton B. Carter and David N. Schwartz, eds., *Ballistic Missile Defense* (Brookings, 1984), pp. 296–301, 308.

and avoiding the nuclear devastation of Russia became the governing objective in the new hierarchy. In order not to lose a world war, the Soviets would have to defeat NATO in Europe and evict U.S. forces from the Continent. If meanwhile they were to avoid the nuclear devastation of Russia, they would somehow have to stop the United States, when faced by defeat in Europe, from striking at Russia with nuclear weapons. Clearly, missile attacks could not be prevented by an antiballistic-missile system, then or in the foreseeable future, and the Soviets would have to rely primarily on deterring such attacks with the threat of instant retaliation.

Holding America deterred in such circumstances was an immensely demanding requirement, and it could only succeed if the scale and certainty of the Soviet response were beyond question. Thus the Soviet Union would have to be sure that it could launch an ICBM force, even if it was undergoing attack. They also had to be certain that once launched, the ICBMs would reach North America. These considerations meant the arms control implications of the 1966 decision were different for offensive and defensive systems.

Intercontinental Strike Systems

There had never been any disagreement in the Soviet Union about the basic importance of intercontinental systems capable of bombarding the United States. Before 1967 the systems served two somewhat different wartime objectives: the offensive one of destroying the citadel of capitalism, including its forces in being; and the defensive one of limiting the damage that the intercontinental component of those forces could to do Russia, by striking them before they could be launched. The requirement to target all U.S. strategic delivery systems, as well as other military, political, and economic targets, translated into a requirement for strategic superiority, and in this context, more was better.

That requirement changed as a consequence of the adjustment in doctrine. The governing objective was now to avoid the nuclear devastation of Russia, and the primary purpose of the ICBM force was to deter America from striking at Russia in the course of a world war. The size of the Soviet ICBM force and its deterrent effect on America were not directly related. Beyond a certain fairly small size there were diminishing returns to scale, and instinct suggested that the curve would soon flatten out. On the other hand, the size of the U.S. ICBM force and the devastation it could wreak on Russia were directly related. Should deterrence fail, the smaller the U.S. ICBM force, the less the devastation to Russia.

The logic of these two relationships meant that Soviet objectives would be served best if mutually agreed-on limits on ICBM numbers were kept as low as consistent with wartime deterrence. It was true that, if deterrence failed, the 1960s hierarchy of objectives would take effect; the requirement to strike at military, political, and economic targets in North America would therefore have to be brought into the Soviets' calculation of optimum force levels. However, the situation would be different from that in the 1960s. In those days Soviet strategy was predicated on achieving intercontinental nuclear preemption. In the 1970s the priority of avoiding escalation meant that it had to be assumed that Soviet ICBMs would be launched, at best, on warning. This policy greatly reduced their targeting possibilities and thus their requirement for weapons.

The revised requirement was to match the U.S. inventory so that the United States would not be able to dominate in the postexchange phase of a war. Once parity was achieved, the Soviets would work step by step to achieve mutual reductions.

The need to match the U.S. capability was as much a political requirement as a military one and was necessitated by the priority that the United States attached to negotiating from a position of strength. If mutual reductions would allow the Soviets to gain a relative advantage in war-fighting capability, so much the better. But that was not the primary objective, and it had to be weighed against the general benefits of reducing U.S. missile inventories and the wider political benefits of the arms control process.

Concrete evidence that Soviet policy had changed in favor of reducing the number of ICBMs emerged in the spring of 1970, when work was halted on missile silos then under construction. At this same period the Soviets began to deploy missiles that were nominally ICBM but in fact were targeted on the continental periphery of the Soviet Union in order to remedy a shortage of regional-range missiles. Western intelligence was aware of these developments, but the shift in policy was obscured by the Soviet military's obsessive secrecy, which prevented the Soviet negotiators from explaining, except very obliquely, which of their missiles were seen as constituting an intercontinental missile force. Meanwhile the Soviet style of negotiation was not such as to dispel the Western belief that the Soviets still sought strategic superiority, even though the new doctrine had shifted the focus to equivalence.

To appreciate the effect of the December 1966 doctrinal decision and of the SALT agreements in 1972 and 1979, one must be aware of the missile production and deployment plans that were already in place at those dates. The plans can be inferred from the Soviet pattern of missile deployments and silo starts and from the evidence of missile tests. The evolving plans for the Soviet ICBM force in the 1961–80 period are reconstructed in appendix D and serve as the basis for the following account.

LAND-BASED INTERCONTINENTAL BALLISTIC MISSILES. During the mid-1950s the Soviets apparently decided that the most cost-effective way of dealing with the steadily growing number of political, military, and economic targets in the United States was for them to use large warheads to destroy all facilities in a given area rather than develop the capability for striking individual targets. To this end, the Soviets steadily increased the size of their warheads. As originally planned in 1957–58, they probably intended to deploy 480 5-megaton (MT) second-generation ICBMs (SS-7 and SS-8) in 1961–65, and 480 20-MT third-generation ICBMs (SS-9 and SS-10) in 1966–70, followed by an unknown number of missiles in the range of 50–100 MTs in the 1971–75 period. This fifteen-year program of heavy missiles would be supplemented by a ten-year program of mobile, 600-kiloton missiles; 240 SS-13s in 1966–70, followed by 240 SS-16s in the 1971–75 period. The combined program would have resulted in a force of 1,200 ICBMs by the end of 1970, with deployments in the 1966–70 period running at 144 missiles a year. (Table D-2, p. 488, in appendix D details the Soviet Union's changing plans for producing and deploying ICBMs in the period 1955–80.)

The original plan was thrown off track in the early months of 1961 when President John F. Kennedy decided to rapidly deploy a large force of Minuteman ICBMs. To appreciate the Soviets' response to this new development one must remember that their ICBM programs were largely a response to the nuclear delivery capability already embodied in the 1,700 bombers of the U.S. Strategic Air Command. Besides being an addition to this existing capability, the Minuteman force was to be deployed in hardened silos in the mid-West, far away from the majority of the unhardened political, military, and economic installations in the existing target set that the original Soviet programs were intended to cover. Responding to the Minuteman force was therefore an additional requirement.

The initial Soviet response to this new requirement was to match the Minuteman buildup with the 1-MT SS-11 program. In 1961 Minuteman production had been programmed at 360 missiles a year, but the final size of the U.S. ICBM force had yet to be decided. The U.S. Joint Chiefs of

Staff favored 1,600 (the Strategic Air Command was lobbying for "thousands") and during 1961–63 the "approved" size of the force fluctuated between 800 and 1,300. Soviet production of the SS-11 was therefore programmed to provide for the deployment of 240 a year, beginning in 1966; this roughly matched the rate at which Minutemen were brought into service in the period 1962–65.

The more measured response to the new requirement was to target the Minuteman launch control centers (there was one for every ten launchers) with the 20-MT SS-9s. This approach was probably decided in 1962–63 and had taken effect by the time the deployment of SS-9s began in 1965, the deployment date having been advanced by one year at the expense of SS-7 production. The SS-8 and its successor, the SS-10, had meanwhile been canceled, since their nonstorable liquid fuel meant that they were unsuitable for a strategy predicated on intercontinental preemption.

This all meant that in 1965, when the Soviets were finalizing the programs for the Eighth Five-Year Plan (to be approved in spring 1966), they were already committed to the production of ICBMs at a rate that would allow the deployment of 336 missiles a year: 48 SS-9s, 240 SS-11s, and 48 SS-13s, although development of the SS-13s had fallen behind schedule. The evidence suggests that the production run of the third-generation missile systems was extended from five years to ten, and that the Soviets planned that fourth-generation systems would begin replacing them in about 1975. These programs, as projected in 1965, would have resulted in a Soviet ICBM force of more than 3,300 missiles, with about 1,800 in place by the end of 1970.

A further change to the planned production program was decided in 1966–67. By then the size of the U.S. Minuteman force had been fixed at 1,000 missiles and 54 Titans, for a total of 1,054 missiles. This defined the counterforce requirement and meant that at least 40 percent of the planned force of 480 SS-9s would be available to cover the Soviets' original area-devastation target set.[3] This, in turn, meant that 80 percent of current SS-11 production could be redirected to remedying the shortfall in regional-range missiles that had resulted from the sudden surge in the requirement for ICBMs in 1961. At this same period the Soviets probably also decided to cancel the requirement for a superheavy missile in the 50- to 100-MT range, following the logic of the 1970s hierarchy of objectives.

---

3. If each Minuteman launch control center were targeted with two SS-9s, from 65 to 100 control centers would be destroyed. See Robert P. Berman and John C. Baker, *Soviet Strategic Forces: Requirements and Responses* (Brookings, 1982), table 3-8.

However, none of this need have affected the underlying plan to provide for the deployment of 336 missiles a year.

This plan would have come under renewed scrutiny by the end of 1969, when the Soviets would have been reviewing production programs for the Ninth Five-Year Plan. By then the SALT negotiations were already under way, and the logic of the 1970s hierarchy of objectives was driving Soviet arms control policy. Consequently, in the first half of 1970 the Soviets decided to curtail the deployment of ICBMs targeted on North America at a number that would roughly match the size of the U.S. force. The SS-9 program was cut short at six years, with 288 missiles deployed, and the SS-13 was canceled with only 60 missiles deployed. Another 60 SS-11s were deployed, but these were all targeted on the Eurasian periphery. If it is accepted that 360 SS-11s were assigned to such regional targets, then there would have been 1,018 third-generation ICBMs targeted on the United States.

This total of 1,018 ICBMs was comparable in numbers to the U.S. total of 1,054 ICBMs, although the Soviet force still lagged in quality. The Soviet total does not include the second-generation SS-7 and SS-8, most of which were not housed in silos and whose capability was just not comparable with the U.S. systems.[4] When the Soviets claimed in November 1971 that "the number of Soviet ICBM silos is approximately the same as the number of U.S. ICBM silos," they were referring to third-generation systems.[5]

In other words, the Soviets reached a decision in early 1970 to round off the intercontinental element of the strategic rocket forces at about 1,000 missiles, roughly matching the number of U.S. ICBMs. This meant that it was also possible to cut back on the planned production of fourth-generation missiles. As forecast in 1965, to replace the third generation of missiles with these new and much more effective systems would have required a deployment rate of 336 a year for ten years. That rate could now be cut to 144 a year, since it would now only be necessary to replace about 1,000 missiles targeted on the United States, the 360 missiles already targeted on the regions surrounding Russia, and perhaps another 60 for new regional targets that would include those in China.

4. U.S. Department of Defense, *Soviet Military Power, 1983,* 2d ed. (Government Printing Office, 1983), pp. 19–20. (Hereafter *SMP.*) Only 78 of these missiles were housed in silos, the remaining 131 were emplaced on unhardened launch pads.
5. This point was made in a private conversation between N. S. Kishilov and Raymond Garthoff during the SALT I negotiations. See Jack Anderson, "Soviets Seem Eager for Arms Pact," *Washington Post,* December 27, 1971.

The agreement from the first series of strategic arms limitation talks (SALT I) was signed in May 1972 and imposed a ceiling of 308 on the number of heavy missiles (the SS-9 and SS-18) that the Soviets could deploy. The United States also asserted that the deployment of land-mobile ICBMs would be inconsistent with the objectives of SALT. This, combined with problems in developing the SS-16 and the possibility of using its components for a medium-range system to replace the obsolescent SS-4 and SS-5, led to the cancellation of the SS-16 program. Considering these constraints, it is likely that the Soviets planned in 1972–73 to deploy 308 SS-18s, 650 SS-17s, and 480 SS-19s in the ten-year period, 1975–84. However, the treaty signed at the end of the second series of the strategic arms limitations talks (SALT II) in June 1979 imposed new limits on ICBMs. A ceiling of 820 was placed on the number of missiles whose warheads included multiple independently targeted reentry vehicles (MIRVs), and all three of the fourth-generation systems were covered by that restriction. As a result, the Soviets' production was curtailed about 600 short of the planned total and the conversion of about one hundred SS-11 silos to SS-17 and SS-19 was aborted. This meant a 40 percent cut in the planned production run. The final totals for the missiles were 308 of the heavy SS-18s, and 150 SS-17s and 360 SS-19s.

These developments reflected the logic of the doctrinal decision made in December 1966, combined with the demands of the arms control process. By early 1970 the Soviets had concluded that they only needed about 1,000 ICBMs targeted on North America, which would match the U.S. ICBM force, and they planned to deploy the fourth generation of ICBMs at 144 a year. Compare these numbers with the program in place in 1965, which could support the deployment of 336 missiles a year, for a total force of more than 3,300 in ten years. At SALT I in 1972, the Soviets accepted a ceiling of 308 heavy missiles, compared with the 480 projected in 1965 for the third-generation SS-9, and the SALT process contributed to the cancellation of the SS-16 mobile missile. At SALT II in 1979, the Soviets accepted a ceiling of 820 MIRVed missiles. This required them to limit the deployment of fourth-generation systems to less than 60 percent of the planned number and to forgo the replacement of more than 500 SS-11s.

SUBMARINE-LAUNCHED BALLISTIC MISSILES. However reliable the early warning of a missile strike and however effective the hardening of the ICBM silos, there was always the possibility that the United States would succeed in developing the means to render the land-based deterrent impotent, through greater missile accuracy, by confusing the early warning system, or in ways that had yet to be devised. As originally conceived, the solid-fuel mobile SS-13 and its successor, the SS-16, might have been able to provide the necessary insurance against the possibility that fixed-silo ICBMs could be technologically outflanked in some way. In any event, the Soviet inability to develop a land-mobile ICBM meant that they had to put the insurance force (and strategic reserve) to sea; it explains the Delta ballistic-missile submarine (SSBN) program, which was an adaptation of the Yankee hull-propulsion system.

The attraction of lower force levels as a means of reducing the nuclear devastation of Russia applied as much to submarine-launched ballistic missiles (SLBMs) as to ICBMs. But the SSBN force, besides providing insurance under the 1970s hierarchy of objectives, was also the primary component of the Soviet war-fighting arsenal and strategic reserve under the 1960s hierarchy for use in the wake of an intercontinental exchange. In this context, there was an obvious advantage in having a larger number of these missiles than one's opponent; such a margin of advantage would also go some way toward compensating for the reusable nuclear delivery capability of carrier-borne aircraft. These considerations would explain why, in 1969–70, when the construction of launch silos for land-based ICBMs was being curtailed, the construction of SSBNs was, if anything, accelerated. The end result was that SALT I codified a Soviet ceiling of 62 modern SSBNs carrying 950 missiles, compared with a U.S. ceiling of 44 SSBNs carrying 710 missiles.[6]

The SALT I ceiling was generous, but it was lower than the number of Soviet SSBNs that had been planned in 1961 for delivery in the 1968–77 period: 35 Yankee Is carrying 16 missiles, followed by 35 Yankee IIs carrying 20 missiles. To this would be added the original 10 Hotels, for a total of 80 SSBNs and 1,290 missiles by 1978. Without the SALT I agreement, the Soviets would not have had to dismantle Yankee and Hotel SSBNs to compensate for the later units of the Delta program and the Typhoons. The second phase of the SALT II agreement could have had the effect of lowering further the ceiling on Soviet SLBMs by another 100. This would not, however, have removed the Soviets' numerical advantage, since the new ceiling on MIRVed missiles would have had the effect of limiting the number of U.S. SLBMs to 450.[7]

6. At that date the Soviet Union was credited with 740 submarine-launched ballistic missiles (SLBMs) on 48 modern ballistic-missile nuclear submarines (SSBNs). The additional 210 SLBMs would require trading in SS-7s, SS-8s, or SS-N-5s.

7. By 1980 all U.S. SLBMs would be MIRVed. The planned inventory of 750 MIRVed

Strategic Defense Systems

Before 1967 the objective of ensuring the survival of the socialist system required the Soviets to give high priority to all types of defense against nuclear delivery systems, both air breathing and ballistic. A Soviet operational policy that was premised on strategic preemption and had as a minimum requirement the capability to launch on warning gave priority to the protection of centers of government and industry over the defense of ICBM fields. This pattern emerged in the 1950s and 1960s, including the deployment of a first-generation antiballistic-missile (ABM) system around Moscow.

The 1966 decision to work toward adopting the objective of avoiding the nuclear devastation of Russia introduced a new consideration. Nuclear attacks on Russia could not be physically prevented, only deterred, and the credibility of deterrence depended on the certainty that Soviet missiles, once launched, would strike North America. The absence of an effective U.S. ballistic-missile defense system was therefore of much greater importance to the Soviets than any advantage that might be gained from a partially effective ABM system for the USSR. Given the American capacity for making large technological leaps, it was therefore much more important to the Soviets to halt the development of U.S. ballistic-missile defense than to deploy a Soviet ABM system.

This conclusion apparently prevailed in Moscow by mid-1968, though only after significant debate.[8] When the SALT negotiations began in November 1969, the Soviets pressed for the maximum ABM limitation. They were even prepared to accept a complete ban. When it became clear that there would be difficulties in reaching agreement on offensive systems, the Soviets sought to restrict negotiations to ABM defense systems and favored deferring discussion of offensive systems until after the conclusion of an ABM treaty.[9] This behavior highlights the underlying shift in Soviet

---

ICBMs (550 Minuteman III and 200 MX missiles) allowed 450 MIRVed SLBMs for a ceiling of 1,200.

8. The difficulties being experienced in developing an effective ABM system would obviously have influenced the debate. Nevertheless, it was out of character for the Soviets to desist in their efforts to deploy some form of defense, however inadequate, while they persisted in trying to develop a better one. A reason other than the technical difficulties must be found for the uncharacteristic change in policy.

9. The compromise reached was the decision to work out interim limitations on offensive systems to serve as the basis for a comprehensive treaty at some future date. Meanwhile the Soviets would press for a permanent treaty to limit ABM systems.

doctrine. Previously, the Soviets had insisted on the inescapable interaction of defensive and offensive forces.

The Soviets' decision in 1968 to pursue an ABM treaty did not imply that they would cease research and development on ballistic-missile defense. The optimum military situation would be to have a certain deterrent capability backed by a fall-back defense system. In any case, the Soviets had to cover against a future shift in U.S. policy. Nevertheless, the ABM Treaty did reflect the new precedence being given to deterring nuclear strikes on Russia, over the traditional policy of "preempting" or "defending against" such strikes.

In general, the ABM Treaty reinforced the effectiveness of the Soviets' wartime deterrent. But one seemingly innocuous provision could undermine the effectiveness of the Soviet deterrent during phase II of a world war. That was the requirement that radars for early warning of ballistic attack must, in the future, be deployed on the periphery of national territory and oriented outward.

The Soviets' shift from a policy of strategic preemption to one of launch on warning, as required by the 1970s hierarchy of objectives, had underlined the importance to them of effective early-warning radars. Of itself, that was nothing new, since ballistic-missile early-warning systems (BMEWS) had always received the highest priority. What was new was that the vital importance of BMEWS was no longer limited to the onset of war and its initial stages. Under the 1970s hierarchy, early warning would be a critical factor for the whole course of the conflict.

Assuming that the Soviets defeated NATO in Europe and evicted U.S. forces from the Continent, a worse-case contingency in phase II of a world war would be for the United States to make arrangements by which it could mount an invasion of Russia through Sinkiang in northwest China. Such an offensive would outflank eastern Siberia and the Central Siberian Plateau, and the Soviet General Staff had to think in terms of being forced to give up these sparsely populated areas and concentrate on securing the industrially important West Siberian Plain. Terrain and other factors suggest that this fall-back defense perimeter would run roughly north-south, to the east of the line of the Yenisey River.

Military prudence would argue that all major facilities should be located to the west of that line, except for those that were specifically directed toward the Asian-Pacific region. And that is, indeed, the general pattern.[10]

10. *SMP, 1986,* 5th ed., pp. 23, 100, 101.

Location to the west of this defense perimeter was particularly important for the early-warning radars. Guaranteed early warning of a U.S. nuclear strike was an essential element of a deterrent posture that relied on launching the land-based ICBM force on warning of attack.

This new constraint on the location of early-warning radars emerged at about the same time as the requirement to deploy additional BMEWS to cover a new arc of threat that was opened up by the U.S. Trident SSBN program. The Polaris and Poseidon systems had lacked the range to strike at central Russia from the Pacific. However, both the projected Trident missile systems would be able to do so and would even be able to reach Moscow from those waters. As if to highlight this new arc of threat the U.S. Navy announced that a new submarine base would be built on the West Coast of the United States, specifically for Trident SSBNs.

To cover the new arc of threat, the Soviets set about building two new early-warning radars. The one at Pechora, which looks out across the Arctic toward the north and northeastern parts of the North Pacific, would also cover the Minuteman ICBM fields. The other radar was at Abalakova, near Krasnoyarsk, and would cover the north and central parts of the North Pacific.[11] The Krasnoyarsk radar lies inside the Yenisey defense perimeter. By the same token, it is also about 750 kilometers from the periphery of the Soviet Union; it is not oriented outward but looks northeast across about four thousand miles of Soviet territory. It is therefore in breach of the technical provisions of the ABM Treaty.

The Soviets may not have realized this future conflict at the time they signed the ABM Treaty. Even if they had, there was no obvious escape from their predicament. To explain why the early-warning radar had to be located west of the Yenisey would reveal the new strategic concept to their potential opponents. The Soviets therefore claimed that the early-warning radar was intended for space tracking.

Wartime Requirements—Theater Weapons

The decision to work toward adopting the objective of avoiding the nuclear devastation of Russia meant that ground and air forces in the continental TVDs had to be completely restructured. In the European theater,

---

11. The Trident threat from the Indian Ocean is covered by a radar being built near Astrakhan, which looks south. See *SMP, 1986*, pp.43–45.

the requirement was for deep disarming strikes against NATO's in-theater nuclear capability and for massive blitzkrieg operations, relying in both cases on conventional means only. In the Far East, Soviet forces had to be able to repel a Chinese offensive, again relying only on conventional weapons. Consequently, the Soviets spent most of the 1970s upgrading the conventional capability of their ground and air forces, both in respect to quality and numbers of men, weapons, and equipment.

The Soviets were therefore unresponsive to the proposals made by NATO, initially in 1968 and more formally in 1970, that the two sides should discuss mutual force reductions in the central region of Europe. This unresponsiveness occurred despite the potential political gains to be had from such negotiations.[12] However, by 1972 the restructuring of Soviet forces was well in hand, and the political dividends of agreeing to negotiate were more clearly defined. In 1973 discussions finally got under way on what was by then referred to in the West as mutual and balanced force reductions (MBFR).

The Soviets did not, however, begin to negotiate seriously at these negotiations until January 1976. They were then responding to a NATO offer in December 1975 to withdraw 90 "long-range" nuclear delivery systems (together with 1,000 nuclear warheads) if in return the Soviets would withdraw a Soviet tank corps, reduce tank strength by 1,700, and agree in principle to bring Warsaw Pact and NATO ground force manpower into balance at reduced levels.[13] Such a withdrawal of Western assets would directly support the Soviet operational objective of eliminating NATO nuclear delivery systems during the conventional phase of a war, and the Soviets therefore responded promptly to the initiative by proposing to match and extend that part of the U.S. offer.[14]

---

12. See Jane Sharp, "Are the Soviets Still Interested in Arms Control?" *World Policy Journal*, vol. 1 (Summer 1984), pp. 820–1.

13. This limited and conditional NATO offer was intended to break the deadlock at Vienna and was seen by the West as a way of trading nuclear systems for Soviet tanks. See Lothar Ruehl, *MBFR: Lessons and Problems*, Adelphi Paper 176 (London: International Institute for Strategic Studies, 1982), pp. 9, 15.

14. The 90 delivery systems included 54 F-4 Phantoms, which represented a significant proportion of this type of tactical aircraft in the area of mutual and balanced force reductions (MBFR), and 36 Pershing Is, representing one-third of the 108 deployed with U.S. forces. Ibid., p. 16. The Soviets responded to the U.S. offer within a month, after having spent almost five years refusing to discuss MBFR and the next three years stonewalling in the negotiations. They offered to trade 54 Su-7s (Fitter) aircraft and 54 SS-1cs (Scud B) missiles, and an unspecified number of surface-to-air missiles (SAM-2) to be matched by U.S. Nike-Hercules SAM systems. In all three cases, the Soviet systems were significantly less capable than the U.S. ones. Ibid, p. 19.

The Soviets could not agree to the reduction of 250,000 men that was called for by Western calculations of the NATO-Warsaw numerical balance, nor could they agree to a sizable reduction in their tank force since they needed a significant margin of superiority if they were to be able to carry out a successful blitzkrieg in the event of war. But the painless elimination of 90 NATO nuclear delivery systems was too attractive to pass up, so the Soviets decided to fudge the issue. Although Soviet negotiators had never specifically admitted that they enjoyed conventional superiority in Europe, their broader arguments had implicitly acknowledged such an advantage. Now the Soviets came up with some figures designed to demonstrate that the opposing ground forces were already in rough numerical balance, a claim that was just not credible to Western governments.

The two components of the Soviet operational concept in Europe (eliminating NATO nuclear delivery systems and pursuing conventional blitzkrieg operations) generated contradictory requirements in terms of the negotiations on mutual and balanced force reductions, and the result was a stalemate since NATO could not accept the Soviet figures. Only in 1979, by which time the restructuring of Warsaw Pact forces was largely complete, were the Soviets in a position to adopt a more constructive negotiating posture.[15] The Soviets' new approach may also have promised a possible way of extricating themselves from the problem they had created by claiming in 1976 that Warsaw Pact ground force numbers were lower than they actually were.

The MBFR negotiations illustrate Soviet priorities in the European theater. Despite the political attractions of reaching a final postwar settlement in Europe, the Soviets were not prepared to discuss the possibility of arms control until the restructuring of their forces was virtually complete, and even then they refused to negotiate seriously. Yet after eight years of stonewalling, the Soviets responded within a month to an offer from the United States to withdraw 90 nuclear delivery systems from the theater. They tendered in exchange, not the 1,700 tanks that had been specified by NATO, but 90 of their own theater nuclear systems, and they suggested further mutual cuts of this kind.

15. For the change in negotiating style see Jane Sharp, "Arms Control Strategies," in Edwina Moreton and Gerald Segal, eds., *Soviet Strategy toward Western Europe* (London: George Allen and Unwin, 1984), p. 256. Although this development coincided with the start of the Soviet diplomatic offensive against the upcoming NATO decision to deploy Pershing II and ground-launched cruise missiles (GLCMs), the unilateral commitment to withdraw 20,000 men and 1,000 tanks was a clear break with the previous negotiating stance.

Negotiations on Nuclear Weapons: 1981–83

The ABM Treaty and SALT I accord were signed by President Richard M. Nixon and General Secretary Leonid I. Brezhnev in May 1972 and endorsed by Congress that October.[16] Negotiations were under way on SALT II within a month, but it was not until June 1979, almost seven years later, that a treaty was ready to be signed. The plan was then to move on to SALT III as soon as the SALT II treaty had been ratified by the U.S. Senate. However, following the Soviet invasion of Afghanistan, President Jimmy Carter shelved the treaty, which was already in dire trouble, and the "process" petered out.

It had been intended that the scope of SALT III would be extended to include forward-based systems capable of striking Russia, and all inter-mediate-, or medium-, range nuclear forces (INF) that could be brought to bear on the European theater.[17] The Soviets had been pressing for negoti-ations on INF since May 1978, hoping to head off a NATO decision to deploy the Pershing II intermediate-range ballistic missile and the newly developed ground-launched cruise missile (GLCM). In December 1979 the NATO nations agreed to engage in such negotiations, with the under-standing that if substantial progress had not been achieved by December 1983, the deployment of new U.S. INF systems would proceed as planned.

The U.S. decision to shelve the ratification of SALT II removed SALT III as the vehicle for INF negotiations, and although Soviet and U.S. offi-cials met for informal talks on INF systems in October and November 1980, these went nowhere. Meanwhile Ronald Reagan was elected to the presidency. He represented an influential body of opinion in America that condemned the SALT accords as "fatally flawed" and a much broader con-sensus that the first priority should be to build up U.S. military strength or, as some argued, to restore U.S. superiority and only then to consider negotiating with the Soviets.

But the realities of alliance politics caused the United States to initiate talks on controlling INF in November 1981. Meanwhile the freeze move-ment had become influential enough in the United States to persuade the Reagan administration to embark in June 1982 on strategic arms reduction

16. The agreement at the first series of strategic arms limitation talks (SALT I) limiting offen-sive weapons was an interim agreement slated to last five years, and not a treaty.

17. The Soviets refer to these same systems as medium range, and both intermediate and medium range are used in this discussion according to context.

talks (START), which was a third round of the SALT negotiations in all
but name. Since the proposals advanced by the Soviets at the START negotiations reflected the priorities that have already been identified, those
negotiations are considered first, and the INF talks, which broke completely new ground, are analyzed next.

The Soviets made substantive proposals at the strategic arms reduction
talks, conforming to the approach that had been established in the SALT
negotiations and reflecting their traditional interests in arms control. The
aggregate ceiling on central strategic systems that had been agreed on at
SALT II was 2,400, reducing to 2,250 by the end of 1980. At the START
negotiations the Soviets proposed a further reduction to 1,800, which was
also the ceiling proposed by President Carter in March 1977. The Soviets
also proposed reducing the limit of MIRVed ICBMs from 820 to 680. (The
inferences that can be drawn from these proposals are discussed in appendix D, p. 516.)

These proposals would have continued to provide for the 1,000 missiles
targeted on the United States, but only if the Soviets replaced the ICBMs
that were targeted on the regions surrounding Russia with medium-range
systems that did not come within the SALT counting rules. The Soviets
would also have to reduce their existing fourth-generation systems by 138
missiles. By contrast, the proposals required no cuts by the United States
and even accommodated future plans. The ceiling of 680 MIRVed ICBMs
would allow for the existing 550 Minuteman IIIs, and the 100 MX missiles
that had been requested by President Reagan. The ceiling on bombers
armed with cruise missiles was the same as for SALT II.

The implicit ceiling on SLBMs was 20 higher than SALT II and was
apparently designed to accommodate the Delta SSBN force, with 280
single-reentry vehicles carried by the Delta I and II, and 400 MIRVed missiles in the Delta III and IV and Typhoon.[18] As was true for the ICBMs,
the Soviet proposal accommodated existing U.S. plans. At the cost of 2
ICBMs, the United States would be able to build 18 Trident SSBNs, the
same number allowed by SALT II.[19] The Soviet proposal required the dismantling of the remainder of the Yankee force, but would have preserved
the Soviet advantage in "survivable" systems, unless the United States

18. In 1982 the Soviets may have envisaged a MIRVed force of 14 Delta IIIs (224), 4 Typhoons (80), and 6 Delta IVs (96).

19. Trident carried 24 SLBMs $\times$ 18 = 432. At the second series of strategic arms limitation
talks (SALT II), with 200 MX missiles planned, the implicit SLBM ceiling was 450. By the time
of the strategic arms reduction talks (START), with only 100 MX missiles planned, the implicit
ceiling was 430.

chose to build a new class of SSBN carrying single reentry vehicle missiles.

The START negotiations provide an insight to Soviet concerns in relation to emerging U.S. programs. The Soviets apparently accepted the MX ICBM and Trident SLBM programs as part of the normal replacement and upgrading process, although they would have tried to prevent the development of the Trident II-D5 missile.[20] Cruise missiles were a different matter. Air-launched missiles had been permitted by SALT II within limits. However, the deployment of long-range ground- and sea-launched cruise missiles (SLCMs) had been banned by the protocol to the treaty, although at American insistence that protocol would only remain in force through the end of 1981. Soviet persistence in seeking to extend the ban on these missiles suggests how they assess the relative advantage in this area, given that in 1983 comparable Soviet systems were within a year or so of entering service.

Although the United States has exposed coastlines, its defense problem is simplified because detecting the missile over water is much easier than over land. It would not be difficult or terribly expensive to deploy a lookdown, shoot-down system, perhaps using dirigibles. The United States can also counter Soviet launch platforms, and Canadian territory covers the northern arc of the Soviet threat. In contrast, potentially hostile states offer emplacements for ground-launched cruise missiles around most of the Soviet Union's extended periphery. The SLCMs carried by U.S. naval units must be added to the threat. About one-third of the cruise missiles are forward deployed, frequently within striking range of Russia but shielded by friendly airspace.

Intermediate-Range Nuclear Forces

Soviet leaders were probably genuinely surprised when NATO claimed that the planned deployment of GLCMs and Pershing IIs was a direct response to the Soviet SS-20 intermediate-range ballistic missile (IRBM), which first became operational in late 1977. There seems little doubt that the Soviets had considered the SS-20 a routine, if rather belated, replace-

20. In the fall of 1982, the Soviets proposed a ceiling on large SSBNs of 4–6 units. At that date the United States had laid down or launched 6 Tridents and the Soviets 4 Typhoons. This can be explained as an attempt to get some benefit from a decision made in the second half of the 1970s to curtail the Typhoon program. See appendix B.

ment for the obsolescent SS-4 and SS-5. The Soviets saw deployment of the SS-20s as fully in accord with both the spirit and the letter of the SALT agreements.

In terms of the Soviets' military objectives, their readiness to reduce the overall number of these intermediate-range missiles emplaced in the western parts of Russia, once they recognized the linkage between the SS-20 and the deployment of the new U.S. "Euromissiles," was most interesting. The offer was first advanced by Brezhnev in October 1979, who spoke as chairman of the Defense Council.[21] It was made specific in the course of the INF negotiations, with a formal proposal in December 1982 to reduce the number of SS-20s to 162, which would match the combined inventory of British and French strategic missiles. The number was further reduced to "about 140" in October 1983.[22] An informal proposal in November would have had the effect of bringing this down another 15 missiles. Meanwhile the walk-in-the-woods formula arrived at by Ambassadors Paul Nitze and Yuli Kvitsinsky in July 1982 suggests that the Soviets were prepared to at least contemplate going well below that figure.[23] These numbers must be compared with the 600 medium-range missiles in range of Western Europe during most of the 1960s and 1970s, and the 423 in place at the end of 1983, of which 243 were SS-20s.

This readiness to make concessions is even more noteworthy because of the extreme position that the United States maintained throughout the negotiations. This was based on the so-called zero-zero option, a proposal to forgo the U.S. deployment of Pershing IIs and GLCMs in return for complete dismantling of the SS-4, SS-5, and SS-20 systems. Even in the opinion of the U.S. secretary of state, "It was absurd to expect the Soviets to dismantle an existing force of 1,100 warheads . . . in exchange for a promise from the United States not to deploy a missile force that [it] had

21. See "Further Reportage on Brezhnev Visit to GDR," Foreign Broadcast Information Service, *Daily Report: Soviet Union,* October 9, 1979, p. F4.

22. General Secretary Yuri V. Andropov made the offer on October 26, 1983, and the exact number was probably 144, since SS-20s are deployed in multiples of nine. The number of SS-20 warheads (432) would equal the number of British and French warheads as calculated by the Soviets. National Academy of Sciences, *Nuclear Arms Control: Background and Issues* (Washington, D.C.: National Academy Press, 1985), pp. 116–22.

23. The package would have imposed a common ceiling of 75 missile launchers in the European theater, where 1 GLCM launcher (carrying 4 single-warhead missiles) would equal 1 SS-20 (carrying 3 warheads); the Pershing II would have been banned. Medium-range aircraft on both sides would be limited to 150, and the British and French systems would not count. John Cartwright and Julian Critchley, *Nuclear Weapons in Europe* (Brussels: North Atlantic Assembly, 1984), p. 27.

not yet begun to build."[24] Yet the Soviet proposals went more than half way toward just that. What was it about the proposed deployment of Euromissiles that prompted the Soviet response, involving both a well-orchestrated diplomatic offensive and a readiness to make unequal military concessions?

The Soviet objective in the negotiations was explicit: to sidetrack the planned deployment of GLCMs and Pershing IIs. There was also a flood of Soviet pronouncements during the 1979–82 period that nominally spelled out the reasons why the Soviets objected to the impending INF deployment. The Soviets started from the assumption that the SS-20 was a belated replacement for Soviet missiles that had been in place for the best part of twenty years. Their diplomatic offensive against the new U. S. weapons systems hammered at three aspects of the deployment, each of which the Soviets claimed endangered détente and increased the risk of nuclear war.[25]

One, deployment would represent a qualitative escalation in the nuclear arms race and, if not matched, would dangerously upset the existing military balance, both in the European theater and in global terms. It was also part of a larger U.S. plan to regain military superiority and achieve the politico-military encirclement of the Soviet Union. Two, deployment would circumvent SALT II and, by posing a dangerous new threat to the Soviet Union, would violate the agreement reached by Carter and Brezhnev in Vienna. It was part of a general shift in U.S. military doctrine toward a preemptive counterforce capability against Soviet intercontinental systems. Three, the Euromissile deployment would provide America with the means to fight a nuclear war against Russia that would be limited to the European continent, while avoiding or at least minimizing nuclear destruction in the United States. This would allow the United States to threaten nuclear war as a means of diplomatic coercion.

The first two points, at least, had a certain validity, even if the conclusions regarding U.S. objectives were overstated. The Soviet claims con-

---

24. Alexander M. Haig, *Caveat: Realism, Reagan and Foreign Policy* (Macmillan, 1984), p. 229. Richard Allen, then the president's national security adviser, publicly derided a less sweeping version of the zero option for the same reason. Strobe Talbott, "Behind Closed Doors," *Time* (December 5, 1983), p. 19.

25. These points are based on the analyses by William V. Garner, *Soviet Threat Perceptions of NATO's Eurostrategic Missiles* (Paris: Atlantic Institute for International Affairs, 1983), pp. 11–44; and Raymond Garthoff, "The Soviet SS-20 Decision," *Survival,* vol. 25 (May-June 1983), pp. 110–14.

cerning the existing balance and the provisions on SALT were similar to criticisms of NATO policy being made in the West. Although there is little doubt that these points reflected genuine policy concerns in Moscow, in themselves they were insufficient to explain the scale and type of response that the impending deployments evoked. Clearly, the new weapons systems touched a raw nerve. While it is impossible to be certain of what lay at the core of the Soviet response, an analysis of Soviet military objectives helps to clarify the issues.

The objectives affected are likely to be those that support the military objective of not losing a world war, rather than the first-order national objective of avoiding such a war. The issue of crisis stability is not as salient in Soviet thinking about the likelihood of war as it is in the West's. It is therefore unlikely that Moscow was primarily influenced by those arguments that harked on the destabilizing effects of the Pershing II's short flight time. And while the Soviets probably did see the INF deployments as initiating a new round of the arms race, the extent to which the deployment would make armed confrontation more likely in the near future was largely in Soviet hands. Yet the Soviets chose to launch a diplomatic offensive aimed at NATO's electorates that combined intimidation with reason and sharply increased tension by playing on the electorates' fear of war.

In respect to not losing a world war, the key supporting objectives are evicting NATO from Europe while avoiding the nuclear devastation of Russia. Some indication of how the Soviets see the achievement of these objectives being threatened by the NATO deployment can be inferred from their arms control proposals. These must reflect to some extent how the Soviets perceive the calculus of the benefits that their own INF systems would yield compared with the costs that NATO systems could impose. In 1976 the Soviets had been ready to take up and match the U.S. offer to withdraw 56 nuclear-capable F-4 aircraft and 38 Pershing I missiles. In 1982 the Soviets' initial INF proposal was for a combined limit of 600 medium-range missiles and aircraft by the end of 1983, of which 300 to 400 would be aircraft; the aggregate ceiling would drop to 300 by the end of 1990. The ceilings would include all systems "in or intended for use" in Europe, with British and French forces counting toward U.S. totals. Between December 1982 and November 1983, the Soviets made successive offers to limit the number of SS-20s, starting at 162 and coming down to 129. The earlier walk-in-the-woods formula would have brought the aggregate ceiling down to 225, including 150 aircraft and 75 missiles, which would have allowed the United States the advantage of a four to three ratio in missile warheads.[26]

Combined with what is known about Soviet force structure and operational concepts, these proposals would seem to reflect the following Soviet considerations about the European theater. In regard to aircraft, the balance of Soviet advantage lay with excluding a nuclear capability at the level of frontal aviation (for example, the SU-24), but the Soviets would want to retain a nuclear capability for strategic aviation (for example, Backfire). In regard to missiles, the threat posed to Soviet plans by the new Euromissiles outweighed any advantage that would accrue from a substantial deployment of SS-20s; nevertheless, the Soviets could not dispense completely with the medium-range missile. The Soviets had also for a long time wanted to bring the relevant British and French systems and longer-range U.S. fighter bombers into the arms control account, including U.S. aircraft that are not permanently based on land in Europe but can be deployed to the area, either directly or aboard aircraft carriers.

The Soviets also proposed a "real zero option" that would have eliminated all (U.S., Soviet, British, and French) medium-range and tactical nuclear systems in Europe. This may only have been a negotiating ploy designed to counter the U.S. version of zero option, but it also accorded with the Soviet military interest in holding offensive operations in Europe below the nuclear threshold, as required by the 1970s hierarchy of objectives.

The Requirement for Medium-Range Missiles

The evidence of Soviet requirements for medium-range missiles is distorted because at the time of the INF negotiations the Soviets were in a process of transition from one targeting concept and related weapons system to another.[27]

About 730 medium-range ballistic missiles were deployed in the period 1958–66; the preplanned target set consisted largely of military facilities on the Eurasian continent, particularly those that could support nuclear strikes against Russia. More than 600 of these missiles were SS-4s (1,000-nautical-mile range), and it seems likely that the 100 or so SS-5s (2,000 nautical miles) that entered service was a much smaller number than had

26. National Academy of Sciences, *Nuclear Arms Control*, pp. 115, 122, 128.
27. For a detailed analysis underlying this conclusion, see appendix D.

originally been planned. About 650 of these SS-4s and SS-5s were deployed facing Europe, and the last 135 were emplaced in silos, suggesting an important subset of targets. Established practice would have been to start replacing the whole force in the late 1960s with the SS-14s and SS-15s. Development of these solid-fuel systems was not, however, successful and the force of SS-4s and SS-5s had to continue in service.

In about 1967 a review of ICBM requirements resulted in the reallocation of 360 SS-11s from the intercontinental target set to the regional one, and these were deployed in 1969–73, largely compensating for the shortfall in the original SS-5 deployments. About 60 of the force of SS-4s and SS-5s emplaced in southwestern Russia had been targeted on the U.S. Sixth Fleet in the Mediterranean, a task that was taken over by a corresponding number of these SS-11 variable-range ballistic missiles (VRBMs). Subsequently, the role of the SS-11 in the regional missile force evolved to cover those targets that could not be included in the preplanned set covered by the SS-4 and SS-5 force because the targets were relocatable. Such targets might be naval groupings, redeployed forces, airlifted or seaborne reinforcements, and extemporary or newly established bases.

When it came to replacing the medium-range missile force with fourth-generation systems in the mid-1970s, the distinction between the roles of the SS-11 VRBMs and the SS-4 and SS-5 force was perpetuated. The SS-19 VRBM replaced the SS-11 in southwestern Russia, covering relocatable targets, and the SS-20 took over the preplanned set of fixed targets.[28] That set, however, had roots in the 1959–66 period, when strategic nuclear preemption was the cornerstone of doctrine and the regional missile force had a target list of over a thousand. By the mid-1970s, that target set was no longer relevant. The December 1966 decision had led to a restructuring of objectives and reshaping of operational concepts that changed the nature of the requirement for medium-range missiles.

Apparently, this change only came into focus during the 1976–77 defense review, which evaluated the effectiveness of the policies and concepts adopted during the 1967–68 decision period. A salient characteristic of the post-1975 situation was the concurrent existence of two different hierarchies of objectives. One hierarchy, which had been in existence since at least 1959, covered the contingency that an East-West conflict might escalate to global nuclear war involving an intercontinental exchange. The other hierarchy, formulated in 1967–68 and effective from about 1975, had

---

28. SALT II limits on MIRVed ICBMs meant that the SS-19 could not replace SS-11 in the eastern parts of Russia.

avoiding the nuclear devastation of Russia as its governing objective. The strategy that flowed from this objective was to avoid, if possible, the use of nuclear weapons in the European theater, but if resort to them became inevitable, the Soviets would use them in such a way as to minimize the chances of escalation to an intercontinental exchange.

This second hierarchy was the preferred one, but the Soviets had to be prepared to shift to the 1960s hierarchy, should escalation become inevitable. A logical corollary of having two separate hierarchies of objectives was to develop two separate lists of nuclear targets that would reflect these hierarchies. In other words, the determinant for inclusion in one or the other target set would be the level of nuclear conflict rather than the target's geographic relationship to Russia. Instead of separate regional and intercontinental target sets, the distinction would now be between theater warfare and global war.

The target set for theater nuclear war would cover those facilities and formations that were directly related to military operations and the conduct of war in the theater and were less likely to precipitate escalation. The targets would not include centers of government or economic resources, nor would they include the British, French, and Chinese strategic nuclear forces.

The set for global nuclear war would include all targets in North America, military, political, and economic, and those targets on the Eurasian continent that were excluded from the theater warfare target set. This arrangement would simplify command and control in war. It would also provide greater flexibility in the use of intercontinental systems in circumstances short of global nuclear war.

The theater warfare target set imposed stringent operational demands: it would mainly be composed of military targets; speed of response would be critical; and often the target's exact location or even existence would not be known beforehand. To some extent these requirements were already being addressed by the VRBMs, but those systems were adaptations and not purposely designed to fit the requirements. Furthermore, they counted as ICBMs in the SALT negotiations. Meanwhile a significant proportion of the targets covered by the SS-20 medium-range missile belonged properly to the global war set. With a few exceptions, such targets were neither time critical nor hardened and could well be covered by slow-response sea-based systems. The exceptions, including the British and French strategic nuclear facilities, did not need to be covered by medium-range missiles but could be targeted by ICBMs or some other rapid-response system.

Apparently, the requirement for a medium-range missile to cover a newly defined theater nuclear war target set emerged from the 1976–77 review.[29] The operational specifications would have been exacting. Because of the emphasis on conventional operations in Europe and the priority given to avoiding escalation, these missiles would probably be the only ones to be kept at immediate readiness to respond to the use of nuclear weapons by NATO. These systems would need to be relatively invulnerable to preemptive attack, by virtue of mobility or hardening. They would need the capacity for flexible targeting, preferably including some capability for guidance in the terminal phase. Development of such a missile was initiated, and the system was programmed to start delivery in the second half of the 1980s.

This explanation, involving a reordering of target sets to bring them into line with the restructuring of objectives that stemmed from the 1967–68 decision period, would resolve the apparent paradox of the Soviet position at the INF talks in 1982–83. In the mid-1970s the Soviets had almost 800 medium-range missiles deployed facing Europe, and after the full SS-20 deployment the Soviets would still have been left with about 420 systems (and 1,200 warheads) deployed within range.[30] Yet at the INF talks the Soviets indicated their willingness to accept a ceiling of about 135 SS-20s in range of Europe. One way of explaining this apparent contradiction is as follows.

The Soviets' decision in 1976–77 to work toward a restructured target set and to develop a medium-range missile system to meet the new requirement did not of itself mean that plans to deploy the SS-20 should be abandoned. The obsolete SS-4 and SS-5 force was more of a hindrance than a help to the post-1975 strategic plan, and there were strong operational reasons for replacing it with a system that was more responsive, accurate, and survivable. However, deployment of the SS-20 was placed in a different light when it became clear that it was being used by NATO as the primary justification for deploying Euromissiles and that the only chance of derailing Pershing IIs lay in major concessions on the number of SS-20s within range of Europe.

In mid-1979 the Soviets apparently decided to curtail the production of the SS-20 and to indicate a willingness to negotiate limits on its deploy-

29. Testing of a new generation of medium-range missile was first reported in April 1985. Michael J. Bonafield, "Successor Ruins SS-20 as a Bargaining Chip," *Washington Times,* April 10, 1985.

30. The systems would initially comprise 180 SS-11s and more than 600 SS-4s and SS-5s, and then 180 SS-19s and 243 SS-20s.

ment. The negotiating floor of about 135 would have had to cover the Soviets' minimum requirement for the new missile that was still in development. But it would also have had to allow for the existing role of the SS-20, which would remain valid for five to ten years. In this context, the 135 SS-4s and SS-5s emplaced in hardened silos may be relevant. In the 1960s the strategic concept was premised on achieving nuclear preemption, but it was always possible that the Soviets might suffer surprise attack. It is plausible that the 135 hardened launchers covered a core of vital targets whose value did not depend on successful preemption and whose destruction was critical to achieving the Soviet's broader objectives in Europe in the circumstances of global nuclear war. Key strategic targets of this type change slowly, if at all, and they may have been important in determining the Soviet negotiating floor at the INF talks. The SS-20 would have to continue covering this subset of the global war target set until alternative arrangements, particularly the necessary command, control, and communications, could be put into place.[31]

Soviet Medium-Range Aircraft

Although three quarters of the existing inventory of bombers was composed of Badgers and Blinders, which date back to the 1950s, during the INF negotiations the Soviets were clearly more concerned to protect the existing force levels and future deliveries of medium-range aircraft than to protect the number of SS-20 missiles. This is not surprising since these aircraft have a major role to play in the conventional air operation that supports the ground offensive in the Western TVD, and if war in the theater should go nuclear, they provide the means for striking at a kaleidoscopic target set.

The importance of these offensive roles has to be balanced against the threat that a corresponding number of NATO aircraft can pose to Soviet plans, but the Soviets can counter that directly by improved air defenses. The Soviets indicated that 300 to 400 aircraft would have been included in the ceiling of 600 delivery systems they proposed for the end of 1983. It seems likely that the limit of 300 delivery systems the Soviets proposed for 1990 would have included as many as 200 aircraft and possibly more.

---

31. Although the SS-20 has three warheads, their total yield (a maximum of 1.5 megatons (MTs) is less than that of the SS-4 (2 MTs) and the SS-5 (4–6 MTs).

This figure would accommodate the present production rate of medium-range aircraft.[32]

The U.S. Deployment of Intermediate-Range Nuclear Forces

How the new U.S. deployments could jeopardize Soviet plans in the event of a world war is best answered in terms of the two critical objectives. First, consider the Soviet requirement to evict NATO from Europe. The immediate effect of the new U.S. deployment was to increase the number of nuclear delivery systems that have to be targeted for conventional deep strikes at the onset of war. This would be an increase of 41 discrete targets at maximum, and in practice it could be as low as 12, and possibly less.[33] The new deployments would, however, increase the number of INF launchers available to NATO by more than half, while the number of INF warheads would increase by about one quarter.[34]

More serious, the new deployments would more than double the number of quick-reaction INF systems that were under the direct control of the U.S. commander in Europe, from just under 500 to well over 1,000.[35] Almost half of these systems would be the GLCMs, which are likely to be more accurate than manned aircraft against fixed targets. The GLCMs would allow a density of attack that would saturate Soviet air defenses, even if the latter possessed the means of countering these terrain-hugging missiles, which as yet they do not. The GLCMs would also pose a new threat to the VRBMs emplaced in southwestern Russia, moving them into the use-or-lose category of weapons. In other words, if the Soviets were unable to avoid escalation in Europe, their offensive might be halted by the increased number of intermediate-range nuclear systems, and they would then be unable to achieve their objective of evicting NATO from Europe.

32. The walk-in-the-woods formula allowed a two to one ratio of aircraft to missiles, but if the Soviets could make do with only 75 SS-20s, that would allow 225 aircraft in the 300 total. In Vienna, Brezhnev confirmed that Backfire production would not exceed 30 aircraft a year. Half of the deliveries go to the naval air force.

33. Leon V. Sigal, *Nuclear Forces in Europe: Enduring Dilemmas, Present Prospects* (Brookings, 1984), pp. 28–31.

34. These numbers do not allow for any reloads that would be deployed with the new launchers. Existing NATO capabilities are drawn from Cartwright and Critchley, *Nuclear Weapons in Europe*, p. 25; and William W. Kaufmann, "Nuclear Deterrence in Central Europe," in John D. Steinbruner and Leon V. Sigal, eds., *Alliance Security: NATO and the No-First-Use Question* (Brookings, 1983), p. 39, table 3-1.

35. The Soviets count 164 F-111s, 265 F-4s, and 63 FB-111s deployed from bases in the United States.

At first sight, this sharp increase in the long-range air threat might seem to justify the scale and style of Soviet response to NATO's proposed INF deployment, and their own proposals did imply an interest in limiting the air threat in the European theater. However, the threat of air interdiction in the Soviet rear is nothing new, and it is only in the last five to eight years that the Soviets have come near to acquiring the capability to counter this NATO capability, which was always seen in the West as compensating for Soviet strength on the ground.

Meanwhile there were reports from Geneva that Pershing II, rather than the GLCMs, concerned the Soviets. This priority of concern is supported by the walk-in-the-woods formula, by which the Soviets would have retained only 75 SS-20s, carrying 225 independently targeted warheads facing Europe, while the United States would have been able to deploy 300 GLCMs with 300 warheads, but no Pershings. To identify the roots of Soviet concern, one must focus on the Pershing II, with its long reach, short time of flight, high accuracy, and ability to destroy well-hardened targets.

The Threat from Pershing II

In the context of evicting NATO from Europe, the most demanding requirement is to carry out a conventional blitzkrieg offensive under the shadow of nuclear weapons. At the same time the capability to switch instantaneously to a nuclear mode if NATO should choose to escalate must be retained. As discussed in earlier chapters, the danger that resort to nuclear weapons could lead to intercontinental escalation led the Soviets to renounce their former doctrine of seeking to preempt in such circumstances in favor of only launching nuclear weapons on warning.

Such a doctrine had obvious dangers, but the level of risk was inversely related to the effectiveness of command, control, communications, and intelligence(C^3I). Soviet C^3I was the most seriously threatened by Pershing II. In the best of circumstances, changing from a conventional to a nuclear mode in the middle of a theaterwide offensive would mean massive problems. But if NATO's use of nuclear weapons in the combat zones was preceded by Pershing strikes on Soviet and Warsaw Pact command centers and communication nodes, the situation mght be rendered irretrievable.[36]

36. I owe this point to Matthew Evangelista.

Similar considerations would apply to the objective of avoiding the nuclear devastation of Russia. The most demanding aspect of this requirement is to deter the United States from launching an intercontinental strike in a last desperate attempt to avert the defeat of its forces in NATO. A perennial Soviet concern is that in some way the United States will develop the capability to render the Soviet deterrent force impotent, and in this respect the Soviets could perceive Pershing II as threatening Moscow and its associated C^{3}I centers. That raises the possibility of a successful decapitating strike, which could neutralize both the land-based ICBMs and the Delta SSBN force.

While this possibility exists in theory, there may have been some disagreement in Moscow on the reality of the threat, the difference of opinion being suggested by a divergence in the ranges attributed to the Pershing II. Some statements credited it with a range of about 1,500 nautical miles, which brings Moscow in reach of its bases in West Germany. Others used the official U.S. range of about 1,000 nautical miles, which covers much of western Russia, including the headquarters of the Western and Southwestern TVDs, but does not reach as far as Moscow.[37]

It is difficult to know how seriously the Soviets saw the threat of strategic decapitation at the time of the INF negotiations. One must be chary of taking their statements at face value, since they are adept at exploiting the sensitivity of the Western arms control community to developments on either side that could be seen as destabilizing. However, a persuasive case could be made that when the Pershing II IRBM was added to the MX ICBM and Trident D-5 SLBM programs, which were initiated in the wake of SALT I, an ominous pattern emerged that could be read as evidence of a U.S. plan to achieve the capability for a disarming strike. Pershing would have the critical role of paralyzing the Soviet C^{3}I system for long enough to ensure that all Soviet ICBMs were still in their silos when the U.S. MX and D-5 missiles struck home. The SSBN force would meanwhile be rendered impotent by the destruction of submarines in port and of the means of communicating with the submarines at sea.

This threat did not depend upon the United States being willing to launch a premeditated "bolt from the blue" attack. The capability could plausibly come into play in at least three types of situation, two arising

---

37. Raymond L. Garthoff noticed this discrepancy about Pershing's range in fifteen Soviet sources in the period late 1979 through early 1981. See Garthoff, "The Soviet SS-20 Decision," p. 116.

from conflict and the third involving peacetime behavior. One would stem from conventional war in Europe, with NATO forces about to go down to defeat; instead of resorting to nuclear weapons in the theater, which would expose it to continental escalation on Soviet terms, the United States might prefer to risk attempting a disarming strike. Another situation would be a Soviet-U.S. crisis confrontation that seemed irrevocably set on the road to world war, when the possibilty of a successful disarming strike might seem the lesser of various evils facing America. The peacetime threat would stem from a U.S. perception that it possessed a first-strike capability, encouraging the type of coercive behavior that would threaten the Soviet capacity for independent international action and make armed confrontation inevitable.

On the other hand, it could also be argued that, whatever the Pentagon's plans, they were still a long way from fruition. The first D-5s were not due to go to sea until 1989, and the fate of the MX program was still uncertain. Even if Pershing II was capable of carrying out a successful strategic decapitation, the United States was still a long way from acquiring the means with which to disarm the Soviet retaliatory capability.

But whatever the military threat from Pershing II, it represented the reversal of a twenty-year trend in the strategic posture of the two superpowers toward each other. After the Cuban missile crisis, partly by design and more as the result of changing circumstances, there had been a gradual drawing back on both sides from posing immediate threats to each other's forces and territories. During the 1950s and early 1960s U.S. forces had been deployed close-up to the Soviet periphery. Thereafter, there was a progressive withdrawal of strategic missiles from Britain, Italy, and Turkey, the relinquishment of SAC staging bases, the withdrawing of carrier aircraft from the initial strike, and a general slackening of the drawstrings of military containment. While the buildup and perfection of central strategic systems also took place during this period, the raw numbers had been capped by 1972 and the first steps toward reduced ceilings had been taken in 1974. Although these intercontinental systems continued to pose a mortal threat to the other side, the danger was from a distance and was held in stasis by the opposing capability.

The deployment of Pershing II was seen by the Soviets as the most threatening of a series of developments that seemed to signal the reversal of a favorable trend and a return to the confrontational posture of the 1950s when global nuclear war was seen as a real possibility.

The Strategic Defense Initiative

The unexpected announcement at the end of March 1983 of the U.S. intention to develop a multitiered ballistic-missile defense (BMD) system that would be likely to include a vital space-based component, tended to support the idea of an underlying long-term plan to hold Russia at risk. The Soviets' ingrained belief that the U.S. military-industrial complex is a powerful force in American government made it easy for them to conclude that the sudden emergence of the Strategic Defense Initiative was not accidental.

President Reagan's proposals had a direct impact on the two main Soviet objectives served by arms control. Whether or not the United States was successful in establishing a space-based BMD system, the attempt to do so would inevitably initiate a second round of the nuclear arms race just when a framework for controlling, and even disarming, the first round had been laboriously agreed on after twenty years of negotiation.

The attempt would also move the arms race into a new arena, with unforeseeable consequences. The notion that superpower competition in space would be limited to defensive weapons systems was inherently implausible. The argument that even so, military jousting in space was preferable to nuclear war on earth, relied on the most primitive genre of science fiction and ignored the more probable and cataclysmic scenarios.

Whatever the Reagan administration might suppose about the Soviet response to the Strategic Defense Initiative (SDI), Moscow could be in no doubt as to what would be involved. Obviously, the Soviets would have to follow suit, and the high expenditures required to develop and deploy such a system would require the emerging threat to be painted by both sides in ever harsher terms to ensure public acceptance of the diversion of scarce resources, which would have a serious impact on the standard of living in the Soviet Union. Since the United States could be expected to develop the relevant technology much more rapidly than the Soviet Union, the Soviets would need to develop offensive means of neutralizing or outflanking the U.S. capability. As the race took hold, and each side's weapons programs fulfilled the other side's prophesies of aggressiveness, tension would rise and the danger of war would increase.

The objective of avoiding world war would also be threatened in another more direct way. From the Soviet viewpoint the SDI could be seen as an attempt to recapture the unique advantage of territorial invulnerability that

America had enjoyed for the first sixty years of this century, an attempt admitted by the U. S. secretary of defense.[38] The Strategic Defense Initiative was just one piece of the accumulating evidence that the United States was seeking to restore the type of worldwide military preponderance that it had enjoyed for twenty-five years after World War II, including a first-strike nuclear capability.[39] Indeed, U.S. leaders were open in their belief that an American military buildup would constrain Soviet foreign policy behavior and allow the United States once more to operate from a position of strength. This situation posed a direct challenge to the Soviet capacity for independent international action, another first-order objective that is in tension with the objective of avoiding world war.

If the Strategic Defense Initiative went ahead, the adverse effect on the objective of avoiding world war would be immediate and would become increasingly pernicious as the new round of the arms race gathered momentum. The adverse effect on the objective of not losing the war was longer term, but it was also much more concrete.

Soviet sensitivity to U.S. missile defenses had been demonstrated at the end of the 1960s by the high priority they gave to concluding an ABM Treaty. The stated objective of the SDI was to develop a BMD system that would be "a thoroughly reliable defense against incoming Soviet missiles."[40] Such a system could render impotent the existing Soviet deterrent, providing the United States with the option of striking at Russia at any stage of a world war, without fear or retaliation. Even a partially effective BMD system, combined with a partial capability to achieve a disarming strike, would make it more likely that the United States would launch a nuclear attack on Russia in an attempt to avert the impending defeat of its forces in NATO.

However, the BMD aspects of the Strategic Defense Initiative were only one part of the threat implicit in these developments. Weapons designed for use in space could be adapted for use from space, for example, lasers

38. In congressional testimony on February 1, 1984, Defense Secretary Caspar Weinberger noted, "If we can get a system which is effective and which we know can render their weapons impotent, we would be back in a situation we were in, for example, when we were the only nation with nuclear weapons and we did not threaten others with it." *Hearings on Military Posture,* Department of Defense Authorization for Appropriations for Fiscal Year 1985, before the Senate Committee on Armed Services, 98 Cong. 2 sess. (GPO, 1984), pt. 1, p. 89.

39. For example, a U.S. Air Force booklet, which outlined basic doctrine, included the requirement to gain and maintain superiority in space. This requirement had been established in 1982, at the latest. Fred Hiatt, "Air Force Manual Seeks Space Superiority," *Washington Post,* January 15, 1985.

40. *Hearings on Military Posture,* pt. 1, p. 55.

against aircraft. Similarly, the underlying research programs would generate new ways of exploiting the potential of space, such as the kinetic energy of orbiting bodies. The move into space would lead to a completely new species of offensive weapons that could be directed at Soviet territory and armed forces, against which the Soviets would have to contrive new defenses.

Arms Control as a Process

A disturbing feature of President Reagan's Strategic Defense Initiative was its implications for the arms control process. To the Soviets, the negotiations were important because of their role in enabling détente. But they were also important as an ongoing diplomatic process. Arms control negotiations were the only means available to the Soviet Union of capping the arms race and effecting a reduction in the size of the U.S. strategic arsenal. Such a reduction was only likely to be achieved through a series of agreements that built up a body of accepted negotiating principles and procedures and registered the accumulating concessions from one set of negotiations to the next.

This process had finally gotten under way in 1969, and the treaty framework was codified in the "Joint Statement of Principles and Basic Guidelines for Subsequent Negotiations on the Limitation of Strategic Arms" that was agreed on by President Gerald Ford in 1974 and signed by General Secretary Leonid I. Brezhnev and President Jimmy Carter in June 1979. The first treaty to emerge from the process had been the agreement to limit ABM systems that was signed in May 1972. It was of unlimited duration, but there was a right to withdraw if a signatory decided "that extraordinary events related to the Treaty jeopardized its supreme interests."[41] The treaty allowed research and development for land-based ABM systems, but it specifically prohibited the development and testing of components for space-based systems.

The Strategic Defense Initiative thus set the United States on a path that was explicitly intended to breach these provisions of the treaty. This was not the result of some "extraordinary event," nor were the United States' "supreme interests" suddenly in jeopardy. Rather there had been a change of mood in the country and a change of fashion in strategic thought.

The ABM Treaty was the only strategic arms limitation treaty to have

41. United States Arms Control and Disarmament Agency, *Arms Control and Disarmament Agreements* (GPO, 1982), p. 142.

been ratified by the U.S. Senate and the SDI could be seen as part of a general unraveling process. For domestic political reasons the treaties on a Nuclear Threshold Test Ban (signed by Richard Nixon in July 1974) and Peaceful Nuclear Explosions (signed by Gerald Ford in May 1976) had never been submitted for ratification; in July 1982 the Reagan administration sought to renegotiate the terms of both.[42] SALT II, which had been negotiated under three presidents, two of whom had committed their signatures to the process, also remained unratified, and it had been described by the incoming president as fatally flawed. The Reagan administration had refused to commit itself in advance to abide by the terms of the treaty, which was due to expire at the end of 1985.[43]

The U.S. approach to the INF negotiations and to START reinforced the impression that the Reagan administration was not interested in arms control agreements unless they required the Soviet Union to make major, unlikely concessions. In the opinion of Secretary of State Alexander Haig, the so-called "zero option" proposed by the United States at INF negotiations raised the suspicion that the United States "was disingenuously engaging in arms control negotiations simply as a cover for a desire to build up its nuclear arsenal." Richard Burt, Haig's principal arms control deputy, described the purpose of the INF negotiations to be the "maximum political advantage. It is not arms control we are engaged in, it's alliance management." The U.S. START proposals conformed to this pattern and were subsequently described by Haig as a "non-negotiable package" and a "two-faced proposal." The proposals ignored the agreed-on guidelines for negotiations and required the Soviets to reduce their number of existing warheads by 60 percent and dismantle almost 70 percent of their modern MIRVed missiles. American plans would meanwhile remain unaffected.[44]

In the circumstances, why were the Soviets prepared to even embark on the START negotiations? Obviously, a Soviet readiness to negotiate would support the political campaign against the deployment of Pershing IIs and

42. Judith Miller, "U.S. Confirms a Plan to Halt Talks on a Nuclear Test Ban" and "U.S. Said to Decide Against New Talks to Ban All A- Tests," *New York Times*, July 21 and 20, 1982.

43. The SALT II limits would not affect the United States until late 1985, when the seventh Trident SSBN was due to start sea trials. This would take the United States past the ceiling of 1,200 MIRVed missiles.

44. Haig, *Caveat*, p. 229; Talbott, "Behind Closed Doors," p. 19; Alexander Haig, who was then secretary of state, later described the U.S. START proposals as a "non-negotiable package . . .[the United States] came up with a two-faced proposal which was clearly going to fall of its own weight and did." Roy Gutman, "Bad Tidings: The World According to Haig," *Newsday*, August 12, 1984. See also Haig, *Caveat* p. 223; and National Academy of Sciences, *Nuclear Arms Control*, pp. 74–75.

GLCMs. More directly, the Soviets believed that their best hope for checking the threatened arms race was American domestic pressure. If that pressure was not to be undermined, Soviet readiness to negotiate in good faith was essential. But the importance attached by the Soviets to the arms control process as a means of reducing international tensions should not be underestimated. Brezhnev, in his last year of life, was hanging on desperately to the belief that East-West détente was not quite dead, and the START negotiations offered the only hope of salvaging strategic arms control in which he had invested so much political capital.

The abortive negotiations on INF and START suggest that if the immediate objective is sufficiently important, the Soviets will enter negotiations, even when faced by U.S. disinterest and the likelihood that failure will rebound to their disadvantage. Derailing the deployment of Pershing II was such an objective. The far-reaching implications of the Strategic Defense Initiative places it in the same category.

The Soviet Approach to Arms Control

The preceding analysis allows various conclusions to be drawn about the Soviet approach to arms control. The underlying objectives of avoiding war, while preserving the capacity to fight one if necessary, can be traced back to early Soviet history, but the 1967–68 period was a watershed in Soviet arms control policy. Analyses that lean heavily on the uniformity of Russian arms control behavior during the first fifty years of the Soviet state may catch the style of Soviet negotiations, but they miss the fundamental change in substance.

One must distinguish between strategy and tactics in arms control policy. The tactics of Soviet arms control are not that different from those of the United States. Over the years, the Soviets have made arms control proposals that were designed to halt or sidetrack military developments that were unfavorable to their interests, such as the rearming of Germany in the 1950s, the deployment of neutron warheads in the 1970s, or the introduction of new weapons like the long-range cruise missile. Similarly, once they are embarked on the negotiating process, the Soviets are skillful in pursuing relative advantage: capping Western capabilities and fencing off dangerous new developments whenever possible while seeking to protect their own programs and the possibilities for future development. The two sides' negotiating styles may be different, but the nature of their tactical objectives is similar.

The Soviet Union and the United States do differ in their strategic approaches. The reasons for this include the different origins and intellectual location of their theorizing about nuclear weapons and arms control and the fact that the two sides are pursuing different kinds of objectives. Furthermore, the Soviet Union has persisted in the traditional approach to arms limitation, while the United States introduced novel criteria for arms control in response to the new challenge of nuclear weapons.

The Implications of Nuclear Weapons

For the Soviets, the advent of nuclear weapons did not represent a clear break with past experience. The western parts of Russia had been laid waste by war before the atom bomb was ever used, and the devastating effect of aerial bombardment had been demonstrated throughout Europe and Japan. For at least the first half of the 1950s, the Soviets faced the possibilty of a "preventive" air attack by the United States. Nuclear weapons therefore came within the purview of established military doctrine, and the Soviet approach to the problem has been evolutionary. Even their responses to the radical change in military affairs that was brought about by the marriage of nuclear weapons and ballistic missiles was evolutionary.

In contrast, the American approach was revolutionary. The idea that American territory could be laid waste in a foreign war was something completely new and became a live possibility only at the end of the 1950s. The U.S. approach was also revolutionary in that theorizing on the implications and use of nuclear weapons became the preserve of a new breed of academic strategist—one who reasoned from first principles and used game theory and axiomatic logic. The end product was nuclear deterrence theory.

To oversimplify, deterrence theory focused on how to prevent Soviet aggression by threatening to inflict unacceptable punishment on the Soviet homeland, a problem that dominated Western strategic theorizing during most of the 1950s. A credible deterrent depended on the certainty of U.S. retribution, and toward the end of the decade, as the Soviets began to acquire the capability to strike directly at the United States, American attention turned to guarding against the danger of a premeditated disarming strike, of the kind attempted by the Japanese at Pearl Harbor.

The emerging Soviet capability also directed attention to a new danger that stemmed from the nature of nuclear weapons and did not depend on aggressive intentions. In a confrontational situation, the advantage of getting in the first blow with nuclear weapons was so great that a prudent national leader might be prompted to launch a nuclear strike on the mere suspicion that the other side was contemplating war. This inherent pressure to preempt in a crisis introduced a new concern for the "stability" of the emerging strategic balance. The simple requirement that Soviet aggression be deterred came, for some, to be qualified by the somewhat contradictory requirement that Russia be reassured that the United States would not initiate preemptive nuclear war.

The Source of Arms Control Policy

The U.S. arms control establishment had its intellectual origins in the recognition of the need for mutual reassurance, but it also accepted the tenets of deterrence theory. Thus strategic stability was to be achieved by both sides having an assured "second strike" (or, more properly, strike second) capability, which would ensure that enough weapons could survive a first strike to be able to inflict unacceptable damage on the initiator. The "deterrers" and the "reassurers" both thought in terms of guarding against a surprise Soviet attack, although they disagreed over what was most likely to prompt it: aggressive urge or reciprocal fear. Thus a primary impulse of U.S. arms control policy has been to cover the danger of sudden attack, whether it be a bolt from the blue during Thanksgiving dinner or a preemptive strike in the course of a crisis.

Western deterrence theory grew out of the U.S. atomic monopoly and the overwhelming preponderance of U.S. nuclear delivery systems during the 1950s; reassurance theory emerged in response to the erosion of that monopoly. In contrast, the Soviets lacked the capability to deliver nuclear weapons against the United States for ten to fifteen years after World War II. Deterrence of Western attacks on Russia had therefore to rely on the traditional method of possessing the demonstrated capability to absorb any such attack and then go on to repulse the aggressor and win the war.

By the early 1960s, when the Soviets were beginning to acquire the capability to strike directly at the United States, they had largely discounted the threat of a premeditated Western attack. The more serious danger was now seen as inadvertent war, something that could not be deterred; it could only be avoided. If war should prove unavoidable, then Soviet strategy was predicated on a successful preemptive strike against the

United States. Within such a doctrine there was no place for the ratiocinations of Western deterrence and reassurance theories. In any case, the Soviets were not persuaded by U.S. claims for the benevolence of deterrence, and their attention was caught by U.S. weapons programs, which seemed to argue otherwise.

The Soviet Interest in Arms Control

Before the 1967–68 period, the Soviet Union had a limited interest in arms control. It favored treaties that fenced off various areas from competition, such as Antarctica and outer space, and constrained developments such as the proliferation of nuclear weapons. The Soviets had also consistently promoted treaties banning the testing of nuclear charges, which would prevent the development of French and Chinese weapons, as well as constraining the further development of U.S. strategic and theater systems. But in most aspects of military capability, the Soviet Union lagged behind the United States. Its primary objective was to draw level and, if possible, to move ahead.

These priorities changed radically after the doctrinal shift in December 1966 about the likely nature of a world war and the consequential restructuring of strategic objectives. Initially, the change only affected intercontinental systems and strategic defense, but the evidence of a vital new interest in nuclear arms control was impressive. Most strikingly, long-established policy regarding the need for ABMs was reversed. The requirement for ICBMs was sharply reduced to produce a force that would match the number of U.S. missiles, and annual production was cut by almost 60 percent. Then, in the course of the SALT negotiations, the Soviets accepted a cap on "heavy" ICBMs that was probably 40 percent less than they had originally planned. In 1979 they curtailed the deployment of fourth-generation missiles at less than 60 percent of what is likely to have been intially intended.

These cuts, which affected current Soviet production and deployment, were unilateral and involved no concessions on the U.S. side, except for a limited agreement on "counting rules," which continued to favor the West. The United States accepted no constraints on the two main new types of program it was developing: the MIRVing of ballistic-missile warheads during SALT I; and long-range cruise missiles during SALT II. Neither agreement had any effect on existing U.S. plans for modernization, and the first time that the limits would bite would be in 1985; the U.S. Navy would then have to deactivate a twenty-year-old sixteen-tube Poseidon SSBN to allow a twenty-four-tube Trident SSBN to enter service.

The Soviets' interest in nuclear arms control did not diminish in the 1980s, and they impressed their readiness for negotiations on the Reagan administration.[45] When the INF talks finally got under way, the Soviets were prepared to make concessions of a kind that had been dismissed as unthinkable by the president's national security adviser and by the secretary of state. Similarly, at the START negotiations, the Soviets offered to make substantial cuts in the ceilings agreed on at SALT II, leaving totals that would require the Soviet Union to reduce its existing inventory of ICBMs, while permitting planned U.S. programs.

Soviet behavior since 1968 has conformed to the logic of the doctrinal decision in December 1966. In the 1967–68 period, the Soviets engaged in a major internal debate about strategic arms control, whether such arms control would promote Soviet interests and, if so, how this could best be achieved. Once the question was decided in the affirmative, Soviet policy swung into line, and since 1968, a basic tenet of Soviet foreign and defense policy has been that nuclear arms control is clearly in the best interests of the Soviet Union.

In contrast to these clear-cut Soviet positions, the U.S. interest in arms control has been ambivalent. From the earliest arguments concerning the use of the atomic bomb in 1945, the American body politic has been afflicted by deep divisions and contrary impulses about the desirability of arms control rather than military superiority. Despite lip service to the idea that defense programs and arms control should work together to advance U.S. security, the reality has been very different.[46] This ambivalence has impaired the coherence and consistency of U.S. arms control policy over the years. Even with administrations that were mainly predisposed to seek agreement with the Soviets on arms control, divisions in the body politic constrained the possibilities for wide-ranging negotiations. While the Soviets were tough negotiators, it became a truism that the most difficult negotiations on arms control took place back in Washington. In the 1980s, with a U.S. administration that distrusted arms control, there was sufficient

45. Former Secretary of State Alexander Haig notes, "The Soviets were eager to enter into arms control talks with the United States. Dobrynin raised the subject in his first talk with me [in January 1981] and never failed to mention it in subsequent encounters. The Soviets were willing to talk on almost any basis." Haig, *Caveat*, p. 228.

46. This conclusion draws on the Council on Foreign Relations book by Michael Krepon, *Strategic Stalemate: Nuclear Weapons and Arms Control in American Politics* (St. Martin's Press, 1984), particularly pp. 1–2, 108–20.

political support to bring the process, in effect, to a halt. In the American body politic the doubts over its value steadily increased through the 1970s. The spectrum of American views on arms control has been characterized as comprising opposing camps of arms control strategists and nuclear weapons strategists. While the ideologically minded wings of the two camps were never able to communicate with each other, the pragmatic policy-oriented wings had been able to work together. These pragmatic wings were the same as the "reassurers" and "deterrers" referred to earlier, and the amalgam of these two viewpoints formed the basis of U.S. arms control policy through the 1960s. But as America gradually lost the clear nuclear preeminence it had long enjoyed, so did this political center steadily erode. The nuclear weapon strategists became increasingly influential and, within that camp, the ideological wing became increasingly important. Arms control negotiations came to be seen, increasingly, in zero-sum terms: not as a cooperative endeavor with the Soviet Union and an end in itself, but as a contest in which one side wins at the expense of the other.[47]

The Objectives of Arms Control

U.S. ambivalence over arms control has meant that American policy has lacked consistent and clearly defined objectives. The inconsistencies were amplified during SALT I by Henry Kissinger and Richard Nixon's disinterest in the negotiations as a means of limiting the arms race, and "their view of SALT as simply one key piece on the political chess board."[48] The inconsistencies steadily increased during SALT II, as the arms control and nuclear weapons strategists drew further apart. By the time of the START negotiations and the INF talks, the clear purpose of the negotiations was to placate domestic and allied opinion rather than to reach agreement on reducing the level of armaments.

However, despite the ambivalence of U.S. arms control policy, the underlying U.S. arms control theory did have a coherent set of objectives. Criteria were derived from these objectives and were then used to judge Soviet weapons programs and arms control proposals. Because of differences in how the two sides see the purposes of arms control, this has led to misunderstanding. Furthermore, the official U.S. approach to the prob-

47. Ibid.
48. Raymond L. Garthoff, *Détente and Confrontation: American-Soviet Relations from Nixon to Reagan* (Brookings, 1985), p. 149.

lem is theoretical and technical. The Soviet approach is more traditional and practical and is based on both political and military considerations.

THE DANGER OF WAR.   Both sides see avoidance of world war as a primary objective, but there is a significant difference in the level of concern about the likelihood of such a war and the type of response that danger evokes. There is an implicit assumption in the American body politic that world war is only likely to come about through some Soviet initiative that has to be countered by the West, leading to conflict. It is also assumed that the way to prevent such Soviet initiatives is to make certain that the Soviet Union is aware of the scale and certainty of the U.S. response. This reflects the lessons of Munich and World War II. The more certain and more comprehensive the retribution, the less likely the war. This thinking formed the essence of nuclear deterrence theory as it emerged in the 1950s, and it continues to undergird Western defense policy.

The United States sees war as something that can be prevented by the threat of dire punishment. In contrast, the Soviets emphasize the need to avert war by political means.[49] This more traditional approach to the problem is informed by the experience of World War I and Sarajevo. It reflects the belief that war is most likely to come about from a chain of events that become uncontrollable. The Soviets' view is inherently less sanguine than the American one, and the distinction is reflected in their different approaches to arms control.

The Soviets do not share the United States' confidence in being able to manage events, and they see the danger of war as related to the level of East-West tension. Arms racing is a source of tension and is therefore inherently dangerous, as well as costly in economic terms. Arms control negotiations can therefore serve a useful political purpose. Moreover, arms control agreements are intrinsically valuable, even though their impact on the weapons equation may be limited.

Many Americans are ambivalent about arms racing and do not see it as inherently dangerous. For the arms control strategist, only some kinds of racing are destabilizing and hence undesirable. For the nuclear weapons strategist, qualitative arms racing is a way to preserve the U.S. advantage by exploiting America's technological capability. Theorists in general point to the lack of conclusive evidence that arms racing leads to war. Instead, they focus on the danger of sudden attack. The U.S. emphasis on sudden attack distinguishes the two sides' approach to arms control most sharply.

49. See Garthoff, "BMD and East-West Relations," p. 308.

THE CONCEPT OF STABILITY. Emphasis on the danger of sudden attack focuses U.S. attention on the stability of deterrence. For the reassurers, this requires that both sides should have the capability to ride out an attack on their retaliatory forces and still have the capacity to inflict unacceptable punishment. The deterrers originally had a more modest definition of such "assured response," namely, the capacity to launch on warning or even under attack, but they gladly adopted the reassurers' more demanding requirements. In due course the improved accuracy of Soviet fourth-generation ICBMs provided two new reasons to worry about the stability of deterrence.

Given the inadequacies of Soviet third-generation missiles, it was to be expected that there would be improvements in the accuracy of the fourth generation, conforming to the normal Soviet practice of product improvement. However, in Western strategic theory, greater accuracy implied a readiness to attack hardened targets such as U.S. Minuteman silos. In conjunction with improvements in Soviet theater weapons during the 1970s and combined with outdated evidence of Soviet military thinking in the 1960s (which failed to take account of the December 1966 watershed), the case was made that the Soviets believed victory to be possible in nuclear war and were actively preparing to achieve such a victory, should a war occur.[50] Western strategic theory decreed that in such circumstances only a comparable capability would deter the Soviets from initiating such a war, and this was a major rationale for Presidential Directive 59 in July 1980.

The other new reasons for Americans to worry about the stability of deterrence concerned the vulnerability of the U.S. ICBM force. Nuclear weapons strategists argued that the Western deterrent position was being undermined because the Soviets were acquiring the capability to disarm the U.S. Minuteman force by using only a proportion of their own ICBMs. Some claimed that the capability was already embodied in Soviet fourth-generation MIRVed systems, and it was widely accepted that the fifth generation of ICBMs would provide such a capability. The Soviets could therefore deprive the United States of its "prompt hard-target kill capability," namely, the means of attacking the remaining Soviet ICBMs.[51] According to the nuclear weapons strategists, this vulnerability meant that the president would be unwilling to retaliate by striking at Soviet cities, knowing that U.S. cities would be struck in return. The ideological wing went

50. Leon Sloss and Marc Dean Millot, "U.S. Nuclear Strategy in Evolution," *Strategic Review*, vol. 12 (Winter 1984), p. 24.
51. The U.S. SSBN force would not acquire a hard-target kill capability until the D-5 system went to sea in the 1990s.

on to argue that the deterrence of Soviet attack was being undermined and was making America vulnerable to Soviet nuclear blackmail.

For the U.S. policymakers, arms control has been largely about fine tuning the stability of deterrence, which is defined in technical and theoretical terms. The Soviets do not share this concern and are skeptical of the underlying reasoning.[52] In part, the Soviets feel this way because U.S. practice has not always followed theory, and the criteria for stability have been prone to change. For example, the United States ignored the destabilizing potential of MIRV until the Soviets acquired the capability. The United States also reversed itself several times on the merits of mobile land-based systems and is now ambivalent on the issue.[53] However, the Soviets' perception of the sources of war and their very different strategic experience are most important.

A major reason for the Soviet shift in doctrine in December 1966 was the conclusion that, given the size and diversity of the U.S. arsenal, strategic nuclear preemption could no longer yield any meaningful military benefit and would certainly ensure the nuclear devastation of Russia. As the number of nuclear warheads continued to grow, the logic of this argument became harder to refute. Having trodden that path themselves, the Soviets concluded that the "pressure to preempt," which underlay the American concern about crisis stability, was a theoretical construct that had no practical relevance to a situation of massive nuclear inventories and diversified delivery systems.

Similar considerations argued against the possibility of a successful bolt-from-the-blue attack by either superpower on the other, a threat that, in any event, the Soviets had largely discounted by the end of the 1950s on the basis of their political analysis. Nor were the Soviets persuaded by the newest concern of the U.S. arms control strategists, namely, that the process of bringing strategic forces to alert in a crisis could acquire its own momentum and lead to a nuclear exchange.

This is not because the Soviets are insensitive to the inherent risks in a situation in which, as Andrey Gromyko noted in July 1969, certain aspects of decisionmaking are delegated to a computer.[54] Rather the Soviets differ

52. A systematic survey of Soviet writings relevant to doctrine for theater nuclear war found no evidence of interest in "the stability of deterrence" or "destabilizing actions." Robert O. Weinlander and others, *The Soviet Navy Declaratory Doctrine for Theater Nuclear Welfare*, Defense Nuclear Agency, Report 4434T (Washington, D.C.: BDM Corporation, 1977), p. 21.

53. Although theory favored the SSBN as a secure second-strike capability, drawing down the Soviet SSBN force has long been a high-priority mission of the U.S. Navy, even when that mission dropped from public discussion during the 1970s, and during the SALT negotiations the United States would not address Soviet concerns over antisubmarine warfare.

54. Gromyko was addressing the Supreme Soviet about Soviet foreign policy and the impor-

with Westerners on the nature of the problem. The central problem is not how to ensure crisis stability, but how to prevent crisis situations that are inherently uncontrollable from arising. Furthermore, the unintentional use of nuclear weapons in a crisis is a lesser danger than their threatened or actual use to shape the outcome. In the Soviet view, the U.S. emphasis on crisis stability is misplaced, and priority should be given to the broader concept of strategic stability, defined in terms of balance and the absence of military advantage.[55] The primary requirement is not to be able to control crises but to devise ways of averting them. Hence the importance attached to the arms control process as a means of relaxing international tensions.

THE SIZE OF OFFENSIVE FORCES. Differing perceptions about the danger of war and the concept of stability have led to differing strategic requirements and different types of pressure on force levels. Both deterrence theory and reassurance theory provide upward pressure on U.S. force requirements. Concern for the credibility of deterrence provides arguments for more, different, or better offensive weapons systems. The reassurers' requirement to be able to ride out an attack links the forces of the two sides in an upward spiral. Both theories provide justification for those who seek to restore U.S. strategic superiority. In other words, the theoretical bases of both wings of the nuclear weapons strategists and of the pragmatic wing of the arms control strategists combine to produce upward pressure. The ideological wing of the arms control strategists is a source of downward pressure, but they have little influence on policy. The primary constraint on U.S. force levels is therefore budgetary.

During the 1950s and 1960s, the primary impulse of Soviet theory on their strategic force requirements was likewise upward. The number of warheads needed to achieve the area devastation of North America was finite, but the hardening of U.S. military targets and the proliferation of unhardened targets outside such areas meant that the requirement for additional warheads steadily increased. Meanwhile the Soviet doctrine of qualitative military superiority implied the upward spiral of an arms race.

The doctrinal shift in December 1966 and the logic of the 1970s hierarchy reversed this situation and introduced a downward pressure on Soviet strategic force levels. The primary purpose of Soviet intercontinental mis-

---

tance of beginning SALT. See Coit D. Blacker and Gloria Duffy, eds., *International Arms Control: Issues and Agreements* (Stanford University Press, 1984), p. 243.

55. These points about the unintended use of nuclear weapons and crisis stability were made at a seminar in Moscow in mid-1984. Information from Ambassador Jonathan Dean, who was a participant.

siles was no longer to destroy the capitalist system, but to deter the United States, in the event of war, from launching a nuclear strike on the Soviet Union when faced by the defeat of U.S. forces in Europe. Should this wartime deterrent prove ineffective, then the smaller the size of the U.S. intercontinental inventory, the less extensive the nuclear destruction of Russia. In the context of the 1970s hierarchy, the lower limit on Soviet intercontinental systems is therefore determined by the level of destruction that would be needed to dissuade Washington from striking at Russia in such circumstances.

Soviet force planners have to allow that wartime deterrence may fail and that the political leader would then revert to a modified form of the 1960s hierarchy of objectives. Although the force planners have to cover this contingency, they do not have to meet the same requirements for intercontinental delivery systems that existed in the 1960s. First, intercontinental nuclear preemption is no longer the Soviets' central strategic concept. Second, the 1970s objective of avoiding the nuclear devastation of Russia has precedence in determining force levels. This precedence would have been reinforced in 1981 by formal acknowledgement that victory in nuclear war was impossible. This acknowledgement implies that low priority will be given to weapons that are primarily intended for use in the post-exchange phase of a global nuclear war, which is the focus of the 1960s hierarchy of objectives.

Given these general considerations and considering the way that Soviet missile programs were curtailed in response to arms control negotiations, it seems likely that Soviet requirements for strategic nuclear forces are primarily determined by politico-military considerations rather than by the type of force exchange calculations that underlie U.S. strategic requirements. The logic of the 1970s hierarchy argues that, as long as the Soviets can maintain a rough strategic equivalence with the West, the lower the level of nuclear inventories the better.

In regard to military operations in Europe, there is no minimum essential target set that has to be covered by nuclear weapons. By the mid-1970s, the Soviets had concluded that their own resort to nuclear weapons would hinder rather than help a blitzkrieg offensive in Europe. The Soviets are concerned that resort to nuclear weapons in the theater by either side would likely escalate to an intercontinental exchange. It follows that the Soviets would see the denuclearization of Europe as being in their interest. But so would lesser measures, such as the mutual withdrawal of all medium-range nuclear systems. These would not necessarily have to include the British and French strategic nuclear forces. Despite some of the things they have said, it seems likely that the Soviets do not see these forces as part of the theater-war problem, but as part of the more challenging requirement to avoid escalation to global nuclear war.

The Soviets hope to avoid escalation to global nuclear war by deterring the United States from striking at Russia. There is, of course, no way of knowing what threatened level of destruction would be required to dissuade Washington from intercontinental escalation if faced by the defeat of NATO in Europe. Common sense suggests that if the president could not be deterred from such action by the prospect of losing America's twenty largest cities, then the threat of destroying two or three hundred is unlikely to be more effective. The actual numbers are not important. The point is that such wartime deterrence would either work at a fairly low level of threatened devastation, or it would not work at all.

This minimum essential requirement for intercontinental systems is not immediately relevant since the factor that currently determines the minimum size of the Soviet force is the need to match the U.S. capability, as was demonstrated in the Soviet START proposals. The requirement has both political and military dimensions. The Soviets believe that their achieving rough strategic equivalence underlay various favorable political developments in the late 1960s and much of the 1970s. The impending military parity of the Soviets persuaded the United States to negotiate on arms control and to treat the Soviet Union somewhat as an equal in international relations. Without strategic equivalence, the United States would again be able to negotiate "from a position of strength."

The Soviet military requirement to match the U.S. capability relates to the contingency of world war. In the 1970s hierarchy of objectives, Soviet medium-range systems have a role in deterring NATO escalation in the theater, as well as a war-fighting role. The intercontinental systems are relevant to the 1960s hierarchy and to global nuclear war. Despite the Soviet belief that there can be no winners in such a war, they are not prepared to allow the United States an advantage in weapons that might allow it to dictate the outcome.

Thus the interaction of two different forces determines the size and shape of the Soviets' strategic weapons inventory: the constraining force of arms control and the maximizing force of the Soviet war-fighting requirement. Under the constraining force of arms control the Soviets accept restrictions on their own capability, as a way of limiting the American capability, among other objectives. Under the maximizing force of the war-fighting requirement, the Soviets seek to embody the most effective military capability within the restrictions of the arms control agreements.

Recognition that two different forces are at work is important when seeking to draw inferences from the physical characteristics of the Soviet ICBM force. It is argued, for example, that the size of the SS-18 missile and the number and accuracy of its MIRVs indicate that it has a counterforce mission. This is taken to demonstrate that the Soviets plan strategic preemption, using only a proportion of their ICBMs to disarm the Minuteman force. The argument is circular and ignores the substantial evidence that the Soviets have discarded the concept of strategic preemption, both because of its escalatory potential and its military impracticality.

Since the first half of the 1970s the primary mission of the Soviet ICBM force has been wartime deterrence. According to Western theory, to be credible, such a force has to be capable of inflicting unacceptable punishment on the United States, even after the force has been subjected to a first strike. Given the steadily increasing accuracy of U.S. missiles, both land- and sea-based, and given that the number of ICBMs was limited by SALT I and could be expected to drop further, the best way of meeting this deterrent requirement was to build missiles with heavy payloads carrying a large number of MIRVs. This would maximize the striking power of those ICBMs that did survive the U.S. first strike, thus improving credibility as well as meeting the war-fighting requirement, should deterrence fail.

Of course, the Soviets probably decided the basic parameters of the SS-18 (but not its MIRV load) in the mid-1960s, and its large size was originally specified to support the 1960s hierarchy of objectives. But that says nothing about its mode of employment under the 1970s hierarchy for which one must turn to later evidence, such as the SALT II negotiations in 1977–78. The priority given by the Soviets to preventing U.S. development of the MX over allowing the development of their own SS-24, both MIRVed missiles, argues against the thesis that the Soviet ICBM force has an offensive, damage-limiting mission and a preemptive strategy.

PARITY OR SUPERIORITY.   Strategic parity does not sit well with the American people. Having achieved strategic superiority during World War II, it was understandable that the United States should seek to preserve that advantage. Although President Nixon, in effect, accepted the concept of parity in 1969, he had campaigned on the promise to restore clear-cut military superiority. During the 1970s there was tenacious resistance to the idea of sufficiency, parity, or equivalence among the nuclear weapons strategists, and in the 1980s the Reagan administration explicitly sought to regain some measure of superiority. These deep-seated attitudes have been reflected in U.S. arms control policy. From the time of the Baruch Plan, arms control negotiations have been used, in practice if not in theory, as a way of capping and, if possible, reducing Soviet inventories in areas in which they were catching up or moving ahead. Meanwhile the United States excluded other areas in which assymetries in force structure or advanced technology would allow the United States to retain an advantage. The SDI is only the latest variation on this theme.

The Soviets have sought to use arms control as a way of denying the United States strategic superiority. There are, however, limits to this approach. Experience since World War II has shown that the United States will not accept limits on weapons systems that give it a unique advantage. For example, the United States resisted negotiating on MIRVed warheads and long-range cruise missiles. So far, space-based defense systems have been another example. In the past, in order to persuade the United States to negotiate limits on such systems, the Soviets have had to develop a matching capability. The Soviets themselves no longer have a requirement for strategic superiority in a world war as a result of the doctrinal decision in December 1966. The theoretical basis for accepting strategic parity rather than superiority as an objective was reinforced by practical considerations. If the United States had been unable to retain its advantage over the technologically backward Soviet Union, what chance did the Soviet Union have of achieving superiority over the United States?

ALTERNATIVES TO NEGOTIATION. A final difference between the two sides is that Soviet objectives provide no alternative to negotiations, but U.S. objectives do. The Soviet objectives of reducing the size of the U.S. strategic arsenal and preventing the development of ballistic-missile defenses can only be achieved through successful negotiations leading to agreements. The U.S. objectives of ensuring the stability of deterrence can be achieved either through arms control or through new weapons programs and innovative basing modes.

Negotiations and Compromise

The record shows that, since 1968–69, the Soviets have been ready to make significant adjustments to their strategic weapons programs in the interests of reaching agreement on arms control. Their own proposals, while few, have on balance been reasonable. They have generally accommodated existing U.S. capabilities, allowed for projected programs, and incorporated the substance of earlier U.S. proposals, thereby maximizing the chances of agreement. Yet the impression persists that the Soviets are not really interested in arms control and are unwilling to compromise. The reasons for this impression go beyond Western preconceptions.

One is the Soviet emphasis on consistency and incrementalism in the negotiating process. The United States is prone to sudden and sweeping initiatives, and the instinctive Soviet reaction is to resist them, particularly if they are introduced with public fanfare. Another is the lack of openness. American negotiating objectives are discussed in the press. The Soviets, while ready to declaim on their objective of avoiding world war, are chary of disclosing those military objectives that come under the rubric of not losing such a war.

The picture is further confused by the Soviet use of arguments from Western arms control theory to advance a case whose military rationale is quite different from that of the West. Then there is the Soviet approach to weapons procurement, in which they seek to compensate for their technological deficiencies by a process of product improvement. The policy of successively replacing whole generations of missiles until qualitative improvements draw abreast the U.S. capability creates a misleading impression of developmental dynamism that seems to belie the professed Soviet interest in limiting weapons inventories. However, the main reason for Western misunderstanding is a failure to grasp the nature of Soviet negotiating objectives.

Soviet arms control policy is largely shaped by the politico-military objective of avoiding world war and by the military-technical objective of not losing such a war. The details of arms control agreements are mainly important at the military-technical level, where specific provisions can improve or impair the Soviet capability to achieve the objectives that are necessary not to lose a world war. For example, limitations on nuclear forces can work to improve the chances of avoiding the nuclear devastation of Russia. The ABM Treaty has enhanced the credibility of the Soviets' wartime deterrent, and should deterrence fail, the smaller the size of the U.S. nuclear inventory, the less the devastation of Russia. Meanwhile the denuclearization of Europe would remove the first rung of the ladder of escalation. Conversely, limitations on conventional forces could prevent the Soviets from defeating NATO and evicting U.S. forces from Europe.

Soviet obduracy and dissembling on specific issues can be traced to objectives at this level. The unproductive nature of the negotiations on mutual and balanced force reductions during the 1970s reflected the Soviet requirement to restructure their forces for a conventional blitzkrieg in Europe in the event of war being unavoidable; until that had been achieved they could not afford to negotiate mutual limitations. The construction of an early-warning radar near Krasnoyarsk, which appears to breach the ABM Treaty, probably reflected the prudential military requirement that such radars be located inside the Yenisey defense perimeter. The response to the Strategic Defense Initiative reflects, in part, the threat it could pose to the credibility of the Soviet wartime deterrent. These issues are seen as strategic imperatives that warrant this type of response.

On other issues, such as reducing the number of ICBMs, military-technical objectives can justify unilateral concessions, at least in theory. For example, it can be argued that the primary military purpose of the Soviet ICBM force is to deter America from striking at Russia when faced by the defeat of U.S. forces in Europe; such deterrence will be achieved either by threatening the destruction of twenty, or even fewer, U.S. cities, or else not at all. If deterrence fails, the extent to which Russia is devastated will be related to the number of U.S. missiles. Therefore, the Soviets should be prepared to offer asymmetrical reductions in ICBM numbers as a way of persuading the United States to reduce the size of its existing inventory. As an optimal bargaining strategy over time, there are obvious drawbacks to this approach. Nevertheless, reasoning along these lines may have justified the asymmetrical concessions agreed to by the Soviet Union at SALT I and II and proposed by the Soviets at the START negotiations. The objective was a series of arms control agreements that would ultimately lead to a reduction in U.S. force levels.

This brings into focus the politico-military objective of avoiding world war. During the first half of the 1970s, the Soviets saw the arms control process as contributing to détente and hence reducing the likelihood of war. This justified making significant military concessions in order to reach agreement and sustain the process. For example, the ground rules for calculating the Soviet-U.S. strategic balance that were accepted at Vladivostok excluded forward-based U.S. systems targeted on Russia, as well as the British and French strategic nuclear forces.[56]

However, by the first half of the 1980s, the arms control process had become an arena for acerbic confrontation, and the United States insisted

---

56. Forward-based forces had been included in the U.S. strike plan since at least 1961. After SALT I Henry Kissinger publicly acknowledged the fact, implying that about 330 units were targeted on the Soviet Union. Raymond L. Garthoff, *Perspectives on the Strategic Balance* (Brookings, 1983), pp. 20–21; and John Prados, *The Soviet Estimate* (Dial Press, 1982), p. 121, table 2.

on excluding from consideration its plan for a space-based defense system. In consequence, Soviet arms control policy was no longer the most fruitful means of pursuing the objective of avoiding world war, and the negotiating focus could be expected to shift to the objective of not losing such a war, should it be unavoidable.

There were, of course, significant arms control objectives to be pursued at the military-technical level. There were also the immediate economic benefits of averting another round of the existing arms race and the longer-term benefits of avoiding a new arms race in space. While the Soviets were in a position to make significant concessions to achieve these objectives, the United States appeared to have lost interest in trading. The United States saw the move into space as a technological stimulus rather than an economic burden, and American concern about the Soviet capability for a disarming strike had largely evaporated.

The very importance of the Soviets' arms control objectives and the fact that they have no other way of achieving them has put the Soviets in a weak negotiating position, while the domestic ambivalence about arms control has strengthened the American hand. The United States has also succeeded in focusing public attention on ICBMs. The impression has been created that the Soviet emphasis on that means of delivery is particularly threatening and somehow unfair; unilateral concessions are therefore in order. True or not, the Soviets have to take account of this impression when dealing with world opinion, particularly the Europeans, who attach considerable importance to arms control negotiations and are predisposed to the American viewpoint.

All of this places the Soviet leadership in a difficult position. If it adopts a tough negotiating posture, the Soviet Union will be accused of intransigence, and the blame for failed negotiations will be laid at its door. If the Soviets make concessions, that reinforces the argument, prevalent in some American circles, that the Soviet Union will always back down under pressure. There is no obvious middle road.

Meanwhile the Soviet leaders must take account of their own domestic constituency and the argument that the effects of arms control negotiations have been one sided. Arms control agreements have required the Soviets to curtail existing missile production and deployment programs, scrap modern submarines, and forgo the replacement of 40 percent of the ICBM force. In contrast, the constraints on U.S. programs have been almost wholly budgetary and, in some cases, arms control arguments have been used to justify new programs.

CHAPTER 12

The Changing International Environment

SIGNIFICANT international developments, including a deterioration in the relationship between the superpowers, have occurred since the Soviets adjusted their military doctrine in 1966 and reviewed subsequent policy in 1976–77. Have the more recent developments prompted changes in the underlying direction of foreign and defense policy? If so, have the earlier Soviet decisions, with all their implications, been affected by a new evaluation? The clearest indication that there may have been a basic reevaluation of Soviet policy in the aftermath of the death of Leonid I. Brezhnev was the declaration by General Secretary Yuri V. Andropov in September 1983. To perceive its significance, the circumstances that would have prompted such a declaration have to be reviewed.

It is appropriate to speak of Brezhnev's term as general secretary as an era in Soviet military and foreign policy. It saw the shift from a wartime strategy founded on intercontinental nuclear preemption, to one designed to sidestep escalation in Europe and avoid the nuclear devastation of Russia. During this period, Soviet general purpose forces were fundamentally restructured for conventional war. The era saw the waxing and waning of détente and of the arms control process, but during this period the Soviets did achieve strategic parity and the arms race was partially capped. It saw the navy's shift to forward deployment and the progressive development of a policy for a wider but still cautious use of the military instrument in the third world. It saw the development of Sino-American relations based on an anti-Soviet alignment. The period also saw an acceleration during the early years of what the Soviets considered a favorable trend in the correlation of forces and its deceleration in the last five years of the era.

The end of an era is a time for reevaluation, for facing up to old problems that have been left too long and for turning to the new problems that are beginning to emerge. After Brezhnev, it was to be expected that Soviet leaders would address major issues in the field of foreign and defense policy, and this reassessment would be likely to lead to a decision period, whose fruits would become apparent in the years ahead. But the end of the Brezhnev era coincided with the beginning of the Reagan administration, whose stated objectives and initial actions challenged many of the assumptions that underlay Soviet policy in the 1970s. The interaction of these two phenomena and the Reagan initiatives in particular seem likely to have prompted a basic reassessment of Soviet policy.

The significance of Andropov's declaration on September 28, 1983, was subsequently obscured by Reagan's attempt to patch up the appearance of U.S.-Soviet relations in the period preceding the 1984 election, by the Soviet concern to negotiate a ban on weapons in space, and by the suave style of diplomacy adopted by the new Soviet leader in 1985. It seems likely, however, that the Andropov declaration signaled a decision-in-principle in Soviet policy toward the United States.

The focus of this chapter is on Soviet perceptions of U.S. motivations and intentions in the 1978–83 period.[1] As in chapter 2, in which Soviet perceptions in the 1946–48 period were discussed, the emphasis is on U.S. behavior and pronouncements, which are presented as they are likely to have been seen in Moscow. Thus one can identify what the Soviets are likely to have inferred from the evidence.

Rightly or wrongly, the Soviets considered themselves the injured party in Soviet-American relations. From their point of view they had respected the "Basic Principles of Relations" that were signed at the May 1972 summit and had continued to negotiate over limiting strategic arms, despite what they viewed as American foot dragging. In their view, their deployment of SS-20 missiles in Europe was a belated replacement of obsolete weapons, and their reluctant move into Afghanistan was a response to a direct threat to the security of the Soviet state. In Soviet eyes, that intervention was no different from American interventions in the U.S. national security zone in the Western Hemisphere and certainly not a reason to disrupt the superpower relationship.

---

1. This analysis of U.S. and Soviet policy in the 1978–83 period draws heavily on the material assembled by Raymond L. Garthoff for a forthcoming book.

The Carter Administration

The Soviets were uncertain about how Jimmy Carter's election as president in November 1976 would affect them. Carter was an unknown quantity and his immediate use of human rights to attack Soviet domestic policy was not propitious. It, however, could be explained as political provincialism. So could the proposals for deep cuts in the missile totals that had been agreed on so laboriously in the second series of negotiations on strategic arms limitations (SALT II) that had been in progress since 1972. Moreover, the Carter administration was clearly disposed to negotiate on a broad range of arms control and related issues.[2] Apparently, the administration was also ready in October 1977 to bring the Soviet Union back into the Middle East negotiations by a Geneva summit.

Similarly, the Carter defense policy was initially nonalarming. The defense budget for the first two years was marginally below the level established by Gerald Ford in his fourth year, and the B-1 bomber program was canceled on the grounds that the long-range air-launched cruise missile could do the job. The May 1977 decision to deploy a much improved warhead, with ten times the lethality of the earlier version, on about a third of the Minuteman intercontinental ballistic missiles (ICBMs) force could be seen as the normal process of force modernization, and the successful push for a 3 percent increase in NATO defense budgets was not untoward and was, anyway, a carryover from the Ford administration. The decision to proceed with the development of the Pershing II intermediate-range ballistic missile and the ground-launched cruise missile was more worrisome. Both were planned for deployment in Europe, to reach targets in the Soviet Union. Nevertheless, the Soviets could still nurse hopes for "military détente," to which they had come to attach much importance.[3]

Two years into the Carter administration, the picture was much more disturbing. U.S. policy toward the Soviet Union had hardened progressively, reflecting a steady swing in public opinion and the gradual accretion

2. Besides the continuing negotiations on strategic arms limitation (SALT II), discussions were initiated on eight other areas of military détente.

3. The Soviets perceive military détente as critical to political détente. Military détente covers such aspects as arms limitation and control agreements, "confidence-building" measures, and crisis management. It refers to measures aimed at reducing military confrontation. See Raymond L. Garthoff, *Détente and Confrontation: American-Soviet Relations from Nixon to Reagan* (Brookings, 1985), pp. 753–54.

of power by Zbigniew Brzezinski, Carter's national security adviser. Bipartisan groups such as the Committee on the Present Danger were increasingly influential in the U.S. political debate, and the twin assertions that America's foreign policy problems stemmed from military weakness, and that the United States would shortly face a window of "strategic vulnerability," were used to justify a policy of "making America strong," which the Soviets saw as a euphemism for restoring U.S. military superiority.

Although the SALT II negotiations made erratic progress toward the treaty that was signed in July 1979, the negotiations on ancillary arms control issues had virtually ground to a halt because of U.S. disinterest. In the fall of 1978 the United States had declined to resume negotiations on the demilitarization of the Indian Ocean. The talks on limiting the transfer of conventional arms collapsed in December, after an apparent reversal of U.S. policy. In the negotiations on a comprehensive test ban, the Soviets had made significant concessions in late 1977, but the United States responded by continually adjusting its position, limiting the scope of the proposed agreement, and hardening its terms until these talks, too, were broken off in 1980 by the United States.[4]

These failures could have been explained as a by-product of the interagency conflict in Washington, except that they harmonized with a broader picture of American policy that was becoming discernible. The second round of the Conference on Security and Cooperation in Europe at Belgrade (September 1977–March 1978) had been used by the United States to launch an offensive against the noncompliance by Russia and its allies with the human rights' aspects of the Helsinki accords, and no progress was made in other directions. Soviet involvement in the Ogaden war had been seized on by Brzezinski as the opportunity for an, unsuccessful, attempt to rally third world opinion against the Soviet Union, even though the Soviet Union was providing support to the defender (its new protégé, Ethiopia) against the aggressor (its original protégé, Somalia), and the aggression was condemned by the Organization of African Unity. Mean-

---

4. The talks on a comprehensive test ban opened in June 1977. In November Leonid Brezhnev announced a three-year moratorium on peaceful nuclear explosions, with prospects of indefinite extension. The Soviets also agreed to the U.S. proposal for a treaty of indefinite duration and indicated a readiness to accept verification through national seismic stations on the other side's territory and on-site inspections on challenge. On the U.S. side, strong objections to the proposed agreement were raised by the Joint Chiefs of Staff, the weapons laboratories, and (later) Zbigniew Brzezinski. In 1978 the United States first backed away from its own proposal for a comprehensive test ban of indefinite duration, and then from its proposal for a total ban on all tests. This approach continued in 1979, including a new demand that the Soviets use American-manufactured seismographs and provide for real-time satellite read outs. Ibid., pp. 756–58.

while it had become apparent that although Egypt and Israel might originally have been responsible for the failure to convene the Geneva summit Mideast conference after the U.S.–Soviet proposal in October 1977, by mid-1978 the Carter administration clearly welcomed the exclusion of the Soviet Union from the Israeli-Egyptian peace process.

Soviet doubts concerning the U.S. commitment to détente in both its political and military aspects would have been confirmed by five specific incidents during the last two years of the Carter administration, during which the U.S. defense budget rose first by 3 percent and then by a whopping 21.6 percent. First, Carter approved the MX ICBM program, one week before he signed SALT II in June 1979. Second, the Soviets judged the U.S. reaction to a Soviet brigade in Cuba to be a trumped-up furor that effectively prevented ratification of SALT II by the Senate. Third, the Soviets were wary because of the announcement in October 1979 that Secretary of Defense Harold Brown would visit China in January 1980, opening up the possibility of Sino-American cooperation in the military field.

Fourth, Moscow saw what it perceived as an exaggerated American response to the Soviet entry into Afghanistan. The Soviet Union viewed the move as an unfortunate but necessary police action to reestablish control within its national security zone. The Soviets thought their action similar to the kind carried out in Hungary and Czechoslovakia and accepted by the West, though with loud public protest. Furthermore, the United States had not hesitated to use force in its own (hemispheric) national security zone. The Carter administration had chosen to respond as if the Soviet action in Afghanistan was unprecedented. The Soviets believed that the United States was using Afghanistan as an excuse for a range of punitive measures against the Soviet Union, and to justify the activation of plans to project U.S. military power into Southwest Asia that had been gestating since Brzezinski first declared the area an arc of crisis.

Fifth was the leaking of Presidential Directive (PD) number 59 in July 1980. In many ways, the directive provided the logical framework that gave coherence to much of the other evidence. It set forth the basis of a "countervailing strategy" based on a U.S. war-fighting capability which, it was claimed, would enhance deterrence. The strategy, by increasing the U.S. capacity for proportional response and allowing multiple nuclear options, would also allow controlled escalation if deterrence failed. The concept of "escalation dominance" was introduced in PD 59, implying the requirement for U.S. superiority at all levels and including the Soviet structure of political control in the U.S. target set.

Considering the massive capabilities for nuclear deterrence already available to the United States, Moscow is likely to have dismissed the explanation of the strategy as designed to enhance nuclear deterrence as a pretense. The Soviets would have focused on the aspects of PD 59 describing the U.S. capability for war fighting. Within that framework the weapons programs authorized during the Carter administration took on an ominous cast. The new Minuteman warhead, the MX ICBM, and the Trident II D-5 submarine-launched ballistic missile were destined to possess a counterforce capability, while the Pershing II, with its short time of flight and thirty-meter accuracy was ideally suited for "decapitation" strikes against the Soviet political and military leadership. The cruise missile also fitted the picture. Although it would have a response time of several hours, its accuracy gave it a hard-target kill capability, and the United States was talking of deploying thousands of these nuclear weapons around the Soviet periphery, either emplaced ashore or carried by naval units and bombers.

The genesis of PD 59 was as worrying as its stress on war fighting. This directive was not the result of a hurried reevaluation following Iran, Afghanistan, and the shelving of SALT II, but was presented explicitly as a refinement and elaboration of existing strategic doctrine that had roots in the 1974 "Schlesinger doctrine." In other words, this reshaping of U.S. doctrine and associated capabilities had been under way for six years or more, which cast doubts on the true nature of U.S. objectives at the strategic arms limitation talks. Ostensibly, the process was intended to reduce weapons inventories on both sides, which would work toward a situation of "minimum mutual deterrence." But the talks could be read another way. SALT I placed a cap on the Soviet missile buildup, at no cost to U.S. programs. SALT II had been used to reduce the number of Soviet ICBMs, while the United States increased its capability of striking at Russia with systems that were not constrained by the agreements.

The First Reagan Administration

If the trend was disturbing to the Soviets by the end of the Carter administration, eighteen months into the presidency of Ronald Reagan it was downright alarming.[5] On taking office, the new administration followed

5. See Alexander Dallin and Gail W. Lapidus, "Reagan and the Russians: United States Policy toward the Soviet Union and Eastern Europe," in Kenneth A. Oye, Robert J. Lieber, and Donald Rothchild, eds., *Eagle Defiant: United States Foreign Policy in the 1980s* (Little, Brown,

through on its campaign promises by demonstrating distrust of arms control and a determination to restore American military superiority in order to negotiate from a position of strength. The motives that animated the specific policy initiatives were even more disturbing.

The span of opinion in the Reagan administration was concentrated in the right third of the political spectrum, with "essentialists" being represented in unprecedented force.[6] Even when pragmatic considerations prevailed, the hostility toward the Soviets was not mitigated. Three interlocking themes ran through the administration's rhetoric.

One was the assumption that Soviet communism was a political aberration and an evil that was not only destined to fail but should be made to fail. Another was the idea that an important function of the U.S. arms buildup was to force an arms race on Russia that would break its economy. Third was the concept of a "crusade for freedom." As articulated in Reagan's speech to the British Parliament in June 1982, this crusade was to be directed at all people living under Marxist-Leninist regimes, including those in the Soviet Union.[7]

In other words, the Reagan administration denied the legitimacy of the Soviet state and was set on undermining it, one way or another. The American people, meanwhile, were being bombarded with the idea of "relentless Soviet expansion," that would have to be checked with military force if necessary.[8] The Soviets had an "increasing proclivity to support change . . . by rule of force, by bloodshed, terrorism, so-called wars of liberation."[9] There was also a distinct change in the tone of how people talked

---

1983), pp. 191–236. The first draft was completed by July 1982 and indicates how outside observers, including foreign policy analysts in Moscow, would have perceived Ronald Reagan's policies.

6. Dallin and Lapidus distinguish the three main perspectives on the Soviet Union. The essentialists see it as inherently evil, bent on expansion and with no concern for world order. The mechanists see it primarily as a geopolitical threat that must be met with countervailing force. The interactionists recognize America's role in Soviet policy and view the world in multipolar terms. See Dallin and Lapidus, "Reagan and The Russians," pp. 206–09.

7. Reagan admitted the need for caution in "forcing the pace of change." "Address to Members of Parliament," June 8, 1982, Weekly Compilation of Presidential Documents, vol. 18 (June 14, 1982), p. 768. In 1981 Richard Pipes, the senior Soviet specialist on the National Security Council staff had asserted, "Soviet leaders would have to choose between peacefully changing their Communist system . . . or going to war." This statement was repudiated by the administration. "U.S. Repudiates a Hard-Line Aide," New York Times, March 19, 1981.

8. As a typical example see Secretary of Defense Caspar Weinberger's statement on defense policy. George C. Wilson, "Weinberger, in His First Message, Says Mission is to Rearm America," Washington Post, January 23, 1981.

9. Secretary Alexander M. Haig, interviewed for the Wall Street Journal, Department of State Bulletin, vol. 81, no. 2054 (GPO, 1981), p. 25.

about the likelihood of war. The idea that conflict of some kind with the Soviet Union was inevitable began to reemerge for the first time since the 1950s,[10] prompting an upsurge of support for peace and antinuclear movements throughout the West.

Against this background, in May 1982, the substance of the 1984–88 U.S. Defense Guidance was leaked, providing an authoritative view of American military policy, one that was in no way reassuring to the Soviet Union.[11] Certain aspects were particularly significant. The Defense Guidance did the following:

—Reaffirmed the PD 59 policy of being able to prevail in a protracted nuclear war and established a strategy of nuclear decapitation, that is, striking at Soviet political and military command, control, and communications.

—Required the development of special forces to be used, in particular, in Eastern Europe.

—Increased the size of the Rapid Deployment Force.

—Advanced by one year the entry into service of the Trident II D-5 missile system.

—Directed the development of space-based weapons and the opening up of other new areas of weaponry.

—Advocated a peacetime policy of applying the maximum economic pressure on the Soviet Union, directly through trade policies and the denial of advanced technology, and indirectly by developing new weapons that would make existing Soviet inventories obsolete.

During the second half of 1982, U.S. attention was taken up with the war in Lebanon, and the midterm elections required the administration to guard against the charge that its behavior was increasing the danger of war. However, by spring of 1983, a series of developments reaffirmed the thrust of Reagan's policies and painted it in even starker tones.

In late March, the president announced that the United States was to move toward developing a space-based ballistic-missile defense system, notwithstanding the provisions of the Antiballistic Missile Treaty. This sys-

10. In October 1981 Major General Robert L. Schweitzer, the military assistant to the National Security Adviser, was reassigned after making unauthorized public comments that there was "a drift towards war," that the Soviets were "on the move," and "were going to strike." See "Security Adviser Ousted for Talk Hinting at War," *New York Times,* October 21, 1981. Although this statement was extreme, the assumption was widespread in military circles that strategic parity would prompt the Soviets into military adventures that would lead to conflict. See, for example, Fred Hiatt, "Limited War Held 'Almost Inevitable,'" *Washington Post,* June 22, 1984.

11. Richard Halloran, "Pentagon Draws Up First Strategy for Fighting a Long Nuclear War," *New York Times,* May 30, 1982.

tem would be part of the Strategic Defense Initiative, announced in what has become known as the president's "Star Wars" speech of March 23, 1983. This step is unlikely to have caught the Soviets entirely by surprise since the evidence that U.S. policy was moving in that direction has been building up for some time.[12] That did not, however, make the development any less worrisome, and it provided further evidence that the United States was not interested in arms control but was seeking military superiority. One of the more influential U.S. groups advocating the move into space was explicit that its objective was "to implement a basic change in U.S. grand strategy and make a technological end-run on the Soviets."[13]

Two weeks before his speech on the Strategic Defense Initiative (SDI), Reagan had described the Soviet leadership as "the focus of evil in the modern world," the Soviet bloc as "an evil empire," and he also implied that the Soviet Union was comparable with Nazi Germany.[14] In June the secretary of state was reported as saying that changing the internal system of the Soviet Union was a U.S. objective, confirming an earlier newspaper report of a Presidential Directive to that effect. In August the U.S. administration greeted with skepticism and disinterest a revised draft treaty on weapons in space, submitted by the Soviet Union to the United Nations.[15]

The trend worsened sharply at the beginning of September, when the downing of a Korean airliner shortly after it overflew Sakhalin led to bitter recriminations. The Soviets were unpersuaded that the aircraft's wanderings were accidental and were convinced that they had been set up by the United States, which had then pilloried them in world opinion. Three weeks later, Vice-President George Bush made a very tough policy address in Vienna, offering political and economic support to countries such as Hungary and Romania (which he had just visited) if they distanced them-

12. See Malcolm Wallop, "Opportunities and Imperatives of Ballistic Missile Defense," *Strategic Review*, vol. 7 (Fall 1979), pp. 13–21; and Clarence A. Robinson, Jr., "Advance Made on High Energy Laser," *Aviation Week and Space Technology*, vol. 114 (February 23, 1981), pp. 25–27. In May 1982 the leaked 1984–88 Defense Guidance referred to space-based weapons.

13. Daniel O. Graham, *The High Frontier: A New National Strategy* (Washington, D.C.: High Frontier, 1982), p. ix.

14. "National Association of Evangelicals," Remarks at the Annual Convention, March 8, 1983, *Weekly Compilation of Presidential Documents*, vol. 19 (March 14, 1983), p. 369.

15. See Dan Oberdorfer, "Schultz Outlines Policy of Opposing Soviets," *Washington Post*, June 16, 1983; and *United States-Soviet Relations*, Hearings before the Senate Committee on Foreign Relations, 98 Cong. 1 sess. (GPO, 1983), pt. 1, p. 5. In fact the substance of the directive was somewhat more moderate than these press reports, but the Soviet Union was not to know that. The revised draft treaty included proposals for the control of antisatellite weapons, which took account of the critical comments by notable American scientists on the earlier 1981 Soviet draft treaty. Richard L. Garwin, Kurt Gottfried, and Donald L. Hafner, "Antisatellite Weapons," *Scientific American*, vol. 250 (June 1984), p. 53.

selves from the Soviet Union. He also rejected any acceptance of the status quo in Eastern Europe.[16]

Bush also insulted historical Russia and denied its European roots. He noted that Russia had missed out on the three great events of European history: the Renaissance, the Reformation, and the Enlightenment, and he spoke of "brutal murder" when referring to the Korean airliner incident. He was echoing Reagan, who had spoken of a "terrorist act," an "inexcusable act of brutality," and an "act of barbarism," that was "inexplicable to civilized people everywhere."[17] It could be inferred from their remarks that the United States considered the Soviet Union essentially uncivilized. In other words, to the Soviets, American rhetoric suggested that in the eyes of the Reagan administration, the focus of all evil was as much Russia as its Marxist-Leninist form of government.

An acerbic backdrop to these unfolding developments was provided by the arms control negotiations on intermediate nuclear forces and strategic arms reductions. The United States' approach to these talks offered little hope that the verbal assaults of the Reagan administration were just rhetoric. On the contrary, the rhetoric implied deeply entrenched beliefs that were structuring objectives, shaping policy, and animating action. A salient feature of the administration was its ability to implement its policies, gaining congressional support for a large and sustained defense buildup at the cost of domestic programs. Clearly, Reagan was actualizing the mood of the people for a restoration of American strength and a more assertive foreign policy.

By the end of September 1983 the Soviet leaders had endured thirty-two months of "the most aggressive anti-Soviet and anti-Communist rhetoric in 25 years, backed by record [U.S.] defense budgets, an uncompromising stance in nuclear arms control negotiations, and the highly visible commitment of American power to the Middle East and Central America."[18]

The Politburo's response to Reagan's political offensive was one of pa-

16. George Bush explicitly rejected the acceptance of the status quo in Europe that the Soviets saw as the key element of the 1974 Helsinki accords. Citing Hungary and Romania, Bush said that the United States would improve "political, economic and cultural relations" with East European countries that asserted greater independence from Moscow. See "Bush: U.S. Will Aid Maverick Soviet Bloc States," *Washington Post,* September 22, 1983.

17. See "Soviet Attack on Korean Civilian Airliner," Remarks to Reporters, September 2, 1983, *Weekly Compilation of Presidential Documents,* vol. 19 (September 12, 1983), pp. 1193, 1197, and 1199–1200.

18. Coit D. Blacker, "The United States and the Soviet Union," *Current History,* vol. 83 (October 1984), p. 310.

tience. To former Secretary of State Alexander M. Haig, this response was "mind boggling." He has noted that despite the most unprecedented criticism from the United States, "The Soviets stayed very, very moderate, very, very responsible during the first three years. . . . They were genuinely trying."[19] One reason for this patience was the central importance of détente, which had been the cornerstone of Soviet policy toward the United States since 1971 and had to be preserved if possible. Soviet political leaders also wanted to enlist European support in the campaign against the deployment of Euromissiles.

The Soviet military leaders were less patient, and by mid-1981 they were arguing that the likelihood of war had significantly increased. By October 1982 even Brezhnev appears to have reluctantly concluded that the prospects for détente and arms control were dim if not dead.[20] However, the change of political leadership in November 1982 presented the opportunity for a fresh Soviet attempt over arms control and détente. In his speeches on November 22 and December 21, Andropov avoided inflammatory language, reasserted the importance of détente, repeated various proposals for controlling arms, and expressed openness to negotiation.[21] This restraint continued into 1983, but it was met by Reagan's "Evil Empire" and "Star Wars" speeches in March, the same month that the Christian Democrats won the West German elections.

That election removed the main hope of significant domestic resistance to the deployment of Euromissiles. Nonetheless, Foreign Minister Andrey A. Gromyko responded to the setback by arguing strongly for continuing the policy based on détente and negotiation. By June, however, optimism among Soviet leaders had largely evaporated. At the Central Committee Plenum, Andropov characterized the present historical period as "marked by confrontation, unprecedented in the entire postwar period by its intensity and sharpness." The next day, Gromyko spoke of "the confrontation of two lines" and accused the United States of using arms control negoti-

---

19. Roy Gutman, "Bad Tidings: The World According to Haig," *Newsday*, August 12, 1984.

20. Compare Brezhnev's words on October 27, 1982, which make no reference to disarmament, to his earlier address on March 16, 1982. In this later and obviously important speech to military command personnel, Brezhnev noted, "Two lines clash in world politics," the Soviet line being for "détente and strengthening international security," while the U.S. line was for deepening tension and arms racing. "Soveshchanie voenachel'nikov v Kremle" (Meeting of military leaders in the Kremlin), *Pravda*, October 28, 1982. At the 1981 party congress, the Central Committee report had noted only that there was "an intense struggle of two trends."

21. "Rech' General'nogo Sekretarya TsK KPSS Yu. V. Andropova" (Speech of General Secretary Yuri V. Andropov to the CC of the CPSU), *Pravda*, November 23, 1982; and "Shest' desyat Let SSSR" (Sixty years of the USSR), *Pravda*, December 22, 1982.

ations as a cover to deploy new systems in Europe.[22] His reference to the confrontation of two lines was a further hardening of the earlier depictions of "an intense struggle of two trends" and "two lines clash." Thereafter, no senior Soviet official spoke out in detail on relations with Washington until Andropov made his declaration on September 28.[23]

The Andropov Declaration

Andropov made the formal declaration in his capacity as general secretary of the Communist party and chairman of the Presidium of the Supreme Soviet of the USSR.[24] Although the statement came in the wake of the furor over the Korean airliner incident and some reference was made to U.S. accusations, that had not prompted Andropov's declaration. Instead the statement reflected a new evaluation that had been gestating for some time.[25] The thrust of the declaration was significantly different from the statements made by Andropov and Gromyko in June, and the pessimistic tone was striking when compared to Andropov's optimistic assertions about détente the previous November. Equally important was the style of presentation and the fact that it was made.[26]

A large part of the declaration focused on how U.S. policy was threatening world peace, but the essence of its message was the following: the United States had launched a crusade against socialism and was bent on military domination, there was no possibility that the U.S. administration would change its ways, and the Soviet Union would respond as necessary

22. A. A. Gromyko, "V.I. Lenin i vneshnaya politika sovetskogo gosudarstva" (V.I. Lenin and the foreign policy of the Soviet state), *Kommunist,* no. 6 (April 1983), pp. 11–32; "Rech' General'nogo Sekretarya TsK KPSS Yu. V. Andropova" (Speech of General Secretary of the CC of the CPSU Yuri V. Andropov), *Kommunist,* no. 9 (June 1983), p. 5.; and "O Mezhdunarodnom polozhenii i vneshney politike Sovetskogo Soyuza" (On the international situation and the foreign policy of the Soviet Union, speech of the First Deputy Chairman of the Council of Minister of the USSR, Minister of Foreign Affairs of the USSR, Deputy A.A. Gromyko), *Pravda,* June 17, 1983.

23. Blacker, "The United States and the Soviet Union," p. 313.

24. "Zayavlenie General'nogo Sekretarya TsK KPSS Predsedatelya Prezidiuma Verkhovnogo Soveta SSSR Yuri V. Andropova" (Declaration of the General Secretary of the CC of the CPSU, Chairman of the Presidium of the Supreme Soviet of the USSR Yuri V. Andropov), *Pravda,* September 29, 1983.

25. Raymond L. Garthoff, who was told by a member of the Central Committee, contributed this information.

26. The mode of presentation of Andropov's declaration was unprecedented in recent years, although this may have been accounted for, in part, by the fact that Andropov was too sick to appear in public. The front-page article was headlined "DECLARATION . . . of Yuri V. Andropov." The statement was read on television and radio on September 28 and published in *Pravda,* September 29, 1983.

to any attempt to disrupt the existing military balance. This message was a significant departure from the established line that the change in the correlation of forces had caused the United States to accept strategic parity with Russia and to forgo reliance on military force as the primary instrument of foreign policy, particularly in dealings with the Soviet Union.

Considering the sharper tone of the statements in June, the silence during the summer months, and the obvious significance of the declaration on September 28, it is possible that the June plenum sanctioned a formal review of the line that had been established at the party congress in 1971 and reaffirmed in 1976 and 1981. Such a review would have involved a reevaluation of the trend in the correlation of forces, with particular emphasis on the persistent elements in U.S. policy and their amenability to change.

Whatever the underlying process, the format of the Andropov declaration suggested that a major decision-in-principle had been reached by the Soviet leaders about the perennial nature of the Soviet-American relationship, which required a significant change in line. According to one observer, it had an "electrifying and sobering effect" on the Soviet populace and, among at least some of the Soviet populace, it was understood to imply a significant possibility of conflict with the United States.[27]

Fundamental changes in the basis of Soviet policy are relatively rare, and they are usually decided after extended debate and then legitimized at the next party congress. This was true in 1967–71, when the Soviet Union decided to adopt détente and arms control as the basis of its policy toward the United States. The circumstances of the September 28 declaration suggest the beginning of an equally fundamental reorientation of underlying policy, which is even more significant for having been announced outside the five-year cycle of party congresses.

In considering what a reorientation implies for the future, one must look at various types of decision. Decisions would include fundamental doctrinal conclusions about the nature of the Soviet-American relationship and the correlation of forces. Decisions would have to be made about the correct strategic direction of Soviet foreign policy, which could generate consequential requirements to redirect existing policies. Decisions would have to be made about the tactics to be adopted until the necessary redirection

27. This was observed by Raymond L. Garthoff, who was in Moscow when the declaration was made. A regional party chief told Garthoff that after a local party meeting convened to discuss the declaration, several women approached him to ask if it meant that their sons would have go off to war.

had been achieved, as well as the style of policy that would be most effective in achieving Soviet objectives.

The evidence suggests that Andropov's declaration reflected a basic decision-in-principle: the Soviets were facing a situation different from what had previously been assumed, but they still had to evaluate its full implications before deciding on consequential policies.

Elements of the Debate, 1980–84

A major change of policy in the Soviet Union is usually preceded and followed by substantial debate. A surprising amount of the debate is carried by the open press, and although the fundamental questions are reflected obliquely, if at all, the subjects addressed do help to define the central issues of the debate. The following interrelated issues, which are directly relevant to the substance of Andropov's declaration, were being debated in the 1980–84 period.[28]

CAN DÉTENTE BE SAVED? The crucial question was, "Will détente be continued or will it give way to confrontation, to antagonism fraught with conflict?"[29] There was no disagreement over the apparent fact that the Reagan administration rejected détente, was disinterested in arms control, and sought military superiority. The argument was whether conciliatory Soviet behavior, combined with the pressure of allied and domestic politics, problems with the U.S. defense budget, and common sense would force the U.S. administration to reconsider its dangerous policies and return to the path of détente and arms control.

As just noted, the pessimistic answer steadily gained ground. A brief spurt of optimism accompanied the new attempt at conciliation following the change in Soviet leadership in November 1982, but this reaction soon faded. The argument was largely resolved at the end of September 1983 by Andropov's comment that "even if someone had illusions as to the possible evolution for the better in the policy of the present American administration, the latest development [the KAL incident] has dispelled them." But even then, the wording left room for doubt about whether Andropov was referring more broadly to the United States or just to the Reagan administration.

28. The following summary draws on work by Raymond L. Garthoff; see also Bruce Parrot, "Soviet Policy toward the United States: A Fork in the Road?" *SAIS Review*, vol. 5 (Winter-Spring 1985), pp. 107–20.

29. See Vladlen Kuznetsov, "The Voice of Reason," *New Times*, no. 11 (March 1981), p. 8.

IS THE TIME FOR DIPLOMACY PAST? The argument about the value of negotiations had been running for some time. But after the West German elections in March 1983, an article under Gromyko's name strongly defended détente as a policy and provided a lengthy list of agreements reached during the 1970s. In particular, it argued that Lenin's policy of differentiating among the various imperialist powers during negotiations in the 1920s had produced positive results. In a September article that cited the June 1983 plenum, Marshal Nikolay V. Ogarkov adopted a different viewpoint. He noted that Lenin's disarmament proposals in the 1920s came to nothing. Ogarkov chose to quote Lenin only on the need to avoid complacency.[30]

WHAT IS THE TREND IN THE CORRELATION OF FORCES? In the concluding paragraph of an editorial in the May 1982 issue of the main party journal, *Kommunist,* which set forth and promoted the Brezhnev line, the author noted that with the prevailing correlation of forces, a policy of peaceful coexistence corresponded to a policy of détente and "only declared enemies of the principle of peaceful coexistence, who are blinded by class hatred towards socialist progress" could fail to see that progress was being made toward the objective of excluding war from international society. This fitted into the general debate about whether détente could be saved and the value of negotiations, but the broader context suggested that there was disagreement over what the correlation of forces actually was.[31]

HOW LIKELY IS WAR? Six months into the Reagan administration, argument surfaced about the danger of global war. During 1980 there was general recognition that the danger of war had increased, but concern about the extent of that increase did not emerge until mid-1981.[32]

In a major article in the wake of the Twenty-sixth Party Congress, Marshal Ogarkov, then chief of the General Staff, stated that the main trends of Reagan's policy were now clear: the United States was working to wreck existing arms control treaties, seeking military superiority, and had adopted a policy of acting against national liberation movements. He went

---

30. Gromyko, *Kommunist,* no. 6 (April 1983), pp. 11–32; "Ogarkov Article on U.S. and Soviet Arms Policies," in Foreign Broadcast Information Service, *Daily Report: Soviet Union,* September 23, 1983, pp. AA1, 4. (Hereafter FBIS, *Daily Report:SU.*)

31. Editorial, "Posledovatel'naya i chestnaya politika mira" (A consistent and clear policy of peace), *Kommunist,* no. 8 (May 1982), pp. 18, 20.

32. See the report to the June 1980 plenum, "O mezhdunarodnom polozhenii i vneshney politike Sovetskogo Soyuza" (On the international situation and foreign policy of the Soviet Union), *Kommunist vooruzhennykh sil* (Communist of the armed forces), no. 14 (July 1980), pp. 8–10; and the article in the same issue by N.V. Ogarkov, "V interesakh povysheniya boeveoy gotovnosti" (In the interests of raising combat readiness), pp. 24–31.

on to talk about the need for an improved war mobilization capability, and his penultimate paragraph said, "It is necessary to convey to the Soviet people, in a more profound and better reasoned form, the truth about the existing threat of the danger of war. It should not, of course, be over-dramatized, but it is obligatory to show the seriousness of the contemporary international situation."[33] A major statement by Minister of Defense Dmitriy F. Ustinov shortly afterward was equally critical of the United States, but there was a distinct difference in his tone about the danger of war and the possibility of negotiating with the United States.[34]

The difference between Ustinov and Ogarkov persisted after Brezhnev's death although Ustinov placed greater stress on the danger of war than did Andropov when Andropov attempted conciliation on assuming the leadership in November 1982.[35] Although the official depiction of the danger of war became sharply more pessimistic at the end of March 1983, the basic difference in emphasis could still be seen in Andropov's September declaration and in the article four days earlier by Ogarkov. A difference was still evident in late November 1983, by which time Ustinov had joined his voice to those stressing the increased danger of war.[36]

There is a reluctance in the West to accept that Soviet leaders could have genuinely believed that war was more likely, which reflects a view that war could only come about because of some Soviet initiative and a Western move to counter it. This perspective leads to the Western assessment that although the Soviet Union faced a more difficult external environment in 1981–83, there was no reason why that environment should have been more dangerous. Indeed it was argued that assertive U.S. policies had

33. N. Ogarkov, "Na strazhe mironogo truda" (Guarding peaceful labour), *Kommunist*, no. 10 (July 1981), pp. 80–91. In an unpublished paper, Dale R. Herspring documents "Ogarkov's repeated public defiance of generally accepted Soviet positions on issues related to East-West relations."

34. D.F. Ustinov, "Protiv gonki vooruzheniy i ugrozy voyny" (Against the arms race and the threat of war), *Pravda*, July 25, 1981.

35. Compare the statements by Ustinov and Ogarkov with the Ministry of Defense's Party Aktiv, as reported in "Na uroven' trebovaniy partii" (At the level of the party's demands), *Krasnaya zvezda* (Red star), June 22, 1983. See also Ogarkov's article, "The Victory and the Present Day," FBIS, *Daily Report: SU*, May 12, 1983, p. V6. Compare Ustinov's statement to the Moscow military district's Party Aktiv as reported in *Krasnaya zvezda*, December 8, 1982, with Andropov's statements of November 23, 1982, and December 22, 1982, in *Pravda*.

36. Vladimir E. Shlapentokh, "Moscow's War Propaganda and Soviet Public Opinion," *Problems of Communism*," vol. 33 (September–October, 1984), pp. 91–92; "Ogarkov Article on U.S. and Soviet Arms Policies," FBIS, *Daily Report: SU*; and D.F. Ustinov, "Borot'sya za mir, ukreplyat' oboronosposobnost'" (Struggling for peace and strengthening defense capability), *Pravda*, November 19, 1983; and "Zayavlenie General'nogo Sekretarya TsK KPSS (Declaration by General Secretary Yuri V. Andropov of the CC of the CPSU), *Pravda*, November 25, 1983.

made war less likely by forcing the Soviets to be more cautious and by constraining their freedom of action.

This Western view stems from the experience of Munich. The Soviets, however, have a "Sarejevo" viewpoint and believe that war will come about through an unintended chain of events, such as led to World War I. What determines the danger of war is the combustibility of the international environment and not the source of the spark.

ARE SUFFICIENT RESOURCES BEING ALLOCATED TO DEFENSE? The debate on the allocation of resources to defense was somewhat different from the argument about the likelihood of war; it was more directly related to the disagreement over the current correlation of forces. The first signs of this question emerged in 1980, when Ogarkov argued that the United States was seeking "overwhelming military superiority," with the long-term goal of "changing the correlation of forces in the favor of imperialism."[37] This assessment was in the wake of the U.S. secretary of defense's visit to China, the sharp increase in the defense budget, the decision to go ahead with the MX ICBM, and the panoply of reactions to the Soviet invasion of Afghanistan.

The Twenty-sixth Party Congress in March 1981 shifted resources toward the civilian sector, and in July of that year Ogarkov's article, with its powerful arguments about the steadily increasing threat and the need to respond to it, was published in *Kommunist*.[38] In October 1982 Brezhnev addressed directly the military's concern about the allocation of resources to defense in a most unusual meeting in the Kremlin with several hundred leading command personnel.[39] He assured them that the armed forces would get what they needed to do their job, but meanwhile they had to make sure that they were making the best use of what they already had. They should also be receptive to new ideas, operational concepts, and techniques for command, control, and communications. Finally, they would have to generally improve the "readiness condition" of the Soviet armed forces.

Indications of major disagreement on this issue abated in the wake of Brezhnev's meeting with military leaders whose material concerns may have been partly met by decisions taken at the time of the November 1982 plenum.[40] By April 1983 the political leaders apparently accepted that an

37. Ogarkov, *Kommunist vooruzhennykh sil,* no. 14 (July 1980), p. 25.
38. Ogarkov, *Kommunist,* no. 10 (July 1981), particularly the quotation from Lenin (p. 85) and the warning about "any kind of peace is good" (p. 90).
39. *Pravda,* October 28, 1982.
40. Talking to the Party Aktiv of the Ministry of Defense about the June 1983 plenum, Usti-

arms race was inevitable and at the June plenum Andropov promised to "enhance the combat might of the Soviet armed forces."[41] In late November 1983, after listing the actions that were being taken in response to the deployment of Euromissiles, Andropov noted, "Of course other measures aimed at safeguarding the security of the USSR and the other countries of the socialist community will also be taken."[42]

The Soviet Assessment of Threat

There are two aspects to the Soviets' perception of threat. One is the immediate concern about the likelihood of war. The other is more general and largely shaped by their perceptions of the nature of U.S. objectives regarding Russia.

THE DANGER OF WAR. In assessing the likelihood of war, most countries distinguish in some way between the concepts of "political" and "operational" warning of impending conflict. The idea of political warning is based on the fact that, most of the time, most nations assume that the prevailing international situation makes it unlikely that, in the immediate future, the country will be forced to take up arms to protect vital interests. Circumstances can, however, change, and the assessment of how rapidly such a change could come about is embodied in the concept of political warning. It is a planning factor that provides the temporal buffer that allows a nation to go about its daily business, on the assumption that the political circumstances make war unlikely within a certain period.

The planning factor for political warning derives initially from the time needed to move one's country to a war footing from a level of military preparedness that can be sustained permanently in peacetime without undue strain. If that time is the same or less than the time it would take for the international situation to deteriorate and/or for one's opponent to move on to a war footing, then that time can serve as the planning factor for political warning. Of course, how one defines "without undue strain" de-

---

nov referred to the "special place" occupied by the November plenum in "ensuring the needs of defense." *Krasnaya zvezda,* June, 22, 1983.

41. See Shlapentokh's description of the sharp change in the tone of *Pravda* headlines, starting in April. Shlapentokh, "Moscow's War Propaganda," p. 92. "Enhance the combat might" is quoted by D.F. Ustinov in *Pravda,* November 19, 1983. Earlier, the June plenum set "the task of doing everything necessary to safeguard the country's security" in "Ogarkov Article on U.S. and Soviet Arms Policies," in FBIS, *Daily Report: SU,* p. AA4. The work of the June plenum was discussed at the time by the Ministry of Defense's Party Aktiv, which was addressed by Ustinov, Yepishev, and Ogarkov.

42. *Pravda,* November 25, 1983.

pends on competing claims for scarce resources and will be influenced by the view of the international situation. Political warning is not, therefore, something that can be calculated with precision but is a political hunch, reflecting the kind of judgment that underlies most decisions about the allocation of resources to defense.

Political warning is a "most likely case" assumption. The concept of operational warning addresses the "worst case," assumes that the enemy has already decided to go to war, and assesses how soon the operational indications of an impending attack would be detected. The planning factor for operational warning is mainly technical, being based on the ability to detect an enemy's preparations to initiate hostilities. It is, however, linked to political warning time, and if that time has to be reduced in response to a long-term deterioration in international relations, the attention paid to operational warning will increase.

That the Soviets think along these lines is suggested by the way in which they have used the term "period of threat" in the past. The formal definition of this term limits it to the preparatory period immediately preceding conflict, and in time of crisis the government can declare a "threatening situation," thereby initiating the "direct preparation of the country and its armed forces for war."[43] The term has, however, also been used to describe a much longer period, namely, the time from which war becomes ultimately inevitable. In respect to World War I, two hostile camps had existed since 1907, but it was not until 1912 that the contradictions between them had built up to make military conflict inevitable, thereby initiating the period of threat. Similarly, the period of threat preceding World War II began in March 1938, when the Germans invaded Austria. In this formulation, the period is divided into two parts, which are of different length and intensity: an extended period of "general threat," which compares with political warning, and an "immediate threat" period, which equates with the formal definition and compares with operational warning.[44]

The assumptions about political warning that underlie Soviet war plans are not known, but it seems likely that the planning factor for such warning was significantly reduced by the end of 1981. A specific reason for such a reduction can perhaps be found in the Polish situation, which raised the possibility that Soviet troops might have to move in to restore control.

43. *Ugrozhayemyy period* in *Sovetskaya voennaya entsiklopediya (Soviet military encyclopedia)*, vol. 8 (Moscow: Voenizdat, 1980), p. 170. *Ugrozhayemoe polozhenie* in *Slovar' osnovnykh voennykh terminov (Dictionary of basic military terms)* (Moscow: Voenizdat, 1965), p. 231.
44. Major General V. Zemskov, "Voyny sovremennoy epokhi" (Wars of the modern era), *Voennaya mysl'* (Military thought), no. 5 (1969), p. 61.

There was an obvious danger that such military intervention, however limited, could provoke more serious conflict and this, in turn, could lead to war. The style and rhetoric of the Reagan administration added to the danger, and the possibility had to be taken seriously that a deteriorating situation in Europe could progressively escalate to full-blown East-West conflict.

One development that could indicate a change in Soviet assumptions about political warning of a world war was the fourfold increase in the detection rate of submarine incursions into Swedish waters during 1982. Soviet incursions go back to the 1950s, and in the 1970s detections oscillated between two and nine a year, with seven to nine detections in five of those years. In 1980 there were nine, and in 1981 ten, but in 1982 detections jumped to forty.[45] This jump followed a politically embarrassing naval incident at the end of October 1981, when a Soviet ocean-going diesel submarine ran aground far inside the Swedish archipelago.

One, therefore, has to identify the benefits that would have justified the risk of incurring further political costs (both in relation to Sweden and to public opinion in Europe that was then being wooed to resist the deployment of intermediate-range nuclear forces), by sharply increasing the number and boldness of these operations. The idea that the higher level of incursions was designed to apply political pressure on Sweden is unpersuasive, and a more plausible answer lies in the concept of preparing a theater of military action (TVD) in peacetime for the contingency of war.

The Baltic constitutes the northern flank of the Western TVD, which is the main TVD of the main theater, where military success has to be ensured if the Soviet Union is not to lose a world war. The Swedish archipelago defines the northern perimeter of the Baltic maritime TVD, and the Soviets have two kinds of interest in this coastline: to prevent it being used to their disadvantage and to use selected parts of it for their own purposes. Thorough peacetime reconnaissance is important to both missions, which would have to be discharged at the onset of war.[46]

If political warning had been reduced from, say, two years to one year, there would have been a new urgency about ensuring that the Baltic mari-

---

45. Submarine Defence Commission, *Countering the Submarine Threat: Submarine Violations and Swedish Security Policy,* Swedish Official Report Series (Stockholm, 1983), p. 20.

46. The Swedish investigative commission concluded that "the main impression is that this [Soviet] submarine activity represents the preparatory phases of military operational planning." *Countering the Submarine Threat,* p. 74.

time TVD was properly prepared for the contingency of world war.[47] The military importance of the heightened requirement would have justified risking significant political costs. This inference is supported by the emphasis that Ogarkov placed in July 1981 on the problems of moving from a peacetime to a war footing.[48]

Another development was the eviction, during 1983, of 147 Soviet diplomatic officials from eighteen countries for activities "incompatible with their status." Informed members of the espionage scene regarded the expulsions as a result of increased KGB effort rather than the result of a coordinated Western campaign or a by-product of disclosures by defectors.[49] Such Soviet action bolsters the evidence of reduced warning time.

More recent evidence that the Soviets reduced political warning time was provided by a report from the Central Intelligence Agency that was prepared in June or July 1984 and leaked to the press. This document is alleged to have said that "the Soviets have concluded that the danger of war is greater than it was before the [December 1983] INF decision, that Soviet vulnerability is greater and will grow with additional INF emplacements, and that the reduced warning time inherent in Pershing II has lowered Soviet confidence in their ability to warn of sudden attack. These perceptions, perhaps driven by a building [U.S.] defense budget, new initiatives in [U.S.] continental defense, improvements in [U.S.] force readiness, and a potentially massive [U.S.] space program, may be propelling the U.S.S.R. to take national readiness measures at a deliberate pace."[50]

The specific evidence listed in the CIA report can be divided into two categories, reflecting the two types of warning time.[51] Certain of the measures, such as the shift of production facilities from civil to military production and increases in the production of existing items, would have flowed from a reduction in the length of political warning. The remaining measures appear to reflect a reduction in operational warning time.

Further evidence of improved readiness for the contingency of world

47. See also Walter S. Mossberg, "Sweden Says It Believes that Soviet Sub Visits Reflect War Planning," *Wall Street Journal*, June 23, 1983.

48. Ogarkov, *Kommunist*, no. 10 (July 1981), pp. 80–91.

49. See Sallie Wise, "1983: A Bad Year for Soviet Diplomats," *Radio Liberty Research Bulletin*, no. 5, RL 467/83 (December 21, 1983). See John Vinocur, "The KGB Goes on the Offensive and the West Begins Striking Back," *New York Times*, July 24, 1983.

50. Jay Mallin, Sr., "Split Voiced by CIA, Pentagon on Buildup," *Washington Times*, July 27, 1984.

51. Jay Mallin, Sr., "Russia at High Level of Battle Readiness," *Washington Times*, July 26, 1984.

war comes from changes in the ground forces order of battle. In the 1983–85 period, the number of mobilization bases (unmanned divisional sets of weapons and equipment) dropped from seventeen to fourteen, while the number of active divisions in western Russia and Eastern Europe rose from ninety-five to ninety-eight.[52] There is also evidence of efforts to improve the preparedness of the civilian population for war.[53]

These fragmentary indicators suggest that the Soviet Union has adopted new planning factors for both political and operational warning. Initially, political warning appears to have been reduced around the end of 1981, with a further reduction being imposed in the wake of Andropov's declaration, late 1983 or early 1984. Following the deployment of the first Pershing II, it appears that the operational warning factor was applied more rigorously in determining the day-to-day posture of the armed forces.

THE UNITED STATES' OBJECTIVES. In large part, the Soviet perception of threat is based on an assessment of U.S. objectives regarding the Soviet Union. The Soviets have never pretended that there was other than an adversarial relationship between the superpowers, but during the 1970s they thought a modus vivendi had been achieved, defining the nature of the competition and placing limits on the means of waging it. This assessment was reluctantly revised in response to the policies adopted by the Reagan administration and, by April 1983, even Andropov was accusing the United States of seeking military superiority, including the capability for a disarming strike, and of having a flippant attitude toward the issues of peace and war.[54]

By the time of Andropov's declaration in September 1983, disagreement on the seriousness of the threat appears to have been resolved, and on November 11, Marshal Ustinov made an authoritative presentation on U.S. policy. The occasion was a special gathering of generals, admirals, and officers from the Ministry of Defense central apparatus, the Moscow military district, and the Moscow air defense district, which had been convened to discuss the implications of Andropov's declaration for the armed

52. See the U.S. Department of Defense, *Soviet Military Power,* 1983, 1984, and 1985, 2d through 4th editions (GPO, 1983, 1984, 1985), pp. 34, 58, and 66, respectively. It is, of course, possible that these changes reflect changes in internal "counting rules" within the Central Intelligence Agency. Nevertheless, an increase of eight active divisions (4 percent) in three years would seem to have some significance.

53. Shlapentokh, "Moscow's War Propaganda," pp. 88, 92, 94.

54. "Otvety Yu. V. Andropov na voprosy korrespondenta *Pravdy*" (Replies by Yuri V. Andropov to questions from a correspondent of Pravda), *Pravda,* March 27, 1983; and "Otvety Yu. V. Andropov zhurnaly *Spigel* (FRG)" (Replies by Yuri V. Andropov to the journal *Spiegel*), April 25, 1983.

services.[55] Sixty percent of Ustinov's statement was devoted to a structured analysis of U.S. objectives, which echoed less formal assessments that had been made by Marshal Alksey A. Yepishev, Ogarkov, and himself during the summer.

The core of the Soviets' threat assessment was the conclusion that the United States, with the rest of the capitalist bloc trailing along more or less willingly, had embarked on a crusade against communism and was determined to "eliminate socialism as a sociopolitical system."[56] According to the Soviets, this objective drove the economic, political, ideological, and military policies of the United States, and these policies pursued three main lines of attack:

—A serious and sustained attempt to achieve military superiority, including the capability for a disarming first strike against the Soviet Union and its allies. The U.S. administration was not interested in arms control and was determined to break the existing military balance between East and West.

—A general militarization of the international arena, drawing in more and more nations to the U.S. military orbit and encouraging them to build up their forces, and at the same time, steadily increasing the scale, scope, and global diversity of U.S. military exercises.

—A massive "psychological" attack against the Soviet Union and the socialist community aimed at preparing the people of the capitalist bloc for the possibility of military action against socialist states and at subverting the peoples of the socialist bloc.

Soviet statements were explicit on the nature of the threat that faced them, but the extent to which these statements reflected the beliefs of Soviet leaders is a different matter. However, concrete evidence had accumulated in the form of U.S. policy pronouncements, budgetary decisions, and operational behavior that the Soviets could interpret as confirming the existence of these three lines of attack. Although it could be argued that this Soviet assessment ignored the complexities of the American political system and the ability of Congress and public opinion to hold the executive branch in check (and there would have been a number in Moscow, though fast diminishing, who put forward this viewpoint), one of the striking characteristics of the Reagan administration had been the ability to get its way.

55. "Za vysokuyu boevuyu gotovnost'" (For high combat readiness), *Krasnaya zvezda*, November 12, 1983.

56. See "The Victory and the Present Day," FBIS, *Daily Report: SU*, pp. V1–9; "At the Level of the Party's Demands," *Krasnaya zvezda*, June 22, 1983; and "Ogarkov's Article on U.S. and Soviet Arms Policies," FBIS, *Daily Report: SU*, pp. A1–6.

It could also be argued that the American people were basically anti-Soviet, and that they therefore approved of a confrontational policy as long as it didn't actually lead to war. There is, therefore, every reason to assume that the characterization of three main lines of attack as just summarized was generally accepted as a planning assumption and that it will animate Soviet policy until there is evidence to disprove it.

Support for the core assessment of U.S. intentions may, though, have been less than universal, particularly in the higher echelons of government. Although the Soviets saw significant evidence that the Reagan administration had indeed embarked on a so-called crusade against communism, this was not quite the same as a U.S. objective of "destroying socialism as a sociopolitical system." The extent to which that aim had to be taken at face value is likely to have been one of the central questions facing the Soviet leaders.

CHAPTER 13

A Potential Decision Period: 1983–85

FROM 1978 to 1983, coinciding with the last five years of the Brezhnev era, a shift in the American mood led to greater U.S. assertiveness and a growing disenchantment with the concept of East-West détente and the idea of strategic equivalence. After Leonid I. Brezhnev's death, the confrontational style of U.S. policy persisted and even worsened, while the Strategic Defense Initiative complicated the question of arms control. The deterioration in the relationship between the United States and the Soviet Union was accompanied by a growing internal debate about the underlying issues. General Secretary Yuri V. Andropov's unusual declaration at the end of September 1983, with its pessimistic evaluation of international affairs in general, and the Soviet-American relationship in particular, was followed by Minister of Defense Dmitriy F. Ustinov's formal assessment that the objective of the United States was to eliminate socialism as a sociopolitical system.

If Andropov's declaration and Ustinov's threat assessment reflected a decision-in-principle, then the following two to three years (1983–85) would be a decision period. During that period the consequential policies would be worked out and the implementing decisions would be made, although the evidence of such decisions might not emerge for many years. Consequently, rather than poring over the tea leaves of current events, Western understanding of a possible new trend in Soviet foreign policy is best served by an attempt to identify the basic questions that are likely to have concerned the Soviets at that period.

The Debate about the Imminence of War

The Soviets distinguish between the military threat and the danger of war. In 1983 few Soviets would have disagreed with the proposition that the military threat to Russia had increased over the previous five years and had to be responded to. The more contentious question was the extent to which the danger of war had increased. If war was imminent, the Soviet Union should move its economy to a war footing and adopt an intransigent international demeanor, both to deter and to avoid conceding anything to the enemy. On the other hand, if the likelihood of war had increased, but it was still not imminent, then precipitous action would achieve the worst of all worlds. Of itself moving to a war footing would increase the danger of war and might prompt competitive mobilization. It would certainly damage the domestic economy, while denying the military the future fruit of ripening research and development. It would force Russia to forgo the potential gains of negotiations.

There is little doubt that the Soviet leaders did conclude that war had become significantly more likely and did take certain precautionary measures. Political warning time appears to have been reduced between 1981 and 1984, and some, if not all, of the Soviet armed forces were placed on a higher level of day-to-day readiness. A radical shift also occurred in the tone of Soviet internal propaganda following President Ronald Reagan's Star Wars speech in March 1983. For the first time since Josef Stalin's death, the threat of war rather than the likelihood of avoiding war became Moscow's dominant theme.[1] However, it could still be argued that the immediacy of the danger was being underestimated.

In April 1984 General Secretary Konstantin U. Chernenko had found it necessary to reassure the Soviet people that the danger of war was not serious enough to justify extending the five-day work week, suggesting that a significant body of influential opinion felt that more far-reaching measures were required.[2] An extreme position would have been to advocate declaring a "threat situation," but it seems unlikely that those favoring more stringent measures in 1983–84 actually considered war imminent. However, between the situation pertaining in the spring of 1984 and the

1. Vladimir E. Shlapentokh, "Moscow's War Propaganda and Soviet Public Opinion," *Problems of Communism*, vol. 33 (September-October 1984), pp. 89, 91–92.

2. "Rech' tovarischa K. U. Chernenko" (Speech of Comrade K. U. Chernenko), *Pravda*, April 30, 1984.

extreme of placing the country on a war footing, there was clearly room for more extensive preparatory measures. These could have included shifting additional resources and assembly lines from civil to military production, increasing the number of shifts worked, and improving the readiness of army divisions.

The call for increased readiness is likely to have been supported by those who argued that the conciliatory posture adopted during the previous three years had worked against the Soviet Union's interests and had emboldened the United States. At the end of 1983 the Reagan administration was describing the Soviet withdrawal from the Geneva negotiations as a passing huff or sulking in a corner, and assuring the American people that the Soviets would soon be back as *demandeur,* now that they realized that the administration intended to play "hard ball." In view of these circumstances, Soviet hardliners could have argued that the Soviet Union must take the political offensive. At issue were not only Soviet interests but national pride and self-respect.

The two bodies of Soviet opinion can be labeled "tough negotiators" and "intransigent alarmists." The policy that ultimately prevailed reflected the judgment that war was not imminent, although the immediate danger had increased significantly and favored negotiation over intransigence in dealing with the United States. The distinction was, however, relative, and the diplomatic approach of the mid–1980s would resemble that of the 1970s more in style than in spirit or substance. Neither body of Soviet opinion considered a conciliatory approach appropriate in the short term. The Soviet response to the deployment of Euromissiles was to withdraw from the negotiations on intermediate-range nuclear forces and strategic arms reductions and to make offsetting deployments of their own. They also reduced Soviet-American contacts and business to a trickle.[3]

It took time for the negotiators to prevail in the debate, which explains the somewhat mixed signals that emanated from the Soviet Union for about nine months following its withdrawal from the arms control negotiations. The mixed signals were due, in part, to a change in the outward style of American policy in January 1984. In pursuit of reelection, Ronald Reagan had agreed to adopt a more conciliatory approach to the Soviet Union. This opened up the danger that, by responding in kind to the U.S. initiative, the

3. Raymond L. Garthoff was told by knowledgeable Soviet officials that the decision to withdraw from the negotiations, and to take offsetting deployments and publicize them, was finally taken in November 1983. This chapter draws on material assembled by Garthoff for a forthcoming book.

tough negotiators would expose themselves to the charge of dancing to the president's tune.

Reopening a Dialogue

In June 1984, doubts in the U.S. Congress about the arms control implications of testing the U.S. antisatellite (ASAT) system provided a crucial opening for those in Moscow who favored negotiation. The U.S. ASAT program was important because of the inherent relationship of such programs to space-based defense systems and the opportunity it offered the United States for evading the provisions of the Antiballistic Missile Treaty.[4] Halting the development of the U.S. antisatellite system was therefore a high-priority Soviet objective, both in its own right and as a means of checking the momentum behind the Strategic Defense Initiative.

On June 11 Konstantin Chernenko reaffirmed the Soviet Union's continued adherence to the unilateral moratorium on ASAT testing declared by Andropov ten months earlier.[5] This move elicited a vote in the House of Representatives to block ASAT testing for a year, and at a subsequent news conference Reagan stated that he hadn't "slammed the door" on talks with the Soviets.[6] On June 29 the Soviets proposed that the two sides should meet to discuss how to prevent the militarization of space by banning the testing or deployment of antisatellite and other weapons. Although the Soviets declared that the U.S. response, which added the resumption of strategic arms reduction talks and negotiations on intermediate-range nuclear forces to the agenda, was tantamount to a rejection, the process of reestablishing a dialogue had begun.

The intransigent alarmists could still argue that the United States was not prepared to negotiate in good faith and that any discussions would be

4. The Antiballistic Missile Treaty allowed research into defense against ballistic missiles but forbade the testing and development of weapons or components. The type of antisatellite system favored by the United States would, however, allow the development and testing of components that could be used in a ballistic-missile defense system, without breaking the letter of the law.

5. This was first announced by Yuri V. Andropov in a private meeting with a group of Democratic party senators on August 19, 1983. The next day Gromyko proposed an amended draft treaty at the United Nations, which was a considerable improvement on the original 1981 version. The Soviets own antisatellite program, which had been under way since 1967, was much more primitive and had virtually no potential for ballistic-missile defense.

6. Paul B. Stares, *The Militarization of Space: U.S. Policy, 1945–85* (Cornell University Press, 1985), p. 234. This was not the only sign of a new U.S. flexibility. Soviet proposals had been ignored by the Reagan administration during 1981–83, but Secretary of State George P. Shultz began to discuss the weaponization of space with Ambassador Anatoly Dobrynin in spring 1984.

manipulated to Soviet disadvantage in world opinion. This contention was reinforced by President Reagan's speech to the Irish Parliament, also in June 1984, in which he recalled the appeal he had made for "a crusade for freedom" when he had addressed the British Parliament two years previously. In August, on the fortieth anniversary of the Warsaw uprising, Reagan declared that the United States would not accept "the permanent subjection of the people of Eastern Europe" and rejected "any interpretation of the Yalta agreement that suggests American consent for the division of Europe into spheres of influence."

Further support for the alarmists' point of view was provided by the Republican platform adopted in August 1984, which stressed the need for U.S. military superiority. In September, a Central Intelligence Agency memorandum was leaked that concluded that the Soviet empire had "entered its terminal phase."[7] Nevertheless, the intransigent alarmists could not deny the vital importance of derailing the Strategic Defense Initiative. That objective justified resuming negotiations and even incurring significant diplomatic costs until it was beyond doubt that the United States could not be made to yield on the issue.

Defeat of the Intransigent Alarmists

The evidence emanating from the Soviet Union continued to be contradictory because, despite this success by the tough negotiators, the alarmists were able to persist in their intransigent approach in less important areas.[8] They were not finally driven from the field until early September, when Marshal Nikolay V. Ogarkov was relieved of his positions as first deputy minister of defense and chief of the General Staff.

It appears that the alarmists' political leverage derived mainly from the thrust and urgency of their arguments about the danger of war, rather than from their share of high-level political support. The three successive general secretaries (Andropov, Chernenko, and Mikhail S. Gorbachev), as well as Foreign Minister Gromyko and Defense Minister Ustinov were on

7. "Dublin, Ireland," Address to a Joint Session of National Parliament, June 4, 1984, *Weekly Compilation of Presidential Documents*, vol. 20 (June 11, 1984), p. 833 and "Fortieth Anniversary of the Warsaw Uprising," August 17, 1984 (August 20, 1984), pp. 1132–33; John B. Oakes, "The G.O.P. Platform – Grounds for Worry" *New York Times*, September 25, 1984; and "CIA Says Soviets in Terminal Phase," *Washington Times*, September 21, 1984.

8. For example, officially inspired harassment of American officials and visitors in Leningrad, which had started in mid-April, continued through the beginning of August. John M. Goshko, "Harassment in Leningrad Leads to U.S. Warnings for Travelers," *Washington Post*, August 7, 1984. Leningrad was Grigoriy Romanov's fiefdom.

the negotiators' side of the debate, and this viewpoint had preponderant support in the Politburo. Nevertheless, the negotiators had to proceed carefully to avoid accusations that they were helping Reagan's reelection. Within the Politburo, at least Grigoriy G. Romanov, who supervised the defense industries, seems to have favored the alarmist point of view. However, the main strength of that viewpoint lay in its support by the military, which had a legitimate concern about the core issues and contributed its professional authority.

Press statements at the time of Ogarkov's removal, and his assignment as the commander in chief of the Western theater of military action (TVD) clarified the central issues of the debate. Although it would be necessary to divert resources to strengthening the country's security, the broad social programs that had been outlined by the 1981 party congress would not be curtailed.[9] These statements put the military firmly in its place regarding the allocation of resources, but its operational concerns were addressed directly by setting up in peacetime the high commands that would be needed in the event of war. The alarmists had lost on the matter of economic mobilization for war, but they won on the question of operational readiness for war.

The creation of wartime command and control organs in peacetime had been one of Ogarkov's most persistent demands, and it was appropriate that he should be sent off to establish such a structure. He undoubtedly annoyed the Politburo with his emphasis on the military-technical to the neglect of politico-social factors and his alarmism about American intentions and the growing danger of war. But his talents as a professional soldier do not seem to have been in question, and his energy and intellect could be usefully applied to this operational problem about which he felt so strongly.

The Need for Decisions

One must distinguish between the hiatus in major decisions on domestic issues that characterized Leonid I. Brezhnev's later years and persisted through the succession process, and the decisions which had to be and were taken on defense and foreign policy during this period. Similarly, one must distinguish between the complex process of domestic decisionmaking

---

9. "Dlya Sovetskogo Cheloveka" (For Soviet man), *Pravda,* September 5, 1984; and "Dlya blaga, naroda" (For the good of the people), *Krasnaya zvezda* (Red star), September 6, 1984.

that Gorbachev embarked on when he became general secretary in March 1985, and a 1983–85 decision period affecting defense and foreign policy.

General Secretary Gorbachev had to come to grips with serious internal problems stemming from an array of causes, including secular changes in the world economy and in the economies of the Eastern bloc, and the steady ossification of the Soviet political economy during the preceding ten years. These problems had been compounded by the domestic paralysis induced by the prospects and realities of a generational change in leadership. Many of the issues were fundamental, affecting major institutional and regional interests. The debate about how best to proceed had to be an ongoing process, reflecting the need to build coalitions in support of particular policies as well as the inherent complexity of the issues.

In the domestic sphere the difficulties lay as much in agreeing on the nature of the problems as on how to solve them. In the sphere of national security the issues were more clearly defined, and decisions could not be deferred. The developments that led to the Andropov declaration constituted an external threat to the well-being of the Soviet state. While there might be argument about the nature of the response, the need for one could hardly be disputed. Despite the succession process and despite the evidence that decisions in the domestic sphere largely lay ahead, the concept of a 1983–85 decision period affecting defense and foreign policy is, therefore, valid. This conclusion holds true partly because foreign policy decisions are driven by the press of external events, but also because a consensus within the collective leadership and the relevant bureaucracies on the need to respond to U.S. pressure would have existed.

A 1983–85 decision period means that any change in the thrust of Soviet policy would have been largely decided before Gorbachev became general secretary. It would be difficult for Gorbachev to change that strategic direction until he had consolidated his hold on the leadership.

The Backdrop to Decisionmaking

The defeat of the intransigent alarmists should not obscure the basic shift in the ground of the Soviet debate about policy toward the United States. In 1980–82 the main divide had been between those who believed that diplomacy and détente were not dead and that a collaborative relationship was still possible, and those who rejected this view and favored what has been characterized as a unilateralist approach.[10] While the two sides of the debate continued to draw on roughly the same constituents, many of the original "diplomatist" positions were abandoned after September 1983 as hopelessly optimistic, and the parameters of the Soviet debate moved sharply toward obduracy and intransigence. Gromyko's reference in his September 1984 speech at the United Nations to the "period of détente" as something in the past was not accidental.[11]

The relatively conciliatory style of Soviet policy that emerged in September 1984 says nothing about the strategic thrust of that policy. Having decided that war was not imminent, the Soviets were able to consider which style of diplomacy would best further their interests. The choice of style was a matter of tactics.[12] The strategic thrust of Soviet policy would have been determined by decisions the Soviets had reached on basic questions about the structure of international relations.

The outcome of a policy reevaluation is shaped by the perceptions of those involved, and these perceptions are colored by emotion as well as rational argument. It is necessary to remember that, at least during 1983 and 1984, the Soviet establishment was permeated with a sense of resentment toward the United States and anger at the way the Soviet Union was being treated by the Reagan administration. There was also frustration at the apparent success of Reagan's policies and the relative failure of their own.

Of several reasons for this feeling of anger and resentment, four were probably paramount. One was the emotional response to the substance of Reagan's rhetoric, which disparaged Russia's national culture, as well as its social system, and depicted the Soviet Union as both threatening to take over the world and bound for the ash heap of history. There were also three substantive reasons. One, détente, a relationship that had been the cornerstone of Soviet foreign and domestic policy for fifteen years, and represented a major political investment, had been ruptured. Two, the Soviets believed that, in the short term, Reagan's policies had increased the like-

10. Dan L. Strode and Rebecca V. Strode, "Diplomacy and Defense in Soviet National Security Policy," *International Security,* vol. 8 (Fall 1983), pp. 91–116.

11. "Vystuplenie A. A. Gromyko na xxxix sessii General'noy Assambley OON" (Address by A. A. Gromyko at the thirty-ninth session of the U.N. General Assembly), *Pravda,* September 28, 1984.

12. Gromyko is alleged to have said that one of the greatest weaknesses in U.S. foreign policy is that Americans do not comprehend the Soviets' final goals and that they mistake tactics for strategy. Arkady N. Shevchenko, *Breaking with Moscow* (Alfred A. Knopf, 1985), p. 279.

lihood of war; in the longer term, the Strategic Defense Initiative would open a Pandora's box. Three, these and other negative developments threatened the economic well-being of the Soviet Union and its people.

A reasonable approximation of how the Soviets perceived the threat to their interests can be obtained by combining their assessment of U.S. objectives, as spelled out by Ustinov in November 1983,[13] with the Soviets' three first-order objectives: retention of power by the Communist party, independence of international action, and avoidance of world war.

As viewed from Moscow in the fall of 1983, the retention of power by the Communist party was being threatened by the massive "psychological attack" that the United States had mounted against the Soviet Union and the socialist community, aimed at subverting the people of the socialist bloc. Soviet independence of international action was being undermined by the U.S. attempt to reestablish military superiority and by the prospective U.S. capability for a disarming strike, accompanied by a more active geopolitical policy. The avoidance of world war had been made more difficult by the shift from détente to confrontation; the steadily increasing scale, scope, and diversity of U.S. military exercises and operational deployments; and the general militarization of the international arena, drawing in ever more countries to the U.S. military orbit and encouraging them to build up their military strength.

In other words, developments in the 1970s had allowed, and perhaps fostered, the emergence of a U.S. policy that actively undermined the Soviet Union's three first-order objectives, thereby endangering the overarching national objective of promoting the well-being of the Soviet state. This situation raised fundamental questions about the appropriateness of the policies pursued by the Soviet Union during that period.

The Structure of International Relations

In the 1978–83 period the Soviets had been extremely reluctant to question, let alone jettison, the tenets that had shaped their foreign policy since the late 1960s. But by the end of September 1983, Andropov had concluded, "If anyone had any illusions about the possibility of an evolution

13. D. F. Ustinov, "Za vysokuyu boevuya gotovnost'" (For high combat readiness), *Krasnaya zvezda*, November 12, 1983.

for the better in the policy of the present American administration, recent events have dispelled them once and for all."[14]

Assuming that a policy reassessment took place during the summer of 1983, the Soviet review would have had to acknowledge that developments in the international arena during the 1978–83 period challenged key Soviet assumptions about the structure of international relations. In particular, questions would have been raised about the trend in the correlation of forces, the immutability of détente, and the nature of the superpower relationship.

The first issue to be resolved concerned the central tendency of the relationship between the superpowers. Did the conflictual thrust of U.S. policy in the 1978–83 period represent a right-wing deviation from the trend toward a more collaborative relationship? Or was it on trend, with the collaborative thrust of the 1969–75 period being a left-wing deviation from a consistently conflictual relationship between the two social systems?

If one looked back forty years to 1943–45, a strong argument could be made that American policy toward the Soviet Union in 1978–83 period conformed to the general thrust of U.S. policy since World War II, whereas the years of relatively sustained détente in 1969–73, and the few brief periods before that, were atypical. The argument became even more persuasive if one surveyed the sixty-six years since the Russian Revolution and the formation of the Soviet state. For most of that period, the United States had demonstrated hostility toward communism and the Soviet Union, and the collaborative relationship during World War II was a relatively brief exception to that norm.

The move from collaboration to confrontation in the postwar era bore a distinct resemblance to what happened in the 1970s, although the 1970s' process was more drawn out. By March 1946 the Anglo-Saxon powers had concluded that Russian behavior was such as to preclude the possibility of normal relations. They started girding themselves for a sustained struggle with the Soviet Union and world communism, although this was not formally announced until the Truman declaration of March 1947.[15]

---

14. "Zayavlenie General'nogo sekretarya TsK KPSS, Predsedatelya Prezidiuma Verkhovnogo Soveta SSSR Yu. V. Andropova" (Declaration by General Secretary Yuri V. Andropov of the CC of the CPSU, chairman of the Presidium of the Supreme Soviet of the USSR), *Pravda,* September 29, 1983.

15. The Truman doctrine was characterized as giving "the impression that the policy of attempting to cooperate with the Soviet Union had been given up, and that an eventual war between the two alternative ways of life . . . was inevitable." See John C. Campbell, *The United States in World Affairs, 1945–47* (Harper, 1948), p. 480.

It was not, however, until July 1947, after Foreign Minister V. M. Molotov had withdrawn from the meeting to discuss the European Recovery Program (the Marshall Plan), that the Soviets finally acknowledged the rupture with the West.[16] It was formally announced at the organizing conference of the Cominform in September 1947. Similarly, in more recent times, the United States had concluded by 1978–79 that the détente relationship was no longer tenable, although the breach did not finally come until the Reagan administration. The Soviets, meanwhile, kept asserting that détente was irreversible. They blamed the deterioration in the superpower relationship on "certain influential forces" in the United States, rather than acknowledging it to be administration policy. It was not until the plenum in June 1983 that the Soviets formally admitted the split.[17]

It may well have been argued in Moscow that Reagan's policies were substantially the same as U.S. policies in the 1920s and 1940s, that capitalist attitudes were immutable, and that America, the bastion of capitalist imperialism, was simply not prepared to accept the legitimacy of the socialist system or of its leader, the Soviet Union. There are indeed striking similarities between the circumstances of September 1947 and September 1983. Andrey Zhdanov's statement and Andropov's declaration both announced the defeat of the cooperative tendencies in the West and the victory of those who sought confrontation with the Soviet Union, and they both marked the end of a period of East-West collaboration or détente. Both Soviet statements depicted the world as having been split into two camps, with the capitalists embarked on a sustained offensive intended to destroy the socialist system.

In the wake of Zhdanov's two camps doctrine, Soviet policy became assertively confrontational, the process of installing pro-Soviet regimes in the states of eastern Europe was hastened, and the constraints on the communist parties of western Europe were lifted. In other words, in response to Harry S. Truman's declaration of a crusade against communism and the depiction of the world as an unconstrained struggle between free people and those who sought to subjugate them, the Soviets moved over to the offensive.

16. Previously, the official Soviet line had been that there were two tendencies in Britain and America, one of which was prepared to continue with the decisionmaking system based on tripartite compromise and agreement that developed during the war, while the other sought world domination for the Anglo-Saxon powers. William Taubman, *Stalin's American Policy: From Entente to Détente to Cold War* (W. W. Norton, 1982), pp. 120–21.

17. See Gromyko's reference to the "confrontation of two lines" in his speech, "Omezhdunardom polozhenii i vneshney politike Sovetskogo Soyuza" (On the international situation and the foreign policy of the Soviet Union), *Pravda*, June 17, 1983.

Forty years later the Soviets may have reached similar conclusions about the appropriate response to what they saw as Reagan's crusade against communism and his depiction of the world as divided between the forces of good and evil. In the 1940s the means available to the Soviet Union were restricted and somewhat crude, and their experience of international relations was limited. As a result, their offensive largely backfired. Forty years later the Soviets have gained considerable diplomatic experience. They also have new leaders who are more flexible and subtle and less constrained by the early experiences of the Soviet state.

The Concept of Détente

Soviet policy throughout the 1970s was premised on the argument that détente was irreversible. It was seen as part of a historic trend that was driven by the acceleration in the movement of the correlation of forces in favor of the socialist system and by a new realism in the United States that recognized the objective situation. The ideological struggle would continue, but collaborative relationships would be encouraged and, most important, the resort to war as a way of settling disputes between the superpowers was ruled out. By 1983 this whole analysis was in doubt.

The best that could be argued regarding the irreversibility of détente, was that it was a ratchet process and, while progress had halted for the time being, and even suffered some reverses, most of the structural gains made in the 1970s were still secure. Most Soviets, however, are likely to have drawn more pessimistic conclusions and to have acknowledged that the détente of the 1970s was a thing of the past and many, if not most, of the benefits had been dissipated.

That would still leave the question of whether détente was a desirable long-term objective that ought to be pursued or whether it had worked against Soviet long-term interests by raising false expectations and encouraging complacency.[18] It could be argued that the nature of the superpower relationship was predominantly conflictual, therefore periods of cooperation were bound to be transitory and could not provide the basis for long-term policies. It could also be argued that the period of détente had

18. Besides the developments of the previous fifteen years, the Soviets would have had available to them as evidence the memoirs by leading members of successive administrations, spelling out their view of détente. For example, Garthoff notes that Nixon and Kissinger saw détente as a strategy rather than an objective, as a means rather than a goal. Raymond L. Garthoff, *Détente and Confrontation: American-Soviet Relations from Nixon to Reagan* (Brookings, 1985), p. 29.

brought problems at home and few benefits abroad and was therefore inherently undesirable.[19]

Peaceful coexistence was a sine qua non in a nuclear world, but that did not necessarily imply détente. It could be argued that a policy of détente embodied the subjective yearning for a collaborative relationship with the other superpower, a relationship that was ruled out by objective factors. By definition détente imposed constraints that in the past had incurred costs in terms of opportunities forgone, while the restraint itself went unrewarded. Soviet restraint in the Greek civil war in the latter 1940s had not prevented the Soviets from being portrayed as the instigators. Soviet restraint in the Western Hemisphere in the 1970s did not prevent the Soviets from being blamed for various upheavals in Central and South America.

The Soviets could argue that the first three years of the Reagan administration had demonstrated that the United States mistook moderate and conciliatory behavior as weakness. If America was emphasizing the role of military force in its global policy, then the Soviet Union should be prepared to respond in kind.

The Correlation of Forces

A separate question about the correlation of forces impinged directly on the question of whether or not the restoration of détente should be a policy objective. In the 1970s it was regularly asserted that détente had been made possible by the increasingly favorable trend in the correlation of forces. What, then, did the failure of détente imply?

Did it mean that the assessment of the 1970s situation had been too optimistic, resulting in a premature turn to détente, and that it was only necessary to wait for a further improvement in the correlation of forces for sustained détente to be possible? Was it that the calculation of the correlation of forces had been correct, but that the Reagan administration was so blinded by anticommunism that it was unable to draw what the Soviets considered "realistic" conclusions from the situation? Or was the long-term trend in the correlation of forces not as favorable as had been assumed? Had the crisis of capitalism been exaggerated so that the Soviets

19. At the height of détente Salvador Allende was brought down in Chile, Richard M. Nixon achieved rapprochement with China, and the Soviets were squeezed out of the Middle East by Henry Kissinger. From the Soviet viewpoint, it was not a period of net gain in world influence, and the gains made were not a by-product of détente.

could not just sit and wait for capitalism to fail but must take more vigorous action to improve the strength of the communist system?

If the third explanation was the right one, then what was the proper balance between matching the Reagan administration's military buildup and investing resources in the Soviet economy?

Historical Inevitability

Soviet policy toward the third world had been based on the assumption that history was clearly on the side of socialism. This meant that the Soviets could afford to "win some, lose some," and to pay heed to the risk of local conflicts getting out of control and precipitating global war. Two developments during the early 1980s undermined this relatively relaxed approach. One was a growing concern about the decelerating trend in the correlation of forces. The other was the evidence that the United States was becoming increasingly intolerant of the emergence of Marxist (or even socialist) regimes and was ready to use military force to protect perceived American interests.

The coincidence of these two developments meant that the Soviet Union faced the possibility of a serious setback in the competition between socialism and capitalism in the third world. Its ability to meet its war-related requirements would also be prejudiced. Should the Soviet Union therefore adopt a more assertive policy in the third world, using a wider range of instruments? Should the Soviets be more active in supporting liberation movements, in providing help to consolidate the power of socialist regimes, and in protecting them from internal and external threats? Should they adopt a more active policy in Latin America where previously, in general, they had been sensitive to U.S. special interests? Was there even a political advantage to be gained from provoking the United States to coercive intervention in Central and South America?

If the answer to these questions was in the affirmative, then what did that imply for Soviet military force, latent or applied, as an instrument of policy in the third world? In the past, its use to support Soviet interests had been severely constrained by the fear that it would lead to superpower confrontation and then escalate to global nuclear war. This cautious approach had been challenged unsuccessfully in 1969–74 but, ten years later, the terms of the debate would have been very different.

In 1983–85 it could be argued that the Soviet Union had to choose between two evils. Inaction could result in a serious setback to its position in the third world and in the competition for world influence. Action would risk military confrontation, which could conceivably escalate to nuclear war. However, the Soviets by then had a better idea of how the United States was likely to respond to their intervention in distant parts of the globe. Evidence had also accumulated of American reluctance to risk devastation to save Europe, or even its own troops in Europe. Although this reluctance could not be counted on in the event of war in Europe, reassuring inferences could be drawn about the risk of escalation in possible confrontations in other parts of the world.

However, others could argue that the real choice lay in different instruments of policy. It was not necessary for the Soviet Union to counter U.S. military intervention, since the American use of force to support its clients or to overthrow progressive regimes would inevitably estrange third world opinion. It was therefore far more important to concentrate on ensuring the economic development of the Soviet Union so that it could serve as a showcase for socialism and provide the necessary economic support to its protégés.

Current Diplomacy

Decisions on the structural issues just discussed would largely determine the strategic thrust of Soviet foreign policy, but three questions of current diplomacy needed to be addressed in their own terms.

ARMS CONTROL. The primary Soviet objective was to derail the Strategic Defense Initiative, but this aim left several questions. What should the Soviets be prepared to concede to achieve a treaty banning weapons from space? What should they do if the United States refused to negotiate constraints on weapons in space? What would be the costs and benefits of staying at the negotiating table in the face of such refusal? Would the succeeding administration be more likely to negotiate on this central issue, even if it were Republican? To what extent could Western public opinion be brought to bear on halting the move into space, and what did this require in terms of the Soviet negotiating stance?

NON-U.S. MEMBERS OF THE CAPITALIST BLOC. The deployment of Euromissiles had surfaced new evidence of the relative strengths and alignments of latent political forces both within the countries of the Western bloc and among them. What did the evidence imply for the long-term Soviet policy? Was it realistic to think of detaching all or some of the Europeans from the American fold? If not, was it realistic to think of Europe and Japan as able to restrain the military emphasis in U.S. policy? If so, what kind of Soviet behavior would be most likely to elicit such initiatives within the Western alliance? Would it be conciliatory behavior toward the West as a whole, including the United States? Or should special efforts be directed at Japan and at some or all the Europeans while adopting a harsh and obdurate policy toward America? Or was the best approach to stimulate public concern about the danger of war by adopting intransigent policies across the board? Should the Soviets adopt some mix of all three, orchestrated as appropriate over time?

CHINA. The relationship with China was of perennial importance in its own right, but it was also affected directly by structural decisions concerning the ongoing struggle between the two social systems. If the Soviets decided that détente with the United States was not a realistic long-term objective, it would then become very important to reduce the conflictual element in the Sino-Soviet relationship, seek areas for collaboration, and if possible achieve some kind of rapprochement with China.

Military Issues

Unless it requires a new emphasis on the role of force in peacetime, a reassessment of the superpower relationship need not affect the structure of the Soviet armed forces. That stucture is shaped by the worst-case contingency of world war. A change in the assessment of the likelihood of war would, however, have implications for the level of resources allocated to defense. Although the alarmist view did not prevail, there is little doubt that the Soviets concluded that the possibility of war increased significantly during the first Reagan administration, and they took a range of measures designed to improve the country's readiness for such a contingency. But the needs of the military had to be balanced against the broader requirements of the Soviet economy.

A successful economy is important to the overarching objective of promoting the well-being of the Soviet state and to two of the three first-order supporting objectives. By demonstrating the advantages of socialist planning and raising the standard of living of the individual Soviet citizen, a vibrant economy enhances the legitimacy of the Communist party and thereby contributes to its retention of power. The same effects increase the Soviet Union's capacity for independent international action, an objective that is also served by being able to use trade and aid as instruments of foreign policy and by having an economy that does not depend on the capitalist bloc for key commodities or technologies.

The guns or butter argument is therefore a permanent feature of the policy debate. It goes back to the earliest days of the Soviet state, and its salience steadily increased following the 1956 doctrinal revision that war with the capitalist bloc was no longer fatalistically inevitable. It is a mistake to assume that the Soviet military gets everything it asks for, and many examples demonstrate that this is not true.[20] Nevertheless, the security of Russia ranks high as a national priority that is accepted by the people at large. In 1983–85, given the general perception that both the threat and the danger of war had increased, there would have been considerable support throughout the political establishment for improving the Soviet Union's preparedness for war.

There remained the question of the best way of achieving this state. Some would have favored Josef Stalin's approach in the 1930s, which was successfully tested in the Great Patriotic War. Others would have argued that mass production was insufficient in itself to meet the requirements of a future war and that emerging technology and new ways of using forces would be the critical factors. The Soviets would have debated the relative priority to be accorded the competing requirements to wage conventional war in the continental TVDs, and to match the United States' strategic nuclear capability, particularly in the field of ballistic-missile defense. They would have disagreed over the scale of investment in very long-range research and development as opposed to shorter-range projects with a higher probability of success but lower probability of technological breakthroughs. Controversy about the imminence of war is unlikely to have evaporated, leading to argument over what resources should be shifted to the defense sector at the expense of the domestic economy.

These arguments would have merged with the broader debate over improving the efficiency of the Soviet economy. That debate was still in its early stages in 1985, but in respect to defense allocations, there were various questions that had to be answered in the relatively near future.

Intercontinental Missiles

In the 1950s the Soviets had determined the number of missiles they needed by reference to the targets or target areas to be covered. In the 1960s the sudden buildup of the American ICBM force introduced an

20. See appendixes B and D.

added requirement to target that force. By the 1970s the logic of the Soviets' new hierarchy of objectives argued for much lower numbers, but the requirement to match the U.S. arsenal for political, as well as military, reasons remained. By the 1980s, as Ogarkov noted in May 1984, both sides had sufficient warheads to destroy all the important targets many times over. These numbers denied either side the possibility of achieving a disarming strike and made nonsense of the concept of limited nuclear war.[21]

Such statements were not new and merely made explicit the reasoning that had led to the doctrinal shift at the end of 1966 away from a strategy of intercontinental preemption, which could no longer serve to limit the nuclear devastation of Russia. Implicit in Ogarkov's statement was the question of how important it was to match the impending U.S. buildup and whether scarce resources would be better spent on conventional weapons that incorporated emerging technologies.

Besides aggregate numbers, questions about intercontinental systems would fall into three general categories. The Soviets were concerned about the optimum proportions between missiles intended for the initial exchange against preplanned fixed targets, for which MIRVed warheads would be most cost-effective, and those missiles for use at a later stage of the war, for which single warheads would be most often appropriate. (Existing policy is suggested by the Soviet proposals at the strategic arms reduction talks, which are analyzed in Appendix D.)

Another category of question would be the appropriate mix between ballistic missiles and cruise missiles and aircraft. From the time the intercontinental ballistic missile entered service in the early 1960s, the Soviets had allowed the United States a virtual free ride in respect to continental air defense. Was such a policy sensible, particularly with the prospect of U.S. ballistic-missile defenses looming in the future? If it was desirable to pose a substantial air-breathing threat, what would be the optimum mix of launch platforms? For example, submarines could be used to strike at the United States from arctic waters.

But the most interesting category of question would have concerned the mix of basing modes for ballistic missiles. The Soviets would have to choose between mobile and fixed launchers and between land-based and sea-based launchers. There is evidence that in the wake of the 1976–77

---

21. Interview with Marshal of the Soviet Union N. V. Ogarkov, "Zashita sotsializma: opyt istorii i sovremennost'" (The defense of socialism: Experience of history and the present day), *Krasnaya zvezda*, May 9, 1984.

defense review, the relative importance of the Arctic Ocean as a region for basing intercontinental missiles was downgraded. This move prompts the thought that the Soviets might be intending to change the proportion between land- and sea-based systems, and if this had seemed a desirable development in 1976–77, it would have been even more attractive in the 1983–85 period. By then it would have been clear that the U.S. Navy was seeking to develop a specialized capability for antisubmarine operations in arctic waters. Meanwhile the Soviets demonstrated that large land-based mobile systems were a practical option.

Ballistic-Missile Defenses

Questions about ballistic-missile defense would pertain to what the Soviets should do to develop their own defenses and how they should respond to U.S. attempts to develop a space-based system. The primary reason the Soviets reversed their policy on antiballistic-missile defense in 1967–69 was the newly perceived possibility of deterring the United States from striking the Soviet Union in an attempt to save U. S. forces in Europe from defeat. The means of deterrence would be the intercontinental component of the strategic rocket forces, and this reliance explained the pressure to conclude a treaty limiting the deployment and further development of antiballistic-missile defenses. The 1972 Antiballistic Missile Treaty allowed the protection of the national capital area and of one area containing ICBM launchers. Each area could be defended by one hundred antiballistic missiles deployed within a radius of 150 kilometers. The treaty did not allow the defense of the national territory as a whole, nor of any region other than the two designated areas. In 1974 the treaty was amended to allow only one ballistic-missile defense site, with the Soviets choosing to defend Moscow and the United States preferring to defend its ICBM fields.[22]

The military logic of 1972–74 was still valid ten years later. The defense of Moscow continued to make good strategic sense, and it also responded to visceral concerns that were immune to the argument that any defensive system could be swamped.[23] The Soviets could meanwhile accept the ballistic-missile defense of American ICBM fields. Such defenses would not

22. The Soviets had originally proposed this arrangement in 1972, but it was turned down by the United States. Congress would not, however, fund the antiballistic-missile defense of Washington, and the Soviets agreed to a protocol amending the treaty in this way. Garthoff, *Détente and Confrontation*, pp. 146–54.

23. In any case, that argument was only valid for the U.S. capability and did not apply to the minor nuclear powers.

affect the credibility of their wartime deterrent, which depended on the capability to devastate the United States. In any case, the concept of a preemptive intercontinental strike was no longer central to Soviet strategy. In fact, given the progressive improvement in Soviet ballistic-missile defense capability,[24] there could have been arguments in favor of providing a third-generation system for Soviet ICBM fields, since such defenses would provide additional insurance against the United States developing the capability for a disarming strike.

Except as a possible response to a U.S. move toward territorial defense, the Soviets are unlikely to have favored developing a system to protect the whole of Russia, or even the western parts of the Soviet Union. Quite apart from the extremely high cost and fairly low effectiveness of such a system, a Soviet initiative in that direction could be expected to prompt the United States to follow suit. Given America's awesome record of achieving clearly defined objectives against apparently insuperable technological odds, the end result would undoubtedly be unfavorable to the Soviets. The United States could be expected to have an operational system in place long before the Soviet Union, which would then face an extended future in which U.S. defenses placed the Soviet deterrent in doubt.

The Soviets would also have to consider their response to U.S. attempts to develop a space-based defense system. They could try to acquire the means of evading the new systems by developing types of ballistic missile that could not be readily intercepted and by adopting delivery vehicles other than ballistic missiles, for instance, cruise missiles. They could also decide to try to counter the space-based defenses directly, either by reducing the vulnerability of ballistic weapons to such systems or by developing the means of neutralizing the systems themselves.

The Soviets would not be able to wait for a crisis or a war to neutralize the U.S. system since they would be placed at a massive disadvantage if a fully operational U.S. system were to be successfully deployed. Could the Soviet leaders afford to allow the United States to proceed unimpeded? Indeed the Soviets could argue that the most prudent and sensible course was to challenge immediately the right of the United States to use space in this way. Perhaps they should issue an ultimatum that any attempt to weaponize space would be resisted (in space) with force.

24. The Soviet ballistic-missile defense system defending Moscow has now achieved the capability of the Sprint system that was discarded in the United States in the mid-1970s. See Sayre Stevens, "The Soviet BMD Program," in Ashton B. Carter and David N. Schwartz, eds., *Ballistic Missile Defense* (Brookings, 1984), pp. 209–13.

The Land-Air Battle

In most cases, the questions that the Soviets had to resolve about land-air operations were of long standing but had been sharpened by the developments of 1981–83, with the partial exception of command and control. The U.S. Pershing II now deployed in Europe had the capability to disrupt C^3 at the TVD level. This disruption would occur at the critical moment that Soviet forces in the European theater would be executing the complex process of changing from a nonnuclear to a nuclear posture, even as the battle was in progress. This emerging NATO capability, the assessment that the likelihood of war had increased significantly, and perhaps the postmortem on the shooting down of the Korean airliner would have been a powerful combination, pressuring the Soviets to streamline the arrangements for moving from peace to a war footing. In the fall of 1984 three new high commands were staffed and activated for the conduct of operations in the Western, Southwestern, and Southern TVDs; the Far Eastern TVD had had its own high command since the latter half of the 1970s. There may also have been other changes affecting arrangements for the Supreme High Command in Moscow.

Other questions requiring resolution would have become more salient with the increased likelihood of war. The future shape of the land-air battle and what changes would be needed in weapons, equipment, and operational concepts confronted the Soviets. Once clear of Vietnam, the vast intellectual energy and technological ingenuity of the American military establishment had been refocused on the problems of war in Europe. The United States' short-term preoccupation was to reequip the U.S. armed forces to restore the ravages of Vietnam and match the buildup in Soviet conventional capability that had taken place in the 1970s. This modernization got under way at the beginning of the 1980s.[25]

The United States' longer-term approach was to develop new operational concepts that would exploit emerging technologies in surveillance and target-acquisition techniques, and in precision-guided munitions. The immediate objective was to be able to strike at Soviet second-echelon forces, as well as those already committed to battle. But, as Ogarkov noted, these developments also meant that conventional weapons were ap-

---

25. Modernization included the deployment of F-15 and F-16 fighters, the M-1 Abrahm tank, the M-2 Bradley infantry fighting vehicle, the Apache advanced attack helicopter, the Blackhawk helicopter, and the Patriot air defense system.

proaching the effectiveness of nuclear weapons in reach and lethality, which would have major implications for activities in the deep rear in the initial stages of a war. Furthermore, in the future lay the prospect of "even more destructive and previously unknown types of weapon based on new physical principles."[26] How should the Soviets respond?

It will be some time before the answers to that question can be discerned, but the Soviet response is likely to involve major innovations. When addressing senior officers from the Moscow area on the implications for the armed forces of Andropov's September declaration, Ustinov emphasized the need for "high creativity" and insisted that the military could not rely on established methods and the inertia of past progress to solve the problems that faced it.[27] Although this particular exhortation applied to combat training for the contingency of world war, it echoed others that Soviet leaders had made in more general contexts.[28]

Questions about the use of nuclear weapons in a future war would also have been at the center of a debate. The Soviets were concerned about their ability to disable NATO's theater nuclear capability with conventional means, and they had to assess the capacity of their ground forces to break through NATO's defenses by using conventional fire only. A separate question was whether the judicious use of nuclear weapons in the theater would risk escalation to an international exchange.

Naval Forces

Although questions about the land-air battle would merely have been sharpened, in the matter of naval developments, new ones are likely to have been introduced and old ones reopened. Debate on the role of force as an instrument of Soviet policy in the third world would have prompted the new questions. The old questions related to phase II of a world war, and the debate in the first half of the 1970s about the navy's role in a global conflict in which the opponent would be a coalition of maritime powers. Both sets of questions had implications for future naval force requirements. The answers would have been conditioned by the decisions made in 1976–77 to place an increased emphasis on the Far East as an area for

26. Interview with Ogarkov in *Krasnaya zvezda,* May 9, 1984.
27. The words Ustinov used were "rabotat' po starinke, dvigat'sya po inertsii, my ne mozhem" in *Krasnaya zvezda,* November 12, 1983.
28. For example, Brezhnev's meeting with command personnel on October 27, 1982, described in *Pravda,* October 28, 1982.

deploying ballistic-missile submarines (SSBN) and to reduce the relative importance of the Arctic.

The original 1970s concept had been to establish command of the Norwegian Sea, making the Arctic Ocean a secure haven for the deployment of the SSBN insurance force. This plan resulted in demanding new requirements for naval forces. It is clear that the 1967–68 decision period led to the provision of additional naval construction capacity and that these plans may have been further increased in 1973–74. The justification for the process of restructuring was, however, subsequently largely removed by the decision to relax the requirement to gain command of the Norwegian Sea. Although force requirements in the Far East would rise, and it would still be necessary to deny the West command of the arctic approaches, the concept of operations was much less demanding in terms of forces. The question would then have arisen of whether to go ahead with the programs as planned or to cut them back.

The evidence, which is still fragmentary, indicates that one of the outcomes of the 1976–77 decision period was the decision to cut back on several naval programs.[29] The one precedent of such a cutback suggests that other programs may have been affected in the longer term. When the threat of maritime invasion was discounted in 1953–54, the Sverdlov cruiser and medium-type submarine programs were halted within two years. Although the delivery of destroyers, escort ships, and submarine chasers ran its full course through 1957, a virtual four-year hiatus of surface ship deliveries occurred thereafter.[30] One cannot, therefore, be certain of the full scope of the 1976–77 decision regarding naval programs, but the 1953–54 precedent does indicate that when the domestic economy is being emphasized (as it was at that time and was again in the second half of the 1970s), there is a readiness to shift resources if the opportunity offers.[31]

29. The Ivan Rogov landing ship and Berezina under way replenishment ships were both canceled. The Oscar SSBN and Typhoon ballistic-missile submarine programs were either curtailed or canceled. The aircraft carrier program may have been modified, and if the allocation of naval nuclear reactors had been increased in 1973–74, this was rescinded. See appendix B.

30. Halting the Sverdlov program required the scrapping of at least 4 partly completed hulls. The submarine program was delivering 72 Whisky submarines a year and had just started the assembly of the first Romeos. This hiatus appears to have been imposed in order to wait for the 1961 "vintage" of weapons systems. It was not complete because of the 4 Kildins (which used Kotlin hulls from the 1952–57 delivery period) and 8 Krupnys. See Michael MccGwire, "Soviet Naval Procurement," in The Soviet Union in Europe and the Near East: Her Capabilities and Intentions (London: Royal United Service Institution, 1970), pp. 77–79.

31. The 1953–54 decision is not an exact precedent in this context since it was possible to use the cruiser building ways to build fish factory and merchant ships, and the canceled submarine

In 1976–77, the concept of closing off the Norwegian Sea had been discarded, creating a surplus of programmed naval capability over actual requirements. In 1983–85 a new requirement to project military force in distant sea areas may have emerged, and it could have been largely covered by that surplus. If, therefore, the surplus was retained or restored, the Soviets would possess a more capable and more flexible navy, able to secure Soviet interests in peacetime and to discharge a wide range of missions in phase II of a global war. It would also yield benefits in phase I of a war.

In essence the question that the Soviets had to address in 1983–85 was whether to restore the cut in the allocation of resources to naval construction that had been imposed in 1976–77. To some extent the Soviets would have been able to capitalize on the resources that had already been invested before the cutback, and a crucial consideration would have been the actual increment of new investment that would be required. Three factors are likely to have been important in their assessment of the relative priority of this revised requirement, compared with other demands on the economy. One would have been their assessment of the likelihood of world war. Two would have been their assessment of the importance of seapower to the Soviet Union; this is an area in which the change of political leadership could conceivably have altered the established bias. The third would have been how the Soviets read naval developments in the West.

When the 1976–77 decisions were made, it appeared that the U.S. Navy would stabilize at about 475 ships with 12 carrier battle groups; the successor to the 688-class of nuclear submarine had yet to be decided; and the desirability of being able to attack Soviet SSBNs was not part of Western public discourse. By 1983 the U.S. Navy seemed well on its way to being a 600-ship force with 15 carrier battle groups and was promoting the concept of horizontal escalation and the idea that war at sea would inevitably be worldwide. The SSN-21 class of submarine had been programmed to succeed the 688 and would be faster and quieter and carry about twice as many weapons. U.S. discussion of the need to draw down the Soviet SSBN force was now commonplace, and submarines from the United States and the United Kingdom conducted joint exercises of under-ice operations in the Arctic. The U.S. Navy did not dispute that a mission of the SSN-21 was to hunt Soviet SSBNs.

In 1978–83 the maritime threat had grown. The wartime threat to the

---

programs released about 220 heavy-duty diesel-generators a year. Contemporary building programs would not allow a comparable reallocation of resources.

SSBN insurance force was now explicit and would increase sharply when the SSN-21 started entering service in 1994. The concept of horizontal escalation had made the likelihood of naval encounters outside of a world war significantly greater. The Soviets believed that the threat of "imperialist aggression" against socialist regimes in third world countries had meanwhile increased markedly. The "Vietnam syndrome" had been a passing phase, the United States had demonstrated its readiness to project coercive force against such regimes and had improved its capability to do so, including a steady buildup of naval strength.

Aircraft carriers and amphibious forces were still the primary instruments of U.S. policy in the third world and, if such intervention was to be countered directly, it would have to be done by Soviet naval forces. How the Soviets have chosen to respond will become clear in the years ahead.

Overview

Because of the distortions introduced by the efforts to derail the Strategic Defense Initiative and by the generational change in the Soviet leadership, it will be hard to distinguish the early stages of a secular shift in Soviet policy from other evidence of change. If such a shift means an increased role for military force in distant parts of the world, then the Soviets would have an interest in obscuring those intentions until they had the necessary capability to implement such a policy.

From the viewpoint of the West, a critical question is what the Soviets concluded about the underlying trend in American attitudes toward the Soviet Union. It would be particularly important if the Soviets decided that Reagan's policies were merely a slight exaggeration of fundamental American beliefs that could be traced back to 1917. The Soviets' assessment of the correctness of the policy they embarked on in 1953–55, which saw the progressive redefinition of peaceful coexistence until, in the 1970s, it became full-fledged détente is also significant. Although the Soviets continue to assert that the objective circumstances dictate that there is no alternative to peaceful coexistence, that concept can be interpreted in a wide range of ways.

In addressing these structural questions, the Soviets are unlikely to have given much attention to the outward change in U.S. policy as Reagan moderated his rhetoric in preparation for the 1984 election, nor to the less confrontational stance of his second administration. These adjustments to U.S.

policy had little bearing on the central tendency in American attitudes toward the Soviet Union.

The Soviet answers to the various questions are likely to be shades of grey rather than black or white. Three factors would have been driving the decisions in the direction of a greater emphasis on military strength and of intransigence toward the United States: the increased danger of war, the concern for independence of action, and the national sense of anger and resentment. Two factors would have worked in the opposite direction: the demands of the domestic economy and the need to derail the Strategic Defense Initiative. The objective of derailing the Strategic Defense Initiative would have been crucial in determining the style of Soviet international behavior, and the tactics of Soviet policy should not be taken as an indication of underlying goals and strategy.

Shaping the whole process of decisionmaking would be the three first-order national objectives. All three were directly threatened by the policies of the Reagan administration. The U.S. move from détente to confrontation and the sharp rise in tension increased the danger of world war. The attempt to disrupt the existing military balance and to achieve U.S. superiority, including the capability for a disarming strike, threatened the Soviet capacity for independent action. The "psychological" attack on the legitimacy of the Soviet state threatened the retention of power by the Communist party. In these circumstances, the objective of preserving the capacity for independent international action would have assumed a new salience.

This increased salience is likely to have a significant impact on Soviet foreign policy. It also means that the danger of war will increase, since the objective of preserving independence of action tends to work against the objective of avoiding world war. This internal impulse toward war will reinforce the external impulse that is seen to stem from what the Soviets view as the confrontational policies of the United States. If the Soviets consider war more likely, they will accord higher priority to providing the means to fight such a war, and this priority would cover both the allocation of resources to defense and the preparation of TVDs for the contingency of world war.

If one moves down from the national to the strategic hierarchy that is headed by the objective of not losing the war, the governing objective of avoiding the nuclear devastation of Russia remains viable for the foreseeable future. The Soviets are adamant that it is no longer possible for either power to develop the capability for a "disarming strike,"[32] and a leakproof strategic defense for the United States lies in the twenty-first century, if anywhere. The concept of deterring nuclear strikes on Russia remains, therefore, operationally valid, and Soviet assessments of the psychological effectiveness of such deterrence are likely to be much more optimistic than they were in 1966, given the general tenor of the Western debate.

Apart from questions of the country's readiness for the contingency of world war, the immediate impact of the 1983–85 decision period is likely to be on the development of strategic delivery and defense systems. The Soviets will also urgently review once more the "methods and forms of armed struggle," brought about by new means of command, control, communications, and intelligence; the increased range, accuracy, and destructiveness of conventional weapons; and the emergence of weapons based on new physical principles. In other areas it seems likely that the decisions made as the result of the reevaluation in the wake of Ustinov's appointment as minister of defense (the 1976–77 decision period) are still working their way through the system. Again, there is no obvious reason why the upper levels of the 1970s hierarchy of objectives should have changed, but experience in the intervening period may have suggested modifications to objectives at lower levels and certainly to the methods of achieving those objectives.

Only time will tell, but it would be prudent to cover the possibility that 1983–85 will turn out to be a major turning point in Soviet foreign and defense policy. In respect to Marxist-Leninist doctrine and foreign policy goals and strategy, the circumstances suggest that it could be of comparable significance to the 1947–48 decision period, when Stalin faced up to the irreparable breakdown of the wartime collaborative relationship. For military requirements, it echoes the 1961–62 decision period, which was triggered by the style and substance of the defense initiatives introduced by President John F. Kennedy in the first six months of his administration. That decision period resulted in significant adjustments to the Krushchevian policies accepted in 1959–60 and included rescinding the 1.2 million cutback in military manpower, the restructuring of the strategic missile programs, and the Soviet navy's shift to forward deployment.

For future Soviet policy, much will depend on the extent to which the

---

32. Interview with Ogarkov in *Krasnaya zvezda*, May 9, 1984; and in "Ogarkov Article on U.S. and Soviet Arms Policies," Foreign Broadcast Information Service, *Daily Report: Soviet Union*, September 23, 1983, pp. AA1,4.

new leaders subscribe to the view of international relations as a historic struggle between the two social systems. If they genuinely believe this formulation and in the Marxist-Leninist framework of analysis, then the impact of the 1983–85 decision period could be as fundamental as the one in 1953–55 following Stalin's death, but with an important distinction. The post-Stalin review led to a shift away from harsh, intransigent policies in which overriding priority was given to military strength toward a more flexible policy that, although still adversarial, emphasized the possibility of peaceful coexistence and shifted resources from defense to the domestic economy. The kind of questions that would have been addressed in the 1983–85 decision period argue that any shift in underlying policy is likely to have been toward greater intransigence and an increased emphasis on countervailing military power.

Intransigence does not imply gratuitous confrontation or a return to cold war rhetoric. Indeed the objectives in the field of arms control and relations with the non-U.S. members of the capitalist bloc place a premium on diplomatic skills and responsible behavior. But intransigence does imply that the Soviets will be less willing to back down when their interests are at stake, and the Western belief that the Soviets will always behave cautiously in crises may have to be reassessed.

CHAPTER 14

Overview and Implications

THIS BOOK has described how a subtle adjustment in Soviet military doctrine about the nature of a world war led to a major restructuring of Soviet military objectives in such a war. The changes in Soviet strategic concepts, force structure, and operational patterns that were required to move from the old 1960s hierarchy of objectives to the new 1970s hierarchy explain many of the developments in Soviet defense policy and clarify various aspects of Soviet foreign policy.

Although the buildup of Soviet forces increased the apparent military threat to Russia's neighbors, the restructuring of Soviet objectives had generally favorable implications for peaceful coexistence. These implications were not appreciated in the West because of prevailing assumptions about Soviet motivations. This study illuminates some of the difficulties the West has in understanding Soviet motivations. These difficulties are central to the problem of living with the Russians.

A Summary of the Argument

Current Soviet plans for the contingency of world war have roots in the 1948–53 period, when the Soviets took the threat of premeditated Western attack very seriously. The Soviet response to that threat was to plan for an offensive into Western Europe that would defeat NATO and deny the United States a bridgehead, a strategic concept reflecting the bias of Soviet military theory as well as the Soviets' recent experience in World War II.

Although the Soviets had largely discounted the threat of deliberate attack by the end of the 1950s, the possibility of world war was inherent in the international system, and the requirement remained to be able to mount a successful offensive into Western Europe, should such a war prove un-

335

avoidable. What did change over time was the underlying strategic concept of operations, which was successively refashioned to accommodate new weapons and technology and changes in NATO doctrine.

The 1950s strategic concept can be characterized as "improved World War II," with nuclear weapons being treated like just another increase in firepower. The 1960s saw a radically different strategic concept, explicitly recognizing the revolutionary nature of nuclear-missile warfare and responding to the doctrinal assessment that a world war would inevitably be nuclear and escalate to massive strikes on Russia. The Soviet response was a strategy predicated on intercontinental nuclear preemption. A decision that war was unavoidable would, at least in theory, trigger a Soviet strike on North America, as well as a ground offensive in Europe and preemptive nuclear strikes on targets located on the periphery of the Soviet Union.

The 1970s saw another fundamental change, but one that moved back toward the relatively traditional strategy of the 1950s and did not extend the radical concept of the 1960s or strike out in a new direction. This change stemmed from a doctrinal decision reached in December 1966. It reflected the conclusion that, given the appropriate Soviet strategy, there would be a significant possibility of avoiding escalation to nuclear strikes on Russia in the event of world war. It might even be possible to prevent NATO from resorting to nuclear weapons in the European theater. In the 1950s and 1960s, the Soviets had had to accept that decisions taken by NATO and the United States would determine the nature of a world war. By the mid-1970s, the Soviets hoped to be in a position to impose their own preferences on how such a war would be fought.

The crucial implication of the doctrinal decision that it was no longer inevitable that a world war would escalate to nuclear strikes on Russia was that it became logically possible to adopt the strategic objective, in such a war, of avoiding the nuclear devastation of Russia. Once possible, it then became necessary to adopt that objective in order to support the overarching national objective of promoting the well-being of the Soviet state. It also became necessary to forgo the parallel strategic objective of destroying the capitalist system. That would require nuclear strikes on North America, which could only lead to retaliation and the nuclear devastation of Russia.

Adopting a new requirement to avoid the nuclear devastation of Russia and relinquishing the requirement to destroy North America also implied a fundamental change in the political nature of a world war. No longer would it be a fight to the finish between two social systems, with defeat meaning extinction. Rather world war would be a crucial campaign in the ongoing struggle. This had important implications for the priority accorded military demands for scarce resources.

The effects of these various changes were amplified by their coinciding with political developments in U.S.-Soviet relations that led to the period of détente in the first half of the 1970s, but it is doubtful if the political developments could have taken place without the shift in military doctrine. It was the consequential changes in the requirement for intercontinental ballistic missiles (ICBM) and in the cost-benefit calculus of arms control that allowed the Soviets to halt the buildup of their ICBM forces, which was a prerequisite to any kind of relaxation in U.S.-Soviet relations.

Strategic Implications of the New Hierarchy of Objectives

The governing objective in the 1970s hierarchy is to avoid the nuclear devastation of Russia. To have any hope of achieving that objective, North America must be spared nuclear attack. The Soviet strategic concept of operations flows from these two considerations.

If North America's military-industrial base was to be left undamaged, it became essential that the United States be denied a bridgehead in the Eastern Hemisphere that would allow it to build up the military capacity for a ground offensive against Russia. The defeat of NATO in Europe and the eviction of U.S. forces from the Continent was therefore a strategic imperative. It was also essential that U.S. forces be prevented from establishing a new bridgehead at some subsequent stage of the war.

The Soviets had to think of world war as having two phases. Initially, in phase I intense operations leading to the defeat of NATO forces in Europe would take place. If it were not possible to make an acceptable peace at this stage, the Soviets would move to occupy key areas throughout the rest of Europe and establish an extended defense perimeter. This first phase could last three to four months, although the Soviets would hope that the initial stage of intensive operations, primarily in the Western theater of military action (TVD), would last no longer than three weeks and preferably less than that.

Phase II of such a war was likely to be long-drawn-out and its course was impossible to predict. A primary Soviet objective would be to prevent the United States from establishing a viable bridgehead in the Eastern Hemisphere from which to mount a land offensive against Russia. This requirement implied an extended defense perimeter. The need to economize force by exploiting natural defensive barriers suggests the Sahara Desert as the southern boundary of the defense perimeter, which would then angle down to meet the Indian Ocean at the Horn of Africa. To the west, there would be some kind of "Atlantic Wall," this time to include Iceland and the British Isles. To the east, the defense perimeter would run north past the inhospitable shores of the Arabian Peninsula, up through Baluchistan to Afghanistan, and then along the Chinese border to the Pacific.

The problem remained of how to defeat NATO in Europe without precipitating nuclear strikes on Russia. One aspect was the danger that NATO's use of nuclear weapons would escalate to an intercontinental exchange, a danger the Soviets responded to in two ways. In 1967–68 they set out to develop the military capability, using conventional means only, to launch preventive strikes against the means of nuclear delivery and related facilities for NATO command and control and to mount a blitzkrieg offensive into Western Europe. Such operations would make NATO's resort to nuclear weapons much more difficult, and, even if the Soviets were not fully successful, NATO's nuclear capability would be greatly reduced and the escalatory momentum would be lessened. This military response to the danger of escalation was reinforced in the second half of the 1970s by a political campaign that had two objectives. One, the Soviets wanted to persuade NATO to declare a policy of no first use of nuclear weapons. The other was to persuade the United States that resort to nuclear weapons in NATO Europe would inevitably escalate to an intercontinental exchange and lead to the nuclear devastation of North America.

The other aspect of the problem was the danger that, when faced by the impending defeat of NATO in Europe, the United States would strike at Russia. There was no way of defending against such a strike and the only means of preventing it was deterrence: the threat of massive nuclear retaliation on North America. The impending availability of the necessary ICBM capability had been one factor underlying the Soviet doctrinal decision in December 1966. Such wartime deterrence required a much higher level of credibility than deterring a premeditated or preemptive strike in time of peace. As a consequence, besides being able to ride out a surprise attack, the Soviets had to insure against the possibility that the United States would devise some way of rendering the Soviet fixed-silo deterrent force impotent. Problems in developing mobile land-based missiles meant that this insurance had to be embodied in ballistic-missile submarines (SSBNs).

Besides these fundamental changes in strategic concepts, the 1970s hierarchy of objectives required a major change in how the Soviets thought of nuclear preemption. The 1960s strategic concept had been predicated on preemption, both intercontinentally and against targets on the periphery of the Soviet Union. The idea stemmed in part from the nature of nuclear-missile conflict, but it also reflected the Soviet emphasis on surprise as a principle of war: both the danger of being surprised oneself and the advantage of surprising the enemy. Soviet military doctrine had, therefore, placed a high value on nuclear preemption, both against the enemy's strategic delivery systems and within the European theater, should war start with a conventional phase.

This value changed with the adoption of the 1970s hierarchy, since the emphasis was now on avoiding escalation, both within the theater and intercontinentally. Under the 1960s hierarchy, one could characterize the Soviet military posture as leaning forward, poised to preempt. Under the 1970s hierarchy, the Soviets had to lean backward, avoiding any suggestion of first use that might precipitate a NATO decision to resort to nuclear weapons or a U.S. decision to strike at Russia. This change does not mean that, in theory, the Soviets have formally renounced the option of preemption under all circumstances. In practice, however, the probability that a preemptive Soviet attack could succeed in preventing the launch of enemy missiles is slight, and this reality reinforces the constraints imposed by the need to avoid escalation. As a consequence, Soviet operational concepts are no longer predicated on nuclear preemption, and it appears that Soviet forces are prepared for NATO and the United States to launch first.

The Restructuring of Soviet Forces

The process of restructuring Soviet forces began in 1967–68 and continued through the 1970s. By 1976 the process was far enough advanced to allow the full adoption of the 1970s hierarchy of objectives and the associated operational concepts. Adopting the new hierarchy did not mean that the Soviets attached a high probability to being able to avoid intercontinental escalation in the event of a world war. Rather the attraction of avoiding the nuclear devastation of Russia was sufficient to justify the high costs of such a fundamental shift in military posture, even though the chances of success were relatively low. Meanwhile the 1960s hierarchy of objectives had not been discarded. Rather it was held in reserve, in case intercontinental escalation could not be deterred. The Soviets hope to be able to implement the 1970s strategic concept, but they are prepared to revert to the 1960s concept if necessary. The two concepts mesh to produce a strategy designed to respond to changing circumstances in a world war.

In 1976–77 the Soviets evaluated the results of restructuring their forces and reviewed developments in NATO's capability and doctrine. This period probably saw decisions on reviving the requirement for a long-range bomber, on the need for a new type of medium-range missile, and on reintroducing the operational maneuver group to ground force operations. Other far-reaching decisions affected the navy. In 1967–68 the Soviets had planned to use the Arctic Ocean as the primary deployment area for the insurance force of SSBNs, closing it off by establishing command of the Norwegian Sea. By 1976–77 the costs of this ambitious concept had become clear in terms of the necessary naval forces and the ground and air operations in Norway and elsewhere that would be required to support such a concept of operations.

As an outcome of the review, the Soviets downgraded the importance of the Arctic, and emphasis was shifted to the Sea of Okhotsk as a deployment area for SSBNs, since it was inherently more defensible. Meanwhile additional insurance against technological outflanking would be provided by mobile land-based systems, whose full potential had yet to be exploited. Rather than establishing command of the Norwegian Sea, the Soviet navy could revert to its traditional and less demanding mission of denying command to NATO, a change that had far-reaching implications for force requirements.

The resultant cutback in naval building programs was part of a larger downturn in the navy's institutional fortunes, which had greatly benefited from the 1967–68 decisions. Besides the new requirement to provide for the security of the SSBN insurance force, the likelihood that a world war would include a long-drawn-out second phase had generated a range of potential naval requirements related to the extended defense perimeter and to carrying the war to the enemy. However, whatever gains the navy may have made as the result of the debate in the first half of the 1970s appear to have been largely reversed by the end of the decade.

These developments do not imply any adjustment to the December 1966 doctrine on the likely nature of a world war or any changes in the main structure of the 1970s hierarchy of objectives, which continue to be valid. The logic of the 1970s hierarchy was reflected in statements at the Twenty-sixth Party Congress in 1981 concerning the impossibility of victory in a nuclear war, and in the 1982 declaration that the Soviets would not be the first to resort to nuclear weapons. Nor is any change implied by the renewed discussion of nuclear operations in the TVDs; or by the nascent debate on the far-reaching implications of the "emerging technologies," both for operations in the theater and throughout the rear. The Soviets must be able to conduct all types of military operation, should war prove inescapable. The Soviets would strongly prefer to avoid escalation to nuclear weapons, both in the theater and intercontinentally; but they are prepared for both contingencies. The 1970s hierarchy continues to embody their preferred objectives; but should intercontinental escalation occur, the military is prepared to revert to the 1960s hierarchy.

What is somewhat new is the insistence that there can be no victors in a nuclear war. This insistence suggests an unwillingness to allocate resources to implementing the 1960s hierarchy of objectives, beyond those needed to make sure that the United States could not dictate terms in the wake of an intercontinental nuclear exchange. Soviet political leaders may be increasingly reluctant to accept the military logic of reverting to the 1960s hierarchy, should escalation seem inescapable. The political leadership may prefer to follow the U.S. lead of limited nuclear options rather than the military logic of a full-scale escalation.

Strategic Forces and Arms Control

The 1970s hierarchy of objectives changed the cost-benefit calculus of arms control from negative to positive. Constructive arms control negotiations would reinforce the movement toward détente and hence make war less likely. Such negotiations were now practical because mutual limitations on strategic systems would, within the 1970s hierarchy, work to support the objective of not losing a world war. These considerations fundamentally altered the Soviet requirement for strategic systems.

The most immediate effect of the move to a new hierarchy was on the requirement for ballistic-missile defense. By 1968–69 the Soviets had reversed their long-standing position on the need for such systems, which derived from the dialectical relationship of offense and defense. The new requirement for a credible wartime deterrent meant that the Soviets had not only to be certain that their ICBMs could be launched under all circumstances, but that the missiles would strike home on North America. Limiting the deployment of U.S. antiballistic-missile (ABM) systems took precedence over deploying Soviet ABM systems, a priority that was enshrined in the Antiballistic Missile Treaty.

Should wartime deterrence fail and the United States strike at Russia, then the scale of devastation would be directly related to the size of the U.S. arsenal; the smaller that arsenal, the better. Meanwhile the requirement to deter the United States could be met by a relatively small number of Soviet missiles. If the president were not deterred from striking at Russia by the threat to destroy the twenty largest cities in America (or even fewer), then he was not likely to be deterred by the threatened destruction of two hundred or even five hundred U.S. cities. Deterrence would either be effective at a fairly low level of threat, or not at all.

It can be seen, therefore, that the 1970s hierarchy completely changed the basis for calculating Soviet ICBM requirements. As long as the Soviets could persuade the United States to make comparable reductions in its arsenal, their interests would be best served by fewer rather than more missiles. This interest was strong enough to justify, in theory, making unequal concessions in order to cap the arms race and start the process of force reduction. However, the Soviets had to consider the need to retain negotiating leverage. They also faced the military requirement, should wartime deterrence fail, of being able to match the U.S. arsenal in the postexchange phase of a global nuclear war.

The immediate decision was to curtail the deployment of ICBMs so as to match the U.S. capability with an equivalent number (about one thousand) of third-generation systems targeted on North America. Since these missiles were significantly inferior to their U.S. counterparts, the Soviets planned to go ahead and replace them with fourth-generation systems, but that replacement program was cut somewhat short of fulfillment by the signing of the treaty on strategic arms limitations (SALT II) in 1979. The importance of arms control and its potential contribution to détente justified accepting constraints. Some evidence suggests that, if SALT II had been ratified and negotiations on reductions had continued, the Soviets would have been willing to accept a standstill on new deployments and to live with this mixed inventory of third- and fourth-generation missile systems.

The 1970s hierarchy also changed the requirement for medium-range missiles. Under the 1960s hierarchy of objectives, strategic targets had been divided on the basis of location into intercontinental and regional target sets, and medium-range missiles covered the regional set. The introduction of the 1970s hierarchy argued that target sets should reflect the logic of the different hierarchies. The distinction was now between targets that would be struck in the event of nuclear escalation that was limited to the continental theaters, and those that would be struck in the event of escalation to global nuclear war. The target set for theater nuclear war would mainly be composed of military targets whose exact locations (and even existence) might not be known in advance, and speed of response would be critical. This would require a new type of medium-range missile that would have a flexible targeting capacity and be relatively invulnerable to preventive conventional attack.

The logic of the two hierarchies of objectives extends to Soviet arms control policy. There is a natural distinction between those systems that would be needed in theater nuclear war and those for use in global nuclear war. In a global nuclear conflict, the Soviets have an interest in the lowest ceiling on offensive forces that is compatible with deterring the United States from striking at Russia, either with nuclear weapons or with those embodying new physical principles; the need to deter attack by these futuristic weapons implies some floor to the level of nuclear arsenals. On its own, this interest would justify Soviet concessions in order to achieve mutual limitations, as was the case in the first phase of the strategic arms limitation talks (SALT I) and in SALT II. But in 1983 the United States introduced a new factor to the negotiations in the shape of the Strategic Defense Initiative (SDI).

The SDI works against the Soviet Union's interests and threatens its main arms control objectives. By initiating an arms race in space, it makes war more likely; and by undermining the Soviet deterrent, it might cause the Soviet Union to lose such a war. The Soviets could restore the credibility of their wartime deterrent, at some cost, but there are other negative factors, including the offensive potential of space-based systems and the opportunity costs of an arms race in space. The only negotiating lever available to the Soviets in this area is American worry over the first-strike capability of Soviet ICBMs. The Soviets can not afford to make concessions on offensive systems except in return for constraints on the SDI.

In respect to limitations on theater weapons, Soviet military interests would be served by the elimination of all nuclear weapons in the European region. This would improve the chance of success of a conventional blitzkrieg, while removing the danger that NATO's resort to nuclear weapons would precipitate intercontinental escalation. The practical difficulties of achieving such a situation are immense, but the thrust of these interests was clearly indicated by Soviet proposals at the talks on intermediate-range nuclear forces (INF). These continental interests are not bound up directly with Soviet interests in limiting the weapons for use in global war, except that the British and French arsenals could be counted under either target set, although they properly come within the target set for global nuclear war.

In the event of world war, China comes within the same global target set. Outside that contingency, the situation faced by the Soviet Union in Asia is not unlike that faced by NATO in Europe in the early 1960s. The role of nuclear weapons in Soviet plans for the contingency of war with China in the 1980s is likely to be comparable with the role of nuclear weapons in NATO plans for war with Russia in the 1960s. Soviet interests in the limitation of theater nuclear weapons are different in Europe and Asia.

The Regional Impact of the New Strategic Concept

One purpose of this study has been to show how Soviet foreign policy behavior has been influenced by the need to prepare for the contingency of world war. The new objectives that stemmed from the doctrinal decision in December 1966 changed the cost-benefit calculus of strategic arms control, and this change was a prerequisite for improving Soviet-American relations. The implications for Soviet force posture at the theater level worked in the opposite direction. To Russia's potential opponents, the restructuring of Soviet forces that was required to support the 1970s hierarchy of objectives appeared as a major and unprovoked military buildup with aggressive implications. Public awareness of this restructuring did not emerge in the West until the second half of the 1970s and, just as the curtailment of Soviet strategic forces in the early 1970s reinforced the Western trend towards détente, so did the buildup of Soviet theater forces contribute to the move away from détente.

Although the 1970s hierarchy of objectives was not formulated until 1967–68, the process of restructuring Soviet ground and air forces was facilitated by procurement decisions taken during the previous ten years, and by the acceptance in the mid-1960s that a nuclear war might start with a conventional phase. First Secretary Nikita S. Khrushchev's downgrading of ground forces and manned aircraft had been reversed in the 1961–62 period, which meant that new aircraft for frontal aviation were already under development and a radical new type of infantry fighting vehicle was ready to enter service. The development and production of tanks had never been interrupted, because the 1959–60 concept of operations, if anything, increased their relative importance. The lessons from Vietnam on the military potential of helicopters were already being digested. To these weapons and equipment that were already in the procurement pipeline were added those justified by the 1967–68 decision period. They began to enter service in the mid-1970s. The combined result of these different flows was an impressive buildup in the fighting power of Soviet ground and air forces during the 1970s, as new weapons and equipment were introduced and the number of weapons (tanks, infantry fighting vehicles, guns, helicopters) per ground force formation was significantly increased.[1]

In restructuring their naval forces, the Soviets did not have the same advantages. The 1970s hierarchy of objectives required radical changes in warship design criteria, and there was relatively little in the procurement pipeline that was relevant to the new concept of operations. Two changes were particularly important, one concerning sustainability, the other the use of nuclear weapons. Under the 1960s hierarchy, the navy's primary mission was to counter the strategic strike capability of Western aircraft carriers and SSBNs. This was discharged in part by the peacetime deployment of Soviet naval units within weapons range of these sea-based nuclear-delivery systems. These forward-deployed units had to be able to survive a preemptive attack by Western forces long enough to launch their weapons, after which they were expendable. Nuclear warheads were essential to the mission and since the logic of Soviet strategy required a preemptive strike against North America, escalation was not a concern.

Under the 1970s hierarchy, the danger of escalation became a central consideration and authority to use nuclear weapons might well be withheld as long as the war did not escalate to major strikes on Russia. Naval forces had to carry a full load of conventional weapons as well as nuclear ones, implying much larger magazines. Meanwhile naval constructors could no longer design ships for short, sharp operations in the initial stages of a war, but had to think in terms of protracted war at sea and the requirement for sustained operations of the kind needed to gain and maintain command of large areas such as the Norwegian Sea. This added up to a requirement for a significant increase in the size of the different types of surface ship (escort and above) and of submarines, and these new classes of larger unit began to enter service in 1980–82. As the number of these larger units

---

1. This evidence does not contradict the CIA assessment that annual Soviet investment in weapons procurement leveled off in 1977 and remained flat through 1982. That estimate covers the whole defense establishment and does not distinguish among different branches of service or type of weapon. Meanwhile the level of procurement remains high and may well exceed the requirements for bare replacement. See Richard F. Kaufman, "Causes of the Slowdown in Soviet Defense," *Soviet Economy*, vol. 1 (January-March 1985), pp.9–31.

built up, the Soviets' capability for waging conventional war at sea would markedly increase, and so would their capability for projecting force in peacetime.

THE EURO-ATLANTIC REGION.   The 1970s hierarchy of objectives generated new and demanding strategic requirements in the European theater. In the event that world war became unavoidable, NATO had to be defeated and U.S. forces evicted from the Continent. These aims were to be achieved, if possible, without either side resorting to nuclear weapons. If it were not possible to negotiate peace on satisfactory terms at that stage, Warsaw Pact forces would need to complete the subjugation of Western Europe and establish an extended defense perimeter within a few months. The restructuring of Soviet forces to meet these new requirements caused understandable concern among NATO nations about Soviet intentions, a concern that was heightened by the Soviet deployment of the SS–20 medium-range ballistic missile.

The SS-20 was not, however, a response to the requirements of the 1970s objective and comes more properly under the 1960s hierarchy, although it would contribute to deterring escalation in the theater. Its deployment in 1977 was apparently coincidental and stemmed from the availability of components of the SS-16 ICBM, the miltary inadequacies of the first- and second-generation SS-4 and SS-5, and the failure of plans to replace them with third-generation medium-range systems at the end of the 1960s. When the Soviet leaders woke up to the political and military costs that were being incurred by the SS-20 deployment, they moved to curtail it, but their response was too little and too late. An undesirable consequence of the resulting imbroglio was to link the deployment of medium-range missiles facing China with those facing Europe.

The European theater of war is the main theater of war. The main TVD in that theater is the Western TVD, and it has overriding priority. In the Soviet contingency plan for world war, success in this TVD (the eviction of U.S. forces from Europe) is essential if the Soviets are not, ultimately, to lose. They must, of course, allow for the possibility that their offensive could bog down. But in considering the Soviet response, which might include political negotiation, it is important to remember that a Soviet offensive would not stem from some urge to aggression, and its failure would not reflect a miscalculation of the costs of opportunistic expansion. An attack on Western Europe would constitute a strategic imperative, stemming from a Soviet conviction that world war was inevitable. To meet their military objectives in the Western TVD, the Soviets require a sufficient margin of superiority to allow them to contrive the local preponderance that would be needed to breach NATO's defenses. The concept of a strategic imperative and the need for local preponderance form the basis for the Soviet posture in the Western TVD.

The Southwestern TVD stands second in importance to the Western TVD, providing direct support to operations in that TVD and pinning down forces in the southern parts of NATO. It is also important because of the Turkish Straits, control of which becomes critical in the event that the Soviet offensive in the Western TVD bogs down. As a minimum, the Soviets would want to be able to deploy naval forces to attack the seaborne flow of supplies from North America to ports on the Mediterranean coast of France. But the primary concern would be to thwart any Western attempt to shift the strategic center of gravity away from the central front. The only feasible way of doing that would be a northerly thrust out of the Black Sea toward the Baltic. If NATO held the Turkish Straits it would be in a position to mount a seaborne invasion of the northwestern Black Sea coast and then launch a major land offensive up through Romania, Moldavia, and the Ukraine, toward Poland. The Soviets must therefore plan to seize the Turkish Straits during phase I-1 of the war.

The Northwestern TVD comes a poor third in importance, the Danish Straits and southern Scandinavia lying within the boundaries of the Western TVD. The overriding priority accorded that TVD implies that the Soviets are unlikely to commit substantial ground forces in the north until they are assured of success on the central front. It would, however, be necessary to take over sparsely populated Finmark, in order to facilitate operations in the Norwegian Sea, enhance the defense of the Northern Fleet area, and provide a 250-mile buffer between NATO and the Kola base complex. If the requirement to gain command of the Norwegian Sea has been relaxed, control of the coasts surrounding that sea would not be necessary, and the military advance in the north could stop well short of the main NATO defense line in Troms province. Once NATO forces had been defeated in the Western and Southwestern TVDs, the surrender of Norway could be expected without the need for military occupation.

If Soviet operations in the Euro-Atlantic region were successful in phase I-1 of a world war, the central problem in phase I-2 would be how to deal with Britain and France without precipitating nuclear strikes on Russia. In phase I-3, the dominant concern would be to establish an effective defense perimeter to prevent the return of Western forces. In this respect, the obvious pitfall is overextension, but the German experience in World War II must have highlighted the fatal danger of allowing enemy control of North Africa. The advantages of including Southwest Asia and the Horn of Africa within the perimeter are several. The area would encompass a large proportion of the petroleum resources in the Western Hemisphere. It covers the southern sea route to the Soviet Far East, and it provides military access to the Indian Ocean. The problems of occupation would be minimized, since the perimeter would run through desolate areas, remote from population centers; in any case, many of the states involved are favorably disposed toward the Soviet Union. In military terms it would be easier for the Soviets to defend this extended perimeter than to defend NATO's erstwhile southern boundary.

THE ASIAN-PACIFIC REGION.   Under the 1960s hierarchy of objectives, a Soviet decision to launch nuclear strikes on North America would have implied the parallel decision to attack China with nuclear weapons to prevent it from emerging the undamaged victor of a Soviet-American conflict. Under the 1970s hierarchy, the need to avoid any action that might encourage the United States to strike at Russia barred such a simple solution. Instead the Soviets had to rely on conventional weapons to cover the contingency that China might seize the opportunity of Soviet involvement in a European war to seek military gains in Asia. This change coincided with the deterioration in Sino-Soviet relations and resulted in a buildup of Soviet forces facing China from 20 to 45 divisions by 1975.

A further adverse trend in the region was the normalization of Sino-Japanese relations and the growing Sino-American rapprochement, which was extending into the defense field. These developments may have accounted for the addition of another 10 Soviet divisions in the first half of the 1980s. The extra divisions may also have been related to the decision in 1976–77 to develop the Sea of Okhotsk as a secure area for deploying SSBNs. This move required that the Kurile Islands be reinforced against amphibious assault and removed the possibility of negotiating the return of the four southern islands to Japan. It also required a further buildup of the Soviet Pacific Fleet, which had already been strengthened in the late 1960s and early 1970s to support the naval deployment in the Indian Ocean.

In phase II of a world war, the Pacific defense perimeter would be likely to encompass an intimidated but unoccupied Japan, the Korean and Liaotung Peninsulas, and Manchuria. The Soviets must, however, cover the worst case that three or four years into the war (when there might be no satellite surveillance), the United States would somehow manage to mount a successful invasion of Russia through northwest China, outflanking the bulk of the Soviet forces in the Far Eastern TVD. In such circumstances, the Soviets would have to consider giving up central and eastern Siberia and concentrate on defending the West Siberian Plain, with this inner defense perimeter running to the east of the line of the Yenisey River. This contingency requires the Soviets to locate as many as possible of their main military facilities within this defended core. The requirement is particularly important for those installations that contribute to the credibility of the wartime deterrent, such as ballistic-missile early warning radars.[2]

THE INDO-ARABIAN REGION. The Southern TVD assumed a new importance with the adoption of the 1970s hierarchy of objectives. Under the 1960s hierarchy, the military interest in the region was limited to its potential as a deployment area for SSBNs carrying Polaris and Poseidon missiles. Under the new hierarchy, the Horn of Africa became a strategic fulcrum of the extended defense perimeter. This changed the geostrategic significance of the region and affected diplomatic calculations concerning the states within the perimeter.

The 1970s hierarchy also reinforced the importance of the southern sea route linking western Russia to the Soviet Far East. This had assumed a new salience following the Sino-Soviet border clashes in 1969. An incidental by-product of the invasion of Afghanistan was an improved Soviet capability to supply this route overland through Chah Bahar. But such potential benefits are minor compared with the mounting costs of that invasion.

Similarly, the Iranian revolution removed an American client from Russia's southern border, but it led to dangerous turbulence in the gulf region, and the final outcome is unpredictable. The revolution meanwhile spurred the United States to develop a new capability to project military force into the area. This has complicated the problem that would face the Soviets in the event of a world war or war with China.

WAR-RELATED REQUIREMENTS IN THE THIRD WORLD. The 1970s hierarchy of objectives fundamentally changed the nature of Soviet war-related requirements in the third world. Under the 1960s hierarchy, which was predicated on the inevitability of an international nuclear exchange, the focus was on the threat posed by U.S. sea-based strategic delivery systems deployed in peacetime within strike range of the Soviet heartland. It was necessary to maintain Soviet forces within weapon range of these stra-

---

2. The radar at Abalakova, near Krasnoyarsk, is inside this defense perimeter.

tegic strike units, forces that would be in a position to attack them at the onset of a war. The areas of primary concern were the eastern Mediterranean and the northwest quadrant of the Indian Ocean, and the requirement was for access to airfields and naval support facilities in at least one country bordering those waters. By the end of the 1960s, this access was being provided by Egypt and Somalia.

Under the 1970s hierarchy it would no longer be possible to use nuclear weapons against U.S. strategic strike units at the onset of war, for fear of precipitating escalation. The carrier could threaten the success of operations in the Southwestern TVD during the early stages of phase I of a war, hence a peacetime naval presence in the Mediterranean continued to be necessary. But war-related requirements in the third world were now mainly concerned with establishing the extended defense perimeter and with phase II of a world war. This focus introduced a new factor into Soviet deliberations concerning which third world nations it was important to have influence with. Arms supply to the third world would acquire an additional purpose. Besides raising the costs of Western military intervention and, in some cases, earning hard currency, arms supply to the third world could also serve as a way of prepositioning heavy equipment in what would become forward defense areas. The buildup of the Libyan tank force may, in part, reflect such Soviet considerations.

The possibility of a long-drawn-out phase II required the Soviet navy and long-range air force to gain experience in operating in far distant waters and changed the cost-benefit calculus of access to shore facilities in such areas. In the Indian Ocean and South China Sea, the possibility of war with China and the importance of the southern sea route reinforced this tendency.

The Military Strand in Soviet Foreign Policy

This study shows that Soviet military requirements have an appreciable effect on the Soviet Union's peacetime foreign policy. It does not, however, show that the Soviets attach undue importance to the role of military power and the use of force as an instrument of that policy. Indeed the analysis suggests the opposite.

It is commonplace to claim that because of the economic and social failures of their political system, the Soviets rely on military power as their primary instrument of foreign policy. It is asserted that because of the amount of military power available to the Soviet leadership, they must be set on world military domination. Both claims ignore the nature of Soviet military requirements.

It is Soviet policy to cover against the worst case of world war, the possibility of which is inherent in the arsenals and antagonisms of the opposing blocs. This is contingency planning on the grand scale and represents prudent precautions, not paranoia. The Soviets do not have the advantage of 3,000 miles of ocean on one side and 5,000 on the other, nor do they enjoy the luxury of overwhelming predominance in their own hemisphere. The Soviet Union covers about half the Eurasian land mass, the traditional enemies on its border are now all ranged against it, and it is without significant or reliable allies. Facing west, with their back to the Urals, the Soviets see the NATO alliance curving round their flanks, with a fully restored Germany in the center. Turning east, they see 4,500 miles of border flanking 1 billion Chinese, and beyond that their traditional enemy, Japan. In both directions they see U.S. forces deployed forward in considerable strength. To the south, they have the worry of Muslim irredentism.

The military must plan for the contingency of world war, the objective being not to lose. In the Euro-Atlantic region this requires the Soviets to defeat NATO on land, evict U.S. forces from the Continent, and establish a defense perimeter that could run from the Norwegian Sea to the Cape Verde Islands and east across North Africa. In the Asian-Pacific region China must be deterred from taking advantage of Soviet involvement in Europe, Japan must be neutralized, the United States must be held at bay, and Soviet forces must be ready to seize Manchuria once victory is assured in Europe. In the Indo-Arabian region the Soviets must establish themselves securely in the Bab-al-Mandeb/Horn region, and be ready to seize Chah Bahar at the head of the Arabian Sea and perhaps to drive south from Azerbaijan to Tabriz in Iran.

Just to list these requirements gives a sense of their scale, and the history of World War II argues that they are not overstated. These requirements have determined the structure of the Soviet armed forces, namely, their composition and deployment and their supporting infrastructure. The strength of these forces depends on the relative priority of the varied requirements and the likelihood of war. Because of the central importance of the Western TVD, the structure of forces in this TVD has always been fully formed and well fleshed out with troops and equipment. But even in this vital region the strength of their forces is not sufficient to give the Soviets great confidence that they would be successful in war.

This relative restraint supports the conclusion that the restructuring of Soviet forces facing NATO during the 1970s was seen as a military necessity and that the Soviets were aware that the political consequences would be negative. The threat implicit in that buildup adversely affected Soviet relations with Western Europe and ensured that the Soviet deployment of the SS-20 would be seen as political intimidation. This deployment was instrumental in preventing the split in NATO that would otherwise have been likely as the United States moved away from détente in the second half of the 1970s and reversed its position on arms control in the early 1980s. Similarly, the buildup of Soviet forces in the Asian-Pacific region has contributed to the deterioration of relations with Japan.

Rather than seeing military power as a primary instrument of policy, the Soviets are aware that it only has political utility in a limited range of circumstances. Its threatened use or even existence in other situations can be counterproductive. This consciousness has not prevented them from resorting to military threats in situations of that kind, but that decision has usually reflected short-term frustrations rather than long-term policy. Military power, backed by the readiness to use force if absolutely necessary, has obviously been essential in retaining political control throughout the Soviet national security zone. But the more interesting role of military power has been in the Soviet-American relationship. The Russians, at least, are convinced that their matching military power persuaded the United States both to view the Soviet Union as a superpower with worldwide interests and to negotiate with it on limiting strategic weapons systems.

The role of military force is distinct from that of military power. The reluctance with which the Soviets have resorted to military force in their national security zone demonstrates their sensitivity to the political costs of coercive intervention. Outside their national security zone, the Soviet use of military force has been limited to supportive intervention and the force has been protective, not punitive. In the past, the use of force has also been constrained by the danger that superpower confrontation in the third world could escalate to global nuclear war. This cautious view persisted after 1974, following a debate on the role of force in the third world that was prompted by the new hierarchy of strategic objectives. A similar debate in the 1983–85 period could easily have yielded the opposite conclusion.

In the first half of the 1970s, the Soviets believed that the United States was reconciled to the trend in the correlation of forces. As a result of Vietnam, America would be increasingly reluctant to intervene militarily to prevent the emergence of progressive regimes. By 1983, not only had that assumption been proven false, but the United States was moving to a policy of promoting and supporting armed rebellion against established Marxist regimes. Meanwhile a separate body of evidence suggested that in the past, the danger that superpower confrontation in distant parts of the world would escalate to a nuclear exchange had been grossly exaggerated. In the circumstances, a powerful argument could be made that the Soviet Union should respond to U.S. military intervention with countervailing force. It so happened that the naval building programs to support such a response were already in place.

Problems of Understanding

This book uses the evidence of change in Soviet military doctrine and strategy to probe the motivations underlying Soviet behaviour. The attempt to discern overall Soviet motivations does not come naturally to military analysts, who tend to shy away from broader assessments of Soviet policy. Significantly, to the extent they do make such assessments, well-informed military analysts tend to reach generally sanguine conclusions about Soviet intentions. However, problems arise when, as often occurs, crude measures of Soviet military strength or details of weapons capabilities are used as the basis for assertions about the motivations shaping Soviet foreign policy. When that happens, distortion is unavoidable.

Analytical Methods

How does one choose among different explanations of Soviet foreign policy? The most practical approach is to evaluate the analytical structure of each explanation and progressively discard those with significant flaws. For a start, the explanations can be ordered on a continuum between those that rely on moral judgments about the competing social systems and largely disregard Soviet behavior, and those that rely on evidence of Soviet behavior and disregard moral considerations. This process allows one to discard the more obviously ideologically based explanations, such as beliefs that the Soviet Union is inherently evil or that the problem lies in the U.S. military-industrial complex.

THE SELECTIVE USE OF EVIDENCE.   Some explanations are ideologically driven, but proponents claim them to be based on evidence of Soviet behavior. The test here is whether the proffered explanation accounts for all the evidence or whether it uses evidence selectively to advance a particular viewpoint. Take, for example, the frequent claim that Soviet communism seeks military domination of the world.[3]

How does that explanation account for the following Soviet behavior at the end of World War II: withdrawing forces that, in the process of driving back the Germans, had advanced about 250 miles into Norway; withdrawing from Finland, Yugoslavia, and Czechoslovakia; agreeing to four-power control of Berlin, a city captured by the Russians and well behind their lines; causing Bulgaria to withdraw its army from Thrace and the Aegean coast; and refusing help to the grassroots communist insurgency in Greece. How does the claim explain the following behavior in the 1950s: relinquishing military bases in Porkala, Finland, and Port Arthur, China; withdrawing from Austria; and failing to occupy Afghanistan, even when the formation of the Central Treaty Organization in 1958 linked Iran and Pakistan in an anti-Soviet alliance, an alliance that could be seen as breaching the Soviet-Iranian treaty of 1921. The failure to act against Afghanistan is particularly telling since it was at this time that the United States and Britain intervened militarily in Lebanon and Jordan.

If the Soviets have been seeking military domination of the world, how does one account for the structure and deployment of their forces since World War II? Such an objective would argue for deploying no more forces facing NATO than were necessary to secure the European borders of the Soviet empire. These deployments would be designed to tie down Western military resources while freeing the maximum number of Soviet forces for use elsewhere. One would have expected the Soviets to exploit the advantage of their adjacency to the Persian Gulf area, which is also the weakest part of the U.S. girdle of containment, rather than giving the Southern TVD the lowest priority in men, arms, and equipment. Why did the Soviets not develop a worldwide capability to project force, comparable with that of the U.S. Navy and Marines? And, having developed a limited naval capability to operate, if not survive in distant waters by the end of the 1960s, why were these deployments cut back in the second half of the 1970s?

If the Soviets believe in territorial expansion, why didn't they take over

---

3. See, for example, statements by Secretary of Defense Caspar Weinberger: "Face the Nation," CBS television, March 13, 1983; interview in *USA Today*, August 11, 1983; and Fred Hiatt, "Pentagon Sees Space Buildup by Soviets," *Washington Post*, April 11, 1984.

Sinkiang in the mid-1960s, while China was embroiled in its cultural revolution? In the late 1960s, with more than half a million Americans tied down in Vietnam, the British committed to withdrawing from east of Suez, but the U.S. tilt to China and the arming of Iran yet to come, why didn't the Soviets use their military preponderance to achieve gains in Iran? The idea that they were waiting to "take advantage" of some Vietnam syndrome five or more years in the future is not plausible. During the time that syndrome did still have a restraining influence on U.S. policy, why didn't the Soviets take the opportunity presented by the Somalian invasion of Ethiopia to establish military dominance of the Horn of Africa?

TENDENTIOUS TERMINOLOGY. The problem of understanding Soviet motivations is complicated when analysts describe the evidence in emotive terms. Reference to "the relentless buildup" of Soviet military capability is an example. Certainly, a buildup in capability occurred in the 1970s as the Soviets restructured their ground and supporting air forces to bring them into line with the 1970s hierarchy of objectives. But having achieved that restructuring, the Soviets resumed their policy of reequipping their forces on a routine, continuous basis. Given the size of the force, large quantities of ordnance are involved, but the actual buildup had largely ceased by the end of the 1970s.

The term "relentless buildup" is even less appropriate to describe events in the other branches of service. For example, in the strategic rocket forces, the deployment of fourth-generation ICBMs was curtailed to conform to SALT II and, compared with earlier generations, the development and deployment of fifth-generation ICBMs has lagged. In the case of medium-range missiles, the long-delayed replacement of the obsolescent first- and second-generation systems by the fourth-generation SS-20 was finally achieved in the first half of the 1980s, about twenty years after the original deployment of SS-4s and SS-5s.

Production of the medium-range Backfire bomber has been running at about 30 aircraft a year since the mid-1970s, divided equally between the long-range air force and the naval air force. To reequip those forces with Backfire will take some twenty years, at the end of which time both forces will be significantly smaller than they were in the 1970s. The adaptation of the long-range turbo-prop Bear (first deployed in the late 1950s), as a platform for the Soviet version of the air-launched cruise missile (ALCM), can be seen as a matching response to the arming of U.S. B-52 bombers with ALCMs.

In the Soviet navy, the new classes of surface ships entering service in the 1980s were much larger than their predecessors, with greater endurance and combat sustainability. But the replenishment and landing ship programs were curtailed in the late 1970s, and a sharp reduction occurred in the delivery rate of SSBNs, which had been running at a lower rate in the second half of the 1970s than in the first. Nor was there a compensating increase in the delivery rate of nuclear-powered attack submarines, whose production appears to be running well below capacity.

When one analyzes the evidence, it becomes clear that the development of Soviet forces during the last twenty-five years has been a more complex process than the single-minded purposefulness implied by "a relentless buildup," which the Soviets decided on following the Cuban missile crisis.[4] The development of the Soviet intercontinental delivery capability is more accurately described as the costly and laborious process of catching up and then remaining abreast of the United States, initially, in numbers, then quality, and, finally, in the diversity of delivery systems. This development involved the wasteful process of deploying and replacing successive generations of missiles until, finally, they approached the capabilities of U.S. systems. The buildup of Soviet ground forces in the 1970s and naval surface forces in the 1980s can be described as the costly restructuring of forces to allow the adoption of a new concept of operations. The Soviets were moving away from the inherently unstable strategy of intercontinental nuclear preemption to one that forwent nuclear strikes on North America, except in retaliation, and sought to avoid the resort to nuclear weapons in Europe.

The assertion of a relentless Soviet buildup of offensive forces is intended to support the claim that the Soviets seek military domination of the world, but even that connection is hard to sustain. By far the largest buildup took place in the Far Eastern TVD, where the number of divisions nearly trebled and a sixfold increase in the number of tactical aircraft occurred. No one suggests that the Soviets are planning the military invasion of China. If a military buildup on that scale does not imply expansionist intentions in Asia, then why should smaller buildups imply them elsewhere?

SUSPECT THREATS. It is fairly simple to marshal the evidence that undermines large claims such as a Soviet drive for military world domination. Lesser claims are sometimes more difficult to challenge but two kinds are automatically suspect. One involves a definition of threat that has

4. See CBS, "Face the Nation," and interview in *USA Today*. In the CBS statements, Weinberger talked of the process as having lasted "over 21 years" and in *USA Today* "for 21 years."

evolved over the years in an attempt to retain plausibility. The idea that Western Europe is threatened by Finlandization is a good example.

The capabilities threat to Western Europe posed by Soviet forces is self-evident, but the more important question is what led the Soviets to develop that capability. During NATO's first decade it was generally asserted and perhaps widely believed that the capability was explained by an urge to incorporate Western Europe into the Soviet empire. As that idea became increasingly implausible, attention shifted to NATO's flanks and a Soviet temptation to seize northern Norway or the Turkish Straits. The question of intentions became less salient in the latter 1960s when the threat of Soviet expansionism was seen to move away from Europe. Attention returned to the central front when the buildup of Soviet forces facing NATO became apparent in the mid- to late 1970s. By then, the notion that this buildup reflected a Soviet urge to military aggression was even less plausible and resort had to be made to the idea of politico-military intimidation, or so-called Finlandization. Nuclear blackmail is another example of an evolving threat. Now used to justify the British independent deterrent, it has emerged because the threat of a premeditated Soviet attack on Britain has been discredited.

The other kind of suspect threat is the "cry wolf" type. The same threat is postulated repeatedly, only to be disproved by subsequent events. A simple example concerns the capability for overseas military intervention, which many Westerners have been expecting the Soviets to develop since the late 1950s. When the Soviets started building the Moskva class of air-capable ship in the first half of the 1960s, some analysts jumped to the conclusion that the Soviets were aping the helicopter assault capability of the U.S. Marines. The Moskva turned out to be a helicopter-carrying antisubmarine cruiser. Western analysts imputed the same interventionist role to the Kiev class when it was identified as under construction in the early 1970s. However, the primary role of the Kiev was to contribute an air capability to the defense of the SSBN bastions. Now there is a third class of air-capable ship building whose mission is a subject of debate.

The assertion that the Soviet Union is poised to seize the oilfields surrounding the Persian Gulf, which dates from the mid-1950s and assumed a new salience in the early 1980s, is a more important cry-wolf threat. Soviet inaction in the past, the absence of material evidence that the Soviets have developed the necessary capability, and the inherent problems in such an endeavor argue against such a claim. Of course, one cannot rule out that such threats might materialize in the future, hence the cry-wolf label. But to substantiate that claim one must specify what has changed that would justify the shift in established Soviet policy. In the case of Soviet policy on military intervention overseas, the grounds for such a change have been suggested in chapter 10. There are no obvious grounds for a change in Soviet policy toward the Persian Gulf oilfields.

THE PERTINENCE OF DATA.   A different kind of analytical problem concerns the pertinence of data as evidence. Take, for example, the role of collateral evidence in deciding among different missions that can be imputed to the large throw-weight SS-18 ICBM and the smaller, but still large, SS-19. Focusing on American vulnerabilities and the U.S. fear of sudden attack, the potential of these relatively accurate Soviet missiles supports a conclusion that they are first-strike weapons. Their mission is to disarm the Minuteman force, using only a proportion of the Soviet ICBM arsenal. A different explanation emerges if one assumes that the United States will be the one to escalate. Then the Soviet Union is vulnerable to a disarming strike. The Soviets, therefore, have to cover the possibility that they will be unable to launch their ICBMs on warning and the whole Soviet force will suffer attack. Large missiles with heavy payloads would maximize the striking power of those ICBMs that did survive a U.S. attack. They are necessary for wartime deterrence and, should deterrence fail, to meet the war-fighting requirement after the initial exchange.

How does one choose between these competing explanations? Soviet writings are advanced in support of the counterforce, damage-limiting explanation, statements that stress the importance of preemption and the decisive nature of the initial strikes by the strategic rocket forces. However, such writings date from the 1960s or earlier, when the 1960s hierarchy of objectives was still in force. The 1970s hierarchy has been operative since the mid-1970s and under the new strategy the strategic rocket forces have a different mission. The shift from a strategy of intercontinental preemption to one of launch on warning was clearly reflected in Soviet writings in the 1970s, and more recently, the emphasis in Marshal V. D. Sokolovskiy's *Military Strategy* (1962, 1963, 1968) on waging war with nuclear weapons was authoritatively repudiated.[5]

The analytical problem is slightly complicated by the initial specifications for the SS-18 and the SS-19, which were drawn up in the mid-1960s when the 1960s hierarchy of objectives was still in force. It is therefore correct to say that the missiles were originally designed for the offensive

5. M.A. Gareev, *M.V. Frunze - voennyy teoretik* (M.V. Frunze - Military theoretician) (Moscow: Voenizdat, 1985), pp. 239–40.

counterforce role. But the shift in doctrine did not necessitate a change in general specifications,[6] which met the requirements for a second-strike capability. The latter role is supported by the absence of any urgency to introduce fifth-generation systems whose counterforce capability could be further improved.[7] Furthermore, the significant characteristic of the SS-19 successor is its solid-fuel propulsion, which allows mobility and hence improves survivability, but may reduce accuracy.

CHANGES IN DOCTRINE. If there has been a significant change in policy or doctrine, data from before that change cannot be used to explain or interpret the new policy. Data in the wake of a decision period must also be treated with caution, depending on how long it would take to fully implement the change. A breach of this rule led to the incorrect assessment in the late 1970s that the Soviets were actively preparing to achieve victory in a nuclear war. Obsolete doctrinal statements from the 1960s were melded with contemporary evidence of Soviet weapons development to produce this alarming picture.[8]

A dwindling but influential school of analysts still asserts that Soviet military doctrine and strategy have changed little since the basic tenets were formulated in the 1953–60 period.[9] They note that in the 1960s, through the medium of open publications, the Soviet Union took steps to ensure that the West was aware of its strategy for world nuclear war. They go on to argue that the cutback of such informed discussion in the 1970s was part of a Soviet disinformation campaign, designed to conceal from the West that the 1960s strategy continued in force.[10] This flouts common sense. Surely, the cutback is additional evidence that the Soviets were then undertaking a major restructuring of strategic concepts, something they

6. There is no merit to the argument that the improved accuracy of the SS-18 indicates a preemptive counterforce role. Note that the accuracy of U.S. ICBMs and SLBMs is steadily being improved.

7. At the second series of the strategic arms limitation talks (SALT II), the Soviets were prepared to sacrifice the successor to the SS-19 in order to prevent the development of the MX missile. The development of a successor to the more threatening SS-18 did not follow the established product-improvement pattern and may only have been initiated when it became clear that the MX would go ahead.

8. For the type of analysis that was influential in shaping the new appreciation see Joseph D. Douglass, Jr., and Amoretta M. Hoeber, *Soviet Strategy for Nuclear War* (Hoover Institution Press, 1979). Of the eighty-seven articles listed in the bibliography, 40 percent were published before 1967 and none were published later than 1969.

9. For example, Richard Pipes, "Why the Soviet Union Thinks It Could Fight and Win a Nuclear War," *Commentary*, vol. 64 (July 1977), p. 28. The most recent and comprehensive exposition of this viewpoint is advanced by William T. Lee and Richard F. Staar, *Soviet Military Policy Since World War II* (Hoover Institution Press, 1986), p. 29.

10. Lee and Staar, *Soviet Military Policy*, pp. 31–32.

did not wish to disclose to the West, at least until they were ready to implement the new concept. The longer they could conceal the change in strategy, the better their chance of achieving operational surprise in the event of war. It was not until 1985 that the Soviets openly admitted that Sokolovskiy was outdated, by which time Western military writings had demonstrated a reasonable understanding of the new operational concepts underlying Soviet plans for conventional warfare, the Western TVD, and the SSBN bastions.

PARTIAL HYPOTHESIS. ˙Military analysts are vulnerable to the temptation to extrapolate large explanations, such as Soviet strategic concepts, from specialized evidence. The case of the SS-18 and SS-19 is an example. Naval analysis is particularly prone to this pitfall because of traditional preconceptions about the role of naval power. The misperceived threat in the early 1950s of a global war on commerce is discussed in the next section. In the late 1950s, responding to the U.S. carrier threat, Soviet naval emphasis was shifted from the Baltic to the Arctic. The West saw this move as a precursor to seizing northern Norway, one of NATO's flanks. In the mid-1960s, the Soviets deployed a small number of highly vulnerable forces in the eastern Mediterranean in a vain attempt to counter the threat to southern Russia from U.S. carriers and Polaris submarines. The West saw this as signaling the Soviet adoption of a Mahanist policy of projecting military power into the third world. In the 1970s, the buildup of naval forces to protect the SSBN bastions in the Arctic and in the Pacific was interpreted by the West as intended to intimidate.

The Perceptual Lens

The prevalence of these analytical flaws can be partly explained by the perceptual lens through which the West views Soviet behavior. It is difficult to avoid these distortions but a sensitivity to their existence can mitigate their effects at least in three areas.

THE ANALYTICAL VIEWPOINT. There is a natural tendency to analyze the evidence of Soviet behavior in terms of Western vulnerabilities, rather than Soviet requirements. The conflicting interpretations of the mission of the SS-18 and SS-19 exemplify how these opposing viewpoints yield completely different inferences.

Focusing on Western vulnerabilities distorts the intelligence estimate and can lead to a misallocation of resources. The West's response in the early 1950s to intelligence that the Soviets were embarking on the construction of 1,200 submarines serves as an early example; the submarines began delivery in 1952 and the program was originally planned to continue through 1965. Having recently experienced the Battle of the Atlantic against a much smaller German force, Western analysts jumped to the conclusion that these Soviet submarines were intended for war on Western shipping around the world. This conclusion led to the construction of large numbers of convoy escorts by the members of NATO. It also diverted resources to counter the spurious threat of surface raiders implicit in the Soviets' cruiser building program.

In fact, more than one thousand of the Soviet submarines were intended to defend the four Soviet fleet areas against the threat of Western maritime assault and invasion.[11] Significantly, the details of the submarines' armament and the overall structure of the emerging Soviet postwar navy provided evidence that undermined the commerce war explanation and supported area defense.[12] The belief in Soviet aggression was, however, too firmly ingrained for the defense explanation to even cross the Western mind.

In 1961, at the height of the Berlin crisis, the Soviets broke their self-imposed moratorium and carried out a series of nuclear tests, including a 57-megaton (MT) weapon and the triggering device for one in the 75–100 MT range. Many observers in the West saw this as a brutal attempt at political intimidation, intended to affect the course of negotiations over Berlin. A different explanation emerges when one views the tests in the context of the Soviets' missile programs, and against the background of the debate in Moscow sparked by the Kennedy defense initiatives and the planned surge in Minuteman production. The tests were necessary if the deployment of the third-generation SS-9 ICBM was to be brought forward and if the Soviets were to develop the very large missiles which, at that date, were still in the program.

The Cuban missile crisis in 1962 provides a variant of this problem. The traumatic effect of the crisis led to a widespread assumption in the West that Cuba was a watershed in Soviet defense and foreign policy, with

11. Staff exercises at Frunze naval academy in the 1945–48 period focused on defense against maritime invasion.

12. The large-type Zulu class carried air defense weapons that would have been needed if the submarine had to surface in the mid-Atlantic. The mass-produced medium-type Whiskey class carried no air defense weapons but mounted a 100-millimeter gun. This combination would have been useless against ocean commerce but would be very effective when operating within range of shore-based support against amphibious assault forces, particularly at night. Similarly, the cruiser/destroyer surface action groups that were then building had a role to play in the fleet areas, but the cruisers had little chance of surviving as ocean raiders, the role ascribed to them by the West.

all that implies for the motivations underlying subsequent Soviet behavior. In fact, the watershed had occurred more than a year earlier, when decisions were taken in response to the Kennedy defense buildup. The Soviets badly miscalculated the nature of the American response to their action, but the crisis and its outcome reinforced the conclusions that had led to the 1961 decisions.

DIFFERENT TYPES OF SOCIETY.   A more intractable problem is the difference between the two sociopolitical orders. The Soviet Union is a monoorganizational society, in which a complex pattern of bureaucracies strive to achieve centrally formulated goals. This "goal-achieving" type of society contrasts with those of the Western democracies, which belong to the "rule-applying" type. They are multiorganizational and the predominant role of the bureaucracy is to apply a system of rules within which the mass of mainly independent social units pursue autonomous goals.[13] The difference is most evident in the United States, with its emphasis on the individual and its constitutional separation of powers.

The structured Soviet approach to analyzing sociopolitical problems and planning social activity, including war, is inherently improbable to the West. A frequent Western metaphor for the Soviet conduct of foreign policy is the brilliant chess player, even though that metaphor is not borne out by the record of Soviet achievements since World War II. Rather than the analogy of a grand master who manipulates inanimate pieces on a global chessboard, reality is better described by the image of an intelligent central planner, frustrated by the unpredictability of world events and the perversity of live human actors. But whether the Soviets are successful or not, their structured way of thinking and the importance the Soviets attach to establishing objectives are central to understanding the motivations that underlie their behavior.

THE REALITY OF WAR.   From the inception of the Soviet state in 1917 until the mid-1950s, the Soviets lived either with war or with the expectation that war must come to their territory. Since then a more sanguine estimate has prevailed, but the dread of war remains. What they now fear is not some deliberate decision to start a war, but the unpredictable "Sarajevo factor," the uncontrollable chain of events, the slippery slope into the abyss of world war.

The United States, bolstered by its European allies, views the possibil-

13. This characterization draws on T. H. Rigby, "Introduction: Political Legitimacy, Weber and Communist Mono-organizational Systems," in Rigby and Ferenc Feher, eds., *Political Legitimation in Communist States* (St. Martin's Press, 1982), pp. 10–11.

ity of war through the lens of Munich and assumes that war would only come about as the result of some Soviet initiative that the West had failed to deter. Following this line of reasoning, American officials dismissed Soviet claims during the first Reagan administration that the confrontational style of U.S. policy was making war more likely. They argued that these claims were propagandistic and did not reflect genuine Soviet beliefs, and that the Soviets could not help but recognize that war was in fact less likely, since deterrence had been enhanced.

But the disjunction in perceptions goes beyond the difference between the precedents of Munich and Sarajevo. In 1981–83 significant numbers of Europeans clearly believed that war was more likely, and there is now concrete evidence that the Soviets had concluded likewise and took steps to increase their preparedness.[14] But it was inconceivable to most Americans, including those in the administration, that the Soviets could really believe this to be true, despite the circumstantial evidence (described in chapter 12) that the Soviets were taking precautionary measures.

This fundamental disjunction in the two sides' perceptions of the danger of war is the root of much misunderstanding. If one thinks war unlikely, then the image of foreign policy as a game like football is not unreasonable. The game is composed of a series of plays that are won or lost, and the approach to problems is zero sum. This imagery pervades U.S. commentary on the superpower relationship and means that deepseated Russian concerns about war are dismissed as rhetoric. But Yuri V. Andropov was not indulging in rhetoric when he accused the Reagan administration of having a flippant attitude toward the issue of peace and war.[15] The Soviets' frustration at their inability to get across their concern is reflected in the comment by a senior Soviet advisor that "the danger of war [in U.S. policy] lies in the fact that politics are carried on as if there were no danger of war."[16]

This disjunction in perceptions makes it particularly hard for Americans to understand the Soviet approach to limiting nuclear weapons. Soviet objections to the Strategic Defense Initiative do not stem only from the pos-

14. Oleg A. Gordievskiy, the former chief of the KGB station in London who defected in July 1985, provided information how, in 1981–83, the KGB had been required to divert assets to seeking evidence of preparations for war and monitoring tactical warning indicators. Murrey Marder, "Defector Tells of Soviet Alert," *Washington Post,* August 8, 1986.

15. "Otvety Yu. V. Andropova na voprosy korrespondenta *Pravdy*" (Replies by Yuri V. Andropov to questions from a correspondent of Pravda), *Pravda,* March 27, 1983.

16. The comment was by Georgiy Arbatov, director of the Institute for the Study of the USA and Canada. Cited in Charles Kiselyak, "Round the Prickly Pear: SALT and Survival," *Orbis,* vol. 22 (Winter 1979), p. 833.

sibility that it could undermine their wartime deterrent or the threat that such a U.S. capability could pose the Russian homeland. The objections stem also from the Soviets' belief that "the weaponization of space" (as they call it) is inherently dangerous and may of itself lead to war. For Americans, the SDI represents a technological opportunity on a par with the Apollo manned space program. For the Soviets, the SDI threatens to open a Pandora's box with unforeseeable consequences. A failure to side-track this development in the 1980s will be as portentous as the failure to agree on the control of atomic weapons in the 1940s.

Paradoxically, while the United States discounts the possibility that an assertive foreign policy could lead to inadvertent war, American concern about some "window of vulnerability" has never been far below the sur-face, reflecting a belief that the Soviets could see global war as serving their interests.[17] For this and other reasons, U.S. arms control policy has continued to focus on the danger of sudden attack, whether a preemptive strike during a crisis or a premeditated bolt from the blue. The threat of sudden attack is not, however, a primary focus of Soviet arms control pol-icy. To the Soviets mutual assured destruction is an inescapable fact. They plan on the assumption that the United States understands that any attempt to disarm Russia would result in the nuclear devastation of North America.

Anticipating Change

Understanding past and present Soviet policy and motivations is one problem. Recognizing a major shift is another. The analytical requirement is for a model of what is "normal" Soviet behavior, ranging from diplo-matic initiatives to weapons production, so that the anomalies that indicate change can be recognized. As can be seen from this study, a fairly minor change at a high level of policy can create major changes throughout the lower levels. However, this study also shows that major changes at these lower levels of policy do not necessarily imply a Soviet reassessment of the basic structure of the international system and of the fundamental re-lationship between capitalism and communism. The opposite is equally true. The absence of evidence of change at the operational level of policy does not exclude the possibility that a reassessment of structural relation-ships has taken place.

Consequently, two kinds of hypothesis are required. One focuses on the

17. Pipes, "Why the Soviet Union Thinks It Could Win," pp. 26–34. In 1981 Pipes was President Reagan's senior adviser on Soviet affairs.

Soviet view of the structure of the international environment, where the struggle for socialism is taking place. The other focuses on the objectives the Soviets are pursuing in that environment and the operational policies that flow from these objectives.

A change in how the Soviets view the structure of the international environment is unlikely to affect the hierarchy of strategic objectives in a world war, although it may affect Soviet estimates of the likelihood of war. Such a change is, however, likely to affect the objectives and policies that relate to the peacetime competition between social systems, although the evidence may take several years to emerge. This is why it is important to have a separate structural hypothesis and to be sensitive to the types of development that are likely to provoke change.

A predisposition to expect change is essential. A well-publicized failure to foresee change was the U.S. national intelligence estimates projecting Soviet ICBM deployment in the second half of the 1960s.[18] These estimates were based on projections of established deployment rates in the early 1960s, but were thrown off track by the production of SS-11s at a rate that would allow deployment of 240 of these ICBMs a year.

One could not expect analysts to have foreseen that the Soviets would adapt this ballistic missile that had been gestating at a design bureau specializing in naval cruise missiles. But one could expect them to have asked how the Soviets would respond to a U.S. procurement program of some 350 Minutemen a year, a program that initially gave no clear indication of the total number to be deployed.

One can also expect analysts to be attuned to the fact that in a goal-achieving type of socioeconomic system, a crop of seemingly unconnected anomalies in patterns of production and deployment are all likely to stem from the same underlying cause. For example, a fixed allocation of nuclear reactors can explain a whole series of major and apparently unrelated anomalies in the submarine building programs that stemmed from the 1961–62, 1967–68, and 1976–77 decision periods. This example also illustrates how the reverberations from sucessive decision periods can interact to produce a complex wave pattern in which the evidence is hard to disentangle. This makes it all the more important to try and find an organizing principle that will bring order to the data.

To foresee how the Soviets are likely to respond to unfolding events, whether initiated by the West or not, one must try and view the world from

18. Albert Wohlstetter, "Is There a Strategic Arms Race?" *Foreign Policy*, no. 15 (Summer 1974), p. 13.

Moscow. This means forgoing the assumption that the benevolence of U.S. intentions is self-evident. In late 1960, when Deputy Foreign Minister Vasiliy Kuznetsov expressed his concern to Walt Rostow about the "missile gap" issue in Kennedy's election, Rostow replied to the effect that any Kennedy rearmament would be designed to improve the stability of the deterrent, and that the Soviet Union should recognize this as being in the interests of peace.[19] Kuznetsov warned that the Soviets would respond in kind, but Washington was not listening.

Twenty-five years later, this same attitude was reflected in comments by Paul Nitze on the Strategic Defense Initiative. He is quoted as saying that the Reagan administration hoped that "the Soviets will come to see the merits of our position—that it will serve their national interests as well as ours." Once again, the Soviets have warned that they do not see it as serving their interests and again it appears that the United States is not willing to listen.[20]

Many of the difficulties in foreseeing Soviet military requirements have stemmed from the Western belief that it has a superior understanding of nuclear strategy and the theory of arms control, but to view the world from Moscow one must avoid a sense of Western superiority. For the future, a patronizing perception of the Soviet socioeconomic system will cause the West to misjudge the Soviet response to the challenge of the SDI.

Policy Implications

A common feature of many Western explanations of Soviet behavior is the reliance on worst-case assumptions about Soviet intentions. In many cases, worst-case assumptions are appropriate. But an important conclusion of this analysis is the high cost to the West and to the world of basing

19. Arthur M. Schlesinger, Jr., *A Thousand Days: John F. Kennedy in the White House* (Houghton Mifflin, 1965), p. 301.

20. In rebutting an assertion by the Soviet ambassador to Washington that the U.S. development of space weapons would lead to a buildup of Soviet offensive systems, Secretary of the Navy John F. Lehman said that the Soviets, with time, would come to view the SDI as "in our mutual interests." Gary Lee, "Dobrynin Renews Attacks on SDI," *Washington Post*, April 13, 1985. Lieutenant General James A. Abrahamson, the Defense Department official in charge of the SDI, is quoted as saying "The Russians are afraid of our technology. . . . When they see that we have embarked on a long-term effort to achieve an extremely effective defense, . . . they will give up on the development of more offensive missiles and move in the same direction." Robert G. Kaiser, "A Disarming Lack of Candor," *Washington Post*, March 10, 1985. This article also contains the Nitze quotation.

U.S. foreign policy on unfounded worst-case assumptions about Soviet intentions.

The Cost of Worst-Case Assumptions

Worst-case assumptions have respectable origins, and they provide the basis for all contingency plans whose focus is one's own vulnerabilities. At this, the military-tactical or "colonel's" level of threat analysis, the concern is properly for an opponent's capabilities, with hostile intentions taken for granted. But while worst-case analysis is appropriate to contingency planning, it is wholly inappropriate at the politico-strategic or "ministerial" level of analysis that should underlie foreign policy.

At this higher level, the primary concern should be for the most likely course of events. An opponent's military capabilities are not ignored, but they are measured against his security requirements to discover whether there is the type of surplus that would indicate an aggressive plan of action. The primary focus is on the opponent's interests and intentions, which are major elements of national motivations. It is difficult to determine any country's interests, even one's own, but it is relatively easy to identify what is against an enemy's interests. One thereby avoids assuming that what is bad for oneself must be good for one's opponent.

Soviet intentions must be examined directly. To claim that they should be ignored is to fall into the "colonel's fallacy." At the national level, intentions are remarkably consistent, and radical change only comes with political shifts of a kind that have not occurred since the Bolshevik Revolution. After more than sixty-five years of Soviet behavior and pronouncements, a fairly clear picture emerges of Soviet intentions, particularly concerning peace and war.[21]

The Soviet Union undoubtedly sees the United States as an adversary, a relationship that stems as much from the global status of the two superpowers as from the ideological struggle for socialism in a world dominated by capitalism. Nor is there any doubt that communist theory predicts that in the long run socialism will prevail. In the decade following World War II, the dominant Western belief was that the Soviets were committed to territorial expansion through military aggression. This belief was under-

---

21. Malcolm Mackintosh, an assistant secretary in the British Cabinet and a special adviser to the government on Soviet military affairs for more than twenty years, concludes that "the Russian people are not and never have been a militaristic nation devoted to the solution of their problems or the achievement of their goals by war." Mackintosh, "The Russian Attitude to Defence and Disarmament," *International Affairs*, vol. 61 (Summer 1985), p. 393.

standable, given the experience with Adolf Hitler's Germany. Expectations were not, however, matched by Soviet behavior. Nor was this surprising, given the Soviet experience of war during the previous thirty years, their doctrinal confidence in the course of history, and the communist belief that in the last analysis economic developments and not violence determine history's course. The Soviets believe the main motivating force of history is the broad masses of the people, not armies.[22]

That explanation for Soviet behavior is not, however, persuasive to those who believe that the Soviet Union has an urge for military aggression. They believe that Soviet restraint has been the direct result of the Western policy of conventional containment and nuclear deterrence. But even those who acknowledge that the hypothesis of a Soviet Union set on military world domination is not supported by the evidence that has accumulated since 1945,[23] are prone to argue that "it is better to be safe than sorry." An implication of this argument is that worst-case assumptions are cost free. That is not true.

The costs of worst-case assumptions are pervasive. The assumptions affect everything from NATO military strategy to U.S. foreign policy, and from the domestic allocation of resources to attitudes toward arms control. The costs discussed here are not the economic ones, although those are obvious enough. Rather the unjustified worst-case assumptions introduce distortions into Western policies, whether domestic, military, or foreign.

For example, the assumption that the Soviets had an urge to seize Western Europe led NATO to adopt the doctrine of flexible response in 1967. Its purpose was to increase the credibility of the Western deterrent by replacing the policy of automatic resort to nuclear weapons with one in which NATO would initially use conventional weapons to check a Soviet assault on Europe. The conventional phase would serve the double purpose of allowing NATO to be certain that it was facing a major attack, while giving the Soviets the opportunity to see the error of their ways and withdraw.

Because the central assumption was ill founded, adoption of this doctrine had the paradoxical effect of both increasing the level of the military threat on the central front and making war just that more likely. A Soviet drive into Western Europe would be responding to a strategic imperative,

22. S.A. Tyushkevich, N.Ya. Shushko, and Ya. S. Dzyuby, eds., *Marksizm-Leninizm o voyne i armii* (Marxism-Leninism on war and the army) (Moscow: Voenizdat, 1968), p. 61.

23. See Ken Booth, *The Military Instrument in Soviet Foreign Policy, 1917–72* (London: Royal United Services Institute for Defence Studies, 1973).

and not to some "urge to aggression" that could be deterred by a threat of punishment. A Soviet offensive would be a by-product of the momentous decision that world war was unavoidable. That decision became slightly less unthinkable once the NATO doctrine of flexible response opened a window of conventional opportunity.[24] If skillfully exploited, that window might allow the Soviets to prevent NATO from resorting to nuclear weapons in the theater and, if that were not possible, at least U.S. escalation to strikes on Russia might be made less likely.

Flexible response was a particular application of the policy of deterrence, which has been a mainstay of U.S. policy since the early 1950s. It has also been one of the most powerful means of perpetuating worst-case assumptions. For deterrence to have any meaning, it must be assumed that the temptation exists to take the action being deterred. A Soviet urge to aggression became a cornerstone of Western policy, an assumption that dispensed with the need to analyze Soviet intentions.

The requirement that nuclear deterrence be credible encouraged a particular style of U.S. foreign policy. Even in the days of the U.S. atomic monopoly, if the American electorate were to support a policy of deterrence, the public had to perceive the Soviet Union as an enemy that deserved such brutal punishment. As the United States was brought within range of Soviet strategic systems, the American people had to be persuaded that they were willing to suffer massive devastation in defense of Europe, which meant that the issues were painted in stark moral terms. The result is a policy that tends toward intransigence (as a demonstration of resolve) and is suspicious of negotiations and the search for compromise.

Worst-case assumptions also work to restrict the flexibility of foreign policy and the choice of objectives. The assumption that the Soviet Union is bent on military world domination requires that physical containment be the primary U.S. objective. The objective of containment requires that the Soviets be excluded from involvements around the world, and the possibility is ignored that Western interests would be better served by enlisting Soviet collaboration.

A broader U.S. objective such as "securing cooperative Soviet behavior" would open up more constructive policy options. With the primary

---

24. The same reasoning would apply to a NATO policy of no first use of nuclear weapons. While such an initiative could be politically important as part of a package designed to reduce tension in Europe, in military terms it is just what the Soviets want. It would increase the likelihood that resort to nuclear weapons in the theater could be avoided.

objective at a higher level of the hierarchy, containment continues to be an important supporting objective, but it can be flanked by positive objectives such as fostering consultation on matters of mutual interest, increasing trade interdependence, and even encouraging rising expectations in Russia by improving the Soviet standard of living. A higher-level objective would accommodate collaborative policies such as joint exploration of space or combining with the Soviet Union to stifle dangerous international developments before they become unmanageable.[25] These various options are incompatible with containment as the principal objective.

During the period of détente in the early 1970s, the United States relaxed its worst-case assumptions and implicitly adopted a higher-level objective, which allowed a broader range of initiatives. These brought benefits that extended beyond the Soviet-American relationship and contributed to the improvement in East-West relations in Europe. But the worst-case assumptions of Western deterrence theory were incompatible with those of a policy of détente, and the pressure to return to more restrictive policies could not be resisted.

Harm also arises from a systematic misunderstanding of the other superpower's motivations. Serious Soviet proposals are not taken seriously, and everything is seen as propaganda. Worst-case assumptions close the mind to the possibility of changes in Soviet policy that could be in Western interests, or to the emergence of cooperative tendencies. Opportunities are missed.

Opportunities have almost certainly been missed in arms control. Worst-case assumptions and the Western focus on its own vulnerabilities combined to blind the West to the tangible evidence that had been accumulating since 1970 that the Soviets had a serious interest in reducing the level of nuclear armaments and were prepared to make major concessions to reach agreement. It did not even enter Western minds that the Soviets might have been willing to cap the arms race with the weapons deployed at the signing of SALT II, and that they might have been ready not to go ahead with fifth-generation ICBMs, except perhaps the small single-warhead replacement for the remaining third-generation systems. Yet the evidence suggests that these possibilities were at least worth exploring.

Worst-case assumptions about Soviet eagerness to seize any chance,

25. A successful example was South Africa's halting of its planned nuclear test in 1977 in response to U.S. diplomatic pressure. The Soviet Union had drawn U.S. attention to this development. A missed opportunity was the initial stage of the Iran-Iraq war.

however slight, to destroy the United States make it almost impossible to ratify an arms control treaty that does not enshrine U.S. superiority. Assumptions about the pressure to preempt focus attention on the control of crises rather than on how to prevent them, although by the time one is in a crisis in which thoughts turn to preemption it is probably already too late. But the most insidious effect of worst-case assumptions about Soviet intentions has been to breed a false complacency about the danger of inadvertent war.

If one believes that war can only come about through some Soviet initiative that the West has failed to deter, then anything that enhances deterrence should make war less likely. The trouble with that approach is that measures intended to improve deterrence, such as the deployment of Euromissiles are likely to raise international tensions, and in the process, make war more likely. Because, as tension rises, so does the likelihood that intentions will be misread and that one side will set off a dangerous chain reaction in which each side will feel compelled to demonstrate its resolve to the other.

"Better safe than sorry" has strong appeal, and it was to be expected that policymakers would tend toward the colonel's fallacy in the years following World War II. But the fallacy has persisted, and the costs continue to accrue. This persistence can be explained partly by the fact that the threat perceptions of the 1948–53 period were institutionalized by the policy of deterrence and by the NATO staff structure. It may also have something to do with democracies, particularly a coalition of democracies, and the difficulty of securing political support for sustained expenditure on defense.

The situation is somewhat ironic since the West has prided itself on the sophistication of its strategic theorizing, while it is the Soviets who are said to be paranoid. Yet the Soviets appear to be better at avoiding this fallacy. They structure their forces for the contingency of world war and make worst-case assumptions about the nature of such a war, but that is appropriate at the military-technical level of analysis. The fallacy is to use this same approach at the politico-strategic level, the ministerial level where the broader issues of foreign and defense policy are decided.

The Soviets have been reasonably successful in keeping the two levels of analysis distinct. Once clear of the 1948–53 period, they steadily moved away from the idea of a premeditated Western attack. By the 1960s, although the potential opponent was still the West and its objective in a war would be to overthrow the Soviet system, the danger was seen to be inadvertent war. If it came, it would be the result of some Western action, but it was not assumed that the West had an urge to go to war.

Living with the Russians

The harsh facts of the adversarial relationship—massive nuclear inventories, opposing forces deployed around the world, and forces facing each other directly across the European divide are daunting. But even these facts become somewhat less intractable when the focus is on the *why* of Soviet behavior rather than the *what*.

CONFRONTATION IN EUROPE.   Undoubtedly, the Soviet military posture facing NATO denotes an offensive concept of operations. In the event of war the Soviet objective is to defeat NATO on the ground, evict U.S. forces from the Continent, and establish control of Western Europe. To execute that offensive concept, the Soviets must be able to achieve a preponderance of force at key points on NATO's central front as high as six or eight to one, which almost certainly requires overall superiority in the theater, perhaps as much as three to two.

There is, therefore, an inherent asymmetry between the two sides' requirements. If the Soviets are not, ultimately, to lose the war, they have to carry out a successful offensive in Europe; whereas for NATO not to lose, it has only to check that offensive. These conditions might seem to imply that NATO must either reconcile itself to living with a significant margin of inferiority or else be prepared to engage in a permanent conventional arms race, as the Soviet Union strives to preserve the relative advantage needed for a successful offensive. That, certainly, is the logic of the situation, but reality is mitigated by two important considerations.

The occupation of Europe is not something the Soviet Union desires for its own sake. The offensive is contingent on the decision that world war is unavoidable, and avoiding that contingency is one of the Soviet Union's first-order national objectives. Second, the Soviets distinguish between the way they structure their forces for the contingency of world war, and the resources they apply to fleshing out that structure to make those forces fully capable of carrying out their assigned missions. In the latter context, the forces in Europe clearly have the highest relative priority. Nevertheless, the less likely the Soviets consider war, the less importance they will attach to having the necessary margin of advantage permanently in place in the European theater.

This seems to have been the situation in the late 1970s. The adoption of the 1970s hierarchy of objectives meant a fundamental restructuring of Soviet ground and air forces facing Europe. Although the restructuring greatly increased their capacity for conventional deep strikes and blitzkrieg offensive, the actual force levels were not sufficient to guarantee success. That, certainly, appears to have been the opinion of various Soviet military writers, and it was also the judgment of many Western analysts. That this level was the result of conscious policy rather than miscalculation is suggested by the Soviet readiness in 1979 to begin negotiating seriously on mutual and balanced force reductions. As long as arms control negotiations are seen to be promoting the objective of avoiding world war, the lower-order objective of not losing once engaged will tend to yield precedence.

SIZE OF THE NUCLEAR INVENTORIES.   The change from the 1960s strategic concept of intercontinental nuclear warfighting to the 1970s concept of wartime deterrence removed the theoretical requirement for numerical superiority in strategic nuclear inventories, a change reflected in the Soviet missile programs. Two factors work strongly in favor of smaller strategic inventories. One is the demands of the Soviet economy. The other is the wartime objective of avoiding the nuclear devastation of Russia. Since the late 1960s, the Soviets have consistently demonstrated their interest in negotiating limits on strategic weapons.

The problem in this area is not an asymmetry of military requirements but of psychological needs. The Soviets have lived with U.S. nuclear superiority for about forty years and are willing to settle for approximate equivalence if that places an effective cap on the arms race. Americans have so far been reluctant to accept the idea of equivalence with the Soviet Union, even an equivalence tilted in favor of the United States and its allies, as was provided for by SALT I and SALT II. This problem is as much one of U.S. domestic politics as of Soviet-American relations.

COMPETITION IN THE THIRD WORLD.   Since Western influence predominates in the third world, it might seem that a Soviet attempt to advance the cause of socialism must lead inevitably to East-West military conflict. But this supposition views the present situation through the historical lens of the European imperial competition and takes no account of Soviet doctrine or the changed political circumstances. During the empire-building phase of the colonial period, the European competitors believed that history waited on no one. They used military and commercial instruments to establish their domain over large areas that often lacked formal structures of government, and they did not hesitate to use force against their competitors. Conflict was endemic.

The present situation is different. The third world is now composed of independent states. The Soviet Union believes that historical processes will inevitably move these states toward socialism, when the conditions are appropriate, and since the Soviets also believe in the inherent superiority of their socioeconomic systems, the primary instruments of Soviet policy are not military ones but political, social, and economic ones.

This world view has encouraged the Soviet Union to adopt a fairly relaxed approach to the competition for influence in the third world. They take advantage of opportunities as appropriate, but they are still prepared to win some, lose some. Military support to third world countries has been provided in the shape of arms, equipment, and training. The Soviets' aim is to enhance the countries' capacity for self-defense, as well as increase Soviet political influence. Support was also provided to national liberation movements, but these movements are now relatively scarce. The use of Soviet military forces in direct support of clients has been strictly limited, a major reason being the concern that a superpower confrontation in the third world could escalate to a world war.

Soviet confidence in historical inevitability, the belief in the primacy of socioeconomic instruments of policy, and the military's limited role of preventing capitalist intervention play directly to America's comparative advantage. In a competition waged with socioeconomic instruments, the United States must win hands down. The Soviet Union's inability to exploit the European nations' withdrawal from empire argues that history is not running its way. And reducing the threat of U.S. military intervention (an activity in which geography places America at a comparative disadvantage) will reduce the pressure in Moscow to involve Soviet forces in the third world.

Prognosis

With hindsight, one can see that in 1976–77, Soviet policies were moving in a direction that was generally favorable to improved East-West relations. The Soviets had largely completed the restructuring of their theater forces, and investment in defense procurement had leveled off. They were ready to accept a treaty on limiting strategic weapons along the lines of SALT II and keen to move on to a third round of negotiations. The likelihood of war was seen to be low, and the Soviets may even have been considering forgoing their fifth generation of ICBMs. Important elements of their naval building programs were to be curtailed. The argument for direct Soviet military intervention in the third world had been lost; and the concept of Soviet-American détente was at the center of Soviet foreign policy.

By 1984–85 the prospects were very different. The Soviets now believed that the likelihood of war had increased significantly. Some resources had been switched from the civilian to the defense sector, the output of certain armaments had been raised, and the number of active divisions had been increased. The production of two of the fifth-generation ICBMs had been authorized, and the development of a third, the replacement for the heavy SS-18, was going ahead. Although the relationship with the United States continued to be at the center of Soviet foreign policy, the future nature of that relationship was uncertain. Both the value of détente and its very possibility were in question. Besides these immediate manifestations there could be other unfavorable changes that would only become apparent in future years.

The prognosis is not rosy. But in dealing with the Soviets the West is fortunate in several respects. The Soviets' belief in historical inevitability makes their vision of the world much less dangerous than that of the great empire builders, whether Arab-Muslim, European-Christian, or Aryan-Nazi. It removes the sense of urgency and the need for a crusade or jihad to achieve one's ends.

The West is also fortunate in the Marxist belief in the primacy of socioeconomic factors, both domestically and in the struggle between social systems. The fact that the mass of Russians will always place the security of their homeland above their personal comfort does not imply that guns always have precedence over butter within the Soviet economy. The relative priority depends on the likelihood of war. The overriding priority that was given to the defense industries in the 1930s, and again in the late 1940s and early 1950s when the danger of war was seen to be high, should not obscure the continued attempts from 1953 onward to increase the relative share of the civilian sector, including shifting resources from the defense sector.

A third respect in which the West is fortunate is the way in which the Soviets view world war. They are serious about the real danger that war will come about, and they are serious about doing their best to avoid such a war if at all possible. This seriousness is clearly in everyone's best interests, but the corollary is that they are also serious about not losing such a war, should it prove inescapable.

The structuring of their forces for the contingency of world war appears threatening to their potential opponents. But the actual level of the threat posed by this force structure is to some extent within Western control, since the resources that the Soviets allocate to fleshing it out reflect their perception of the danger of war. It was unfortunate that the demonstration of this point in the second half of the 1970s and early 1980s was obscured by the reequipping and restructuring of Soviet forces that had gotten under way in the late 1960s. It was also unfortunate that U.S. policies in 1981–84 made nuclear war seem appreciably more likely to major sections of world opinion, including the Soviet Union at whom the policies were explicitly directed.

Prescription

The challenge facing the West can be expressed in the form of three questions. Is the West politically mature enough to distinguish between the structuring of Soviet forces for the contingency of world war (including plans to take over Western Europe) and Soviet intentions for the use of military force as an instrument of policy? Is the West politically astute enough to perceive that the level of the capabilities threat it faces is directly related to the probabilities the Soviets attach to the outbreak of war, and that U.S. attitudes and behavior are the most important factors in the Soviet estimate of the likelihood of war? Is the West wise enough to appreciate that attempts to solve its security dilemma by military means alone can only make the problem worse?

On the basis of this study, one can conclude that NATO has no alternative to living with Soviet forces that are structured for offensive operations against Western Europe, but that the assertiveness of the threat will diminish as the Soviets think war less likely. One can also conclude that the Soviets have good military reasons for negotiating reductions in their arsenal of strategic nuclear weapons, and they have even stronger reasons for resisting or countering the deployment of weapons in space. For practical policies, the most important conclusion to be drawn from this analysis of Soviet objectives is that ill-founded worst-case assumptions about the Soviet Union's broader intentions generate U.S. policies whose results are the opposite of what the United States desires.

The colonel's fallacy is costly because it calls for military responses to problems that are primarily political. So far, the fallacy has not led the West into war, but it has caused significant damage. It has encouraged the steady buildup of armaments. The cyclical fluctuations of the arms race have been a major source of friction in the superpower relationship and have caused serious discord in the Western alliance. The colonel's fallacy has encouraged the West to view the competition for world influence through a military lens and in zero-sum terms, neglecting the West's comparative advantage in socioeconomic instruments of policy. The colonel's fallacy also ignores the fact that militarizing the competition imposes heavy costs in current human suffering and jeopardizes future world order.

PART FOUR

Appendixes

Identifying the December 1966 Decision

THIS APPENDIX outlines the methodology for identifying decision periods and details the evidence for the change in Soviet military doctrine in late 1966 that is discussed in chapters 2 and 3. The process of coming to a decision on the need for a major change in policy can be visualized in the form of a wave. The rear slope of the wave represents the period when perceptions of the need for change build up to the crest of a top-level agreement-in-principle. The front slope of the wave represents the series of implementing decisions that stem from this acceptance of the need for change and constitutes what can be called a decision period.

By working back from the end product of these individual implementing decisions, the analyst is able to date a decision period. In this respect the introduction of new weapons systems (or modifications to existing ones) is particularly helpful.[1] Because the different lead times required in such programs are now reasonably well established, he or she can date the separate decisions that resulted in these new or modified systems entering service. When the decision also involves cancellation of an existing program, "pipeline inertia" may allow him to bracket the date with greater confidence.[2] The clustering in time of these individual design decisions defines the decision period,[3] which is usually expressed as a pair of years, both because the estimates of lead time can never be precise and because

1. For an early discussion of this analytical approach, see Michael MccGwire, "The Turning Points in Soviet Naval Policy," in MccGwire, ed., *Soviet Naval Developments: Capability and Context* (Praeger, 1973), pp. 176–209.

2. "Pipeline inertia" describes the combination of economic and operational factors that justifies the continued production of weapons platforms or systems for a substantial period after the decision not to proceed with the program.

3. A "design decision" defines the date when an operational requirement was identified and the wheels were set in motion to do something about it. A design decision could be in response to some new aspect of the threat being perceived, reflect the adoption of a new operational concept, or indicate approval to introduce or apply some newly developed capability. The term implies that authority has been given to apply funds and development effort to meet a specific operational requirement.

Figure A-1. *Decisionmaking as a Wave Form*

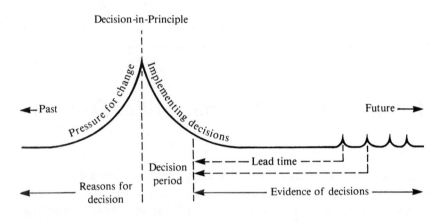

the implementing decisions are likely to be spread over a year or more as the implications of the original decision-in-principle are analyzed in ever increasing detail (figure A-1).

In some cases the analyst can infer that a decision-in-principle has been reached from the nature of public pronouncements at the time. This was true in September 1947, when Andrey Zhdanov announced the "two camps" doctrine, and probably also in September 1983, when General Secretary Yuri V. Andropov made his "Declaration" (see chapter 12). In other cases, the existence of a decision period may be publicly announced, as when First Secretary Nikita S. Khrushchev set out his revised defense policy in January 1960.[4] But more often, awareness of a decision period emerges retrospectively; even when there are clear indications at the time that a decision-in-principle has been reached, understanding what was involved depends largely on hindsight.

Identifying a decision-in-principle can therefore be seen as an iterative four-stage process. First comes the alert that something has changed. The signals may be shifts in established procedures, perturbations in weapons programs or production processes, or the emergence of operational patterns and concepts that flout the logic of established objectives. The second stage is to establish the decision period from which these various changes emanated. The analyst needs to examine each change separately to deter-

4. N. S. Khrushchev, "Razoruzhenie—put'k uprocheniyu mira i obespecheniyu druzhby mezhdunarodomi" (Disarmament for durable peace and friendship between peoples), *Pravda*, January 15, 1960.

mine the date it must have been decided, using estimates of lead time, pipeline inertia, and other types of evidence. The clustering of these dates will locate the front slope of the decisionmaking wave in time.

The third stage of analysis is to cross over to the rear slope of the wave in search of an explanation of why the underlying change in policy was decided. All kinds of circumstances have to be reviewed, including technological opportunities and setbacks, international developments, changes in enemy capabilities or in Soviet threat perceptions (which are not synonymous), and, of course, the domestic competition for resources. To produce the necessary impetus to overcome the inertia of established policies, the conjunction of a range of circumstances is usually required unless there is some clear-cut imperative, for example, the need to react to the Kennedy defense initiatives in 1961.[5]

As a result of such a review, the analyst should be able to identify a cause, or a series of causes, that could have led to the effects that triggered the awareness of change. He can then move to the final stage of the analysis and postulate the nature of the central decision-in-principle. Once he has some idea of its substance, he is then in a position to repeat the four-stage process, with the advantage that he now knows where to look for evidence of change. The second round allows him to date the decision period more precisely, to look more perceptively at the surrounding circumstances, and to refine the formulation of the decision-in-principle.

On this first iteration it may also be appropriate to expand the scope of the fourth stage to include an analysis of Soviet pronouncements and writings over the period of the decisionmaking wave to see if there are indications of a watershed. Whether to widen the inquiry in this way will depend on the nature of the decision, but analysis of various texts will sometimes allow the analyst to date the actual decision with greater precision, as was possible for 1961. The analyst may also be able to identify a consistent pattern of minor but significant additions and omissions that, taken together, clarify the substance of the decision-in-principle.

Having dated the decision-in-principle and postulated its nature, the analyst can then move on to teasing out the implications of this decision.

5. The Soviet response to the Kennedy initiatives illustrates the importance of dating the decision period correctly. Identifying mid-1961 as the time of the key decision-in-principle, rather than 1963 (post-Cuba) or late 1964 (post-Khrushchev), was essential to the correct interpretation of Soviet developments in the naval field during the 1960s and in the strategic rocket forces in the 1960s and 1970s. John McDonnell, "Khrushchev and the Soviet Military–Industrial Complex: Soviet Defense Policy, 1959–61" (Halifax, Nova Scotia, Dalhousie University, Center for Foreign Policy Studies, 1979), pp. 73–82.

These are testable hypotheses, which can be verified by analyzing subsequent weapons programs, operational concepts, and doctrinal statements. A fruitful approach to uncovering the full range of implications is to establish the effect of the central decision on the existing hierarchy of policy objectives and its supporting mission structure. That approach is demonstrated in chapter 3 and provides the analytical framework of this book.

This book focuses on the implications of the decision periods in 1967–68 and 1976–77 and postulates another decision period in 1983–85. In the twenty years before 1967, there is firm evidence of another five significant decision periods in Soviet defense and foreign policy.

1947–48. This period followed Stalin's final acceptance that the wartime collaborative relationship was irretrievable, an acceptance that was formalized in the Zhdanov "two camps" doctrine. It involved a shift in threat perceptions from the expectation of war with Germany in fifteen to twenty years, with perhaps Japan in the rear, to the likelihood of war within five to seven years against a capitalist coalition led by the Anglo-Saxon powers. The evidence includes the halting of the postwar run-down in Soviet forces, the decision to build a force of 1,200 submarines, and the organization of national air defense as a separate service.

1953–54. There was a major review of defense and foreign policy following the death of Stalin, the results of which included downgrading the threat of invasion and a shift in resources from defense production to the domestic economy. Evidence included the midcourse cancellation of warship building programs, notably, the cruiser and medium-type submarine programs and the reallocation of naval construction facilities to the merchant fleet and the fishing industry.

1957–58. The development of longer-range ballistic missiles was sufficiently advanced to allow the decision to concentrate on these systems for strategic delivery rather than on aircraft and submarines. Aircraft production was switched to the civil air fleet, while nuclear submarine hull-propulsion units were reallocated to the mission of countering the U.S. carrier threat (see chapter 5).

1959–60. The so-called revolution in military affairs brought about by the advent of nuclear warheads and missile means of delivery prompted a defense review. This resulted, among other things, in the strategic rocket forces being established as a separate service and the decision to cut the armed forces by a further 1.2 million men. The broad lines of the review's conclusions were announced by Nikita S. Khrushchev in January 1960.

1961–62. The defense initiatives taken by the Kennedy administration on assuming office in January 1961 prompted a debate in the Soviet Union, which built on existing dissatisfaction with the Khrushchev defense review. A decision-in-principle was reached in mid-1961, resulting in adjustments to, and the reversal of, several of the 1959–60 decisions. The revised policy was announced at the Twenty-second Party Congress in October (see chapter 2). Evidence included the first edition of Sokolovskiy's *Military Strategy* and the navy's shift to forward deployment.

The 1967–68 Decision Period

For the 1967–68 decision period, the fourth stage of the analytical process proved particularly fruitful. The analysis of Soviet pronouncements over the period of the decisionmaking showed the nature of the central decision-in-principle—a change in military doctrine—and bibliographic evidence indicated that it must have been agreed on in the final months of 1966.[6] The analysis also provided conclusive evidence that the change did not emanate from the Twenty-third Party Congress in March–April of that year. That congress merely reaffirmed established policy, whereas the doctrinal shift occurred several months later.

The first three stages of the analysis can be briefly summarized. The initial alert was sounded by new developments in the structure of the Soviet navy that gradually became apparent during the 1970s.[7] There were the ungainly characteristics of the new Delta class of SSBNs that started delivery in 1973 and the anomalies in the testing of its missile, the SS-N-8. There was the evidence of ballistic-missile submarines (SSBNs) being deployed in defensible "bastions" adjacent to Soviet home waters in the Arctic and the Pacific. In 1980 a new family of surface warships started delivery, whose characteristics indicated a fundamental change in the underlying operational concept.

These developments (discussed in chapter 5) were related to the security of the SSBN force and coincided with a clear indication in the literature that the Soviets viewed the Deltas as distinctly different from the earlier

6. In Soviet parlance, military doctrine is an officially adopted system of views on fundamental questions to do with war, including the nature of a future war and the method of waging it.

7. The evidence is summarized here in a neat package, but the awareness of change built up only over time. The series of articles by Admiral Sergey G. Gorshkov published in the 1972–73 period indicated a major debate on defense matters, and by 1978 a new decision period affecting the navy had been tentatively dated to 1967–68, although its scope was still unclear.

Yankee force.[8] The surface warship program argued a design decision not later than 1968–69, a cutoff date that was supported by the Delta SSBN program.[9]

Meanwhile the mission structure of frontal aviation had swung "dramatically in the direction of deep offensive interdiction [ground attack] and its supporting missions."[10] In dating this change, one must distinguish between aircraft from existing production programs that were adapted for the new missions and aircraft from programs that were specifically initiated to meet this requirement. Two aircraft fit the second category. The twin-engined SU-24 Fencer, which entered service at the end of 1974, is generally considered to have been designed for deep interdiction with the use of conventional ordnance. And the ground-attack MiG-27 Flogger D, which entered service in 1975, is a major reconfiguration of the MiG-23 Flogger B air-superiority fighter.[11] A standard seven-year lead time puts the design decision for these two aircraft in 1967–68.[12]

The developments in frontal aviation reflected a shift from nuclear to conventional delivery systems and were part of a general reorientation of the Warsaw Pact's ground and air capability toward a conventional blitz-krieg capability.[13] On the whole, this reorientation of the ground forces did not yield clear design decisions, since much of the equipment stemmed from the 1961 decision period; the new threat from China that emerged at the end of the 1960s also had a distorting effect. Artillery was an important exception: its strength was significantly increased in the first half of the 1970s, both by more tubes per unit and by the introduction of improved

8. For example, Sergey G. Gorshkov, "Voenno-morskie floty v voynakh i v mirnoe vremya" (Navies in war and peace), *Morskoy sbornik (Naval journal)*, no. 2 (February 1973), p. 21, paras. 2–3. The distinction between the Yankee and Delta forces is discussed in chapter 5.

9. A 1968–69 design decision would allow the qualitatively new surface ship design to emerge from the routine planning-production process, as seems to have been the case with the Udaloy class of large antisubmarine ship. The Delta program yields two types of evidence. One is the requirement to modify the Yankee II to carry the much longer SS-N-8 missile and to order the necessary launch systems and command and control equipment. The other is the developmental history of the SS-N-8, which was first flight tested in 1969 at about 3,000 nautical miles, but was then withdrawn and the range increased. See appendix B.

10. Joshua M. Epstein, *Measuring Military Power: The Soviet Air Threat to Europe* (Princeton University Press, 1984), p. 4.

11. *Jane's All the World's Aircraft, 1982–83* (London: Jane's Publishing Co., 1982), pp. 210, 225.

12. Since the MiG-27 was a reconfiguration, the lead time would have been less, which suggests that work on this redesign did not start until 1970, when the first preseries aircraft were delivered to the air force.

13. Phillip A. Petersen and John G. Hines, "The Conventional Offensive in Soviet Theater Strategy," *Orbis*, vol. 27 (Fall 1983), pp. 705–24.

weapons.[14] This development too was compatible with a 1967–68 design decision.

After this second stage of the analysis, which identified 1967–68 as a decision period, the third stage was to review the 1964–67 period to discover what might have justified these fundamental changes in military posture. This process is set forth in chapter 2, where I conclude that the catalyst of change was probably the announcement by France in March 1966 that it planned to withdraw from NATO at the end of July. The fourth stage, the textual analysis, is described in the following sections.

The Central Decision-in-Principle

With 1967–68 identified as the decision period, the analysis focused initially on the third (revised) edition of Marshal Sokolovskiy's book *Military Strategy*,[15] which was sent for typesetting in late November 1966, released to the printers one year later, and published in 1968. In most respects, the general thrust of the book remained unaltered from the second edition;[16] most of the changes involved updating the information on Western military strategy and capabilities. Harriet Fast Scott, who made a detailed comparison of the successive editions, concluded that the third edition's "similarity to earlier editions may be more striking . . . than the differences. . . . The positions taken on Soviet military strategy and doctrine did not change substantially. . . . This third edition . . . is nevertheless remarkably similar to the first edition."[17]

There were, however, a number of amendments that touched on Soviet strategic concepts, and taken together, these implied a fundamental shift in underlying military doctrine.

14. See Kurt Hoffman, "An Analysis of Soviet Artillery Development," *International Defense Review,* vol. 10 (December 1977), pp. 1057–61; Charles J. Dick, "The Growing Soviet Artillery Threat," *RUSI Journal for Defence Studies,* vol. 124 (June 1979), pp. 66–73; and Davy Isby, "Soviets Refurbish Artillery for Deeper Attack Missions," *Defense Week,* vol. 4 (December 5, 1983), p. 12.

15. Marshal V. D. Sokolovskiy, ed., *Voennaya strategiya,* 3d ed. (*Military strategy*) (Moscow: Voenizdat, 1968). The book was sent to typesetting on November 23, 1966, and was released to the printer on November 30, 1967.

16. The first edition was published in 1962 and the second in 1963. In the context of the present analysis, there were no significant differences between the first and second editions.

17. Analysts owe their detailed knowledge of the changes between the three editions of *Military Strategy* to the invaluable work of Harriet Fast Scott. Harriet Fast Scott, ed. and trans., *Soviet Military Strategy* (Crane, Russak, 1975). Quotations are from p.xvi. Hereafter source notes show page/paragraph in the H. F. Scott translation (HFS) and in the relevant edition of the Russian original, by Sokolovskiy (Sok). References may appear in text or in footnotes.

The Evidence from Military Strategy

The changes to the second edition (1963) suggested a shift in doctrine away from the conclusion that war with the West would inevitably be nuclear, which implied the need to preempt with strikes on the United States, and toward the conclusion that it might be possible to limit the geographic scope of such a war and to deter an intercontinental exchange.

INTERCONTINENTAL NUCLEAR PREEMPTION. The assertions emphasizing the absolute necessity of destroying the enemy's strategic weapons, the importance of surprise, and the need to preempt were deleted from the third edition. They were partially replaced by comments that recognized the potential importance of striking the enemy's vital centers but allowed that victory could also be achieved by the traditional means of theater warfare.

In the second edition two specific references had been made to the need to "annihilate or neutralize" the enemy's strategic weapons. Without such action, the book claimed, it would be impossible either to achieve the politico-military objectives of a world war or to protect one's own population centers.[18] The book also claimed that surprise depended on taking the initiative against the enemy's strategic forces and weapons and that if victory depended on destroying the enemy's forces, then the strategy must provide for "preventive action."[19] In a different context it was noted that general mobilization could not be initiated before the initiation of military action, because the enemy would detect it; that is, surprise would be forefeited (*HFS* 460/10; *Sok* 411/10). All five of these assertions were deleted from the third edition (1968). The first two were replaced by the more benign comment that nuclear strikes against the enemy's vital centers and means of armed combat were the quickest and most certain way to victory, but the author did not dismiss the "former" way of waging war in the theater, noting only that it was a lengthy way to victory (*HFS* 276/5; *Sok* (1968) 332/4).

THE PRACTICALITY OF LIMITED WAR. A significant change of focus occurred in the discussion of limited war, which had been dismissed as impractical in the first two editions. The third edition described the U.S. concept as envisaging a war in which both Russia and America would be

18. *HFS* 451/7, 452/2; *Sok* (1963) 366/3,5.
19. *HFS* 390/6; *Sok* 88/1; and *HFS* 390/7; *Sok* 88/2. The discussion concerned U.S. military thinking.

spared nuclear strikes and in which the conflict would be geographically restricted but would include Europe. Other changes shifted the emphasis from the inevitability of escalation to an intercontinental exchange to the possibility of avoiding it.

In the earlier editions, two and a quarter pages were devoted to ridiculing the concept of limited nuclear war, while stressing the inevitability of escalation to an intercontinental exchange. (*HFS* 393–95; *Sok* (1963), 93–96). In the 1968 edition the emphasis was in the opposite direction. Seven new pages were devoted to a reasoned discussion of the subject, noting first that this Western concept excluded strategic bombardment of both America and Russia and second that the United States envisioned a limited war as being waged within a restricted geographic framework, which would include Europe but exclude North America.[20] The discussion extended to cover NATO efforts to reduce the likelihood of escalation from limited to general war (*HFS* 69/2; *Sok* 89/2). In the chapter "Methods of Waging War," the author decoupled the use of strategic weapons from frontal operations by dropping a reference to preparing the way to the fronts with strategic weapons.[21] A reference to using operational-tactical nuclear weapons to ensure a rapid advance by the ground forces was also dropped.[22]

EFFECTIVE DETERRENCE. The third edition made specific reference to Pentagon estimates of the level of damage that "any industrial country" would find unacceptable; the capability to inflict that damage would therefore "serve as an effective deterrent."[23] Three pages earlier a short addition to the text had the effect of emphasizing the survivability of such a Soviet deterrent. In a discussion of U.S. counterforce strategy that had been new to the second edition, a comment that (in American opinion) one should not count on the complete destruction of Soviet strategic weapons was reinforced by adding a reference to the growing number of mobile launch platforms (*HFS* 61/1; *Sok* 78/2).

PROTRACTED WAR. Omissions from the key chapter on "Preparing the Country to Repel Aggression" put more emphasis on the need to prepare for protracted war. This was the only chapter attributed to a specific author in the first and second editions.[24] It was substantially unchanged in the

20. *HFS* 64–69; *Sok* (1968) 82–89; and *HFS* 64/3; *Sok* 82/3.
21. *HFS* 452, note 183; compare *Sok* (1963) 368/2 with *Sok* (1968) 339/2.
22. *HFS* 452, note 184; compare *Sok* (1963) 369/2 with *Sok* (1968) 340/2.
23. *HFS* 63/1; *Sok* (1968) 81/1 (*posluzhit effektivnym-faktorom ustrasheniya*).
24. General-Lieutenant A. I. Gastilovich (later promoted to general-colonel) whose article "The Theory of Military Art Needs Review" led the "Special Collection" of articles in

third edition except for those omissions. They consisted of five passages totaling less than 400 words, all of which had dealt with the specific implications of nuclear war.

The longest deleted passage (about 250 words) had stressed the devastating effects of a nuclear exchange on the people and material base of the country and used that fear to support the argument that concentration on strategic delivery systems, as the most cost-effective means of war, was justified.[25] In sum, this main passage had downplayed the need for a broad military-industrial base, while another passage had noted the lowered requirement for conventional munitions. Removing these passages, particularly the longest one which set the tone for the whole discussion, gave this chapter a more natural emphasis on the need to prepare for the long haul. A further deletion concerning reserves reinforced this effect.[26]

Supporting Textual Evidence

A shift in doctrine toward the conclusion that it might be possible to avoid an intercontinental exchange would generate new assumptions about the possible length of such a war and about the need to allow for a protracted conventional war, which might or might not escalate. Two other dectrinal works show that such a change in assumptions was being made at this time.

A cursory comparison of the fourth (1965) and fifth (1968) editions of *Marxism-Leninism on War and the Army* reveals some significant alterations.[27] The term "contemporary war" replaced "nuclear war" in the relevant section headings, references to the inevitability of nuclear war were changed to possibility, and a reference to the initial period of the war as being "the time in which nuclear strikes will be carried out" was deleted.[28] A comment that "water and medications, food products and electricity

---

the top secret editions of *Military Thought* in 1960. See Scott, *Soviet Military Strategy,* pp. xx, 304.

25. *HFS* 460; compare *Sok* (1963) 408/4–409/6 with *Sok* (1968) 369.

26. *HFS* 461/1; *Sok* (1963) 420/1; and *HFS* 460 note 196; compare *Sok* (1963) 413/2 with *Sok* (1968) 373/3.

27. S. A. Tyushkevich and N. Ya. Sushko, eds., *Marksizm-Leninizm o voyne i armii,* 5th ed. (Marxism-Leninism on war and the army) (Moscow: Voenizdat, 1968). The fifth (1968) edition went to typesetting on April 25, 1967, to printing on April 18, 1968; the fourth (1965) edition (by the same authors) went to typesetting on April 29, 1965, to printing on September 14, 1965. Hereafter referred to by *ML* (year) with page/paragraph when appropriate.

28. Compare *ML* (1965) 257, 292, 313 with *ML* (1968) 254, 283, 316. In the third case "nuclear war" was dropped and the heading reworded. The wording of the adjacent paragraphs was also amended. Compare *ML* (1965) 260/1, 293/5, 300/3, 337/7 with *ML* (1968) 257/1, 284/4, 304/2, 350/6. Compare *ML* (1965) 338/5 with *ML* (1968) 351/2–3, cited by H. F. Scott.

could prove more necessary than certain types of weapons and military equipment" was omitted from the 1968 edition, and the role of the economy was upgraded.[29]

The fifth edition also put a new emphasis on conventional operations in the shadow of nuclear escalation. For example, "The war can begin as non-nuclear and only subsequently escalate to nuclear; in certain circumstances the belligerents could find the means of carrying out extended war." (*ML* [1968] 257/1). Further, "The troops while engaged in intense, mobile action, must be ready at any moment to use nuclear weapons to defend against them. The transition from one type of military action to the other, from non-nuclear operations to nuclear, requires vast moral steadfastness" (*ML* [1968] 316/2). In contrast, the comparable passage in the 1965 edition talked of the special responsibility of the strategic rocket forces and other troops equipped with nuclear missiles (*ML* [1965] 314/2).

Comparable changes occurred between successive editions of the book *Methodological Problems of Military Theory and Practice*.[30] The 1966 edition was 328 pages long, whereas the 1969 edition had 510 pages and (according to the introduction) had been completely restructured, including the addition of several new chapters.

Chapters 6 (1966) and 15 (1969), both called "The Dialectics of the Development of the Methods and Forms of Armed Struggle," showed a significant difference in their third sections. Much of the text of the 1969 edition was new. That edition had a completely different approach to the experience of World War II and put a new emphasis on the need to study history, which was "important and necessary."[31] The paragraphs that discussed operations in a nuclear war were the same in both editions, but in the later one the discussion was followed by the statement that it would be "nondialectical" to assume that the revolution in military affairs involved the rejection of old methods of war.[32] One of the "regularities" (*zakonomernosti*) of developments in military affairs, the new edition said, is that

29. Compare *ML* (1965) 260/1 with *ML* (1968) 257/1.

30. N. Ya. Sushko and T. R. Kondratkov, eds., *Metodologicheskie problemy voennoy teorii i praktiki* (Methodological problems of military theory and practice) (Moscow: Voenizdat, 1966); and A. S. Zheltov, T. R. Kondratkov, and E. A. Khomenko, eds., *Metodologicheskie problemy voennoy teorii i praktiki*, 2d ed. (Moscow: Voenizdat, 1969). Hereafter referred to by *MP* (year), with page/paragraph when appropriate.

31. Compare *MP* (1966) 137/4 with *MP* (1969) 356/2. In 1973, after a twenty-year hiatus, the training of military historians was resumed at the General Staff Academy. Marshal V. G. Kulikov, *Akademiya general'nogo shtaba* (The General Staff Academy) (Moscow: Voenizdat, 1976), p. 202. Although histories were being written in the 1955–60 period, the Soviets were not analyzing the historical experience in the way they began doing in the 1970s. Compare *MP* (1966) 137/3 with *MP* (1968) 358–59.

32. Compare *MP* (1966) 135–36 with *MP* (1969) 358–59.

new methods do not automatically displace old, which are usually capable of further developments (*MP* [1969] 359/3–4). Similarly, the style was less didactic than the 1966 edition; for example, "contemporary war might," or "contemporary means of combat allow" (*MP* [1969] 356/5, 357/2).

Of the new chapters in the 1969 edition, one was called "Economics and Contemporary War," which showed a new emphasis on economics, as was the case in *Marxism-Leninism*. Another new chapter, "The Dialectics of the Correlation of Forces in Armed Conflict," made extended reference to historical experience, particularly World War II, and discussed the factors that determine a change in the correlation of forces. There was also a new section on "the features of limited war" to which attention was drawn in the introduction (*MP* [1969] 91–100).

Further confirmation of a shift in doctrine was provided in a 1968 article in *Military Thought* by Marshal Sokolovskiy and M. I. Cherednichenko, in which the authors commented that "military affairs are entering or have already entered the next stage of their development."[33]

The textual extracts referred to in this section are drawn on, and the substance of the changes in military doctrine are summarized in table 2–1, in chapter 2. It can be seen that the omissions of established doctrinal tenets are as significant as the adjustments in wording.

Dating the Central Decision

The nature of the shift in doctrine was established, but the question remained of when it took place. Since military doctrine is ordained by the Soviet political leadership, any change in doctrine would be authorized by them. The analytical requirement was to bracket the central decision with two cutoff dates: the earliest that the evidence allowed the decision to have been taken and the latest.

The Early Cutoff

The fourth (1965) edition of *Marxism-Leninism on War and the Army* was written in the wake of Khrushchev's ouster. The preparation of a fifth edition within nineteen months of its predecessor's being sent to press in-

33. Marshal of the Soviet Union V. Sokolovskiy and Major-General M. Cherednichenko, "Military Strategy and Its Problems," *Voennaya mysl'* (*Military thought*), no. 5 (October 1968), p. 40.

dicated, therefore, that the change in doctrine was not related to the leadership change in October 1964. The change must have come about after the fourth edition went to press in September 1965 and after the implicit reference to it and to *Methodological Problems* in the agenda for theoretical research on military affairs that was outlined in the February 1966 issue of *Military Thought*.[34]

The first edition of *Military Strategy* was published after the Twenty-second Party Congress, held in October 1961. It can be viewed in part as a by-product of the debate that took place in the first half of 1961 on the implications of the Kennedy defense initiatives, which resulted in significant modifications to Khrushchev's "new look" in defense and a greater emphasis on traditional military principles. Its open publication also served as a deterrent statement, since it demonstrated that the Soviets had thought through the problems of waging nuclear war.[35] A second edition of *Military Strategy* was published fifteen months later, and though it did not differ in substance from the 1962 edition, the changes suggested that the first edition had been produced in a hurry and without extensive consultation. This haste can also be inferred from the foreword to the second edition.[36]

It was to be expected that a substantially revised third edition would appear after the Twenty-third Party Congress, held in March 1966. Significant developments in Western military strategy and capabilities had occurred since the second edition was published, and equally if not more important, First Secretary Khrushchev had been ousted and the new leadership would not necessarily share his biases about the nature of war in the nuclear age.

There was, however, no hint in the relevant speeches at the Twenty-third

34. "Under the Banner of the Great Lenin," *Voennaya mysl'*, no. 2 (February 1966), pp. 13–14. This article listed "the most important trends of theoretical research" as defined in an order of the minister of defense dated November 6, 1965, "On the Journal *Military Thought*." The second item on the agenda was "the propaganda of Marxist-Leninist teachings concerning war and the army" and "the explanation of questions of methodology." The rest of the agenda reflected the established doctrine, with a predominant emphasis on nuclear weapons.

35. Such a purpose was indeed implied by Marshal R. Malinovskiy, the Soviet minister of defense, who asserted that "the best method of defense is to warn the enemy of our strength and readiness to smash him at his very first attempt to commit an act of aggression." This statement was quoted in the introduction to the second edition of *Military Strategy*. See R. Ya. Malinovskiy, *Bditel'no stoyat' na strazhe mira* (Vigilantly standing guard over the peace) (Moscow: Voenizdat, 1962), p. 25.

36. See Scott, *Soviet Military Strategy*, pp. xli–xliii. See also, for example, Admiral V. A. Alafuzov, "K vykhodu v svet truda voennaya strategiya" (On the appearance of the work *military strategy*), *Morskoy sbornik*, no. 1 (January 1963), pp. 88–96.

Party Congress of the change in military doctrine that has been identified here.[37] Nor were there any indications of this shift in the journal article, coauthored by Marshal Sokolovskiy, which was timed to coincide with the party congress.[38] The article noted that a new world war "will use weapons of unprecedented destructive force, such a war will inevitably acquire global scope, it will be short and swift moving"; it also asserted that "simultaneous action with nuclear weapons on vital centers and on the armed forces of the enemy is the basic method of waging nuclear-missile war."[39]

This kind of assertion was missing from an article by the same authors on the same general subject that was published thirty months later, although the two articles had many similarities.[40] The later article did not ignore the likelihood of nuclear war, but stressed the possibility of conventional and protracted (limited) nuclear war. It also put a new importance on the problems of mobilization and on economic factors.[41] The emphasis was on the sheer complexity of emerging strategic problems, and one can perhaps detect a wistfulness for the former certainties and simplicities of inevitable nuclear war. In other words, the October 1968 article reflected the shift in doctrine, whereas the April 1966 one did not.

The doctrinal changes were not implied in a journal article by Voznenko, published in June 1966, which noted, "It is now possible to accomplish the main missions, and achieve the goals of the war or of strategic operations, by striking all the main enemy objectives simultaneously. . . . Strategic operations will primarily be decided by strategic nuclear strikes."[42] Nor were the changes found in a newspaper article by Grudinin in July, which stated that "the requirement for [the all destroying] blow has become the most important law of the methods of waging world war."[43] Both these articles continued to reflect the old doctrine, providing persuasive evidence that the doctrinal decision was taken after July 1966.

37. *XXIII S'ezd kommunisticheskoy partii Sovietskogo Soyuza: Stenograficheskiy otchet* (The twenty-third congress of the Communist party of the Soviet Union : Stenographic report) (Moscow: Politizdat, 1966), vol. 1, pp. 18–47, 408–17; vol. 2, pp. 62–67.

38. Marshal of the Soviet Union V. Sokolovskiy and M. Cherednichenko, "O sovremennoy voennoy strategii" (On contemporary military strategy), *Kommunist vooruzhennykh sil* (Communist of the armed forces), no. 7 (April 1966), pp. 59–65.

39. Ibid., pp. 63, 64.

40. "Military Strategy and Its Problems," *Military Thought,* no. 10 (October 1968), pp. 32–43.

41. Ibid., pp. 37, 39.

42. V. Voznenko, "Dialektika razvitiya i smeny form i sposobov vooruzhennoy bor'by" (The dialectics of development and change of form and methods of armed conflict), *Kommunist vooruzhennykh sil,* no. 11 (June 1966), pp. 42–48; the quotation is from p. 48.

43. I. A. Grudinin, "On the Question of the Essence of War," *Krasnaya zvezda* (Red star), July 12, 1966.

Two later articles suggested that the decision had still not been taken by the end of September. Although these articles had the same thrust as the three already mentioned, the evidence was somewhat weaker, since their focus was such that they would not necessarily have reflected the change in doctrine. But both repeated formulas from the established doctrine. One noted, "Under the influence of the nuclear missile and the other latest means of destruction, the importance of the initial period [of a war] is increased, and the possibility of changing the correlation of forces in the course of the actual war is much more difficult."[44] The other noted, "Great gaps . . . made by nuclear weapons . . . will create the prerequisites for maneuver at the very beginning of combat action."[45]

Further negative evidence of this kind was provided by an article published in November 1966 and written by Colonel-General Lomov, who had been announced as the author of a book on military doctrine.[46] The book had been due for publication at this period, but, as discussed later, it never appeared. In the second part of the article, Lomov addressed the effect of nuclear-missile weapons on tasks and missions and hence on the structure of the armed forces. He focused on the role of nuclear weapons at all three levels, especially the strategic, and offered no caveats about conventional weapons. To the extent they were mentioned they were used as points of comparison. For example, "Just as in its time the development of tanks and aircraft became the basis for fundamentally restructuring the separate arms of the armed services, so now has the adoption of nuclear-missile weapons and of nuclear [propulsion] plants in the fleet effected a fundamental contemporary military-technical revolution in our armed forces."[47]

The conclusion that the doctrinal decision had still not been reached in October was supported by several pieces of textual evidence. The evidence suggested that the relevant changes to the third edition of *Military Strategy* were made at the last moment, either shortly before the manuscript was

44. Lieutenant-Colonel V. Bondarenko, "Voenno-tekhnicheskoe prevoskhodstvo—vazhneyshiy faktor nadeshnoy oborony strany" (Military-technological superiority—the most important factors for the defense of the country), *Kommunist vooruzhennykh sil*, no. 17 (September 1966), p. 8.

45. Colonel N. Miroshnichenko, "Izmeneneiya v soderzhanii i kharaktere sovremennogo boya" (Changes in the form and character of contemporary war), *Voennyy vestnik* (Military herald), no. 10 (October 1966), p. 26. This article and the two preceding ones were identified in William R. Kintner and Harriet Fast Scott, eds., *The Nuclear Revolution in Soviet Military Affairs* (University of Oklahoma Press, 1968).

46. General-Colonel N. Lomov, "Osnovy i printsipy stroitel'stva sovetskikh vooruzhennykh sil" (The bases and principles for structuring the Soviet armed forces), *Kommunist vooruzhennykh sil*, no. 22 (November 1966), pp. 7–15.

47. Ibid., p. 14.

sent for typesetting on November 23 or after it was set in type and before it was released for printing one year later.[48]

First, although the third edition was similar to its predecessors, the changes noted earlier in this appendix had the effect of removing the more glaring contradictions to the new doctrine and, with one exception, all the major changes involved deletions of material in the second edition. The exception was the completely new discussion of limited war, but this was part of the chapter describing Western strategy and capabilities. As such, changes could have been made without creating problems of internal consistency. In any case, that chapter would have been substantially revised earlier to reflect the 1964–65 conclusion that a world war might well start with a conventional phase, so that the further changes would have been relatively minor.

Second, this assessment of last-minute changes was strongly reinforced by a minor amendment to the first chapter ("General Concepts") of the book. The amendment constituted the only substantive addition to the thirteen-page lead section entitled "General Information on Military Strategy." After an italicized forty-three word definition that remained unchanged in all three editions and that stated, "Military strategy under conditions of modern war becomes the strategy of deep nuclear-missile strikes . . . ," a new paragraph was added to the third edition: "Quite naturally, we are talking here about the strategy of nuclear-missile war, and this definition does not reflect the character and laws of war without the use of nuclear weapons." (*HFS* 11; *Sok* 20).

In other words, the authors of the third edition of *Military Strategy* had to meet two different requirements. The first was to provide an updated revision of the 1963 edition. The implications of the doctrinal changes that were decided at this time would not begin to have an effect at the operational level for five years or more, and the new doctrine could not be fully implemented until the mid-1970s. But meanwhile the reasons that had led to the revision of the 1963 edition remained valid, and the third edition would continue to serve an important purpose for the next five to seven years. The second requirement was to remove various categorical state-

48. There does not appear to have been a general update of the book during this one-year hiatus. A couple of references to NATO's capabilities in "early 1967" (*HFS* 103; *Sok* (1968) 132) appear to have been derived from the 1965 edition of *The Military Balance* by the International Institute for Strategic Studies (London).

ments that emphasized the primacy of strategic weapons in the old doctrine, in order to leave room for new doctrinal formulations to be phased in gradually.

The Late Cutoff

The weight of evidence therefore argued that the new doctrine must have emerged after October 1966, perhaps during November, and it was possible that *Military Strategy* could even have been amended much later, while in galleys. There were, however, no comparable reasons for suspecting that *Marxism-Leninism* was amended at such a late stage, which argued that the doctrinal decision was taken before April 1967.[49]

This conclusion was supported by an article by General-Lieutenant Zav'yalov, "On Soviet Military Doctrine," that was published at the end of March. The article reflected the specific changes that have been identified between successive editions of the three books analyzed here and concluded with the unusual injunction: "Soviet military doctrine is being enriched with new theses. This is why officers, generals and admirals who study military doctrine must attentively follow these developments."[50]

An editorial in *Red Star* in January, "On the Nature of War," did not address the subject, but focused on the theoretical debate about war as a continuation of policy.[51] But a footnote to an article by Admiral Gorshkov in the February issue of *Morskoy sbornik* defined a "well-balanced navy" as one that was able to discharge its assigned mission both in a nuclear-missile war and in a war that did not involve such weapons.[52] Not only was this the first time this definition had appeared, but General Zav'yalov said the same thing about both the army and the navy in his March article (see note 60).

---

49. *Marxism-Leninism* was sent for typesetting on April 25, 1967. The Arab-Israeli war in June 1967 was, however, added to the chronology on page 387.

50. General-Lieutenant I. Zav'yalov, "O sovetskoy voennoy doktrine" (On Soviet military doctrine), *Krasnaya zvezda*, March 31, 1967.

51. Editorial, "O sushchnosti voyn" (On the essence of war), *Krasnaya zvezda*, January 24, 1967.

52. This was the sole explanatory footnote in an article by the commander in chief of the navy. S. G. Gorshkov, "Razvitie sovetskogo voenno-morskogo iskusstva" (The development of Soviet naval art), *Morskoy sbornik*, no. 2 (February 1967), p. 20. The article would have been sent for typesetting in mid-December, but the footnote could have been added in galleys.

The December Plenum

If one relies on the evidence of the Zav'yalov article, the doctrinal decision must have been formally agreed upon sometime between November 1966 and March 1967. If the Gorshkov footnote is accepted as pertinent, the bracket would be narrowed to November and January. Within these parameters, the most obvious occasion for the doctrinal decision to have been approved was the Central Committee Plenum held December 12–13, 1966.

This plenum was addressed by, among others, Marshal Grechko, who was then commander in chief of the Warsaw Pact Forces and would soon be appointed minister of defense.[53] The allocation of resources to defense was thought to have been discussed at the 1966 plenum, which would be expected, given the substance of the new doctrine.[54] The doctrine had major implications in terms of the volume of ordnance needed to support a conventional blitzkrieg, the need to completely reshape the navy and the ground and air forces, and the need to restructure the nation's military-industrial base to be able to compete with an undamaged United States in a protracted conventional war.

Zav'yalov's Article

The article by General Zav'yalov, "On Military Doctrine," in March 1967 was important both because of its substance and because it could be compared with another article by him in July 1966 that was specifically tied to the Twenty-third Party Congress.[55] Although the earlier article recognized the possibility that war might start with a conventional phase,[56] it assumed that escalation was inevitable and emphasized the need to be able to fight a nuclear war.[57] Not only was Zav'yalov reflecting established doc-

---

53. *Pravda,* December 13 and 14, 1966, cited by John McDonnell, "The Organization of Soviet Defense," in Michael MccGwire and John McDonnell, eds., *Soviet Naval Influence: Domestic and Foreign Dimensions* (Praeger, 1977), p. 98.

54. Roman Kolkowicz, "Generals and Politicians: Uneasy Truce," *Problems of Communism,* vol. 17 (May-June 1968), p. 75.

55. General-Lieutenant I. Zav'yalov, "XXIII s'ezd KPSS i voprosy dal'neyshego ukrepleniya vooruzhennykh sil" (The twenty-third party congress and questions concerning the further strengthening of the armed forces), *Voennaya mysl',* no. 7 (July 1966), pp. 3–11. The references that follow show page and paragraph.

56. Ibid., 4/6.

57. For example, ibid., 8/5, 11/1–2.

trine, but he also noted that "at this time we are of one mind on all the basic questions of military affairs."[58]

This wording and the substance of the article confirmed the evidence already discussed that at the time of the Twenty-third Party Congress in March and April 1966 (and for some time thereafter) Soviet military doctrine still considered that war with the West would inevitably involve nuclear strikes on the USSR. The 1959 doctrine had been modified to recognize that NATO might choose not to resort to nuclear weapons immediately (see chapter 2), but the inevitability of nuclear escalation remained the basic assumption on which all plans were based.

The July 1966 article was clearly an authoritative statement. So too was the March 1967 one. It was long enough to be published in two parts in successive issues of *Red Star* and was printed across the bottom of pages 2 and 3, the usual location for major theoretical statements.[59] As significant as the inclusion of new assertions particularly relevant to the postulated shift in doctrine was the absence of most of the routine assertions about nuclear war that were characteristic of the earlier articles referred to in this analysis.

The positive evidence included Zav'yalov's assertion that "a pivotal question of military doctrine is the definition of the character of a future war" (KZ 30/5/2). Although a truism, this comment was significant because the position on the nature of future war had been firmly established at least seven years previously and was reasserted at every opportunity. Determining the nature of a future war had therefore ceased to be a pivotal question of doctrine, and in his July article Zav'yalov had claimed that the military "was of one mind on all the basic questions." Reopening this issue implied a fundamental revision of prevailing assumptions.

The article presented other examples of the shift. "Military doctrine cannot be indifferent to the price of achieving victory." This attitude is different from the previous acceptance of the mass devastation arising from the inevitable intercontinental exchange. "All military structuring and methods of waging war are under the determining influence of the nuclear-missile weapon. . . . However, one should not . . . make a fetish of nuclear weapons." "For waging modern war, such armed forces are required as would be able to wage a worldwide nuclear war and any other war. The army and the navy must be . . . well trained for acting both with the use

58. Ibid., 10/1.
59. "On Soviet Military Doctrine," *Krasnaya zvezda*, March 30 and 31, 1967. Hereafter the references that follow show date/column/paragraph in *KZ*.

and without the use of nuclear weapons." And finally, "The achievement of victory in war . . . demands the preparation of reserves of trained personnel and stockpiling reserves of material-technical equipment."[60] This last quotation echoes the change to chapter 7 of *Military Strategy* and the new emphasis in *Marxism-Leninism*.

On their own, these assertions are suggestive. Placed in the context of Zav'yalov's injunction that "Soviet military doctrine is being enriched with new theses" and that "officers, generals and admirals who study doctrine must follow these developments attentively," the evidence becomes persuasive (*KZ* 31/9/4). But when the March article is compared with the one published the previous July, the evidence of doctrinal change would seem conclusive: two articles, both by the same author and both clearly authoritative, but each reflecting different assumptions about the nature of a future war.

Bibliographic Confirmation

If the changes in *Military Strategy, Marxism-Leninism,* and *Methodological Problems* were the result of a doctrinal decision that was formalized in December 1966, one would expect other reverberations to be detectable in the publication process. Indeed there were several anomalies at this time. Each of them could possibly be explained individually, but taken as a set, they suggested that after the December 1966 decision the publication of military books was put on hold and the program substantially revised.

The Hiatus in Military Publications

One anomaly was that at least forty-three military books were published between 1965 and 1969,[61] but for one year after November 1966 no books on military doctrine were sent to the printer.[62] In November 1967, four books were sent to the printer, three of them within ten days, including the

60. *KZ* 30/5/4; 30/6/2–3; 31/7/1; and 31/8/3.

61. Harriet Fast Scott, *Soviet Military Doctrine: Its Continuity, 1960–70,* SSC-TN-8974-28 (Stanford Research Institute, June 1971), p. 92. The twenty-two books referred to here are mainly those that are tied into the Officers' Library series. See H. F. Scott, *Soviet Military Doctrine: Its Formulation and Dissemination,* SSC-TN-8974-27 (Stanford Research Institute, June 1971), pp. 81–91. I have made considerable use of the bibliographic data in these two publications.

62. *Military Psychology* (one of the books in the Officers' Library series) breached the one-year hiatus; it was sent to the printing press in September 1967, but it had already been held up for forty-nine weeks between typesetting and printing.

third edition of Sokolvskiy's *Military Strategy*. It is sometimes argued that the printing demands of the fiftieth anniversary of the Russian Revolution swamped the capacity of Voenizdat, the military publishing house. But even if Soviet forward planning is not faultless, the advent of the fiftieth anniversary was hardly a surprise, and the 1965–67 publication schedule for the Officer's Library series had been long established and well publicized and had the personal support of the minister of defense. Meanwhile, a naval book, which had no particular relevance to the anniversary and, more important, had no doctrinal significance, was sent for typesetting in October 1966 and released to the printer on May 25, 1967; 25,000 copies of this 592-page book were published.[63] This hardly suggests a printing bottleneck.

This publishing hiatus was reflected in the pattern of excessive delay between the time military books were sent for typesetting and sent to the printer. Looking at the 1965–68 period, one finds a distinct difference over time in the books that were delayed thirty weeks or more. Before December 1966 there were four such books, and all were noncontroversial: *The Bases of Soviet Military Law*, forty-two weeks; *M. I. Kalinin on Communist Indoctrination and Military Duty*, thirty-eight; *Organization and Armaments of the Armies and Navies of Capitalist States*, thirty-three; and *Military Pedagogics*, thirty. Any important book was released to the printer more quickly. After November 1966 all important books suffered inordinate delay: *Military Strategy*, fifty-three weeks; *Marxism-Leninism on War and the Army (1968)*, fifty-one; *History of Naval Art*, fifty-one; *Military Psychology*, forty-nine; and *50 Years of the Armed Forces of the USSR*, forty-four. The two noncontroversial books did not suffer these delays: *Party-Political Work*, nineteen; and *The Officer's Handbook for Quartermasters*, thirty-one.

That the delay to *Military Strategy* was imposed and not planned was suggested by the first sentence in the introduction to the third edition: "Four years have elapsed since the second edition . . . appeared in print." In practice, it was closer to five years; the publication dates were 1963 and 1968. And whereas the third edition of *Military Strategy* took fifty-three weeks to go from typesetting to printing, the first had taken only eleven and the second nineteen weeks. Similarly, the fifth edition (1968) of *Marxism-Leninism on War and the Army* took fifty-one weeks, whereas the fourth (1965) had taken only twenty weeks.

63. N. A. Peterskiy, *Boevoy put' sovetskogo voenno-morskogo flota*, 2d ed. (The combat path of the Soviet fleet) (Moscow:Voenizdat, 1967).

The Missing Book on Doctrine

A second anomaly was the nonappearance of the book *Military Doctrine,* which had been scheduled for publication in 1966 as one of the seventeen books in the Officer's Library series. In December 1964 the military publishing house Voenizdat had announced a list of seventeen authors and book titles that would be published in the series during 1965–67. The purpose of the series was "to arm the reader with a knowledge of the fundamental changes that have taken place in recent years in military affairs."[64]

Of the seventeen titles, ten were released for printing between 1965 and November 1966; six were released for printing after the 1967 hiatus, two of them being four and six years behind schedule, and one, *Military Doctrine,* did not appear at all. One title, *50 Years of the Armed Forces of the USSR,* appeared without the series insignia, while an unannounced title, *The Officer's Handbook for Quartermasters,* appeared carrying the series insignia.[65]

A fundamental change in doctrine, such as the one postulated here, would make obsolete a book on military doctrine that had been projected and perhaps written before the change was decided. Therefore, the nonappearance of the original edition of *Military Doctrine* supports the hypothesis. It seems likely that a revised edition was published in due course but would not have been released to the public.

The Officer's Handbook, one of the two books in the series to suffer inordinate delays, provided a synopsis of relevant information appearing in other books of the series. Under the announced schedule, it should have been published in 1967–68. It was sent for typesetting in February 1968, but was not released for printing until the end of November 1970; it was published in 1971, three years after the other books in the series. Meanwhile *The Officer's Handbook for Quartermasters,* which was not one of the original seventeen titles and whose scope and subject matter were atypical of the series, was published in 1968. Its publication may have been intended to obscure the withdrawal of the original book from publication—temporarily, as it turned out.

The third chapter in the *Officer's Handbook* included a section on Soviet military doctrine, which must have presented the Soviet authorities with a dilemma. Although they had decided to work toward the objective of avoiding nuclear strikes on the Soviet Union, this aim was not something

---

64. See Scott, *Soviet Military Doctrine: Its Formulation and Dissemination,* p. 82.
65. Ibid., pp. 81–84, 87–91.

that could be achieved overnight; it had to be assumed that for the next five years or so any war with the West would inevitably escalate to a nuclear exchange. That assumption had to be reflected in the *Officer's Handbook,* which was intended to help junior officers solve present-day problems. In addition, there is every reason to suppose that the Soviet leadership would not have wished to advertise the advent of such a fundamental change in doctrine by providing a succinct summary in such a general circulation publication. On the other hand, the leadership was about to embark on a major restructuring of the Soviet forces to allow the adoption of the new doctrine in due course, and the result of this restructuring would become apparent by the early to middle 1970s.

In the version of the *Handbook* that finally appeared in 1971, statements about the nature of war were suitably ambiguous, but clearly fell on the side of the new doctrine. The book explained that "arguments pertaining to problems of preparing and waging universal nuclear war occupy the most important place in Soviet military doctrine" because, of all the possible kinds, "the most dangerous is a world nuclear war."[66] A one-paragraph statement reflected the emerging doctrine: "Contemporary world war is characterized by its vast spatial scope. Armed combat under conditions of nuclear war acquires an intercontinental character." Here the authors clearly distinguish world war from world nuclear war, with its inevitable intercontinental exchange.[67]

The other book to suffer inordinate delay, *Scientific-Technical Progress and the Revolution in Military Affairs,* appeared six years behind schedule.[68] The change in doctrine—from the position that war with the West would inevitably be nuclear to the position that escalation to an intercontinental exchange could possibly be avoided—would obviously require a different thrust to a book that dealt mainly with the methods of waging contemporary war.

New Editions of Key Books

A third anomaly was that new editions of two key books appeared unduly soon after their predecessors, the publication of the successive editions falling before and after December 1966. The first edition of *Meth-*

66. General-Major S. N. Kozlov, ed., *The Officer's Handbook: A Soviet View,* translated for the U.S. Air Force (Government Printing Office, 1977) and published as number 13 in the U.S. Air Force series Soviet Military Thought, pp. 62–63.

67. Ibid.

68. Colonel-General N. A. Lomov, ed., *Scientific-Technical Progress and the Revolution in Military Affairs: A Soviet View,* translated for the U.S. Air Force (GPO, 1977), and published as no. 3 in the U.S. Air Force series Soviet Military Thought.

odological Problems of Military Theory and Practice was released for printing on October 1, 1966 (two months before the doctrinal decision) and appeared shortly thereafter. A substantially revised and enlarged second edition was ready for typesetting within two years (September 27, 1968). All twenty members of the authors' collective that prepared the first edition were involved in the second (plus two newcomers), and the same colonel-general signed the introduction to both editions. Since the 1966 edition was explicitly a first attempt to interest officer cadres in the methodological (that is, Marxist-Leninist) problems underlying military theory and practice, a revised edition was to be expected in due course. But a new edition of 60,000 copies (the first run was 45,000) within three years seems rather soon. The second edition reflected the changes in doctrine that have been identified and developed the methodological rationale for the new emphasis on conventional war and the study of history. There were thirty-seven weeks between typesetting and release for printing, and the introduction was not put in final form until just before the book was printed.[69]

As for *Marxism-Leninism,* the evidence is much more clear-cut. The 1961 edition came out in the wake of the new look in defense policy announced by Khrushchev in January 1960. The 1962 edition (which paralleled the first edition of *Military Strategy*) came out in the wake of the Twenty-second Party Congress, which reestablished the military verities. The 1965 (fourth) edition came out in the wake of Khrushchev's ouster. This edition was one of the titles in the Officer's Library series and was nominated for the Frunze prize. Nevertheless, within thirty-two months a fifth edition had been prepared for typesetting in the wake of the December 1966 plenum.

Conclusion

A limited textual comparison of successive editions of *Military Strategy, Marxism-Leninism,* and *Methodological Problems* indicates that during 1966 and 1967 a fundamental shift occurred in underlying assumptions regarding the likely nature of a world war and how it would be fought. These books provide a more stable base for comparison than do journal articles, whose doctrinal status is often hard to define.

69. A reference to the June 1969 plenum appears in *Methodological Problems,* p. 7.

A partial analysis of Soviet pronouncements and writings during this period indicates that at the time of the Twenty-third Party Congress, March–April 1966, and for several months thereafter, the 1959 doctrinal, assumptions (with minor modifications) remained in force. Such analysis also indicates that the new assumptions were not accepted until the last months of the year. The most likely occasion for their formal adoption was the Central Committee Plenum held on December 12–13, 1966. The fundamental nature of the change in assumptions is shown by the one-year hiatus imposed in November 1966 on the release to the printer of books about military doctrine. The revised assumptions that can be inferred from this analysis are summarized in table 2-1, chapter 2, and provide sufficient reason for the changes in force structure and operational concepts that drew attention to this decision period.

A full understanding of what took place in the second half of 1966 must await a systematic analysis of the articles and books published around that time. But one must also bear in mind that debates were going on in this same period about the allocation of resources to defense, the proper locus for decisions and planning on strategic matters, and the scope of military strategy as a science.[70] One problem that will tend to create contradictory evidence is that military "doctrine exists primarily for *the present and the immediate future* [my emphasis]. It determines the practical tasks of military development for some relatively limited period."[71] In 1967–69, and for the next several years, the Soviets still had to assume that war would escalate to a nuclear exchange, even though they were working toward escaping that cul-de-sac. Depending on the targeted readership, the emphasis on the inevitability of nuclear war was likely to vary during this period.

70. For a very extensive definition see Sokolovskiy and Cherednichenko, *Kommunist vooruzhennykh sil* (April 1966), p. 63, para. 5.
71. Kozlov, *Officer's Handbook,* p. 65.

Operational Requirements and Naval Building Programs

THE FIRM identification of a major decision period stemming from the doctrinal decision taken in December 1966 and the new understanding of the implications of that decision allow a reinterpretation of Soviet naval developments over the last twenty-five years. This appendix focuses on the evidence that can be derived from naval construction, with particular emphasis on the submarine building programs. It provides the detailed analysis needed to support the broader discussion in chapter 5 and is not intended to be comprehensive. It should be read in conjunction with that chapter, which concentrates on the doctrinal changes that drove Soviet naval developments.

The analytic process also unearthed persuasive shipbuilding evidence that a further major change in naval policy occurred in the second half of the 1970s. The effects of that change are discussed in the final section of this appendix, in which future submarine building programs are also examined.

The Genesis and Development of the Soviet Ballistic-Missile Submarine Force

As it exists today, the Soviet ballistic-missile submarine force reflects three distinct developmental periods: the search for strategic reach (1947–58), the requirement for a "matching force" (1961–67), and the emphasis on an "insurance force" (1968–present). In each period, the submarine's capability for the intercontinental delivery of nuclear weapons was meant for a significantly different strategic purpose. Between the first and second of these periods, the navy actually lost the mission of strategic strike.

Strategic Reach

The evidence suggests that the Soviets originally planned to build 36 Zulu-class diesel-powered torpedo-armed submarines (SS), with delivery running from 1952 through 1957, and that these would be followed by the Foxtrot program, with 144 units planned for delivery between 1958 and 1965.[1] All or some of these large-type submarines were intended to carry nuclear-armed torpedoes.[2]

In about 1947 the Soviets decided to allocate nuclear propulsion to the navy's strategic delivery mission; the November class was projected to begin delivery in 1958 at 6 units a year,[3] and to run parallel to the Foxtrot program, which was to be built at 18 units a year. In about 1949–50, the Soviets decided to develop a missile-firing variant of both types of submarine. A ballistic missile was first test fired from an adapted Zulu in 1955, and the design of the Zulu was modified to allow 2 SS-N-4 surface-launched ballistic missiles with a range of 350 nautical miles to be carried to the fin. Six of these Zulu V ballistic-missile submarines (SSBs) were delivered in 1956–57.

Meanwhile the design of the Foxtrot was modified to allow 3 SS-N-4s to be carried, the result being the Golf SSB, with delivery of 6 units a year due to begin in 1958. In the same way the design of the November-class nuclear-powered torpedo-attack submarine (SSN) was modified to allow 3 SS-N-4s to be carried in the fin, the result being the Hotel-class ballistic-missile submarine (SSBN), with 15 units planned for delivery in the 1958–62 period, along with 15 November SSNs.

The Soviets have tended to make public claims for a military capability about two years before it was scheduled to become operational, which suggests that nuclear-armed torpedoes first went to sea in 1955–56,[4] with mis-

1. Michael MccGwire, "Soviet Naval Procurement," in *The Soviet Union in Europe and the Near East: Her Capabilities and Intentions* (London: Royal United Service Institution, 1970), pp. 76–78.
2. The Russians have traditionally linked the mission of the submarine to its type, which is a function of size.
3. This delivery rate of nuclear submarines was not quite achieved, probably because of reactor constraints. By 1949 the planned program had split into 3 Novembers and 3 Hotels a year.
4. In "Statement of the Soviet Government concerning President Eisenhower's Address of 8 December 1953," a reference to "torpedoes with atomic heads" was linked to "rocket weapons which . . . can cover thousands of kilometers." *Pravda,* December 22, 1953. On January 19,

sile-armed units being due to deploy starting in 1959. Between 1955 and 1958 the Soviets made a steady flow of references to a naval capability for attacking bases and other strategic targets. By 1957 the stock formula was a capability for "delivering powerful strikes on objectives situated in other continents."[5]

This formula was reasserted as late as Armed Forces Day in February 1959, and a Zulu V was sighted off Iceland in May 1959. However, none of the Navy Day articles in July of that year laid claim to a strategic strike capability for the navy, which implied that it no longer had such a mission.[6]

Change in Mission Priorities

The formal deletion of the navy's strategic delivery mission appears to have been delayed until the spring of 1959. But the constraints of lead time argue that in the 1957–58 period, the Soviets decided to concentrate on intercontinental ballistic missiles (ICBMs) for strategic delivery and to re-deploy naval resources to counter the qualitatively new threat posed by long-range nuclear-strike aircraft aboard carriers.

The 1957–58 decision period resulted in major changes to naval building programs. It included the decision that nuclear hull–propulsion units that had originally been intended as ballistic-missile submarines should be reconfigured as guided-missile submarines (SSGNs) carrying long-range cruise missiles for use against the carrier. In consequence, the last 5 units of the Hotel SSBN program emerged as Echo I SSGNs, each armed with 6 surface-to-surface missiles (SSMs). The follow-on SSBN program that was due for delivery in 1963–67, and which would have carried the SS-N-5, was reconfigured to yield the Echo II SSGN, armed with 8 SSMs. Both classes of the Echo used the elevating launchers and missile systems that had already been ordered for the Juliet-class diesel-powered guided-missile submarine (SSG). Meanwhile the November SSN was given the new task of trailing aircraft carriers to provide target data on their location.

The Hotel SSBN and Golf SSB were scheduled for retrofitting with the second-generation SS-N-5 submerged-launch ballistic missile with a range

---

1954, an article in *Izvestiya* noted that contemporary developments of aviation, missiles, and the submarine fleet made it possible to deal crushing blows across a distance of many thousands of kilometers. Quoted by H. S. Dinerstein, *War and the Soviet Union: Nuclear Weapons and the Revolution in Soviet Military and Political Thinking* (Praeger, 1962), p. 71.

5. Robert W. Herrick, "Soviet SSBN Roles in Strategic Strike," Report KTR 119-79 (Arlington, Va.: Ketron, 1979), p. 4

6. Ibid., pp. 5–6.

of 650 nautical miles, and 9 Hotel IIs reentered service between 1964 and 1968. The Foxtrot SS may have retained its limited role in strategic delivery at least until after the Cuban missile crisis, when 6 Foxtrots deployed off the American coast were forced to the surface by U.S. antisubmarine forces. That there was a subsequent change of role for the Foxtrot is suggested by the absence of large-type submarines from the force based on Albania between 1958 and 1961, although they participated in the deployments to the Mediterranean that started in 1964.

One of the Soviet decisions that emerged from the 1957–58 period was to place primary reliance on nuclear submarines at the expense of large surface units.[7] The decision was prompted by the requirement to attack U.S. carriers before they launched their nuclear strikes from the eastern Mediterranean and south Norwegian Sea, and by the West's domination of those seas and the air above them. This decision set in process a two-thirds increase in the Soviet nuclear submarine production capacity, in terms of both yard capacity and critical components, particularly nuclear reactors. Submarine deliveries between 1968 and 1977 indicate a production rate of 20 reactors a year, but most likely the planned configuration mix, as envisaged in 1957–58, was very different from the mix that actually started delivery in 1967–68.

Lead time requires that the Yankee hull-propulsion unit stemmed from this same 1957–58 decision period, but the anomalies in the submarine building programs that accompanied the delivery of 7 Yankees a year, starting in 1968, make it virtually certain that annual construction of this unit had originally been set at a much lower figure. It is argued later in this appendix that the Soviets originally planned to build only 2 a year, plus 4 Victors and 4 Charlies.

The question remains of how the Yankee hull-propulsion unit would have been configured. Possibly, the Soviets always planned it to be a 16-missile SSBN, comparable with Polaris. Arguing against that intention is the checkered history of the navy's participation in the strategic delivery mission. If these hull-propulsion units had always been intended for strategic strike, it made no sense to delete that naval mission in 1959 and then restore it in 1964, when the 3-missile Hotel IIs began to enter service. It seems more likely that the Yankee hull-propulsion unit was originally intended as the platform for a battery of SS-NX-13 tactical ballistic missiles

7. This decision was publicized by First Secretary Nikita S. Khrushchev during his visit to the United States in September 1959. See Robert Waring Herrick, *Soviet Naval Strategy: Fifty Years of Theory and Practice* (Annapolis, Md.: U.S. Naval Institute, 1968), p. 67.

to be used against carriers.[8] This anticarrier system, perhaps using a radar satellite (which first became operational in 1967) to provide target data for the 400-nautical-mile, terminally guided SS-NX-13, would have complemented the SS-N-7 horizon-range submerged-launch cruise missile to be carried by the Charlie SSGN. It would also have sidestepped the obvious deficiencies of the long-range cruise missile systems carried by the Echoes and the Juliet.

The Need for a Matching Force: The Yankee Program

The design and development of the nuclear hull-propulsion unit that was used for the Yankee SSBN stemmed from the 1957–58 decision period, but the requirement for a force to "match" the emerging U.S. capability stems from the period 1961–62. This dating is based on the anomalies in naval construction patterns and procedures, and on the evidence that the ballistic-missile system was itself an adaptation, as well as the possibility that the hull-propulsion unit was originally intended to have a different configuration.

In the 1957–58 period the requirement for a matching force had yet to be perceived. There was public skepticism about Polaris in the United States, and on the basis of their own unsatisfactory experience with SSBs and SSBNs, the Soviets had small reason to foresee the success of either the concept of Polaris or the system. Besides this consideration, many assumed that Polaris was intended to fill the polar arc of the strategic delivery capability that was then being deployed around the Soviet periphery.[9] Only in 1961, by which time the first Polaris SSBN was at sea and President John F. Kennedy had announced the sharp increase in building rates, did the Soviets seem to have addressed the threat from Polaris seriously.

Having recognized a renewed requirement for an SSBN force, the Soviets were able to overcome the problem of the lead time needed to develop the appropriate missile by building on work already in progress at Chelomey's design bureau, which specialized in naval systems. The 1,350-

8. This was also suggested by the chairman of the Joint Chiefs of Staff, in General George S. Brown, USAF, *United States Military Posture for FY 1978* (Government Printing Office, 1977), p. 16.

9. It seems likely that the Moskva program of helicopter-carrying antisubmarine cruisers, which stemmed from 1957–58, was originally intended to cover the threat from Polaris submarines operating in arctic waters. Only 2 units were actually built, but most likely 12 were originally projected, the 10 remaining weapons outfits being used to reconfigure the Kresta hull from a missile ship (Kresta I) to a large antisubmarine ship (Kresta II).

nautical-mile SS-N-6 system that went to sea aboard the Yankees in 1968 appears to have incorporated components from two other missiles that were then being developed by the Chelomey design bureau. The SS-NX-13 tactical ballistic missile would have been under development since 1957–58 and was designed to fit the Yankee missile tubes. The original version of the SS-11 would have been under development from at least that date, if not earlier, and was designed as a land-based regional range system that may have been primarily intended for naval targets.

On the basis of the 1968–72 delivery rate and the total number of Yankees and Delta SSBNs, the Soviets probably planned to build 70 Yankee SSBNs. The shipbuilding practice at that period was a ten-year production run, with some improvements to the hull-propulsion unit and a substantial upgrading, by a factor of two or more, of the primary weapons system after five years. The average production rate of Yankees was 7 a year, 5 at Severodvinsk and 2 at Komsomol'sk, although the Komsomol'sk yard was slow in getting started.

Granting that the Delta I used the hull-propulsion units intended for the second half of the Yankee program,[10] the Yankee II probably would have carried 20 missiles; some twenty-one feet longer than the Yankee I, it could carry at least two extra rows. There would therefore be a total of 1,260 missiles for the 70 boats (35 carrying 16 missiles and 35 carrying 20), as against the roughly 1,200 delivery systems (missiles and aircraft) planned for the U.S. naval inventory at this period, plus the 64 missiles planned for the British Polaris force.   •

Established procedures suggest that a successor to the Yankee SSBN would have been projected to begin delivery in 1978 and, as explained later, possibly the hull-propulsion system used for the Oscar SSGN may have originally been designated for this role. Before 1967, the Soviets may also have intended that, as this successor to the Yankee SSBNs entered service, some Yankee Is would be retrofitted to carry a refined version of the SS-NX-13 tactical ballistic missile and thus revert to the anticarrier role. In any event, the SS-NX-13 was never deployed, perhaps because of counting rules under the Strategic Arms Limitation Treaty. But the more important reason was probably that the system was designed for use with a nuclear warhead. It would not be able to achieve the accuracy or have the payload needed for its use with a conventional warhead, as required by the 1970s concept of operations.

10. As late as 1974 naval analysts were still referring to the Delta as a "stretched Yankee" or as Yankee II.

THE FORWARD DEPLOYMENT OF SSBNS. Deployment of SSBNs within closing range of the American coast started in 1964, coinciding with the availability of the first Hotel SSBNs to be refitted with the SS-N-5 missile. The Hotel IIs were replaced by Yankees when the latter became available in 1969–70.[11] Various explanations have been offered for these deployments, none of them satisfactory.

U.S. analysts initially thought that the Yankees' mission was to carry out strikes on bomber bases and command, communications, control and intelligence (C^3I) installations in the forefront of a surprise ICBM attack. Although that idea has now been discredited, the perceived threat did prompt the United States to increase both the number of satellite bases for its bombers and the ground-alert component of the bomber force. More recently, analysts have suggested that the Yankees' mission was to explode a limited number of missiles three hundred miles above the continental United States so as to cause electromagnetic pulses that would disrupt electrical and electronic equipment and land-line communication systems and power grids. The remaining missiles could be launched at one-minute intervals to explode about one hundred miles over the Minuteman fields so as to achieve "X-ray pin down" of those missiles.[12]

In theory, either mission would make sense if the Soviets assumed that a world war would inevitably be nuclear and if they planned to launch a preemptive strike on North America in the event that war became inescapable. In both cases, it would, of course, be extremely difficult to ensure timely communications, and in the second, the Yankees would have to close the coast in order to discharge their mission. Such a movement, even if it could be successfully accomplished, would alert the United States and prejudice preemption. But one can argue (if not persuasively) that either mission could have supported the 1960s objectives, on the principle that a possible contribution was better than none at all. However, once the Soviets moved to adopt the 1970s hierarchy of objectives and thereby renounced the option of strategic preemption, they had to face the question of whether they could realistically expect their forward-deployed Yankees to be available to discharge this type of mission in the event of escalation to an intercontinental exchange. More likely, the Yankees would succumb

11. The deployment of Delta ballistic-missile submarines (SSBNs) in 1983, when the submarines transited the Iceland-Faeroes Gap on the surface, was a political response to the deployment of Pershing II in NATO Europe, and not part of the Hotel/Yankee pattern.

12. John Steinbruner, "Launch under Attack," *Scientific American*, vol. 250 (January 1984), pp. 39–43.

during the conventional phase of the war or as they moved into a firing position.

A more plausible explanation for these SSBN deployments goes back to the initial deployment of Hotel IIs and builds on that development to explain the subsequent pattern. Despite the precedent of the attempt to emplace missiles in Cuba in 1962, the Soviet deployment of SSBNs in 1964 is unlikely to have been related to the large disparity in the size of the superpowers' ICBM arsenals. In 1965 the Soviets had 209 of the second-generation SS-7s and SS-8 ICBMs in service, with third-generation missiles due to start deploying at a rate of more than 300 a year. The 3 to 6 missiles carried by the forward-deployed Hotels[13] would not have been a significant increment to that capability. These facts suggest that the deployment of the Hotels stemmed from the 1961–62 decision period and was driven by the same requirement that underlay the Yankee building program, namely, the need to match the U.S. sea-based strategic strike capability.

There were two ways of achieving such a match: by building up one's own capability and by drawing down the enemy's. It is therefore most likely that the Hotel SSBNs were intended to strike at any aircraft carriers and Polaris submarines that were in port at the onset of war.[14] This mission would also explain the deployment of Golf SSBs at this period within closing range of the Polaris bases at Holy Loch, in Scotland, and Rota, in Spain. As a subsidiary benefit these forward-deployed units might also provide early warning of a surprise attack on the Soviet Union. If the United States were to attempt a disarming strike (a capability America seemed to be developing in the first half of the 1960s), it would have to neutralize the Hotels off the American coast. To do so would require that U.S. forces be positioned ahead of time, and probably the Soviets would be able to detect the preparatory moves.

Such a mission makes sense for the 1964–75 period; it both fits the known mission structure and had a good chance of success, since it did not depend on the split-second timing that would be needed to participate in a preemptive strike. More important, the mission of striking at carriers and submarines in port remains plausible in the post-1975 period in a way that

13. It probably took at least 3 Hotel SSBNs to maintain 1 on station. Two Hotel IIs became operational each year from 1964 through 1968.

14. The SSBNs would have available to them the reports from the intelligence ships that were stationed off these ports from 1961 on. It may also be relevant that 1964 was the year in which the Soviet navy began marking Sixth Fleet carriers in the Mediterranean.

the preemptive missions do not. Because timing would not be critical, the forward-deployed Yankees could concentrate on survival through conceal-ment and would have to expose themselves only after an intercontinental exchange had taken place. By that time, it could be assumed, the U.S. antisubmarine warfare (ASW) capability would be severely degraded.

The U.S. decision to request funds in 1978 for a completely new mid-ocean acoustic surveillance system suggests that the Yankee submarine may be having some success in "vanishing" once deployed to its patrol area. Two factors would contribute to that success: improvements in sub-marine quieting and an operational policy to seek out the acoustic shad-ows of the bottom-mounted sound-surveillance system, such as would be caused by the mid-Atlantic ridge. Except for the 2 or 3 units deployed one thousand miles off the U.S. coast, the Yankees would remain sheltered in home waters until after the nuclear exchange, when they would deploy as required to within range of target areas, as designated by Moscow. The ASW environment would be relatively benign, since most Western shore-based facilities would have been destroyed in the intercontinental ex-change, but the Yankees would need combat support against ASW forces afloat, particularly as they sought to transit defensive barriers manned by Western submarines. Such support would have been one of the tasks of the surface units that were designated as large antisubmarine ships (BPK) in the 1964–75 period.[15]

In 1976 the Hotel SSBNs and Golf SSBs were apparently reassigned to cover targets in the theater-war (as opposed to the global-war) target set,[16] and probably sometime afterward the Yankee force was progressively reas-signed to the same target set,[17] while still retaining the forward deployment mission. Starting in 1978, the Soviets also needed to deactivate Yankee SSBNs in order to remain below the SALT I limits of 62 SSBNs. By 1985, 12 Yankees had been taken out of service, their missile-launching hull-

15. Robert Weinland develops a good argument for this position, but carries it too far in his conclusion that it was the SSBN's requirement that prompted the introduction of the BPK desig-nation, starting in 1964. See Robert G. Weinland, *The Evolution of Soviet Requirements for Naval Forces—Solving the Problems of the Early 1960s*, Professional Paper 368 (Alexandria, Va: Center for Naval Analyses, 1982), pp. 31–34.

16. For the distinction between these two target sets, which is temporal rather than spatial, see appendix D. The dating of this shift derives from the redeployment of 6 Golf-class SSBs from the Northern Fleet to the Baltic in 1976. See Floyd D. Kennedy, Jr., "Theater Nuclear Encircle-ment: Soviet SLBMs Targeted on Western Europe," *National Defense* (February 1980), p. 43.

17. U.S. Department of Defense, *Soviet Military Power, 1984*, 3d ed. (GPO, 1984), p. 25 (Hereafter *SMP*); and see *SMP, 1985*, 4th ed., p. 32. Both of these publications refer to this reassignment, and Kennedy, "Theater Nuclear Encirclement," demonstrates how it fits in with Soviet doctrine.

sections having been removed to comply with the SALT provisions. Some of the hull-propulsion units were reconfigured as SSNs, but others are being converted to SSGNs, carrying the new SS-N-24 land-attack cruise missile.[18]

An Insurance Force: The Deltas and Typhoons

The requirement that emerged in the 1967–68 decision period was for an SSBN that could remain secure within the protection of home waters while carrying missiles with the range to strike at North America from those waters. The adaptation of existing programs to meet this new requirement was typical of established Soviet procedures and a classic indication of a major change in policy. Following normal practice, the Soviets programmed an initial, an interim, and a final response.

In 1967–68 the Yankee program was in full production, the first unit having been delivered to the navy in the fall of 1967, just before ice closed Severodvinsk for the winter. A somewhat longer Yankee II was due to begin delivery in 1973, carrying a missile with about twice the range of the Yankee I's 1,350-nautical-mile SS-N-6. A successor to the ten-year Yankee program would have been in the early stages of design, due to begin delivery in 1978. The successor-class of SSBNs would have had to be significantly larger than the Yankee II in order to carry the fifth-generation missile. The extra size of the hull would bring advantages in higher speed. This was an important attribute for the matching force, both to evade Western ASW lines and to close distant target areas after the initial nuclear exchange. The missile for this SSBN would also have been in the early stages of design, and in the normal process of incremental product improvement it would have had a range of 4,000 to 4,500 nautical miles.[19]

THE INITIAL RESPONSE. The Soviets needed at least the beginning of an "insurance force" to be in service by 1976, when the 1970s hierarchy of objectives came into full effect. The hull-propulsion units that had been projected for the Yankee II program were available as launch platforms; the missing element was a missile that could reach North America from Soviet home waters. The initial response to this requirement was to with-

18. *SMP, 1985*, p. 35.
19. The trend in product improvement was consistent in the twenty-year period 1958–77: 1958 (Hotel I), 350 nautical miles; 1963 (Hotel II), 750 nautical miles; 1968 (Yankee I), 1,300 nautical miles; 1973 (Yankee II), 2,100 nautical miles; 1978 (Delta III), 4,300 nautical miles.

draw the missile intended for the Yankee II from testing in order to increase its range by adding extra fuel tankage.[20] To fit the Yankee launcher tubes, the missile's diameter had to be about the same as its predecessor's.[21] Extra tankage meant extra length, and the final version of the SS-N-8 was about one-third longer (approximately eleven feet) than the SS-N-6. Its length even exceeded the diameter of the submarine's hull, so that the missiles had to protrude high above the pressure hull, the result being the ungainly humpbacked Delta.[22]

Twenty-two of these SSBNs were built, the first 18 (Delta I) carrying only 12 SS-N-8s, and the last 4 (Delta II) carrying 16 missiles. This odd pattern, particularly the production run of only 4 Delta IIs undermines the argument that it was topweight that limited the Delta I to 12 launchers and suggests that there was a production constraint related to the missile-launch system.[23] The SS-N-8 was a much heavier missile than the SS-N-6 and would therefore have needed significantly larger launch generators, which perhaps explains why 12 launcher tubes in the Delta take up about the same space as 16 of the same size tubes in the Yankee. The Delta was built at about 6 units a year, and the production of these larger gas generators may have been limited to 72 a year for the first three years. A 33 percent increase in production capacity could have come on line in the fourth year, to produce a total of 96 gas generators a year thereafter, which would allow 16 launchers to be fitted in the 18 Delta IIs and IIIs.[24]

20. This missile was the original version of the SS-N-8, which ultimately went to sea aboard Delta I with a range of 4,200 nautical miles. It was, however, originally tested at a much shorter range. At that stage it was reported in the West as a standard midterm improvement of the SS-N-6 carried by Yankee I, even to the extent of sharing the same NATO code name, Sawfly; its range was estimated at about 3,000 nautical miles. After a delay the missile reappeared for further testing, with the range being progressively increased. *Jane's Weapon Systems, 1983–84* (London: Jane's Publishing Co., 1983), p. 25; Robert P. Berman and John C. Baker, *Soviet Strategic Forces: Requirements and Response* (Brookings, 1982), p. 131, note 45; and Edgar Ulsamer, "A Searching Look at 'The ICBM Challenge,'" *Air Force Magazine* (July 1973), p. 70.

21. One can assume that the basic Yankee design allowed for the introduction of an improved missile at the five-year midpoint, without requiring major changes in hull or weapons installations.

22. In 1972, when discussing the likelihood that the Yankee hull would be modified to carry the SS-N-8, John S. Foster, director of defense research and engineering in the Department of Defense, said, "It probably could be done, but our guys wouldn't do it." Michael Getter, "Russian Missile Puzzles Analysts," *Washington Post,* March 22, 1972.

23. The Juliet SSG program offers a clear-cut example of the effects of a production constraint on delivery rates.

24. Large generators of this kind were probably planned for the successor to the Yankee program, which would have carried the SS-N-18, but the requirement was now advanced by five years. To avoid assembly holdups, the Soviets schedule the production of components well ahead

THE INTERIM RESPONSE. At the same time as the Soviets were striving to adapt the existing missile-launcher hull-section of the Yankee to take a stretched SS-N-8, they also had to work out a less extemporaneous solution. There were two options. One was to design a completely new hull section that would accommodate the even larger SS-N-18 (1.15 meters longer and 0.15 meters greater in diameter), which had already been programmed to enter service in 1978 aboard the Yankee successor. The other was to develop a solid-fuel missile that would be compact enough to fit the Yankee II missile launchers without major adaptation.

The Soviets pursued both approaches.[25] They developed a solid-fuel missile, the SS-N-17, which had the same diameter as the SS-N-6 and was only 1.5 meters longer. They began flight testing the SS-N-17 in 1975, but were unable to achieve the necessary range. This was, however, a serious attempt: an existing Yankee was converted to carry 12 of the SS-N-17s, and the system was undergoing some kind of trials at sea in 1977.[26] The liquid fuel SS-N-18, which also started flight testing in 1975, shortly after the SS-N-17, did have the necessary range. The first launch from a submarine was carried out in November 1976, and by early 1979 the missile had been deployed aboard the Delta III.

The result of this further adaptation of the Yankee hull-propulsion system was an even more ungainly SSBN, 14 of which were built, making a total of 36 Deltas. These, added to the 34 Yankees, account for all 70 of the hull-propulsion units that were originally planned for delivery under the ten-year Yankee program, from 1968 through 1977.

THE FINAL RESPONSE. At the same time as work was proceeding on the initial and interim responses to the new requirement for an insurance SSBN force, design would have started on the Typhoon, which represents the final response.[27] A great deal is still uncertain about the Typhoon's characteristics, particularly the arrangement of pressure hulls, the weapons and

---

of requirements; doing so would have helped meet this new demand, but there would still have been a lag.

25. The chart on p. 40 of *SMP, 1985*, shows the SS-N-17 as starting technological development in 1968–69, whereas the SS-N-18 is shown as starting in the 1963–64 period.

26. The Soviets may, however, persist in their attempt to develop a missile with the parameters of the SS-N-17, but with a greater range. The 280 single warheads carried by the 22 Delta Is and IIs are the "postexchange" component of the SSBN force (see appendix D), and the ungainly configuration of the launch platform is an operational handicap.

27. Work on the massive construction halls that were needed to build the Typhoon appears to have been started by the end of the 1960s. See references to the Severodvinsk shipyard in *SMP, 1981*, 1st ed., pp. 9–10; *SMP, 1983*, 2d ed., p. 74; and *SMP, 1984*, p. 93.

sensor outfits, and the type of propulsion. One can, however, specify the primary requirement the Typhoon would have been designed to meet: to survive attempts by Western naval forces to draw down the Soviet SSBN force in the event of war.

The Typhoon's mission of insuring the ICBM deterrent force against technological outflanking meant that survivability was particularly important in a war that did not escalate to an intercontinental exchange, and an intact SSBN force would, of course, contribute to deterring such escalation. But should a nuclear exchange take place, the requirement to survive would still persist as the role of the force changed from insuring the Soviet ICBM force to matching the remaining U.S. nuclear capability, and the SSBNs became available for immediate use or for holding in reserve, as the Supreme High Command might decide.

The requirement to survive while still remaining mission capable argues that the Soviets would have placed even greater emphasis than usual on unsinkability.[28] To minimize the chance of detection, the Soviets would have concentrated on reducing all types of signal, including noise; if detected, in order to evade attack, the Typhoon would need to go deeper and faster than Western attack submarines. If evasion were not possible, the Typhoon would have to be able to defend itself at least with antisubmarine weapons and perhaps also with antiaircraft weapons.

The Typhoon's war-fighting role in the wake of an intercontinental exchange generates the requirement that each unit carry as many ballistic missiles as possible. Yet this submarine, which is at least 1.35 times as large as the U.S. Trident SSBN, has only 0.83 the number of missile launchers. The Typhoon may therefore be designed to carry 2 missiles for each of its launcher systems.[29]

There may also have been a third requirement: to maximize the return on the massive investment represented by the Typhoon hull-propulsion unit and associated self-defense systems. The Typhoon may have been designed with a significant general purpose capability, so that it can be used in a combat role once it has launched all its ballistic missiles or in phase II

28. Soviet SSNs are double hulled and have 35 percent reserve buoyancy, whereas U.S. SSNs have single hulls and about 14 percent reserve buoyancy. Cortana Corporation, "Submarine Capabilities: A Prognosis of Technologies," Report prepared for the U.S. Congress, Office of Technology Assessment (Falls Church, Va., 1984), pp. 17–24.

29. There are various ways this capacity could be achieved. It has, however, been reported that the SS-N-20 is loaded in clips of two. "Washington Roundup: Typhoon Missiles," *Aviation Week and Space Technology*, vol. 119 (November 28, 1983), p. 17.

of a war that does not escalate to an international exchange. Considering the Typhoon's surface displacement of about 22,500 tons (comparable with that of the Kirov-class battle cruiser), the Soviets' emphasis on double hulls, and their habit of locating sensors and weapons systems outside the pressure hull, a wide range of possibilities opens up. And the Typhoon's 90-foot sail with its massive 130-foot-long rounded base is significant. The Typhoon may have been designed to operate with the sail clear of the water and the hull trimmed down below the surface, as has been the Soviets' intermittent practice with other classes of submarines.[30]

Given the capacity of the vast new construction sheds at Severodvinsk and the projected size of the U.S. Trident program, and bearing in mind the SALT II ceiling of 380 submarine-launched ballistic missiles (SLBMs) with multiple independently targeted reentry vehicles (MIRVs), which during the strategic arms reduction talks (START) the Soviets proposed adjusting to 400, one would expect the Typhoon program to have been originally projected at 20 units, with deliveries running 2 a year for ten years. In practice, deliveries of Typhoons (which started in 1982) have been running at barely 1 a year; that anomaly is discussed later in this appendix.

The Changed Requirement for Surface Forces

Unlike the relatively clear-cut requirements for SSBNs that emerged in the 1967–68 period, the requirement for general purpose forces was open to disagreement over the scope of the Soviet navy's roles and missions and over the type of forces required to discharge such missions. The substance of that argument is analyzed in appendix C. Further decisions about general purpose forces appear to have been reached in 1973 and 1974 as the result of that debate. But the basic decision to restructure the surface force stems from the 1967–68 period, and this restructuring was provided for in the Ninth Five-Year Plan (1971).

30. See, for example, the pictures of the Oscar, *SMP, 1983*, pp. 104–05. During the last twenty years there have been many pictures of Soviet submarines with only their sails above water, which have been explained as inadvertent broaching because of bad depth keeping. In some cases this explanation may have been true, but one should remember the German submarine tactic in the early years of World War II of closing to attack on the surface, with the hull trimmed down and only the conning tower exposed to view.

The Implications

The 1970s hierarchy of objectives had three major implications for surface forces. One was a new requirement for sustainability. In the 1960s, the concept of operations envisaged inevitable escalation to global nuclear war, and forces needed to survive only long enough to be able to discharge their primary mission. In the case of forward-deployed naval units, that mission was to deny the United States the option of withholding carriers and SSBNs from the initial exchange and, if possible, to prevent them from actually launching their strikes.

Under the new concept of operations, which was premised on the ability to deter escalation to a nuclear exchange, SSBNs, from the onset of war, had to be held secure against attempts by Western navies to draw down the force. To do so required surface ships capable of sustained operations in a hostile environment, implying greatly increased endurance and survivability and much larger weapon loads. The Soviet response was to scale up the size of the next generation of surface ship-types, which would start entering service at the beginning of the 1980s.[31] The light cruiser-sized ship jumped from about 8,000 to 9,000 tons to 12,000, and the destroyer-sized jumped from 4,000 to 5,000 tons to more than 8,000.[32] A second and larger escort type of almost 4,000 tons was added to the inventory by reclassifying the Krivak as an escort ship (SKR) in 1978.[33] The addition met the new requirement for ocean escorts that was a corollary of the concept of a two-phase war. At the same time, the existing 1,200-ton escort-sized classes (the Riga, Petya, Mirka, and Grisha), which had been recategorized in the 1960s as small antisubmarine ships (MPKs), had the SKR designator restored, except for the latest class (Grisha), which continued as an MPK.

The need for a specialized ship to exercise command and control had already emerged in response to the original forward deployment, and apparently this requirement was supposed to be met (at least initially) through the conversion of Sverdlov-class cruisers.[34] However, the new concept of

31. This requirement for larger surface ships was partly responsible for a 30 percent increase in building way area (more than 125,000 square meters of new building ways) after 1970. *SMP, 1984*, p. 93.

32. It has been found that type size is the most useful descriptor, since these remained remarkably consistent for thirty-five years after the war and continued the prewar practice.

33. The Krivak, at 3.7 thousand tons, originally filled the destroyer-sized slot in the type inventory.

34. As an expedient, the Soviets had initially made use of Sverdlov-class cruisers and Ugra-

operations justified the reintroduction into the fleet of the heavy cruiser category of ship, which had been in abeyance since the mid-1950s. Such ships would combine the command function with that of serving as platforms for longer-range "force" weapons, hence the 23,000-ton Kirov class.

A second implication of the new concept of operations was that as long as war on land remained conventional, nuclear weapons would probably not be released for use at sea. In other words, Soviet naval forces had to be prepared to engage U.S. carrier battle groups relying solely on conventional weapons, the best available being the cruise missile, with the submarine torpedo as a supplementary system. To disable a carrier, several missiles would have to strike home, which meant that the navy would need a much larger number of missiles at sea aboard many more platforms.[35] This requirement was reflected in the design of the new family of surface types that began delivery at the beginning of the 1980s.

In addition, land-based ballistic missiles could not be used against carriers as long as the war remained conventional, a restriction that was particularly important in the Mediterranean. The interim response to this restriction was to fit horizon-range cruise missiles to the destroyer-sized units whose task was to remain in close company with the U.S. carriers when they were in the eastern Mediterranean. In the 1970–76 period, 3 Kildin and 5 Kashin were modified in this way, protection against preemptive attack being strengthened at the same time.[36] The final response may be embodied in the Slava class of missile cruiser that is now being built at Nikolaev on the Black Sea. With its very strong air defense capability, including the SA-N-6 vertical launch system, and its 16 SS-N-12 long-range SSMs, it seems designed for the Mediterranean mission.

A third implication was that naval operations would revert to being more general and less task specific, and direct support of ground forces would once more be a major mission. This change in the nature of naval operations, combined with the need for sustainability, restored the value of the gun, whose place as the primary surface-to-surface weapon had been usurped by the homing missile. Shells could be carried by the hundreds,

---

class tenders as command ships. In the 1967–72 period, 2 Sverdlovs were extensively modified and reconfigured as specialized command ships.

35. In those cases in which launchers doubled as missile stowage, or in which there was no provision for changing warheads once at sea, ships would have to load out with a mix of nuclear and conventional missiles, further increasing the requirement for larger numbers.

36. It is pertinent that the fourth Kildin, stationed in the Far East, was not so modified.

and improvements in range and accuracy (including the possibility of terminal guidance) gave gun systems a renewed importance. This was reflected in the decision to modify the design of Krivak, which had begun delivery in 1970, to carry two new-type 100-mm single mountings in place of the twin 76-mm systems.[37] The first of these Krivak IIs was delivered by the end of 1975, and the same system was incorporated in the design of the Udaloy, which began delivery in 1980, and (as an expedient) in the lead ship of the Kirov class.[38] The Soviets also developed a 130-mm twin turret, and this system was incorporated in the design of the Sovremenny-class destroyer, the Slava-class light cruiser, and the Kirov-class heavy cruiser.[39]

A Shift in Primary Focus

The effect of these various changes was to shift the balance of the distant-water surface force from a predominantly antisubmarine configuration to one that was primarily antisurface, although with a significant ASW capability. The shift reflected the change in mission structure. During the 1950s, the Soviets shaped the surface force to deal with the surface threat, initially that of seaborne invasion and then the threat from attack carriers. In the wake of the 1961–62 decision period, the Soviets reconfigured the force for the antisubmarine role as they sought to extend their defense perimeter to exclude Polaris from the eastern Mediterranean and the Norwegian Sea. This reconfiguration was manifested by the characteristics of the new construction units that began delivery in the 1969–70 period, by the conversion or major modification in the 1964–70 period of existing units to improve their ASW capability (SAM Kotlin and Kanin), and by the introduction in 1964 of "large antisubmarine ship" (BPK) as a type designator. The BPK designator was ultimately applied to all surface ships equipped with ASW systems of Kashin-design vintage (1962) or later, in other words, almost the whole distant-water surface force.

37. The 76-millimeter (mm) system was 1962 vintage and primarily intended for the antiair role.

38. In the postwar period, the design of gun systems had moved sharply away from the prewar design 100-mm and 130-mm weapons, which had been primarily antisurface systems, to 57-mm and 76-mm weapons with much higher rates of fire, which were primarily antiair. This new 100-mm system therefore represented new, rather than incremental, development, which would account for the five-to-six years' lead time.

39. Development of this new 130-mm system appears to have run into problems, since it was not ready for fitting in the lead ships of the Kirov and Sovremenny classes, which were delivered in 1980.

By the mid-1970s, the pendulum was already swinging back. In the Mediterranean the counter-Polaris mission had lapsed, and the Soviets focused on how to deal with the carriers and amphibious force in war while withstanding the air and submarine threat posed by the ever-present U.S. Sixth Fleet. In the Northern and Pacific Fleet areas they focused on establishing command of the approaches to the SSBN bastions, or at least denying command to the U.S. Navy. In these areas, the primary role of the Soviets' surface forces was to ensure a "favorable operating environment" for their submarines, which would be the main defense against enemy SSNs seeking to draw down the SSBN force. In all areas, surface forces would be required to provide gunfire support to operations on land along the maritime axes of advance. This reorientation of the surface force was formalized in 1977 and 1978, when there was a further change in type designators, with the classification of BPK being limited to those classes that had been designed primarily for the ASW role (Kashin, Kanin, Kresta II, Kara, and the new-construction Udaloy).

The 1973–74 Adjustments

As discussed in appendix C, the 1970–73 period saw a major debate on naval roles and missions, and the evidence suggests that among the outcomes was a modest increase in the allocation of resources to surface warship construction. The problem is to distinguish between what had already been planned by 1971 and what was approved subsequently. The structure of the discussion in Admiral Sergey G. Gorshkov's February 1973 article in *Morskoy sbornik* provides some clues to the answer.[40] As part of a section describing the prevailing situation (*Msb* 73/2/21/2), Gorshkov listed the characteristics required for naval operations in the nuclear era: long-range at high speed for surface ships, large radius of action for aircraft, nuclear propulsion for submarines, and sufficient afloat support to sustain distant-water operations (*Msb* 73/2/22/5, 22/10). Although all these attributes were not yet available in 1973, they were characteristic of the forces that were already programmed to join the fleet from 1977 on. The design decisions must therefore have predated 1971.

The two paragraphs that immediately preceded this descriptive section

---

40. This was the final article in the eleven-article series by Sergey G. Gorshkov, called "Voenno-morskie floty v voynakh i v mirnoe vremya" (Navies in war and peace), published in *Morskoy sbornik* (*Naval journal*) between 1972 and 1973. Hereafter *Msb* year/month/page/paragraph (if appropriate); reference may be given in text.

in Gorshkov's article were clearly advocacy. Having noted that the Central Committee had supported the development of an ocean-going fleet based on nuclear-powered submarines (*Msb* 73/2/20/7), Gorshkov went on to argue that a modern navy could not "only be an underseas navy" and noted the need for many kinds of surface ship, each with its own specific weapons outfit. He commented that attempts in many countries to create "universal" ships to discharge all (or many) missions, had been generally unsuccessful (*Msb* 73/2/20/8–21/1).[41]

There are two surface programs that could have been authorized as a result of this argument. One is the Sovremenny-class destroyer, which is an adaptation of the Kresta hull-propulsion system (the class that immediately preceded Sovremenny at the Zhdanov yard) and hence could stem from a decision taken as late as 1973–74. Furthermore, its 130-mm gun system and its SS-N-22 surface-to-surface missile (SSM) system apparently were not ready to be fitted in time to meet the 1980 delivery schedule, but were fitted on return from sea trials. However, within the context of Gorshkov's argument, the Sovremenny destroyer and the Udaloy large antisubmarine ship are best considered as a pair of weapons' platforms, and the final allocation of weapons between the two (and hence the final configuration of Udaloy) could also have been decided in 1973 and 1974. In its present configuration, the Udaloy is the lineal successor to the Kresta II and Kara BPKs, but it may originally have been intended to cram much more into that single hull.

The other program that could have been authorized in the wake of the Gorshkov debate was the aircraft carrier,[42] but one must be clear about which aircraft carrier is being talked about. At the time of the debate, the Kiev program was well under way and is unlikely to have been an issue. It can be seen as an interim response to the requirement to establish command of the sea approaches to the SSBN operating areas.

The Kiev hull-propulsion system was probably conceived originally as a double-sized version of the Moskva ASW cruiser, since the Moskva would carry too few helicopters for distant-water ASW operations. The requirement for this ship would have stemmed from the 1963–64 debate, when the navy won its case for more surface forces to support its forward deployment. It was probably then that the Moskva program was canceled

41. The Russian word was *universalniy,* which was mistranslated as "general purpose," a term that has a misleading connotation in Western naval parlance.

42. The decision to build a new carrier is thought to have taken place no earlier than 1974. John Jordan, "Soviet Destroyers-Part 3: The Sovremenny and Udaloy," *Defence,* vol. 14 (May 1983), p. 253.

(its weapons suit being used to reconfigure the Kresta as a BPK) and work started on the basic design of the Kiev.

This process would have been overtaken by the doctrinal adjustment in December 1966, which generated the requirement to provide for the protection of the SSBN force during the conventional phase of a global war, a requirement that would become operative in the second half of the 1970s. Therefore, the final design of the Kiev, including its angled deck and vertical takeoff and landing (VTOL) capability, was probably very different from the original concept. But because much of the ground work had already been done and perhaps long lead items already ordered, the Soviets were able to finalize the design in time for the keel to be laid in September 1970.

Assuming that the Kiev program was the interim response to the new requirement that emerged from the 1967–68 decision period, then a final response would also have been projected. And most likely it was the type of ship being pushed as the final response to the new requirement that was the object of Gorshkov's criticism of "universal ships." Of course, the Kiev was an example of such a ship. It carried long-range SSMs, long- and short-range SAM and gun systems, long- and short-range ASW weapons and associated sonars, and both helicopters and VTOL aircraft. But the Kiev was an expedient, an interim response, and in the circumstances the mixture could be justified. To design such a ship from scratch would be a different matter.

One can infer from the Gorshkov series and from other material published about this period (see appendix C) that Gorshkov had been arguing for an aircraft carrier that could achieve air superiority over an area such as the Norwegian Sea, which suggests a specialized ship on the lines of an American conventional takeoff and landing (CTOL) carrier. His opponents appear to have been arguing for a universal ship, a warship that would combine the attributes of a Kirov-class heavy cruiser and those of a much enlarged version of the Kiev aviation cruiser, all within a single hull.

Possibly, Gorshkov's advocacy was successful at this earlier stage. By March 1979 U.S. intelligence analysts were convinced that construction of a CTOL carrier was under way at Severodvinsk, and in December, Defense Department officials were reported as having confirmed that a nuclear carrier was under construction in the north, which would be about 75,000 to 80,000 tons and carry about 85 aircraft.[43] Subsequently, it be-

---

43. Charles W. Corddry, "Soviet Said to Construct Huge Warship," *Baltimore Sun*, March

came clear that the aircraft carrier was being built not in the north but at Nikolaev on the Black Sea. The possible implications of this development are discussed in the last part of this appendix.

The Requirement for Attack Submarines

In considering the effects of the 1967–68 decision period on the general purpose submarine force, one must distinguish between the new programs that would have been generated by the new requirements and those programs that were already planned or in progress at that date. In the 1967–68 period the second-generation nuclear submarines had just begun delivery. The Yankee SSBN was being built at the rate of 7 units a year, and the Victor SSN and the Charlie SSGN were each being built at the rate of 2 units a year.

The effect of the 1967–68 decisions on the SSBN program has already been described, including the initial and interim response to the new requirement, which involved the reconfiguration of the Yankee II hull-propulsion system to produce the Delta I, II, and III. As for the attack submarine program, the interim response was to alter the configuration mix of the second-generation submarines that were then being built, with a sharp shift in emphasis away from SSGNs and toward SSNs.

Attack Submarine Programs, 1968–82

The Charlie SSGN had been designed specifically for launching nuclear strikes against aircraft carriers. It carried the 30-nautical-mile, submerged-launch, surface-skimming SS-N-7 SSM that had been developed to bypass the major operational limitations of the 300-nautical-mile SS-N-3 system carried by the Echo II and Juliet. The drawback of the SS-N-7 under the new concept of operations, in which nuclear weapons might never be released at sea, was that it relied on a nuclear warhead. Not only could this not be changed once embarked, but the missile's payload was too small to carry a conventional warhead of the size needed to disable a carrier. There

---

15, 1979; John F. Fialka, "Soviets Apparently Building a Nuclear Aircraft Carrier," *Washington Star,* March 16, 1979; and Richard Halloran, "Soviet Navy Building Its First Nuclear Powered Carrier," *New York Times,* December 17, 1979.

were, of course, the intervening five to eight years before the 1970s hierarchy of objectives came into full effect, during which time the 1960s concept could still apply. But, clearly, to have too many eggs in that type of submarine basket would limit future operational flexibility.

The outcome of the decisions taken in the 1967–68 period was the construction of 41 Victor SSNs (built at three different yards) and only 17 Charlie SSGNs.[44] This shift in emphasis was added to the more fundamental change in programs that stemmed from the 1961–62 decision period, and to understand the contemporary implications, one must go back to 1957–58, which saw the genesis of the Charlie class.

In that period the Soviets came to appreciate that the U.S. nuclear strike carrier would need to be countered in distant waters that were controlled by Western surface and air forces, and they made the decision to rely primarily on missile-armed submarines and aircraft. Priority in the allocation of nuclear propulsion would be switched from the role of strategic delivery to that of countering the carrier. The annual production of nuclear reactors would be increased to 20, to allow the construction of 10 submarines a year, with deliveries planned to start in 1968.[45]

THE 1957–58 DECISIONS. Given the production constraint of 20 reactors a year, it is possible to reconstruct the submarine building plan that stemmed from successive decision periods (see table B-1). In 1957–58 the evident threat was from nuclear-strike carriers, along with a potential threat from the Polaris submarine if its development was successful.[46] All 20 reactors were allocated to countering these threats, and on the basis of actual deliveries in 1968–77 the original configuration mix planned for annual delivery during the 1968–72 period was apparently as follows: 4

44. They were built mainly at Admiralty Yard, Leningrad, but also at Komsomol'sk and Gorky. *Jane's Fighting Ships, 1984–85* (London: Jane's Publishing Co., 1984), pp. 508–09.

45. The actual rate of production in the 1958–67 delivery period averaged about 11 reactors a year, but the layout and capacity of shipyard facilities suggests that the planned annual rate may have been 12. The increase to 20 is a solid figure. In 1969 U.S. analysts asserted that the Soviets had the capability to build 20 submarines a year. *Status of Naval Ships,* Report by the Seapower Subcommittee of the House Committee on Armed Services, 91 Cong. 1 sess. (GPO, 1969), p. 419. This number was unrealistic in terms of yard capacity and probably reflected the assumption that the Soviet submarines, like their U.S. counterparts, were powered by only 1 reactor, whereas they usually have 2. The allocation of 20 reactors a year was confirmed in 1981 by an intelligence source, who was reported as saying that the Soviets could not build more than about 10 nuclear submarines a year unless they increased their reactor production facilities. *Norwich Bulletin* (Connecticut), April 19, 1981, p. 4.

46. Given their own experience with submarine-launched ballistic missiles, the Soviets are unlikely to have anticipated the speed with which the Polaris system was developed, or its operational success.

Table B-1. Planned and Actual Delivery of Nuclear-Powered Warships, 1968–82[a]

Classes of warship	1957–58 decision period Delivery planned for:		1961–62 decision period Delivery planned for:			1967–68 decision period Actual deliveries:		
	1968–72	1973–77	1968–72	1973–77	1978–82	1968–72	1973–77	1978–82
Tac-Yankee	10	10	..	..	..	0	0	..
Yankee I, II	..	..	35	35	..	34	0	..
Successor SSBN[b]	..	..	..	..	10	..	..	0
Delta (Yankee II)[c]	..	..	..	..	..	1	35	..
Typhoon[b,c]	..	..	..	..	..	..	..	6[d]
Victor I, II	20	..	10	10	..	10	13	..
Victor III	..	20	..	..	20	..	0	18
Charlie (½)	..	..	10	10	..	10	7	..
Charlie	20	..	..	..	..	..	..	..
Papa[b]	..	20	..	..	15[e]	..	1	0
Alpha[b]	..	..	..	..	5[e]	..	..	..
Oscar[b,c]	..	..	..	..	..	..	..	9[d]
Kirov[b,c]	..	..	..	..	..	..	..	2
Addenda: number of reactors[f]								
1968 model	100	60	100	100	40	100	139	..
1973 model	..	40	..	..	60	..	60	..
Total	100	100	100	100	100	100	199	..

a. It is assumed that the navy was allocated 20 nuclear reactors a year during this period.
b. These units have 1973 model reactors.
c. Because of their size, the date of launch is used for Typhoon, Oscar, and Kirov rather than the date of delivery.
d. Only 3 Typhoons and 3 Oscars were actually launched in this period as the result of decisions made in 1976–77.
e. Lead units of Papa and Alpha were built in the preceding delivery period.
f. All units have 2 reactors except for Typhoon, which has 4, and Charlie (½), which has 1.

Victor SSNs, 4 Charlie SSGNs, and 2 of the original tactical versions of the Yankee hull-propulsion system.[47] The same proportions of basic types would have been maintained in the second half of the ten-year period (1973–77), but because Charlie was only the interim response to the countercarrier requirement, its place in the program was to be taken by a new class of SSGN.

In other words, the Echo II SSGNs, 28 of which were delivered in the 1963–67 period, had been the initial response to the carrier threat, with the 5 Echo Is as just a hurried expedient. The Charlie was to have been the interim response, with 20 units being delivered in the 1968–72 period. And a third class, representing an extension of the concept embodied in Charlie, was planned for delivery in the 1973–77 period. This three-stage development process would have followed established Soviet practice, but it was not allowed to run its course. One must, however, be aware of the original plan dating from 1957 to 1958 if one is to understand the apparent anomalies of the solitary Papa SSGN, the single reactor in the Charlie, and the strung-out pattern of Charlie deliveries.

THE 1961–62 DECISIONS. In the wake of the Kennedy defense initiatives, there arose the completely new requirement for an SSBN force to match the U.S. sea-based strategic delivery capability. The Soviets met this requirement by reconfiguring the Tac-Yankee hull-propulsion system as an SSBN and programming it for construction at 7 units a year, with deliveries starting in 1968 and running for ten years. This SSBN program would usurp 70 percent of naval reactor production, leaving only 6 reactors a year for attack submarines throughout the 1968–77 delivery period. It would also usurp the assembly ways at Severodvinsk, requiring the Victor SSN to be built at Admiralty Yard, Leningrad. The Soviets would have to rely heavily on the use of floating docks for assembling the submarines.

The Soviets responded to this problem in two ways. One was to fit only 1 reactor in the Charlie SSGN, the rationale being that the stand-off capability provided by the missile system made the reduced speed somewhat less of a handicap. It was therefore better to have two twenty-knot Charlies than a single thirty-knot one, an argument that did not, however, apply to the torpedo-armed Victor SSN.

The other response was to halve the building rate for the first half of the attack submarine program and to deliver the planned 40 units over a period of ten years rather than the normal five. At the end of those ten years the

47. The presence of the Tac-Yankee in the 1957–58 plan enabled the short lead time on the Yankee SSBN program.

SSBN force would stand at 70, and the original allocation of reactors to the attack submarine program could be restored. This would then allow the construction of 4 SSNs and 4 SSGNs a year, both types having 2 reactors. The usual midpoint upgrade would therefore be deferred for five years, but thereafter the second half of the program would run according to plan, delivering a combined total of 40 units of the "improved" versions of both types in the five years, 1978–82.

For the SSNs—the Victor III—this upgrading would involve a marked improvement in overall performance, but the basic Victor hull-propulsion system would be retained. For the SSGNs the change would be more fundamental. As mentioned before, the Charlie was only the interim response to the countercarrier requirement, and the class that would represent the final response was already under development, the Papa. Whereas the Charlie and Victor shared the same basic hull-propulsion unit (as was standard Soviet practice), the Papa would use a new and significantly improved system. It was designed for sustained operations in distant sea areas such as the Mediterranean, where it had to remain undetected within weapon range of a carrier, and it would be larger and more capable than Charlie and carry more offensive weapons. And it would, of course, have 2 reactors, so a carrier would not be able to outrun the Papa as it could the Charlie.

Although series construction of the Papa would now be delayed until the 1978–83 delivery period, the Soviets decided that, since the class would incorporate a new hull-propulsion system, they ought to build the lead unit according to the original schedule. Doing so would allow operational evaluation of the new hull-propulsion system and the incorporation of improvements into the design of the series-production units. Construction of this lead ship took place at Severodvinsk, and delivery was made somewhat ahead of the original schedule, in 1971.

THE 1967–68 DECISIONS. It is against this background of a seriously distorted plan for building attack submarines in the 1968–82 period that the effects of the 1967–68 decision period must be assessed. As already explained, the new concept of operations undermined the projected role of the Charlie and Papa SSGNs, which relied on the use of nuclear weapons to discharge their mission. Plans for the series production of the Papa were therefore canceled. The Charlie program had already started delivery in 1968; the Soviets then had to decide whether to let the program run its full course or to reconfigure some of these units as Victor SSNs.

The final decision to complete 17 Charlies would have been determined

in part by pipeline inertia, that is, by the number of missile launcher systems that had already been delivered or were well along in the production
pipeline.[48] Although the total of 40 hulls (23 Victors and 17 Charlies)
matched the 1961–62 plan for the first half of the program, reconfiguring
Charlie hull-propulsion units as 2-reactor Victors caused an overexpendi-
ture of 3 in the reactor account. This was adjusted in the second half of the
program, when 18 of the improved Victors were delivered, rather than 20
as planned, leaving 1 reactor left over.

These and other changes produced a confusing pattern of production
which is best described in terms of three five-year delivery periods, the
first two constituting the first half of the original program. Production that
was delivered during the first period (1968–73) ran according to plan, with
10 SSNs and 10 SSGNs being delivered. A year or so into production for
the second period (1973–77), a modification to the design of the original
hull-propulsion system was introduced during construction. This change
involved inserting an additional section forward of the fin and increasing
the Victor's length by about twenty feet and the Charlie's by about thirty.
All 7 of the stretched SSNs (Victor II) were completed during this second
five-year period, but delivery of the 6 Charlie II SSGNs extended well into
the third period (1978–83), reflecting the SSN's priority in the allocation
of nuclear reactors.[49]

The modifications were introduced to both types at the same period, and
since they share a common-design hull and since most of the Victor IIs
(perhaps as many as 5) were actually built at Gorky (the only yard to build
Charlies), it is probable that similar weapons or equipment were being
fitted to the two classes. The additional ten feet in the Charlie II could
indicate extra fire control equipment for a longer-range missile.[50] These
were modifications to the original design and were incorporated in about
one-third of the submarines that were built in the first half of the attack
submarine production run. They should not be confused with the improved

48. The Charlie and Victor program used 1 reactor and 2 hulls less than provided for in the
original plan, which supports the conclusion that the number of launcher systems available determined the number of Charlies. The concept of pipeline inertia also considers cost-effectiveness
and operational requirements. Examples of the available number of weapons' outfits determining
the number of platforms are the Juliet SSG, the Kresta, the Kanin and SAM Kotlin conversions,
and (less certainly) the Golf SSG.

49. An earlier example of "trickle delivery" was the Juliet program, which delivered 16 units
over six years, paralleling the production of the Echo SSGN and using the same paired launchers.

50. The Charlie II is reputed to carry a submerged launch version of the sixty-nautical mile
SS-N-9 SSM system. This entered service aboard Nanuchka in 1969 and therefore could have
been available in time.

design that was introduced at the halfway mark, according to normal practice. That was the Victor III, 18 of which had been delivered by the end of the final period (1978–82).

Completely separate to these mainstream submarine attack programs was the Alpha class of high-speed, deep-diving titanium-hulled submarine. Although work on the development of these general capabilities probably goes back to the 1957–58 period, the specifications for the Alpha stem from the 1961–62 decision period. Most likely this class was originally intended to trail Polaris and its successor, a task that demanded high speed and deep diving and generated formidable new requirements in submarine design.[51] The prototype of this radical design was scheduled for delivery at the start of the 1970s, and delivery of 5 series-construction units was planned for the 1978–82 period. In the wake of the 1967–68 decision period, the counter-Polaris task yielded precedence to protecting the SSBN force; however, the Alpha's characteristics suited it for the role of a hydrospace fighter in defense of SSBN bastions. The Soviets therefore persisted with the development of this radical new type of submarine, and by 1982, 6 of the class were operational.[52] They had a speed of more than 40 knots, and their hulls could withstand pressures down to three thousand feet.

The Reactor Account, 1973–82

Reconstructing the planned and actual building programs for attack submarines allows one to postulate the shape of the remaining programs. With the focus on the ten-year period 1973–82, and the pattern of deliveries as planned in 1961–62, the first five years, 1973–77, would have seen the delivery of 35 Yankee II SSBNs, as well as 10 Victor SSNs and 10 Charlie SSGNs. The second five years would have seen the emphasis swing back, with the delivery of 40 attack submarines and (probably) 10 of a larger SSBN than the Yankee, built around the Oscar hull-propulsion system. The configuration mix of attack submarines would have conformed largely to

51. Gorshkov refers to the use of submarines in this role. *Msb* 73/2/20/1. In 1961–62, for the near future, this was the only practical way of providing data on the location of Polaris submarines. This trailing would be the submarine equivalent of the Soviet surface ships' shadowing the U.S. carriers in the Mediterranean. Trailing would be active, hence silence would not be important. The Alpha prototype went to sea in 1971, a lead time that was consistent with the main 1961–62 decision period.

52. The prototype was dismantled or scrapped in 1974. A new lead ship was delivered in the mid-1970s and became operational in 1978. Another 5 units became operational in the 1978–82 period. The prototype's reactors could have been incorporated into another new construction unit.

the second half of the original ten-year plan (as formulated in 1957 and 1958), in that 20 Victor IIIs would have been delivered, but only 15 Papa SSGNs would have been built in order to provide for the construction of 5 Alphas.[53]

The 1967–68 decision period caused major changes to the building plans for those ten years. Except for the lead unit, the Papa program was canceled. Delivery of Yankee hull-propulsion units (reconfigured as Delta I, II, III) was reduced from 7 a year to 5 or 6 and ran on well into the second half of the period.[54] Reconfiguring the Charlie hull-propulsion units as Victor SSNs reduced the total number of submarines delivered by 2, but did not materially affect the reactor account. Meanwhile development of the Alpha prototype had been successful and 6 production units were delivered in the second half of the period.

The number of reactors available for use in this ten-year period was 200. The maximum number that can be accounted for by the programs listed so far is 155 (Victor–62; Charlie–7; Delta–70; Papa–2; and Alpha–14). Three programs have not been mentioned: the Kirov heavy cruiser, the Oscar SSGN, and the Typhoon SSBN. What does the availability of 45 reactors suggest about the shape of these three new programs as they were envisaged in the 1967–68 decision period?

In terms of the reactor account, 2 Kirovs were "delivered" in the 1973–83 period, each with 2 reactors.[55] Given lead time, the complexity of the ship, and building way constraints, it is unlikely that more were originally planned. This leaves 41 reactors for submarine construction or 43 if one allows that the reactors from the Alpha prototype (which was dismantled) were used to power one of the production units.[56] The Oscar needs 2 reactors, the Typhoon needs 4, and there could be different ways of apportioning these reactors between the two programs. However, in postulating the 1967–68 plan, a plausible approach is to build on the earlier assessment. In 1961 and 1962 the Soviets had planned that, after the construction of 70 Yankee-size SSBNs, a much larger SSBN would be built at 2 a year.

53. This assumes that the Papa and Alpha use the same reactor, which is different (and five years more advanced) than that used in the Victor and Charlie.

54. This description does not allow for the fact that Komsomol'sk deliveries invariably lagged behind the Severodvinsk schedule, but treats them as if they ran level.

55. Because the Kirovs spend about two and a half years fitting out, the date of launching is used as a surrogate for actual delivery to the navy.

56. The prototype was delivered in 1971 and dismantled in 1974, so the reactors were only about four years old. The dismantling (or scrapping, as reported in the West) of this unit went against normal Soviet practice but can be explained by the fact that it allowed the construction of an extra Alpha. These results are shown in table B-1.

Allowing three-years' worth of Typhoon and Oscar deliveries during this accounting period, there were enough reactors to build 2 Typhoon SSBNs a year (24) and 3 Oscar SSGNs (18), for a total over the three years of 42 reactors. That would leave 1 reactor over, which was the odd one left over by the reconfiguration of 3 Charlie SSGNs as Victor SSNs in the 1973–78 period.

EVIDENCE OF A CHANGE IN PLAN. Although deliveries of Typhoon and Oscar actually ran at about 1 a year during this period, there are several reasons for concluding that in the 1967–68 period the Soviets did plan to build at the higher rates just mentioned. The most persuasive reason is the power plant of the Kirov class, which combines 2 nuclear reactors with two oil-fired boilers. Such a propulsion system is distinctly suboptimal; normal practice would have been to fit 4 reactors to a ship. One can only assume that the Kirov system was an expedient, forced on the designers by the limited availability of reactors. Nuclear propulsion is a virtual necessity in modern submarines, whereas in surface ships it is more of a convenience.

Another reason for believing the higher figures is the 80 percent increase in shop space at Severodvinsk, including a vast new construction hall.[57] This space was in addition to the extension of construction facilities in the first half of the 1960s that was required for the Yankee SSBN, which the yard built at an average rate of 5 units a year. A third reason is the strong probability that as far back as 1961–62 the Soviets had planned to build 2 large SSBNs a year in the wake of the very rapid buildup of the Yankee force, and the logic of that requirement had not changed.

A fourth reason is the numbers of Oscar SSGNs that would be needed if the operational requirements that emerged from the 1967–68 decision period were to be met. The naval objective was to establish command of the sea approaches to the SSBN deployment areas, and the main surface threat was the aircraft carrier. Since 1955, the American attack carrier force had consistently stood at about 15 units, which were split roughly 10 and 5 between the Atlantic and Pacific Oceans; in addition, the British had three fixed-wing carriers and the French had two. Ten years of Oscar construction at three a year would yield 30 units, which could be split 21 and 9 between the North Sea and the Pacific Ocean. When one considers the limitations of conventional warheads, the difficulty of penetrating the air defense of a carrier battle group, and the problems of distinguishing the

57. *SMP, 1984*, pp. 92–93.

carrier from all the other possible targets in the group, the requirement for large numbers of missiles arriving simultaneously is clear. Given that each submarine must carry a mix of nuclear and conventionally armed missiles, the postulated force levels are in no way overgenerous.

That the reactor account works out so neatly at the higher delivery rates is probably not accidental; the possible implications of this below-plan construction are discussed in the last part of this appendix. It might also be more than coincidental that the Soviets were able to plan the construction of two nuclear icebreakers at this period.[58] That the one reactor left over came from the Victor-Charlie program suggests a further inference that can be drawn from the account, one that concerns the reactors themselves.

REACTOR DESIGN. The first half of the Victor-Charlie program built 23 Victors and 17 Charlies rather than 20 of each as planned. There were therefore 3 more reactors used than had been allocated. But 4 fewer reactors were used in the second half of the program (1978–82), when only 18 Victor IIIs were built rather than the 20 in the original program. By that time, however, there were spare reactors from the Oscar and Typhoon programs, perhaps as many as 16. One must therefore ask why 3 of these spare reactors, plus the 1 already left over, were not used to power the last 2 Victor hulls, which in all other respects had been provided for by the plan. The most likely answer is that different models of reactors were involved.

Supporting this conclusion is the distinction that was drawn earlier between the Victor III and the Papa programs. Both were originally planned for delivery in the 1973–77 period, but they differed in their relationship to the preceding program. Victor III was the usual midprogram upgrade of the basic Victor-Charlie hull-propulsion system. Papa, however, was the final response to the countercarrier requirement (Charlie having been the interim one), and its hull-propulsion system represented a design that was perhaps as much as five years more advanced. In other words, there were two separate reactor accounts that could not be cross-traded. One account dealt only in 1968-vintage reactors, which totaled 240 over fifteen years, providing for the Victor, Charlie, and Yankee. The other account dealt in 1973-vintage reactors, and its 60 units had in 1961–62 been intended for the Papa (30), the Alpha (10), and the large SSBN (20). But in 1967–68

58. Rossiya was laid down January 1981, and a second ship in November 1983. Another two nuclear-powered icebreakers are to be built in Finland, the reactors being provided by the Soviet Union.

when the Papa program was canceled (the lead unit being completed), the account was reallocated to provide for the Kirov, Oscar, and Typhoon, plus an extra Alpha. These results are shown in table B-1.

The Next Generation of Attack Submarines

By 1985 the lineaments of the new family of nuclear submarines were beginning to emerge. The first Typhoon SSBN was delivered in 1982. In the same year, the first Oscar SSGN appeared, and 1982–84 saw the delivery of another three new classes of attack submarines: the 8,000-ton Akula SSN, being built at Komsomol'sk; the 9,700-ton Mike, being built at Severodvinsk; and the 8,000-ton Sierra, being built at Gorky. A fifth type of attack submarine, the small-sized Uniform, was also under construction, probably at Sudomekh, and there was possibly a sixth as well.[59]

Combining this evidence with the analysis in the two preceding sections allows one to postulate the requirement for attack submarines that would have been established in 1967 and 1968. But while the basic submarine designs would have been formulated at that stage, the number of different configurations and the final building rates may not have been agreed on until 1972–73. This possibility is suggested by the emphasis in Gorshkov's articles, "Navies in War and Peace," on the battle for sea communications in World Wars I and II. As discussed in appendix C, his analysis of why the blockade of Germany was effective in World War I but not in World War II can be read as justifying the blockade of North America in phase II of a world war. His analysis of the German attempt to disrupt Allied shipping stressed the importance of having large numbers of submarines at the outset of the campaign.

Whatever its genesis, the final requirement appears to have been for one very large kind of SSBN, which would also have a residual general purpose capability, and five different kinds of attack boat. The core of the attack submarine force would comprise three kinds, all in the range of 8,000 to 10,000 tons and of a size to carry large weapon loads and, insofar as was practical, designed to permit the changing of warheads at sea. One of the three would perhaps be optimized for operations against carrier battle groups and be able to rely, if necessary, on its own sensors for target

59. *Jane's Fighting Ships, 1985–86* (London: Jane's Publishing Co., 1985), p. 528, describes the Uniform as a small submarine, probably intended for research and development purposes. The Uniform may therefore be a program comparable to the earlier Alpha, where a development prototype was built, to be followed in due course by series production.

information. Another would be optimized for operations in defense of SSBNs against enemy SSNs. The third would be a more general purpose submarine, combining reasonable ASW performance with a reasonable capability against surface combatants other than carriers and battleships.

Given the difference in size between the Papa and the Victor III (and between the Charlie II and the Victor II), the Mike is the likely candidate for the antisurface role, a likelihood that is also supported by the absence of a pod on its vertical stabilizer.[60] Of the other two kinds of attack submarine, the Sierra may be the general purpose one and the Akula the one that is optimized for ASW.

Beyond the Mike's self-contained antisurface capability, which of necessity would be limited in its reach, the concept of establishing command of areas such as the Norwegian Sea (or at least denying command to the enemy) raised the requirement for a much larger SSGN. This submarine would carry a large number of longer-range weapons that could be launched from well outside the defensive reach of the carrier battlegroup and achieve the concentration of force required to saturate its air defenses. The result was the Oscar, which carried 24 long-range SS-N-19 missiles and whose hull-propulsion system may already have been projected in the 1967–68 period as the successor to the original Yankee SSBN program.

At the other end of the scale, one can envisage a requirement for a submarine that was much smaller than the three basic types (8,000–10,000 tons). Such a submarine could be a development of the Alpha hydrospace fighter and could be optimized for antisubmarine operations in congested or shallow waters. This may be the intended role of the Uniform class now under development or construction. But the constraints of reactor production capacity suggest that this unit may be a prototype, with production not scheduled until the next five-year delivery period (1988–92). This pattern would conform to the precedent of the Alpha program.

The capabilities of this family of submarines would show a marked advance on the Victor, whose basic hull-propulsion system began delivery in 1968. One would also expect a full-generation improvement on the capabilities of the Papa system, which had been due to begin delivery in 1973, and the incorporation of much that was learned from the Alpha in terms of high-speed operations and automated controls.[61] These capabilities would

60. There is no such pod on the Delta III, the Typhoon, or the Oscar, all of which overlapped the Victor III program. The pod's external configuration suggests a water jet propulsor, which would increase stealth when in close contact with the enemy. The absence of the pod would indicate a stand-off capability.

61. The hull strength that allows the Alpha to dive to great depths translates into resistance at

represent an enormous advance in hull and propulsion design, including a new type of reactor.

A family of five attack submarines, plus the Typhoon SSBN, the Kirov heavy cruiser, and an aircraft carrier would need a large number of nuclear reactors. Unless the Soviets planned to build most classes at a rate of 1 unit a year, they would have needed to increase reactor production, perhaps by 50 percent, that is, from 20 to 30 reactors a year. It is possible that the original plan that stemmed from the 1967–68 decision period did not provide for an increase in reactor production. If that were so, allowing 8 reactors for the Typhoon and 6 for Oscar would leave only 6 reactors a year for the attack program, the same number as was available in the sparse years of the 1968–77 delivery period.

If that were the attack submarine program approved at the Twenty-fourth Party Congress in the spring of 1971, it would explain why Gorshkov focused on the effects of naval blockade on the outcome of wars and devoted so much space to discussing the feasibility of disrupting sea communications, which led to his conclusion that success depended on the availability of sufficient submarine forces at the outset of the campaign. It is therefore possible that the original attack submarine building program as authorized at the Twenty-fourth Party Congress in 1971 did not meet the requirements for the next generation of attack submarines that have just been outlined. Rather the program was increased as the result of Gorshkov's demarche in 1971–72, with additional resources being allocated to allow additional type configurations and higher delivery rates. The idea of an out-of-plan increase is appealing, since its reversal in the second half of the 1970s would explain an apparent anomaly in the deliveries of this new family of attack submarines that began delivery in the 1983–84 period.

The 1976–77 Decision Period

As discussed in the final sections of chapters 3 and 5, in the 1976–77 period the Soviets probably reviewed the concept of gaining and maintaining command of the Norwegian Sea in order to turn the Arctic Ocean into an enclosed sea for the deployment of SSBNs. That process would be ex-

---

lesser depths to overpressure from underwater explosion, thereby increasing the submarine's survivability and its value as a combat unit. See Cortana Corporation, "Submarine Capabilities," pp. 19–22, 136, 139.

tremely costly because of the operations needed to seize key islands and stretches of coast and because of the naval and air forces needed to maintain command of the sea. The question also remained of whether it was operationally practicable to exclude Western SSNs from arctic waters.

Two kinds of evidence suggest that the Soviets moved away from this concept for reasons of practicality as well as cost-effectiveness. One kind is the buildup of military capabilities in the Pacific. For the navy the buildup involved a clear shift in resources from the Northern to the Pacific fleet, with a significant increase in the proportion of naval forces deployed in the Far East, including SSBNs. For the other branches of service, the buildup involved the strengthening of the air and land defenses of the Kurile Islands and a more intransigent attitude toward Japanese claims on the southernmost ones. That evidence is reviewed in chapter 8.

The other kind of evidence comes from the naval building programs that have not run true to pattern, either in terms of what would be expected from the shipbuilding evidence or in terms of what the 1967–68 operational requirements would predict. There is the specific evidence that the Typhoon program is building at a rate that is barely half what might be expected. There is also indirect shipbuilding evidence.

The Surface Programs

Two new construction programs of ships that had been specifically designed to support the new concept of operations in the Norwegian Sea were almost certainly canceled. The delivery date of the lead ships implied that these newly designed units stemmed from the 1967–68 decision period, and there was every reason to suppose that they were intended for series production. However, in one case only 2 units were built (with a five-year gap between them), and in the other case only 1 was built.

AMPHIBIOUS ASSAULT. The Ivan Rogov class of landing ship was three times the size and had three times the range of existing amphibious assault ships and was 40 percent faster. It could carry a battalion of naval infantry and 20 tanks plus support vehicles. This long-range, large-capacity, high-speed lift was not required for operations within the fleet areas, where the smaller Ropuchka class offered the advantages of flexibility and tactical dispersion. It was, however, the kind of lift that would be needed to seize distant islands and stretches of coast in the Norwegian Sea. The Ivan Rogov was built at Kaliningrad, where the Alligator class of landing ship had been built, and in 1979 U.S. naval intelligence assumed it was in series

construction.[62] The first Rogov was delivered in 1978, but the second one
not until 1983. This hiatus cannot be explained by design defects, since
the Soviets normally press ahead with production, making corrections retrospectively. In the light of established shipbuilding practice, one must
assume that this program was canceled.

UNDER WAY REPLENISHMENT. The 35,000-ton Berezina under way replenishment ship was built at 61 Kommuna, Nikolaev; it was laid down in
1973, launched in 1975, and delivered in in 1978. It had a 50 percent
increase in speed and range over its predecessor, the Boris Chilikin, and
could carry 25 percent more stores. This heavily armed unit was the first
under way replenishment ship to have been designed for the role; U.S.
naval intelligence referred to it as the first of its class,[63] yet only one was
built. The anomaly becomes more significant when operational factors are
considered.

The most important feature of under way replenishment is that it allows
the force to maneuver in combat formation. It is therefore an essential
capability when operating in wartime in a hostile environment, but in other
circumstances it is a convenience rather than a necessity. For that reason
the Soviet navy did not invest in an under way replenishment capability
before 1967, since forward-deployed units were operating under "the protection of peace" and could rely on improvised methods of replenishment.
After 1967 a new requirement arose for general purpose forces to establish
command of the sea approaches to SSBN operating areas, particularly the
Norwegian Sea. Maintaining surface forces in such a hostile environment
would require under way replenishment.

The Berezina's predecessor, the Boris Chilikin class, of which 6 units
were delivered in the 1971–78 period, was probably the interim response
to this requirement. The Chilikin was an adaptation of the Velikiy Oktyabr'
class of commercial tanker, which was already being built at Baltic Yard,
Leningrad, the lead ship having been delivered in 1968. The Chilikins
were originally fitted with twin 57-mm dual-purpose mountings, but these
guns were deactivated about 1976–77. The Berezina was much more heavily armed, and besides the guns, carried a SAM system, Gatlings, hull-

62. Statement of Rear Admiral Sumner Shapiro, Director of Naval Intelligence, Office of the
Chief of Naval Operations, *Hearings on Military Posture,* Department of Defense Authorization
for Appropriations for Fiscal Year 1980, before the House Committee on Armed Services, 96
Cong. 1 sess. (GPO, 1979), pt. 4, p. 24. The construction of the Udaloy class at Kaliningrad is
likely to be a result of the Rogov's cancellation and not the reason for it.

63. Ibid., p. 23.

mounted sonar and ASW weapons, and 2 Hormone helicopters. As such, it was a full-fledged warship, and given its designed role, a single copy did not make operational sense. Nor does one ship accord with Soviet warship-building practice. The cancellation of this program and the disarming of the Chilikins at about the same period suggest a change in operational requirements.

THE AIRCRAFT CARRIER. Besides this strong evidence that the Berezina and Rogov programs were canceled, there may also have been a change of plan concerning the characteristics of the aircraft carrier at about this time. As noted earlier, in 1979 the U.S. Navy believed it had good evidence that an aircraft carrier was to be built at Severodvinsk. It is now, however, absolutely clear that an air-capable ship is being built in Nikolaev in the Black Sea, and its characteristics appear to be that of a universal ship, which combines the capabilities of the Kirov and a much enlarged Kiev in a single hull.

The evidence of a change in policy regarding this ship is far more tenuous than in the case of the Brezina or the Rogov. U.S. naval intelligence could have been wrong in its conclusion that construction had been planned in the north. But even if it was right, the Soviets may always have intended to build a universal ship rather than a U.S.-style CTOL carrier, and only shifted the venue because of problems to do with building ships in the harsh northern climate. Nikolaev is obviously not the ideal place to build this ship, since there is no slipway long enough to take it and it has to be built in two halves, which are joined together after launching.

On the other hand, some anomalies could be explained by a major change of plan. One is the excessive lead time of this new air-capable ship, which was not laid down until 1983 and will not enter service before the end of the decade. That will be more than twenty years after the decision to build the Kiev as an interim solution to the command-of-the-sea problem. Another anomaly is the slowdown in the Kiev program that took place sometime in the 1977–80 period, which resulted in the third unit taking almost one and a half times as long to build as the first, and in both the third and fourth units spending 30 percent more time on the building ways than did the first two.[64]

A third development that occurred at about the same time as the various

---

64. *Jane's Fighting Ships, 1984–85*, p. 517. The time (in months) spent on the building way and fitting out was as follows: Kiev I, 27 + 29 = 56; Kiev II, 32 + 30 = 62; Kiev III, 39 + 44 = 83; and Kiev IV, 40 + 32 = 72.

other changes was the redesignation in 1978 of the Kiev class as a heavy aviation cruiser,[65] whereas previously it had been classified as an antisubmarine cruiser, as was the Moskva class, which continues as such. This change may have been just part of a broader reclassification that took place at about this time, but it could also have been the echo of a decision to build the universal ship at Nikolaev. The idea would have been to bypass the legalistic argument that the Montreaux Convention does not permit the passage of carriers through the Turkish Straits[66] by establishing the precedent that the Kiev was an air-capable cruiser. The new ship would be an air-capable battleship, which is clearly allowed passage by the terms of the convention.

The Submarine Programs

The unexpectedly slow delivery of Typhoon has already been mentioned, but equally relevant is the delivery rate of Oscar, which appears to be running at only one-third of what was planned. The Oscar SSGN would be a key player in the battle for the Norwegian Sea, and the slowing down of that program fits well with the other evidence that establishing command of that sea area is no longer a priority mission. Curtailment of the Oscar program would also explain why the Soviets are going to the expense of upgrading the twenty-year old Echo II (delivered 1963–67) to carry the improved SS-N-12 SSM system.

One must assess the series construction of a further Delta-sized SSBN against this general background, since the decision to build this new class is likely to have stemmed from the 1976–77 period.[67] If the Soviets had decided to move away from the concept of an arctic bastion, they would have to place greater emphasis on protecting the SSBNs by concealment and dispersion, in which case the Typhoon's massive size could be a disadvantage. The concentration of cost in a single vehicle might also have become an issue, and the concept of Typhoon as a general purpose combat unit could have been challenged in the more general argument about the navy's role in phase II of a world war.

In the light of these issues, General Secretary Leonid I. Brezhnev's pro-

65. *Tyazhelyy Aviatsionnyy Kreyser.* The term avoids *avianosnyy,* the basis of the Russian word for an aircraft carrier.

66. See, for example, Captain V. Serkov, "Legal Regime of the Black Sea Straits," *Msb* 76/7/83–86.

67. Two units of this new class were launched between the spring of 1984 and the spring of 1985, and it is currently referred to as Delta IV. *SMP, 1985,* p. 32.

posals for mutual limitations on Typhoon and Trident assume particular significance. At the Twenty-sixth Party Congress, in February 1981, he floated the idea that their deployment, or development, should be limited.[68] And in the fall of 1982, at the strategic arms reduction talks (START), the Soviets proposed that the number of these large SSBNs should be limited to 4 to 6 units. (At the date of the Soviet proposal, a total of 6 Ohio-class SSBNs were operational or under construction. The seventh unit was not laid down until March 1983.)

It is therefore possible that the Soviets decided to curtail the Typhoon program and make do with a combination of Typhoon and Delta. The Delta III carries missiles with MIRVs, which are most useful against preplanned targets and are therefore likely to be used in the initial nuclear exchange. If the Soviet START proposals of 400 MIRVed SLBMs are taken as a possible ceiling, the Soviets might have decided to build only 4 Typhoons and to add 6 Delta IVs to the existing 14 Delta IIIs.[69] If so, the rescission would probably stem from the 1976–77 decision period and could have been justified by the changed concept of operations and the reduced importance of the SSBN bastions in the Arctic. But the decision could also have been influenced by the serious shortfall in the planned production of civilian nuclear reactors that became apparent about this period.[70]

In addition to the anomalies in the Oscar SSGN and Typhoon programs, the delivery of the new family of 8,000-ton to 10,000-ton attack submarines appears to be running more slowly than one would expect. The lead unit of each class seems to have appeared on schedule, but an annual building rate of 2 of each type would have resulted in an additional 4 Mikes and 4 Sierras being delivered by mid-1985. There is no indication that they were. The explanation that Mike and Sierra are development prototypes is not plausible because of the maturity of Soviet nuclear submarine programs, the obvious shortage of modern attack submarines, and the Soviets' past readiness to move ahead with series production of relatively new de-

68. *XXVI s'ezd kommunisticheskoy partii Sovetskogo Soyuza: Stenograficheskiy otchet* (The twenty-sixth congress of the Communist party of the Soviet Union: Stenographic report), vol. 1 (Moscow: Politizdat, 1981), p. 47. The exact meaning of the proposal was ambiguous, since *razvertivanie* can mean both deployment and development.

69. In 1985 U.S. official sources said that 3 Typhoons had been built and 3 or 4 more were probably under construction. *SMP, 1985*, p. 31. However, it is unlikely that more than 2 units would be visible fitting out alongside, and the number inside the construction halls is largely a matter of conjecture. There are 320 MIRVed missiles aboard Delta hulls and 80 aboard Typhoon hulls.

70. See Lesley J. Fox, "Soviet Policy in the Development of Nuclear Power in Eastern Europe," in Joint Economic Committee, *Soviet Economy in the 1980s: Problems and Prospects, Selected Papers*, 97 Cong. 2 sess. (GPO, 1983), pt. 1, pp. 473, 480–81.

signs.[71] In the light of past experience, the most likely explanation for the anomaly is the availability of nuclear reactors.

If one assumes that the Mike, Sierra, and Akula were originally planned for series production with deliveries starting in 1983 (according to the established pattern), then by 1973 (at the latest) the projected nuclear-powered naval building program would have comprised five classes of submarines (including the Oscar and Typhoon) and two surface classes (the Kirov and the carrier). This program could not have been sustained by the existing allocation of 20 reactors a year; it therefore seems likely that the Soviets planned to increase the production of naval reactors. This is a reasonable assumption, given the very large increase that was planned at this period for civilian reactor production,[72] and a 50 percent increase in the existing naval allocation would have yielded 30 reactors a year. If there is now some holdup in the construction of the new family of attack submarines, despite the slowdown in Typhoon and Oscar construction, it may be that the increase was rescinded and that the constraint of 20 reactors a year continues to apply, but with certain complications.

If one works on that assumption, the following explanation covering the 1983–87 delivery period would account for the fragmentary evidence that is now available. In the 1978–82 delivery period, the annual quota of 20 units had divided between eight 1968-vintage reactors and twelve 1973-vintage units. The new requirement to increase reactor deliveries was met by raising the output of both these production lines by 50 percent, the 1968 model being replaced by a significantly improved 1983 model. The original plan for the 1983–87 delivery period stipulated that the 1973 model would continue to power the Oscar and Typhoon programs (14 a year), the remainder (20 reactors over five years) being used in 2 Kirovs and the first 2 of the new carriers.[73] The 1983 model (12 a year) would power 2 each of the 3 new 8,000-ton to 10,000-ton attack classes (table B-2).

The response to the rescission of the increase in the allocation of reac-

71. One would, however, expect these lead units to be operated as if they were prototypes, even if they had not been intended as such, in order to reap the benefits of improving the original design before full production got under way.

72. Robert Weinland pointed out to me that this increase included the construction of the heavy machine building plant *Atommash* for the production of 1,000-MWe reactors on an assembly-line basis. See Fox, "Soviet Policy in the Development of Nuclear Power," p. 473.

73. The third Kirov was laid down in late 1982, which allowed a fourth to be laid down in late 1985. The first carrier was laid down in January 1983 ("Satellite Pictures Show Soviet CNV," *Jane's Defence Weekly,* August 11, 1984, p. 171) and is expected to be launched by mid-1986, when a second unit could be laid down. Richard Halloran, "Soviets Speeding a Big Carrier," *New York Times,* May 10, 1984. It is assumed that these carriers will have 8 reactors each, as did the U.S.S. *Enterprise,* but this assumption is not critical to the argument.

Table B-2. *Planned Delivery of Nuclear-Powered Warships: Effects of a Decision in 1973–74 to Increase the Allocation of Reactors by 50 Percent, Followed by a Decision in 1976–77 to Rescind the Increase*

| | | Number of hulls planned for delivery | | |
| | | 1973–74 decision to increase allocation | 1976–77 decision to rescind the increase | |
Class of warship	Reactors per hull	1983–87	1983–87	1988–92
Typhoon	4	10	1–2	
Oscar	2	15	1–2	
Kirov	2	2	4[a]	
New Carrier	8	2	3	
Total 1973 reactors		90	38–52[b]	
Delta IV	2	. . .	6	. . .
Akula	2	10	10	10
Sierra	2	10	10	10
Mike	2	10	16	25
Uniform	2	. . .	. . .	5
Total 1983 reactors[c]		60	84[d]	100

a. Kirov might be fitted with 4 reactors if they were available.
b. These would comprise 4 reactors not used in the 1978–82 delivery period and pipeline inertia of the original 1983–87 allocation of 18 reactors a year.
c. The 1983 model replaced the 1968 model in the reactor production process.
d. These would comprise 12 a year for the period 1983–84 and 20 a year for the period 1985–87.

tors to naval propulsion was to persist in the planned production of twelve 1983 models a year, but to cut back the output of the other line to eight a year and rejig it to produce the 1983 model. The new models from that line would not, however, be available in time for fitting in submarines scheduled for delivery in the first two years of the 1983–87 period, and perhaps even longer. Twelve reactors a year would still have allowed the production of the three new attack classes, each at two a year, except that the revised plan required the construction of 6 Delta IVs, which would need to be powered by the 1983-model reactors.[74] As a result, there were only enough reactors during the first two years of the period to build the Akula as planned at 2 a year and the lead ships of the Mike and Sierra.

If this reconstruction is correct, and if the overall naval allocation has

74. There are obvious operational attractions to fitting the 1983 reactor model in these units, but there may also have been technical reasons why the 1973 model could not be fitted in the Yankee-Delta hull. Both Yankees and Deltas were powered by the 1968 model.

not dropped below 20 reactors a year, then the hiatus in Mike and Sierra construction would be only temporary, and the plans for these submarines would probably be backfilled as soon as the 1983-model reactors became available from the other facilities. Furthermore, one would expect the production rate of the antisurface type (assumed to be the Mike) to increase sharply. In part this increase would be to compensate for the Oscar SSGN (assuming that program has been curtailed), and in part to correct the gross imbalance between the SSNs and SSGNs that emerged in the 1968–83 period, when 47 SSNs were delivered but only 18 SSGNs, 17 of them with single reactors. If the other reactor source became available for deliveries starting in 1985, the 1983–87 period could see the construction of 10 Akulas, 10 Sierras, and 16 Mikes, plus 6 Delta IVs.

The estimate assumes that the requirement for 1973-model reactors to power the Kirovs and aircraft carriers in the 1983–92 period (estimated at 32 or 40 reactors) will have been covered by the deliveries from those production facilities before their rejigging to produce the 1983 model. Whether that is so will depend on the answer to the following questions: How many Typhoons and Oscars will be built and hence how many reactors will be left over from the 1978–82 account? How far advanced was the process of increasing reactor production capacity at the time of the policy reversal, and had the facilities for 1973-model production started building reactors at the higher rate of 18 a year by then? Assuming that the full allocation of 20 reactors a year will be available for submarine production in the 1988–92 period, annual deliveries might be composed of 2 Akula IIs, 2 Sierra IIs, 5 Mike IIs, and 1 high-performance Uniform.

Overview

Although considerable uncertainty exists as to exactly what was decided in the second half of the 1970s and why it was decided, there is sufficient evidence to indicate that major changes to existing plans did take place at that period, including the cancellation of some programs and the slowing down of others. This was the same period in which the Soviet navy lost its bid for greater doctrinal autonomy, and in which the U.S. Navy was being shaped for a reduced strength of only 12 carrier battle groups. It was also a period when the Soviets considered that détente was irreversible.

These developments occurred at the same time that Dmitriy F. Ustinov became minister of defense and Nikolay V. Ogarkov became chief of the General Staff. One cannot know whether there was some causal relationship here, or whether the changes came about through a routine process of reevaluating long-range plans when their implications had had time to emerge. There is, however, little doubt that certain decisions were taken at this period that had a fundamental effect on naval programs. Without more concrete information, 1976–77 is a reasonable estimate of the decision period, which can be confirmed or refined as more evidence accumulates.

The evidence already available supports the assessment that at this period the Soviets downgraded the importance of the Arctic Ocean as a safe haven for SSBNs and in consequence discarded the requirement to establish command of the Norwegian Sea in phase I of a world war. Having done so does not mean that they were prepared to concede command to the West, and the modified mission would be to deny command to the enemy. That mission would be much less costly in terms of forces and the ground-air operations required in support, yet it would be a sufficient response to the more limited requirement to provide for the security of the smaller proportion of SSBNs that will now be sheltering in northern waters.

This analysis has focused on decisions stemming from the 1976–77 period. Of course, further changes may have been made in response to subsequent decisions. In this respect, the collapse of arms control negotiations in the 1979–83 period is of particular relevance, as is the possible decision period of 1983–85 that is discussed in chapter 13. The decisions taken in the 1976–77 period were reached at a time when détente was still considered irreversible and when it looked as if the U.S. Navy would stabilize at 12 carrier battle groups. It is therefore possible that the breakdown of détente and the resurgence of U.S. naval power may have caused the Soviet leaders to reassess the conclusions they reached in 1976–77. The allocation of reactors to new naval construction would be included in such a reassessment.

The Debate over Naval Roles and Missions

THE RESTRUCTURING of Soviet objectives that stemmed from the doctrinal decision in December 1966 generated a major internal debate about the consequential strategic and operational concepts and the roles and missions of the five branches of service.[1] Although the 1967–68 decision period resulted in a substantial increase in the resources that would be allocated to warship construction, in late 1970 the navy was apparently still unhappy with the provisions of the Ninth Five-Year Plan, which was due for approval at the Twenty-fourth Party Congress in the spring of 1971.[2] In February 1972 the first of a series of eleven articles entitled "Navies in War and Peace" was published in *Morskoy sbornik* under the name of Fleet Admiral Sergey G. Gorshkov.[3]

This was the first time in fifty years of military publication that a commander in chief had captured his own professional journal for such a sustained exposition of the role of his branch of service.[4] Coming from such

1. John Erickson, "Soviet Defense Policies and Naval Interests," in Michael MccGwire, Ken Booth, and John McDonnell, eds., *Soviet Naval Policy: Objectives and Constraints* (Praeger, 1975), pp. 60–61.
2. See A. A. Grechko, "Prikaz ministra oborony CCCP" (Order of the defense minister of the USSR), *Pravda,* February 23, 1971; V. M. Zakharov, *Sovietskaya Rossiya,* January 19, 1971; and A. G. Kavtaradze, *History of the USSR,* November–December 1970 issue, cited in Robert W. Herrick, "Gorshkov Announces Soviet Naval Expansion to Continue and Advocates Urgent Construction of 'A Navy without Equal,'" Working Paper 651-73 (Arlington, Va., Center for Naval Analyses, 1973), pp. 36–38.
3. Sergey G. Gorshkov, "Voenno-morskie floty v voynakh i v mirnoe vremya" (Navies in war and peace), *Morskoy sbornik* (Naval journal), no. 2 (February 1972). Hereafter references will read *Msb* year/month/page/paragraph (as appropriate); reference may be given in text. The article by N. Aleshkin, "Nekotorye tendentsii razvitiya voenno-morskikh sil" (Certain tendencies in the development of naval forces), *Msb* 72/1/24–30, was probably a precursor to the series, even though it was explicitly based on material from foreign sources.
4. Erickson, "Soviet Defense Policies," p. 60.

a source, the substance of the articles was obviously important to Western analysts, but a prior and more critical question was that of authoritativeness. Was the Gorshkov series a concrete expression of doctrine, announcing an officially accepted body of views? Or was it an exercise in advocacy, arguing that the role of the navy in the 1970s concept of operations was being gravely undervalued by the army-dominated military leadership?

In hindsight it is clear that the primary objective of the series was advocacy, to draw on historical examples to demonstrate the crucial role played by navies in determining the outcome of war, particularly when the opponent was a maritime power. At the time, however, the objective was less clear-cut, and there was major disagreement on the issue among Western analysts, a disagreement that was never finally resolved. The question of authoritativeness is, however, critical to any analysis of Soviet plans for the contingency of world war.

In the first half of this appendix, I concentrate on resolving that question, starting with the empirical evidence that the Gorshkov articles were an exercise in advocacy. In the second half, I summarize the substance of the articles in so far as it is relevant to this study and describe the continuing debate and the reassertion of General Staff control over the development of strategic concepts by the end of the 1970s.

My focus here is on the naval debate which was, however, taking place in a much broader context. This appendix should therefore be read in conjunction with chapter 5, which provides the naval overview, and the relevant sections of chapters 9 and 10, which provide parts of the larger picture.

The Gorshkov Series: An Exercise in Advocacy

Many Western specialists analyzed the Gorshkov series in the 1973–75 period, and most concluded that the articles were an exercise in naval advocacy.[5] They based their views on the style and substance of the series as well as the thrust of the arguments. Gorshkov was contending that navies had an essential role to play in peace and war, that Russia had always suffered when it neglected its naval strength, and that the Soviet Union

---

5. See analyses by Robert G. Weinland, James M. McConnell, and Michael MccGwire in *Admiral Gorshkov on "Navies in War and Peace," CRC 257* (Arlington, Va.: Center for Naval Analyses, 1974). Robert Herrick's perceptive analysis can be found in his "Gorshkov Announces Soviet Naval Expansion."

needed a powerful fleet. Within a few years after the series appeared, there was sufficient empirical evidence to confirm this initial judgment that "Navies in War and Peace" was an important exercise in naval advocacy and not a doctrinal pronouncement. But still not fully clear were the details of what Gorshkov was arguing for and against, and the reasons that had prompted the unprecedented publication of the series.

Publication Anomalies

Much of the evidence that Gorshkov was involved in a major dispute derived from the journal itself. Robert Weinland was the first to draw attention to various aspects of the publication process that argued against the series being a doctrinal statement. These ranged from anomalies in publication dates to the fact that the articles were published without fanfare. Apart from a rather defensive fifty-word editor's introduction to the first installment, *Morskoy sbornik* made no reference to the series in the course of its publication, and its placement within the "lead articles" section varied widely but was never higher than third. (Placement ranged between 3d and 10th and averaged 4.7.) There was no advance notice of the series in *Morskoy sbornik*, nor was it discussed during the period in any of the other major organs of the Soviet military press.[6]

John McDonnell followed up on this initial analysis, going deeper into the question of publication anomalies.[7] All Soviet publications show the dates they were "set in type" and subsequently "released to the press." The period in between is taken up in part by the censorship process, since galley proofs must be approved for publication. McDonnell compared the gap between those two dates (which he labeled "censor days") for the 156 issues of *Morskoy sbornik* from 1963 through 1975 to identify the extent to which it was constant over time. He concluded that there was considerable consistency and in the thirteen-year period could find only two clear-cut examples of a series of three or more issues being substantially delayed by the censor. The first of these "deviant series" (covering four issues) could be tied to the Twenty-third Party Congress in 1966.[8] The second deviant

6. Weinland, "Navies in War and Peace," in *Admiral Gorshkov,* pp. 9–14.

7. John A. McDonnell, *Content Analysis of Soviet Naval Writings* (Halifax, Nova Scotia: Dalhousie University, 1977).

8. The March and May issues were eleven days later than trend; the June and July issues thirteen days later. The May issue carried Gorshkov's "report" on the Congress and the July issue covered Navy Day.

series, involving eight issues, started after the fifth article of the Gorshkov series and continued through the final one, seven issues later.

Besides this specific series of delays, the proportion of censor days that were four or more days later than trend almost doubled in the wake of the Gorshkov articles,[9] suggesting a heightened sensitivity to the political acceptability of the journal's contents. There were also two publication anomalies of a different kind. One was the break in the Gorshkov series in July, the same month that censorship delays began.[10] The other was the one-month gap before the final article appeared in February. The latter raised the possibility that the series was originally planned to comprise the first ten articles only, which made up a coherent whole that was stylistically consistent. The tenth article deployed a powerful argument in support of the Soviet navy's forward deployment in peacetime, and its final section read like a summing up of the series.[11] In contrast, the eleventh article consisted of two separate chapters that were not only very different from each other but differed greatly from the previous ten articles in style, content, and structure of argument.[12]

The Journal's Editorial Board

McDonnell also discovered that *Morskoy sbornik's* editorial board underwent unprecedented turbulence during and after the publication of the Gorshkov articles.[13] The composition of the board, consisting of fifteen to twenty people, was usually quite stable; the first major change in at least six years, including the appointment of a new chief editor, oc-

9. The proportion was 32 percent after the series and 15.5 percent before. This understates the change because there was a lull between the end of the Gorshkov series and the appointment of a new chief editor in February 1974, after which the proportion of "late" issues rose to 40 percent.

10. The July issue did carry an article by Gorshkov on the role of a ship's commanding officer, which had every appearance of being a filler.

11. The tenth article was called "Navies as an Instrument of the Aggressive Policy of the Imperialist States in Peacetime." There was an asterisk break toward the end of the article (the first such break in the ten articles), followed by what could be read as a summing up of the argument of the whole series. The only other asterisk break appeared at the end of the eleventh article and was followed by a 520-word conclusion. Those 520 words would, if anything, fit rather better at the end of the tenth article and would still come within the average length.

12. Forty percent of the final article addressed ocean resource and law-of-the-sea questions. Clearly written by a different author it was irrelevant to the main thrust of the Gorshkov series. About 52 percent of the article consisted of a general review of the Soviet navy's contemporary situation, followed by a brief conclusion.

13. McDonnell, *Content Analysis,* pp. 20–26.

curred at the end of 1969.[14] A year later the Military Council of the navy expressed general satisfaction with the journal's improvement, but within eighteen months the board underwent another big change (*Msb* 71/2/ 33–34).

In June 1972 two members who had served less than thirty months left and five new members joined, including two full admirals, the only instance in which such rank had served on the board.[15] The singularity of this development was highlighted by a further change in May 1974, when eleven members of the board were dropped and ten added. Those dropped included four of the five who had joined in June 1972, the two full admirals among them. Besides these changes to the board, a wholesale turnover of editorial officers took place between the end of 1972 and early 1974 despite the favorable reviews of the journal in early 1971 and 1973.[16]

One cannot be certain just what this turbulence implied, but it is significant that in the nine years before the Gorshkov series, there were only twenty-two changes to the board (including the major revamping at the end of 1969), whereas in the next four years there were forty changes (additions, departures, promotions, and demotions). In other words, the average rate of change jumped from 2.4 to 10.0 changes a year, and this understates the real difference, since the membership of the board stabilized after May 1974.[17] The strengthening of the board in June 1972, including the unprecedented appointment of two full admirals, coincided with the start of the censorship delays,[18] suggesting demonstration of naval solidarity. The large turnover in May 1974 coincided with other indications that a compromise had been reached, as discussed later. But whatever their exact meaning, these unprecedented board changes suggest some kind of conflict over matters of political importance.

14. *Morskoy sbornik* first became available to the public in January 1963. The first major change thereafter occurred at the end of 1969, when a new chief editor was appointed and six board members were dropped and eight added. McDonnell concluded that this change was more likely to have been a shakeup than a routine turnover because of the dissatisfaction implied in the article "About the Journal *Morskoy sbornik*," in *Msb* 71/2/33–34.

15. There was also a vice admiral, who was chief of the Political Department of the Main Naval Staff, and two rear admirals, one of them first deputy chief of the Political Administration of the Navy. McDonnell, *Content Analysis*, p. 24.

16. Ibid, pp. 24–26. The chief editorship changed February 1974, the "political" deputy in July 1973, and the "regular" deputy December 1972 and June 1974. The favorable reviews were by the Military Council and by the chief of the Main Naval Staff.

17. Of the fifteen regular board members in May 1974, eight were still serving in June 1980 and six in March 1985.

18. The July issue went to the censor about May 20. The June issue was released to the press about May 27, at which stage the table of contents (which lists the editorial board) would have been made up.

The Empirical Account

The empirical evidence developed by McDonnell and Weinland can be summarized as follows. The unprecedented publication of a series of articles by the commander in chief of the Soviet navy on the importance of the navy's role in war and peace coincided with a series of unprecedented (or extremely rare) events to do with the publication and management of the journal in which the articles were appearing. These events started occurring after the appearance of the third article, when the scope and thrust of the series were becoming apparent. They included a consistent pattern of delays in clearing the journal for publication; two unexplained breaks in the series, one coinciding with the start of the censor delays and the other preceding the final article; and two major changes to the membership of the journal's editorial board, as well as the wholesale replacement of its senior editorial staff.

These events suggest a major disagreement between the naval leadership and the army-dominated military leadership over the role of the Soviet navy in peace and war. They are not consistent with the use of the articles to announce an officially accepted body of doctrine; rather they are consistent with the presentation of controversial views. Admiral Sergeyev almost said as much in his article in the issue of *Morskoy sbornik* that followed the last of the Gorshkov series, where he stressed that the journal must be allowed to discuss matters of current controversy.[19]

Other evidence of an internal debate was provided by the announcement in April 1973 of a series of theoretical articles to be published in *Red Star* (the official organ of the Ministry of Defense) under the general title "The Defense of Socialism: Questions of Theory." The two articles that appeared did not address Gorshkov's arguments directly, but both took issue with some aspect of what he said.[20] Then the series ceased without any expla-

19. Fleet Admiral N. Sergeyev, "Drug i sovetchik ofitserov flota" (Friend and adviser of the naval officer), *Msb* 73/3/17/3, 19/4–5 (noted by McDonnell). Sergeyev was then chief of the Main Naval Staff. The article, which marked the 125th anniversary of the founding of *Morskoy sbornik*, was complimentary and supportive of the role the journal had played in increasing the professionalism of Soviet naval officers. Although he made some minor criticisms, Sergeyev reaffirmed the generally favorable opinion advanced by the Military Council in 1971.

20. Zav'yalov stressed the primacy of political factors and that the fundamentally political content of military doctrine remained unchanged (compare with Gorshkov, *Msb* 72/2/20/5; 72/4/13/10, 14/4, 15/7). Milovidov emphasized that one could *not* take examples from one historical period to support arguments in the contemporary period, the method that was the explicit basis of Gorshkov's analysis (*Msb* 72/2/23/2,5). General-Lieutenant I. Zav'yalov, "The Creative Nature of Soviet Military Doctrine," in Foreign Broadcast Information Service, *Daily Report: Soviet Union,*

nation.[21] This breakoff coincided with the temporary lifting of censorship delays on *Morskoy sbornik* and had the appearance of an imposed truce, which may have been connected with the appointment of Marshal Grechko to the Politburo in late April.[22]

The Broader Picture

The conclusion that the Gorshkov series was an exercise in advocacy becomes overwhelming when this detailed analysis is placed within the larger picture. As noted earlier, by the end of 1970 there were indications that the navy was dissatisfied with the allocation of resources in the Ninth Five-Year Plan. After the Twenty-fourth Party Congress, which approved the plan in March 1971, there was no article by Gorshkov in *Morskoy sbornik* reporting on the proceedings of the Congress (there had been one in May 1966), but an article by Marshal Grechko appeared in the July (Navy Day) issue.[23] It was unusual for the minister of defense to fill this slot, but more important, the tone and substance of Grechko's article read very differently from Gorshkov's subsequent arguments.

Further evidence that the two men had divergent views was provided by Grechko's 1971 booklet, "On Guard for Peace and Building Communism," which emphasized combat readiness and discussed the Soviet Union's international commitments only in regard to other socialist states.[24] This position was poles apart from Gorshkov's argument for an assertive overseas policy based on military power and for the navy's unique qualifications as an instrument of state policy in peacetime.

So much for the immediate evidence that the naval leadership was involved in an important bureaucratic struggle in the 1971–73 period. By

---

April 24, 1973, pp. M1–7. (Hereafter FBIS, *Daily Report: SU.*); and Major-General A. Milovidov, "A Philosophical Analysis of Military Thought," in FBIS, *Daily Report: SU,* May 23, 1973, pp. M1–6. The planned series was announced on April 19.

21. No article of this type was published in June, but on July 4, without any form of announcement, a new but unrelated series began under the title "Theory, Politics, Ideology."

22. Grechko was minister of defense, but this was the first time since Marshal G. K. Zhukov's ouster in 1957 that a professional military officer was coopted on to the highest party body. Andrey Gromyko (Foreign Affairs) and Yuri V. Andropov (KGB) joined the Politburo at the same time.

23. A. A. Grechko, "The Fleet of Our Homeland," *Morskoy sbornik,* no. 7 (July 1971), in FBIS, *Daily Report: SU,* August 11, 1971, pp. M1–6.

24. A. A. Grechko, *Na strazhe mira i stroitel'stva kommunizma* (On guard for peace and building communism) (Moscow: Voenizdat, 1971).

mid-1974 a compromise appears to have been reached, biased in the navy's favor.[25] In an article published in May, Grechko acknowledged that the "historic function of the Soviet armed forces is not restricted merely to . . . defending our motherland and the other socialist states" and that their external function had now been expanded and "enriched with new content."[26] This statement brought him into line with the policies endorsed by the Twenty-fourth Party Congress.[27]

In July Gorshkov acknowledged that the main naval mission in war would be operations against targets on land rather than combat against the enemy fleet.[28] He thus accepted the formal priority of missions that the military leadership appeared to have been trying to enforce since the 1967–68 period.[29] Nevertheless, the Soviet leadership had approved a significant increase in the future allocation of resources to the navy and authorized the preparation of a book by Gorshkov, which would be called *Seapower of the State*. This book would have to reflect the political interests of those involved in the wider-ranging debate that had prompted, and enabled, the publication of the Gorshkov series.

25. It is possible that the retirement of Kasatanov at the early age (by Russian standards) of sixty-four may have been part of the price exacted by Grechko. Kasatanov (a submariner) could be seen as Gorshkov's most trusted lieutenant and may have provided the seapower thrust to the naval leadership. See MccGwire, "Advocacy of Seapower in an Internal Debate," in *Admiral Gorshkov*, p. 55, note 1.

26. A. A. Grechko, "The Leading Role of the CPSU in Building the Army of a Developed Socialist Society" in FBIS, *Daily Report: SU*, May 30, 1974, p. A10. Weinland compared this with earlier pronouncements, including a comparable article in *Kommunist*, May 1973, and concluded that there was a distinct shift in emphasis. Except for Gorshkov, the military leadership in general, and Grechko in particular, appeared reluctant to discuss, let alone embrace, the expanded "internationalist functions" of the Soviet armed forces endorsed by the Twenty-fourth Party Congress. Weinland, "Navies in War and Peace," p. 17.

27. McDonnell has noted that Grechko's 1974 article followed the same general line as that of A. A. Yepishev (former chief of the Main Political Administration of the Soviet Army and Navy), *Moguchee oruzhie partii: Nekotorye voprosy partiyno-politicheskoy raboty v armii i flote* (A mighty weapon of the party: Several aspects of party-political work in the army and navy) (Moscow: Voenizdat, 1973), which was released to the press at the end of 1972.

28. S. G. Gorshkov, "Morskaya moshch strany sovetov" (Soviet national seapower), *Pravda*, July 28, 1974.

29. The sentence, "Hence, the principal mission of our navy in a modern war will be to combat with enemy forces at sea and at their bases" was deleted from the chapter on the structuring of the armed forces in the third edition of Sokolovskiy's book on military strategy. See Harriet Fast Scott, ed. and trans., *Soviet Military Strategy*, 3d ed. (Crane, Russak, 1975), p. 254, and note 171. This deletion may have been one of the last-minute changes made to the book in the light of the December 1966 decision (see the section "The Early Cut-Off" in appendix A of this volume), and in any case it implied that the disagreement on mission priorities went back several years.

The "Announcement" Fallacy

The most plausible inference that could be drawn from the empirical evidence outlined here was that during 1970–74 the navy was involved in a major bureaucratic struggle within the defense establishment, with *Morskoy sbornik* becoming a focus for that struggle while the Gorshkov series was being published. When the empirical evidence was added to the evidence provided by the substance and tone of the articles, the argument that they were an exercise in advocacy became overwhelming. That explanation had the merit of being able to account for all the evidence, which was not true of the "announcement" hypothesis. But not only did that hypothesis fail as an explanation; there were also serious errors in the analysis that led to the explanation.

The announcement school of analysis considered that the Gorshkov series represented a "concrete expression of doctrine" and that its content reflected "a Soviet political decision to withhold a substantial portion of their submarine-launched ballistic missiles (SLBMs) from the initial strikes in order to carry out 'deterrence' in war, conduct intra-war bargaining and influence the peace talks at the end of the war." Previously, submarine missiles were "intended for the initial salvos," but now the SSBN force would be a "fleet in being," implementing a new Soviet "doctrine of conserving forces."[30]

One might wonder why the Soviet leadership would have thought it either appropriate or necessary to inform the navy at large of such a decision, particularly when the option was inherent in the characteristics of the weapons system. One might also wonder why Gorshkov would need to write 54,000 words in order to convey this rather simple information, and why he would then choose to express the message in such enigmatic terms that its meaning was hidden from the average reader. But beyond these commonsense questions and the failure to address the empirical evidence of a bureaucratic struggle, the more serious objection to the announcement

---

30. James M. McConnell, "Military-Political Tasks of the Soviet Navy in War and Peace," in Committee and National Ocean Policy Study, *Soviet Oceans Development,* 94 Cong. 2 sess. (Government Printing Office, 1976), pp. 183–84. McConnell was the leading exponent of this viewpoint. For a later iteration of his argument, see James McConnell, "The Gorshkov Articles, The New Gorshkov Book, and Their Relation to Policy," in Michael MccGwire and John McDonnell, eds., *Soviet Naval Influence: Domestic and Foreign Dimensions* (Praeger, 1977), pp. 565–620.

hypothesis was that the underlying analysis did not stand up to critical examination.

It is sufficient to summarize the failure of that analysis on three counts.[31] First, the constraints of geography and missile range meant that the vast majority of SLBMs could never have been intended for the initial strike, and therefore "withholding" was not something new. Second, the criteria established by the announcement school for identifying a doctrinal statement were not met by the Gorshkov articles. Third, the textual evidence advanced in support of the purported announcement turned out to be saying something quite different.

The Question of Novelty

There were several reasons for concluding that most of the Yankee nuclear-powered ballistic-missile submarine (SSBN) force had not been intended for the initial salvos. The range of the SS-N-6 (initially 1,350 nautical miles and then 1,600) meant that only those Yankees that were already deployed forward would be able to participate in such a strike. The pattern established by the end of the 1960s was of three or four Yankees on patrol within closing range of North America, meaning that in the most likely circumstances 90 percent of the Yankee force would have been physically unable to join in the initial strike.

It was theoretically possible that if the outbreak of war were preceded by a period of tension, the Soviets would deploy the remainder of the Yankees to within range of North America. But they had powerful reasons for not doing anything so foolish. Deploying the SSBN force in that way would be highly destabilizing, working directly against the objective of avoiding world war. And if war did come about, such deployment would also work against the objective of not losing, since this depended heavily on successful intercontinental preemption by land-based missiles. The deployment would endanger that success and would contribute nothing to the damage-limiting purposes of such a strike.

The Yankees, meanwhile, would be extremely vulnerable while in transit. Most of the forward-deployed SSBNs would probably be sunk at the onset of war and might even be attacked covertly before the war. The role of the Yankee force, however, was to match those elements of the West's sea-based strategic capability that might be withheld from the initial

---

31. For a detailed criticism, see Michael MccGwire, "Naval Power and Soviet Oceans Policy," in *Soviet Oceans Development,* appendixes B and C, pp. 167–82.

exchange. To be in a position to match, the Yankees had themselves to be held back from the initial exchange. They also had to survive Western attempts to draw down the force. This argued strongly against deploying the main body of SSBNs into the open ocean, at least until the West's antisubmarine warfare (ASW) capability had been severely degraded in the initial phase of the war.

In other words, the concept of withholding most submarine missiles and using them to influence the postexchange phase of a war was already firmly established by the end of the 1960s, when the Yankees entered service. The Deltas took on this role in due course, but their primary mission was to prevent such an exchange from occurring, by helping to deter America from striking at Russia when faced by defeat in Europe. What was new, then, in 1972 and 1973 was the concept of SSBNs being used to deter intercontinental escalation,[32] and not the established policy of withholding submarine missiles should such an exchange take place. The concept was part of the larger strategic shift from the 1960s concept of intercontinental nuclear preemption to the 1970s concept of conventional theater war and intercontinental deterrence.

The Question of Authoritativeness

The announcement school of analysis acknowledged that nowhere in the articles did Gorshkov unambiguously state that his work represented either doctrine or an expression of doctrine,[33] but it then went on to claim that the articles nevertheless met certain criteria that qualified them as "concrete expressions of doctrine." The articles did not, in fact, meet those criteria. One criterion was that doctrine covers the present or very near future and does not investigate the past. Yet more than 80 percent of the series was historical analysis, and Gorshkov was explicit about the historical basis of his argument.[34] Another criterion was the use of the doctrinal

32. This mission is specifically referred to in *Msb* 73/2/21/2–3. (The Gorshkov series was subsequently published in translation as *Red Star Rising at Sea,* trans. Theodore A. Neely, Jr., and ed. Col. Herbert Preston, USMC [United States Naval Institute Press, 1974]. References to that English version will hereafter follow the Russian citations, giving page/column/paragraph [after a colon], but the translation used here may not be identical to that in *Red Star Rising*.) See *Red Star Rising at Sea,* 131/1/2–3. The term used is "unleashing nuclear war." The reference clearly distinguishes between the existing capability of the Yankee force and the impending capability of the Delta-Typhoon force.

33. McConnell, "Military-Political Tasks," p. 191.

34. In his 1,500 word introductory section, Gorshkov referred to the relevance of history no less than nine times. McConnell tried to escape that fact by claiming that Gorshkov had explicitly

authenticator "unity of views." But the standard formula is to talk of such views as having already been "developed" and as "proceeding from the general tenets of Soviet military doctrine."[35] There were only two references to "unity of views" in the Gorshkov series. Both spoke of "fostering the development" of such views, and when read in full context, they have no sense of authoritativeness.[36]

Other evidence points in the same direction. The phrase "the will of the CPSU Central Committee" was linked only to the creation of an ocean-going fleet (and its forward deployment in one case),[37] established policy that Gorshkov was trying to preserve and promote. And, unlike the way most doctrinal pronouncements are treated, there was no "echo" of the purported announcement in other publications. The only echoes were of advocacy statements, and these only in naval publications. Final proof that the Gorshkov series was not a "concrete statement of doctrine" came in the reviews of Gorshkov's subsequent book, *Seapower of the State,* all of which stressed the work's contribution to military science, a category that excludes doctrine (see notes 83–85).

The Question of Evidence

Three claims central to the hypothesis of the announcement school of analysis could be inferred from its writings.

—Whenever Gorshkov used the word *oborona* (defense) in a contemporary naval context, he was referring to the role of the ballistic-missile

---

denied any intention of probing the past. This claim was based on the partial quotation of a paragraph that when read in its entirety made it clear what Gorshkov had really said, namely, that while he did not intend to cover the whole history of naval art, he was going to draw on various examples to illustrate his argument. See *Msb* 72/2/23/2:3/2/1.

35. See G. G. Gorshkov, "Bol'shie zadachi sovetskogo flota" (The great tasks of the Soviet navy), *Krasnaya zvezda,* February 5, 1963; and S. G. Gorshkov, "XXIII S'ezd KPCC i zadachi voennykh moryakov" (The twenty-third congress of the CPSU and the tasks of navy men), *Msb* 66/5/8.

36. One reference was in the eight-line editorial introduction to the series, where the "opinion" was advanced that publication of the articles would "foster the development . . . of a unity of views on the role of navies under various historical conditions." *Msb:* 72/2/20. The other reference was by Gorshkov and was even more tentative. *Msb* 72/2/23/2:3/2/1. Both emphasized the historical approach.

37. *Msb* 72/12/20/5:119/1/2; and 73/2/20/7–8:130/2/4. In the second case, a change of tense implied that the Central Committee did not value surface ships sufficiently. The third reference linked the Central Committee to strengthening the nation's defenses, "to increasing its sea power, and to the harmonious, balanced development of the forces of an ocean-going navy." *Msb* 73/2/25/2:134/2/6. The reference to "balanced" echoed the argument in the historical analysis for a balanced fleet.

submarine in deterring attacks from the sea, and their role as a strategic reserve in war.

—Gorshkov's articles indicated that the role of countering Western sea-based strategic delivery systems had been downgraded.

—His historical analyses emphasized the role of navies as a diplomatic instrument during a war and in subsequent peace negotiations.

THE USE OF *OBORONA*. The textual evidence did not support those claims. The most crucial claim for the announcement hypothesis was the linking of *oborona* with the role of the SSBNs. But the articles made only three unambiguous references to that role, and not one was linked to *oborona*. That word was used thirteen times in the last two articles, and in four cases the context yielded nothing. In eight cases the immediate context made it clear that the reference must at least have included general purpose forces, and in at least four of those the broader context made it unlikely that SSBNs were included. Only in one case was it possible to fudge a possible link between *oborona* and the SSBN role, and that at six paragraphs removed.[38]

A major error was to assume that when the navy was linked with the strategic forces, Gorshkov was talking of SSBNs, whereas careful analysis makes it clear that he was talking of general purpose naval forces.[39] In other words, the strategic rocket forces (SRF) in question were not intercontinental systems but regional ones, which could be targeted on the Eurasian periphery.[40] Gorshkov was not talking of the navy's wartime mission, but of the two tasks the navy had to discharge in peacetime: defense of the Soviet Union against attacks *from* the sea, and defense *on* the sea against imperialist aggression. These involved countering Western naval strike forces, deterring imperialistic aggression in distant sea areas, and being prepared to deliver retributory blows in those areas. Only once did Gorshkov speak of strategic nuclear deterrence, and then he did not use *oborona*.[41]

38. For an analysis of these references, see MccGwire, "Naval Power and Soviet Oceans Policy," pp. 171–76. For an example of *oborona* being linked explicitly to countering strategic missile submarines, see Capt. 1st K. Sokolov, "Razvitie voenno-morskogo iskusstva v poslevoennyy period" (The development of naval art in the postwar period), *Voennaya mysl'* (Military thought), no. 10 (October 1972), p. 53, para. 2.

39. See *Msb* 73/2/21/4:131/1/4 in particular, but that paragraph should be analyzed in conjunction with 72/12/15/4:114/2/2 and 72/12/20/5–21/5:119/1/2–6, which also refer to the strategic rocket forces (SRF), and 73/2/21/2:131/1/2, which does not.

40. See note 54 for Grechko's statement, also in December 1972, that identified the use of the SRF in this way.

41. *Msb* 73/2/21/2–3:131/1/2–3.

COUNTERING WESTERN STRIKE FORCES. The claim that the mission of countering Western sea-based strategic delivery systems had been downgraded appeared to depend on linking a comment by Gorshkov on the survivability of missile-carrying submarines with a comment three chapters earlier about the problem that nuclear attack submarines would pose to the defense of ocean shipping.[42]

When taken in context, Gorshkov's own words yielded the opposite conclusion. In his final article he listed the three elements of the basic mission of great power navies in a worldwide nuclear war, the second of which was "blunting nuclear strikes by enemy naval forces from the ocean axes,"[43] which implies direct action against enemy weapon platforms. In the previous article he had described "defending the country against the aggressor's attacks from the oceanic axes" as the navy's main task.[44] He made only one specific reference to the operational aspects of countering Polaris, and that was favorable, when he commented that nuclear submarines were "becoming full-value antisubmarine ships, capable of detecting and destroying the enemy's missile-carrying submarines."[45]

Gorshkov was in fact arguing for the continued importance of countering Western sea-based strategic delivery systems. It is relevant that in a major naval publication that went to typesetting in March 1974 this task was specifically ranked as being "no less important" than that of missile-submarine strikes.[46] In July Gorshkov finally conceded that the task had lower priority in his Navy Day *Pravda* article, although he retained considerable room for maneuver by the way he defined the mission as "fleet-against-shore."

THE FLEET IN BEING. The claim that Gorshkov's historical analysis

---

42. Ibid.; and *Msb* 72/11/26/6–7:101/2/1–2.

43. *Msb* 73/2/21/8:131/2/2.

44. *Msb* 72/12/21/2:119/1/3.

45. *Msb* 73/2/20/1:130/1/6. This assertion is repeated and amplified in *Seapower of the State*, where it is noted that submarines are capable of "detecting enemy missile-armed submarines, tracking them for a prolonged period of time and, when necessary, attacking them." The book notes that "countermeasures against [missile-armed nuclear-powered submarines] had assumed the nature of a national mission." Sergey G. Gorshkov, *Morskaya moshch' gosudarstva*, 1st ed. (Seapower of the state) (Moscow: Voenizdat, 1976), pp. 337–38.

46. "An important task of our fleet in a future war . . . is the launching of nuclear strikes with atomic missiles from submarines against targets in his territory. Another no less important task of the fleet is the struggle with the nuclear forces of the enemy fleet, with first priority the missile-armed nuclear submarines and carrier strike forces. The successful discharge of this task will significantly weaken the enemy's nuclear strikes against the territory of the Soviet Union." L. T. Yemilov and A. E. Karasev, eds., *Boevoy Put' sovetskogo voenno-morskogo flota* (*The combat path of the Soviet navy*) (Moscow: Voenizdat, 1974), p. 491, para. 5. See also Sokolov, *Voennaya mysl'*, no. 10 (October 1972), p. 53, para. 2.

emphasized the role of navies as a diplomatic instrument during a war and in subsequent peace negotiations was based on a highly selective reading of the articles. The bulk of the historical review concentrated on the conduct of naval operations in various wars. Apart from his analysis of operational trends, Gorshkov placed most emphasis on the navies' capacity to *enable* the actual conduct of war against nonadjacent states. He also stressed the navies' contribution to the outcome of war. Drawing on a broad range of examples from 1703 through 1945, many of them not involving Russia, Gorshkov's dominant theme was that naval operations were important to the outcome of wars and that countries paid a price for their naval inferiority or defeat.

Since wars are fought for political goals, it was natural for Gorshkov sometimes to mention the terms of peace, but that was not a major theme of his presentation. And if his primary purpose had been to propound a doctrine of "conserving forces," he could have chosen better examples and presented them in a more pointed fashion.

In fact, Gorshkov refers to only one occasion in which the belligerents' "naval forces in being" were critical to the subsequent peace talks, and that was after the Crimean War, when Anglo-French naval dominance of the Black Sea allowed them to dictate the terms of the Treaty of Paris (1856). He also gave two examples of nonbelligerents having the ability to affect the terms of peace by virtue of their naval power: at the Congress of Berlin (1873), and after the Sino-Japanese war (1895).[47]

However, in none of those three cases was Gorshkov focusing on the concept of conserving forces and "navies in being," and in the two Black Sea cases, he was referring to the ability of naval forces to project effective military power into distant sea areas. The main thrust of his conclusion on the two wars with Turkey was that as soon as "the major capitalist powers" became concerned over Russia's attempts to gain egress to the Mediterranean, "the relative weakness of the Russian Navy was immediately manifested," and Russia was not only unable to profit from its victories on land, but was sometimes forced to concede defeat.[48]

---

47. At the Congress of Berlin, Britain was able to reverse many of the gains won by Russia in its war with Turkey. In 1895 Russia, Germany, and France forced Japan to relinquish its claim to the Liao-tung Peninsula by threatening its sea lines of communications. *Msb* 72/4/17/9:31/1/3.

48. *Msb* 72/4/15/4–5:29/1/4. This discussion was all part of the special emphasis that Gorshkov placed on the Black Sea and the Mediterranean. Between them they accounted for about 10 percent of the total text, a figure that does not take account of their appearance in discussions of naval operations in World Wars I and II.

The Question of Circularity

The Gorshkov articles illustrate rather well the difficulty of interpreting Soviet pronouncements. It has taken more than ten years after their publication to gain a reasonable understanding of the thrust and substance of the articles, and, undoubtedly that understanding is still incomplete. Meanwhile the announcement hypothesis highlights certain pitfalls in the analytical process. One of these is making interpretations from Western practice. The assumption that before the Delta SSBN, submarine missiles were "apparently intended for the initial salvos" would seem to have reflected the pattern of Polaris operations, rather than that of the Yankee. Another pitfall is inverting the proper order of analysis. Focusing first on *what* Gorshkov was saying shaped the conclusion of *why* he was saying it. But the question whether Gorshkov was "advocating" or "announcing" needed to be determined before one could be in a position to understand what was being said, or why it was being said.

Placing the material in its proper context is a problem. Some context is obviously necessary, but the wrong one can skew the analysis. By 1973–74 it was becoming clear from operational evidence as well as from Soviet writing that the Soviets were placing a new emphasis on the combat support of their SSBN force.[49] This perception helped generate the announcement hypothesis, but one of the problems that Gorshkov was arguing about was the problem of adequate combat support. Finally, there are the dangers of partial quotations and quotations out of context, which completely change the sense of what is being said,[50] and of allowing careless translations to provide evidence in support of the driving hypothesis.[51]

What most of this adds up to is the problem of circularity. Inevitably, some circularity will occur in any analytical process of this kind, but

49. See Bradford Dismukes, "The Soviet Naval General Purpose Forces: Roles and Missions in Wartime," in MccGwire, Booth, and McDonnell, eds., *Soviet Naval Policy,* pp. 573–84.

50. See note 34 for an example, but the best one was provided by *Msb* 72/12/20/5 through 72/12/21/5:119/1/2–6. In its entirety and if read carefully, it provided a clear exposition of what Gorshkov was talking about; a partial quotation, however, was used to support a different conclusion. See the extract on page 466 for the key passage.

51. For example, see Aleshkin's comment in *Msb* 72/1/24–30. "In the circumstances of a non-nuclear start to the war, [SSBNs] will generally be found in the reserve" (p. 25, para. 7) was rendered as "'even in a nuclear war' SSBNs will be found 'in the Reserve.'" And the statement in Yemilov and Karasev, eds., *The Combat Path of the Navy,* that the task of countering the nuclear strike forces of the enemy fleet is "no less important" than that of nuclear strike was modified to say that the task "is evaluated simply as 'important,'" and was then compared with a reference to nuclear-strike forces in another book, to create the impression that this task was of lesser importance.

clearly one must be wary of it; the announcement hypothesis provides a good example of the consequences. Because the concept of withholding SSBNs was thought to be new (false), Gorshkov must therefore have been making a doctrinal announcement (false). Because of the new emphasis on protecting SSBNs (true), Gorshkov must also have been announcing the downgrading of the counterstrike force mission (false–he was resisting its downgrading). Because the SSBNs' mission was now the most important one (true), when Gorshkov used the term *oborona,* he must have been referring to their mission (false), and defense against sea-based strike systems must therefore now depend on the deterrent effect of the SSBN force (false).

Only one of the two *trues* was supported by textual evidence in the Gorshkov series, and then only in part. The importance of providing combat support to submarines in general could be inferred from the articles, but not to SSBNs in particular. Since Gorshkov did not concede the priority of the SSBN mission until July 1974, it was not surprising that no evidence of that new priority was found in his articles. The announcement hypothesis was useful in drawing attention to the SSBNs' role as a strategic reserve and a matching force in the wake of an intercontinental exchange, a role that had been in effect since the late 1960s but that had not been grasped by Western analysts. However, by focusing attention on that one aspect, the withholding thesis obscured the additional new (and more important) role assigned to the Delta force. More serious, it diverted attention from the argument in the Gorshkov series concerning the navy's potential role in phase II of a global war.

The Substance of the Gorshkov Series

The bulk of the series consisted of a selective historical review of the role of navies since the seventeenth century and the development of the Russian and Soviet fleets over those years. Eighty percent of the series covered the period before 1945, and roughly two-thirds of the historical discussion focused on the various wars of the period, half of which was devoted to World War II.

The articles were rich in information. Although the dominant theme was that of advocacy and justification, they contained a strong element of "educating the fleet," and Gorshkov also took the opportunity to score points in the wider debate. The series covered a lot of ground and advanced many detailed arguments, but from this mass of information three major themes could be identified: the military and political importance of the navy's forward deployment in peacetime; the operational requirements for ensuring the security of the SSBN force in war; and the navy's role in phase II of a global war that did not escalate to an intercontinental exchange.[52] Taken together, these added up to a powerful argument for a larger and better balanced fleet.

Forward Deployment in Peacetime

To find the forces needed to ensure the security of the emerging Delta SSBN force, the navy would have to reduce the number of units deployed forward in peacetime. This reduction could be justified if the role of countering Western sea-based nuclear delivery systems was downgraded and if the navy's emerging role as an instrument of policy in peacetime was downplayed. Gorshkov opposed such a reduction on both counts.

DEFENSE OF THE HOMELAND. Gorshkov described the "defense of the country against attacks by aggressors from the ocean axes" as the navy's "main mission."[53] He explicitly linked the Communist party and the Soviet government with the decision to oppose "the forces of aggression on the world ocean with strategic counterforces of defense" (*kontrsily oborony*), one of whose two key elements was the ocean-going fleet.[54] In the final article, when he described the "basic mission" of great power navies in a global nuclear war, he included "the blunting of nuclear attacks by the enemy navy from the ocean axes."[55] And it is relevant that in the *Combat Path of the Soviet Navy*, which was under preparation by the navy at the

52. For more detailed analyses of the series, which, though dated, is still valid, see MccGwire, "Advocacy of Seapower in an Internal Debate," and "Naval Power and Soviet Oceans Policy." See notes 25 and 31.

53. *Msb* 72/12/21/2:119/1/3.

54. *Msb* 72/12/20/5:119/1/2. The other element was the strategic rocket forces and, as just discussed, the full context made it clear that these were regional missile systems, not intercontinental ones, and that the "fleet" consisted of general purpose forces and not SSBNs. This reference to the regional element of the SRF coincided with Grechko's statement that the SRF's mission included the destruction of "naval groupings in . . . the maritime theaters of military action." A. A. Grechko, "Armiya sotsialisticheskaya mnogonatsional'naya" (A socialist multinational army), *Krasnaya zvevda,* December 12, 1972.

55. It was noteworthy that Gorshkov chose not to talk of three separate tasks, but referred only to the "basic mission," which involved "participation in the attacks of the country's strategic nuclear forces, the blunting of nuclear attacks by the enemy from the direction of ocean, and participation in the operations conducted by ground forces in the continental theaters of military operations." *Msb* 73/2/21/8:131/2/2. *Oslablenie,* rendered here as "blunting," literally means "weakening."

same time as the Gorshkov series appeared, the tasks of strategic delivery and countering the enemy's naval strike forces were specifically assigned equal priority, being referred to as "important" and "no less important."[56] The passage went on to stress that successful discharge of those tasks would significantly weaken the enemy's strike against the territory of the Soviet Union.

COUNTERING IMPERIALIST AGGRESSION. Gorshkov argued that the navy also needed to be deployed forward to counter imperialist aggression in distant sea areas, while at the same time demonstrating the Soviet state's economic and military might. He not only brought out in the historical analyses the unique capacity of navies to project military power in peacetime but also devoted a whole chapter to "Navies as Instruments of Peacetime Imperialism" and to the Soviet navy's role in countering such imperialistic aggression. The emphasis in the series as a whole was on the positive benefits that accrued from the use of navies in peacetime to protect and promote state interests, and Gorshkov hinted at direct intervention in local wars, although he never quite said so.[57] Overlying this general advocacy of the navy's peacetime role was a particular concern for the Mediterranean (see note 48), which got disproportionate attention in the series as a whole. Gorshkov was at pains to stress the historical and contemporary importance of the Mediterranean to the Russian homeland and the legitimacy of the Soviet presence in that area.[58]

THE PEACETIME ROLE. The substance of Gorshkov's case on forward deployment was summed up in the overview section of the tenth article, one paragraph of which deserves quotation:

> The creation at the will of the party of a new Soviet Navy, and its emergence on the ocean expanses have fundamentally altered the correlation of forces and the situation in this sphere of confrontation. In the shape of our modern navy, the Soviet Armed Forces have acquired a powerful instrument of defense on the ocean axes, a formidable force for the deterrence of aggression, which is constantly ready to deliver punishing retributory blows and to disrupt the plans

56. See note 46. An article by a navy captain in *Military Thought*, published at the time of the Gorshkov series, made the same point in a different way. Having discussed the new strategic requirement to counter submarine ballistic-missile systems, the author noted that "this new task is now of no less concern to admiralties and committees of chiefs of staff, than the problems of employing offensive strategic nuclear forces." Sokolov, *Voennaya mysl'*, no. 10 (October 1972), p. 53, paras. 3–4.

57. *Msb* 73/2/21/4,9–10:131/1/4, 2/2–3. For the relevance of the Gorshkov series to the wider debate on the role of military force as an instrument of overseas policy, see chapter 10.

58. See MccGwire, "Naval Power and Soviet Oceans Policy" pp. 124–26. The Soviet decision to withdraw from Egypt when opportunity offered may have precipitated the publication of the series. See chapter 9.

of the imperialists. And the navy, along with other branches of the Soviet armed forces, is successfully fulfilling its main mission—the defense of the country against attacks by aggressors from the ocean axes. The ships of our navy are a threat to none, but they are always ready to give a deserved rebuff to any aggressor who dares to infringe on the security of the homeland.[59]

The distinction between "on" and "from" the ocean axes is crucial. Gorshkov was summarizing the role of the Soviet navy's general purpose forces in distant sea areas and describing the two primary missions. The main one (which the navy shared with other branches of the armed forces)[60] was the defense of the country against attack *from* the ocean axes. The navy also served as an instrument of defense *on* the ocean axes, against imperialist aggression. This second mission included both the use of Western naval forces as general instruments of expansionist foreign policy (including the repression of liberation movements) and the aggressive deployment of Western nuclear-strike forces (carrier and submarine), which were used as instruments of nuclear blackmail in peacetime.[61]

Securing the SSBN Bastions

This part of Gorshkov's thesis was not an argument about the desirability of the navy's contribution to strategic nuclear strikes, a topic Gorshkov all but ignored,[62] but about the operational requirements for ensuring the security of the SSBN bastions, with particular reference to the Arctic Ocean. Gorshkov's presentation had several strands, which can be grouped under two broad arguments. One concerned the kind of forces needed for that mission; the other concerned the need to establish command of the Norwegian Sea and what would be involved in that operation.

Gorshkov contended that securing the SSBN bastions demanded not only a strong and well-balanced fleet but also surface ships and aircraft to support submarines. He cited German experience in World Wars I and II to demonstrate the requirement.[63] In his final article, he reiterated the theme, as part of his argument that various kinds of surface ships were

59. *Msb* 72/12/21/2–5:119/1/2–6. In the following paragraph Gorshkov talked of "the former inaccessibility of the continents" [plural], which implicitly excludes an intercontinental contest [that is, North America] and locates the discussion around the Afro-Eurasian periphery.

60. Mainly the regional missiles of the SRF, but also some elements of the long-range air force and PVO strany.

61. *Msb* 72/12/19–20:117–118.

62. There were only three clear references to the strategic strike role, all in the final chapter. The most explicit ran to seventy-two words. *Msb* 73/2/21/2–3:131/1/2–3. The other two were nineteen and eight words long (19/9, 21/8).

63. *Msb* 72/5/17/6:45/1/3; and 72/11/28/6:103/1/1.

needed to provide "combat stability" to all types of submarines, including SSBNs.[64]

The requirement to establish command of the Norwegian Sea was implied obliquely first by Gorshkov's reference to the German seizure of the Norwegian coast in 1940.[65] He also referred to the public rehabilitation of the concept of "command of the sea" in his discussion of naval thinking in the 1930s.[66] A third element was his emphasis on the need for air support to be subordinated to naval command,[67] and coming within this general point was his implicit argument about the need for carrier aviation to help provide command of the air over the sea.[68]

This fragmentary evidence became conclusive when placed within the framework of a 1970 article in the restricted journal *Military Thought*.[69] The article brought out the need to establish command of the sea (and the air above it), noting that it was particularly important in relation to the SSBN's mission (58/5). The article provided an implicit description of the Arctic Ocean and Norwegian Sea as areas (among others) where command was essential (59/3, 60/4), repeatedly stressed that command of the air was a necessary part of command of the sea (for example, 55/5, 56/2), and noted the problem inherent in the limited range of shore-based fighters (56/4). It also discussed the German seizure of the Norwegian coast in the face of British naval superiority (52/7) and stressed the importance of a favorable regime ashore to establishing command of adjacent sea areas (56/1, 60/1).

Phase II of a Global War

Using historical analogies, Gorshkov argued that protracted war at sea was probable.[70] In reviewing the basic tasks discharged by navies in World

64. *Msb* 73/2/20/8–21/1:130/2/5–131/1/1. Note Aleshkin, *Msb* 72/1/24–30.

65. *Msb* 72/9/16/6:79/2/1.

66. Gorshkov explicitly identified two opposing schools of thought, one stemming from the outdated "small war" theory and the other stemming from the theory of "command of the sea." *Msb* 72/8/21/3:71/1/6.

67. The German failure in the battle of the Atlantic is used as the example (*Msb* 72/11/27/3:101/2/5), and Gorshkov returned to this point in the final chapter. *Msb* 73/2/20/8:130/2/5.

68. This argument was heavily camouflaged, but for evidence of it see MccGwire, "Naval Power and Soviet Oceans Policy," pp. 118–19. The most persuasive item was the quotation from Lenin on the foolishness of not mastering all the forms of weaponry available to the enemy. *Msb* 72/6/12/7:55/2/1.

69. Capt. 1st. N. Petrov, "Gospodstvo na more" (Command of the sea), *Voennaya mysl'*, no. 6 (June 1970), pp. 51–61. Hereafter page/paragraph will be given in parentheses in the text.

70. This inference is drawn from my original 1973 analysis. "If Gorshkov's historical examples are analogies . . .[Gorshkov] believes that protracted war at sea is possible. He envisages

War II,[71] Gorshkov grouped all operations under three headings: the battle for sea communications (which constituted 78 percent of his discussion); landing operations (14 percent); and operations to destroy naval forces (8 percent). Since, as he pointed out, the last was almost always integral to the first two types of operation,[72] his argument was focused on those two. From the way Gorshkov handled these subjects, it was originally inferred that they were of particular significance to the case he was making,[73] but their relevance became clear only when the discussion was placed within the context of the second phase of a global war that had not escalated to an intercontinental nuclear exchange.

Two separate arguments could be drawn from Gorshkov's argument: one related to defense against amphibious assault forces, the other to the potential utility of blockading North America. In his analysis, Gorshkov seemed most concerned to draw lessons from the failure of the defense against amphibious operations, noting that not once during the war was a continuous attack mounted against a landing force, from the time of its initial assembly to its entry into the landing area. He ascribed this failure to a lack of prior intelligence and insufficient defending forces (*Msb* 72/11/31). It can be inferred that Gorshkov was arguing that the phase II defense perimeter could be defended against Western seaborne invasion only by carrying the war to the enemy and attacking invasion forces in their assembly areas and on passage to the assault area.

In his discussion of blockade, Gorshkov was concerned about stressing its potential and identifying the reasons why it had sometimes not been fully effective. Gorshkov concluded that the Allied blockade of Germany had had a considerable effect on the course of World War I but had been less effective in World War II, because the Germans had access to the economies and natural resources of almost all the Western European countries.[74] During World War II German attacks on sea communications con-

---

attacking merchant convoys, troop reinforcements and amphibious assault groups, and perhaps the occupation of the Norwegian coast at the outbreak of war." MccGwire "Advocacy of Sea Power," p. 47.

71. This was a 4,840-word chapter, the ninth in the series. *Msb* 72/11/24–34.

72. *Msb* 72/11/31/3. Half the discussion on the destruction of enemy forces was devoted to establishing the sharply rising trend in the number of ships destroyed in port as opposed to at sea, and arguing the need for dispersal.

73. See MccGwire, "Advocacy of Seapower," pp. 49–52.

74. *Msb* 72/5/18/1–4: 45/1/1–4; and 72/11/27/8:102/1/6. Gorshkov also claimed that the reason why a blockade did not make Japan sue for peace was that the United States failed to attack the sea link with Korea, Manchuria, and Northern China. These areas supplied key resources (including basics like iron ore and coking coal) that were essential to the Japanese war economy. *Msb* 72/11/29/3:103/1/4.

siderably weakened Britain's economy and had a definite effect on military operations in the secondary theaters, but for three reasons such attacks had less impact than they had had in World War I: the Germans initially lacked a large enough submarine force; the West therefore had time to build up its merchant fleet and ASW forces; and, in any case, most of Germany's efforts and resources were concentrated on the eastern front (*Msb* 72/11/27–28).

Since Gorshkov implied that the Soviet Union, with access to Europe's resources, would be immune to maritime blockade, one can infer that he was arguing the merits of blockading North America, which depends on seaborne imports for many key resources. Such an operation would be feasible if the Soviet Union had sufficient submarine forces at the outset and did not allow the United States time to build up its merchant fleet and ASW forces. He noted that despite the massive buildup of Western ASW forces in World War II, the diesel submarine was never driven from the sea. Nuclear submarines would be even harder to deal with.[75]

The Continuing Debate

As mentioned before, the public debate over naval roles was cut off in May 1973, and by mid-1974 a compromise appears to have been reached. But compromise does not mean the end of disagreement, and one of the more persuasive bodies of evidence that the Gorshkov series was an exercise in advocacy was the way the disagreement between the navy and the military leadership continued to be expressed in Gorshkov's book, *Seapower of the State*.[76]

Gorshkov's Book

Seapower of the State was officially scheduled for publication during the second quarter of 1976. It actually appeared two weeks before the Twenty-fifth Party Congress, in March. That its schedule was advanced

---

75. "The question of the ratio of submarine to antisubmarine forces is of great interest even under present-day conditions, since if ASW forces, which were so numerous and technically up to date [for that time], possessing a vast superiority, turned out to be capable of only partially limiting the operations of diesel submarines, then what must the superiority be today, in order to counter nuclear-powered submarines." *Msb* 72/11/26/6:101/1/5.

76. *Morskaya moshch' gosudarstva.*

suggested the political clout of those supporting that side of the wider debate.[77] The seventeen weeks the book spent in the censorship process compared favorably with the ten-and-a-half weeks it took to clear the first (1962) edition of Sokolovskiy's *Military Strategy* (which is generally assumed to have been a crash production) and was better than the nineteen weeks it took to clear the second (1963) edition.

The book was almost three times as long as the articles, with significant additions and deletions to the original material. The historical analysis (which made up 80 percent of the Gorshkov series) reappeared as the second chapter of four, with substantial amendments. About 20 percent of the book was devoted to the nonmilitary factors of seapower, an aspect that had been treated cursorily in the articles. Since the broader analysis of the series had suggested that the merchant fleet was probably on the other side of the debate from Gorshkov, it was interesting that a former minister of the merchant fleet (Bakaev) joined the collective of authors who actually wrote the book. As a result, the book had almost 11,000 words on maritime transportation, compared with only 75 words in the articles (*Msb* 73/2/18).

Like the articles, the book criticized the military leadership's preoccupation with the continental theaters of military operation and complained about the leadership's inability to perceive the central importance of the Soviet navy's role in a war in which the primary opponent was a maritime power such as the United States. In the articles, Gorshkov had referred to "Tsarists and fools," who persistently failed to perceive Russia's need for a powerful navy.[78] In the book, he was more direct in the choice of analogy, criticizing Napoleon for blaming his admirals for repeated failure, whereas the fault lay in his own "inability . . . to make a timely analysis of the French navy's capabilities, and to use it in the struggle with the enemy." Napoleon's failure to invade England in 1805 was primarily due not to Britain's unchallenged maritime superiority but to Napoleon's "one-sided strategy . . . , which stemmed from his preoccupation with operations in

77. The 1973 analysis of the series stressed that the cleavage of opinion ran within groups as well as between them. It was inferred that the following institutions and interests were among his potential supporters: the party ideologues, the state security apparatus, the fishing industry, and the ocean science community; on the opposite side to Gorshkov were the main body of defense intellectuals, some of the professional naval strategists, the merchant fleet, and elements of the domestic economic apparatus. In addition, it was inferred that both Brezhnev and Grechko (particularly the latter) were on the opposite side. See MccGwire, "Advocacy of Seapower," pp. 25–28.

78. *Msb* 72/3/20/2, 21/1; and 72/4/9/1, 22/9.

the land theaters and his lack of understanding of the navy, his disregard for its capabilities in war, and as a result, his inability to use it in a struggle with a naval power, such as England was at the time."[79]

In a section of the book that purported to be expounding the new priority of the fleet-against-shore (that is, the pro-SSBN) mission (348–61), most of the space was devoted to illustrating the importance of the traditional fleet-against-fleet role. Gorshkov accomplished this shift by first extending the definition of fleet-against-shore to include landing operations (355/1) and attacks on sea lines of communication (361/3), and then establishing two categories of fleet-against-fleet operation: the "pure" form, intended to gain and maintain command of the sea (352/5, 353/4), and those operations that are "tied to the simultaneous accomplishment of other missions" (352/4). He went on to show that this second category of fleet-against-fleet (which comprises the bulk of all naval operations [354/2]), was in fact supporting operations against the shore.

As a result Gorshkov could define the navy's main objective as "securing the fulfillment of all missions *related* to operations against enemy land targets and to the protection of one's own territory from the attacks of his navy" (354/3, emphasis added). The extensive definition of fleet-against-shore operations allowed discussion of the traditional roles played by navies in World War II, including the importance of carriers as general purpose forces. Under the guise of exceptions to the general role, Gorshkov smuggled in many examples of traditional naval operations that had had strategic significance (351/2) or had even been more important than the battle on land (349/3).

A completely new subsection on "Command of the Sea" (372–80) provided additional arguments in support of the traditional role. It constituted almost half the section "Some Theoretical Questions of Naval Art," which in other respects reproduced verbatim the greater part of an earlier journal article.[80] In the subsection, which contained the first substantial public discussion of "command of the sea" in recent years,[81] Gorshkov tried to

79. Gorshkov, *Seapower*, pp. 356, 355. Hereafter page/paragraph will be given in parentheses in the text.

80. S. G. Gorshkov, "Nekotorye voprosy razvitiya voenno-morskogo isskustva" (Several questions on the development of naval art), *Msb* 74/12/24–32.

81. For an earlier discussion of the concept in a restricted forum, see Petrov's article, "Command of the Sea," in *Voennaya mysl'*. For earlier references to "Command of the Sea," see Peter H. Vigor, "Soviet Understanding of 'Command of the Sea,'" and MccGwire, "Command of the Sea in Soviet Naval Strategy," in MccGwire, *Soviet Naval Policy*, pp. 601–36.

show the continuing validity of the concept rather than the way to achieve it. He stressed its uniqueness to the maritime environment and claimed that it was the most "vital concept" in the art of naval warfare. The discussion provided powerful support to the arguments advanced elsewhere in the book for the continued relevance of the fleet-against-fleet role and the importance of general purpose forces, particularly in the antisubmarine and pro-SSBN role.

The major concession in the book was reversion to the tautological definition of a balanced fleet (413/2) that was first publicized in 1967,[82] whereby "balance" denoted the capability to carry out assigned missions in differing circumstances, but said nothing about mission structure. In his articles Gorshkov had viewed "balance" as stemming from the *choice* of mission, which needed to be defined in as general terms as possible in order to exploit the navy's inherent versatility and allow for unforeseen eventualities. However, except for this definitional retreat, the section "Problems of Balancing Navies" (pp. 411–51), which mainly consisted of a critical analysis of great power fleet structures since 1905 in terms of their capacity to handle the unforeseen demands of war, illustrated the importance of flexibility and provided a range of example that could be used to support most of Gorshkov's arguments.

Seapower of the State was favorably received.[83] Marshal of the Soviet Union Bagramyan noted that "for the first time in our literature, the author convincingly formulates the concept of seapower as a scientific category,"[84] and Admiral of the Fleet Lobov said that "the book will be an important source of developing a correct viewpoint of the seapower of the state."[85] Within four years an expanded second edition had been printed.[86] The military publishers described the first edition as being "for the military reader," whereas the second edition was specifically for "admirals, generals and officers of the Soviet army and navy." Two of the contributing au-

---

82. *Msb* 67/2/20. The importance of the definition at that time was that it was alerting the fleet to be prepared for conventional as well as nuclear war at sea. See the section "The Late Cut-Off" in appendix A.

83. Reviews of the book were analyzed by John McDonnell in a working paper presented to the fourth Dalhousie seminar on Soviet naval developments, Halifax, Nova Scotia, 1977.

84. I. Bagramyan, "Mogushchestvo vo imya mira" (Might in the name of peace), *Izvestiya*, May 22, 1976.

85. S. Lobov, "Seapower of the State and Its Defensive Capacity," *Msb* 76/4/99–105.

86. The first (1976) edition print was 60,000 copies, compared with only 30,000 for the third edition of Sokolovskiy's *Military Strategy*. The second (1979) edition was 12.5 percent larger, and again printed 60,000 copies.

thors were promoted to vice admiral and one to rear admiral. However, as an indicator of the navy's institutional fortunes, this impression of general approval was misleading.

Reassertion of Ground Force Dominance

With hindsight one can see that the increasing influence of naval ideas reached its peak at about the time the first edition of Gorshkov's book was published in early 1976. At about that time it became clear that the United States intended to stabilize its fleet at 12 carrier battle groups and about 475 ships, rather than the 15 battle groups it had averaged since the mid-1950s, with ship numbers in the 900 to 1,000 range for most of the 1960s. And early in 1976 Ustinov became minister of defense, and Ogarkov took over as chief of the General Staff within the year.

The second edition of the book provided evidence that by 1979 the General Staff was regaining control of the strategic debate. First, although it preserved the critical tone of the first edition (including the pointed reference to Napoleon's failure to understand seapower), the second edition had a new ten-page section devoted to affirming that military strategy was a unified whole and could not be divided into separate naval and land components, and to criticizing those who believed in divided strategies, a belief "characteristic to this day of the military theorists of the imperialist states."[87] The book thus paid formal obeisance to the central tenet of unity. One could, however, infer that the author was still dissatisfied with the overall structure and application of the Soviet Union's unified strategy and considered that its maritime aspects were neither properly integrated nor given sufficient attention.[88]

Second, the first edition had slipped in at least six references to "naval science," as distinct from military science, and these references were deleted from the second edition. In 1979 the separate doctorate in naval (as distinct from military) science was discontinued.[89] Final confirmation that

87. Gorshkov, *Seapower of the State*, 2d ed., 1979, pp. 308–17; quotation from 315/6.

88. See ibid., 317/2–3. For an interpretation of these two rather obscure paragraphs, see Michael MccGwire, "Soviet Naval Doctrine and Strategy," in Derek Leebaert, ed., *Soviet Military Thinking* (London: George Allen and Unwin, 1981), pp. 143–44.

89. Both these changes were noted by Charles Petersen. The entry for *Doktor Voennykh Nauk* in the *Voennyy entsiklopedichesikiy slovar'* (Moscow: Voenizdat, 1983), p. 240, noted that the naval doctorate had been discontinued in April 1979, at which date the second edition was in the censorship process. For the removal of "naval science," see Charles C. Petersen, *The "Stalbo Debates": Their Point of Departure*, Professional Paper 404 (Alexandria, Va: Center for Naval Analyses, 1984), p. 4.

the upsurge in naval political influence had been battened down by the end of the 1970s was provided by a series of articles that began publication in *Morskoy sbornik* in April 1981.

There were eleven articles in all, published at intervals between April 1981 and July 1983 on the general subject of the theory of the navy.[90] They can be seen as a cautious, carefully planned, and apparently successful attempt to recover some of what had been lost by the deletion of "naval science" from the Soviet strategic lexicon. The vehicle for this demarche was a structured debate on the need for theory about the development and employment of the navy, a need that was equally relevant to the four other branches of service, and one that had in fact been previously noted in the military press.[91] The debate was initiated by Vice Admiral Stalbo in a rather ponderous double-issue article. Admiral Chernavin, the recently appointed deputy commander in chief of the navy, contributed the fourth article, and Gorshkov summed up the debate in July 1983. In April 1983 the section of *Morskoy sbornik* that had been entitled "Naval Art" since at least 1963 was changed to "Naval Art and Questions of Theory."

The discussion yielded little that was not already present in the Gorshkov series and subsequent book.[92] The only article clearly out of tune with the rest was the penultimate one by Shlomin, who appeared to be presenting the General Staff's point of view. He was also the only contributor to the debate whom Gorshkov rebutted by name, once on the matter of what constituted a "balanced fleet" and once on the scope of the navy's theoretical interests.[93] The points in question suggested that the navy's autonomous tendencies and the further development of the fleet were still matters of contention.

In his articles Gorshkov established that "the *subject* of the theory of the navy is the application of laws and principles of military science to the conduct of warfare in the sea and ocean theaters in all its diversity and in close interaction with the war in the continental theaters, as well as in defense of the USSR's state interests on the World ocean in peacetime" (*Msb* 83/7/31/8). He stated that "naval art" was the most important part of

90. *Msb* 81/4/20–28; 81/5/17–27; 81/11/24–29; 82/1/20–24; 82/3/21–27; 82/4/27–31; 82/7/ 18–24; 82/11/26–31; 83/3/18–23; 83/4/20–27; and 83/7/27–38.

91. *Msb* 81/11/27/2; and 83/7/28/6.

92. The analysis of this 1981–83 series owes a great deal to fellow members of the Writings Analysis Group, led by Theodore A. Neely, Jr., who together with Charles Petersen identified the series and organized its analysis.

93. *Msb* 83/7/27/5, 29/6. Shlomin had proposed that the appropriate subject should be "the theory of the combat employment and the structuring of the navy," a much more restrictive formulation. *Msb* 83/4/22 (chart).

the theory of the navy, but devoted twice as much space to the subtheory of "structuring the navy," the bulk of which discussed the "primary problem" of "balancing" the fleet. He also devoted a disproportionate amount of attention to oceanology and hydrodynamics, which suggested a new threat that the control of these navy-related sciences might be lost.

Overview

The decade of the 1970s saw the rise and fall of a serious naval attempt to achieve a larger voice in the shaping of broad strategic concepts and greater autonomy in determining the best way to conduct war at sea. This attempt was made possible because of the doctrinal turbulence that resulted from the restructuring of objectives in the wake of the December 1966 decision, and the need to rethink a whole range of policies, ranging from the role of military force in the third world to providing for phase II of a global war.

This protracted debate was not just a manifestation of interservice rivalry. Although there were obvious institutional interests at stake, the debate was focused on key issues of strategy and resource allocation, over which there was ample room for serious professional disagreement about the best way of proceeding. In the narrow sense, the Soviet navy lost this internal debate, in that the lessened importance of the Arctic Ocean as a deployment area for SSBNs reduced the overall requirement for naval forces, and the navy also lost its autonomous doctorate in naval science. In the broader sense, the debate made the politico-military leadership more sensitive to the role of navies in peace and war, and in that respect Gorshkov was extremely successful.

Development of the Strategic Rocket Forces

TO ANALYZE the Soviets' objectives in the field of nuclear arms control, as discussed in chapter 11, one must understand the development of their strategic rocket forces (SRF) and the pattern of their missile programs. Knowing what missiles were deployed and how those systems appeared to be targeted is not sufficient. The genesis of each program and changes in requirements between the time of a system's initial conception and operational deployment some years later are important aspects.[1]

The record shows that during this design and development period, a high proportion of major Soviet weapons systems have undergone significant changes in their role, method of employment, and production schedule. This has been the result of changes in requirements that stemmed from changes in the external environment, in internal priorities, or in operational concepts. The turbulence is well documented for naval programs, but it also applies to the other branches of service, except for the ground forces and, perhaps, for fighter aviation. Change has certainly been true for strategic missile programs.

An account of the development of the SRF must therefore distinguish between the requirements that underlay the conception of the various missile systems and the requirements that determined how the missiles were actually deployed. To make such a distinction is more practicable than might at first appear because for most of the postwar period, the Soviets have been faced with fairly clear-cut requirements for strategic delivery

1. U.S. officials estimate about six years for technological development and five years for engineering development, giving a total of eleven years' lead time. U.S. Department of Defense, *Soviet Military Power, 1985,* 4th ed. (Government Printing Office, 1985), p. 40 (Hereafter *SMP, 1985.*) Of course lead time can be shortened to meet urgent requirements, by exploiting what is already available rather than initiating new development.

systems, and shifts in these requirements have resulted in major perturbations in the missile programs. The overall pattern of missile development, the evidence of perturbations caused by changes, and the inferences that can be made about strategic and operational requirements can be combined to develop a robust hypothesis that provides a coherent explanation of how Soviet policy in this area developed.

This appendix represents such a hypothesis. Because the available data consist of relatively limited information on the numbers and characteristics of the various missiles, and on their test and deployment dates, the hypothesis is expressed in broad terms, outlining the general thrust of the programs. The detailed evidence that is available at the classified level would undoubtedly allow a more finely textured explanation. However, the macroapproach has certain advantages, and the data are sufficient to allow the main parameters of the succeeding programs to be discerned and their geneses to be inferred. This analysis builds on the pioneering work of Robert P. Berman and John C. Baker and draws extensively on their explanation in order to develop likely missile production and deployment schedules for intercontinental ballistic missiles as they have evolved since the mid-fifties.[2] It has also been possible to develop new explanations for the contemporary role of the continental, or regional, component of the SRF, based on the apparent anomalies in the proposals advanced by the Soviets in the talks on intermediate-range nuclear forces (INF) in the 1982–83 period.

In the first twenty-five years after World War II, the development of the strategic rocket forces was driven by the military requirement to inflict damage on the enemy while limiting his capacity to strike at Russia with nuclear weapons. These military requirements largely persisted after 1970, although the new priority on wartime deterrence and on avoiding nuclear escalation affected the detailed implications. They were, however, overlaid with a different kind of requirement that emerged from the arms control process. This took two forms. The negotiated limits became an important factor in determining the number of missiles to be deployed. And the possibility of using arms control to restrict the development or limit the deployment of new types of U.S. weapons systems prompted the matching development of Soviet systems. The primary function of such systems (the long-range cruise missiles are a prime example) was to get America to

2. Robert P. Berman and John C. Baker, *Soviet Strategic Forces: Requirements and Responses* (Brookings, 1982).

agree to negotiate on limits rather than to meet a particular military requirement.

In explaining the development of the land-based element of the strategic rocket forces, it is convenient to distinguish between those missile systems with an intercontinental range, and those whose range limits them to use in the regions adjacent to the Soviet Union, that is, the continental periphery. Missiles with an intercontinental range could, in principle, be targeted against facilities in the region, and the Soviets have done so in practice since the beginning of the 1970s. However, it now appears likely that the Soviets are moving to distinguish target sets on the basis of the nature of the conflict rather than on geographic location. If that is true, one set will comprise those targets that would only be struck in the event of escalation to global nuclear war. The other will comprise those targets that would need to be attacked in the event of a nuclear war limited to the Eurasian continent and its periphery. The Eurasian set will mainly comprise military targets and is likely to exclude a range of political-administrative targets in Europe that would come within the target set for global nuclear war.

Despite this likely change in targeting practice, in describing the development of the SRF, it is still most convenient to distinguish between its continental and regional components. In the early 1950s, development of both components started on parallel paths. If anything, design work on the first intercontinental system (the SS-6 ICBM) was initiated prior to that on the first regional missile (the SS-4), but the problems involved in developing these novel weapons were to some extent a function of range.[3] The actual development of ballistic missiles therefore started at the lower end of the scale, the first operational system being the 600-nautical-mile SS-3, which entered service in 1955. The fact that it was easier to develop shorter-range systems was partly responsible for the first regional strategic system (the SS-4) being deployed four years before the first fully operational intercontinental ballistic missile (ICBM) (the SS-7).[4] The immediacy of the threat from U.S. strategic delivery systems on the continental periphery was also an important consideration. Besides the bombers, and

3. Berman and Baker, *Soviet Strategic Forces,* p. 82, figure A-1. Except where otherwise noted, all data on missile characteristics, development, and deployment are drawn from the tables in this book. The initial deployment dates for Soviet intercontinental ballistic missiles (ICBMs) are taken from the chart in *SMP, 1985,* p. 41.

4. The first-generation ICBM (SS-6) was never fully operational. Its test program suggests that it had been hoped to start deploying this missile in 1959–60, but the program was curtailed. In any event, only four missiles were deployed in 1961. Desmond Ball, *Politics and Force Levels: The Strategic Missile Program of the Kennedy Administration* (University of California Press, 1980), pp. 53–55.

later, the missiles already based there, it was planned that the main force of strategic bombers based in the United States would stage through airfields on the continental periphery.

By the end of 1983, four generations of strategic missile had been deployed, with a fifth at the flight-testing stage of development.[5] The first generation comprised the SS-4 and SS-6; the second comprised the SS-5, SS-7, and SS-8; the third comprised the SS-9 through SS-15, without the SS-12, which was not a strategic system; and the fourth comprised the SS-16 through SS-20.

Intercontinental Ballistic Missiles

The requirements underlying the first five generations of intercontinental ballistic missiles (ICBMs) can be explained in decades, starting with the 1950s.

The 1950s: The Initial Approach

In about 1957–58 the Soviets chose the intercontinental ballistic missile in preference to the submarine or the bomber as the means of delivering nuclear weapons targeted on North America. At this period the United States already possessed a massive nuclear delivery capability in the bombers of Strategic Air Command (SAC), and the United States was also beginning to deploy Atlas and Titan ICBMs; a world war was seen as being a fight to the finish between two social systems; and a primary Soviet objective in such a war would be to destroy the United States as a functioning political entity.

The pattern of missile development during the first decade suggests that the Soviet response to this requirement was based on the principle of using large warheads to devastate a large area, destroying all types of target in that area rather than waiting to develop the capability to target individual installations (point targeting). To this end, the Soviets steadily increased the size of their ICBM warheads. The first and second generations of operational ICBMs (the SS-6, SS-7, and SS-8) had warheads in the 5-megaton (MT) range; the third-generation SS-9 and SS-10 had warheads

---

5. Contemporary Soviet practice classifies ballistic missiles with a range of 2,000 kilometers or more as "strategic." Although the range of the SS-4 was slightly less (1,750 kilometers), it was nevertheless classified as a strategic system in 1959.

in the 20-MT range; and the fourth-generation missiles would have had warheads in the range of 50 MTs to 100 MTs. Although this fourth generation never entered service, its projected development can be inferred from the series of nuclear tests that took place in September 1961, which included the testing of a 57-MT warhead and the triggering device for a much larger warhead. As further confirmation, there were Soviet and East European references during the 1960s to Soviet warheads of 100 MTs.[6] It also seems likely that what is now known as the Proton space booster, which was first tested in 1965, was originally intended as the military system to carry this very large warhead.

The concept of using very large warheads to achieve "area devastation" sidestepped the problem of matching an indeterminate but growing number of U.S. intercontinental delivery systems and offered the Soviets a cost-effective solution to the nuclear arms race. The target set would be finite, comprising designated areas of North America, expressed as a predetermined number of square kilometers.[7] Larger warheads would allow the target set to be covered by fewer missiles and would not require additional fissionable material.[8] Large warheads made a virtue of the Soviet lag in miniaturization and avoided the problems of achieving accuracy. A smaller number of missiles mitigated the constraints imposed by the limited Soviet

6. In 1966 the East German defense minister credited the Soviet Union with ICBMs carrying 100-megaton (MT) warheads. Robert Waring Herrick, *The USSR's "Blue Belt of Defense" Concept: A Unified Military Plan for Defense against Seaborne Nuclear Attack by Strike Carriers and Polaris/Poseidon SSBNs,* Professional Paper 111 (Arlington, Va.: Center for Naval Analyses, 1973), p. 1. Soviet references were made to bombs of "20, 50, 100, and more MTs," and "50 MTs and greater." S.A. Tyushkevich and N.Ya. Shushko, *Marksizm-Leninizm o voyne i armii,* 4th ed. (*Marxism-Leninism on war and the army*) (Voenizdat, 1968), p. 294; A. S. Zheltov, T. R. Kondratkov, and E. A. Khomenko, eds., *Metodolodicheskie problemy voennoy teorri i praktiki,* 2d ed. (Methodological problems of military theory and practice) (Moscow: Voenizdat, 1969), p. 62, para. 4. More significantly (since the authors would have been aware of current weapons programs), the first two editions of Sokolovskiy's *Military Strategy* refer to Soviet warheads of "several tens of megatons," but this reference was deleted from the third edition. See Harriet Fast Scott, trans. and ed., *Soviet Military Strategy,* 3d ed. (Crane, Russak, 1975), note 113, p. 431.

7. For example, the area of the eighteen U.S. states having a population density in excess of eighty persons per square mile in the 1950s totaled about 657,000 square miles. About 60 percent of that area could be exposed to blast damage (four pounds per square inch over pressure) and 1.5 times that area to thermal effects (second- or third-degree burns) by using 960 warheads (480×5 MT + 480×20 MT), the number that seems originally to have been planned for deployment in the 1961–70 period. By excluding rural areas, the 960 warheads could certainly cover the fifty-seven cities outside those eighteen states with a population of 100,000, and probably the remaining fifty-one with populations of more than 50,000 as well. Author's estimates using standard references.

8. The requirement for fissionable material increases by some root of the yield, which compensates for the blast effect increasing in proportion to the two-thirds root of the yield. At the period in question, the availability of fissionable material was a constraint. Strobe Talbott, ed. and trans., *Khrushchev Remembers: The Last Testament* (Bantam Books, 1976), p. 55.

capacity for mass producing fine-tolerance components. At that period, most of the population and industry of the United States was still east of the Mississippi, besides which there were very large conurbations on the East and (to a lesser extent) West Coasts and around the Great Lakes. Relatively few military installations lay far from centers of population, and almost all targets were "soft."

By analogy with recent missile programs and Soviet practice in other areas of weapons development, it seems likely that it was originally planned to start deploying the 5-MT SS-7 and SS-8 (designed by Yangel and Korolev, respectively) in 1961. These missiles would have been followed in 1966 by the SS-9 and SS-10 from the same design bureaus, and in the third five-year period (1971–75), the "superheavies" would have been deployed. In regard to warheads the relationship between these three generations of missile was that of the initial, interim, and final responses to a new requirement. It seems likely that Soviet production of missiles for the initial and interim responses was programmed to allow the deployment of 48 of each type a year, with a total of 960 missiles deployed in ten years.[9]

In the second five-year period, the Soviets probably planned to augment the two-track program of heavy ICBMs with a third type, the SS-13 light missile, adding another 240 missiles for a total of 1,200 in the ten years. This solid-fuel mobile missile from Nadiradze's design bureau would constitute the strategic reserve. It would be followed by an improved version in the third five-year period.

The Soviet concept of area devastation as the means of destroying U.S.-based strategic delivery systems, as well as other targets, remained valid into the early 1960s. The existing striking power of the U.S. strategic bomber force had worked against the early development of a U.S. ICBM force. Dwight D. Eisenhower continued to resist the more extravagant demands for the rapid buildup of a very large missile force despite the increased public pressure in the wake of Sputnik in October 1957.[10] Mean-

9. In 1962 the U.S. estimate of future ICBM deployment was 65 to 120 a year. See Albert Wohlstetter, "Is There a Strategic Arms Race?" *Foreign Policy*, no. 15 (Summer 1974), pp. 12–13. The assessment of 48 of each type a year is based on the pattern of deployment depicted in table D-1. The number 48 or its multiple reoccurs in the deployment patterns between 1960 and 1980. (See notes 16, 17, 28, 39.)

10. The original U.S. program intended a force of only 20 to 40 missiles and by October 1957 only 80 ICBMs had been fully funded. At no time before 1958 was an operational force of more than 200 missiles seriously proposed. A total of 255 Atlas and Titan missiles had been authorized through 1960, which was about twice what the administration thought necessary. Eisenhower had,

while the early U.S. plans for deploying Atlas and then Titan were such as to suggest to the Soviets that those missiles would be covered (in the main) by area devastation.

The 1960s: Reshaping the Programs

Two developments at the beginning of the 1960s disrupted the planned progress of Soviet ICBM programs as just outlined. One, the Soviets adopted the strategic concept of international nuclear preemption in the event that world war was deemed inescapable. As discussed in chapter 2, this policy was a logical consequence of the doctrinal decision in late 1959 that a world war would inevitably be nuclear and would inevitably escalate to an intercontinental exchange. A corollary of the concept of nuclear preemption was that any intercontinental missile that was fueled by nonstorable liquids became operationally unacceptable because the necessary response time could not be guaranteed. It is plausible that this characteristic led to canceling plans for the series production of the SS-8 and to curtailing the development of its successor, the SS-10. Both systems were designed by Korolev, who favored nonstorable liquids for rocket motors. As a consequence, the area devastation requirements had to be met by the SS-7 and SS-9, missiles from Yangel's design bureau.

The other development was external to Russia and far more disruptive in its effects, since it forced the Soviets to give up their cost-effective area-devastation policy and to redefine their targeting requirements. The redirection of U.S. defense programs initiated by the John F. Kennedy administration in the first half of 1961 coincided with the impending availability of the solid-fuel Minuteman ICBM. The Minuteman force would be mainly deployed in the remoter parts of the Middle West, and these missiles would be the first to be truly dispersed and hardened. By no stretch of the imagination could the Soviets cover the Minuteman force by the existing plans for area devastation, and this development meant the Soviets faced an additional requirement to target individual missile silos.

THE INSTINCTIVE RESPONSE. To understand the effect of this new development on Soviet missile programs, one must distinguish between the initial Soviet reaction to the problem, which can be inferred from the pat-

---

however, approved plans for a force of 400 Minutemen. Ball, *Politics and Force Levels*, pp. 43–45.

tern of missile production, and the subsequent realization of a more effective way of addressing the problem, which can be inferred from the actual deployment and targeting of the third generation of missiles. One must also remember that the hardened Minuteman silos were an addition to the existing target set and did not replace it. The original list of military, economic, and administrative targets still needed to be covered, including SAC airfields, naval bases, military embarkation ports, and centers of national and local government. In other words, the missile systems that were already in production or under development (the SS-7 and its successor, the SS-9) were fully committed, and the Soviet requirement was for an additional program that would cover the Minuteman deployment.

In looking for an expeditious way to meet this new requirement, the Soviets turned to Chelomey's design bureau. It was primarily involved with naval cruise missiles but was also developing a variable-range ballistic missile for use against U.S. carrier battle groups when they approached to launch nuclear strikes against Russia. The Soviets could adapt the design of this naval missile system to develop the SS-11 ICBM, carrying a 1-MT warhead that could be targeted against individual Minuteman silos. The poor accuracy of the system was less important than the fact that the whole Minuteman force would be put directly at risk.[11] It made sense as an interim response, while development of a more effective hard-target counterforce weapon was proceeding.

Because of its relatively small size, it would be easier to deploy the SS-11 in the large numbers required, but the production rate still had to be determined. In the 1961–62 period the final size of the Minuteman force was still uncertain, and in early 1961 there had even been talk that production capacity was to be doubled to 720 missiles a year.[12] The Joint Chiefs of Staff favored a force of 1,600 missiles while Strategic Air Command was lobbying for "thousands," and during from 1961 to 1963 the "approved" number fluctuated between 800 and 1,300.[13] Given such circumstances, the prudent Soviet response was to install the production capacity to deliver missiles at something approaching the annual rate being pro-

11. The original SS-11 decision was in line with the established Soviet policy of posing some kind of counter to any threat to the Soviet homeland, and of responding to new problems by a series of responses (initial, interim, final) rather than waiting until the final solution is available. The Soviet response was also in line with the warning that Deputy Foreign Minister Vasiliy Kuznetsov gave to John F. Kennedy's emissary, Walt Rostow, in December 1960, that the Soviets would respond in kind to a U.S. buildup.

12. Joseph Alsop, "Shortening The Missile Gap," *New York Herald Tribune,* February 7, 1961.

13. John Prados, *The Soviet Estimate* (Dial Press, 1982), pp. 114–15.

Table D-1. *Deployment Schedules for Intercontinental Ballistic Missiles, Postulated and Observed, 1961–73*

| | Postulated deployment of each type of missile | | | | | | Total deployment of all types | |
Year	SS-6	SS-7	SS-8	SS-9	SS-11	SS-13	Postulated	Observed
1961	4	24	. . .	. . .	. . .	. . .	28	. . .
1962	. . .	48	. . .	. . .	. . .	. . .	76	. . .
1963	. . .	48	12	. . .	. . .	. . .	136	80
1964	. . .	48	11	. . .	. . .	. . .	195	180
1965	. . .	18	. . .	12	. . .	. . .	225	225
1966	. . .	. . .	. . .	48	120	. . .	393	340
1967	. . .	. . .	. . .	48	240	. . .	681	720
1968	. . .	. . .	. . .	48	180	. . .	909	900
1969	. . .	. . .	. . .	48	60	40	1,057	1,060
1970	(−4)	. . .	. . .	48	240	20	1,361	1,350
1971	. . .	. . .	. . .	30	120	. . .	1,511	1,520
1972	. . .	. . .	. . .	6	30	. . .	1,547	1,550
1973	. . .	. . .	. . .	. . .	40	. . .	1,587	1,587
Total	0	186	23	288	1,030	60	1,587	1,587

Sources: The numbers in the "observed" column under total deployment are derived from Albert Wohlstetter "Is There a Strategic Arms Race?" *Foreign Policy*, no. 15 (Summer 1974), p. 13, fig. 1; U.S. Defense Department, *Statement of Secretary of Defense Robert S. McNamara before the House Armed Services Committee on the FY 1968–72 Defense Program and 1968 Defense Budget*, 91 Cong. 1st sess. (GPO, 1967), p. 41; *Department of Defense Annual Report, Fiscal Year 1969*, p. 54; *Fiscal Year 1970*, p. 42; *Fiscal Year 1971*, p. 102; *Fiscal Year 1972*, p. 165; *Fiscal Year 1973*, p. 40; and *Fiscal Year 1975*, p. 50. The initial year of deployment in the postulated deployment columns are from U.S. Department of Defense, *Soviet Military Power*, 1985 (Government Printing Office, 1985), p. 41; for SS-9, see note 22 in text; subsequent deployments are based on author's estimates.

posed for the Minuteman program, the length of the production run being determined by U.S. decisions. Minuteman production never exceeded 360 a year, and Minuteman launchers were brought into service at a rate of 20–25 a month (240–300 a year) between December 1962 and June 1965.[14]

The Soviets' initial response to the sudden surge in U.S. ICBM capabilities can be inferred from their missile programs. There is sufficient information on the deployment of Soviet ICBMs in the 1961–73 period to allow the reconstruction of a plausible production schedule as it would have been decided in the 1961–62 period, and then subsequently adjusted. The schedule shown in table D-1 postulates the notional production rates

14. Ball, *Politics and Force Levels*, pp. 46–53.

that would have been needed for deployment to have taken place as it did.[15] The table shows the broad patterns of production and deployment as they might have been formulated at the central planning level. When this pattern is combined with the details of the individual missile programs, it suggests the following course of events.

In 1961 the Soviets decided to continue with the 5-MT SS-7 and 20-MT SS-9 programs as arranged. The production of both systems had been programmed to allow the deployment of 48 units a year.[16] The SS-7 deliveries would run 1961–65, followed directly by the SS-9 for another five years (1966–70). To this original ten-year program would be added a high-volume five-year program of SS-11s. This 1-MT missile would be produced at 240 units a year, with deployment planned initially for 1966–70, yielding a force of 1,200 SS-11s.[17]

None of this affected the requirement for a superheavy missile as the most cost-effective way of destroying a significant proportion of the governmental, economic, and military targets in North America. In May 1966 the East German defense minister credited the Soviet Union with this capability, and reference was made to warheads in the range of 50 MTs to 100 MTs in books of the Officers' Library series published in 1968–69. This requirement was probably not dropped until the restructuring of objectives that stemmed from the doctrinal decision in December 1966.

THE MEASURED RESPONSE. Some time in the 1962–63 period, perhaps in the course of the reevaluation that would have followed the failure to emplace missiles in Cuba, the Soviets came to appreciate that a more effective way of countering the rapid buildup of the U.S. Minuteman force was to focus on disabling the launch control centers (there was one for every ten missiles) rather than attempting to strike at each individual Minuteman silo.[18] Of the systems then under development or in production, only the third-generation SS-9 had the appropriate mix of payload and accuracy that would be needed for such a targeting concept.

15. Deployment figures can be used as a surrogate for production. Keep in mind that no allowance is made for additional production needed to meet the requirements for spares, testing, and so forth. Focusing on the production rates that would be needed to support known deployment figures allows one to identify evidence of policy changes.

16. A rate of about 50 a year was required by the arithmetic of table D-1. The choice of 48 is based on the following: the total deployment of 288 SS-9s equals six years at 48 a year; there were twenty-four silos started in the first half of 1970, which is equivalent to 48 a year if silo starts are made at six-month intervals; and the numbers 48, 24, and 12 are all divisible by both 3 and 4, the basic missile "unit" for hard and soft deployments respectively.

17. A rate of about 250 a year was required by the arithmetic of table D-1. The SS-11 was deployed in groups of 60, and 240 is a multiple of 48.

18. See Berman and Baker, *Soviet Strategic Forces,* pp. 117–18, and table C-6.

At this period, Soviet strategy for the contingency of world war was firmly based on intercontinental nuclear preemption, and there was considerable urgency to develop a response to the Minuteman. The series production of SS-9 was therefore advanced by about twelve months, and arrangements were made to extend its production run as necessary to cover the final Minuteman deployment. To make room for this production, the SS-7 program was curtailed.[19] To compensate for this change (since at that early stage, numbers were critically important), it was decided to complete the 23 SS-8 units that were available from "pipeline inertia."[20] A total of 186 SS-7s and 23 SS-8s were deployed in the period 1961–64.[21]

The 20-MT SS-9s first entered service in 1965, and deployment continued during the rest of the 1960s.[22] The underlying rate of 48 launchers a year was achieved in 1966. Deployment of the 1-MT SS-11 began in 1966 and reached its planned annual deployment rate of 240 a year in 1967, but in the 1968–69 period there was a hiatus in deployment, roughly equivalent to one year's production of SS-11s. The decision underlying the hiatus would have been taken in 1966–67 and was most probably related to the completion of the Minuteman deployment in 1967, with a total force of 1,054 ICBMs (including 54 Titan IIs), all emplaced in silos. The hiatus in the deployment of SS-11s can be plausibly explained by a decision to reassign 80 percent of SS-11 production to meet the requirements of the continental, or regional, target set, and these requirements necessitated changes in the missile's design and manufacture.

Probably the unforeseen demands of the SS-11 ICBM program had caused the planned production of the SS-5 intermediate-range ballistic missiles (IRBM) to be curtailed in the 1961–62 period, resulting in a serious gap in the coverage of regional targets. This gap could now be filled by assigning SS-11s to that target set, employing them in their originally intended configuration as a regional-range system for use against targets on the continental periphery. In the 1969–70 period the previous deployment rate of 240 a year was resumed, adding about 70 SS-11s to the inter-

19. Both systems stem from Yangel's design bureau and could be expected to use (consecutively) the same production facilities.

20. This would explain why the SS-8 was not deployed until 1963, although the rationale for the program's cancellation should have been apparent in 1960. The "pipeline inertia" of 23 missiles suggests a decision to cancel in 1960–61. (The resources already invested in producing all components of the missile system combine to produce pipeline inertia.)

21. Through the early 1970s, the U.S. officials used to include the 11 missiles at a test site, to make a total of 220.

22. Berman and Baker, *Soviet Strategic Forces,* p. 82, give 1966; *SMP, 1985,* p. 41, gives 1964; reported deployment numbers (table D-1) argue for 1965.

continental missile force, but the main production of 360 SS-11s went to the regional missile force.

Somewhat apart from the SS-9 and SS-11 programs was another third-generation ICBM, namely the 600-kiloton SS-13. This solid-fuel missile came from Nadiradize's design bureau, which specialized in that form of propulsion. Soviet statements leave little doubt that this missile was intended to be mobile, and the survivability that would have provided suggests that the intended purpose of the system was to serve as a strategic nuclear reserve, as well as to provide a hedge against a disarming strike.[23]

The genesis of this program lay in the 1950s, and it was probably originally intended to be deployed on a parallel path with the SS-9s and SS-10s, starting in 1966 at a rate of 48 a year. Although it is possible that the planned production of this system was affected by the superimposition of the SS-11 program, the main problem was probably with the solid-fuel propulsion system.[24] Development of this system seems to have fallen behind schedule, and it did not start flight testing until 1965. It was another four years before it began deployment. Apparently the SS-13 was unsuccessful in the mobile mode, and when deployment started in 1969 it was in fixed silos (table D-2).

THE IMPACT OF ARMS CONTROL. The five-week preliminary session of the strategic arms limitation talks (SALT) in November–December 1969 apparently convinced the Soviets that the United States was serious about negotiating the limitation of strategic arms, and in the spring of 1970 the Soviets decided to halt the buildup of ICBMs targeted on North America. Work was stopped on the construction of eighteen silos for the heavy SS-9 missile, while a total of sixty silos for light missiles (SS-11 and SS-13) were abandoned.[25] This event signaled the end of the SS-9 and SS-13 deployments, the SS-9s completing at 288 in the 1971–72 period and the SS-13s at 60 in 1970, but the SS-11 deployment continued to 1973. In 1971

23. See, for example, Lieutenant-Colonel V. M. Bondarenko, "Voenno-tekhnicheskoe pre-voskhodstvo—vazhneyshiy faktor nadezhnoy oborony strany" (Military-technical superiority—The most important factor of the reliable defense of the country), *Kommunist vooruzhennykh sil* (Communist of the armed forces), no. 17 (September 1966), p. 9.

24. Nadiradize's design bureau was responsible for the medium-range SS-14 and SS-15, which also were unsuccessful. However, while the SS-13, SS-14, and SS-15 were nominally third-generation missiles, their propulsion systems were the first generation of solid-fuel rocket motors.

25. There were twenty-four SS-9 silos starting construction in the first half of 1970; six of these were completed and eighteen abandoned. Similarly abandoned were ten SS-11 silos, twenty SS-13 silos, and another thirty silos about which it was too early to say whether they were SS-11s or SS-13s. (Personal recollection of Raymond L. Garthoff as a member of the U.S. negotiating team at the strategic arms limitation talks [SALT])

another sixty light silos were started in a former SS-4/SS-5 field in south-west Russia,[26] and these were occupied initially by SS-11s, which were subsequently replaced by SS-19s.

The figures provide some insight to the underlying decisions. In the case of the light missiles, the same number of silos were abandoned in 1970 as were started in 1971, the difference being that the 1971 silos were designed to house the SS-19. In other words, the 1970 construction halt reflected the decision that it would be a waste of resources to build silos for the SS-11 and SS-13 if they would shortly have to be refashioned to take fourth-generation missiles, as would be necessary once ceilings were imposed.[27]

For the heavy SS-9, the coincidence was in the fact that only eighteen out of the twenty-four new silo starts were abandoned. The six that were completed brought the total of SS-9s to 288, the equivalent of six-years' production at the notional rate of 48 missiles a year. This last fact and the timing of the abandonments in relation to the five-year planning process (the Ninth Five-Year Plan would start in 1971) suggest that they were part of a longer-range decision on missile numbers that took account of the effect of the new hierarchy of objectives on the requirement for ICBMs, the shape of the arms control agreement that was beginning to emerge, and the demands of the domestic economy. There is little doubt that the SS-9 program was curtailed, and the original plan (as revised in the 1962–63 period) may have provided for a full ten years' deployment of 480 mis-siles.[28] But by 1970 it would have been clear that the requirement to attack the Minuteman launch-control centers could be met by a smaller number.[29]

Similarly, in the 1961–62 period, the SS-11 may have been pro-grammed for an initial five-years' production yielding 1,200 missiles, which was within the bracket of Minuteman numbers then being talked about. The Soviets would have had the option of a second five-year pro-duction run if necessary. Unlike the SS-9 and SS-13 programs, SS-11 pro-duction was not curtailed immediately, and there were new silo starts in

26. Raymond L. Garthoff, "The Soviet SS-20 Decision," *Survival,* vol. 25 (May-June 1983), p. 111.

27. Raymond L. Garthoff suggested this explanation, having noted the coincidence between the number of abandoned silos and the new ones started in 1971.

28. There are two reasons for this conclusion. First, the SS-9 force was deployed in forty-eight six-silo sites. In 1971 (probably as a negotiating ploy) the Soviets added an additional four silos at five of the sites. If all sites had been upgraded to ten silos, this would have yielded a force of 480 SS-9s. Second, the development program of the fourth generation of ICBMs did not pro-vide for deployment to begin until about 1975, ten years after the deployment of the third-generation systems.

29. See Berman and Baker, *Soviet Strategic Forces,* p. 138, table C-8; and Bruce G. Blair, *Strategic Command and Control: Redefining the Nuclear Threat* (Brookings, 1985), pp. 313–20.

Table D-2. Programming Decisions for Deploying Intercontinental Ballistic Missiles, 1957–79[a]

Missile type and design bureau	1957–58	1960–61	1962–63	1965	1966–67	1970	1972–73	1979
SS-7 (Y)	Five years at 48 a year, 1961–65	...	Curtail by one year	...	...	...	...	...
SS-8 (K)	Five years at 48 a year, 1961–65	Cancel	Deploy pipeline inertia	...	...	...	...	...
SS-9 (Y)	Five years at 48 a year, 1961–65	...	Advance one year	Extend five years, 1970–74	...	Curtail at six years	...	...
SS-10 (K)	Five years at 240 a year, 1966–70	Cancel	...	...	...	...	...	...
SS-11 (Ch)	...	Five years at 240 a year, 1966–70	...	Extend five years, 1971–75	Hiatus, retarget on region	Curtail short of five years	...	...
SS-13[b] (N)	Five years at 48 a year, 1966–70	...	...	...	...	Curtail after 60 missiles	...	...

	1957–48	1960–61	1962–63	1965	1966–67	1970	1972–73	1979
Proton (K)	Five years at ? a year, 1971–75	…	…	…	Cancel	…	…	…
SS-16 (N)	Five years at 48 a year, 1971–75	…	…	…	Cancel	…	…	…
SS-17 (Y)	…	…	…	Five years at 336 a year, 1975–79c	…	Ten years at 144 a year, 1975–84	172 in five years, 480 in five years	Curtail after 150 missiles
SS-18 (Ch)	…	…	…	…	…	…	308 in five years	…
SS-19 (Ch)	…	…	…	…	…	…	480 in ten years	Curtail after 360 missiles

Source: Postulated from deployment patterns described in text and shown in table D-1. The design bureaus are designated as follows: Y-Yangel; K-Korolev; Ch-Chelomey; N-Nadiradize.

a. Programming decisions:

1957–48	Original plan
1960–61	Soviet doctrine of strategic preemption; U.S. buildup of ICBMs
1962–63	Target Minuteman control centers
1965	Prepare for Eighth Five-Year Plan
1966–67	Minuteman buildup completes; Soviet doctrinal shift
1970	Arms control takes hold; Ninth Five-Year Plan
1972–73	SALT I
1979	SALT II

b. Problems in development caused delay in deployment.

c. The SS-18s would have been programmed for deployment in the period 1975–79; the SS-17 and SS-19 for the period 1976–80.

1971. These were, however, for missiles covering targets in the continental, or regional, target set, implying that requirements for the intercontinental set had already been met.

If 360 SS-11s were assigned to regional targets, a total of 1,018 third-generation ICBMs were left for targets in North America; 288 SS-9s, 670 SS-11s, and 60 SS-13s. This was comparable in numbers to the 1,054 missiles of the U.S. ICBM force. The 209 SS-7s and SS-8s did not qualify because they were "inaccurate, carried relatively small payloads and required lengthy launch procedures."[30]

The start of work in spring 1971 on the construction of four additional silos at five of the existing six-launcher SS-9 bases remains to be explained.[31] Rather than being an indication of some aborted deployment policy, it seems more likely that this construction was aimed at the arms control negotiations. At this stage the U.S. side was still standing firm on the demand that the Soviets accept a limit of 250 SS-9s,[32] even though more than that number were already deployed. Twenty new silos, by their placement in existing SS-9 bases, implied a Soviet readiness to proceed with the deployment of an additional 192 heavy missiles. The deployment warned America it would either have to settle for a freeze on new silo construction as the basis for an arms control agreement or watch the Soviets continue to increase their inventory of heavy ICBMs.[33]

The 1970s: Consolidation

The fourth-generation systems that entered service in the 1970s stemmed from decisions the Soviets made during the first half of the 1960s. The basic requirement, as it would have been formulated in the 1963–64 period, was to develop follow-on systems to take over from the adjusted family of third-generation missiles that would enter service during the second half of the 1960s: the SS-9, SS-11, and SS-13. A successor to the large throw-weight ICBM presented few difficulties, since Yangel's SS-9 (11,000-pound throw-weight) was a successful system that was itself an improvement on the 4,000-pound SS-7 from the same design bureau. Yangel was therefore assigned to develop the SS-18, with a throw-weight of

30. *SMP, 1983*, 2d ed., pp. 19–20.

31. Raymond L. Garthoff contributed this information.

32. Raymond L. Garthoff, *Détente and Confrontation: American-Soviet Relations from Nixon to Reagan* (Brookings, 1985), pp. 141–42.

33. These twenty silos were completed and occupied in due course by SS-18s, bringing the total of heavy missile launchers to 308. The 288 SS-9s were later converted to SS-18s.

about 16,000 pounds and a range of 8,500 nautical miles. Similarly, Na-diradize was assigned to develop the solid-fuel SS-16 as a follow-on to the SS-13.

The Soviets also needed an accurate missile carrying a relatively small payload for use against dispersed and hardened point targets, a require-ment the SS-11 was not going to be able to meet. Following established practice, the task of developing a successor was given to both contenders: Yangel, as the designated designer of land-based ICBMs, developed the SS-17; and Chelomey, the designer of the SS-11, developed the SS-19. Both missiles had similar characteristics, with a payload of 8,000 pounds and a range of about 5,500 nautical miles, but the SS-19 apparently turned out to be the better system, with a greater potential for modification and improvement.[34]

By the time these systems were due to enter service in the mid-1970s, there had been two major developments. One affected the employment of the different missiles, and the other affected the numbers to be deployed. The availability of multiple independently targeted reentry vehicles (MIRVs) introduced a new flexibility to targeting, making it cost-effective for the large throw-weight SS-18 to be used against hardened point targets. This capacity did not dispense with the need for an area-devastation weapon as the most cost-effective way of dealing with large cities and even larger conurbations. All three of the fourth-generation missiles had single warhead variants, although only the SS-18 and SS-19 were deployed in any numbers. The estimated yield of a single reentry vehicle SS-18 is about four times that of a ten-MIRV version; for an SS-19, yield is about one-third more. Besides their use to devastate large built-up areas, single warheads can disrupt communications with electromagnetic pulse and be used against particularly well-protected targets, such as national com-mand, control, and communications (C^3) centers.[35]

The other development was the initiation of the SALT process, which took hold in 1969. This coincided with the restructuring of Soviet objec-tives that stemmed from the doctrinal adjustment in December 1966 and gave new importance to arms control. The most immediate implication of the strategic arms limitation talks was that the United States was accepting the concept of parity and that a nuclear arms race was therefore no longer

34. The SS-19 was deployed in both the intercontinental and the regional role, replacing the SS-11 variable-range ballistic missile (VRBM) in the latter role.

35. The single reentry vehicle SS-18 is credited with being "capable of destroying any known fixed target with high probability." *SMP, 1981,* 1st ed., p. 56.

inevitable. This major change in prognosis opened new prospects for reducing Soviet ICBM programs, which would yield significant economic benefits.

When the Soviets' fourth-generation systems were originally being projected in the first half of the 1960s, it would have been hard to predict where the U.S. program was going. The speed of the U.S. buildup was awesome. Equally impressive was the short time between successive generations of missiles, and the Soviets had to assume that the Minuteman would soon be replaced by an improved system.[36] It is probable therefore that the Eighth Five-Year Plan that the Soviets accepted in 1966 would have provided for the production of fourth-generation ICBMs to continue at the rate established for the SS-9, SS-11, and SS-13, which was sufficient to sustain a deployment of 336 units a year. However, by the time the Ninth Five-Year Plan was being prepared in 1970, the situation had largely stabilized. The U.S. ICBM force seemed to be fixed at 1,054 launchers, and although a successor to Minuteman I/II had been developed (the MIRVed Minuteman III), Congress was being slow in authorizing its deployment. It seemed unlikely that more than half the force would be replaced by the improved system during the next five years.

Since the rapid buildup of the Soviet missile force was a direct response to the sudden surge in the number of U.S. ICBMs, it could be expected that when the number of U.S. ICBMs stabilized, the Soviets would respond in kind. As discussed, during the first six months of 1970, the Soviets apparently reached a decision to round off the number of intercontinental-range missiles at 1,090 light systems (of which 360 were allocated to regional targets), and 288 heavy ones, the heavy ones being increased by 20 in 1971, as a prod to the SALT negotiations. It can also be inferred that at this time the Soviets decided to cut substantially the projected production of fourth-generation systems, which had likely been set at the notional rate of 336 a year. If the 1,378 third-generation missiles were to be replaced by fourth-generation systems over a ten-year period, that would require an annual deployment rate of only 144 a year.[37]

---

36. The U.S. ICBM force went from a strength of 63 in 1961 to 931 in 1964. The Minuteman force went from 20 in 1962 to 821 in 1965; 698 had been deployed by the end of 1964. Ball, *Politics and Force Levels*, p. 50., table 1. Development of Minuteman III, which is MIRVed and a later generation to Minuteman I and II, was authorized in 1966 and a successful launch was made in mid-1968.

37. The figure 144 is inferred, as $3 \times 48 = 144$. During the 1970s the Soviets did convert "about 150 ICBM launchers a year to new systems." Raymond L. Garthoff, *Perspectives on the Strategic Balance* (Brookings, 1983), p. 15.

The deployment of fourth-generation systems did in fact run at about 140–150 a year during the second half of the 1970s, but it then fell away sharply, and the average rate over some eight years of deployment was only about 100. There seems little doubt that this reflected a further curtailment in production following the signing of the treaty on limiting strategic arms (SALT II) in June 1979. A central feature of that agreement was the ceiling of 820 MIRVed ICBMs, a limit that affected the three fourth-generation programs, all of which had been tested in the MIRVed mode. The Soviets observed that limit, deploying a total of 818 units, comprising the 308 heavy SS-18s, and 510 light missiles. This required abandoning plans for converting at least fifty launch silos for SS-17s and another fifty SS-19s (about one hundred silos in all).[38] The final numbers deployed were 150 SS-17s and 360 SS-19s. This, combined with the initial adherence to the predicted deployment rate of 144 a year and the fall away that followed SALT II, provides persuasive evidence that the program was curtailed.[39]

It would seem that all three of the fourth-generation liquid-fuel missiles were reasonably successful. Apparently this was not true of the solid-fuel SS-16 program, which began flight testing in 1972 but never went into production. It seems likely that problems with the propulsion system and the possibility of using the components to meet another requirement (the SS-20 IRBM) were the main reasons for this decision, which would have been made in the first half of the 1970s. The SALT negotiations would, however, have been a factor. The new Soviet priority on the arms control process to promote détente and reduce the likelihood of war meant that U.S. concerns about the Soviets' land-mobile ICBMs would have been taken into account, even though the Soviets were not prepared to accept U.S. arguments about the destabilizing effects of such systems.

By the end of the 1970s the deployment of fourth-generation ICBMs was essentially complete. The SS-18 had replaced the SS-9, and 510 SS-17s and SS-19s had replaced an equivalent number of SS-11s, including

38. Garthoff, *Détente and Confrontation,* p.793, note 114.
39. The marked imbalance in the numbers of SS-17 and SS-19, the specific evidence of equal cancellations, and the limited evidence on the pattern of deployment that can be derived from various annual issues of *The Military Balance* (London, International Institute for Strategic Studies) over these years can perhaps be explained by an underlying production schedule along these lines. Notional production was planned at 144 a year for ten years of which Chelomey was allocated 48 a year for the SS-19. Yangel had 96 for his two missiles and for the first four years this was apportioned as 72 for the SS-18s and 24 for the SS-17s. The limit of 308 for SS-18s would be reached in the fifth year, when those facilities would become available for SS-17 production at the rate of 96 a year. As originally planned in 1971, the notional production rate of 144 a year would have had to accommodate the SS-16 program as well.

the 180 missiles of the regional force deployed in the southwestern part of Russia. During this same period, the Soviets dismantled the launchers for the second-generation SS-7 and SS-8, but they retained the 60 third-generation SS-13 solid-fuel missiles. The end result was that more than 60 percent of the Soviet ICBM force was composed of fourth-generation systems, which had large payloads and were reasonably accurate. This was comparable with the U.S. ICBM force. By mid-1975 more than half of the U.S. force was composed of Minuteman IIIs. These were solid-fuel systems and more accurate than the Soviet systems, but they had smaller payloads.

The 1980s: Stay Put or Carry On?

The Soviets would have formulated requirements for fifth-generation systems in the first half of the 1970s, and they had to address two kinds of questions. One concerned the type of missiles that might be required in the 1980s. The other concerned the actual need for a family of fifth-generation ICBMs, given the improved climate of international relations and the progress made in arms control negotiations. This second question involved decisions about production rather than design and development, since that would carry on regardless of decisions about production. The answer could be deferred until the flight-testing stage was reached in about 1980, although production requirements would have to be penciled into the long-range plan. The type of missiles required had to be decided on immediately, however, in order to allow design and development to proceed.

SPECIFICATIONS. These ICBM requirements would be the first to reflect the restructuring of objectives in the wake of the December 1966 doctrinal adjustment. The doctrinal change meant a shift from a strategy of intercontinental nuclear preemption in the event that war was unavoidable to one of seeking to avoid intercontinental escalation by holding America deterred, even when its forces faced defeat in Europe. This shift in doctrine did not mean that the Soviets were confident that this deterrence would succeed. They had therefore to be capable of launching a full-scale nuclear attack on the West and to have the forces for waging war after the intercontinental exchange. Between the two extremes of holding America deterred and waging global nuclear war was the possibility of limited nuclear war extending beyond the reach of regional missiles.

All the ICBMs would contribute to deterring escalation, but beyond that, the forces to meet these requirements fell into two main categories.

Some ICBMs would participate in the initial intercontinental strikes against military, political, and economic targets. Others would be needed in the aftermath of the intercontinental nuclear exchange to wage war and to match the West's remaining strategic nuclear capability, whether it was used or not. The major difference between the two requirements was that the target set for the initial strikes was mainly fixed, with location and type known in advance, but the war-fighting target set was unknowable in advance, except in terms of broad possibilities. Missiles carrying a MIRVed warhead were the most cost-effective way of meeting the first requirement to strike a large number of fixed targets in as short a time as possible. Such warheads would, however, be wasteful and less effective against the war-fighting target set, which would probably be dispersed in time as well as space. That requirement could best be met by missiles carrying single warheads of moderate yield but greater than that of the usual MIRV.

The move away from the strategy of intercontinental preemption in favor of avoiding the nuclear devastation of Russia by avoiding escalation meant that at best the Soviets could hope to launch their ICBMs on warning that an American strike had been launched, and more likely when they were already under attack. The United States, meanwhile, was developing the MX ICBM and the Trident II submarine-launched ballistic missile (SLBM), which would have the accuracy and payload to strike directly at hardened silos. The vulnerability of the Soviet ICBM force to surprise attack would therefore be significantly increased, both because of improved U.S. weapons and because of the change in Soviet strategic concepts. There were two ways of responding to that problem: by increasing the hardening of missile silos and control facilities or by mobility and concealment. The problem of survival would be particularly acute for the war-fighting component of the force which, to perform its function, had to come through the intercontinental exchange with its capability unimpaired.

By 1975 it would have been clear that the major deficiency in the ICBM force of the early 1980s would be the lack of a survivable war-fighting component. All fourth-generation systems would be MIRVed, and the single-warhead force would comprise the rather inaccurate SS-11s (and 60 SS-13s) deployed in 1960-vintage silos. The Soviets tacitly acknowledged this unmet requirement when they argued at the 1977 SALT negotiations for a single-warhead missile as the permitted "new type," while the United States argued for a MIRV.[40] Soviet development therefore moved ahead on

40. The final agreement was for one new type, MIRV or non-MIRV.

a fifth-generation solid-fuel missile with a single warhead, which would be road mobile—the SS-25. Although in numerical terms this new missile could be seen as a replacement for the SS-11,[41] in terms of its role the SS-25 was the lineal successor to the SS-13 and the canceled SS-16. The SS-25 was designed to the general parameters of the solid-fuel SS-13 by the same design bureau, allowing the Soviets to claim that it was a replacement and not a new type.

The fourth generation of missiles, the main MIRVed strike component of the ICBM force, would place the force on a strong footing, and if there were to be another generation, the main requirement would be to improve survivability. The successor to the light element of the force (the SS-17 and SS-19) was therefore designated as the new missile, and designed as a solid-fuel system, allowing the option of rail mobility—the SS-24. Apparently the development of a successor to the SS-18 was deferred. This was not because the Soviets undervalued these heavy missiles which, besides their military effectiveness, had potential value as bargaining chips. It probably reflected the fact that the SS-18 was a more mature system than the others, and of course these large missiles were much more expensive.[42] In due course the Soviets did start developing a follow-on system, and the decision to proceed is likely to have been made in the 1978–79 period.[43] It may have been prompted by the U.S. decision to go ahead with the MX. Because of its size and liquid fuel, improved survivability for this missile is likely to have been sought through increased hardness.

The Soviets still had to consider the 360 SS-11s and SS-19s that were deployed in regional fields, covering targets on the continental periphery. The evidence suggests that the Soviets planned to replace these by a new type of medium-range missile that would not count against ICBMs.

PRODUCTION. As already discussed, a decision was apparently made in the first half of 1970 to curtail production of the third generation of ICBMs and to round off the intercontinental component of the force at just over 1,000 missiles, meanwhile increasing somewhat the regional component. Apparently the Soviets also decided to program the production of the fourth generation of ICBMs to sustain a deployment rate of 144 a year,

41. In the spring of 1985, the Soviet Union informed the United States that it intended to start replacing SS-11s with SS-25s, initially by deploying 18 SS-25s and retiring 20 SS-11s.

42. Unlike the SS-17 and SS-19, which were meeting new requirements, the SS-18 was a successor to the SS-9, which succeeded the SS-7.

43. Robert Berman assumed that development of a new system started when the predecessor moved on to flight testing. This yielded a seven-to-eight-year lead time between design decision and flight testing. Berman and Baker, *Soviet Strategic Forces,* p. 82, figure A-1. In mid-1985 the SS-18 replacement was known to be nearing the flight-testing stage of development but had not yet flown. *SMP, 1985,* p. 31.

which was about two-fifths the production rate for third-generation missiles. In 1979, following the signing of SALT II, there was strong evidence of a decision to curtail the deployment of SS-17s and SS-19s to remain within the agreed limits. Assuming a ten-year program of 144 missiles a year, this would have meant curtailing planned production by as much as 40 percent. In the 1970s work on the design of a successor to the SS-18 was apparently deferred by some five years.

This evidence suggests the Soviets are willing to cut programs, forgo production, and even delay development when the appropriate arms control regime is in place. Such a regime appeared to be emerging in the 1970s when the Soviets would have addressed the question of whether it was necessary to move to the production of the fifth generation of ICBMs. A crucial preliminary step was the flight testing of the systems then under development, and it appears that this testing was deferred for at least two years.

It had been Soviet practice to initiate the design of a follow-on system as soon as a new missile entered flight testing. On that basis one would expect the Soviets to have started flight testing the fifth-generation SS-24 in 1980 and the SS-25 in 1981. They did not begin flight testing until 1982 and 1983. The conclusion that this delay was because of a deliberate policy decision rather than technical or other problems is supported by an official U.S. assessment that at least two new ICBMs had been ready for flight testing by the end of 1980.[44]

The SS-24 did begin testing in October 1982,[45] and for analytical convenience the decision will be pegged to the plenum held in June 1982. This decision would have been subsequent to the leaking of the *U.S. Defense Guidance for Fiscal Years 1984–88,* with its emphasis on strategic decapitation and the need to prevail in nuclear war, and the U.S. decision to advance by one year the deployment of the Trident II ballistic-missile submarine (SSBN) carrying the D-5 missile. Apparently, the SS-25 did not begin flight testing until February 1983.[46] The decision to go ahead in this case may have been taken in conjunction with the somewhat unusual meeting that Leonid I. Brezhnev and other members of the Defense Council had had with military command personnel the previous October, shortly

44. This information was provided by a Reagan administration official as evidence that the Soviets might "cut back on their expensive and threatening land-based missile program." See Walter Pincus, "Behind Reagan's Tough Talk, A Unilateral Arms Reduction," *Washington Post,* January 10, 1982.

45. *Defense Daily,* vol. 128 (June 2, 1983), p. 178.

46. "Soviets Test Launch Small ICBM," *Aviation Week and Space Technology,* vol. 118 (February 21, 1983), p. 16.

before Brezhnev died.[47] The testing of the SS-25 would certainly have been approved by the end of the November plenum that confirmed Yuri V. Andropov as Brezhnev's successor.

It is necessary, however, to distinguish between the delay in moving to the flight-testing stage of development and a delay in production and deployment. As noted, it seems likely that it was planned in 1971 and reaffirmed in 1976 to produce and deploy the fourth-generation systems over a ten-year period, 1975–84. This implies that the fifth generation would not be due to start deploying until about 1985. The asymmetry between this ten-year deployment cycle and the established design and development cycle provided about two years' slack during which Moscow could assess whether evidence that the Soviet Union was holding back would evoke some response from the U.S. side. The hiatus in testing was indeed observed by members of the Reagan administration.[48]

1955–85: The Overall Pattern

The Soviets' initial requirement for intercontinental ballistic missiles was to develop a capability to deliver nuclear weapons on the United States, comparable with the then existing capability of U.S. Strategic Air Command. The programming of missile production was sufficient to support a deployment rate of 96 ICBMs a year, rising to 144 a year in the mid-1960s.

At the beginning of the 1960s, a new requirement to match the Minuteman force was introduced, and the Soviets met it by programming additional production equivalent to 240 deployments a year. The governing strategic concept was intercontinental nuclear preemption, and priority in targeting was shifted to counterforce, which evolved to focus on facilities for command, control, and communications rather than on missile silos. This focus allowed the reallocation of SS-11s to cover regional targets.

By the end of the 1960s the Soviets' governing strategic concept had shifted to deterring wartime escalation to an intercontinental exchange, and arms control had become an important factor. In 1970 the intercontinental element was stabilized at just over 1,000 ICBMs (not counting the obsolescent SS-7s and SS-8s), with another 360 missiles assigned to a regional role. Production of fourth-generation ICBMs was set at the equivalent of 144 deployments a year to provide for the replacement of third-

---

47. Reported in "Soveshchanie voenachal'nikov v Kremle" (Meeting of military leaders in the Kremlin), *Pravda*, October 28, 1982, including the text of Leonid I. Brezhnev's speech.
48. See Pincus, "Behind Reagan's Tough Talk."

generation systems in both intercontinental and regional elements of the force over a ten-year period.

At the end of the 1970s, arms control considerations halted the deployment of fourth-generation systems at 818 units. This would have curtailed the planned production program by as much as 40 percent. At this period, the Soviets had still not decided whether it would be necessary to go ahead with the flight testing and production of the fifth generation of ICBMs.

The decision to move ahead with all programs had been made by the end of 1982. The regional element is likely to be replaced by medium-range missiles and, in the absence of further arms control reductions or a major U.S. buildup, the intercontinental force will continue to be about 1,000 strong.

Long-Range Cruise Missiles

Soviet development of long-range nuclear-armed cruise missiles is likely to have been a direct response to the U.S. decision to develop this type of system, a decision that was made immediately after the signing of SALT I. The cruise missile was not covered by SALT I and largely escaped the provisions of SALT II.[49] After the Vladivostok summit in November 1974 and the SALT negotiations that followed, it became clear that the United States was seriously committed to the development of the cruise missile. Experience had taught the Soviets that the United States would not negotiate limits in any area in which it held an unchallenged lead, and the relative timing of the U.S. and Soviet programs suggests that the decisions about developing the Soviet versions of the Tomahawk cruise missile were echoes of U.S. decisions. The three variants of the Soviet missiles entered service two to three years after their U.S. counterparts, and Soviet statements linked the two programs.[50]

The fourth cruise missile program, the naval SS-N-24, is usually categorized as an intercontinental system. However, it seems more likely that it is primarily intended for use in the European theater. It seems likely that

49. SALT II allowed a maximum of 3,360 air-launched cruise missiles (ALCMs). The protocol to the treaty banned the deployment of sea- and land-based missiles with a range of more than 600 kilometers, but the protocol expired at the end of 1981 and would not constrain U.S. development.

50. In October 1984 the Soviets announced that, in response to the deployment of ground-launched cruise missiles (GLCMs) in Europe and the equipping of U.S. strategic bombers and warships with long-range cruise missiles, they were embarking on the deployment of their own long-range cruise missiles on strategic bombers and submarines and were successfully testing ground-based missiles. "V Ministerstve oborony SSSR" (At the USSR defense ministry), *Krasnaya zvezda* (Red star), October 14, 1984.

the concept underlying this system was to exploit the availability of a suitable platform in order to meet an existing requirement in a different way. The requirement was to strike, using conventional means, at NATO nuclear assets and command facilities in the early days of a war. The platform was the Yankee hull-propulsion unit that would become available when newly constructed SSBNs took the force above the SALT limits. The design of the weapons system would build on twenty-five years' experience of naval cruise missiles, and the size of the Yankee SSBN would allow a missile with the necessary speed, range, and conventional payload to be carried in sufficient numbers to justify this role.[51] One Yankee had been converted to a cruise missile attack submarine (SSGN) by the end of 1984, and the system could be operational by 1987.

As discussed in chapter 7, the use of sea-launched cruise missiles in this way would outflank the NATO air defense system and give easy access to targets in Britain and in NATO's far rear. At the same time, the missiles would reduce the demand for long-range interdiction aircraft in the Western theater of military action (TVD). The decision to adopt this concept probably stems from the Dmitriy Ustinov defense review in the 1976–77 period.

Continental, or Regional, Ballistic-Missile Systems

The evolution of the regional component of the SRF does not lend itself to a chronological description tied to succeeding generations of missiles. Instead it is more useful to focus on three separate categories of missiles: the SS-4 and SS-5 medium-range ballistic missiles, the SS-11 and SS-19 variable-range ballistic missiles, and the SS-20 deployment.

The SS-4 and SS-5 Medium-Range Missiles

The original requirement for medium-range missiles[52] would have been made final in the mid-1950s, with the 1,000-nautical-mile SS-4 scheduled to begin deployment in 1959, and the 2,200-nautical-mile SS-5 in 1961.

51. The missile is about twelve meters long and is reported to be supersonic, *SMP, 1985*, p. 35; and Walter Andrews, "Soviets Gain U.S. Cruise Missile Technology," *Washington Times*, November 17, 1983. This missile is likely to have a range of more than one thousand miles.
52. The Soviets use the term "medium range" to describe the forces that are now categorized by NATO as intermediate range.

This medium-range missile force was to cover a preplanned set of targets on the continental periphery of the Soviet Union, with particular emphasis on targets that could be the source of nuclear strikes on Russia or contribute to such strikes.

The Soviets deployed about 730 of these medium-range missiles in the period 1959–66, of which more than 600 were SS-4s. This was probably close to the number of SS-4s originally planned, but there are reasons to suspect that the 100 or so SS-5s that entered service reflect a curtailment of that program. One, the target set that this combined force was intended to cover included about 1,200 or more targets.[53] Two, the number of SS-5s does not conform to the pattern of "minimum" production runs established over time.[54] More persuasive, in the 1962–66 period, the Soviets were faced with a heavy and unforeseen demand for ballistic-missile production facilities.

In 1961, the same year that the SS-5 began deployment, the requirement emerged to respond to the Minuteman program with a capability for point targeting. The Soviets then had to produce the SS-11 at about 240 a year, which was at least 30 to 40 percent higher than the production rate planned for the SS-5 and probably even higher.[55] This increase would have placed heavy demands on existing missile-assembly facilities, even if they had been augmented by adapting manufacturing capacity intended for production of cruise missiles. But the more severe constraints were probably on high-technology components of ballistic missiles and their nuclear warheads.

It was originally planned to replace the SS-4 and SS-5 with the third generation of medium-range missiles, starting in about 1967. The SS-14 and SS-15 were both solid-fuel systems from Nadiradize's design bureau and would have been mounted on mobile launchers. They both started flight testing in 1965 but, like their ICBM contemporary (the SS-13), neither system appears to have been successful. They were never deployed in a fully operational role, nor did they go into series production. Con-

53. Berman and Baker estimated 1,145–1,410 such targets in the early 1960s, and in the latter half of the 1950s there would have been additional Strategic Air Command bases on the list. *Soviet Strategic Forces*, p. 135, table C-3.

54. The existence of minimum production runs was first established in naval construction; anything below that figure suggests that the program had been canceled or curtailed.

55. This is by analogy with the SS-4, whose launchers were deployed at a rate of about 75 a year. If one assumes that reloads were deployed at the same time as the main deployment, the missile deployment rate would increase to 150 a year. But the reloads could also have been supplied by continuing production. The planned deployment rate of SS-11s appears to have been 240 a year. See table D-1.

sequently, the SS-4 and SS-5 were retained despite their manifest inadequacies.

MISSILE DEPLOYMENT. About 650 of the SS-4 and SS-5 launchers were deployed facing Europe. Most of the missiles were in relatively soft sites, with the launchers located above ground in clusters of four. The last 135 missiles were emplaced in silos in groups of three. The vulnerability of surface emplacement was discussed by military writers, and the Soviets demonstrated their awareness of this danger in practical terms by seeking to develop mobile systems. One must therefore ask why they only emplaced 135 of the SS-4s and SS-5s in silos, rather than retroactively hardening the whole force. This question is addressed later in this appendix.

About 60 of these missiles were withdrawn from the missile fields in southwestern Russia at the same time that 180 SS-11 variable-range ballistic missiles (VRBMs) were emplaced in that area in the 1970–72 period. But most of the force did not change until the missiles started being replaced by the SS-20s in 1977.

The remaining 70 or so SS-4s were emplaced during the last two years of the deployment period, 10 of them between the Caspian and Aral Seas, facing the Central Treaty Organization to the south, and the rest in eastern Russia. A handful of the ones in eastern Russia were located on the Chuchki Peninsula (facing Alaska and the Aleutians), but most were deployed in 1966 along the Mongolian border to the east of Lake Baikal, in sites served by the Trans-Siberian railway.[56] It seems likely that these 56 missiles were primarily intended to cover political, military, and economic targets in China and perhaps Japan, whose destruction would ensure that neither country would be able to turn on Russia in the wake of a Soviet-U.S. nuclear exchange. The missiles would also have targeted U.S. military installations in the SS-4's reach, such as the nuclear capability in Korea.

Within three to four years, these SS-4 sites were being deactivated. This took place in the wake of the Sino-Soviet border clashes, suggesting that deactivation was a precautionary move to remove from China's path the temptation to launch a preventive attack against these vulnerable missile sites. They were not replaced immediately,[57] but the early 1970s saw the deployment of silo-based SS-11 VRBMs in the area. It would, however,

---

56. Edward L. Warner III, "Soviet Strategic Force Posture: Some Alternative Explanations," in Frank B. Horton III, Anthony C. Rogerson, and Edward L. Warner III, eds., *Comparative Defense Policy* (Johns Hopkins University Press, 1974), p. 316.

57. There are reports that a small number of SS-14s and SS-15s were deployed at about this period, which may have been a stopgap measure.

have been practical to build silos for the original missile force, and the SS-4 remained operational in western Russia for another decade. Vulnerability to Chinese attack is not therefore a sufficient explanation of this change in the Far Eastern force structure.

The more likely explanation relates to a change in the target set. The intended target set also provides the most plausible explanation of why the Soviets only hardened 135 of some 650 SS-4s and SS-5s in western Russia, an explanation that may also have some bearing on the contemporary role of the SS-20.[58]

The decision to harden the 135 missiles would have been made in the 1962–63 period, at which time it was planned that preemptive nuclear strikes against targets in Europe and North America would be launched in the event that the Soviets believed a world war unavoidable. Soviet strategic rocket forces were therefore not expected to have to ride out nuclear attacks. But surprise was always a possibility, and the Soviets had to cover the contingency that they would be preempted by NATO, rather than vice versa, particularly since the reaction time of these first-generation missiles was too slow to allow the option of launching under attack.

In such circumstances many of the military targets in the original set would lose their importance, since the birds would have (literally) flown. But a hard core of political and military targets would remain, whose importance did not depend upon preemption and whose destruction was critical to the outcome of the war in Europe. It is therefore possible that the 135 hardened missiles, rather than reflecting some quirk of the deployment program, were intended to cover such targets. This core target set would remain much the same over a long period, since key strategic targets of this type, political and military, change very slowly.

The Variable-Range Ballistic Missiles

As already discussed, it can be inferred that by 1967 the Soviets' original concept of targeting each U.S. Minuteman silo with an SS-11 missile had evolved so that it was possible to reassign 360 of the planned produc-

---

58. The argument that only hardening 135 SS-4s and SS-5s was the result of priority being given to building silos for the SS-9 and SS-11 is not persuasive, particularly since work on the ICBM silos began in 1964 and ran on a parallel path with the emplacement of the last 135 SS-4s and SS-5s facing Europe. Paradoxically, hardening of the medium-range missile force stopped in 1966, by which date, the Soviets expected that war in Europe would start with a conventional phase, which meant that the other three quarters of the force, emplaced in clusters of four on surface launch pads, would be even more vulnerable to preemptive attack.

tion run of these missiles from an international to a regional role, reconfiguring them as variable-range ballistic missiles.[59] In the 1970–72 period, 180 of the SS-11 VRBMs were deployed in the SS-4 and SS-5 fields in southwestern Russia, and in the early 1970s another 180 were deployed in the Far East.[60]

At first glance this deployment would seem to fit the pattern established for the original medium-range missiles, with the SS-11 VRBM deployment filling in part of the shortfall created by the curtailment of the SS-5 program (perhaps about 500 missiles) and compensating for the failure of the SS-14 and SS-15 replacement programs. There are, however, anomalies, and any explanation of the role of the VRBM must account for the different deployment patterns in the eastern and western parts of Russia. In the east more than three times as many SS-11s as SS-4s were deployed, and subsequently they were partially replaced by the SS-20. In the west the 180 SS-11s were an addition to the existing medium-range force, since only 60 SS-4s and SS-5s were removed, and the SS-11s were subsequently replaced by an equal number of SS-19s.

VRBMS IN EASTERN RUSSIA. The decision not to build silos for the SS-4, but to remove these missiles in the wake of the border clashes with China in 1969, suggests that the decision to deploy the SS-11s had by then already been made. This makes sense, since the target set for medium-range missiles in the Far East had changed radically in the mid-1960s. By 1967 the United States had well over half a million men in South Vietnam, and in early 1968 American military commanders were calling for another 200,000. U.S. bases from the Philippines to Japan were bulging with ships and aircraft, and the Pacific Rim had become a veritable *place d'armes*. This was well beyond the capacity of the existing Soviet missile force to deal with in a world war, not least because most of the targets were out of range. The 60 SS-4s were therefore scheduled for replacement by 180 SS-11 VRBMs.

By the mid-1970s the situation had again changed. The United States had withdrawn all forces from the Southeast Asian mainland and one of

---

59. The configuration of variable-range ballistic missiles was probably close to the original design, which was intended for use against targets in the peripheral seas.

60. Raymond L. Garthoff "The Soviet SS-20 Decision," p. 111. In each year, 1968, 1970, and 1971, sixty silos were begun. Garthoff gives only 120 for deployment in the Far East. However, Berman and Baker show three variable-range missile bases in the Far East. Berman and Baker, *Soviet Strategic Forces*, p. 16, figure 1-3. *SMP, 1984,* 3d ed., p. 21, also shows SS-11s being deployed at the same three bases. Since the normal base comprises sixty launchers, it seems likely that 180 SS-11s were deployed in the Far East.

two divisions from Korea, and national attention in America had swung back to the NATO area. A slow rapprochement was taking place between the United States and China. China was steadily expanding its nuclear delivery capability and could no longer be counted on to remain neutral in a world war. Therefore, in the number of targets to be covered, China became the primary concern. However, the formulas emerging from the SALT process were making it increasingly unacceptable to cover regional targets with missiles that would count against intercontinental ceilings. Part of the SS-11 VRBM force was therefore scheduled for replacement by the SS-20.

VRBMS IN WESTERN RUSSIA. Despite coming under the SALT counting rules, the SS-11s in western Russia were replaced by the SS-19s, whereas the SS-4s and SS-5s were replaced with the SS-20s, which would only be counted (later) under INF. This distinction implies that by the mid-1970s, if not earlier, the role of the VRBM was somewhat distinct from the role of the SS-4 and SS-5. A clue to the role of the VRBM may be found in the fact that when the 180 SS-11s were first deployed, only 60 SS-4s and SS-5s were removed.[61]

With hindsight it seems probable that the task of those 60 SS-4s and SS-5s was to strike at U.S. carriers in the Mediterranean. In the mid-1960s Western analysts assessed that Sixth Fleet carriers were targeted by medium-range ballistic missiles emplaced in southwestern Russia, that being the only plausible explanation for the close shadowing by gun-armed destroyers that had begun in 1964. The destroyers were acting as forward observers positioned to call down fire on the carriers, whose nuclear-strike capability made them high-priority targets at the onset of war. The SS-4s and SS-5s would have had only a limited capability in such a role, but something was better than nothing.

This arrangement suggests that the deployment of SS-11s was originally meant to supplement the existing force of SS-4s and SS-5s, providing the long-range capability that had been forfeited with the curtailment of the SS-5 program. The original role of 120 of the VRBMs in southwestern Russia was therefore to join in the preplanned nuclear strike. Meanwhile another 60 SS-11s were adapted to replace the same number of SS-4s and SS-5s in the countercarrier role. However, as the implications of the December 1966 doctrinal adjustment worked their way through the system,

61. If the SS-11 was an addition to the regional missile force, then why remove any? If it was a third-generation replacement, then why not remove the same number of the first- and second-generation launchers?

the broader applications of the flexible targeting capability that was an essential feature of the countercarrier version of the SS-11 became increasingly apparent. Thus in December 1972 the Soviet minister of defense made the unprecedented assertion that the wartime mission of the strategic rocket forces, which he described as being equipped with intercontinental and medium-range missiles, included the destruction of "troop and naval groupings in the land and sea *(morskoy)* theaters of military action."[62]

With the target set in the Far East in mind, the statement suggests that during the first half of 1970s, the role of the SS-11 in the regional missile force evolved to cover any targets that by their nature could not be included in the preplanned target set of the SS-4 and SS-5 force because they were "relocatable."[63] Such targets might well be mobile and could include naval groupings, redeployed forces, airlifted or seaborne reinforcements, and extemporary or newly established bases.

This role of the VRBM would become even more important in the second half of the 1970s, when the 1970s hierarchy of objectives came into full effect. Should there be a resort to nuclear weapons in the theater, there was no way of foretelling how NATO forces would be disposed at that moment, and the requirement for a flexible targeting capability increased. It was therefore to be expected that the SS-11 would be replaced in due course by an improved VRBM, the SS-19.[64]

The SS-20 Deployment

An assessment of the intended role of the SS-20 must take account of certain apparent anomalies. As discussed in chapter 11, the evidence suggests that the Soviets had originally planned to deploy about 500 launchers.[65] About 350 were to be located in the western parts of the Soviet

---

62. A. A. Grechko, "Armiya sotsialisticheskaya mnogonatsional'naya" (A socialist, multi-national army), *Krasnaya zvezda,* December 12, 1972. Note the use of the qualifier *morskoy* rather than *okeanskiy*. In the same month, Gorshkov referred to this same mission, linking the strategic rocket forces with forward-deployed naval forces. See appendix C to this book.

63. Such a strike plan was essential for successful nuclear preemption, which was what the SS-4 and SS-5 force was originally designed for.

64. The SS-11 and SS-19 both originated in Chelomey's design bureau, as did the SS-NX-13, a 400-nautical-mile tactical submarine-launched ballistic missile with terminal guidance that was tested in the 1970–73 period but never deployed. If this maneuver capability were incorporated in the VRBM warhead it would greatly increase the missiles' military value.

65. By April 1985, 414 SS-20 launchers had been deployed and work was proceeding on another eight sites of 9 missiles each. "New Soviet Missile Sites Reported," *New York Times,* April 23, 1985. This would bring the total to 486 launchers, which is equivalent to six missile armies of three divisions each. To provide 2 missiles for each launcher, plus 25 percent for main-

Union, in range of NATO Europe. By 1982 deployment sites for 243 launchers had either been completed or were under construction in western Russia. And yet, in the course of the INF negotiations, the Soviets made an official offer to reduce the force facing Europe to 144 launchers (and an informal offer of 129).[66] They also indicated they were willing to dismantle the surplus launchers and destroy missiles. If NATO did not deploy any new missiles, the Soviets would destroy any SS-20s located in western Russia that were in excess of the combined total of British and French missiles.[67] Furthermore, the pattern of deployment in the 1979–82 period and the renewed deployments in 1984–85 suggest that in about mid-1979 it was decided to halt the production of SS-20 systems. But following the Soviet withdrawal from the INF talks, the Soviets decided to resume production of the system.

To explain these anomalies, one must attempt a reconstruction of the original Soviet policy. It is assumed that the routine replacement of the SS-4 and SS-5 by the third-generation SS-14 and SS-15 systems was provided for in the production plans drawn up in the first half of the 1960s, but when these systems proved unsatisfactory the requirement remained on the books. In due course the Soviets met it by adapting the solid-fuel SS-16 ICBM, which had already been programmed for production, to produce the SS-20 mobile IRBM, armed with three MIRVs. In 1977 there were roughly 570 SS-4s and SS-5s still deployed, and all except 10 were facing NATO. These would be replaced by about two-thirds that number of SS-20 launchers, but these missiles would have to meet the targeting requirements of the Southern TVD, as well as covering the existing target set in the European theater. The SS-20 would also replace most of the SS-11 in

tenance replacement, proof testing, and so forth, would require 1,215 missiles. That figure echoes the information available to U.S. officials in 1976 that the Soviets were planning to produce "about 1,200" of these missiles. William Beecher, "Russia's New Missile: A Gray-Area Weapon," *International Herald Tribune*, September 10, 1976.

66. The calculations run as follows. In November 1983 the Soviets had 243 missiles within range of Western Europe, of a total of 351 SS-20s deployed or under construction. At the end of 1983 the Soviet Union claimed that it had reduced the original number of medium-range missiles in the European part of Russia from 600 to 473 and that the SS-5 had been completely withdrawn. The lower total yields 230 SS-4s. In November 1983 the U.S. and Soviet representatives discussed a mutual reduction of 572 warheads, which would have had the effect of reducing the proposed U.S. INF deployment to zero. Subtracting 572 warheads from the Soviet inventory would leave only 129 SS-20 launchers (243 × 3 = 729 SS-20s + 230 SS-4s = 959 warheads minus 572 = 387 warheads yielding 129 SS-20 missiles).

67. This offer was made by Yuri V. Andropov in an interview in "Otveti Yu. V. Andropova na voprosy gazety Pravda" (Answers by Yuri V. Andropov to questions from *Pravda*), *Pravda*, August 27, 1983.

the eastern parts of Russia, but in the western parts, the SS-11 VRBM would be replaced by the SS-19 VRBM.

Deployment of both these new missile systems did get under way in 1977, and the approximate rate of deployment that was planned for the SS-20 can be inferred from the fact that in both 1978 and 1979, work started on new emplacements for eighty-one launchers (or nine missile bases).[68] However, in October 1979 Brezhnev announced his readiness to reduce the existing number of Soviet medium-range missiles, which then totaled about 600 (SS-4s and SS-5s, and SS-20s) and in the event only 378 SS-20s (42 bases) were deployed in the 1977–83 period, 243 of them in range of western Europe.

The final total bears little relation to the various ceilings proffered by the Soviets in the INF negotiations. The temporal pattern of the SS-20 deployment suggests that this figure reflects an arbitrary decision to complete those systems that were already in the production pipeline when it was agreed to curtail the program.[69] The decision appears to have been made in mid-1979.[70] What explains this reversal of policy?

As originally planned the SS-20 program probably stemmed largely from the inertia of past requirements, which would have been reinforced by a need to assuage military concerns that the Soviets had conceded too much in the SALT negotiations. But if there had been any doubts about exploiting the resources that had originally been earmarked for the SS-16 ICBM program, these would have been removed by the realization in November 1974 that the new limits on MIRVed ICBMs would preclude the replacement of about half the SS-11 VRBM force.[71]

68. Garthoff, "The Soviet SS-20 Decision," note 7, p. 118. A notional production run of 72 SS-20 systems a year for seven years seems plausible, based on the deployment figures for the first four years. The higher rate of 81 may have reflected the military's attempt to establish "facts" before the political leadership turned to negotiate. It may not be coincidental that the final deployment of 486 is very close to ten years' production at the "standard" ICBM rate of 48 a year.

69. Deployment started in 1977, built up to a brief plateau in 1980 and 1981, and then fell away over the next three years. The numbers on which this assessment is based are drawn from John Cartwright and Julian Critchley, *Nuclear Weapons in Europe* (Brussels: North Atlantic Assembly, 1984), p. 18, and Garthoff, "The Soviet SS-20 Decision," notes 7 and 18, pp. 118, 119. The deployment pattern was typical of a canceled program, the tailing-off being clues to pipeline inertia.

70. New starts on missile bases fell in 1980 and tapered to a halt in 1982, having reached a plateau of nine new bases in 1978 and 1979. Garthoff, "The Soviet SS-20 Decision," note 7, p. 118.

71. The general parameters of these limits were proposed by Henry Kissinger in Moscow in October 1974 and generally agreed on. Garthoff, *Détente and Confrontation*, pp. 443–44. The SS-11s in southwestern Russia were replaced by SS-19s, but not those in the Far East. *SMP, 1985*, p. 26.

As a replacement for the SS-4 and SS-5, it was natural that the SS-20 should take over the same target set. Indeed as the SS-4 and SS-5 sites were deactivated, one would expect the newly emplaced SS-20s to assume responsibility for covering the assigned targets. However, the SS-4 and SS-5 target set had roots in the 1959–66 period, when strategic nuclear preemption was the cornerstone of doctrine and the regional missile force had a preplanned target list that was originally more than one thousand.

By the mid-1970s that target set was no longer relevant. The December 1966 decision had led to a restructuring of objectives and reshaping of operational concepts that completely changed the nature of the requirement for medium-range missiles. It seems likely that this requirement would have come into focus during the 1976–77 policy review, which evaluated the effectiveness of the policies and concepts adopted during the 1967–68 decision period. Of itself the change did not justify modifying plans for the deployment of the SS-20, since it would take eight to ten years to develop the appropriate response to the new requirement. The SS-4 and SS-5 force was more of a hindrance than a help to the post-1975 strategic plan, and there were strong operational reasons for replacing it with a more responsive, accurate, and survivable system.

It was, however, a different matter when it came to weighing the potential benefits of continued SS-20 deployment against the possibility of halting the deployment of Pershing II. As discussed in chapter 11, the Pershing II, by destroying facilities for command, control, and communications at the TVD and front levels, would put at risk the Soviet capability to respond to NATO's resort to nuclear weapons in the European theater. If the Soviets could prevent the deployment of Pershing II by halting or even reversing the deployment of SS-20s, it was clearly in their interest to make concessions in this area, subject to an important proviso. Any ceiling on medium-range missiles would have to accommodate the revised requirements that would have emerged from the 1976–77 decision period.

This explanation would account for the apparent reversal of Soviet policy in mid-1979, including halting the production and deployment of the SS-20. It is, however, also necessary to explain the actual limits proposed by the Soviets at the INF negotiations, in terms of their military requirements in the 1978–87 period and their requirements in the subsequent period when the response they had purposely designed would be available. Such an explanation requires one to distinguish between the requirement for medium-range missiles in the eastern and western parts of Russia.

Keep in mind that in military terms, these missiles have to cover three separate theaters: European, Far Eastern, and Southern.[72]

MEDIUM-RANGE MISSILES IN EASTERN RUSSIA. The problem of China is likely to have dominated Soviet requirements in the eastern parts of Russia, and not only because the immediate U.S. threat had subsided with the removal of its forces from Southeast Asia and the shift of its attention to the NATO area. The Soviet relationship with China was as acerbic as ever and would deteriorate further with the invasion of Afghanistan at the end of 1979. China was growing close to Japan as well as to the United States, there was a slow but steady buildup in the Chinese nuclear delivery capability, and it seemed likely that China would acquire military technology and support equipment from the United States, if not actual weapons.

As discussed in chapter 8, the operational concept in the Far Eastern TVD was to hold China deterred. Should China seek to profit from a world war to make gains in Siberia while Soviet forces were engaged in Europe, the Soviets would repel the aggression by using conventional means only. The European theater was the main one, and no action would be taken in the Far East that would encourage nuclear escalation in the European theater or escalation to a full-scale intercontinental exchange. Should, however, such an exchange prove unavoidable, then China, as well as the United States, would be struck with nuclear weapons.

Within such an operational concept, the role of medium-range missiles would be similar to their role against European NATO in the pre-1967 period. In both cases their task was to strike, preemptively if possible, against a preplanned set of fixed targets. The difference would be that in the pre-1967 period the strike against NATO would have been triggered by a Soviet decision that world war was inescapable; but in the contemporary period, the strike against China would be triggered by a Soviet decision to launch a full-scale nuclear strike against North America, world war already being in progress.

In other words, the SS-20 had a valid role in the eastern part of Russia. Furthermore, many of the problems that vitiated the capability of the SS-4 and SS-5 force to meet the same type of requirement in the European theater in the 1960s, such as vulnerability to preemption and long reaction times, did not apply to the SS-20 in the Far Eastern TVD in the 1980s. Mobility reduced the system's vulnerability, as did the buildup of Soviet

---

72. The missile bases are roughly on an east-west axis, and the middle third can cover either Europe or the Far East, as well as the South.

forces in the region, and solid fuel allowed an immediate response. Meanwhile the threat of preemptive nuclear strikes by China lay far in the future.

About 135 SS-20s (fifteen bases) were deployed or under construction in the eastern parts of Russia at the end of 1983. A sixteenth missile base was under construction in April 1985, which would bring the total to 144 launchers. These have not replaced all the SS-11 missiles, which presumably are needed to cover U.S. military facilities outside the SS-20's reach.[73]

MEDIUM-RANGE MISSILES IN WESTERN RUSSIA. What would be the role of nuclear-armed medium-range missiles in a concept of operations that prescribed conventional attacks against a significant proportion of the installations that originally belonged in the nuclear target set? Three come to mind.[74] One covers the possibility of nuclear escalation in the theater and the need to strike at any distant strategic targets that had survived conventional interdiction. A second covers the contingency of military disaster in the Western TVD and the need to break up a NATO offensive into Eastern Europe. The third covers the possibility of intercontinental escalation and the need to strike at key politico-military targets in the region.

When these three possible roles are matched against the capabilities of the available missile systems and against the inferred roles of the SS-11 and SS-19 VRBMs on the one hand and the SS-4 and SS-5 force on the other, it can be seen that the first two require the flexible targeting capability of the SS-19 and come within the description of the VRBM's role.

The only role appropriate to the genesis and capabilities of the SS-20 is that of striking at regional politico-military targets in the event of war escalating to an intercontinental nuclear exchange. This highlights the coincidence between the minimum number of SS-20s offered by the Soviets in October–November 1983 (129 informally and "about 140" publicly), and the 135 SS-4s and SS-5s that were emplaced in silos in the 1963–66 period. It was just argued that these 135 missiles could have been intended to cover a hard core of politico-military targets whose importance did not depend on successful preemption and was unlikely to change much over

73. The present number of SS-11s in the Far East is not known, but at the beginning of 1985, SS-11s are shown as being deployed at the three original sites. The availability of SS-19s as a replacement was constrained by the SALT II limits.

74. A fourth possibility is that these missiles are required to match the British and French strategic systems directly. However, this requirement would not have been met by the limits the Soviets were willing to accept in October and November 1983, nor by the walk-in-the-woods formula, which would have allowed the Soviets less than half the British and French total. The Soviet concern to match is directed at those systems that would survive an intercontinental exchange (that is, the SSBNs), and these are matched by the Soviet SSBN force.

time. It may well be that this same target set was one of the factors that determined the Soviets' negotiating floor for SS-20s.

The Requirement for Medium-Range Missiles

In the INF negotiations the Soviets also had to cover their future requirements for medium-range missiles facing Europe, which at the time were met in part by VRBMs, which are not counted under INF. In the first half of the 1970s the combined force totaled more than 750 launchers, and even the proposed limit of only 135 SS-20s would keep the strength at about 300.[75] How, then, could the Soviets manage to make do with 135 or even less? The contradiction was highlighted by the fact that both the SS-20 IRBM and the SS-19 VRBM were adaptations of systems originally designed as ICBMs. The established practice of product improvement would lead one to expect a fifth-generation missile that incorporated the advantages of both fourth-generation systems and was purposely designed to cover both strategic roles in the continental region, that is, unless the underlying requirement for regional range systems had changed.

An explanation of this seeming paradox can be found in the distinction between the roles of the SS-19 and SS-20 that has just been inferred. Since the early 1970s, a distinction has apparently been drawn between missiles that could be flexibly targeted, the SS-11 and SS-19, and those that covered preplanned target sets, the SS-4, SS-5, and SS-20. This distinction may now have been refined to draw the line between systems that would be used to support military operations, should nuclear war be resorted to in the European theater, and those systems that would only be used in the event of escalation to global nuclear war.

This new approach would follow the logic of the December 1966 decision and recognize explicitly that there are two different target sets in the European theater, which are determined by the nature of the conflict and not by the target's geographic location. One target set is limited to the situation in which nuclear weapons are resorted to in the theater, but it is still hoped to avoid escalation to an intercontinental exchange. In other words, the 1970s objectives and strategy apply. This set would mainly comprise military targets, speed of response would be critical, and often the targets' exact location or even existence would not be known much ahead of time.

75. This limit includes 180 SS-19 variable-range ballistic missiles.

The other target set applies to the situation in which conflict in Europe or elsewhere does escalate to global nuclear war. In that case, the 1960s hierarchy of objectives would come back into force, the war would be redefined as a fight to the finish, and the concept of operations as described in chapter 2 would apply. In Europe this set would mainly comprise political targets (military targets would be covered largely by the "theater war" set) and, except for British and French strategic nuclear facilities, response time would not be critical.

What would this categorization imply for overall Soviet requirements for nuclear weapons targeted on Europe and for specific requirements for medium-range land-based missiles? For a start, such missiles are not essential for attacking the targets that come under the category of global nuclear war. Those targets could therefore become an appendage to what used to be thought of as the "intercontinental" target set, but would now constitute most of the global war target set. With a few exceptions these targets in Europe are neither time critical nor hardened, and they could therefore be covered by slow-response, sea-based systems. The exceptions, including British and French strategic nuclear facilities, could be targeted by ICBMs or some other rapid-response system.

This plan would mean that the next generation of medium-range land-based missiles could be developed to respond optimally to nuclear escalation in the theater. This requirement is very demanding. Because of the emphasis on conventional operations and the priority on avoiding escalation, these missiles are likely to be the only systems at immediate readiness to respond to the use of nuclear weapons by NATO. They would need to be relatively invulnerable to preventive attack by virtue of mobility and/or hardening, and to have the capacity for flexible targeting, perhaps including some capability for guidance in the terminal phase. Since the target set would mainly comprise relocatable facilities, either because of their inherent mobility or because the military facilities are likely to have been newly established or relocated after the onset of war, these missiles are likely to have a single warhead.

The Shape of Future Requirements

The logic of distinguishing between strategic systems that are designed for theater nuclear war, and those designed for global nuclear war, extends well beyond Europe. This temporal distinction could therefore replace the natural spatial division between regional and intercontinental systems that is based on range and may already have done so. Wartime command and control would be improved and simplified by establishing as a separate set those targets that would only be attacked in a global nuclear war, whether they be in Europe, North America, or anywhere else in the world. Such an arrangement would also provide greater flexibility in the use of intercontinental-range systems in circumstances short of global nuclear war.

However, the evidence for how the Soviets see their future requirements for strategic missile systems is partly based on their arms control proposals, and these follow the U.S. definition of "strategic" (that is, intercontinental) and "intermediate range" (that is, continental or regional). It is therefore best to persist with the spatial distinction when assessing future Soviet requirements for strategic nuclear forces.

Intercontinental Systems

The launcher limits included in the revised Soviet proposals at the end of round five of the strategic arms reduction talks (START), November 1983, are shown here, with the previous limits agreed on at SALT II.[76]

START	*Types of Launcher*	*SALT II*
1,800	ICBM + SLBM + heavy bombers	2,250
1,200	MIRVed missile + ALCM bombers	1,320
1,080	MIRVed missile (ICBM + SLBM)	1,200
680	MIRVed ICBM	820

The Soviet START proposals represented significant reductions on the SALT II limits, most notably in the aggregate of all launchers (-450) and in the number of MIRVed ICBMs (-140). There were some interesting aspects to the changed totals. One was the coincidence between the limit on MIRVed ICBMs (680) and existing number of SS-18s and SS-19s (668), the most successful of the MIRVed ICBMs. The SS-18 is the fourth generation of heavy missile from Yangel's design bureau and is the primary cause of U.S. strategic concern because it combines a large payload with high accuracy. The SS-19 is the more successful of the two programs that were initiated in response to the new requirement posed by the Minuteman deployment and developed on parallel paths; the SS-19 also has a variable-range capability and can be used in the theater.

76. National Academy of Sciences, *Nuclear Arms Control: Background and Issues* (Washington, D.C.: National Academy Press, 1985), p. 67.

A second point was that the drop in the number of MIRVed ICBMs (140) is close to the number of SS-17s (150), the less successful of the two "parallel development" programs. Third, the START proposals kept the implicit limit on bombers armed with air-launched cruise missiles (ALCMs) at 120 but raised the implicit limit on MIRVed SLBMs from 380 to 400, at the expense of the relative number of ICBMs.

To these figures can be added a conclusion from the first part of this appendix, namely, that it was decided in the first half of 1970 to stabilize the ICBM force at about 1,000 missiles for the intercontinental target set, with another 360 missiles allocated for regional targets. Last is the composition of the SSBN force, with 280 single-warhead SLBMs carried by Delta I and II, whereas Typhoon and Delta III and IV carry MIRVed systems.

The START proposals allowed a minimum of 600 non-MIRVed missiles, which could be either ICBMs or SLBMs. Assuming that the quota for submarine-launched ballistic missiles would be carried by Delta I and Delta II, this would allow 320 single-warhead ICBMs. When this figure is added to the ceiling on MIRVed ICBMs (320 + 680), the total is exactly 1,000. This figure suggests the following breakdown of the Soviet START proposal:

System	MIRVed	Single Warhead	Total
ICBM	680	320	1,000
SLBM	400	280	680
Bomber	120	. . .	120
Total	1,200	600	1,800

Three points about this breakdown need highlighting. An ICBM force about 1,000 strong has been Soviet policy since 1970, and the concept of 400 MIRVed SLBMs may have been latent at the same period.[77] The aggregate totals are similar to those proposed by President Jimmy Carter in 1977. To reach the individual totals, the Soviets would only need to dispose of their SS-17 force (138 MIRVed) and their remaining Yankee SSBNs, which lack the range to strike at North America from home waters.[78] Furthermore, these Soviet proposals provided for the 100 MX

77. See appendix B.
78. Within the SALT limits the Soviets could have retained a maximum of 16 Yankee ballistic-missile submarines. However, these hull-propulsion units may now be needed for conversion

ICBMs that were in Carter's fiscal 1982 budget and would have allowed the construction of the 18 Trident SSBNs in the SALT II limits. This is another indication of their substantive nature.

The 1,080 MIRVed ballistic missiles were intended to provide the primary wartime deterrent. If deterrence failed, they would be used to strike at the target set for global nuclear war since the use of MIRVed missiles is most effective against preplanned sets of static targets. The ICBM would be divided between heavy missiles in superhardened silos (308) and light missiles on mobile launchers (372). The 600 single-warhead missiles were intended mainly for use following an intercontinental nuclear exchange. The single-warhead missiles were primarily for use in a global nuclear war, including being held back in a strategic reserve, but some of them may also have been earmarked for use in the event of escalation that was limited to the European theater or for response to selective strikes by the United States against noncritical targets in Russia.

The 120 ALCM-armed bombers have a multiple role. They would have a range of conventional missions in both phase I and II of a world war that does not escalate to an intercontinental nuclear exchange. If it does escalate, they become "use or lose" systems because of their dependence on airfields. They would therefore participate in the initial nuclear strike, covering strategic targets that were not already covered by the preplanned list for MIRVed missiles because they were new, mobile, or some similar reason.

Continental, or Regional, Systems

The INF negotiations suggested that the requirement for medium-range missiles in the European theater was about 135, assuming that no Pershing IIs were deployed. In the contemporary situation, this number allows for enough SS-20s to cover fixed politico-military targets that would have to be attacked in the event of escalation to global nuclear war. In the future, the requirement is to be able to replace the 180 VRBMs with a medium-range single-warhead system that can respond immediately to nuclear escalation in the theater, striking at targets whose exact location is unlikely to be known much in advance. The reduction of one quarter in the number of missiles considered necessary for this task can perhaps be explained

---

to SSGNs armed with the SS-N-24 land-attack cruise missile, their new mission being conventional interdiction of NATO theater nuclear assets.

by removing the responsibility for attacking the aircraft carrier from the medium-range missile force.

In the eastern parts of Russia, 180 SS-11s were deployed during most of the 1970s, and they may have been augmented and perhaps partly replaced by 144 SS-20s.[79] In a world war, targets in China come within the category of those that would only be attacked in the event of escalation to an intercontinental nuclear exchange. A large number of such targets are administrative and industrial centers that do not require an immediate response. But China has a growing nuclear delivery capability that would need to be struck preemptively. The Soviets also face the separate contingency of a Sino-Soviet war. To meet these varied requirements, a certain number of land-based systems are essential.

When these two parts of Russia are combined, the total requirement is for about 400 medium-range missiles, to which there should now be added another 100 or so to cover the Pershing II deployment. This suggests an overall requirement for at least 500 medium-range systems, which would, in time, take the place of both the SS-20s and the VRBM force.

The requirement for medium-range nuclear delivery systems for use in the continental region relates primarily to waging war and only incidentally to deterring escalation in the theater. It is therefore sensitive to the number and disposition of the forces around the periphery of Russia, and there is every reason for the Soviets to reject arms limitation agreements that omit such forces from the account. By the same token, the Soviets' interest in keeping operations in Europe at the conventional level would favor mutual reductions in nuclear delivery vehicles.

79. In 1985, 144 SS-20s were deployed in the eastern part of Russia and an unspecified number of SS-11s were deployed at three bases, which used to have 60 apiece. The ten-year production run of fourth-generation ICBMs would have allowed the allocation of 440 missiles to regional targets. As early as 1970, it may have been intended to increase the number of regional missiles in the eastern part of Russia from 180 to 260. Development during the 1970s could have further increased the requirement.

Index

ABM (antiballistic missile): development of, 234; early limitations, 92; Soviet and U.S. deployment, 325–26; Soviet importance of limiting U.S. deployment, 341; reversal of Soviet policy, 269. *See also* BMD

ABM Treaty, 242–43, 247, 264, 341;

Addu Atoll, 206

Aden, 202–05; Gulf of, 208

Afghanistan: Soviet invasion of, 188, 228, 247, 284, 349

Air forces: of Soviet Union, 57–58. *See also* Long-range aviation; Frontal aviation

Algeria, 143; Soviet missile-armed patrol craft, 222

America: foreign policy with accession to NATO, 19; navy in World War II, 107; Soviet view of attitudes in, 331; wartime assumptions about, 4. *See also* United States

Andropov, General Secretary Yuri V.: Declaration of September *28, 1983,* 283, 294–306, 307, 311, 317, 382

Arab-Israeli war: *1973,* 219; *1967,* 59–60

Arctic Ocean: control of, 101, 112; deployment area for SSBNs, 340; importance in *1970s* hierarchy of objectives, 329–30; Soviet reassessment of, 110, 148–49

Arctic OTVD, 146–56. *See also* Arctic Ocean

Arms control as a process, 264–66, 321; American ambivalence, 270–71; contribution to détente, 342; differences in U.S. and Soviet approach, 271–79; impact on ICBM development, 490–92; military objectives, 232–82; under *1970s* hierarchy of objectives, 341, 343; and SDI, 343; and worst-case assumptions, 368

Army: dominant element in Soviet military, 121–26. *See also* Ground forces

ASAT (antisatellite system), 310

Asian-Pacific region, 161–82, 348–49

Assured destruction, 23; strategic concept, 31–32. *See also* Mutual assured destruction

Assured second-strike capability, 27, 29, 32, 268

ASW (antisubmarine warfare), 99–100, 414

Atlantic OTVD, 156–60. *See also* North Atlantic

Austria, 141; postwar era, 70

Azores: Soviet control of, 159

Azovtsev, N. N., 63–65

Bab el Mandeb, Straits of: importance to Soviets, 201

Balkans: focus of Southwestern TVD, 139; land attack routed through, 68

Baltic Sea: land attacks on Russia, 68; Soviet naval operations in, 136–38; in the Western TVD, 130

Barents Sea: in Arctic OTVD, 148; control of, 111–12

Baruch Plan: proposal for management of atomic materials, 17

Bering Sea: Soviet control of passage to, 174

Berlin crisis, 361

Black Sea: land attacks on Russia, 68, 141

BMD (ballistic-missile defense): requirements for under *1970s* hierarchy of objectives, 341; in SDI, 262; Soviet concerns about, 325–26

BMEWS (ballistic-missile early-warning system): constraints on the location, 243–44

BPK (large antisubmarine ship), 414

521